HUMAN CONDUCT

Problems of Ethics

SECOND EDITION

HUMAN CONDUCT

Problems of Ethics

SECOND EDITION

JOHN HOSPERS

University of Southern California

HARCOURT BRACE JOVANOVICH, PUBLISHERS

San Diego   New York   Chicago   Austin
London   Sydney   Toronto

ISBN: 0-15-540094-0

Library of Congress Catalog Card Number: 81-86171

Printed in the United States of America

For no light matter is at stake; the question concerns the very manner in which human life is to be lived.

Plato, *Republic*, Book I, 352-D.

Preface

In what way should people conduct their lives? What things in life should count most—pleasure and enjoyment, truth and knowledge, moral courage and acting on one's convictions? What makes some goals worth achieving and others not? What makes some actions right and others wrong? What obligations have we toward others, and why should we perform them? In what circumstances should we be praised, blamed, punished, or excused for our actions? To what extent are we free—to act, to choose, to desire? What kind of social and political order should we endeavor to promote?

It is to such questions that this book is addressed. The proponents of each of the major historical views on these subjects are described and assessed. No attempt is made to consider them in chronological order; instead, they are grouped under the subject-matter headings that deal with their particular type of theory. No previous acquaintance with the literature of the subject is presupposed. Every view discussed is illustrated by numerous examples, including attempts to apply it to problems of today's world: problems of personal morality and of the individual's relation to the social order, involving law, the economy, political authority, and war and peace. Numerous exercises, often involving issues not specifically discussed in the text, appear at the end of each chapter, along with lists of further readings.

Though the general structure of the book remains much the same in this edition as in the first, nearly all of the text has been rewritten. About fifteen percent of the original exercises remain, but only about two percent of the original text remains. The result is actually a new book, which has only the title and a portion of the table of contents in common with the old one.

John Hospers

Contents

1

The Problems of Ethics

Ethics is a branch of the study of human conduct. But there are other subjects which also are concerned with human conduct: psychologists study it, trying to arrive at general laws of how the human mind works and to cure psychological disorders; historians study human conduct as exhibited in historical persons and movements; anthropologists study human conduct, describing the behavior and customs of peoples and tribes around the world.

The aspect of human conduct that concerns ethics is *morality*. Ethics is a study of morality, as biology is the study of life. But there are other subjects that study morality besides ethics. Anthropologists, for example, study the moral beliefs and practices of human beings, but theirs is a *descriptive* study of morality: they do not judge but only survey and describe the moral beliefs and practices of human beings in various cultures. Ethics, by contrast, is a *philosophical* study of morality. It is concerned with such questions as: When is an act right or wrong? What actions are just, and which are unjust, and why? When is a moral practice good or bad? What goals of action are good, worthwhile, or desirable? What kind of character traits are good or bad? For what actions should a person be praised or blamed, punished or rewarded? For what actions should a person be held morally responsible? And most important of all, what *reasons* can be given for or against a position someone holds on these questions?

We speak of human *acts* as right or wrong. By what standards an act should be judged right or wrong will be discussed in Chapters 3–7. But we should notice at the outset that on many, perhaps most, of the occasions when we use the terms "right" and "wrong" we are not discussing moral questions at all. We say, "That's the right answer to the question," and "I always manage to say the wrong thing at parties." In neither case are we talking about *moral* right and wrong.

1

We not only speak of right and wrong acts; we also speak of acts we *ought* (or ought not) to perform, or have a *duty* to do. "You ought to do X" is a somewhat stronger statement than "It would be right for you to do X." To say that it would be right for you to do X is, as a rule, a negative sort of statement; it means only that it would *not be wrong* for you to do X. In many circumstances there might be many things that it would not be wrong for you to do: it might be right for you to express your appreciation for a favor by sending the person money, and it might be equally right for you simply to send a letter of thanks. Calling something right ordinarily carries the meaning of "all right," "O.K.," "permissible." But to say that you *ought* to do X, or have a *duty* to do X, is to say something more than this: if you have a duty to do X, then to do anything other than X would be wrong. Thus, "X is right" means (ordinarily) that it would *not be wrong* to do X; but "You ought to do X" ("You have an obligation to do X") means that it would be wrong *not* to do X. (Like "right" and "wrong," "ought" is often used in non-moral contexts: "There ought to be a road just about here," you might say as you are looking about in the dark, or, when trying to repair a machine, "I think I ought to give it one last try.")

Our use of the words "good" and "bad" in ethics covers an even wider range than "ought" and "right." We speak of good or bad *ideals* and *goals* of action: "Having a little more patience would be a very good thing to aim at." We speak of good or bad *consequences* of actions: "This will cause her lots of distress, and I think that would be a bad thing to bring about." We also speak of a good or bad *person* and of a person's good or bad *character*. We speak of good or bad *motives:* "He did it because he hated and resented her." (A motive is what moved a person to do the act, and in this case we imply it was bad.) We speak, too, of good or bad *intentions:* "What she did had catastrophic results but she did have good intentions." It is only for acts themselves that the terms "right" and "wrong" are reserved. Thus, you can do the right act but have bad motives—such as keeping your word for fear of the law—and you can do the wrong act from good motives—such as acting from love but causing only distress or embarrassment as a result.

"Good" and "bad" are comparative words: good, better, and best, and bad, worse, worst. All these words are used in non-moral contexts more than in moral contexts. We speak of a good watch, a good road, a good car, a good pen, a good horse. When we speak of a good X, whatever the X is, we are saying that X fulfills to a high degree the criteria for that class of goods. Good watches, for example, must run well and keep accurate time; a good car must run smoothly and not require frequent repair. The criteria for a good sports car are not the same as those for a good limousine; the criteria for a good dinner table are not the same as those for a good desk; the criteria for a good office chair are not the same as those for a good easy chair. But each has criteria in virtue of which we call it good. When we speak of a good man or woman—a morally good man or woman, not just "good man for the job"—we are saying that he or she fulfills to a high degree the criteria for moral goodness in human beings. In this case, however, the criteria used are much more varied. In the case of a manufactured object, human beings have made it and human beings use it, and presumably they know for what purpose they made it and use it; but since human beings are not objects of that kind, and there is not any one main thing they can be used for, there is quite a bit of variation in what makes us call someone a morally good person, or a motive a morally good motive (or an intention, etc.). What the principal suggested criteria are for judging moral goodness or badness is something we shall examine in the following chapters. Meanwhile, we need to note at the outset that "good," in persons as well as in watches, has to do with the fulfillment of criteria, whatever they may be.

1. MORAL ISSUES

The term "moral" is used in two different ways. (1) Sometimes we praise someone's action by saying, "I think that was a very moral thing to do," and here the opposite of "moral" is "immoral," as when we condemn a person's conduct as immoral. This first sense of "moral" is a narrow use of the term. (2) But both moral and immoral actions are moral in a wider sense of that term: they *belong in the area of morality.* Where to place the plates on the table and whether to get out of bed on the right foot or the left foot are not questions of morality, but whether to go out of your way to help someone in distress is. Whether infanticide is ever right is a moral question; whether every even number is the sum of two prime numbers is not. The latter is a non-moral question, that is, it has nothing to do with morality, in the wide sense, one way or the other.

What makes something a moral question (in the wide sense) remains a matter of some difference of opinion. The sphere of the moral can be marked off in different ways.

One could attempt to distinguish moral from non-moral issues by saying that if you believe an act is wrong, you are committed to believing that someone else who thinks that the same act is right not only *differs* from you but is *mistaken*. If you believe that cruelty to animals is always wrong, you certainly *disagree* with someone who believes that cruelty to animals is all right. By contrast, if you believe that lobster tastes better than crab and someone else thinks that crab tastes better than lobster, there is only a difference in personal *preference;* you don't really believe that the other person's preference is mistaken, it's just that his preference differs from yours.

There certainly is a difference between statements about right and wrong acts and statements of preference; those who believe that a certain act is wrong believe not only that those who believe it's right *differ* from them in their preference, but that their judgment on the matter is *mistaken,* and that the judgments ("X is right" and "X is wrong") cannot both be true. This does serve to mark off moral matters, on which people constantly disagree, from differences of taste or preference. But it fails to mark off moral differences from countless other non-moral ones, in which there is genuine disagreement concerning matters that have nothing at all to do with morality. For example, if you believe that 6 times 8 is 48, then you also believe that a person who believes that 6 times 8 is 68 is mistaken; and if you believe that colds are caused by a virus and someone else thinks that they result from phases of the moon, again there is genuine disagreement, although neither of these examples has anything to do with morality.

Another attempt to distinguish the moral is by the kind of *experience* that is involved; thus moral experience can be opposed to aesthetic experience, religious experience, and so on. People have a moral experience when they believe they have done a fine or noble act and have a certain feeling of moral satisfaction or triumph. They also have that kind of experience when they believe they have done something wrong and suffer feelings of shame, remorse, and guilt. I may paint my house a color that I later come to dislike, but I do not feel shame or remorse about it, though I may *regret* that I did it. Regret is not necessarily held to be a moral experience, though guilt and shame usually are.

Another attempt to distinguish the moral from the non-moral is by the kind of *situation* involved. Thus, whether you should go out of your way to help someone in need is a moral matter; so too are the questions of whether a woman whose child will probably have a genetic defect should have an abortion, and whether a person should keep a promise at great personal sacrifice. All of these are moral issues in the wide sense—matters of morality. Some people might not *feel* guilt or shame at not acting in certain ways in these situations, but one could say that if they don't, they should, because these are moral rather than non-moral matters.

There is considerable disagreement, however, on which situations are the concern of morality and which are not. In most Western cultures prostitution and homosexuality have a stigma of immorality attached to them, and many people feel guilt and shame if they indulge in them; but in most Oriental cultures they are considered matters of individual taste, with no more moral relevance than a preference for steak or fish, blondes or brunettes. In a religious environment, failure to observe the Sabbath or to eat prescribed foods is attended with guilt and the failures are considered to be lapses in morality, but a nonreligious person will not consider them to be matters of moral relevance at all.

Some contend that morality does not enter the picture until acts affect other people and that to Robinson Crusoe alone on an island, there would be no matters of moral concern at all. Yet to survive he had to develop habits of industry, perseverance, and courage—and aren't these moral qualities? Besides, can't you be said to have duties to yourself—to develop your talents and not waste them, to see to your health and well-being, not to spend your life in idleness and self-indulgence? Many people would say that we indeed do have such "self-regarding" duties.

Even if we say that moral matters concern the interactions of individuals with one another, we can hardly say that *all* such interactions are matters of moral concern. Whether or not to play cards in the evening is (normally at least) not a moral matter; but whether you cheat at cards is. Whether you eat at six o'clock or at seven is not usually a matter of moral right or wrong, but whether you poison your wife's drink is.

We might say that moral issues have to do with *important* matters involving others, but not everyone agrees on what is to be considered important. Presumably concern for other people's lives is important; yet people who would make every effort to save the life of a person in distress often drive recklessly and do not keep their cars in safe condition. Though such acts and omissions greatly endanger the lives of others, they do not think of such things as moral or immoral, but merely as matters of what they can get by with. Yet if helping a person in distress is a moral issue, so, surely, is driving in such a way as not to endanger others.

Probably most people do not consider it immoral to overpark by ten minutes at a parking meter. Such an action does not usually affect others in an important way, though it does keep other motorists from using the space. Most take their chances with it, paying the ticket if they get one but not feeling guilty if they don't. What about parking next to a fire hydrant? Most people don't appear to consider this a moral issue either, though in this case there is an obvious danger: if a fire breaks out in a nearby apartment, the fire truck can't get to a hydrant and lives may be lost. It would appear that most people are not very consistent in their views about what is a moral issue and what is not.

In spite of the vagueness of the term "moral," is there any general criterion for determining which actions are morally right or wrong?

Let us examine several answers that have been proposed to this question.

A. Conscience

"Do whatever your conscience tells you," we sometimes hear, "and whatever it tells you will be right." *Conscience* is a kind of "inner voice" telling us what it would be right or wrong to do. According to some theologians, conscience is the voice of God speaking within, guiding us in our moral decisions. According to some psychologists, conscience is the product of the internalization of external commands: children prefer to be their own authority rather than being told what to do, and yet they will be punished if they disobey parents' commands; so the way out—to obey the commands and yet salvage their egos—is to "internalize" the commands, to act as if they came not from outside but from inside, so that in obeying, the children are only obeying themselves and not really bowing to any outside authority. At the age of two, a little boy sulks at being scolded for spilling soup on the table, but by the age of four, when little sister spills soup on the table, he is full of moral indignation against her. Thus has an external command become internalized.

Whatever your view about how conscience came to be formed, there are some problems in accepting its verdicts as the sure test of what is right and what is wrong.

Different people's consciences vary enormously. Some people's conscience tells them to kill in revenge if a member of the family has been killed or maimed, and other people's conscience tells them never to kill anyone at all, not even in self-defense. Some people's conscience tells them never to take what does not belong to them, and other people's conscience apparently registers no objections to theft. Hamlet's conscience bothered him because he did *not* kill his uncle; but another person's conscience would bother him if he did kill his uncle, even in Hamlet's circumstances.

If conscience is the inner voice of God, it is difficult to explain why God speaks in so many voices, implanting an inner oracle that says one thing to one person and just the opposite to somebody else. But if what our consciences say is determined at least partly by our background and training, then the variation is explained easily: as children, different people receive different commands, and thus a variety of rules become internalized. In that case, however, how can conscience be an infallible guide to right and wrong? If one person's conscience tells him to do X, and another person's conscience tells her not to do X, which is right?

"Both may be right," someone may reply, "for the first person's conscience may tell him what is right *for him* to do. Circumstances differ, and what's right for him in a certain circumstance may not be right for the second person. In fact, what's right for the first to do at one time may not be what's right for him to do at another time."

It is true, of course, that the circumstances surrounding each action by each person are different. Still, it is curious, if conscience is always to be followed, that one person's conscience says that it is always right to wreak revenge against an enemy, and another person's conscience reveals that it is never right to do so. Besides, conscience doesn't just tell what the individual alone ought to do; it tells what *everyone* ought to do. The conscience of pacifists doesn't say (as a rule) that only *they* ought to refrain from taking human life—it tells them that *everyone* should so refrain. Authoritarian parents don't believe that only they should raise their children firmly, but that all parents should do so. So it is still true that different people's consciences speak with different voices, even (sometimes) contradicting one another. And if any two are contradictory, they can't both be right.

If people raised in an orthodox Jewish tradition eat pork (or if orthodox Hindus eat beef), their conscience bothers them, and they have strong feelings of guilt. People raised to observe the Sabbath strictly feel pangs of conscience if they go to a movie on Sunday. To a considerable extent our conscience is a product of our early upbringing. Many adults are more bothered by conscience at minor infractions of rules learned in early childhood than they are at much greater crimes committed in adulthood, concerning which their conscience seems to desert them entirely. This is particularly the case with people who stop thinking at the age of twelve (if they ever started).

They have been told as children not to lie or steal, and, may feel guilt if they do these things, yet as adults they may feel no guilt at robbing the public treasury or driving so as to endanger the lives of others: when they were children, there was no need for the latter commands. They wouldn't steal from their friends, but they feel no qualms about leaving work at three when they are paid to work till five, though this may have much the same effect, and can be called stealing as much as can taking money from the till. But in thoughtful and reflective people, conscience does change and develop: they may no longer feel pangs of conscience at going to a movie on Sunday, even if they did earlier in their lives, but they may be conscience-stricken at any suspicion of racist behavior, although they were not taught anything about racism as children but later concluded for themselves that prejudice is wrong.

"But," someone may object further, "many of these people are just kidding themselves. Hamlet may have *thought* that his conscience told him to kill his uncle, but in fact he was deluding himself: he knew better all the time—knew that killing was wrong—and was just trying to squelch the voice of conscience, since it didn't tell him what he wanted to hear. Hitler knew very well that killing Jews was wrong, but he wanted to kill them, so he tried to still the voice of conscience which told him that it was wrong to do this."

This view is easy to state but not easy to defend. There are many things that you and I might find shocking and monstrous but which many people in many places and times have considered a positive duty and felt pangs of conscience if they did *not* do them. Hamlet's conscience bothered him at the thought that he had *not* yet killed his uncle; there is no basis whatever for saying that he believed that dispatching his uncle would be wrong. Those who believe in a duty of revenge believe it quite sincerely; if they do not seek vengeance, they suffer pangs of guilt and may even lose their appetites and become ill. Those who tortured others during the Spanish Inquisition thought it their sacred duty to do so and would have felt remiss in their duty if they had not done so. If there is anything that seems certain, it is that many people have believed *sincerely* that certain acts which you and I consider wrong were right, and vice versa. If a person would rather die than receive a blood transfusion, that is pretty good evidence of the sincerity of the individual's belief that transfusions are wrong. People can be as sincere in their belief that such acts as receiving transfusions are wrong as we are in the belief that they are right.

"Well then," the objector may continue, "it's not just any conscience that should be followed, but only an *enlightened* conscience." But what is it that makes a conscience enlightened? The Inquisitors believed that their consciences were enlightened and that those they judged had been remiss in their duties. Most people tend to think that their own consciences are enlightened and that the consciences of those who are opposed to their views are not. Every time you say your conscience is enlightened and someone else's is not, the other person is likely to return the compliment.

In his book *Religion and Science,* Bertrand Russell said of conscience:

The diversity in the deliverances of conscience is what is to be expected when its origin is understood. In early youth, certain classes of acts meet with approval, and others with disapproval; and by the normal process of association, pleasure and discomfort gradually attach themselves to the acts, and not merely to the approval and disapproval respectively produced by them. As time goes on, we may forget all about our early moral training, but we shall still feel uncomfortable about certain kinds of actions, while others will give us a glow of virtue. To introspection, these feelings are mysterious, since we no longer remember the circumstances which originally caused them; and therefore it is natural to attribute them to the voice of God in the heart. But in fact conscience is a product of education, and can be trained to approve or disapprove, in the great majority of mankind, as educators may see fit. While, therefore, it is right to wish to liberate ethics from external moral rules, this can hardly be satisfactorily achieved by means of the notion of "conscience." [1]

Besides the diversity of its promptings because of people's varied upbringings, there is still another problem about conscience: its dictates are usually quite vague. Though the conscience of pacifists tells them that it is wrong to kill, that leaves many questions unanswered. Is it wrong to swat flies or to kill a poisonous snake? Some people, such as the great humanitarian Albert Schweitzer, believed that it is wrong to take any life, human or animal; many Hindus consider all life so sacred that they will not kill a cobra, even though the cobra kills their child. Most pacifists, however, believe only that one should not kill human beings.

But even with regard to human beings there is a considerable vagueness. Should we kill a mass murderer who is likely to strike again? No, most pacifists would say, capital punishment is always wrong. Should we kill in self-defense, when it's the attacker's life or ours? No, most pacifists would say, it is better to be killed than to kill; sacrificing one's life is preferable to killing another person. Should we condone an abortion if the fetus is deformed or has a grave genetic defect? Here pacifists might disagree on when a fetus is to be called a human being, but many would say that it is wrong to have abortions under any circumstances. What if the continued growth of the fetus endangers the life of the mother? In that case there is a problem: either the child's life or the mother's life must be sacrificed; most Catholics believe that the mother's life must be sacrificed when only one can live and it's uncertain which, whereas most others believe that it is the unborn child's life that must be expended. If *all* killing is wrong, and we have no choice but to kill either one person or another, it would seem that there is wrongdoing in this situation no matter which alternative is chosen.

There are still other problems in considering the killing of a human being. What, in fact, is to be construed as killing? Parents who allow their child to

---

[1] Bertrand Russell, *Religion and Science* (New York: Henry Holt & Co., 1935), p. 237.

die of exposure or starvation would probably be said to have killed as surely as if they had poisoned the child. If you fail to contribute money to the relief of starving persons in Africa or Asia, are you killing them? If the death of these persons is the result of failure to help them, and could be prevented by helping them, how is this situation different from other deaths brought about by human agency? And what of human deaths brought about *accidentally* through automobile accidents, for example, when brakes suddenly give out? Or what about the individual who, in walking through the forest, gets caught in a trap set for bears, or the foreigner who, through ignorance of American traffic laws, drives on the wrong side of the road and kills himself? Consider, too, the passer-by who is accidentally shot by someone doing target practice, or the person who dies in the collapse of an apartment building that has been badly constructed in some way, though not on purpose and perhaps not in a way that was foreseeable at the time? If these are to be considered cases of killing, then killing can be caused by negligence or inadvertence, which is sometimes avoidable. Can we rightly be condemned for doing something we couldn't help?

The same vagueness attends almost every moral rule which conscience tells us is inviolable. Consider stealing. Are you stealing if you take something that you think belongs to you but, as it later turns out, does not, or if you think you're stealing someone else's pen but it's really your own? Are you stealing if you enter the apartment of someone who has stolen something from you and take an object of equal value? Are you stealing if someone hands you a five-dollar bill, thinking it to be one dollar, and you say nothing about it? Are you stealing if you underpay your workers, or if you have been given ten cents too much change for a purchase at a drugstore a hundred miles away and fail to return it?

If your conscience tells you that it's wrong to tell a lie, does that mean that you're lying if someone makes a false charge against someone else and you fail to deny it? (Can you lie by omission?) We may agree that lying is not just the telling of an untruth, but *knowingly* doing so: if you sincerely believe a statement to be true when it isn't, you're not lying. But is knowingly telling an untruth always wrong? If you tell a lie under torture, is that wrong? If you lie about the whereabouts of friends to a hoodlum who is about to kill them, is that wrong?

There are many more cases that could be cited of the vagueness of the moral rules that conscience dictates. But the important point is that anyone who says "My conscience tells me never to do *X*" needs to state carefully what the *X* is which his or her inner voice is condemning as wrong.

B. Revelation

Another answer to the question of how we determine what's right and what's wrong is *divine revelation*: God has spoken to human beings, usually through sacred books, and in these God issued certain commands which we should obey. It is such commands, and their accompanying prohibitions, that tell us what is right and what is wrong. Conscience may come in secondarily, as God's way of speaking to us personally; but if conscience goes against revelation, it is revelation that must decide what is truly right or wrong. If the verdict of conscience conflicts with revelation, it is conscience that is mistaken and must be amended.

A number of points can be made against this position, however.

1. There are many alleged revelations: the Old Testament is the revealed truth of the Jews; the Old and New Testaments together, of Christians; the Koran, of Muslims; and so on. The advocates of each religion believe that their own "sacred book" contains the one and only divinely revealed truth. Yet a person cannot consistently believe all of them since each one contradicts the others at some points; if one of them contains the one and only revealed truth, the rest of them are frauds. It seems unlikely that God would issue contradictory commands, saying one thing to one nation or tribe and quite incompatible things to another.

Before relying on revelation, then, we had better be sure which of the alleged revelations is the genuine article. But how are we to make such a choice? This ticklish problem takes us outside the realm of ethics, into metaphysics and epistemology. Yet if the correct criterion for right and wrong is to be found in revelation—*the* one and only true revelation—then we must have a way of discovering which one is the true one. The fact that the proponents of one say they have found the true one proves nothing, since the proponents of others make the same claim for their own.

2. Revelation also runs up against the fact that what the sacred books say is often vague, cryptic, and hard to interpret. Indeed, different people often interpret the same sayings in different ways. Does "Thou shalt not take the name of the Lord in vain" refer to taking oaths, as it was once interpreted, or to uttering curse words, as it is currently interpreted? Does "Thou shalt not kill" mean that we shouldn't kill anyone at all, or only that we shouldn't kill fellow members of our own tribe? (We infer from our knowledge of ancient cultures that it did apply to members of the tribe but not to other tribes; but the commandment itself doesn't qualify the prohibition at all.) If our eternal well-being is to depend on following the commandments correctly, it is extremely important to know exactly how broad their application is supposed to be. Yet even thousands of years later, the interpretation of these commands is still a matter of much controversy.

3. Revelation falters, too, in that few sacred books, not even the Talmud, which tries to cover virtually everything, are complete in what they command. There are whole areas of life which are not covered by the directives. What has revelation to say, for example, on such questions as: Should news reporters be required by law to divulge their sources of information, or should these be privileged? Should psychiatrists be required to testify against their patients in court, or attorneys against their clients? Should the arts be censored by government in any way? Should a physician stop to tend an

injured animal along the highway if there is a 50 percent chance that an injured man requires her attention ten miles away? Should children take care of their elderly parents, or should the State or someone else? For countless day-to-day decisions that we all have to make, revelation offers no moral guidance.

C. Reason

Some contend that what's right and wrong must be discovered not by consulting revelation, real or alleged, but by using the human faculty of reason. The word "reason" in this context, however, is extremely vague: if someone said to you, "I'll tell you how to answer questions about right and wrong—follow reason," would you find this advice useful? What specifically would you be enjoined to do in following it?

In one sense "reason" may mean *reasoning*—that is, drawing conclusions from premises. But reasoning may be perfectly *valid* even if the premises from which we reason are *false*. Thus we might argue. All acts committed in the light of the full moon are right; this act is committed in the light of the full moon; therefore, this act is right. Such reasoning would be perfectly valid, but the premises from which the conclusion is drawn are false, because the first premise (acts committed in the light of the full moon are right) is false.

It is true that human beings "possess reason" in the sense that they have the power to think, to deliberate, to weigh alternatives, and to choose. It is probably true that no other animal has this capacity. But it is not clear in what way it is "reason" that tells us what are the moral premises from which we are to draw conclusions. Is it reason that tells you to save your children when their lives are endangered? Is it reason that dictates that it is wrong to inflict needless pain on other human beings? Is it reason that tells you to be kind to animals as well as to people? Is it reason that leads you to believe that you should be grateful to your parents if they have been good to you? Surely none of these acts would be so much as thought of if we did not have certain benevolent *inclinations*. But inclinations, of course, are not the same as reason.

The advice to "follow reason" might be construed to mean something different—that we should always follow that course of actions for which the *best reasons* can be found. Very few people would wish to deny this. The questions arise, however, as to what the best reasons are and how we tell what they are. Many people would say that if someone has injured you, you have an excellent reason for injuring him or her in return; others would say that this is not a good reason at all. If "reason" is to be the arbiter in such a controversy, what specifically is it supposed to do, and how does it help to solve the problem of whether such retaliation is morally justified?

In the study of ethics we constantly employ our faculty of reason, as well

---

as reasoning. We shall consider reasoned defenses of and attacks on a variety of positions concerning what is good and bad, right and wrong. Without the faculty of reason we could not engage in such ethical controversy. Indeed, ethics is *reasoned* discourse about morality, not just unsupported pronouncements. Whether such controversy helps to solve the problems set forth, we shall have to judge for ourselves after we see what can be said for and against the various ethical views that will be scrutinized.

2. RELATIVISM AND ETHICS

That there is a problem in trying to find a standard of right and wrong action is shown by the fact that so many people at so many different times and places have believed very different actions, and kinds of actions, to be right and wrong. Americans generally believe that stealing is wrong and that being caught and punished for stealing is all right, provided the punishment isn't too severe; but the Spartan youth who allowed the fox to gnaw at his vital organs rather than be caught for stealing the animal reflected the then current belief that it wasn't stealing itself but being caught at it that was to be condemned. The Dobu tribesmen of New Guinea believe that growing your own vegetables is honorable, but stealing your neighbor's vegetables is still more honorable. The ancient Romans, unlike the Christians, had more respect for honor than for pity; they could be forgiving if they could gain some advantage from being so, but otherwise they had very little feeling for victims, such as prisoners of war. Courage was prized, but mercy and humility were not. Some desert tribes think it a sacred obligation, when one of their number has been killed or captured by an opposing tribe, to capture and kill a member of that tribe, even if the person caught did not participate in committing the deed. In most eras slavery was an accepted institution; today almost everyone considers it wrong.

All these are examples of *cultural relativism:* in one culture people believe one kind of action to be right, which people in another culture believe to be wrong. In our century anthropologists have been at work all over the world uncovering more and more such differences in what people consider right or wrong. Of course, there are similarities too. No tribe or nation could permit indiscriminate killing among members of the tribe, or there would soon be no tribe left. In almost every culture it is considered the duty of the mother to take care of her children, and every culture prohibits incestuous relations within families. But differences abound even in areas where there seems to be a great deal of agreement: adultery is generally condemned, but not always; and, as we have seen, homosexuality and prostitution are often considered wrong but in many cultures are considered simply matters of taste, not of right and wrong at all. So if cultural relativism is interpreted as the view that moral rules differ from culture to culture, it is surely true. Anthropologists aren't just dreaming it up.

However, there are not only moral *rules* but moral *principles,* and it is far from clear that anthropologists have shown that cultural relativism of principles is true. It is important to keep the distinction in mind.

A *rule* is a "do" or "don't" attached to a certain kind of act: for example, we generally try to follow the rules "Don't steal," and "Do be honest in your dealings with others." No one rule covers every situation that might arise. If morality consists only of a set of rules, we do not yet have any instruction as to what to do in cases that are not covered by the rules. The Ten Commandments consist largely of a set of don'ts, but there are many kinds of behavior that they do not cover at all—for example, whether you should attempt to restore a stray dog to its owner.

A moral *principle,* by contrast, attempts to guide us in all our actions; it is meant to cover not only certain specific types of action but all our actions throughout life. For example, if we were guided by the precept "Always act in such a way as to promote your own long-term advantage," that would be a moral principle (an egoistic one). A nonegoistic one could be, "Always act so that as many people as possible in your group will survive and prosper." We might not know in every case just what to do, because we wouldn't always know what course of action would lead to our own (or our group's) survival or prosperity. Still, we would have a principle, something that would be a guide in all our actions, not just actions of a limited kind.

If we were to ask what moral principles most primitive tribes accept, the question would be difficult to answer because they don't appear to have the concept of a moral principle at all. All they have is a certain set of rules, and no more. Whether there is one principle or several principles from which these rules flow, and which serve to unify the rules and explain why they are held, is a question tribal members may not even understand. We may be able to *infer* some general principle, however, which would explain why they have the rules they do. Many rules—for example, that individuals may not kill within the tribe but may kill those who threaten members of the tribe—can be explained by the principle that people should do whatever contributes most to the survival of their own tribe. Some rules may be explained on the principle that people should be made as happy as possible, though most tribal rules don't seem to have that much regard for individual happiness.

It would seem from what has been said that there is some cultural relativism of principles as well as of rules, though not nearly as much. The evidence is not clear, since most tribes aren't aware of principles as such, and anthropologists have not really addressed themselves to the issue of moral principles. They exhibit for us a wide diversity of moral rules but nothing that would show that the rules are selected on the basis of some underlying principle.

Cultural relativism of rules, however, remains. The differences in moral rules among people living in various times and places seem to be so enormous that reconciling them may seem an impossible task. Yet as far as ethical disagreement is concerned, the case is not as hopeless as it may seem:

1. Sometimes what people believe to be right or wrong depends on beliefs which they have about *non-moral* matters, and without the underlying beliefs on other matters, such as facts of nature and the realm of the supernatural, the differences in beliefs about morality would not exist. In the ancient Greek drama by Sophocles, Oedipus the king was exiled at the age of eighty from his native city of Thebes, although he was blind and nearly helpless and had committed no crime that (we believe) deserved such a punishment. Were the Greeks so morally insensitive that they were happy to consign him to this fate? No, but they had a belief about the gods that we do not share. They believed that if they did not expel Oedipus, the gods would take vengeance on the entire city, and they reasoned that it was better to lose one man than an entire city. Is this so different from what we would have done if *we* had the same belief about the gods that they did?

Some South Sea tribesmen used to kill their parents when the parents reached the age of sixty. We might consider this a cruel, barbaric practice, showing great moral insensitivity. But they believed, as we do not, that the dead will enter the next world in the same body with which they made their exit from this world; if that body is too old, wrinkled, and arthritic, and they have to pass their entire time in the next world with such a body, it would make living quite unpleasant for them. Thus, pushing the old into the next world, while their bodies are still healthy or at least manageable, would be doing them a service. Once you view the moral practice in the light of this belief, the practice becomes more understandable. You might approve the same practice yourself if you had the same beliefs about the next world as they.

Today we are appalled at the tortures inflicted during the Spanish Inquisition, to name just one historical episode. Were the people of that time a bunch of sadists and murderers? There was probably a sprinkling of such individuals in that age as in every other, particularly among those who rose to positions of power. But there were many who legislated such tortures, and others who were appointed to inflict them, who did it with sincere reluctance, and who couldn't stand the smell of charred bodies or even the sight of blood. Why, then, did they do it? Because they believed that the persons who were punished in this way were either infidels or adherents of religious beliefs which would bar them from entrance into heaven and condemn them to an eternity of hellfire. Just possibly persons under torture or while being burned at the stake would recant and "accept the truth," thereby saving their souls; even if they didn't, then other people, seeing such things happen, would think twice before consigning themselves to such a fate. After all, what would a few hours in the flames be compared with a never-ending eternity of such torture? By torturing them now, the Inquisitors might be saving their souls forever; even if there was just a 1 percent chance of last-minute conversion, wouldn't the risk be worthwhile? Even a thousand hours, one hour each for a thousand people, spent burning at the stake would still be nothing compared with a torture that would never end.

If we say merely, "They believed torture was morally acceptable, and we don't," we wouldn't be describing the situation correctly. It would be more accurate to say, "They believed that a little torture was better than eternal torture." And wouldn't we believe that too? Is our *moral* belief all that different from theirs, or isn't it rather the theological basis of their moral belief on which we and they would disagree? There are many such cases in which the disagreement is not on moral beliefs themselves but on theological or other non-moral beliefs.

Today many people disagree about the wrongness of abortion. At least part of this disagreement is the result of differing non-moral beliefs. Many Christians believe that from the moment of conception an immortal soul is brought into existence and that therefore to destroy the fetus is to commit murder, just as much as if an adult human being were to be killed. Others believe, not that an immortal soul has come into existence, but at least that a human being exists, either from the moment of conception or from the time (about ninety days after conception) that the bodily organs have formed. Opinion differs considerably on all these matters, and much of the difference of opinion about the legitimacy of abortion rests on such disagreements about when the fetus can be classified properly as a human being. The parties may all agree that killing a human being is wrong, but they disagree on when or under what circumstances something is to be called a human being. (There are still further differences, of course, such as whether the fetus should be aborted if the life of the mother is endangered, or whether abortion is proper when the mother doesn't want the baby, has been a victim of rape, or has a hereditary disease which is fairly certain to make the baby badly crippled or diseased.)

2. Besides disputes about non-moral matters, many seeming disagreements in moral belief are the result of adaptation to differing environmental conditions. Certain Eskimo tribes have traditionally killed their parents when they reached an advanced age, not for theological reasons but in response to environmental conditions. For survival they must travel a distance of 600 miles between their summer grazing grounds for the reindeer and where they can hole up for the winter without freezing to death. The trip is long and arduous, and if they stopped to tend those who are sick or infirm, none would arrive at their destination and all would die. Those shoved through a hole in the ice would have died anyway, if the others had stopped to take care of them and been overtaken by winter along the way. We are lucky not to face such a situation, but they have had to do so. Might we not favor such a practice also, or a similar one, if we were in their situation? Surely, they would not have engaged in such a practice if they lived under less harsh climatic conditions.

Many moral rules are adapted to the specific conditions of place, and if we were in that place we might live by them too. It's not that certain people believe X is right and we believe X is wrong, but that *both* believe that X in circumstances C_1 is right and that X in circumstances C_2 is wrong. It is surely misleading to speak of this as "moral disagreement."

3. Circumstances vary over time as well as place, and moral disagreements

may seem to arise because the times are different. Among the ancient He-
brews, as well as many other tribes, it was considered immoral to eat pork.
At that time, slow cooking over an even fire was difficult to achieve, and
people who ate pork that was not well cooked could contract trichinosis, a
worm infestation of the animal. From the point of view of health the rule
was doubtless a very sensible one. Whether such a rule is useful today, when
meat can be well cooked, as well as refrigerated, is very doubtful. But many
rules of conduct are preserved for centuries through a kind of moral inertia.
They continue to be observed even though the occasion of their usefulness
has passed, giving rise to differences in moral practice that would not have
occurred but for the resistance to changes in moral habits.

4. It is also true that many moral disagreements are more apparent than
real because what is at issue is not a matter of morality at all. With many
primitive tribes it is questionable whether the customs they practice should
be placed in the category of morality. Some practices are prohibited by the
chief, the tribal elders, or the medicine man, and members may be punished
for flouting them, but this is not the same as saying that the people believe
the practices are morally wrong. Some of them may not have been thought
of for generations and may be nothing but long-held taboos—the kind of
thing that just isn't done. Among the Dobu tribesmen of New Guinea, if a
man wants a wife, he must go to another tribe to obtain her, and the other
tribe is supposed to put up a fuss about it, resisting his attempts by force if
necessary. Apparently things have been done this way from time immemo-
rial; the practice doesn't exactly make for intertribal harmony, but it persists.
Are the tribesmen acting from a *moral* rule—one practiced out of moral conviction, with a deep sense of guilt if the practice is not maintained? It is
difficult to say, but the question is at least worth considering.

5. Sometimes people *would* reach agreement if they were aware of all the
relevant *facts* or *information* concerning the issue at hand. People constantly
make moral judgments on the basis of incomplete information. "I saw him
run down that poor woman! He ought to be killed!" someone exclaims; but
the observer's opinion might change if he became aware that that person was
a careful driver whose brakes suddenly failed to operate at the top of the hill.
Or, one person thinks that in a custody suit the wife should keep the children, because she sees what the wife has endured in the unpleasant marriage;
but she may not see what the husband has endured (perhaps because she
hasn't seen him around much), nor how much he too really cares for the
children—facts which could change her opinion if she knew them. Or again,
a mother condemns her daughter for her rebelliousness but fails to see what
she herself has done, by way of failing to understand her daughter, to bring
about that very rebelliousness; if she really tried to step back from the situation and view it as a psychiatrist would, she might well understand better
and not continue to be so accusatory of her daughter (and the daughter might
do the same in relation to her mother). Aren't most moral judgments that
people make, especially about the behavior of others, based on incomplete

information concerning the facts? Some people, indeed, remain ignorant needlessly. Sometimes they even *want* to remain ignorant, so that they can keep on airing their favorite prejudices just as they always have. ("My mind is made up—don't disturb me with facts.") If all moral judgments were made on the basis of complete knowledge of the situation being judged, how much moral disagreement would there be left? Doubtless there would be some; but it would be ever so much less than it is now.

6. After all the relevant facts are known to all parties, however, there is still room for considerable disagreement. Two judges can be acquainted with the very same set of facts concerning a case and yet arrive at different verdicts: one will favor sentencing the defendant and the other will favor handing down a suspended sentence. Some of this disagreement may occur because people do not imaginatively place themselves in the position of the individuals involved. Though acquainted with all the relevant facts of the case, a man may empathize with a husband's problems, because he is a husband himself, and ignore those of the wife because they "mean less" to him ("What's housework anyway?") and he attaches less weight to them. Similarly, most tribes that enslave others seem to have very little sense of the "inferior tribe" as human beings like themselves. Intellectually they may know that their slaves suffer, but they do not imaginatively identify with the slaves.

Sometimes the inability to identify imaginatively with others has to do with differing *temperaments*. Some people are workaholics and are inclined to believe that everyone should behave likewise, whereas others think that everyone should take life easy, even if that means doing without certain things. One person instantly empathizes with whoever is in trouble or in need, giving even sacrificially in order to be of help, whereas another person believes that people should be self-sufficient and help themselves. The very same set of facts will appear *in a different light* to persons of opposing temperaments. These temperamental differences may be the greatest stumbling blocks of all to agreement in ethics.

Such differences can be transmitted to an entire culture. In our own culture it is a widespread, but far from unanimous, view that it is wrong to mistreat animals, at least those animals (such as nonpoisonous snakes) which are no threat to ourselves. We may not think it wrong to kill them for food, but to treat them with wanton or purposeless cruelty would be viewed with disapproval by most persons in Western civilization. But it is not so in many other parts of the world: among most African and Amazonian tribes, for example, just about anything you do to an animal is considered all right. The same attitude usually doesn't apply to pets, but then it isn't customary for the tribes to adopt animals as pets. Animals are—just animals. If they were thought of as experiencing enjoyment or pain, they might be treated differently, but apparently they are seldom thought of in this way.

It is a matter of opinion, however, whether this difference is a temperamental-cultural one or whether it is rooted in a stark fact of their situation—

that human life is lived there near the subsistence level, and when animals compete with human beings for scarce resources, or when out of sheer necessity they have to be eaten to sustain life, it is simply not possible for people to have the luxury of conceiving of animals only as pets. If the latter is true, then the difference is less one of temperament than one of the basic conditions of existence, and the beliefs of tribal members (or the lack thereof) about mistreating animals might disappear if their situation changed. If you or I had to live solely by hunting, and if we had to do without many meals (or even starve to death) by sparing animals, is it likely that we would spare them?

So much, then, for cultural relativism. But we must now be careful to distinguish it from *ethical relativism*. Like cultural relativism, it can be held (or rejected) with respect to both rules and principles.

Ethical relativism of rules holds that there is no one set of rules that is right for all persons and groups under all conditions. What really is right (not just believed to be right) in one tribe or culture is not necessarily so in another; there is no set of rules that correctly prescribes right conduct for all human beings. Stated thus, ethical relativism appears to be obviously true; surely the rules by which we live have to be adapted to differing situations. In a desert tribe, wasting even a small amount of water is quite rightly considered a grave offense, since lives are lost if the rule is violated, whereas in a second tribe that enjoys a plentiful supply of water, there is no point in having such a rule. Countless examples could be cited to show how a rule is desirable in one situation but not in another.

If ethical relativism seems unquestionably true on the level of rules, is it also true on the level of principles? Relativism of principles is at least more debatable. Both the tribes in the example just given may operate on the principle that the survival of the maximum number of persons within the tribe is desirable. The same principle then yields two different rules in the two different situations; there is relativism of rules, but not of principles. Judging by their behavior, however, some tribes do not seem to operate on this principle. Some tribes, for example, may operate on the principle of "survival of the strongest," so that it wouldn't matter how many died as long as the strongest survived. Thus it would *seem* that not all rules can be placed under the banner of a single principle. Yet it is difficult to say for certain because, as we have already seen, moral principles are seldom made explicit, unless we are consciously undertaking to study ethics.

But that is just what we are doing in this book. Ethics is first and foremost an examination of moral principles, and of rules only insofar as they exemplify those principles. Numerous principles have been advanced in the history of ethics from the ancient Greeks to the present. Our task will be to state them, to analyze them, and to evaluate them. That task will occupy the greater part of this book. Before turning to it, however, we must explore one other important preliminary issue.

3. WHY ACT MORALLY?

The question sometimes arises: Granted that some acts are right and others wrong, why should I act rightly and avoid doing wrong? Practically everybody would believe it wrong to shortchange a blind news vendor by telling him he was being paid with a five-dollar, rather than a one-dollar, bill. Even those who do such things would usually admit that such an act was wrong: cheating anyone is bad enough, but taking advantage of a blind man who is trying to eke out a meager livelihood is even worse. Now what if someone said, "Why shouldn't I do it anyway? What happens if I do?"

A. Divine Will

1. One answer that has often been given to this question is, "Because God will punish me if I do wrong and reward me if I do right." If the statement is true, then it *pays* you to do the right thing in the sense that it is in your long-term interest to do it. The law may not catch you, but God watches always. You may be able to get by with cheating in this world, but there is always the next world, where punishment will be exacted.

Our concern is with ethics, not with the truth or falsity of religious belief. Clearly answers like "God will reward me in heaven" will not appeal to those who do not believe either in God or in heaven. And, of course, there are many different kinds of belief in God—Christianity, Judaism, Islam (not to mention polytheism, the belief in many gods)—each of which has a somewhat different set of moral commands. For this answer to be convincing, therefore, you must not only believe in a God and eternal life but also be convinced that your particular belief in God and an afterlife is the true one. (A Christian God, after all, is not likely to reward a person for believing in Mohammed and keeping his commandments.)

It should be noted that the answer, "God will reward me if I do," is a perfectly *egoistic* one, appealing to the believer's *self-interest:* you shouldn't do this because *you* will be punished if you do. This is not necessarily an objection to the answer, but at least we should be clear what kind of an answer it is. If you do certain things in the here and now that you don't particularly enjoy doing but do anyway out of hope of reward or fear of punishment, you are really no different from workers who collect time-and-a-half at the end of the day. Most religions appeal very strongly to self-interest. "Great will be your reward in heaven" and "Cast thy bread upon the waters and it will come back to thee in many days" are typical scriptural quotations which appeal to the perfectly self-interested concerns of the believer.

It is also worth noting that if this is your only reason for behaving morally, you need not even believe that the God who issues these commands is *good*. If there was a devil or evil spirit who controlled the world and had the power to reward obedience to his commands to rob and kill, and to punish disobedience, you could give the same reason for obeying him as before: "He will reward me if I do, and punish me if I don't." If you lived in a nation governed by a cruel and tyrannical dictator, you could say the same thing; you might not *like* the dictator—might even think he was evil and corrupt— but if he had absolute power, he would still be obeyed out of hope of reward or fear of punishment.

"Do it because I'll punish you if you don't" is an appeal to *power*, not to *goodness*. If the only reason to obey commands is belief in an all-powerful being who punishes disobedience, obedience stems not from the goodness, nobility, or worthwhileness of the commands but from the power of the one who issues them. You may not revere or love him, but obey only out of hope (of reward) and fear (of punishment). You may cringe before him, even while wishing you could get out from under the threatened punishments. In fact, if you believe the commands to be immoral ones, like Hitler's command to destroy the Jews or the Old Testament God's commands to destroy the "wicked" Canaanites (who appear to have committed no crime except that they inhabited the land the Israelites wanted for themselves), then it might be more noble, more courageous, to resist the commands and defy the being who issued them. If I am told that I must do certain things, and when I ask why, I am told that if I don't I'll be punished, I have still not been given a *reason* for obeying them. I have only been threatened. One might well react as English philosopher John Stuart Mill did to such a command:

> When I am told that I must believe this, and at the same time call this being by the names which express and affirm the highest human moral- ity, I say in plain terms that I will not. Whatever power such a being may have over me, there is one thing which he shall not do: he shall not compel me to worship him. I will call no being good, who is not what I mean when I apply that epithet to my fellow creatures; and if such a being can sentence me to hell for not so calling him, to hell I will go.[2]

There is another way of looking at divine commands, however. One may say, not "Do this because God commands it," but "God commands it be- cause it is good." That means that God has a reason for commanding what he does—the reason being that what he commands is good. If the commands were obeyed, for example, people might be better or happier or the world might be a better place.

There is one thing to be noticed about this reasoning, however. If God has a reason for commanding *X,* and you can understand what that reason is, then you could do *X* without God's commanding it; if you thought *X* was good, you might do it anyway, just for that reason, whether God com- manded it or not. Thus your reason for doing it would really be independent of God's command: you would do *X* because *you* thought *X* was a good

[2]John Stuart Mill, *An Examination of Sir William Hamilton's Philosophy* (Boston: Spencer, 1865), p. 131.

thing to do, not because God commanded that it be done. God would be a kind of *enforcer* rather than a *creator* of the right, but X would be right anyway, whether God commanded it or not.

2. It should be added, however, that not all religiously based ethics appeal to divine rewards and punishments. You may obey what you believe to be God's command, not out of fear or a craving for rewards, but from the belief that God should be loved and adored.

People may, of course, do many things out of love or adoration, and sometimes such love and adoration are misplaced. A wife may obey her husband because she loves and adores him, but that doesn't guarantee that what he tells her to do is good for her or for anybody else; he may, in fact, be a stupid fool or a conniving con-artist. We shouldn't love just anybody, and we shouldn't obey just anybody's commands. A woman may love her husband, but that doesn't mean she should obey him when he tells her to sell her body on the streets to augment the family income. Love, devotion, adoration, and esteem can all be misplaced; we must first make sure that the person we love is worth loving and that if we do what that person says, the commands are themselves good. The same applies to God; we may obey God's commands out of love or adoration, but only if it has first been determined that the God we believe in is *worthy* of love or adoration. The ancient god Moloch, who commanded all parents to throw their firstborn children into the flames to prove how much they adored him, hardly seems worthy of adoration. If someone did obey this god out of love and not out of fear, would that make the obedience better?

3. One other religious justification for behaving morally deserves comment. One may say, "I should do what God commands, not because I expect rewards for it, nor even because I love him and obey out of love, but simply because he is the author of my being." As one Christian moralist has noted: "God made us and all the world. Because of that He has an absolute claim on our obedience. We do not exist in our own right, but only as His creatures, who ought therefore to do and be what He desires."[3]

As the argument stands, however, it is flawed. Let us assume that there is a God who created us and that this same being laid down certain moral commandments for us to follow. We can still ask *why* we ought to obey these commands. "God created us; therefore we should do as God commands" is not a complete argument. It requires the additional premise that creatures ought to obey their creator. And whether they should or should not depends, it seems, on what kind of creator it is. What if creatures were created by a malevolent creator who brought them into being only to make them suffer or to play about with them, as children sometimes do with sparrows on a string? Should the commands of such a creator be obeyed, just because he is the source of human life? The fact that a being has the *power* to create and *uses* that power doesn't tell us whether either he or his use of power is *good*,

[3] R. C. Mortimer, *Christian Ethics* (New York: Rinehart, 1950), p. 7.

or whether he is *entitled* to unquestioning obedience. Such a being would have to be good as well as powerful in order to *deserve* obedience. The situation is similar to that of a child who asks her parents, "Why do you tell me to go panhandling in the streets?" and the parents reply, "You are our child, we brought you into this world, and this makes it your duty to do whatever we tell you to do." Such an answer clearly is not sufficient. The child is not questioning the fact that the parents brought her into the world (and are in that sense the authors of her being); rather, she is asking what right they have to issue such a command. The command may be a bad one or a good one, whether they are the authors of her being or not.

B. Morality Pays

The belief in a divine power need not be the only reason for behaving morally. It might be said that, quite apart from any belief in God, there is a perfectly good reason for behaving morally in this world, namely, that in the long run it *pays* to do so. Honesty may be the best policy simply because it pays to be an honest person. Being helpful to others may be advantageous, because, when you need help, others may reciprocate. Also, driving carefully may be a good idea because the life you save may be your own. Believing in God because it brings peace of mind is still another appeal to a personal reward, not in another life, but in this one. In all these cases, you may do certain things which are claimed to be good simply because of the personal profit gained from doing so.

It is possible that leading a good life *does* pay, and that misdeeds do come home to you in one way or another, perhaps when you least expect it. If you deal honestly with other people, they will trust you; if you do not, at least in the long run, they will not care to have dealings with you. If you are kind to others, they are surely more likely to be kind in return. If you pay your debts, you are more likely to be able to borrow again when you need to. If you try to cheat others, you may get by with it for a time but sooner or later it will come out, and even before it does you may live in dread that the deed *will* come out. The idea is that in some way good deeds are rewarded (eventually) and bad deeds come back to haunt you, if only in the lowered opinion others will have of you.

Surely this is a sensible reason, one that anyone can understand, for behaving morally: in the long run, at least, it is personally beneficial to behave morally toward others.

In a variation of this position, the Greek philosopher Plato (427–347 B.C.), in his classic work *The Republic,* alleged that the reasons just given for being moral aren't very good ones. If you deal honestly with others, you will *more probably* be dealt with honestly in turn, but not necessarily and not always; someone may use your honesty to defraud you. Besides, the opinion of others and public esteem are unreliable and changeable. Your neighbors may respect you for things they shouldn't respect you for, or feel contemptuous of you for being good to those who will never be good to you in return. Most important of all, they may respect you for qualities which they *mistakenly* think you have, or hate you for offenses you have never actually committed. Besides, if they approve of you today, they may disapprove tomorrow, though nothing has changed. Personal happiness should not be based on the shifting opinions of others; it should be anchored in what you *are* rather than on what other people *think* you are. Self-esteem, the realization of personal self-worth, should be abiding, something that cannot be touched even by the unfavorable opinion of others, or even their vicious behavior.

Imagine, says Plato, a supremely good man who is thought by others to be immoral and who is hated and ostracized by his former friends for his imagined crimes; and imagine, on the other hand, the blackest villain, a paragon of evil, who is so clever at hiding his villainy that he is thought by those around him to be the best of men and is followed by praise and adulation wherever he goes. If the rewards of goodness were to be found in the esteem of others, then the good man who was mistakenly thought to be bad would be extremely unhappy, and the bad man who was thought to be good would be extremely happy. And yet, contends Plato, this is not the case. The good man, even under the conditions described, is the happy man, because of the awareness he has of his own goodness and the emotional satisfaction that goes with it, and the bad man is unhappy even though others mistakenly call him virtuous. There is no need of heavenly rewards to make the good person happy; he is happy already, now, just because he is good. Happiness has to do with an inner state of the soul, and it can not occur unless one is at peace with oneself and knows one's own worth.

While rejecting the notion that morality pays in public esteem, Plato nevertheless accepts the idea that it pays in another way—in a feeling of inner happiness. His view has seemed strange, even ridiculously false, to many people, who consider it a heroic attempt that fails. But there are two distinguishable positions in it: (1) that being moral is sufficient for being happy; and (2) that being moral is necessary for being happy. Let us examine each separately.

That morality is *sufficient* for happiness is such a strong statement that thousands of plainly evident facts from daily life seem to refute it. Whatever actions we have in mind in calling someone moral, isn't it plain that many people are extremely moral but also extremely unhappy? Some people may be honest to a fault, utterly reliable in their dealings with others, generous, good as parents, and yet be quite unhappy. Some can be happy at least to a degree in spite of ill health or constant pain, but wouldn't they at least be happier if they didn't have constant pain? Yet pain and disease fall to the lot of moral and immoral persons alike. Similarly, some people may be as moral as you please, but loved ones may die and leave them alone in the world, or circumstances may make them unable to earn a decent living, so that life is a constant struggle to have enough to eat; seeing one's family in want would usually make one unhappy. Again, some may be victims of severe mental disorders, so that they are in a constant state of depression or unbearable tension: life may hold no joy, no matter how noble such people are. There are so many things that can make individuals unhappy that it seems highly implausible to say that all a person needs is to be moral and happiness will be assured.

That morality is *necessary* for happiness—that is, that people who are immoral cannot truly be happy—seems more plausible. Consider Plato's example of the man who desires great power over the lives of other people. Having been abused by others, he thinks that once he has attained the pinnacle of power, he will be the happiest of men, issuing orders and having them instantly obeyed, being able at last to bend others to his will as he has been made to do others' will. The power luster is, says Pluto, the most evil of men, enslaving and killing others if it suits his fancy. Once he fights his way to the top and reaches his life's goal, the happiness that he thought he would gain still eludes him. The impulse to power grows and feeds on itself: it is never satisfied. The ruler of a small kingdom is not satisfied until he has a large one; and the ruler of a large one is not satisfied until he rules the world. In addition, the life of the power luster becomes insecure, for he has made too many enemies; he has killed others, and their friends are now equally determined to kill him. He never knows who of his seeming friends may be an enemy; he must surround himself with guards to protect his life, and even among these he hardly knows whom he can trust. At the beginning he thought that power and only power would gratify his desires, but in the end it has only made him miserable.

As far as the tyrant is concerned—whether it be a Caligula, a Nero, or a Stalin—Plato's account is extremely plausible. And the same applies in general to those persons that most people would describe as extremely evil. If we want to find happy people, we will not try to find them among dictators or among habitual criminals. Such persons seldom experience inner peace: they struggle, plot, scheme, and kill, never secure of life and limb, never sure that others won't succeed in doing to them what they do to others, never knowing whom they can trust, full of hostility, aggression, and fear.

But such people represent only the most extreme cases. Aren't there many immoral people who are nevertheless happy, particularly if their immorality is not known to others, or even if it is? Aren't many immoral persons happier than many very moral ones? Plato himself uses the example of "the ring of Gyges," which enables a person to become invisible simply by turning the ring on his finger. A man could thus steal items from stores and get away with countless other things, because no one could discover his crimes. Plato contends that such a person would be unhappy, because of the knowledge that what he is doing is immoral. But is this really true? Is unhappiness so invariably consequent upon believing that one is acting wrongly? Aren't there lots of people who do evil things (even without being invisible) who aren't disturbed a bit as long as they get away with them? Let us consider an assortment of cases.

1. Novels often tell of people who do good deeds for which, at the moment, they do not seem to be rewarded. A man helps many who are down-and-out with money, advice, and valuable time. The recipients seem to be unappreciative. Then, years later when the giver least expects it and most needs it, one of the many persons he has helped turns up suddenly and helps him, as occurs, for example, in Charles Dickens's *Great Expectations*. Such stories are very warm and consoling. But what about those thousands of cases in which the giver does *not* run into one of the recipients of his beneficence, either at a critical juncture or at any other time? Perhaps the recipient dies too soon, never hears of the benefactor's trouble, or is delayed en route to helping and arrives too late. These situations go largely unrecorded, for they do not appeal to our sense of the romantic and our deep-seated wish that things turn out in accordance with our desires.

2. There are two brothers, one hard-working and the other indolent. The older brother cannot have an education because he earns money for his younger brother's education. The younger brother, however, never makes use of his schooling; he is always getting into scrapes, and the older brother constantly must get him out of jail and pay his bills. The younger brother counts on the older one's helping him out and so gets into trouble without worry: "George always helps me in a pinch." A large portion of the older brother's income goes to the support of the younger brother, whom the State will not support as long as there is a member of his family capable of doing so. The older brother's generosity means a lifelong sacrifice from which he gains nothing, not even personal satisfaction. He could have used the money himself to much better advantage, yet he feels that while he is able to, he should take care of his own flesh and blood, even if his benevolence means that he himself will have no savings in his old age. The older brother has been unlucky in love and lives a comparatively unhappy life in spite of his benevolence, while the younger, much more attractive to the opposite sex, has a much better time in life in spite of his laziness, shiftlessness, and constant dependence on the good will of his older brother. It would certainly seem that the one is more moral and the other is happier.

3. There is a young bank clerk who decides, quite correctly, that she can embezzle $50,000 without her identity ever being known. She fears that she will be underpaid all her life if she doesn't embezzle, that life is slipping by without her ever enjoying the good things of this world; she wants to help her crippled sister by buying a suburban house for the two of them, surrounding herself with books, stereo hi-fi set, and various *objets d'art,* and spending a pleasant life, combining culture with sociability; she never wants to commit a similar act again. She does just what she wanted to do—buys a house, invests the remainder of the money wisely so as to enjoy a continued

income from it, takes care of her sister, and lives happily ever after. She doesn't worry about detection because she has arranged things so that no blame can fall on her; anyway she doesn't have a worrisome disposition and is not one to dwell on past misdeeds. The degree of happiness she now possesses would not have been possible had she not committed the immoral act. Apparently, crime sometimes does pay, sometimes very handsomely. Only a small portion of the crimes committed are ever detected. Nor do those who commit crimes always suffer pangs of conscience or fear of detection; they often suffer far less than the unfortunates who fill our mental hospitals and who generally have committed no crimes at all.

4. There is a person of great sensitivity and strong humanitarian feelings who is extremely conscientious in fulfilling what he believes to be his duties to others. Realizing poignantly the state of the human race and the hopelessness of one person's trying to change it, he leads a life that is not nearly as happy as that of the comparatively thick-skinned individual who is less intelligent and less sensitive to the sufferings of other human beings. The latter person may stumble through life seeing only a small part of it, not worrying about evils he cannot understand, happier by far than the first man.

5. In a courtroom the defendant is a psychopath who is extremely clever at inventing stories about her imaginary troubles. She can weep and lie brazenly but with such emotion that the jury is moved to tears and exonerates her from the perfectly true charge against her. There is also a falsely charged man who is genuinely innocent but is not so clever at putting on an act. His story, every word of it true, fails to impress the jury, and he is convicted, even though he is innocent. That justice always triumphs is an aphorism as absurd as it is often quoted. It is a law of human nature that for every aphorism there is an equally true opposite one—in this case, "There ain't no justice."

6. Perhaps the most dramatic illustration of all of evil triumphant is war. Millions of people are killed in wars, and most certainly do not deserve their fate. They are innocent victims of the rapacity of some individuals and of the fact that war, though undesirable to most nations, is nevertheless blundered into time and again. Nothing seems more certain than that those who suffer in war are, for the most part, innocent victims and that they pay with their lives for misdeeds which are not their own.

To one who reflects on the state of the world and the people in it, there seems to be no due proportion between human merit and human happiness. It is difficult to avoid agreeing with the remark by eighteenth-century English novelist Henry Fielding: "There are a set of religious, or rather moral writers, who teach that virtue is the certain road to happiness, and vice to misery, in this world. A very wholesome and comfortable doctrine, and to which we have but one objection, namely, that it is not true."[4]

---

[4]Henry Fielding, *Tom Jones* (New York: Modern Library, n.d.), p. 672.

C. The "Fair Play" Argument

Suppose that you are playing a game and that when you play it you agree on certain rules. You cannot change the rules in a pinch just because the game is going against you. You play the game to win, but to win you must abide by the rules. To the extent that you cheat, you are not playing the game at all. If you are interested enough to play, you probably have an interest in continuing the game. Yet the game can be continued only if you play by the rules.

None of us is forced to play baseball or billiards, but the game of life is one which we all have to play in one way or another. Nor can we play it alone, for we are surrounded by other people who also must play the game. What, then, is the best means of playing it—best for all of us? As long as we are all together on this planet, isn't it better for all of us to find some arrangement whereby we can live together in such a way that we can each pursue as many of our own interests as possible yet not prevent others from pursuing theirs? To live in that way, we all have to stick to certain rules. Those rules—requiring us to consider the safety and welfare of others and prohibiting us from aggression against them—will operate to our *mutual* advantage; that is why we should obey them.

Consider two groups of people, of any size you please. In the first group the people live by certain rules: they refrain from killing, stealing, and committing other acts of aggression against one another. In the second group the people do not wish to be tied down by any rules; they commit acts of aggression against one another with no punishment other than retaliations from the injured party or friends of the injured if they happen to catch the aggressor. The first group, then, accepts certain limitations on the behavior of each member, whereas the second does not. In the second group the result is that people are much worse off than they would otherwise have been: their livelihoods and their very lives are in constant danger, because at any moment they may be victimized by other people without recourse to law. Surely the members of the first group are much better off than those of the second. Thus to live in the first group and behave according to its rules will be in the interest of every member of the group.

At least, to behave according to the rules will be to the interest of every member of the group on *most* occasions. For example, as a member of the group it may be in your interest to be honest, for by being honest you gain the respect of others and they will trust you in personal relations and in business enterprises. It also may be in your interest to refrain from aggression against others, for if you damage others, you will probably be caught and imprisoned, and besides you will have few, if any, real friends. Nevertheless, it may not be in your personal interest to live by the rules on *all* occasions. Suppose, for example, that law enforcement is lax or that you can bribe the appropriate officials; you can thus get away with stealing from others and be quite sure of not being prosecuted for your actions. Why, then, shouldn't you steal? The answer is that you shouldn't commit such a crime, not because it wouldn't work to your advantage (for in this case it would), but because it works against the interests of the group as a whole, that is, "the general interest."

Once we realize that a group in which members obey certain rules is better than one in which they do not, we have a reason for behaving in accordance with these rules even in situations where doing so does not benefit us personally.

> Moralities are systems of principles whose acceptance by everyone as overruling the dictates of self-interest is the interest of everyone alike, though following the rules of a morality is not of course identical with following self-interest. If it were, there could be no conflict between a morality and self-interest and no point in having rules overriding self-interest. . . . The answer to the question "Why be moral?" is therefore as follows. We should be moral because being moral is following rules designed to overrule self-interest whenever it is in the interest of everyone alike that everyone should set aside his interest.[5]

Of course, not everyone will agree on what the rules should be. Most people may agree that certain books or films should be banned, but you may not go along with this prohibition, not just because you believe such material is harmless for you to read or see, but because you believe it does no real harm to others either. So why should you obey such rules? Some of the rules imposed on everyone may, in fact, be harmful—pointless regulations, taxes paid which line the pockets of politicians and bureaucrats but don't achieve the purposes for which they were designed, rules with whose purpose you disagree. Even with regard to the rules that are generally beneficial, what if you want to "resign from society" and not be subject to them? For example, what if you don't want to help others, as the rules say you sometimes must, and you don't want any help from others either? Why should you be bound by rules to which you never agreed and of which you disapprove? Just because most people say you should help others so that you may be helped by them when you need it, why should you do so when you don't want their help and don't even agree with the majority that everyone should be required to help others?

D. "Because It Is Right"

Perhaps we have been on the wrong track all along: many would say that if you assent to the view that a certain action is right, the question of whether or not it works to your advantage is simply irrelevant. If you know that

---

[5] Kurt Baier, *The Moral Point of View* (Ithaca, N.Y.: Cornell University Press, 1958), p. 314. Reprinted by permission of the publisher.

doing the right thing works to your advantage, then this will make you *want* to do it, but it will not have provided a reason why you *should* do it. An immoral act may sometimes work to your advantage too, and that fact would surely not be claimed to give you a reason for doing it.

The question of why I should do something is a request for a *reason;* and the reason why you should do something, many would say, is plain to see. Indeed, you have already admitted it in saying that it's the right thing to do. It's right to give the correct change to the blind news vendor, and *that*—not the fact (if it is a fact) that you will benefit from it—is the reason why you should do it. Perhaps you will be rewarded in heaven, perhaps not; perhaps your act will pay off for you in future benefits, and perhaps it won't; these considerations are irrelevant as reasons for why you ought to do it. The only reason that *is* relevant is simply the fact that it's the right thing to do. Nothing more is needed, and nothing more should be desired.

Certain contemporary moralists have contended that Plato was simply sidetracked on this issue:

> [*The Republic's*] main argument is an elaborate attempt, continued to the end of the book, to show in detail that if we look below the surface and consider what just actions really consist in and also the nature of the soul, and to a minor degree, the nature of the world in which we have to act, it will become obvious, in spite of appearances to the contrary, that it is by acting justly that we shall really gain or become happy.[6]

Plato's opponents, the Sophists, held that being moral doesn't always pay and that when it doesn't pay we have no reason to be moral. Plato argued against them that being moral always pays. But, says Prichard, what he should have questioned is the entire notion of the relation between moral activity and a payoff: an act may be moral and not pay, and it may pay and not be moral. The important issue is not whether an action pays but *whether it is right;* and if it is, one then has the only good reason for doing it, whether it pays or not.

A person may insist there is no reason for doing the right thing unless it pays or is to his or her advantage: "Tell me why I should do *X,* when doing *X* is not to my advantage." Yet the only reason that person will *accept* for doing *X* is that doing *X* is, in some way, to his or her advantage. It is, of course, impossible to give a self-interested reason for doing something that is contrary to self-interest. That would be a contradiction in terms, and in asking for it the individual is making a self-contradictory request. It is no wonder, in that case, that the request cannot be fulfilled. A seeker after square circles would be similarly disappointed.

Why does a reason in ethics have to be a self-interested one any more than in other areas? "Why did you work so long and hard to discover a vaccine

[6]H. A. Prichard, "Duty and Interest," in *Readings in Ethical Theory,* eds. Wilfrid Sellars and John Hospers (Englewood Cliffs, N.J.: Prentice-Hall, 1970), p. 691.

for this disease?" a scientist might be asked. "Because I enjoyed it" and "Because I saw the need for a cure and wanted to spare human beings further agony" would both be accepted as reasons, the one self-interested and the other not. When someone asks, "Why should I do the right thing?" why are only self-interested reasons such as "Because I think I'll get something out of it" acceptable? According to the view we are considering, the shoe should be on the other foot: such a so-called reason is not a reason at all; it only supplies the person with a motive. The *reason* why a person should do something is simply that it's the right thing to do. *X's* being the right thing to do is by itself the only reason you need for doing X.

EXERCISES

1. Which of the following would you look upon as a matter of *moral* concern? Why? (See John Hartland-Swann, *An Analysis of Morals,* Chapter 3.)
   a. Cheating at cards
   b. Cheating on examinations
   c. Jaywalking
   d. Keeping your car washed
   e. Keeping your car in good running condition
   f. Stopping your car in a traffic jam simply for the fun of it and letting the cars behind you try to get past
   g. Eating healthful foods
   h. Doing two hours' work for eight hours' pay
   i. Getting drunk every couple of days
   j. Cheating on your spouse
   k. Beating your dog
   l. Eating cake when your neighbor lacks bread
   m. Letting your garbage accumulate, so that the neighborhood becomes infested with rats
2. What conclusions, if any, do you think the Gospels lead you to adopt on questions of (a) Obeying the law? (b) Divorce? (c) Racial prejudice? (d) Democracy versus totalitarianism? (e) Laissez-faire capitalism versus planned economy? (f) Class distinctions on the basis of blood or wealth?
3. The following practices are usually considered wrong in our society. Do you think you would still consider them wrong if you were living in the social or physical conditions in which they are not considered wrong? Can you think of any general moral principle of which the two rules (in one society, "It's wrong to do this"; in another society "It's right to do this") can be considered applications?
   a. Mass executions without a trial or with only the pretense of one in a country undergoing a revolution.
   b. Tormenting trapped or captured birds and animals for sport.
   c. Eating human flesh, assuming that it will give one strength and virility on the next hunting expedition.
   d. Polygamy, in a country in which (owing to casualties in war) the women outnumber the men by five to one.
   e. Using torture to extract military secrets from prisoners of war.

f. Refusing to eat the flesh of cattle from religious conviction, even when refusal means starvation.

g. Killing those who do not belong to the master race.

h. The moral code of some indigent students, especially with regard to affluent roommates: When I have money, I should share what I have with my roommate; and when he or she has money, it should be shared with me.

i. Stealing, provided that those stolen from are personal enemies, have done me an ill turn, or belong to a class hostile to the people (e.g. the bourgeoisie), but of course not from relatives and friends.

4. Which side of the following dispute are you inclined to agree with? Why?

A: People are always violating in practice what they preach. They believe something is wrong, and yet they do it.

B: I doubt this. People usually do what they *think* is right—at least at the time they do it they have convinced themselves that it is right. No, the trouble is not so much that they act contrary to their beliefs as that they aren't careful enough in arriving at their moral beliefs in the first place.

5. If there was a God who issued moral commands but who had no power to enforce them, would his lack of power make any difference to your view of divine commands as a reason or incentive for being moral? Explain. Suppose, instead, that there was a God who was omnipotent but either evil or morally indifferent. Would that make a difference? Why?

6. The following is an old parlor game, designed to bring out differences in moral opinions based on differences in temperament or situation. After you have read the story presented, give your answers to the question asked at the end, and then compare yours with those of others.

Adam and Eve have been married six years. They live on an island. Adam says one morning, "I'll be back tonight."

There is a man, John, whom Eve has been interested in for some time; he lives across the river. Eve waits until Adam has gone, and then goes to visit John. She tells him of her attraction to him. They go to bed together.

When she leaves John's house, the river has risen. She starts to cross the bridge on foot but encounters a murderer there. She flees and escapes him.

She then goes to the ferry to cross the river. The charge for crossing is ten dollars, and she hasn't got her purse with her.

She runs back to John. She explains the situation and asks for ten dollars from him, to ferry across the river. He refuses, saying, "I did not ask you to come back. Leave me alone."

Paul, who loves her but whom she does not love, also lives close by. She runs to his house, and explains the situation to him. He also refuses her the ten dollars, saying, "I loved you; you chose someone else; now don't trouble me."

She pleads with the boatman to let her cross free of charge. The boatman refuses, saying, "I cannot make any exceptions. If everyone who asked for free passage received it, I would go broke. I cannot let you cross without the payment of ten dollars."

Desperate, she now tries to run across the bridge. Halfway across, the murderer attacks her and kills her.

Rate each of the six characters—Adam, Eve, the murderer, John (Eve's lover), Paul (her rejected suitor), and the boatman—in order of their moral turpitude (in your opinion). #1 is the one you consider, on the basis of the evidence given in the story, the morally *worst* person; #2 is the *second worst*; and so on.

7. In the following passage Aleksandr Solzhenitsyn, the Russian exile and novelist, describes the relation between old people and children in a Siberian labor camp:

> The mess hall at this camp was a plank lean-to not adequate for the Siberian winter. The gruel and the bread ration had to be carried about 150 yards in the cold from the kitchen to the dugout. For the elderly invalids this was a dangerous and difficult operation. They pushed their bread ration far down inside their shirt and gripped their mess tin with freezing hands. But suddenly, with diabolical speed, two or three kids would attack from the side. They knocked one old man to the ground, six hands frisked him all over, and they made off like a whirlwind. His bread ration had been pilfered, his gruel spilled, his empty mess tin lay there on the ground, and the old man struggled to get to his knees. . . . And the weaker their victim, the more merciless were the kids. They openly tore the bread ration from the hands of a very weak old man. The old man wept and implored them to give it back to him: "I am dying of starvation." "So you're going to kick the bucket soon anyway—what's the difference?" And the kids once decided to attack the invalids in the cold, empty building in front of the kitchen where there was always a mob of people. The gang would hurl their victim to the ground, sit on his hands, his legs, and his head, search his pockets, take his makhorka and his money, and then disappear.
>
>   . . .
>
> [The boys'] chief amusement . . . was the slingshot: the index and middle fingers of the hand parted in a "V" sign—like agile, butting horns. But they were not for "butting." They were for gouging. Because they were aimed always at the eyes. This had been borrowed from the adult thieves and indicated a seriously meant threat: "I'll gouge out your eyes!" And among the kids, too, this was a favorite game: all of a sudden, like a snake's head, a "slingshot" rises out of nowhere in front of an old man's eyes, and the fingers move steadily toward the eyes. They are going to put them out. The old man recoils. He is pushed in the chest just a bit, and another kid has already knelt on the ground right behind his legs—and the old man falls backward, his head banging the ground, accompanied by the gay laughter of the kids. . . . Old man T. nourished burning hatred for them. . . . Whenever he succeeded in creeping up on a kid on the sly, he would hurl him to the ground and press down on the boy's chest with his knees until he could hear the ribs crack—but he didn't break them. He would let the kid up at that point. T. used to say that the kid wouldn't survive and that there wasn't a physician who could diagnose what was wrong with him. And by this means T. sent several kids to the next world before they themselves beat him to death. (From *The Gulag Archipelago 1918–1956: An Experiment in Literary Investigation I–II,* Volume One, by Aleksandr I. Solzhenitsyn, pp. 458, 461–62. Copyright © 1973 by Aleksandr I. Solzhenitsyn. English translation copyright © 1973, 1974 by Harper & Row, Publishers, Inc. Reprinted by permission of the publisher.)

Considering the hard work, the bitter cold, the starvation rations, and the rule of brute force at the camps ("Be strong or die"), would you consider the behavior of the old men toward the children, and the children toward the old men, to be right, wrong, or partially justified? How would you behave in circumstances such as Solzhenitsyn describes?

SELECTED READINGS

The Nature of Morality

Baier, Kurt. *The Moral Point of View: A Rational Basis of Ethics.* Ithaca, N.Y.: Cornell University Press, 1958.

Broad, C. D. *Five Types of Ethical Theory* (1935).* New York: Humanities Press, 1960.

Dewey, John. *Human Nature and Conduct.* New York: Modern Library, 1930.

Hartland-Swann, John. *An Analysis of Morals.* London: Allen & Unwin, 1960.

Jarvis, Judith. "In Defense of Moral Absolutes." *The Journal of Philosophy* 55 (1958): 1043–53.

Mackie, J. L. *Ethics.* Baltimore: Penguin Books, 1977.

Mandelbaum, Maurice. *The Phenomenology of Moral Experience.* Chicago: Free Press, 1958.

Nielsen, Kai. "On Moral Truth." *Studies in Moral Philosophy: American Philosophical Quarterly Monograph No. 1* (1968), pp. 9–25.

Nowell-Smith, Patrick. *Ethics.* Baltimore: Pelican Books, 1954.

Rashdall, Hastings. *Theory of Good and Evil.* 2nd ed. 2 vols. New York: Oxford University Press, 1924.

Sidgwick, Henry. *The Methods of Ethics.* 7th ed. New York: Macmillan, 1874.

Taylor, Richard. *Good and Evil.* New York: Macmillan, 1970.

Relativism

Bambrough, Renford. "A Proof of the Objectivity of Morals." *The American Journal of Jurisprudence* 14 (1969): 37.

Brandt, Richard B. *Ethical Theory: The Problems of Normative and Critical Ethics.* Englewood Cliffs, N.J.: Prentice-Hall, 1959. See Chapter 11.

Edel, Abraham. *Ethical Judgement: The Use of Science in Ethics.* New York: Free Press, 1955.

Ginsberg, Morris. *On the Diversity of Morals.* New York: Macmillan, 1956.

Ladd, John, ed. *Ethical Relativism.* Belmont, Calif.: Wadsworth Publishing, 1973.

———. *The Structure of a Moral Code.* Cambridge, Mass.: Harvard University Press, 1957.

Nielsen, Kai. "Ethical Relativism and the Facts of Cultural Relativity." *Social Research* 33 (1966): 531–51.

Stace, Walter T. *The Concept of Morals.* New York: Macmillan, 1937.

Sumner, W. G. *Folkways.* Boston: Ginn & Company, 1907.

Wellman, Carl. "The Ethical Implications of Cultural Relativity." *Journal of Philosophy* 60 (1963): 169–84.

Westermarck, Edvard A. *Ethical Relativity.* New York: Harcourt Brace Jovanovich, 1932.

*Dates in parentheses are dates of first publication.

Histories of Ethics

Bambrough, Renford. *An Outline of the History of Ethics.* 6th ed. London: Macmillan, 1937.
MacIntyre, Alasdair. *A Short History of Ethics.* New York: Macmillan, 1966.
Sidgwick, Henry. *A History of Ethics.* London: Macmillan, 1886.
Warnock, Mary. *Ethics Since 1900.* London: Oxford University Press, 1960.

Anthologies of Ethics

Brandt, Richard B., ed. *Value and Obligation.* New York: Harcourt Brace Jovanovich, 1962.
Feinberg, Joel, ed. *Moral Concepts.* New York: Oxford University Press, 1970.
————, and Henry West, eds. *Moral Philosophy: Classic Texts and Contemporary Problems.* Belmont, Calif. Dickenson Publishing, 1977.
Frankena, William, and John Granrose, eds. *Introductory Readings in Ethics.* Englewood Cliffs, N.J.: Prentice-Hall, 1974.
Johnson, Oliver A., ed. *Ethics: Selections from Classical and Contemporary Writers.* 4th ed. New York: Holt, Rinehart and Winston, 1978.
Melden, Abraham I., ed. *Ethical Theories.* Englewood Cliffs, N.J.: Prentice-Hall, 1955.
Munitz, Milton K., ed. *A Modern Introduction to Ethics.* New York: Free Press, 1958.
Oldenquist, Andrew, ed. *Moral Philosophy: Text and Readings.* Boston: Houghton Mifflin, 1978.
Rachels, James, ed. *Understanding Moral Philosophy.* Belmont, Calif.: Dickenson Publishing, 1976.
Sellars, Wilfrid, and John Hospers, eds. *Readings in Ethical Theory.* Englewood Cliffs, N.J.: Prentice-Hall, 1970.
Singer, Marcus G., ed. *Morals and Values: Readings in Theoretical and Practical Ethics.* New York: Charles Scribner's Sons, 1977.
Taylor, Paul W., ed. *Problems of Moral Philosophy.* Belmont, Calif.: Dickenson Publishing, 1974.

2

The Good

How does the idea of good arise?

Imagine that the world was entirely uninhabited by any form of life. It could be ugly or beautiful—that is, the kind of world that would be *called* beautiful or ugly by sentient beings if there were any; as long as no one was there to respond to it, it would make no difference what qualities it had. We could not speak of one state of the world as better than any other, for there would be no one to whom any state could appear better or worse than any other.

But now suppose that there are inhabitants. Let us assume that they are intelligent beings, with the ability to think and to reason. Let us assume further, as one writer has, that these beings have the following characteristics:

> [They] can perceive what is going on around them, distinguish between true and false, and make various inferences; but they are machine-like in that nothing *matters* to them, nothing *makes any difference* as far as their *needs and purposes* are concerned, because they *have* no needs or purposes, they do not care about anything. If it is raining, they observe that it is raining, but they seek no shelter, for they have no interest in being dry. If it is bitterly cold, then again they note this fact, but make no attempt to warm themselves because they care not whether they are warm or cold. If one of these beings observes another moving with great speed and force toward itself, it infers that a collision is impending, but makes no attempt to step aside, because it has no purpose that would be frustrated by such a collision. It has not even the desire to perpetuate its own existence, because it has no desires whatever.[1]

[1] Richard Taylor, *Good and Evil* (New York: Macmillan, 1970), p. 124. Reprinted by permission of The Macmillan Co.

35

In other words, nothing would be good or bad for them, because nothing would either promote or threaten their interests. Nothing would matter to them: they would be incapable of *caring* about anything, including their own continued existence. They would have intellects but no feelings or wills. A world populated by such beings would be just as much a world without good or evil as the world which had no inhabitants at all.

But now consider a world populated by beings such as ourselves, with not only minds but needs, desires, and interests. They would be beings who *care* what happens, whose desires can be fulfilled or frustrated, whose interests can be promoted or threatened by what they do and by what happens to them. In such a world the concepts of good and bad would be applicable. Even if there were only *one* such inhabitant, there would be situations that could be good for that person, such as finding water to quench thirst or shelter to keep out the cold. "Good" and "bad" have meaning only in the context of beings who have interests which can be furthered or threatened by what happens.

But in what does such goodness or badness consist? What things are good or bad in relation to such beings, and why?

1. INTRINSIC VERSUS INSTRUMENTAL GOOD

"If you want to retain your health, you should eat nutritious foods." "If you want to get along with other people, you shouldn't keep on hurting their feelings." "If you want people to trust you, you should tell them the truth." Such statements are constantly made in advising other people; and each of them is *conditional,* or dependent, on what it is that we want.

But isn't it better to want some things than others? Aren't there some things we can think of as good, desirable, worthwhile, worth trying to achieve? If so, we would do well to know what they are, so that by our actions we can pursue those things.

Most of the time, when we speak of something being good or bad, we mean good or bad as a *means* to something else. Going to a dentist when you have a toothache is good, because you will be relieved of the pain and also cured of the condition that caused it. Concentrating on your courses is good, because you will get more out of them and will also get better grades. Eating nutritious food is good, because you will stay healthier and live longer.

But is everything we consider good merely a means to something else? If we do *A* as a means to achieve end *B,* we presumably attach some value to *B;* if we use *B,* in turn, as a means to a further end *C,* we consider *C* in some way worth achieving or pursuing. But does the series keep on going forever? Is everything done as a means to something beyond itself? Aren't there things we consider good in themselves, that is, good because of what they *are* and not because of what they lead to?

Suppose you go to see a physician (*A*) in order to cure some ailment (*B*);

you do *A* merely as a means to *B*. Suppose the ailment is cured, and the goal of restoration of health has been achieved. But now suppose someone asks you, "What's so great about health?" That is a rather peculiar question, because people generally take the value of health for granted. But if someone asked it, what would you say? You might say, "Health is a good thing to have, just for its own sake." On the other hand, if pushed, you might say, "In general, healthier people are happier people—at least, people can't be as happy if they are in constant pain or anxious about their health. But if you ask me why I value health, I'd say it's because I want to be happy and live a long, happy life, and if I'm in poor health I'm not so likely to be able to do that."

But the questioner might then pursue the issue and ask, "Why do you want to be happy? What's so great about happiness?" What would you answer in that case? The question sounds strange, not just because it is one that is rarely raised, but because the answer to it—that being happy is worthwhile for its own sake—is generally taken for granted. Other things may be worthwhile as a *means* to it, but being happy is worthwhile as an *end,* as a goal to be cherished and pursued, not because it leads to something else but for its own sake alone. This is what philosophers mean when they say that something is *intrinsically good:* it is good or worthwhile in and for itself, not merely as a means to something else. It can, indeed, turn out to *be* a means to something else. For example, a happy person is likely to be a more productive person, easier for others to live with, and so on; in the chain of causes and effects everything is probably at some time or other a means to something else, but the happiness enjoyed is nevertheless considered good or worthwhile in itself. It would be worth having even if it had no consequences beyond itself. By contrast, that which *leads to* intrinsic good is considered *instrumentally good.*

Not everyone agrees on what things, if any, are intrinsically good, and that is the subject of this chapter. We might say, for example, that *life,* or just the process of living, is itself intrinsically good. But we would then be faced with the question: Is *any* kind of life desirable for its own sake? If someone has been given three months to live and that three months is filled with intense pain and depression, is such a life, or what remains of it, still intrinsically good, just because that individual is alive and not dead? If you were to become blind, deaf, and dumb, would you still consider it worthwhile to live, just because your heart was still beating? You might say, "Yes, because I can still think: my brain is still functioning." But what if you were a living vegetable, alive but aware of nothing, or living on intravenous nourishment, hopelessly withered and deformed? What if you could not control any of your bodily movements or were unconscious for life, aware of nothing? Almost everyone would agree that at least *one* of these conditions, and perhaps more (people wouldn't always agree on which), would be a condition under which life was not worth living, and it would be preferable to be dead. In other words, it's not just life—continued heartbeat and cerebral activity—that is worthwhile; what is worthwhile has something to do with the *quality* of life. Being alive may be a *necessary condition* for whatever is good for its own sake, but just being alive, no matter under what conditions, hardly seems desirable for its own sake.

What kind of life is it, then, that is worth living? Here we may get an array of different but overlapping answers: "a pleasant life"; "a happy life"; "a virtuous life"; "a life in which most of one's desires are satisfied"; "a life full of knowledge and wisdom"; "a life filled with a variety of rewarding experiences." We might consider not only our own lives, but the lives of everyone else to be worthwhile if they contained those things. But we must be careful to distinguish what we consider worthwhile *instrumentally* from what we consider worthwhile *intrinsically* (for its own sake): some people, for example, consider knowledge to be worthwhile only if it leads to happiness, whereas others consider knowledge to be worthwhile for its own sake alone, that is, even if it does not lead to happiness.

At any rate, there is a considerable consensus that only *states of consciousness* can be intrinsically good and that without consciousness there could be nothing of value (either good or bad) at all. Let's go back to the world described at the beginning—the one uninhabited by any conscious being who can have an experience of it. In fact, let's consider, as contemporary British philosopher G. E. Moore has done, two such worlds: "Let us imagine one world exceedingly beautiful. Imagine it as beautiful as you can . . . and then imagine the ugliest world you can possibly conceive. Imagine it simply as one heap of filth."[2] Which of these two worlds is better and thus should come into existence? We are tempted to say that the first world would be more worth creating, because beautiful scenes usually *cause* people to experience pleasure more than "heaps of filth" do. But if neither world is ever going to be experienced by anyone, could it matter whether either one was created? Still, you yourself, in contemplating these two imaginary worlds, may experience pleasure in *imagining* the first world; so there is some experience of it after all, at least in the imagination of the would-be creator. Moreover, *calling* it a "heap of filth" is not merely a description of it but a reaction as well; the same can be said for the word "beautiful." It is, then, almost impossible to keep out a reference to our *experience* of such a world even in the act of describing it as existing unexperienced. However, if we rigidly exclude the pleasure in contemplating the one world and the displeasure in the other, and keep in mind that no one will ever experience either, then it becomes clear that as far as value goes, there is nothing to choose between them.

2. HEDONISTIC THEORIES

Hedonism (from the Greek *hedone,* meaning "pleasure") is a theory about what is intrinsically good. The hedonist says that pleasure, enjoyment, satisfaction, or happiness is good in itself. The terms the hedonist uses to de-

[2] G. E. Moore, *Principia Ethica* (Cambridge: Cambridge University Press, 1903), p. 8.

scribe what is intrinsically good are not the same, and we need to examine the differences. Let us begin with pleasure. The thesis of hedonism is divided into two parts: (1) that *all* pleasure (and enjoyment, etc.) is intrinsically good, or good for its own sake; and (2) that *nothing but* pleasure is intrinsically good. The second is much more controversial, so let us begin with the first.

It is important to keep clear exactly what the hedonist is saying in maintaining that all pleasure is intrinsically good. Let us, then, look at several misunderstandings.

A. Pleasure as Intrinsic Good

1. It is easy to jump from "All pleasure is intrinsically good" to "All pleasure is good." The hedonist would assert the first but strongly deny the second. Many things other than pleasure may be good; even pain may be good, but only instrumentally. If your foot is in the fire and you feel pain, the pain may cause you to remove your foot from the fire, and this is a good thing because if you didn't your foot might burn off without your knowing it. If you feel pain and go to a doctor, the condition causing the pain may be corrected. Pain may then be good as a means, particularly when the end cannot be achieved in any other way. But to aim at pain as an *end*—to inflict pain or enjoy the pain of others if doing so served no worthwhile end or purpose—would be, according to the hedonist, a monstrous evil. Even masochists don't really consider pain an end: the self-infliction of various kinds of punishment, resulting in pain, is for them a means to achieve their peculiar kind of enjoyment. A strange kind of enjoyment, we may say, but it is still the enjoyment they're after, and the infliction of pain is a means to that end. Masochists don't enjoy run-of-the-mill pains like headaches and toothaches any more than others do.

2. Nor does the hedonist say that pleasure is the only thing we should desire. We should desire many things, such as peace and liberty, but the reason is that living in peace is (as a rule) more pleasant than living in war, and being free is more pleasant than being in bondage (since people cannot fulfill most of their desires when they are enslaved). Enhanced enjoyment of life is the reason that liberty and peace are desirable, but they *are* extremely desirable—as means.

It is not even true that liberty and peace are never desirable as ends: activities of various kinds can be conducive to these, and such activities are thus means to achieve peace as an end. But peace is not the *ultimate* end; the enjoyment of living is, and peace is desirable because it is on the whole conducive to this end.

3. We should also not confuse pleasure with the *sources* of pleasure. Pleasure is good for its own sake, but in different people pleasure may have many different sources. Some people enjoy reading books, some don't; some people enjoy going to ball games, while others, don't; some people are very gregarious and enjoy the constant company of others, and some enjoy many

hours of each day spent alone. Thus the sources of pleasure vary enormously from person to person. This point is obvious enough, but people tend to get it confused by saying such things as "Your pleasure is in family life; mine is in the freedom that comes with nonattachment." What is really being said here is that the *sources* of pleasure or enjoyment in the two persons are different. As to the sources of pleasure, one man's meat is another man's poison. One person finds pleasure in *X,* another in *Y;* but the pleasure isn't the same as *X* or *Y,* nor need the pleasure be different (though it probably is to some degree) just because the sources of it are different. Confusion of pleasure with the sources of pleasure exists not only among college undergraduates but among numerous writers:

> Let us imagine a moment of the most intense pleasure we have ever known. . . . Now imagine that moment of experience continued without change and without further activity for the whole span of a normal lifetime. If it is pleasure and pleasure alone that gives to experience its character of intrinsic goodness, then such a life span should, as a whole, have the greatest intrinsic good imaginable in any life span. But, I think, few of us will agree that it has. We would gladly exchange some of the pleasure content for a little variety, for an opportunity for genuine activity.[3]

The author contradicts himself here: he speaks of intense pleasure but then says that continued pleasure would no longer be pleasurable. In that case, however, it wouldn't be pleasure any more: Pleasure has to be pleasurable! What the author should be saying is that when something is a continuous *source* of pleasure, we grow tired of it so that it is no longer the source of pleasure it once was; our sources of pleasure change with time, as we grow tired or bored and want some other source of pleasure. This is very different from saying that pleasure itself becomes other than pleasurable, which is self-contradictory. The hedonist would gladly exchange one continuous, unchanging source of pleasure for a variety of sources, precisely because the most pleasure in the long run is obtainable from the variety.

4. Another kind of misunderstanding of hedonism is to be found in the following quotation: "A man is not morally good because his career has been marked by extraordinary cases of unexpected good luck, nor is the life of the lower animals to be reckoned morally good because it may contain a vast number of pleasant moments."[4]

The misunderstanding here is the confusion of *intrinsic* goodness with *moral* goodness. It is true that a person's moral goodness is not estimated by how many pleasant moments he or she has experienced; but according to the hedonist, moral goodness is always *instrumental.* Why are some things considered morally good, others bad? Why are some considered virtues, others

[3] A. C. Garnett, "Intrinsic Good," in *Value: A Cooperative Inquiry,* ed. Ray Lepley (New York: Columbia University Press, 1949), p. 85.
[4] A. E. Taylor, *The Problem of Conduct* (New York: Macmillan, 1901), p. 327.

vices? A life of constant indulgence of appetites tends to make people (and others around them) miserable in the long run; addiction to drugs produces pain and early death; and on an interpersonal level, people are happier if they deal peacefully and honestly with one another. Like going to the dentist, being honest, courageous, or productive isn't always the most pleasant at the time, but the sum of human happiness (both one's own and that of others) tends to increase if all people practice those virtues, and human misery certainly increases if they don't.

For example, if people are to have a decent standard of living, they must work. Work, therefore, is instrumentally good: people would certainly have an unhappy life, and indeed they wouldn't live long, if they didn't work at all. But it doesn't follow that work is therefore intrinsically good. *Enjoyable* work is, not because it is work, but because it is enjoyable. But work without enjoyment would have no point if it did not lead to more intrinsic good later: if you work and save, you have security and the hope of an enjoyable and more disturbance-free old age. Work is important as a means to an end, but unenjoyable work—drudgery—has nothing to recommend it if it does not contribute to a worthwhile end. And what makes an end worthwhile in the final analysis is its conduciveness to happiness. "Why do you work so hard?" An acceptable answer would be, "Because it's necessary to make my business succeed" (assuming that a successful business, in turn, leads to happiness). "Because I enjoy it" would also be acceptable—if enjoying it means that it's intrinsically worthwhile, not merely productive of good effects. But if it is *neither* enjoyable in itself *nor* conducive to enjoyment later, the hedonist would ask, "What's the point?"

5. Still another misunderstanding of hedonism is that people should be *seeking* pleasure constantly. On the contrary, they should seek many things—knowledge, beauty, anything that will lead to an increase of happiness. To be seeking happiness constantly and consciously is usually not the best way to get it. This is the *hedonistic paradox:* "Pleasure to be got must be forgot." But it isn't really a paradox, just a plain fact of life. Some things are best obtained by forgetting about them, at least most of the time. In a poem by Maurice Maeterlinck the bluebird of happiness turned black when it was touched. *How* pleasure is to be maximized in any person's life varies considerably from individual to individual; but most conscious pleasure seekers become rather frantic in the search, tense and apprehensive as they go partying or bar hopping, lest they miss out on some enjoyable experience. If you go about your daily work, not thinking too much about yourself *or* about being happy but losing yourself instead in work and play, and in people and causes outside yourself, you will wake up and realize one day that you are quite happy—much happier than the conscious happiness seekers who find the achievement of happiness elusive because they are always thinking about it. Saying that something is intrinsically good is not at all the same as saying that it must be pursued constantly. If it comes, by whatever route, it is intrinsically good.

B. The Quantification of Pleasures

British philosopher Jeremy Bentham (1748–1832) believed that pleasure and pain were the sole measures of intrinsic goodness. But if they are to be compared, it should be possible to measure them. Bentham held that (1) between two pleasures which are otherwise equal, the more intense is to be preferred to the less intense; (2) between two pleasures otherwise the same, the one of longer duration is to be prefered to the one of shorter duration (and between two pains, of course, the one of shorter duration is to be preferred); (3) between a pleasure certain to occur and one with a probability of occuring of less than 100 percent, the first is to be preferred to the second; (4) between a pleasure that is likely to lead to more pleasure ("has greater fecundity"), and an equally great pleasure that is likely to lead to pain, the first is to be preferred to the second, for obvious instrumental reasons; and (5) between two equal pleasures, one "pure" (unmixed with pain) and the second not, the first is to be preferred.

Bentham also believed that of two pleasures otherwise equal, the one with greater *propinquity* (nearness in space or time) is to be preferred to the more distant one. But it is likely that the criterion of propinquity can be reduced to that of probability (3 above), for promised pleasures in the distant future are less likely to occur than those that will occur immediately. If the probability of the two were the same, many persons wouldn't mind waiting (and having the pleasure of anticipation besides). Most persons would probably rather receive a promised gift today than a year hence because the promisor may be dead or have changed his mind, the recipient might no longer care for it as much, and so on.

In presenting these criteria Bentham was attempting to lay the foundation for a "calculus of pleasures," which would enable people to measure pleasures precisely against one another. Quite certainly, however, no such attempt has ever been successful. Of all the criteria, duration is the only one that can be calculated with any precision. Intensity doesn't seem to be similarly measurable. We can say, not that this pleasure was 15 times as intense as that one, but only (sometimes) that it lasted 15 times as long. If I told you with a straight face that I enjoyed my bacon and eggs this morning exactly 2.7 times as much as I enjoyed them yesterday morning, you would be understandably skeptical, perhaps asking me, "How do you know it isn't 2.6?" In comparing pleasures we have to give up exact quantification (sometimes called a "cardinal value") for a more indefinite measurement (sometimes called an "ordinal value"): "I enjoy chocolate ice cream much more than I do vanilla; and I enjoy vanilla so much more than I do cherry"—and so on. I want a new stereo more than I want a new rug, but I can't tell you exactly how much more; nevertheless, in the absence of such knowledge I can still get the stereo. As one author has put it: "A man knows that some pains are terrible, some slight; that some pleasures are great, some small; although he cannot measure either the pleasure or the pains."[5]

[5] W. T. Stace, *The Concept of Morals* (New York: Macmillan, 1937), p. 132.

It was only the total *quantity* of pleasures—as measured by intensity, duration, and the like—that, according to Bentham, determined the amount of intrinsic good. Bentham's follower, John Stuart Mill (1806–1873), muddied the waters somewhat by adding to the notion of quantity of pleasures the idea of *quality* of pleasures. How is one to determine, as between two pleasures (e.g., playing darts vs. artistic creativity), which is of higher quality? Mill answered:

> If I am asked what I mean by difference of quality in pleasures, or what makes one pleasure more valuable than another merely as a pleasure, except its being greater in amount, there is but one possible answer. Of two pleasures, if there be one to which all or almost all *who have experience of* both give a decided preference, irrespective of any feeling of moral obligation to prefer it, that is the more desirable pleasure. If one of the two is, by those who are completely acquainted with both, placed so far above the other that they prefer it, even though knowing it to be attended with a greater amount of discontent, and would not resign it for any quantity of the other pleasure which their nature is capable of, we are justified in ascribing to the preferred enjoyment a superiority in quality, so far outweighing quantity as to render it, in comparison, of small account.[6]

According to many of Mill's critics, however, this qualitative principle is a blunder: if one experience is less pleasurable than another, and yet intrinsically better, it would seem as if it is not just pleasure but something else that is being smuggled in here—some criterion of worth other than pleasure itself. How can the lesser pleasure yet be intrinsically better, from a hedonistic point of view? If Mill was trying to defend certain pleasures (such as that of artistic creativity) against others (such as cheating people successfully), he could have done so for *instrumental* reasons, without saying that the lesser pleasure, in addition to being instrumentally preferable, is also *intrinsically* better. By sticking to his guns on the qualitative principle, he may have been forced to abandon his hedonism, that is, the view that pleasure is the only criterion of intrinsic good, for, as Richard Taylor notes:

> To say that pleasure is the supreme good, and the only thing good for its own sake, that it is the only thing that lends value to anything else that is good, and then to declare that some pleasures are intrinsically *better* than others, is quite obviously to appeal to some standard of goodness other than pleasure, some standard by means of which even pleasures can be evaluated as better and worse. . . . It would be no worse to declare that some yardsticks are longer than others.[7]

[6] John Stuart Mill, *Utilitarianism* (1863), Chapter 2.
[7] R. Taylor, *Good and Evil*, pp. 93–94. Reprinted by permission of The Macmillan Co.

C. Pleasure and Happiness

Already in speaking of pleasure or enjoyment, we have mentioned happiness. But surely the two are not the same. A happy person isn't the same as a pleasant person or even a pleased person. I can have lots of pleasures and not be happy, though it would be strange to say that I am happy without ever having any pleasures. Many people think ill of pleasure yet value happiness. What is the difference between pleasure and happiness?

The word "pleasure" itself covers more than one kind of thing. In the physiological sense, "pleasure," refers to what we feel at certain places in our bodies, such as the feeling we have in being tickled or stroked, or in experiencing sexual orgasm. But there is a much more general sense of the word "pleasure," which refers to just being *pleased* by something: listening to music, reading a book, or walking in the woods can cause me pleasure in this sense. Here we don't ask, "Where did you feel the pleasure?" Pleasure in the second sense is a general state of consciousness. We may say "we felt it all over," but that wouldn't exactly be correct. When walking along the beach or looking at the starry sky, for example, I wouldn't say I felt the pleasure in every part of my body, including my big toe. Rather, I had a kind of experience that didn't produce feelings in any particular place. It is this second sense, the *general hedonic affect,* that hedonists particularly have in mind when they say that pleasure is intrinsically good.

If you ask most people what is the opposite of pleasure, they will say "pain." And pain is the opposite of pleasure in the first sense: it too is a physiological state (or the conscious effect of a physiological state) having to do with stimulation of the nerve endings. "Where did you feel the pain?" we ask. And the answer is, "In my tooth," or "In my stomach," or "I had a headache," and so on. There are, in addition, many states of consciousness which we find extremely unpleasant: we feel worried, distressed, depressed, bored, tense and anxious. Should we describe these states as pain as well? Opinion is divided. Some authors contrast pleasure with *dis*pleasure and call all these states—worry, boredom, pain, and so on—types or forms of displeasure, but not pain. Others call all such states forms of pain, though not necessarily physical pain. In this usage they are extending the physiologist's use of the word "pain," but on the other hand they are also preserving such common locutions as "I was deeply pained to hear of your sister's death." Probably the limitation of the word "pain" to its physiological sense is preferable, and we shall use it that way most of the time. But some writers we shall consider, such as Bentham, use "pain" in the more extended sense.

Now, what is the difference between pleasure and happiness, between displeasure and unhappiness?

Happiness is, compared with pleasure, a long-term affair. I might say, "I felt a stabbing pain at 11:03, and by 11:05 it had subsided, though it commenced again at 11:57." I could also clock in a similar way the times at which I felt certain pleasures. But it would be very strange to say, "I was happy from 11:05 to 11:15, unhappy for ten minutes, then happy again." Happiness is a kind of enduring "state of the soul," which may vary upward or downward through a lifetime—I can be happier now than I was the year before—but not from moment to moment. Happiness is more an enduring disposition than an evanescent state. "Are you happy?" someone asks. I may ponder and reply, "Ask me in six months." But I would never reply, if someone asked me if I had a toothache, "Ask me in six months." Consider an analogy: we say the *weather* changed at 11:05, when it started to rain suddenly, but we never say that the *climate* changed at 11:05; the climate is the weather over a considerable period of time. Happiness is like the climate, pleasures like the weather.

But this is not the only difference. A pleasure or a pain is an episode in one's life; it is an *occurrent state*. You know at any given moment whether you are in pain, or whether you feel sleepy, or whether the taste of the ice cream is pleasant to you. But if you are asked, "Are you happy right now?" the answer would not be as obvious. You can't tell just by introspection whether you are happy or not; and the reason is not only that happiness is more long term, but that "happiness" does not name an occurrent state, as does pain. When you are happy, it is not merely the case (as with pleasure and pain) that you are experiencing a certain conscious state at that moment; it is also the case that you are disposed to *behave* in certain ways in which you would not if you were unhappy. If you say you are happy, but everyone notices that you are full of worries and tensions (you are trembling, you snap back at people's remarks, etc.), it is clear to them that you are not happy. You may not be lying but instead may actually have deluded yourself into believing you are happy; or perhaps you were so unhappy previously that your present state is preferable. Still, people can have a pretty good suspicion that you don't measure up to the standard of happiness, as evidenced by your behavior. Indeed, you may misjudge your own happiness at a given moment. You yourself, later in life, may be so happy that looking back you may say, "I *thought* I was happy then, but I was mistaken. I didn't know then what it was to be truly happy."

Generally, though, to the extent that happiness is an occurrent state you yourself are the best judge of whether or not you are happy. But to the extent that, unlike being pleased or pained, happiness is a disposition to behave in certain ways, others who are careful observers of minimal cues in behavior can judge whether you are happy as well as or better than you can—just as others can judge whether you are vain without your suspecting you are (though being vain, unlike being happy, is *entirely* a disposition to act in certain ways and not at all a matter of *feeling* vain). Happiness, thus, has both an "inner" an an "outer" aspect, on the first of which you are the final judge and on the second of which you are not.

What, then, is the relation of pleasure to happiness? The simplest view is that happiness is just "the sum of pleasures"; pleasures are the *ingredients* of happiness, just as the strawberries, cake, and cream in strawberry shortcake are the ingredients of that dish. The more pleasurable states of consciousness a person experiences, the happier he or she is. The relation of pleasures to happiness is that of parts to a whole. Happiness is the aggregate of pleasant states. The degree of happiness we have thus depends on the number and duration of pleasures we have. The pleasant states, of course, may have a variety of causes—music, socializing, playing chess—but whatever their source, the more pleasant states we have during a year or a decade, the happier we are during that period. We may be happy without certain sources of pleasure, but we cannot be happy with no pleasures at all. One swallow does not a summer make, and one pleasure does not constitute happiness. Many pleasures do, however, constitute happiness; for it is of individual pleasures that happiness is constituted, just as it is out of individual stars that constellations are made. One star in a constellation may grow dimmer, but as long as others grow brighter to replace it, the constellation itself remains radiant; the same can be said for pleasures and happiness.

Can animals other than human beings be happy or unhappy? According to this view, they can be, since they experience pleasant and unpleasant states of consciousness. The difference is that the *sources* of their pleasure (and displeasure) are much more limited, so that the degree of happiness they can attain, as well as the degree of unhappiness, is also more limited.

But there is another view of the relation of happiness to pleasure, which is described by the ancient Greek philosopher Aristotle (384–322 B.C.) in his *Nicomachean Ethics.* "Happiness," runs the usual translation of the first sentence in Aristotle's ethics, "is that at which all men aim." But "happiness" is not a very satisfactory translation of the Greek word *eudaimonia,* for which there is no satisfactory English equivalent, but which has to do with a state of personal well-being. Physicians have standards for physical health—feeling good, having all one's bodily parts functioning well together, not feeling much bodily discomfort. Similarly, there are standards (though more vague) for mental health—having a feeling of self-worth or self-esteem, setting goals and trying to achieve them, feeling a zest for life, radiating energy, being a "positive" kind of person. These would be more modern formulations of what Aristotle had in mind in speaking of *eudaimonia* (having a "good spirit").

Such a condition is possible only to human beings, because it depends on our peculiarly *human* nature. What distinguishes human nature and *homo sapiens* from all the other animals is *rationality,* the power of reason. Rationality is the distinguishing virtue of our species. "Virtue" isn't quite the word either: the Greek word *arete* means something like "peculiar excellence." The *arete* of a knife is that it cuts; the *arete* of a clock is that it tells the time. What, then, is the *arete* of humankind? Not the fact that we are alive, for life is something we share with all animals, as well as plants. Not the fact that we are sentient (can perceive the world through our senses), for animals, though not plants, have this power also. Our *arete* lies in something that we alone possess—our rational faculty, or power of reason. Human beings are rational animals; that is a proper definition of our species. To say that is not to contend that we always *use* our rational powers; it is only to say that, unlike other creatures, we have such powers and the potentiality for using them.

Happiness (again, an inadequate translation of *eudaimonia*) is not the same as pleasure, according to Aristotle. Animals can feel pleasure and pain, but they cannot be happy. Your dog may be pleased or glad when you come home, but it cannot be happy, or for that matter unhappy. Happiness and unhappiness alike are impossible to animals, just as pain and pleasure are impossible to sticks and stones. Happiness, in Aristotle's view, is a state that accompanies typically human activities, such as thinking, weighing alternatives, deliberating, choosing, and acting on the basis of the choice. Other animals do not think, deliberate, choose; only human beings do this. Animals are on the whole programmed to do what they do; they don't have to think things out for they respond instinctively to stimuli in their environment. (To say the behavior is instinctive means only that it doesn't have to be learned.) A three-month-old puppy can survive pretty well on its own if there is food around; a three-month-old human baby is helpless, for his or her particular tool of survival, the rational faculty, is not yet developed. As human beings we have to use our minds in order to do even the simplest things, such as find (or grow) food, build shelter against the elements, and discover when to prepare for snowstorms and how to cultivate each different type of plant for food. We cannot rely on our instincts for this; we must rely on our minds to weigh alternatives and make decisions. In such capacities, which only human beings have, lies our potential for *eudaimonia,* a kind of well-being that only human beings can attain.

But a potential for happiness (or well-being) also carries with it a potential for unhappiness (ill-being). If it is true that only human beings can learn a language, read books, or enjoy the arts, it is also true that only human beings become depressed and miserable, fear death years ahead of its happening, plan revenge against an enemy for twenty years and finally carry it out, or become schizophrenic. Rationality brings all these negative potentialities with it. It carries with it the possibility for both great happiness and great unhappiness, both well-being and ill-being.

Eudaimonia is a state of the soul (psyche) that exists when a person's faculties are all working together in harmony; will and emotions need not and should not be suppressed, but they must be subordinated to reason, which must be in the driver's seat. A people who are "enslaved by their passions" and consistently go in for one kind of behavior, even though their reason tells them that another kind of behavior would be much better for them, are not in a state of *eudaimonia.* Nor are people who have "paralysis of the will" and don't or can't act in accord with their reason. The feeling of "being happy" is the consequence of this *eudaimonic* state of the soul.

Pleasure, by contrast, is experienced, as far as we can tell, by all sentient beings, as is pain. It is perfectly obvious that animals feel pain when they sustain bodily injury—as is also the case with a newborn human. But neither the animal nor the infant can be happy, the animal because it does not have

the human potential and the baby because he or she hasn't yet developed it.
It is true that we sometimes *say,* "The dog was unhappy because its master
left him alone at home," but such comments, Aristotle would say, are pro-
jecting human feelings into the dog: the dog certainly is displeased (could
one also say distressed?), but unhappiness occurs when, for example, planned
or hoped for goals have not been realized, and human beings are the only
creatures who can plan or hope.

"What difference does this really make?" you might ask. "Some say that
dogs can be happy or unhappy, others that they can only be pleased or displeased, content or discontent. We both agree that they can experience pain,
so their pain is intrinsically bad; we both agree that their sources of pleasure
and pain are more limited than ours. What's the difference, aside from all the
differences in terminology that have been uncovered?"

The answer is, it makes a considerable difference, if not in our treatment
of animals at least in our ideals as human beings. Consider the following
possibility. Every hour you can take a pleasure pill. The pleasure pill gets
you into a state of mild euphoria, gives you a "high." If it wears off you can
take another pill and sustain the high by taking as many pills as you like,
over your whole life span. Others may feel sorry for you because you don't
enjoy reading books or traveling, but you don't mind it at all; you are getting
more pleasure this way than you would otherwise. Of course, if you sit in a
corner and enjoy yourself, without being productive, others will have to do
the world's work while you have the high, even providing you with pills.
But that's only an instrumental consideration. The question is: Isn't a
drugged state as *intrinsically* good as the state of a happy and productive person? If happiness is the sum of pleasures, well, you get lots and lots of pleasure—admittedly from the same source, but that doesn't count against the
drugged state if you continue to enjoy it. Yet isn't there a great deal that you
might be missing? Aren't we right to feel sorry for you, and to urge you on
to other things? Wouldn't your life contain more intrinsic good if you didn't
live it in this way?

If happiness is just the sum of pleasures—and your sum is admittedly a
very high one in this case—then you must be said to be happy. But Aristotle
would disagree, contending that you are not living the "life proper to man."
Yours would be a subhuman life, filled with pleasures as a pig's might be. If
happiness is the accompaniment of the activities characteristic of a rational
being, then your enjoyments, great though they may be when you add them
all up, don't add up to happiness.

Mill, though a hedonist, admitted in a famous statement that "Socrates
dissatisfied is better than a pig satisfied." [8] But if satisfaction is the only intrinsic good, how can this be? The reason it is not good for a human being
to live like a pig is surely that the life of a pig does not *satisfy* humans.

[8] Mill, *Utilitarianism,* Chapter 2.

According to Bertrand Russell, "If you try to make yourself content with the happiness of a pig, your suppressed potentialities will make you miserable."[9] Another philosopher, Brand Blanshard, responded to Mill's statement this way:

> What is it that makes the life of Socrates more worth living than that of the pig, whether pleasanter or not? Surely not the quality of his pleasure, whatever that may mean, but something more obvious. It is simply that in the mind of a great thinker we have a richer fulfillment of the faculties that make us men.[10]

D. Pleasure and Happiness as Intrinsically Good

Now let us return to the hedonist, who, on the basis of our previous discussion, seems to be saying that pleasure, satisfaction, enjoyment, and happiness are all intrinsically good, and their opposites intrinsically bad. Many other things can be good and bad, but only as a means to the achievement of these states, in oneself or others. Let us examine that contention in light of a few examples that offer objections and see how a hedonist might respond to them.

Example 1. There are pleasures and pleasures, happiness and happiness. Let's say two people get an equal amount of pleasure from two different things—one from breaking a roomful of expensive crockery, and the other from experiencing a great work of music, painting, or literature. Isn't the latter more worthwhile than the former? Or again, what if one man has a fairly happy life working at a job to which he doesn't have to give much thought and spending the evening in drinking beer and watching TV, while a second person has an equally happy life as a kind of Thomas Edison, inventing things like phonographs and electric light bulbs. Isn't the second life more worthwhile than the first?

HEDONIST: Do you mean intrinsically or instrumentally? In our daily discourse we tend to mix the two. Breaking a roomful of crockery is, of course, destructive: the crockery is either lost or replaced, and someone must make up the loss. It also sets a bad precedent for future behavior and reinforces some bad habits. But the pleasure obtained from this activity is instrumental. The enjoyment one gets from the arts tends to grow with time; that is instrumental also. So the two experiences have very different instrumental potential. But if you can look at them without their causal connections, considering just the pleasure of the two experiences, I would say that intrinsically they are equally good, even though instrumentally they are of greatly different value.

[9] Bertrand Russell, *Human Society in Ethics and Politics* (London: Allen & Unwin, 1954), p. 238.
[10] Brand Blanshard, "The Impasse in Ethics and a Way Out," in *Readings in Ethical Theory,* eds. Wilfrid Sellars and John Hospers (Englewood Cliffs, N.J.: Prentice-Hall, 1970), p. 299.

The real difficulty comes when we have to weigh a miserable but instrumentally worthwhile life as against a happy but instrumentally worthless one. The paintings of Vincent Van Gogh have been the source of much pleasure, even happiness, to many people over the years and will probably continue to be. But Van Gogh, who created those masterworks, is the one who paid the price of desperation and unhappiness. Possibly he would have been even unhappier if he hadn't painted; but the point is that we are, in a way, the ones who profit from his misery. Would I want someone to go through such misery to make others happier? I think not. But if you consider the total intrinsic good involved (happiness vs. unhappiness), there is surely more happiness in the world because Van Gogh painted, even though *he,* the creator of it all, did not reap any dividend of happiness from it. I regret the fact that he was unhappy, yet I am sure there is more intrinsic good (happiness) in the world because he lived and painted.

I would make similar remarks about the other case. The life of an Edison is of much greater instrumental value to the human race than that of the other man; at the same time, don't discount the instrumental value of the worker who helps keep our lights burning in the long night. Both have their instrumental value, though doubtless the inventor's is greater. But as for intrinsic value, it seems to me they are the same: each is happy in his own way, and his way would be unwelcome or impossible to the other. Instrumental values aside, who are *we* to say that the quality of the first man's happiness is inferior? Perhaps if he had trained himself, he would have derived greater pleasure from other things than from beer and television. But if you tell me that the total pleasure of these two people is the same and ask me to judge the *intrinsic* goodness, keeping the instrumental strictly out of the picture, I would have to say that they have the same amount of intrinsic worth.

Example 2.   Doesn't the *kind* of happiness one derives make any difference? Consider the situation in Mark Twain's story *The Mysterious Stranger:* an angel promises perfect and unalloyed happiness to an old man. The angel then fulfills the promise by making the old man insane. In an asylum the old man sees his friends and relatives who visit him, and he ecstatically confers on them (imaginary) kingdoms and dominions, delighted at being able to do for his children what circumstances had always prevented him from doing before. He is radiantly happy in the belief that he is doing his best for his children; he has no worries in the world, since he is able to fulfill all his wishes. Yet wouldn't we view such a situation with horror? We might even say that he was better off sane and unhappy than insane and happy. Surely the happiness of insanity can't be called intrinsically good? We don't say, "How happy I am for him!" but rather "I'm sorry for him"—which indicates that we think his present state is bad, not good.

HEDONIST: There are various points involved here. First, I would say that his present state of happiness as an insane man is better, intrinsically, than his previous state. Perhaps for most people the world is so full of tensions, frustrations, and insoluble problems that only those who can escape it in some way are happy. Anyway, we are considering his present state *without* regard to its causal conditions or consequences: that's what we are talking about when we speak of intrinsic, as opposed to extrinsic, value. Second, however, it must be admitted that extrinsically his state—viewed in its full context of causes and consequences—is deplorable. Consider the distress of family and friends, the wrench in the lives of those around him who can't communicate with him as they used to. Also, as an insane person, he can do no constructive labor, though he must be given a share of the world's goods: he must be fed and clothed and waited on, and other people will have to contribute to his upkeep with their earned resources. Even though he doesn't know it, his happiness is parasitic on the labor of others, and they know it. If everyone was as deranged as he is, who would provide for him, who would grow the crops that feed him? Their well-being must in some measure be sacrificed in order to make his possible.

Besides all that, I would have to express grave suspicions about his really being happy. For most mentally deranged people, the escape into an imaginary world is a desperate way out of problems in the real world that they can't solve. And deep down they know this; sometimes, in moments of insight, the realization of what has happened is terrifying. So the happiness, if indeed there really is any, is precariously balanced on a melting ice block. It is not without reason that we wouldn't trade places with the man. He knows really that his happiness is a state of desperation. Anyone who thinks that the man's happiness is anything like that of the *eudaimonia* that Aristotle describes should read some books on psychiatry. So I say, *if* it's happiness, it's intrinsically good—but I doubt that there's much happiness in the whole mix.

Example 3. Happiness isn't always intrinsically good. It depends on the kind of happiness (or pleasure, etc.) that it is. Suppose that a murderer gets a big thrill out of killing people, so much so that he does it over and over again. Isn't this enjoyment an intrinsically bad thing? Suppose he never gets caught and that he has a feeling of positive triumph and achievement when he reflects on his cleverness in eluding the law and being free to kill again. I don't deny that much, perhaps most, happiness is intrinsically good; I am denying only that it always is. For example, *undeserved* happiness is intrinsically bad; it is worse than if the person had no happiness at all.

HEDONIST: Your charge exhibits the usual confusion between intrinsic and instrumental good. I agree that murderers shouldn't be free to kill again; but that is because by assaulting and killing people, they are diminishing the happiness of their victims, and by killing them, they are permanently removing all possibility of their happiness. The evil is to be found in the *consequences* of their being happy, not in the happiness itself. The happiness that murderers feel on completing their deed is instrumentally very bad, because it leads them to kill again. But when we are speaking of intrinsic good, we are talking about what is good in itself, not good because of what it leads to. What it leads to is admittedly bad, but we aren't talking about what it leads to but about what it is, considered apart from any consequences. And abstracting from any consequences, I have to say that happiness, under whatever conditions it is experienced, is intrinsically good. If the murderer's life were about to end in five minutes, and it was quite certain that no harm could come of his feeling happy—that he could never kill again, nor could anyone see him happy and thus be encouraged to commit crimes—I'd say that I'd rather see him happy than unhappy. Divorce the state from its consequences, and there is no reason to object to it; your objection is based entirely on its *instrumental* badness. But once again, intrinsic isn't instrumental. Once you keep the two distinct, there can be no objection to saying that a murderer's happiness (very temporary in this case) is intrinsically good. It's just one additional bit of happiness in the world, out of which (in this case) no harm will come, so the world is just that much better for containing it.

If two bitter enemies lived in different countries, and each was in ecstasy because each one believed falsely that the other one was being tortured, the ecstasy would be intrinsically good. In our actual world, where everything has consequences, we would say that this situation is (instrumentally) very bad. But why? Because pleasurable states tend to reinforce behavior: if you get pleasure out of doing something you are more likely to do it again. If the enemies were *actually* being tortured, the pain of the torture would far outweigh the pleasure of believing they are being tortured. But by our very hypothesis, neither of them is being tortured; in reality there is all pleasure and no pain. In this case the pleasure is harmless. As long as we're sure it doesn't lead to anything bad (as it usually does), there is a hedonic gain: more pleasure enters the world and no pain results from the two individuals' false belief.

3. PLURALISTIC THEORIES

Once the misconceptions of it have been pointed out, the hedonistic view is both simple and plausible. But many philosophers who have pondered the matter have not been convinced. They do not usually deny that any addition of pleasure, satisfaction, or happiness to the world makes it intrinsically better. But they have resisted the hedonist's contention that *nothing but* pleasure is intrinsically good. They contend that there is, rather, a *plurality* of intrinsic goods—that other things in the world are good, not just instrumentally but intrinsically.

There is a temptation when we believe something to be highly desirable or worthwhile to call it desirable in itself (intrinsically good). For example, freedom is of enormously great value to human beings; it is better to be free than in chains, better to act in accordance with our own choices than to have those choices dictated by others. The instrumental value of freedom seems unquestionable: as a rule we are happier in circumstances of relative freedom than when we are crushed under the heel of a tyrant or a totalitarian state.

(Even so, freedom can be used for evil purposes as well as good: people who are free can either develop their talents or waste them; they can use their freedom to help others, but also to harm them.) But is freedom an intrinsic value?

Most persons have concluded that though freedom is on the whole a great good, it cannot be called an intrinsic good. Freedom is rather a *necessary condition* for the achievement of intrinsic good. It is not a state of consciousness like happiness, but it is necessary to have some of it in order for happiness to exist. It is much more difficult to be happy under a repressive dictatorship than in a nation where a high degree of personal freedom exists. But this fact, of course, does not make freedom an intrinsic good, but only an important instrumental one: freedom would seem to be instrumental to the existence of intrinsic good without itself being an intrinsic good. But there are other things besides freedom that some have claimed to be as intrinsically good as pleasure. Let us turn to some of those other candidates now.

A. Fulfillment of Desire

One view, closely related to hedonism yet not the same, is that what is intrinsically good is the *fulfillment of desires or wants*. True, getting what we want often (though not always) makes us happy, and usually makes us happier at the time because we feel frustrated if our desire is not fulfilled. But fulfillment and happiness are not the same. Our desire may be, not for happiness, but for something of which we have no idea whether it will make us happy or not. For example, an adopted daughter may desire a reunion with her natural parents, not knowing whether the fulfillment of that desire will bring her happiness.

The fulfillment of a desire, of course, may at the same time be instrumentally bad. The cake you desire may give you indigestion. Or you may desire some food that disagrees with you or in the end poisons you, but the desire is fulfilled. As fulfillment of desire it is good, but as leading to indigestion or cramps or death it is bad, since these events lead to a frustration of *other* desires you have, such as health and life.

According to this view, then, the fulfillment of any desire is intrinsically good, and the frustration of any desire is intrinsically bad. The problem, of course, is that desires can conflict with one another. Your desire for an exotic dish may conflict with your desire for sustained good health. If one is fulfilled, the other cannot be. The same holds true on an interpersonal level. As one author states:

> The desire of a family to dwell in safety may conflict with the desire of one of their children to play with explosives. The latter is plainly the lesser desire, as it conflicts with others of far greater importance; these,

accordingly, should be fulfilled at the cost of the other. The desire of the child, although in no sense either bad or wrong in itself, is bad in relation to the more pressing desires of others, with which it conflicts.[11]

(Exactly what should be *done* about conflicts of desires is a matter dealt with in discussions of theories of right, and at the moment we are discussing only theories of good.)

To many the difference between happiness-as-intrinsically-good and fulfillment-of-desire-as-intrinsically-good may seem picky or trivial. But the two theories aren't the same: fulfillment of desire may or may not lead to happiness, that depending on what is desired. At the moment that we desire food, we desire that and not happiness (though we do not desire unhappiness either). The more desires fulfilled during our lifetime, the more intrinsic good our lives contain, even if some of the desires are for things that are instrumentally bad. As fulfillment, they are still intrinsically good, even though it might be better, instrumentally, if some of them (such as the desire to frustrate the desires of others) were not fulfilled.

This view of intrinsic goodness can be combined with the hedonistic one to form a kind of double-header theory of intrinsic good. One exponent, Brand Blanshard, writes of it this way:

> Take any case you will of experience regarded as intrinsically good, and ask yourself whether its goodness does not turn on two facts about it—first that it brings satisfaction in the form of some degree of pleasure, and second that it fulfils a want. Try it with any experience of love, of friendship, of intellectual insight, of sex, of beauty, of victory in contest, of success in skill or creation. . . . Both these characters, and only these, will be invariably there.[12]

There are times when fulfillment of desire occurs without satisfaction. The poet Goethe, for example, wanted to write great literature and did, but apparently it gave him little satisfaction. "At the bottom," he said, "it has been nothing but pain and burden, and I can affirm that during the whole of my 75 years I have not had four weeks of genuine well-being."[13] The same is often true of creative artists. Suppose that their total satisfaction in life was small but that the fulfillment of their desire to create was great. Don't we believe that this condition is not as good intrinsically as one in which they had both fulfillment and satisfaction?

There are times as well when satisfaction occurs without fulfillment of desire. There are those who, according to Blanshard,

[11] Taylor, *Good and Evil*, p. 137. Reprinted by permission of The Macmillan Co.
[12] Brand Blanshard, *Reason and Goodness* (London: Allen & Unwin, 1961), pp. 316–17.
[13] Quoted in William James, *The Varieties of Religious Experience* (New York: Modern Library, n.d.), p. 137.

live in a state of perpetual euphoria, cackling and cooing with idiot's delight over the little nothings of their daily round. . . . If the hedonists were right, such a state would be highly desirable. But we certainly do not so regard it. We think, rather, that for an experience to be genuinely good, there must be not only satisfaction, but something worth taking satisfaction in.[14]

Hedonists, for their part, would say that only the satisfaction is intrinsically good and that the fulfillment of desire is good only insofar as it contributes to the satisfaction. Thus they would contend that Goethe's life was mostly intrinsically bad (if he really was unhappy most of the time) but instrumentally good (for the human race). (They might add that there is an ambiguity in the word "fulfillment," since in one case it is used to mean the realization of a desire and in the other to mean that the end in question was in some way worth realizing.)

In any case, it is only experiences, hedonists would say, which can be called intrinsically good or bad. Facts about the physical world, such as earthquakes, are good or bad only instrumentally, insofar as they produce intrinsically good or bad experiences.

Take any experience you wish that at once fulfills a drive of human nature and brings pleasure or happiness with it, ask about this experience whether it is intrinsically worth having, and we suggest that you have the answer already. The experiences you would naturally think of as meeting the requirements—the experiences of beauty, friendship, sex, play, creation, knowledge—are those about which it is least possible to have any genuine question as to their goodness.[15]

They—the experiences, not the things that produce the experiences—are satisfying in quality, and they are also fulfillments of universal human impulses.

B. Beauty

In the familiar philosophical triad, there is not only goodness but beauty and truth. Isn't beauty, both in nature and in art, intrinsically valuable?

We already have given reason to believe that, even if beauty is a quality of objects quite independent of human perception, beauty cannot be a thing of intrinsic value: if the beautiful things were on an uninhabited planet and therefore could be seen and appreciated by no one, they would be of no value to anyone. It is not beauty itself but the appreciation of it by sentient beings that is a more plausible candidate for intrinsic value. And as far as we know

[14] Blanshard, *Reason and Goodness,* p. 337.
[15] Ibid., p. 320.

only human beings are capable of appreciating the beauties of nature or art; animals, no matter how much they may be influenced by human beings, never look at or listen to anything in their environment for anything other than practical purposes. But here the views of hedonists and pluralists diverge. Consider the following dialogue between them:

HEDONIST: Pleasure, satisfaction, enjoyment, happiness are all, in my view, intrinsically good. (If you want to add fulfillment, I won't cavil about that point.) Aesthetic satisfaction is just one *kind* of satisfaction, and as such it is also intrinsically good. Enjoying works of art is intrinsically good just as any enjoyment is. Insofar as the experience is an enjoyable one, it is intrinsically good.

PLURALIST: Do you mean that the experience of a person who has a full and enjoyable appreciation of an artistic masterpiece is just as worthwhile as the experience of a novice who enjoys a piece of trash or a cheap imitation?

H: If the two experiences contain equal enjoyment, yes. They differ only instrumentally: if something is a cheap imitation or an artistic fraud (and I am not questioning here, though I could, your assumption that some works of art are objectively better than others), this fact will come out in subsequent experience. A masterpiece you can enjoy for years, going back to it again and again with renewed enjoyment. Your average jukebox tune wears itself out after a few hearings and hasn't much potential for repeated, much less permanent, enjoyment. So the difference lies, not in the single experience itself, but in the future experiences that this experience will (or will not) lead to—which is an instrumental consideration from the point of view of the initial experience.

P: What of two people who both equally enjoy, say, an acknowledged masterpiece like Bach's Mass in B Minor—but the first person is fully appreciating it, listening carefully, aware of every harmonic and contrapuntal feature in the music, the development, the interweaving of melodic elements, and so on, while the second person is not really listening at all, just using it as a background for his or her own private reveries or a springboard for some irrelevant associations having nothing to do with the music, fulfilling George Santayana's ironic definition of music as "a drowsy reverie interrupted by nervous thrills." Surely the first person's enjoyment is much more to be valued than the second, whose enjoyment is superficial and not really a specific response to the music at all?

H: Assuming that their experiences are equally enjoyable—which doesn't really seem likely from your description—I would say again that intrinsically they are equally worthwhile. The difference between their appreciations comes later, on repeated hearings; the first type of experience persists and becomes richer, while the second tends to vanish.

P: But what if the superficial listener never gets over the habit and always enjoys music in this way, really paying very little attention to it?

H: Then the experiences of the two musical works are equally valuable intrinsically. But a continued rehearing of the music is very unlikely to produce such equality of enjoyment. An advantage of really listening to the music in all its formal complexity, as opposed to just letting it roll over you, is that you have a firm basis for continued enjoyment. Besides, the appreciative listener has the capacity both to enjoy careful listening *and* to use it as a springboard for a reverie if he or she is tired or depressed, while the superficial listener can do only the second—again a great difference in the potential for future enjoyment.

P: I think you are being oversimplistic in reducing all intrinsic value to enjoyment. When you appreciate great art there is much more than enjoyment going on (though far be it from me to knock enjoyment). There is appreciation, which isn't merely enjoyment. Great art can move you, make you sad, shock you, change the mode of your awareness, give you insight into the world and the nature of people's attitudes toward it; it isn't a vehicle merely for enjoyment.

H: I don't question that. But the other values which it affords are instrumental. That great literature helps you understand the world or human motivation is all to the good, but it is an instrumental good, not an intrinsic good.

P: I don't see why, if enjoying art is intrinsically worthwhile, being deeply moved by it in a way that would not be described as simply "enjoying" it is not also intrinsically worthwhile. I don't think that an appropriate response to Picasso's *Guernica* or Goya's *Disasters of War* or Solzhenitsyn's *The First Circle* or Penderecki's *Auschwitz Oratorio* would be to say "I enjoyed them." You'd be missing a great deal—and I don't see why other aspects of the experience aren't just as intrinsically worthwhile as the enjoyment. For that matter, not only the *appreciation* of art but the *creation* of it seems to be intrinsically valuable: even if we can't characterize the "divine agony of creation" solely in terms of enjoyment, it is still eminently worthwhile—just one of the great things human beings do; and I would say that artistic creativity is intrinsically worthwhile even if it produces nothing of value to others, even if it isn't seen by others, but just for its own sake alone. I think that both the appreciation of art and the creation of it involve not only enjoyment (and often not much of that) but understanding. And understanding is as much an intrinsic value, I would say, as enjoyment is.

We must cut short the dialogue here, but it leads us naturally to the next candidate for the position of intrinsic value.

C. Knowledge

Is it intrinsically better to believe what is true than to believe what is false? There must be countless truths about which nobody yet knows. There could be all sorts of truths about the world which would be of value to human beings *if* they knew about them, but as long as no one knows about them, they are of no value to us whatsoever. It is not truth by itself, but awareness of truth—knowledge—which is the plausible candidate for being considered intrinsically valuable.

Knowledge, says the value pluralist, is just a good thing to have; it is better to be knowledgeable about something than ignorant. Even if the knowledge brings no greater happiness than before, isn't it better to know? Undeniably, happiness is an intrinsic good, but knowledge is also an intrinsic good. Between two equally happy people, one with considerable knowledge of the world and the other ignorant of almost all of it, isn't the state of the first person intrinsically preferable to the state of the second?

Hedonists would object to this portrayal. Let us pick up the dialogue at this point.

HEDONIST: Knowledge is good or worthwhile *only* to the extent that it serves the cause of human happiness; in other words, it is strictly an instrumental good. Not all knowledge is worthwhile; some knowledge can be positively bad, if it produces misery rather than happiness. For most people, at least, knowing in advance the exact day of their death would not be desirable, because no matter how far away the date was, they would tend to start counting the days and might be miserable the whole time. I know I'll die sometime, but since I don't know the exact time, I go on living, more happily than if I knew exactly when death would occur. Or again, knowledge of how to make thermonuclear bombs may be a bad thing to have; it may some day mean the extermination of life on this planet. I could say the same of destructive weapons of any kind—adding that if some people have them and some don't that situation would also be bad, since the first group then would probably wipe out the second. But in all this I am speaking of what is good or bad *instrumentally*. The value of knowledge must be judged instrumentally, by what it leads to. In itself it is neither good nor bad.

Thus, between two persons, one ignorant and the other having knowledge, is the state of the second preferable to the first? Yes, *instrumentally* better: when we have knowledge we can deal with situations in a way that we can't if we don't. A person may have invested in the stock market and may get satisfaction from the belief that the stocks have gone up; her broker doesn't tell her that they have gone down. Now *intrinsically* the satisfaction she has, like all satisfactions, is good; but instrumentally it is very bad, because even if she was depressed at the unwelcome news, she could then make her own decision as to what to do—to take a loss and pull out, or sit out the crisis and hope that they'll go up again. That's better than if she waits until her broker tells her she's been wiped out. But what is the nature of this "better"? It's instrumentally better, of course. Her state of distress at the bad news is intrinsically bad, but since it may lead to better things, or at least prevent worse, it is instrumentally better if she knows, because in the end more happiness (or at least less unhappiness) will occur that way. If she has knowledge, she can deal with the situation in a way she can't do if she is ignorant. It is not true that ignorance is bliss; ignorance is, as a rule, instrumentally disastrous. If an epidemic breaks out and you know how to keep from contracting the disease (e.g., by a vaccine), then you are prepared to deal with the situation; if you are ignorant, you are not. Again, it is not true that ignorance is bliss; if you don't know how to grow crops or build a shelter against the elements and your life depends on it, your ignorance also will mean death—and so on in countless other situations. Even when ignorance doesn't lead to death, it leads to less happiness and more misery than you otherwise would have had.

In the case when knowledge is not instrumental to survival, it is instrumental to other things. Consider purely theoretical knowledge, with no practical application: for many people, at least, it's simply satisfying to have it, to know about the universe, even if nothing can be done about some aspects of it. (Anyway, much so-called theoretical knowledge is extremely practical at a later date, though its application was not suspected at the time of its discovery.) Or consider knowledge of philosophy: it probably won't furnish you a livelihood unless you teach it, yet to many people knowledge of it is extremely satisfying. It is satisfying to know its problems even if not its solutions and to know something about our place in the universe and the difficulties we have in our quest for knowledge. Even the excitement of *searching* for it can be satisfying: if you offered me a choice between knowledge and the search for knowledge, I might well prefer the search. But either way, it's the happiness it brings that is desirable; the value of knowledge, whether practical or theoretical, is always instrumental to happiness, not intrinsic.

It is true that you may be a Romantic and say with Lord Byron, "The tree of knowledge is not that of life." Knowledge may not be as great a source of happiness as is adventure, love, or challenge. Many people would gladly let some knowledge go in order to scale Mt. Everest. Also, it is true that if a subject matter is difficult, and you can't quite grasp it, particularly when other people do grasp it, you feel inferior and uncomfortable; the feeling of confusion and "not knowing where you are" when you first study philosophy, for example, can produce a lot of unhappiness. You might think you'd be better off doing something else; more likely, however, you'd be better off in the long run by sticking with it, for as the confusion gradually gives way to clarity, you'll be glad you didn't stop trying. Few things can be more frustrating than mental confusion, or more satisfying than confusion giving way to clarity and the satisfaction that "now finally I've got it licked." But it is because of this "satisfyingness" that the experience of learning has value. The value of knowledge is never itself intrinsic; only the satisfaction is. If studying philosophy *never* produced anything but confusion and unhappiness, it would not be worth pursuing.

Of course, there are lots of cases in which knowledge is not even instrumentally good. Consider just four of them. (1) A certain child is exceptionally intelligent, but if she is reminded of this, she may become arrogant and conceited, which she has a tendency toward already. Surely it is better not to tell her, at least for the time being. (This doesn't mean, of course, that she shouldn't be given encouragement.) (2) If you tell the parents of a certain child about his misdeeds, you know they will beat him, so you keep knowledge of the offense to yourself. Their knowing will only harm the child. (3) A person works on a research project for months, not knowing that someone else was also working on the same thing until the other person publishes his results. The first person wouldn't have had the stamina to finish his project if he'd known; yet he may say afterward that he was glad he didn't know, since the experience of doing it and finishing it successfully was of immense value to him and would help him in his future projects. (4) An insecure person gradually learns to live with certain rationalizations and unconscious defenses which give her a tolerable degree of happiness. If someone were to inform her that she was kidding herself, she would be miserable. Of course, it depends: if being frank with her would help her get her act together and, after some distress, cause her to be a better person, more honest with herself, then the knowledge would be of help. In all these cases knowing the truth isn't *always* helpful. If it makes someone miserable *and* doesn't have any happiness-producing aftereffects, then it's better for that person not to know. Once again, whether knowledge is good in a given case depends on the facts of that case. But in every case, the knowledge isn't intrinsically good; when it is good, it is instrumentally so.

PLURALIST: I put the following to you. Case 1: a man is happy in the *true* belief that his wife loves him. Case 2: a man is happy in the *false* belief that his wife loves him. I submit that it is intrinsically better for the first situation to exist than the second.

H: Of course it is better, but again instrumentally so, because in the second case the man will probably find out the truth one day and be more miserable than if he had known the truth in the first place. But intrinsically—that is, considered *without* regard to their consequences—the two cases are exactly the same. Your error is that you take our perfectly correct conviction that the first situation is better than the second—which is true enough in daily life because the second has potentially explosive consequences—and transfer it to the quite different situation in which only intrinsic good is under discussion; you say that Case 1 is still preferable to Case 2 even after the consequences are removed! I believe the reason you say that is that you are still, in the back of your mind, thinking of the ordinary situation, where the consequences have to be considered (as they do in daily life). Once you get that out of your mind, there is no barrier left to concluding that the two situations are—intrinsically but not instrumentally—equally good.

P: There is a tendency to do this, but I don't believe I'm guilty of it. I say, take two situations and look at them without regard to their possible aftereffects or consequences: a person happy in a true belief is just preferable intrinsically to a person who is happy in a false belief. This doesn't mean that happiness isn't intrinsically good; it just means that knowledge of the truth is *also* intrinsically good and, other things being equal, is always to be preferred to ignorance. There may be cases in which the happiness factor *outweighs* the truth factor, as possibly in some of the examples you cite, such as the one about the superintelligent but arrogant child. But that doesn't begin to show that knowing the truth isn't intrinsically good; one could conclude equally well that knowing *and* being happy are *both* intrinsic goods, and that sometimes the first outweighs the second—just as, I would contend, the second sometimes outweighs the first. (Knowledge of nuclear fission may turn out to be a bad thing for anyone to have had.) Thus, I would say that a smaller satisfaction obtained from a true belief is better, even intrinsically, than a greater satisfaction obtained from a false belief. Indeed, I would go further and say that dissatisfaction obtained from a false belief is intrinsically better than *any* satisfaction at all obtained from it. The combination of satisfaction and falsehood is intrinsically worse than the combination of dissatisfaction and falsehood.

H: That's ridiculous. You are just taking your reactions to the situation in which something does have consequences and transferring them to a situation in which, by your very hypothesis, consequences are not relevant.

P: What of falsehoods which are never discovered? Are those, then, all right as far as you're concerned?

H: Well, you never know when falsehood is going to be discovered. If you live with falsehood, you're sitting on a time bomb. That's the trouble with lies and falsehoods: the truth will out, or at least you can never be sure that it won't. Just wondering and dreading whether or when it will is enough to make falsehood (instrumentally) a big minus.

P: What of a falsehood that never can be discovered? I have to make this hypothetical, but assume (for purposes of the example) that I know that there is no life after death. Suppose, too, there is someone who has had an unhappy life, and the one thing she clings to is the hope that the next life will be happier. When she dies she will never wake up again to discover that she has been deluded. Right now she believes fervently in a happy hereafter. Would you try to take that belief from her?

H: If the question is whether I would try to take the belief away, that would depend. If she is old and can't change her habits and attitudes, I would leave her in her belief; she's happier that way and no one else is harmed. But if she can arrange her life in accordance with the unwelcome truth, she might well be happier *that* way, depending on how adaptable she is to new situations. If, the question is, however, which of the states is intrinsically better—being happy in a true belief or being happy in a belief whose falsity will never be discovered—I'd say that intrinsically it makes no difference at all.

P: Alas, you have respect for truth only if it makes people happy; but I have respect for truth itself, or at least knowledge of it. I say it is intrinsically better to believe what's true than to believe what's false, whether or not the falsity will ever come out and therefore have any consequences.

H: Alas, it is you who have no respect for instrumental considerations. It unsettles you to see one person living on the basis of a comforting delusion, because you think this will reinforce the tendency to believe something only for its consolation or comfort rather than for the evidence that it is true.

P: But according to you, as a hedonist, I suppose that's all right—to believe something, no matter what, as long as it makes a person happy?

H: If it makes someone happy *and* does not cause that person or others any unhappiness, then yes. But that's a big "if." If the individual in question once suspects that the belief isn't true, he or she will have more mental anguish from that than from believing an unpleasant truth in the first place. And even if the individual never suspects the belief to be false, others may know or suspect it, and if they care for him or her, they won't be exactly happy about the situation; it may even make them suspicious of whatever sources of happiness they themselves have, even if their own beliefs are well founded. You see how complex the instrumental aspects of the situation are. All I insist on is, don't get the instrumental mixed up with the intrinsic, even unconsciously. Viewing something in the light of its consequences and viewing it by itself apart from its consequences are two entirely different things.

P: I grant that, of course. But I still think you resist the fundamental insight that knowing the truth is something that has great value, which is partly instrumental (in guiding your actions), but also partly intrinsic. It's just better to have truth around than falsehood, that's all, even if there are no consequences. A world that contains X amount of happiness *plus* knowledge is better than one that contains X amount of happiness *without* knowledge.

D. Moral Qualities

By far the most controversial candidates for intrinsic goodness are moral qualities. As a rule the opponents of hedonism do not deny that pleasure and happiness are, at least sometimes, intrinsically good: it is better for people to be happy than to be unhappy. But they say that it is *also* intrinsically good for a person to be noble, to be animated by noble motives, to do things in a certain way, or to feel a certain way about others. For example, happiness associated with a benevolent frame of mind toward others is intrinsically better than happiness felt as a result of the suffering of others.

Hedonists, for their part, don't deny that there are morally virtuous qualities, good motives, and so on, but they say there is an important difference between *moral* good and *intrinsic* good: moral good has to do with means (in general, ways to increase happiness), and intrinsic good has to do with ends, that is, what the moral qualities are *for* or what purpose they serve. This said, let's pick up the dialogue again.

HEDONIST: Moral qualities are all instrumental. Kindness, honesty, benevolence, fairness, generosity, fidelity—these, I do not deny, are admirable qualities. If people are kind, they thereby usually bring more happiness into the world than if they are cruel; so kindness is, in general, instrumentally good. But it is *only* instrumentally good (as if that weren't enough). Aristotle made a good point when he said that the gods don't need most of the conventional virtues. They have no financial or other dealings with one another, so what need have they of honesty in such dealings? They don't need to be beneficent because in paradise there are no unfortunates in need of their beneficence. They do not need courage, for they have no battles to fight, no causes to be won. Virtue presupposes an imperfect world in which those qualities are exercised. If everyone in our world were beneficent and wise, there would be no need here for many of the so-called virtues; they are instrumental goods in our imperfect world. In heaven they would be useless.

PLURALIST: That only shows that in *our* imperfect world such qualities are intrinsically good. If a person acts courageously in a cause in which he or she believes, people think of this courage, or the exhibition of it, as "good in itself," even if it achieves nothing, even if it in no way contributes to anyone's happiness. If a person is loyal to an important cause, such loyalty is a valuable quality in itself, even if we do not sympathize with the cause to which the loyalty is shown. If a person conscientiously does his or her duty and conquers all temptation to do otherwise, this is admirable in itself. The eighteenth-century philosopher Immanuel Kant thought that the only thing good in itself was "the good will"—the tendency to do something solely out of a sense of duty, and not because of anything it achieved.

H: It is easy, again, to confuse intrinsic with instrumental value in all this. When witnessed by others, courage, loyalty, conscientiousness (acting out of a sense of duty), and other qualities may set an example or be an inspiration to them, thus resulting in much good; but that only shows that those qualities have instrumental value. The question is whether such qualities have intrinsic value as well. I say they do not. We should value qualities like these only instrumentally, as leading to happiness: even in cases where they do not, we may value them as in general *tending* to increase happiness; but that reason for valuing them is still instrumental. What's so good, after all, about the loyalty of fanatical Nazis to their party? That sort of loyalty got people killed. What's so marvelous about a person who conscientiously believes that he has to exorcise the devils from his children by beating them with hot irons? What's so great about the sense of duty of parents who won't permit their child to have a blood transfusion, with the result that the child's life is lost? I say that these so-called moral qualities can be either good or bad: instrumentally good if they increase the total quantity of happiness, and instrumentally bad if they decrease it. But in either case, their value is entirely instrumental.

P: I agree that conscientiousness can be instrumentally bad as well as good. But that does not prevent it from also being intrinsically good. Sometimes the instrumental badness of its consequences outweighs the goodness of the conscientiousness itself, but the manifestation of this quality can still be good, as Kant said, "shining like a jewel by its own light." And manifestations of an *evil* will are, I say, intrinsically bad—bad in themselves, not merely because they lead to evil consequences. Happiness combined with virtue is intrinsically good, and happiness combined with vice is intrinsically evil, just as pleasure taken in a true belief is good but pleasure taken in a false one is intrinsically bad. The goodness of such things as pleasure, satisfaction, and happiness, is, I would say, *conditional:* it depends on what they are combined with. Pleasure taken in the misfortune of others is intrinsically worse than sorrow at the misfortune of others; sorrow is a fitting emotion at such misfortune, whereas delight or glee in such circumstances is intrinsically evil, even if no bad consequences result. Let me quote to you the thoughts of the philosopher C. D. Broad on this point:

> Consider the state of mind which is called *malice.* Suppose that we perceive or think of the undeserved misfortunes of another man with pleasure. Is it not perfectly plain that this is an intrinsically bad state of mind, not merely *in spite of,* but *because of,* its pleasantness? No doubt malice is a state of mind which on the whole tends to increase human misery. But surely it is clear that we do not regard it as evil simply as a means. Even if we were quite sure that all malice would be impotent, it seems clear to me that we should condemn it as intrinsically bad. . . .
>
> Malice is not intrinsically bad simply because it is pleasant; many pleasant states are intrinsically good. And it is not intrinsically bad simply because it is a cognition of another's undeserved happiness: the sorrowful cognition of such an object would not be intrinsically bad. The intrinsic badness of malice depends on the *combination* of being pleasant with having this particular kind of object. We must therefore be prepared for the possibility that there is no single simple characteristic which is necessary and sufficient to make an experience intrinsically good or bad. It may be that intrinsic goodness or badness always depends on the combination of certain characteristics in the same experience. Any experience which combined the characteristics $c-1$ and $c-2$ might be intrinsically good; any that combined $c-2$ and $c-3$ might be intrinsically bad; whilst experiences which combined $c-2$ and $c-1$ might be neutral.[16]

H: You know what I think of all that. It's taking things that I agree are instrumentally good and acting as if they were intrinsically good as well. We are taught to accept as virtuous those qualities which (on the whole) promote human happiness; and now we are asked to consider them good entirely apart from this fact, even in situations where there will be no such consequence. The momentum of their instrumental value is supposed to carry over to make us admit their intrinsic value. But I don't buy it.

P: Every time you come across some counterexample to your theory, you

[16] C. D. Broad, *Five Types of Ethical Theory* (London: Routledge & Kegan Paul, 1935), p. 234.

dismiss it as something only instrumentally good. But I think you should reconsider. Sir David Ross puts it this way:

> If we compare two imaginary states of the universe, alike in the total amounts of virtue and vice and of pleasure and pain present in the two, but in one of which the virtuous were all happy and the vicious miserable, while in the other the vicious were all happy and the virtuous miserable, few people would hesitate to say that the first was a much better state of the universe than the second.[17]

It is *fitting* that happiness should attend virtue, and not vice versa. As Ross concludes:

> Four things seem to be intrinsically good—virtue, pleasure, the allocation of pleasure to the virtuous, and knowledge. . . . Of the three elements, virtue, knowledge, and pleasure are compounded all the complex states of mind that we think good in themselves. Aesthetic enjoyment, for example, seems to be a blend of pleasure with insight into the nature of the object that inspires it. Mutual love seems to be a blend of virtuous disposition of two minds towards each other, with the knowledge which each has of the character and disposition of the other, and with the pleasure which arises from such disposition and knowledge.[18]

Your oversimplified theory that only pleasure or happiness is intrinsically good ignores the fact that when we reflect carefully, we learn that if the universe contains these other things we find it intrinsically better than if it contained pleasure or happiness or want fulfillment and not these other things.

When G. E. Moore surveyed what hedonism implies, he wrote that hedonism "involves our saying . . . that a world in which absolutely nothing but pleasure existed—no knowledge, no love, no enjoyment of beauty, no moral qualities—must yet be intrinsically better—more worth creating—provided only that the total quantity of pleasure in it were the least bit greater than one in which all these things existed *as well as* pleasure."[19] This seemed to him the *reductio ad absurdum* of hedonism. It seems so to me also.

The controversy concerning intrinsic good is one on which disagreement persists. The importance of the controversy for deciding what course of action to pursue, however, is not as great as it might first seem. The very things that hedonists deny to be intrinsic goods are soon incorporated into their list of instrumental goods; and, however lengthily people may dispute

[17] Sir David Ross, *The Right and the Good* (London: Oxford University Press, 1930), p. 138.
[18] Ibid., p. 140.
[19] G. E. Moore, *Ethics* (London: Oxford University Press, 1912), pp. 237–38.

in the ivory tower about what is good apart from its consequences, in daily life everything that occurs does have consequences that it is necessary to consider. Whether knowledge is an intrinsic good which sometimes has bad consequences, or whether it is an instrumental good which sometimes does not achieve a worthwhile end, is of less importance in daily life than it is as a distinction in moral philosophy.

We must now survey the bearing of hedonistic and pluralistic theories on human conduct. Regardless of what is or is not intrinsically good, the question must be raised: What should we do about the theories? What actions are called for in light of them? Chapter 3 will focus on the view that only an individual's own good should be considered, and Chapter 4 will concentrate on the view that nothing less than the good of all should be our aim.

EXERCISES

1. Indicate as carefully as you can what you would consider to be the differences among the following concepts: pleasure, satisfaction, contentment, happiness, well-being.
2. Is Mill's saying that "Socrates dissatisfied is better than a pig satisfied" compatible with hedonism? Can you say Socrates dissatisfied is instrumentally better but intrinsically not? Does your result change if you substitute happiness for satisfaction? Explain.
3. Discuss the following passage from the opening pages of Ralph B. Perry, *Realms of Value:*

   To say that something is *valuable* to me is to say that I take some kind of *interest* in it, positive or negative. And to say that I take an interest in it is to say that I like it, or that I desire it, or that it gives me pleasure or satisfaction or arouses my curiosity . . . (or the opposite of these). . . . The silence of the desert is without value, until some wanderer finds it lonely and terrifying. The cataract is without value until some human sensibility finds it sublime, or until it is harnessed to satisfy human needs.

4. Discuss the following passage from Clarence Darrow, *The Story of My Life,* p. 240:

   Is it at all necessary that a person should be of any value to the world? The justification for living is that you are alive and do not want to die. If one cannot justify life in that way, then it cannot be justified. It would be very dangerous to be able to declare that a man could be executed because he was of no value to the world. If a trial of this sort should be fairly decided, most of the class who advocate such ideas would be found wanting, and therefore guilty.

5. Comment on the following suggestions. What bearing have they on the question of what is intrinsically good?
   a. "If something is true, it should be told to people regardless of whether it's going to increase their happiness. Knowledge is an intrinsic good."

b. A few astronomers discover that an opaque star is hurtling toward the solar system and will strike the earth in four days' time, shattering it to bits. There is nothing that anyone can do about it. Since no action will be of any value instrumentally, what should people do in their last hours?

6. In the quotation from C. D. Broad in this chapter, malice was presented as a candidate for intrinsic evil. Would you say that envy is also intrinsically evil or is it only instrumentally evil (or perhaps neither)? Consider, in your answer, the following quote:

The ugly girl cannot legislate good looks in her favor. She may resent the good-looking girl, but nothing she can do will ever get those good looks transferred to her. . . . How does the ugly girl vent her wrath? By throwing acid in the face of the better-looking girl. By hacking her to pieces. This is exactly what happened to a girl at Warren Wilson College in North Carolina . . . her unattractive ex roommate literally hacked her face up with a hatchet. Why? At the first hearing, she claimed it was envy that drove her to do it. There's even a book about this sort of envy: *Facial Justice,* published in Britain in 1960. It's a *1984*-type book about a future society in which envy is made illegal, and good-looking people are required by law to get face lifts (face drops?) to make them appear average.

Here's another crime that is almost always associated with envy: arson. The arsonist resents the prosperity of others. He gets joy from the fire, true enough. But the old question is "Why?" He likes pretty lights? He likes to see flames? He can see flames in his fireplace. Yet how many times have you ever heard anyone refer to the arsonist as envy-dominated? The arsonist gets joy from seeing other people's property, hopes, and visible signs of success being consumed by the flames. (From Gary North, "The Politics of Envy," *Remnant Review,* August 15, 1980, pp. 3–4. Reprinted by permission of Gary North.)

7. Discuss pro or con the issue raised in the following dialogue:

A: I don't think there is any such thing as intrinsic good. There are things we pursue as means (such as going to the dentist), and there are things we pursue as ends (such as going fishing if we enjoy it). But that doesn't imply that there is anything we can call *good in itself.* I can say that when I do something just because I enjoy it, I pursue it as an end and not as a means to something else, *without* saying that this end is intrinsically good.

B: In other words, you say (correctly) that you pursue something as an end, without making the further judgment on it that it is *intrinsically good.* But isn't that what the whole controversy is about—that some things are worthwhile as means to other things, and other things are worthwhile not because of what they lead to but because of what they are? In fact, I don't see what remains of the controversy according to you. To say that something is intrinsically good is to say that it is good in itself, considered apart from its surrounding conditions (causes and consequences). To say that it is instrumentally good is to say that (1) it does in fact lead to something else and (2) that something else is intrinsically good. So if you throw out intrinsic good, you have to throw out instrumental good too.

A: Indeed I do. I throw out instrumental good by that definition, at any rate. What I don't throw out is that A may be adopted as a means to B, and that B may in turn be a means to C, and so on.

B: But that's just ordinary empirical science; I thought we were doing ethical theory.

A: Let me put it this way: in life we examine every act and every situation in the context of its causes and its consequences. But sometimes we don't wish to consider consequences, but only the qualities of the thing or action we are considering. The child wants to swing, which she finds enjoyable, just for its own sake; but before we say O.K. to the child, we want to be sure that the rope is strong enough to hold her, that she won't catch cold, that she doesn't have homework to do, and so on. Once we've determined all that, then nothing any longer *stands in the way* of saying, "Go ahead and swing!" I can say that without saying that the enjoyment of the child swinging is intrinsically good.

B: But why do you pick on enjoyment as something for which "nothing stands in the way"? Suppose the child wanted to multilate herself; would you first make sure that the knife was sharp and the child really meant it and so on, and then say, "Nothing stands in the way—go ahead and cut yourself"? Surely not, because you believe that enjoyment is good as an end and self-mutilation is not. (See Monroe C. Beardsley, "Intrinsic Value," *Philosophy and Phenomenological Research* 26(1965):1–17.)

SELECTED READINGS

Aristotle. *Nicomachean Ethics*. Many editions.

Austin, Jean. "Pleasure and Happiness." *Philosophy* 43 (1968): 51–62. Reprinted in James M. Smith and Ernest Sosa, eds. *Mill's Utilitarianism: Text and Criticism*. Belmont, Calif.: Wadsworth Publishing, 1969.

Baylis, Charles A. "Grading, Values and Choice." *Mind* 67 (1958): 485–501.

Beardsley, Monroe. "Intrinsic Value." *Philosophy and Phenomenological Research* 26 (1965): 1–17. Reprinted in Wilfrid Sellars and John Hospers, eds. *Readings in Ethical Theory*. 2nd ed. Englewood Cliffs, N.J.: Prentice-Hall, 1970.

Blake, Ralph Mason. "Why Not Hedonism? A Protest." *International Journal of Ethics* 37 (1926): 1–18.

Bradley, F. H. "Pleasure for Pleasure's Sake." In his *Ethical Studies*. London: Oxford University Press, 1927. Reprinted in James M. Smith and Ernest Sosa, eds. *Mill's Utilitarianism: Text and Criticism*. Belmont, Calif.: Wadsworth Publishing, 1969.

Brandt, Richard B. *Ethical Theory: The Problems of Normative and Critical Ethics*. Englewood Cliffs, N.J.: Prentice-Hall, 1959. See Chapter 12.

Cowan, J. L. *Pleasure and Pain*. London: Macmillan, 1968.

Edwards, Rem B. *Pleasures and Pains: A Theory of Qualitative Hedonism*. Ithaca, N.Y.: Cornell University Press, 1979.

Fried, Charles. *An Anatomy of Values: Problems of Personal and Social Choice*. Cambridge, Mass.: Harvard University Press, 1970.

Gosling, J. C. B. *Pleasure and Desire: The Case for Hedonism Reviewed*. London: Oxford University Press, 1969.

Lewis, Clarence Irving. *An Analysis of Knowledge and Valuation*. LaSalle, Ill.: Open Court Publishing, 1946. See Book 3.

Mill, John Stuart. *Utilitarianism* (1863).★ Many editions.

★Dates in parentheses are dates of first publication.

Moore, George Edward. *Ethics*. London: Oxford University Press, 1912. See Chapter 6.

———. *Principia Ethica*. Cambridge: Cambridge University Press, 1903. See Chapter 6.

Penelhum, Terence. "The Logic of Pleasure." *Philosophy and Phenomenological Research* 17 (1957): 488–503.

Perry, David L. *The Concept of Pleasure*. The Hague: Mouton, 1967.

Perry, Ralph Barton. *Realms of Value*. Cambridge, Mass.: Harvard University Press, 1954. See Chapter 1.

Plato. *Gorgias; Philebus; Protagoras*. Many editions.

Rashdall, Hastings. *Theory of Good and Evil*. 2 vols. New York: Oxford University Press, 1924. See Volume 1, Book 1, Chapter 7.

Ross, Sir William David. *Foundations of Ethics* (Gifford Lectures, 1935–1936). New York: Oxford University Press, 1939.

Ryle, Gilbert. "Pleasure." *Proceedings of the Aristotelian Society* 28 (1954): 135–46. Reprinted in Joel Feinberg, ed. *Moral Concepts*. London: Oxford University Press, 1970.

Sesonske, Alexander. *Value and Obligation: The Foundations of an Empiricist Ethical Theory*. New York: Oxford University Press, 1964. See Chapter 4.

Von Wright, Georg Henrik. *The Varieties of Goodness*. New York: Humanities Press, 1963. See Chapters 4 and 5.

3

Egoistic Theories

1. PSYCHOLOGICAL EGOISM

The view that is called *psychological egoism* is not itself a theory of ethics; that is, it is not a theory about good or bad, right or wrong, or any other moral concept. It is a theory of human motivation. As such, it would seem to belong in psychology rather than in ethics. And so it does, but it is closely related as well to a theory of ethics called *ethical egoism*. Since the two are often confused, and since the truth of the first would have important consequences for the second, it is desirable to discuss psychological egoism first.

Psychological egoism can be formulated in a variety of ways, but the following statements, often heard in ordinary conversations, are typical:

1. People always look out for No. 1 first.
2. People act so as to benefit themselves, whether or not they also benefit others.
3. People always do what they want to do, or if that is impossible, what they dislike doing the least.
4. People always act in such a way as to maximize their own pleasure or happiness, that is, they do what they think (at the time) will bring them the most happiness.

Since these statements overlap in meaning, we shall consider only the last two.

A. Doing What One Wants

The statement that people act from some *specific* egoistic motive such as to get as much wealth as possible, could easily be proved wrong by pointing to many who don't care about wealth at all and cheerfully give it up for other things, such as power or a relaxed and easy life. The statement that people act from love of power also could be proved wrong: many are indifferent to power and care nothing about it. But the statement that people act from motives of personal desire, that is, that everyone does what he or she wants to do (*whatever* that might be), would not be so easy to refute. This, in one version, is what psychological egoists say.

Yet there are many apparent exceptions. I don't want to wash the dishes, but I do so anyway. Of course, someone may reply, you don't want to do the dishes, but you want to see a dirty kitchen even less, so you do the thing you dislike less and wash the dishes. Or, I don't want to obey the commands of the dictator but instead want to do my own thing and be left alone; in obeying them I'm doing what I don't want to do. In any usual sense this is true. Yet I obey them; and psychological egoists would say I do so because I like disobeying them (and taking the consequences, such as prison) even less.

Will psychological egoism cover all cases? Suppose you are half dead from lack of sleep, and a friend phones you on a rainy night and asks you to drive ten miles to help her repair her stalled car, and you do it. Can you really say that you are doing what you *want* to do? It seems obvious that what you *want* more than anything else is to stay in bed and that by going to help the person you are acting against your strongest desire. What could the psychological egoists say to this? They might say, "Well, as a friend you felt you owed it to her, and you would have felt guilty if you hadn't done it." But what if you didn't owe her anything (you had done more for her than she had ever done for you), and what if you would not have felt guilty at not doing it? (And even if you did feel guilty, that might not be strong enough to counteract your desire to stay in bed.) They might say, "Well, if you wouldn't have felt guilty at not doing it, then you wouldn't have done it." But you did do it, and it is up to psychological egoists to prove that you did it to avoid feeling guilt. How do they know this? In fact, aren't they assuming the very point they are trying to prove—that what you did is what you really wanted to do? What is obvious is that you wanted to stay in bed; it is not obvious that you wanted to go out in the middle of the night. Psychological egoists have to prove that the second is what you really wanted, more than you wanted the first. They can't do that by just *assuming* it to be true, for that would be committing the logical fallacy of "begging the question."

The fact that you did get up to help in the middle of the night, psychological egoists would say, shows that that's what you really wanted to do. But how do they know what you really wanted to do? Do they know more about you than you do yourself? If you sincerely say that what you wanted most was to stay in bed and that the last thing you wanted was to get up sleepily on a rainy night, are they really in a position to say that what you said isn't true? If they say, "You *must* have really wanted to, because that's what you did," they are not giving an *argument* for the view that people always do what they want to do but are *assuming* it, and thus are begging the question.

Consider another case. A policeman tracks down a murderer, dreading the moment he will find him because the murderer is his brother. Is the policeman doing what he really wants to do? Psychological egoists would say that he wants to catch him, otherwise he wouldn't try to do it. But if the policeman says, "I don't want to, but I have to (or I should)," are psychological egoists in a position to call him a liar? "I do it because it is my duty, and duty sometimes goes contrary to desire," the policeman says. "No," say the egoists, "you want to do your duty more than you want your brother to go free." But again, how do the egoists know this? Aren't they again just assuming it? Do they know the policeman's motives more than the policeman himself does? (Remember they say the same not only for the policeman, whom perhaps they know slightly, but for perfect strangers and people yet unborn and people long since dead. How can they know all their motives, since they don't know the persons at all?) What evidence have they that the policeman wants to catch his brother, in view of the policeman's sincere statement that he doesn't? Do the egoists *know* that desire always triumphs over sense of duty?

Egoists might say, "Sense of duty does sometimes triumph over desire, but that only shows that one has a stronger desire to act from duty than to act from other desires. Among the desires one has is the desire to do what one believes one ought. In some people this desire is very strong. Apparently it is strong in the policeman, so he acts in accordance with this, his strongest desire. So one always acts from the strongest desire after all." But is acting from a sense of duty a case of acting from desire? It certainly doesn't *feel* the same. What if the policeman says it is *not* his strongest desire? How do the psychological egoists know that this *is* the strongest desire? Only, it would seem, from the fact that this is how the person acts. You always act from the strongest desire, but how does one tell what the strongest desire is? Why, it's the one you act on. But then their statement comes to this: "Your strongest desire (the desire on which you act) is the desire on which you act." This is an obvious tautology, utterly trivial in its content: if you do *A,* you do *A.* Is this the statement that psychological egoists are trying to get us to accept?

We could go on, with case after case. A woman attends her sick cousin, knowing her to have a communicable disease. After attending the cousin for a few days, she herself contracts the disease and dies. She knew in advance that this might happen. Her desire to attend her cousin wasn't all that great, but she thought simply that it was "the proper thing to do." She did it. But how could it be shown that she was acting in accordance with her strongest desire, unless the matter is already settled by definition in *calling* whatever action she did the one that was motivated by the strongest desire?

No matter what examples we choose, we can always raise the following issues with the psychological egoists:

1. When you say that people always do what they want to do, aren't you overgeneralizing? People often do what they most want to do, but how do you know they *always* do? "She'll do what she wants to do," we say of someone who follows her desires; "you may reason with her but she'll end up doing what she wants to do anyway." There would be no point in saying this of her if it were not contrasted with what other people do, people who do *not* always follow the path of desire. Psychological egoists take what is true of some people some of the time, perhaps even most people most of the time, and, without evidence, say it is true of all people all of the time. But they don't even know all the people of whom they are saying this; and even of those they do know, do they have more insight into motivation than anyone else does? They can *assert* that thesis, but they certainly are not doing anything to *establish* it.

2. The statement of psychological egoism can easily be interpreted as a disguised tautology, true but empty of factual content. If someone says, "All persons always act from the strongest motive," and it turns out that what is meant by "the strongest motive" is the motive from which one acts, then the statement becomes simply, "The motive from which you act is the motive from which you act." In exactly the same way, "People always act from the strongest desire" becomes "People always act from the desire from which they act." Moreover, nothing has been offered to show that this desire is necessarily an egoistic one; indeed, nothing has been offered to show that a person necessarily acts from desire at all. What if people do something simply from the conviction that they ought to do it?

3. Psychological egoism often takes the very fact that Jones performed a certain act as the sole evidence that this was the act Jones most wanted to perform. No other evidence is forthcoming: since psychological egoists know no more about Jones than anyone else, if they are so sure that Jones is always acting from the desire to do *X* it is only because *X* is what Jones actually does. However, the fact that the desire to do *X* is Jones's strongest desire doesn't yield the conclusion that Jones will do *X*, unless there is inserted into the argument a premise stating that people always do what they most strongly desire to do; and this statement is the theory of psychological egoism itself. You can't prove a conclusion by assuming that very conclusion in the course of arguing for it; to do so is to assume the point at issue (beg the question).

Sometimes the theory undergoes a subtle alteration, from saying that all people always do what they consciously desire to saying (as some psychologists do) that all people always do what they *un*consciously desire. Consider a woman who constantly picks quarrels with her husband by reminding him of an infidelity that occurred many years before. Every time he wants to do something, she reminds him of it and never lets him forget it. Why is she doing it? She doesn't really enjoy the constant quarrels; she says, sincerely, that she would much rather do without them. Why, then, does she constantly precipitate them? Because it gives her a certain power, something to hang over his head so that she can always be in command or cow him into submission. Her psychologist says she doesn't give up the behavior because she enjoys wielding the power more than she would enjoy ending the quarrels. Unless there is some psychological "payoff," he says, she would not keep on dredging up ancient history. He tries to convince her that if she would drop the subject and live in harmony with her husband once again, her payoff might be greater. This is an appeal to abandon one kind of egoistic motivation for another, and possibly a more fruitful, kind.

Suppose she says that she doesn't consciously enjoy wielding this power over him. He would probably reply that she may not enjoy it *consciously,* but that she certainly does enjoy it *unconsciously,* or that if she doesn't consciously desire to do what she is doing, she is unconsciously desiring it. But now the theory that "one always does what one wants" has changed: it has been abandoned at the conscious level but retained at the unconscious level.

Therapists constantly give explanations of this kind. Wash-compulsion, agoraphobia, and many other conditions are not consciously enjoyable to people; they wish they didn't have the constant impulse to wash their hands or the fear of going out into open places. Psychological egoists who say that people do what they want to do will have a hard time handling such cases as long as it is conscious desires that they say are followed. But, therapists may say, such behavior fills a deep unconscious desire and that is why it is continued.

A woman's husband is a perpetual drunk, and she is miserable; he is out every evening and doesn't come home until he is thoroughly intoxicated. Then she takes care of him, puts him to bed, tries to see to it that he is at work on time the next morning. She attempts to change him but without success and goes to a psychiatrist to ease her pains. But the psychiatrist reminds her that deep down she is doing what she really wants to do. She knew of his habit before her marriage and also that he was a somewhat passive type—a man who wants a mother and seeks a motherly type in his wife. She, for her part, was the "mothering kind," and thus they were unconsciously drawn to one another. Doesn't she really *enjoy* this role of mothering him? In spite of her conscious misery, isn't there an unconscious satisfaction (perhaps *some* conscious satisfaction too) in playing mother to the big baby that her husband is? The psychiatrist tells her that nobody continues for any considerable period a certain habit pattern without some psychological payoff.

What are we to say of this version? It is easy to hold that people do whatever they unconsciously desire, even when it isn't what they consciously desire, when some bit of behavior can't be explained by a conscious desire. If an action doesn't fit the first formulation of psychological egoism, it can always be made to fit the second: one can simply invent unconscious desires, unconscious fears, unconscious pleasures, and so on to salvage the theory.

However, the matter is not as simple as that. That persons are driven by unconscious drives, which they know nothing about consciously and cannot reach by introspection, is a commonplace of psychiatry. Fears and desires that are so hard to live with that they must be suppressed, though they still motivate actions, are often excellent explanatory tools for behavior that otherwise would remain puzzling and unintelligible. The unconscious is not simply an *ad hoc* device invoked to defend a theory; it is part of a systematic body of knowledge with the power to explain many widely divergent aspects of human behavior.

But even psychiatrists would be hesitant to say that *all* acts are egoistically motivated, even unconsciously. What of actions not motivated by desire but by "unconscious accusations" against authority figures (or the "superego," as psychiatrists call it)? Moreover, some behavior seems to be simply the result of habit: it is done from neither conscious desire nor unconscious desire. In *Beyond the Pleasure Principle,* when Freud was discussing the repetition compulsion (the urge to reenact actively what one has once been subjected to passively), he wrote that the compulsion appeared to be so basic in human nature that it was "beyond the pleasure principle"—not motivated by either conscious or unconscious desires. If that is true, it would appear that even some professional psychiatrists are not psychological egoists.

Besides, even if one believes that all acts are dictated by unconscious egoistic urges, it must be remembered that this is a different theory from the one with which we began, which held that "people do what they want to do" in an ordinary, garden-variety *conscious* sense of "want." To say that the desire is unconscious is already to commit oneself to a considerable body of psychological theory.

B. Doing What Brings Pleasure

A second version of psychological egoism, called *psychological hedonism,* says that people always act to maximize their own pleasure, satisfaction, or happiness—which need not be the same as doing what they want. (Doing what they desire may sometimes be disastrous for their happiness.)

When someone says, "People always do what they desire," there is nothing in this statement to indicate *what* it is that they desire: they may desire fame, fortune, or recognition for themselves, or they may desire the well-being of others. The person is the *subject* of the desire, but the *object* of the desire may be anything at all.

Psychological hedonists, by contrast, say that the object of a person's desire is some future state of that person, specifically pleasure, satisfaction, or happiness. I may do all sorts of things—even help other people—but if I do so it is only in order to get pleasure for myself: I wouldn't help others if it didn't give me pleasure to do so. My act may be altruistic, but my motives are always egoistic.

There is one problem with this view at the outset: even if our motives are always self-seeking, it doesn't seem to be true that they always have as their object personal pleasure or satisfaction. If I want a glass of wine, is it the wine I want or the pleasure I get from drinking it? Perhaps I want the wine *because* I get pleasure from drinking it, but still *what* I want is the glass of wine. Someone might still insist that it is the pleasure I want, and only because of its pleasure-producing potential do I want the wine. But what of the case of a man who is starving and wants food more than anything else? Is it plausible to say that what he wants is not the food *per se* but the *pleasure* he will get from eating it? If he is very hungry, he will take the food whether he gets pleasure from it or not; give him a choice between the food and the pleasure, and he will take the food. (He will take it even if the taste of it is unpleasant to him.) It certainly seems that the food is what he wants and that the pleasure he gets from eating it (if any) is just a fringe benefit.

Anyway, that he gets pleasure from it *presupposes* that he first wants it. Some people, but not all, want fame; it is fame they want, not necessarily the pleasure they get from having it. (Sometimes they get little or none, and still keep craving it.) If they didn't already want fame, they wouldn't get any pleasure from achieving it; those who don't want it don't usually care much about it if they do get it. So it is the fame that is really the object of the desire: they also want the pleasure, of course, but that doesn't take away the fact that they do want fame. It is not true, then, that the only thing they want is pleasure, since they also want the fame that (they hope) will lead to it. This, it would seem, is enough to refute the view that personal pleasure (or satisfaction, etc.) is the sole object of human desire.

Apparently, Abraham Lincoln once did make the mistake of believing this false position, though:

> Mr. Lincoln once remarked to a fellow-passenger on an old-time mud-coach that all men were prompted by selfishness in doing good. His fellow-passenger was antagonizing this position when they were passing over a corduroy bridge that spanned a slough. As they crossed this bridge they espied an old razor-backed sow on the bank making a terrible noise because her pigs had got in to the slough and were in danger of drowning. As the old coach began to climb the hill, Mr. Lincoln called out, "Driver, can't you stop just a moment?" Then Mr. Lincoln jumped out, ran back and lifted the little pigs out of the mud and water and placed them on the bank. When he returned, his companion remarked, "Now Abe, where does selfishness come in on this little episode?" "Why, bless your soul Ed, that was the very essence of selfishness. I should have had no peace of mind all day had I gone on and left that suffering old sow worrying over those pigs. I did it to get peace of mind, don't you see?" [1]

[1] F. C. Sharp, *Ethics* (New York: Appleton-Century-Crofts, 1928), p. 75.

The following reply to Lincoln is appropriate, however:

If Lincoln had cared not a whit for the welfare of the little pigs and their "suffering" mother, but only for his own "peace of mind," it would be difficult to explain how he could have derived pleasure from helping them. The very fact that he did feel satisfaction as a result of helping the pigs presupposes that he had a pre-existing desire for something other than his own happiness. Then when *that* desire was satisfied, Lincoln of course derived pleasure. The *object* of Lincoln's desire was not pleasure; rather pleasure was the *consequence* of his pre-existing desire for something else. If Lincoln had been wholly indifferent to the plight of the little pigs as he claimed, how could he possibly have derived any pleasure from helping them?[2]

There are other problems with psychological hedonism. The first one is to formulate it carefully.

If someone said, "People act in such a way that they bring themselves the maximum pleasure (satisfaction, enjoyment, or happiness)," this would be demonstrably untrue. People get married in order to be happy, and sometimes they turn out to be miserable. The career that some think will bring happiness brings primarily unhappiness. People constantly misjudge what will make them happy. The view that people always do what *actually* makes them happy is too obviously false to require further comment.

But someone could say, "People act in a way that *they think* (at the time of acting) will bring them the most happiness (or least unhappiness)." This would take care of the miscalculation problem. The bride and groom think they will be happy, but in a year they are involved in constant bitter quarrels and recriminations. But they *thought* they would be happy; they just miscalculated. And surely this often happens: people by and large tend to act in whatever way they think will make them happiest, but what they thought at the time would bring them happiness fails to do so.

Another question also needs to be clarified: When we say that people act so as to maximize their own happiness, what time span are we talking about?

It might be said, "People always act in a way that they *think* will maximize their pleasure (enjoyment, happiness) in the long run." But this is demonstrably untrue. Many (most?) people don't think much about their long-run happiness at all; they think only of today or perhaps today and tomorrow. They will throw away all kinds of possibilities for happiness over a lifetime in order to enjoy life now. They will spend a fortune, even knowing that they will be poverty-stricken as a result in a year. To say that everyone acts out of long-term self-interest (prudence) is attributing too much farsightedness to people. Rather than say they calculate their long-term happiness, it

[2]Joel Feinberg, "Are All Human Actions Motivated by Self-Interest?" in *Understanding Moral Philosophy,* ed. James Rachels (Belmont, Calif.: Dickenson Publishing, 1976), p. 71.

would be more accurate to say that they don't think much about the long term at all.

Well, then, let us try another formulation. "People always act in a way that (in their opinion at the time) will bring them short-term happiness." But this isn't true either; many people forgo short-term happiness and make great sacrifice in the present in order to have a happier life later. They scrimp and save for a rainy day; they study law or medicine for years while others are having a good time, in order to have a reliable source of income (as well as a satisfying career) later on.

In order to make the formulation at all plausible, we will have to leave the time span elastic: "People act to produce maximum pleasure for themselves, either in the short run or in the long run, or anything in between." In this more elastic formulation, is the theory of psychological hedonism true? Let us try a few cases.

A man says to his wife, "I love you so much that if you really wanted to be with someone else, and would be happier that way, I'd let you go, even though I'd be unhappy about it." It certainly looks as if he is more interested in *her* happiness than in his own; he certainly doesn't seem to be the kind of man who would do anything to get happiness for himself. But psychological hedonists will try to turn this argument against its proponents: they will say that it gives him greater *happiness* to see her happy (even with someone else) than to see her less happy (with him). Or, some will say, this is really a ploy to get her to stay with him and be happy doing so. But what if he says it quite sincerely? Does he have to be lying or deluding himself? He seems to think more of her happiness than of his own. How do psychological hedonists know he is mistaken?

Consider another case. A woman, with all the comforts of civilization, goes to a faraway place in a leper colony to live among the lepers and minister to their needs, knowing that she will probably contract leprosy herself in time and die a horrible death. Perhaps, you may say, she is just trying to escape an unhappy situation at home; even if this was so (which it may not be), it would certainly seem as if prospects in a leper colony would be even more unpromising and that if she wanted to leave home she could choose another place to go where she would be happier.

But maybe she is attracted by the idea of doing good for other people, especially those who need and can't easily get help. Isn't that a really unselfish desire? Not at all, say the psychological hedonists. What's really going on is that she is turned on by the prospect of doing good for others as well as by the plaudits she will receive from others—the fact that others will think of her as a hero or saint. But suppose that others don't know, that she gets no praise for her action, but does it anyway? Then it must be that just the *thought* of going to the leper colony gives her satisfaction, a special kind of satisfaction that comes from helping others in need. So she is really doing it for the sake of the pleasure after all, the "warm inner glow" that comes, at least to some people, from helping others or from the belief that one is doing so.

It is tempting to leave it at that and say, "Well, isn't that all right? If she gets satisfaction from helping others, more power to her. Would you have her help others and get *no* satisfaction from it? She differs from other people in that many others get satisfaction only from helping themselves, whereas she gets it from helping others. Ordinarily we'd say the others are egoistic and she is not. But if you want to say they're all egoistic, more power to the second kind of egoism! Would that more people got satisfaction from helping others!" Perhaps so, but the psychological hedonists' point is that she doesn't do it really to help others; rather, she does it for the satisfaction she gets. If she didn't get that satisfaction from doing it, she wouldn't do it. So her motivation is egoistic after all.

Psychological hedonists are making claims, but they have not proved them by their argument. The fact that someone does X *and* gets satisfaction from doing X doesn't prove that he or she did it *for the sake* of the satisfaction. I may get some satisfaction from helping you out of a jam, but that isn't why I did it. (I can get much cheaper sources of satisfaction than that, if satisfaction is what I want.) I did it, quite simply, to help you out; the satisfaction is just a fringe benefit, and I wouldn't have done it if I had *not* thereby helped you out.

Moreover, I don't always get satisfaction: I may get much more enjoyment staying at home on a rainy night rather than helping you repair your car five miles away, but I do it anyway. It was an unpleasant job, I felt I should do it, I did it, and I was glad when it was over. I can't remember feeling any particular satisfaction in doing it.

"But," psychological hedonists might reply, "if you felt you ought to do it, you would have felt guilty if you had *not* done it." Sometimes that's true, but is it always true? Usually people feel guilty when they believe something is a duty, is expected of them, and they fail to do it; but I don't always do something because I feel it's my duty. If no one expected it of me or thought less of me for it, and I didn't even consider it a duty, I would not normally feel guilty if I didn't do it. Yet I did it. Did I do it for the satisfaction? No, I didn't get any particular satisfaction out of doing it at all. Neither might the woman in the leper colony, though she might continue with her activities anyway, perhaps because she saw how great the need was and saw too that there was no one else to fill the need (even if she didn't get any particular pleasure from filling it).

"But you must have got satisfaction from doing it, or else you wouldn't have done it," the psychological hedonists might persist. But to say this is to beg the question. How do they know that if I hadn't got satisfaction from doing it, I wouldn't have done it? This is pure assumption on their part. Sometimes a person does something and gets satisfaction, even though he or she didn't particularly do it *in order* to get the satisfaction; and sometimes a person does it and doesn't get any satisfaction from it at all, not even the moral satisfaction or "inner glow" of feeling that a duty was fulfilled. (Don't many people do what they feel they ought to do, without getting any "zip" or "kick" at all out of it themselves?)

The same kind of objection that was made to the "doing what you want" version can also be made to this one: How do you know that everyone, everywhere, at all times, acts to maximize his or her own happiness? Do you know that much about human beings, including people you have never known and people who are not yet born, to be able to say that in every one of their actions they try to maximize their own happiness? Once again we confront the fallacy of hasty generalization—generalizing from some cases in which it seems clear that people act to maximize their own happiness to other cases in which we have no such evidence.

The other mistake mentioned in connection with the first version also confronts this version. No matter what a person does, egoists will say it was done to maximize his or her own happiness. A man used his medical degree to make a lot of money? Of course, I told you so—money makes him happy, or at least he thinks it will, so he acts to maximize his happiness by raking in as much money as he can. (It may not bring him happiness after all, but if he *thinks* it will at the time, that's all the theory requires.) What if the same man decides to give it all up and to labor for no financial reward among the poor? Well, the hedonists will say, then that is what (he thinks) will make him happier. The very fact that a person does something, whatever it is, is taken as proof that he or she does it to maximize personal happiness. If a person does X, whatever that is, it is taken as proof of the theory; and if he or she does *not* do X, that's taken as proof of it also. But, of course, in contending this, the hedonists are not *proving* their theory; they are merely *assuming* it, and thus once again begging the question.

If we look at the matter empirically, it seems that, far from acting for their own happiness, some people follow life patterns which make them miserable; not only this, but they know that their way of life will make them miserable, yet they continue in it. Consider the gambler who can't quit while he's winning and never quits till he's hocked everything he owns. He knows that if he continues, he'll be miserable and broke all his life, and yet he keeps on. This too could be attacked: perhaps the excitement of the roulette wheel is so great that it more than makes up for his constant bankruptcy. But what if he weighs the alternatives and sees that though the roulette wheel is exciting it won't bring him as much happiness as a life without gambling, all things considered, and does it anyway?

The force of habit is very great and can be used against the position of psychological egoists. A smoker knows that smoking will injure her health and yet she can't make herself stop; a husband keeps starting quarrels with his wife and feeling sorry afterward. Habits are hard to break: it's easier just to stay in the same rut and do what you've always done, even when you know that you're working *against* your own happiness by doing so. Breaking a habit is very difficult and involves lots of self-discipline and sacrifice, and that's why it's easier to continue in the same old ways. But if egoists rely on this fact, they have shifted their position: they are no longer saying that people always act for their own happiness, but rather that they always do what is *easiest*. That too is a generalization that is clearly true in some cases but doesn't seem to be true in all, surely not for those who do the difficult thing, bite the bullet, steel their resolve. The theory that people always do the easiest thing is just as questionable as the theory that people always act for their own maximum happiness. In fact, for some people the easiest course of action seems to be to do something for someone else, so that the easiest course is not always the egoistic course.

It also seems most unlikely that all persons go through calculations of happiness versus unhappiness for themselves before embarking on most of their actions. Consider the suicide pilot who dives his plane into an enemy ship; he kills many of the enemy, which he wants to do, but in so doing he also knowingly kills himself. It might be said that he would feel guilt if he didn't do it; but if no one expected such an action of him, this is most unlikely, or if he did feel a twinge of guilt at not doing it, it would soon pass. And, would the guilt be so great that it would make his whole subsequent life unhappy if he did? "He probably had nothing to live for," it might be objected. But what if he did—if he had a promising career ahead of him, and he did it anyway? It is most unlikely that he had (or thought he would have) more happiness in that one moment of diving his plane into the ship than he would have had in fifty more years of life had he lived.

The fact is that most of us do most of our actions without any such calculations of future happiness and unhappiness as psychological hedonism requires. Once in a while we say "I'll do this, because I'll be happier if I do," but most of the time we just do what we do without thinking very much, if at all, of the possible future happiness that will result. We go about our work from day to day without calculating whether each act we perform will maximize our happiness.

Psychological egoism in all its forms holds that no matter what action is undertaken, it is always done with an egoistic motivation. Let us imagine an opposite theory of motivation and call it *psychological altruism*—the view that every person in every action has an altruistic (unselfish) motivation. But there are many people, we might object, who appear to have perfectly selfish motivations: they want to see themselves famous, wealthy, recognized, or loved, and they act in accordance with these egoistic desires. "Not at all," say the psychological altruists, "all actions are *really* motivated by concern for the welfare of others." But what of a person who rides roughshod over other people in order to achieve personal ends? "That's only a superficial account," say the psychological altruists; "if you look deeper, you will find some altruistic motive." But we look and look, and still we find none. "Well then, that only shows you haven't looked deeply enough. Look deeply *enough,* and you'll find an altruistic motive behind every act." When have we looked deeply enough? When we've found one! And suppose we never find one? That only shows we haven't looked deeply enough.

Most of us would find such a theory ridiculous, but it is not all that different from psychological egoism. Consider an action which appears to be, and is believed by the agent to be, against the agent's own interests and entirely devoted to the interests of others. (Whether such an action should be done is another question which is not our concern at the moment.) Let's say a woman makes a great sacrifice in order to contribute to the welfare of people starving in Somalia, whom she has never seen and who will never thank her personally for helping them. She has been saving up to buy something she wants or needs for herself, but instead she gives her savings to help others. Just how is such an action egoistically motivated? It is not done for recognition, fame, love of gain, nor even to assuage a feeling of guilt if she didn't (since no one would have reprimanded her for not doing it, not even herself). It was done because she felt it would be the right thing to do (not necessarily her duty), or simply because it would be "a good cause to contribute to." Is it really plausible to say that she did it to maximize her own satisfaction, or to make herself happier?

To insist that it is, is surely to deny a plain fact in order to support a dubious theory—particularly when psychological egoists claim it for *all* actions by all people, including all those who have ever lived on the earth and all those who ever will. Psychological egoists are impressed by the fact that so many people, including those who say they're not, *are* egoistically motivated, and they jump from this true assertion to another (and unproved) one—that *all* people in *all* of their actions are so motivated. In doing that, they are guilty of the fallacy of hasty generalization. And when made to discuss cases in which the evidence goes against them, they say that the very fact that a person behaved in a certain way proves that he or she was egoistically motivated in doing so, which begs the very question at issue. This, in the current idiom, is a cop-out.

At least two plausible conclusions emerge from our discussion of psychological egoism:

1. Human beings are not exclusively egoistic; they also have benevolent impulses, what we might call "limited benevolence." People do sometimes do things for other people, when there is nothing in it for themselves. The "impulse to help," especially in times of crisis, is very strong in many people, though not in everyone.

2. Besides the impulse to benevolence, people sometimes do things out of a sense of duty, against their inclinations. They do what they think they ought, whether or not this coincides with their "natural inclinations." They "do the right thing," or what they think is the right thing, sometimes getting satisfaction from doing it and sometimes not, but in any case not necessarily doing it for the sake of personal satisfaction. (If the other person weren't helped, they wouldn't experience any satisfaction.) Someone could say, in opposition, that in doing so, they are acting in response to their strongest desire (even though that desire is not for their own well-being). But then that opponent must admit that their desire is not always for their own well-being (i.e., other people's welfare may be the object of the desire, not their

own personal welfare); moreover the opponent could only say that people are motivated by the strongest desire by assuming (not proving) that the desire they acted from was always the strongest. This is typically done by using the fact that a person did X as the sole proof that X is what the individual most wanted to do—a conclusion that follows only if one begs the question by assuming that people always do what they most want to do.

2. ETHICAL EGOISM

Unlike psychological egoism, *ethical egoism* is a theory about what one *should* do, not about what people actually do. And since most people, most of the time at least, can't change their *motives* voluntarily (they can obey the command "Give money" but not "Give money out of good will"), ethical egoism is a theory about right actions, not motives. It is about what people should do, how they should act. It says that individuals should act *for their own self-interest*—that is, that the only reason people should do something is to promote their own interests.

It is easy to say, "You should pursue your own interests," but it is not always easy to do it. A person may have a wide variety of interests which conflict with one another. Consider just two cases:

Case 1: Is it to your interest to continue with your medical training? You are already in the first year of medical school, and your parents expect you to finish, but you seem to see the handwriting on the wall that tells you medicine is not for you, that you have other talents you want to exercise, that you'd rather do something more creative even though you will earn less money. What is it really in your interest to do? You want to do what is best for yourself in the long run, but it's terribly difficult in the circumstances to know what this is. How do you know what your preferences will be ten years from now? And yet you have to make the crucial decisions now.

Case 2: Ms. *A* is anxious to get married, and she's very much in love with a fellow graduate student, Mr. *B*. The trouble is, he's gay, or at least bisexual. Perhaps he will change after they're married, though her counselor tells her he probably won't, and if she marries him she will just have to live with it. At the same time another young man, Mr. *C*, is passionately devoted to her, and he has no such conflicts; from all appearances he would make an excellent husband. The trouble is he doesn't turn her on all that much. She likes to be with him, and she does enjoy their times together, but that certain spark just isn't there. But does it have to be there? Perhaps she can learn to love him. Maybe in time she'll even be able to forget Mr. *B*, though she doubts it now. She could live for a while with each in turn, but if she did it with one she would probably lose the other. Of course, she could just wait and not marry anybody. But time is rolling by, and perhaps in the future she won't meet anyone she cares for as much as she does for both of these two. After all, how is she to know? She wants to do what's really in her interest, but how is she to know what that is? What is *really* in your own interest is often very difficult to know, even without taking into consideration the interests of other people.

Besides the difficult empirical problem of how at one time people are to determine what their long-term interests will be at future times, there is the conceptual problem of what exactly is involved in saying that something is in one's interest. Some would give a comparatively simple and obvious answer—that what promotes a person's long-term interests is whatever makes him or her *happiest* over the longest time span. Thus, if pursuing a certain career will make me happier than pursuing any other, choosing that career is to my interest. This we may call the *hedonistic* interpretation of "interest."

But the term "interest" can also be related to what a person wants or desires. If I desire more knowledge of philosophy and have a great intellectual hunger to pursue it, then that is where my interest lies. Frustrating that interest will doubtless make me (for a time, at least) unhappy, but the central point of this interpretation of "interest" is not that pursuing philosophy will make me happier but that I want or desire it. Possibly the pursuit of philosophy will not make me any happier; I may not even have thought of its effect on my happiness or considered one way or the other whether it will make me any happier. I may not know anything about that, but I do know that I want to study philosophy, since that is what is a central interest (at the time, anyway) in my life. What I want may or may not make me happier, but I still want it, and wanting it is what makes it true to say that I have an interest in it.

The trouble is that many of the things I want may make me unhappy and may work to the detriment of my other wants. If I am a heroin addict, my desire for heroin is greater than my desire for anything else, and I have an enormous interest in getting my next fix. I *have* the interest, but in the long run, fulfilling this constant want is not *in* my interest. Why not? Because my life span will be shortened, and because my interest in this one thing will put an end to the fulfillment of many other interests I may have, such as saving money, pursuing knowledge, and so on. Something is *in* my (long-term) interest, then, not necessarily if it makes me happiest in the long run, but if it fits into (is coherent with) a pattern of my desires that promotes my long-term ends. Addiction to heroin certainly does not do this; it is incompatible with the fulfillment of almost all my other interests, and therefore, in the pattern of my *total* desires over the long term, the addiction is not *in* my interest, although it now may be a very strong interest of mine.

When ethical egoists say that people should pursue their (long-term) interests, or that they should do what is in their (long-term) self-interest, they need not specify which meaning of "interest" they are using; that is left open. As a rule, of course, what fits into a coherent pattern of your interests is also what makes you happiest, but it doesn't necessarily have to be so: even your long-term pattern of interests, cohering into a certain whole, may not turn out to be what makes you happiest. It all depends on what your interests are: they may, for example, all center on one kind of career, whereas another kind of career, of which you may not even have thought, may (had you chosen it) have made you happier.

One further word about self-interest: in its common meaning it is broader than the term "selfish." We usually think of a selfish person as one who pursues his or her own ends regardless of the well-being of others, as someone who will take advantage of others or even do them injury in order to get what he or she wants. But a person who acts out of *self-interest* need not be behaving *selfishly*. A person who is sick and goes to the doctor out of self-interest (to be cured) is not thereby treading on the interest of others or ignoring their well-being in order to further his or her own. Developing your creative talents is done from self-interest, but we do not ordinarily call such activity selfish. Selfish acts are included in the class of self-interested acts, but they are not the whole of that class. There are, apparently, many people who do behave out of self-interest (at least most of the time) but who seldom or never engage in selfish acts (i.e., self-interested acts which are harmful to the interests of others). Ethical egoism says only that people should behave self-interestedly and is not committed to saying (though it may include saying) that people should act selfishly; certainly it never says that one should always act selfishly—only self-interestedly.

What, then, is it that ethical egoists believe? It depends on the degree of generality with which they hold their position. Three types of ethical egoism can be distinguished by degree of generality—personal, individual, and universal.

A. Personal Ethical Egoism

If a man says, "I'm going to pursue my self-interest," this statement has nothing to do with ethics at all; it simply expresses a determination to act in a certain way, which may be instructive to a psychiatrist. But if he says "I *ought* to behave self-interestedly," that puts him on record as a *personal ethical egoist*. He is saying what he thinks he ought to do; but when he is asked what other people ought to do, he says nothing. He might say, "I don't presume to say what other people ought to do; I am saying only what I believe *I* ought to do. My theory is about myself only, not about everybody." As such, it lacks generality and is not a general ethical theory at all. It tells us something about how someone thinks he or she should behave, but ethical theories are considered to be theories about how everybody ought to behave, not just the speaker.

B. Individual Ethical Egoism

Suppose that an egoist says instead, "I am saying what everyone else should do. They should all serve my interests." The position then being advocated is that *A* should promote *A*'s interests, *B* should promote *A*'s interests, and everybody else should promote *A*'s interests.

There are not many people who would actually state such a view openly, but there are many who *act* as if they believed it; they act as if other people didn't exist or as if other people existed only to serve them and minister to their interests. Such people are usually referred to as not only egoists but *egotists.* "She's a very egotistical person" means that the individual uses others to serve her ends, that she thinks of herself first and thinks of others only as people who can fulfill her needs (without thinking of fulfilling *their* needs in return); if she can't use them she drops them.

This position, termed *individual ethical egoism,* rests on a very shaky foundation. Suppose that *A* is an individual ethical egoist who believes that everyone should serve him, but *B* is also an individual ethical egoist who believes that everyone should serve her. They are clearly on a collision course with one another. And only one of them can be correct in his or her belief: if everyone should serve *A*'s interests exclusively, it cannot also be true that everyone should serve *B*'s interests exclusively. The individual ethical egoism of two or more people cannot both be true, any more than you can have two or more chairs in this room each of which is the only chair in this room.

We can ask: Why should one person's interest be paramount over all others? If *A* says, "My interests are the only ones that count," *B* can respond with, "No, *my* interests are the only ones that count." They can't both be right, and nothing has been said to show that either one of them is right. Similarly, if *A* says, "My interests are the only ones that count *to me,"* *B* can respond, "And mine are the only ones that count *to me,"* and so on for everyone else.

Why should there be only one person in the world whose interests "count"? A person might say, "I am so good, or so important, or so handsome, or so (you fill in the adjective), that I am entitled to exclusive attention; others should pay no attention to their own interests, but to mine." But how is it that being famous, important, handsome, intelligent, or whatever entitles that person to exclusive attention? Even if he or she is the most intelligent person in the world, how does that merit the service of everyone else?

Also, the individual ethical egoist is playing a dangerous game: if a man says, "I deserve exclusive attention because I am the most intelligent person," and a woman arose who was more intelligent, then he would, to be consistent with his theory, have to say that she, and not he, was entitled to the exclusive attention and service of everyone, including himself. And if he said, "Well, I may not be the smartest or handsomest person in the world, but I am myself, I am I," then any other person could in equal truth respond, "Yes, and I am I too." The fact that "he is he" doesn't distinguish him from anyone else, and in no way does that entitle him to exclusive attention from others.

There seems, then, to be no basis whatsoever for holding to individual ethical egoism. As a result, it is quickly transformed into the third version, by far the most plausible one.

C. Universal Ethical Egoism

If I should pursue my interests, why shouldn't you be entitled to pursue your interests, and Jones pursue Jones's interests, and so on for everyone else? There is then, no one person who should be the recipient of everyone's service, but all should act in the service of themselves. If it is right for me to promote my own interest, by the same token it is right for you to promote yours. People should serve the interests of others only to the extent (if any) to which doing so promotes their own. "You cultivate your garden, I will cultivate mine." Nor should people do something if doing it doesn't in some way promote their own interests—which doesn't mean necessarily winning them money or fame, but simply giving them desire fulfillment, pleasure, or happiness. Thus if helping you makes me happier, then I should do so, for the sake of my own happiness. This view is known as *universal ethical egoism*.

A person may be egoistic simply as a means to some nonegoistic end: for example, an individual may believe that if each person pursued his or her happiness and left other people alone, everyone would thereby be happier; but in that case "everyone being happier" is the end, and this is the ideal of the theory to be considered in the next chapter—utilitarianism. Such a person is egoistic only in order to promote the general happiness (the happiness of society or of everyone) and is using egoistic recommendations as a means to a nonegoistic ideal; such a view does not belong to egoism, properly speaking.

On the other hand, someone may be nonegoistic as a means to egoistic ends: I may compliment you so that you will like me, or be honest with you so that you will trust me and lend me money, or contribute extensively to charity so that I will be known as a good person and be elected to the Board of Trustees or the City Council. In that case, my altruistic behavior is only a means to reach my egoistic ends. Universal ethical egoism, properly speaking, is not egoism of means but of ends: each person acting from self-interest is an ultimate end, not just a means to some nonegoistic end.

3. IDEALS OF PERSONAL WELL-BEING

Let us now examine some ideals of personal life that have been held in the history of ethical theory. They are not all 100 percent egoistic, but they all emphasize how individuals are to attain their own happiness, satisfaction, or personal well-being. And all are in the tradition of universal ethical egoism, holding egoism in one form or another to be a guide to human conduct that applies to everyone.

A. Epicureanism

According to egoistic hedonism, all people should attempt to maximize their pleasures and minimize their displeasures (i.e., pain, distress, worry, boredom, and all other unpleasant states of consciousness). But over what time span should individuals go about doing this? As a rule egoists believe that pleasures and displeasures should be calculated in advance, with consideration given not only to today or to today and tomorrow or to next week, but to the long run—that is, a person's *whole life span.*

Egoism as practiced over a whole lifetime is, of course, quite different from what could be called "egoism of the present moment." According to egoism of the present moment, I should do, at any moment, whatever will give me the most pleasure (and least displeasure) at that moment. I should behave at each moment as if there were not going to be any future moments.

For a baby or a small child to behave in this way seems natural enough; but one sign of growing up is increased ability to think ahead to future moments and to forgo pleasures that may be had in the present in favor of greater ones in the future. The baby survives by being fed and taken care of by others; but no adult could be self-sufficient for long if he or she were an egoist of the present moment. If you thought only of the present moment, you would not do work now (at least if the work was unpleasant) in order to get paid later so that you could have food and shelter. If you thought only of the present moment, you might imbibe a pleasant-tasting poison, and a moment later you would be dead. If only the present moment counts, this would be a perfectly consistent thing to do.

Although no one could live long as an egoist of the present moment, some people, including some adults, are egoists of the present week or the present year. Many people don't think very far ahead: they eat a delicious-tasting food now although they will suffer the pangs of indigestion within a few hours, and the pain of indigestion will far outweigh the pleasures of eating the food. Many people who do think a few hours of a day ahead don't think ahead much further than that: they get drunk, even though that means they won't be able to pay the rent and will be evicted from their apartment a few days later; they leave home on an impulse, not thinking how they will survive a week or month afterward. The time span varies, of course; some people can think a year ahead but not much more, some people think ten years ahead, and some people (e.g., those who make payments on life insurance policies that won't come due for forty years) think ahead even more than that. They give up certain enjoyments now in order to have greater ones later. Thus you should think ahead for your entire life span so as to maximize your pleasure throughout that entire period. It would be most unwise for you to have all your enjoyments during the next ten years and then be miserable forever afterward: the displeasures of the later time would greatly outweigh the pleasures you had in the present. Even your present pleasures would be clouded by the knowledge that you wouldn't be having them after the ten years had passed.

Of course, you don't know how long your life is going to last. But if you are twenty years old, it is highly probable that your life will go on for quite a few years more, and it would be wise to plan accordingly. *If,* however, you have reason to believe that your life isn't going to last long—for example, if the doctor has given you three months to live—then there isn't going to be any long run for you, and in that case it would be perfectly sensible for you to plan ahead only for those three months and get as much enjoyment out of that limited time as you could. "Eat, drink, and be merry, for tomorrow you die" is a saying that is often, though incorrectly, associated with hedonism; but *if* it is true that you are going to die tomorrow, and you know it, then of course there would be no point in doing things like making down payments on a house or enrolling for a course in mathematics. (Even so, eating and drinking might not be the activities that would give you the most pleasure, even if you were going to die tomorrow.)

Since the ideal is to have the maximum total pleasure, the best thing for you is to have a pleasant life but also a long one (so that you can have a longer time in which to enjoy pleasures). But planning your pleasures over a life span will often require you to do without certain pleasures now. If you want a secure and rewarding life, you will have to prepare for a trade or profession, which means going to school, sticking to a schedule, and studying even if you don't feel like it and would get more immediate pleasure from going out on the town. If you want to be secure when illness or old age overtake you, you will be wise to prepare for it by taking out medical insurance, for example, even though this involves having less money to spend and perhaps doing without certain things that would give you pleasure now. If you want to start a business, you will have to sacrifice a great deal of enjoyment in the present, hoping to have still more later on. You must be able to forgo many present enjoyments in order that the future will provide you even more of them.

But you have to strike a balance. Just as it would be unwise to "put all your eggs in one basket" by having all your enjoyments now and ignore the miseries that might come later, so also you would be unwise to sacrifice continually for the future until age seventy-five, for by then a more pleasant future will probably never come. Either way, you get less than the maximum total enjoyment possible to you. In the first case, you get pleasures now and displeasures for years thereafter; in the second case, you get displeasures now and few or no pleasures later to make up for them. Either extreme provides you less pleasure than you would have had if you had planned your pleasures wisely.

Let's consider an example of the first extreme. An immigrant laborer has to change his habits if he is to work in industry. He must learn to be more efficient, less disposed to spend half his time chatting or lying down on the job; he must learn to obey orders precisely. Yet he doesn't change his ways and, predictably, he is dismissed. His life in the past has been so insecure that promises of greater financial rewards in the future just don't move him very much. He accepts the loss of a job and consequent poverty with resignation, since he has experienced similar misfortune constantly in the past. In this case he could have done better for himself by exerting some effort. But doing so would make the present uncomfortable for him, and he is unable to project his imagination very far into the future. So, by failing to put forth a little effort now, he makes future benefits impossible.

Now let's consider an example of the second extreme. A business executive has spent most of her life working sixteen hours a day so that she can retire on her income and enjoy her later years. (Of course, if she enjoyed working sixteen hours a day, then it was no displeasure for her and no sacrifice as long as she enjoyed doing that more than anything else.) Now that she has achieved her goal and has all the money she can ever use, one would think she could take things easier, put the business in someone else's hands, and enjoy her leisure (again, assuming that she would enjoy leisure more than working, which isn't always the case). But instead she keeps on working overtime as if she were still fighting poverty and had to ensure she would have enough to live on. Sacrificing the present to the future may once have been a wise policy; but now it isn't any longer. Still, she may keep on doing it.

What is wrong with both these extremes is that they do not result in the maximum pleasure over the long run. The best policy is to have as much pleasure as possible all along the way while still preparing for future pleasure. If you study hard now in order to have a secure future in your profession later, *and also* enjoy studying hard now, then you have the best of both worlds: you are enjoying your work now (so that if something happened to you and it turned out that you had no future, you still would have enjoyed the present); thus preparing for the future is no great sacrifice, and by doing the preparing now you will also have a more secure (and hopefully pleasant) future.

Epicureanism is a form of egoistic hedonism that would hold to the policy just described. But the insistence on calculating pleasures over the long run is not what is the most distinctive of Epicureanism: many non-Epicureans would agree that one should do that. What characterizes the Epicureans specifically is their view on how people should go about obtaining the most pleasure in the long run.

It is here that the historical picture of Epicureanism is almost the very opposite of what Epicurus (342–270 B.C.), the founder of this school of thought, said. The words "epicure" and "Epicurean" today bring to most people's minds images of someone who gorges on food and drink, of a rank indulger of sensual appetites, or of a decadent wastrel who is either a dilettante or a slob. This was the sort of thing the poet Geoffrey Chaucer meant when he characterized his franklin, in *The Canterbury Tales,* as "Epicurus' owne sonne," and it is what the restaurateur today has in mind when he names his establishment "The Epicurean Restaurant." The Epicureans, however, believed just the opposite. They condemned a life of sensual indulgence; they believed that long-term pleasures could be maximized by strictly controlling physical appetites and by cultivating the mind. They were convinced that the pleasures most easily attained, and most intense at the time, were "hedonistic booby traps" which would produce the most distress and misery in the end. So studious were the Epicureans in avoiding these tempting pleasures of the moment that they went a long way toward asceticism, the systematic suppression of these pleasures.

Concerning the pleasures of food and drink, the historical Epicurean was at the opposite extreme from the popular conception of the Epicurean who wants ever more exotic delicacies to titillate the palate. Epicurus wrote:

> Plain fare gives as much pleasure as a costly diet, when once the pain of want has been removed, while bread and water confer the highest possible pleasure when they are brought to hungry lips. To habituate one's self, therefore, to a simple and inexpensive diet supply is all that is needful for health, and enables a man to meet the necessary requirements of life without shrinkings, and it places us in a better condition when we approach at intervals a costly fare and renders us fearless of fortune.[3]

If you cultivate a taste for rare or expensive delicacies, you will be embarking on a road which ends not in continued pleasure but in an unfulfilled and unfulfillable desire. The more taste combinations you try, the more you are likely to want; your palate, increasingly jaded, will crave ever more exotic taste combinations. If you cultivate a taste for peacock's tongue, you may find that nothing else compares with it in taste, but in that case you will want ever more of this impossibly expensive delicacy. You would be better off if you had never come to have that craving in the first place. Besides, such indulgences can bankrupt you, and the pain of doing without what you have become accustomed to is greater than the pleasure of enjoying them while you have them.

On the pleasures of sex Epicurus had similar advice. He did not think such pleasures evil in themselves, but he considered them extremely evanescent and not worth getting "hooked" on since they would provide much more pain than pleasure. Nature entraps us: the pleasures we tend to want most, such as food, drink, and sex, are those which are most likely to make us miserable in the end. They give us a high degree of momentary pleasure, and we anticipate the immediate pleasure so strongly that we tend not to think of possible long-term consequences. But if we indulge in a life of sexual abandon, we soon become miserable: we always want more such satisfaction than we can have, and we come to desire many more sources of this pleasure than are available to us, thus suffering pangs of frustration which are usually more intense than the possible pleasures. Our tastes become so overrefined that nothing really satisfies us, and we wind up in a frantic search for the unattainable. We would do well never to start on that fateful road. It is not that we should not indulge in sex at all, but rather that we should not be-

[3] Epicurus, "Letter to Menoeceus," in *Epicurus: The Extant Remains,* trans. Cyril Bailey (Oxford: Oxford University Press, 1926). Reprinted by permission.

come so used to it that we become miserable when we have to do without it, or bored when we have constantly indulged in it.

When we get emotionally involved with others, our chances of long-term pleasure and freedom from misery are even worse, according to Epicurus. Two people often become tired of one another; jealousies, conflicts, and quarrels arise as each makes the other miserable. The costs in distress and misery of one single attack of jealousy, or one good-sized quarrel, amount to more than the satisfactions of many pleasant encounters. The wisest course, if we truly wish to maximize our own pleasures in the long run, may be the most difficult one at the outset, namely, not to get involved in the first place.

This more "detached" life will provide us with what we could not have if we became involved in life's turbulence—calm and peace. It will provide much greater satisfaction than the stormy involvements to which we would otherwise fall prey. As Epicurus wrote:

> When we say that pleasure is the end and aim, we do not mean the pleasures of the prodigal or the pleasures of sensuality, as we are understood to do by some through ignorance, prejudice, or willful misrepresentation. By pleasure we mean the absence of pain in the body and of trouble in the soul. It is not an unbroken succession of drinking-bouts and of revelry, not sexual love, not the enjoyments of the fish and other delicacies of a luxurious table, which produce a pleasant life; it is sober reasoning, searching out the grounds of every choice and avoidance, and banishing those beliefs through which the greatest tumults take possession of the soul.[4]

The pleasures of food, drink, and sex are classified as "lower" pleasures, because in the long run they produce not so much pleasure as distress and misery. What pleasures, then, did Epicurus recommend? He endorsed the "higher pleasures," which are chiefly aesthetic and intellectual. To appreciate great works of art requires some training and cultivation, but once we have acquired a taste, they are enduring sources of satisfaction year after year, and they are not followed by distress and misery. We may tire of them for a time, but we return to them again with satisfaction. The acquisition of knowledge requires an initial expenditure of time and effort, but once this hurdle has been leaped, there is enduring pleasure unaccompanied by pain: the enjoyment grows with the passage of time, and unlike being involved with other people, no one can take the experience away. Art and learning are acquired pleasures; like coins which do not shine until you rub them, the more you know and appreciate, the brighter the pleasures of such knowledge. Accordingly, these "higher" pleasures are much more worthy of cultivation, even though our nature impels us to seek the "lower" ones, which

---

[4] Ibid. Reprinted by permission.

require no cultivation or training and which in anticipation present them-selves as most inviting, but which, when all is said and done, are a snare and a delusion.

But much of what Epicurus recommended cannot be brought under the heading of higher versus lower pleasures. For above all else Epicurus valued the achievement of peace of mind, of a state of inner calmness and tranquil-lity, of the absence of distress, worry, and conflict. Indeed, it seems that Epicurus' ideal of maximizing pleasures is more one of minimizing pain and distress than of actively pursuing pleasures, even the "higher" pleasures. Above all he wished to avoid those things that would disturb inner tranquil-lity and calm.

Among the things that people fear and dread most is death. According to Epicurus, however, this fear is the most irrational of all:

Death is nothing to us. Good and evil imply sentience, and death is the privation of all sentience; therefore a right understanding that death is nothing to us makes the mortality of life enjoyable, not by adding to life an illimitable time, but by taking away the yearning after immortality. For life has no terrors for him who has thoroughly apprehended that there are no terrors for him in ceasing to live. Foolish, therefore, is the man who says that he fears death, not because it will pain when it comes, but because it pains in the prospect. Whatever causes no annoy-ance when it is present, causes only a groundless pain in the expecta-tion.[5]

Leaving aside any criticism of hedonism in general, which we considered in Chapter 2, and of egoism in general, which we shall consider later in this chapter, let us examine a few critical comments that could be made about the specific form which egoistic hedonism takes in Epicureanism.

Epicurean claims about the higher versus the lower pleasures are the most frequent targets of attack. Are the "lower" pleasures as self-defeating as the Epicureans believed? Most people doubtless would say that they are not. The pleasures of love, for example, are admittedly fraught with dangers—fear of the loss of the beloved, danger of disaffection with its accompanying bitter-ness and sorrow, danger that love will diminish and that the relationship will develop into a tragicomedy of mutual recriminations. Still, most people ap-parently believe that the experience is worth the risk, even after they have suffered such consequences. " 'Tis better to have loved and lost than never to have loved at all," wrote poet Alfred Lord Tennyson. Besides, people don't always lose: many marriages last, and even when conditions are less than ideal, both parties usually testify that they enjoy life more together than they would alone.

The same may be said of other sources of pleasure. Indulgence in food and

[5] Ibid., p. 30. Reprinted by permission.

drink is not as dangerous as Epicurus believed. But he was so anxious to avoid all unpleasant consequences of such indulgence that he erred by rec-ommending the opposite extreme—asceticism. But wasn't the simple diet he recommended unnecessary, as well as monotonous? Moderation, as well as not getting hooked on expensive or unhealthful foods and drinks, would seem to be a wiser course than the degree of abstemiousness recommended by the Epicureans. "I would rather gratify my natural wants," one may say, "though in moderation, than to deny them entirely and have the peace of abstinence—if indeed it is peace and not just frustration." Epicurus was con-fident that once people became aware of the risks involved, they would not indulge themselves; but perhaps all of us would do better, as far as long-run egoism is concerned, to take some risks while proceeding with caution. Risks themselves can be enjoyable, and gamblers love them even while knowing full well the possible consequences.

"The lower pleasures are more transitory," Epicurus insisted. But are they? The pleasure of eating a juicy steak is more transitory than that of listening to Brahms, in that you can't eat *this* steak again whereas you can listen to the same Brahms composition. But then, if tomorrow you can have a steak just like the one you had today, what's the difference? As long as both are available, what does it matter if the object enjoyed is numerically the same object as before? Anyway, it's not always true that we tire of the "lower" pleasures more quickly. Many people tire of art and learning very quickly, if indeed they ever enjoy them at all, but they never seem to tire of food, drink, and sexual satisfaction. If you were to eat your favorite food once every day or listen to your favorite musical composition once every day, which would you tire of sooner? Even lovers of the arts would often admit that the repeated pleasure of enjoying their favorite food or drink would endure longer than their enjoyment of the same work of art.

Moreover, the "higher" pleasures usually depend on the previous satisfac-tion of the "lower" ones, not the other way round. If you have to do with-out a few meals, the most intense source of aesthetic or intellectual satisfaction probably will bring no satisfaction at all. It is difficult to study when you have hunger pangs, though admittedly some works of art have been appreciated, and even composed, on something less than a full stomach.

The "higher" pleasures also take a great deal of time to cultivate. Often they require years of preparation, involving considerable labor and energy, expenditure of money, and initial confusion of mind. And some may not enjoy great works of art even after all this preparation. Far from the "lower" pleasures being the risky ones, it may be that the "higher" ones are much more risky because they tend to be acquired tastes, which some persons will never acquire at all.

It is probably true that *constant* indulgence in the "lower" pleasures usually brings distress or misery; but the same may be true of constant indulgence in anything. In any case, moderate indulgence in the "lower" pleasures may bring considerable satisfaction, often much more than that derived from the "higher" ones. People differ so much in what they consider pleasurable that it is dangerous to generalize; but someone could argue quite plausibly that the "lower" pleasures do more to make life tolerable, even enjoyable, than all the "higher" ones put together. W. E. H. Lecky, the distinguished nineteenth-century British historian, who was acquainted with the "higher" pleasures firsthand throughout a lifetime, wrote:

> No painter or novelist, who wished to depict an ideal of perfect happiness, would seek it in a profound student. . . . Bodily conditions have in general more influence upon our enjoyment than mental ones. The happiness of the great majority of men is far more affected by health and temperament, resulting from physical conditions, which again physical enjoyments are often calculated to produce, than by any mental or moral causes, and acute physical sufferings paralyze all the energies of our nature to a greater extent than any mental distress. It is probable that the American inventor of the first anesthetic has done more for the real happiness of mankind than all the moral philosophers from Socrates to Mill.[6]

Critics have also pointed out that the Epicureans appeared to be less interested in the achievement of positive enjoyment than in the elimination of pain and distress. They seem to have identified pleasure with a state of quiescence and tranquillity—the absence of disturbances, not the positive enjoyment of anything. At least they talked more of avoiding than of seeking, of refraining more than of doing. But a state of tranquillity and peace, while highly valued by those who do not have it, seems somewhat "vanilla-flavored" to those who do: they seek more positive things in life than the passive pleasure of tranquillity. They can achieve more happiness by active involvement than by sitting contemplatively by the side of the road and watching the bustle of human activity pass by.

B. Stoicism

The Stoic movement was founded by the Greek philosopher Zeno (c. 336–264 B.C.) and was carried from Greece to Rome, where it flourished for several centuries into the Christian era alongside Christianity. Its influence can be seen in many Christian writers such as St. Paul, through whom it has put an indelible stamp on Western thought. St. Paul was raised in Stoicism, and even after his conversion to Christianity the influence of Stoicism was dominant in his Epistles, giving the Epistles of Paul a more severe moral cast than the Gospels.

Stoic ethics has an elaborate underpinning in metaphysics, but we shall

---

[6]W. E. H. Lecky, *A History of European Morals* (New York: Braziller, 1955; first published in 1869), p. 88.

restrict ourselves here to a brief description of the ethics alone. It is not entirely egoistic—for example, the Stoics, though they did not seek involvement in the world's affairs, believed it their duty to assume political office if it "fell to one's lot" to do so—but first and foremost Stoicism was an ethics of personal salvation. In practice it had much in common with Epicureanism, and often the one would be indistinguishable from the other in observations of the behavior of adherents. Still, the reasons for recommending certain modes of behavior were different in the two ethical views.

It has been said that happiness is the ratio of *what you have* to *what you want.* If you have everything you want, you are completely happy. If you have half of what you want, you are only 50 percent happy, and so on. With most people, however, "the more you have, the more you want." As one desire after another is fulfilled, more desires arise to take their place. Someone with one car wants two, and someone who is famous wants to be twice as famous. Wants always seem to increase faster than the ability to satisfy them, and so you remain unhappy no matter how much you have. But, according to the Stoic, this is not the way to happiness: instead of constantly increasing your wants, which always exceed what you have, you should *pare down* your wants. Want little, and you won't be disappointed. If you can succeed in extinguishing your desires entirely, you won't be unhappy even if you have nothing.

How did the Stoics recommend that this be done? First of all, live simply and abstemiously, as the Epicureans recommended. Your nutritional needs can be met simply and inexpensively; the rest you don't need. Restrict your wants to only the minimum that you need. Everything other than food and water, required for life, is superfluous. Second, don't rely on external things at all, such as fame, fortune, the adulation of others, even their love or affection or respect. All those things are quixotic and undependable. You fall in love, and the loved one finds another or is struck down by death or disease. You become involved in noble causes, and your best efforts are frustrated by others who wish to bring you down. The hopes and dreams of youth turn to dust; to depend on them is only to invite disappointment and endless frustration. How many hopes at age twenty are realized by age forty? "Vanity of vanities, all is vanity," said the author of *Ecclesiastes,* who was nine-tenths a Stoic. If you rely on fame, it will desert you sooner or later, and the attempt to retain it while you have it is so wearing as not to be worth the trouble. If you rely on money or material things, they do not make you happy anyway, and if they are taken away, through war or depression, you will suffer more by being without them than you ever enjoyed having them. If you rely on the esteem or affection of others, this too may be taken away, or you yourself will change your feelings toward those who care for you. You should rely only on what lies *within the control of your own will.*

But you may be carried away by your own passions and emotions. To prevent that, you place your emotions totally under the control of your will. Your will is the key to your happiness; with sufficient willpower you can overcome every barrier to happiness, even sickness, disease, and slavery.

None of these things matters; only your will to withstand them does. You cannot control events, but you can control how you react to them. Nothing in the external world is good or bad; what is good or bad is *your response* to them, and how you respond to events *is* within your control.

From the Greek word *apatheia* we derive the English word "apathy." We think of people as apathetic when they are bored or listless, as at a dull cocktail party. But this is not what the Stoics meant when they spoke of *apatheia*. To them it was kind of steeling of the will by which to master whatever hand fate dealt by refusing to be emotionally crushed or hurt by it. To achieve *apatheia* is to extirpate from life the whole array of desires implanted by nature, which only lead to endless nonfulfillment. Desires are nature's booby traps. If you desire nothing in the external world, you will not be adversely affected at not having it. The will can control natural appetites, so that whatever happens will not disturb your inner peace.

It doesn't matter what your position in life is, whether rich or poor, well or ill, king or slave. Since all that matters is the state of will, you can be equally happy whether you are king or slave. Indeed, misfortune may be an excellent opportunity for cultivating *apatheia,* whereas a life of continuous good fortune would lead you *not* to cultivate it, and thus make you the more vulnerable to ill-fortune when it comes. The two most famous Stoics, who wrote books on the subject, were Marcus Aurelius (121–180 A.D.), an emperor, and Epictetus (c. 50–135 A.D.), a slave. Since all human beings are fellow sufferers from the desires implanted by nature, and all human beings alike can achieve personal salvation only by overcoming these desires, all distinctions of social class and rank are of no consequence: the slave is as free as the emperor if he or she has developed *apatheia* and ruthlessly expunged all desire. Freedom is having what you want, and if you want nothing except what is in your own direct control, your freedom is assured, no matter what your station in life is. A king without *apatheia* is worse off than a slave with it. This may have been solace to the slave, but on the other hand it afforded no incentive to change any social institutions, such as slavery, since these were mere external conditions which were, according to the Stoic, of no consequence. The slave Epictetus wrote:

> Ask not that events should happen as you will, but let your will be that events should happen as they do, and you shall have peace.
>
> What disturbs men's minds is not events but their judgements on events. For instance, death is nothing dreadful, or else Socrates would have thought it so. No, the only dreadful thing about it is men's judgement that it is dreadful. And so when we are hindered, or disturbed, or distressed, let us never lay the blame on others, but ourselves, that is, on our judgements. To accuse others for one's own misfortunes is a sign of want of education; to accuse neither oneself nor others shows that one's education is complete.
>
> Ask not that events should happen as you will, but let your will be that events should happen as they do, and you shall have peace.

Sickness is a hindrance to the body, but not to the will, unless the will consents. Lameness is a hindrance to the leg, but not to the will. Say this to yourself at each event that happens, for you shall find that though it hinders something else it will not hinder you.

Never say of anything, "I lost it," but say, "I gave it back." Has your child died? It was given back. Has your wife died? She was given back. Has your estate been taken from you? Was not this also given back? But you say, "He who took it from me is wicked." What does it matter to you through whom the Giver asked it back? As long as He gives it to you, take care of it, but not as your own; treat it as passers-by treat an inn.

It is silly to want your children and your wife and your friends to live forever, for that means that you want what is not in your control to be in your control, and what is not your own to be yours. In the same way if you want your servant to make no mistakes, you are a fool, for you want vice not to be vice but something different. But if you want not to be disappointed in your will to get, you can attain to that.

Exercise yourself then in what lies in your power. Each man's master is the man who has authority over what he wishes or does not wish, to secure the one or to take away the other. Let him then who wishes to be free not wish for anything or avoid anything that depends on others; or else he is bound to be a slave.

Remember, that you must behave in life as you would at a banquet. A dish is handed round and comes to you; do not stop it. It has not reached you; do not be impatient to get it, but wait till your turn comes. Bear yourself thus towards children, wife, office, wealth, and one day you will be worthy to banquet with the gods. But if when they are set before you, you do not take them but despise them, then you shall not only share the gods' banquet, but shall share their rule. . . .

When you see a man shedding tears in sorrow for a child abroad or dead, or for loss of property, beware that you are not carried away by the impression that it is outward ills that make him miserable. Keep this thought by you: "What distresses him is not the event, for that does not distress another, but his judgment on the event." Therefore do not hesitate to sympathize with him so far as words go, and if it so chance, even to groan with him; but take heed that you do not also groan in your inner being.

Remember that you are an actor in a play, and the Playwright chooses the manner of it: if he wants it short, it is short; if long, it is long. If he wants you to act a poor man you must act the part with all your powers; and so if your part be a cripple or a magistrate or a plain man. For your business is to act the character that is given you and act it well; the choice of the cast is Another's.[7]

[7]From *The Manual of Epictetus,* trans. P. E. Matheson (Oxford: Oxford Library, 1916). Reprinted by permission.

The early Stoics wrote in such praise of *apatheia* that we might well conclude that they considered it an end in itself. On the other hand, it also seems plausible to believe that they considered happiness to be the end and *apatheia* the sole means to attain it. Such a view is always likely to become popular when conditions in the external world are such as to frustrate most desires. As the Roman Empire began to crumble and the external world came to be more unpredictable from day to day, it was only natural that many people should attempt to rely entirely on their own inner resources rather than place any trust in the external sources of happiness. Stoicism is the kind of view that comes to be practiced only when the external world has ceased to be a source of happiness, and then, as a second line of defense, people try (often without success) to find their entire source of happiness within themselves.

Yet external conditions do not always have to be unfavorable to the fulfillment of desires in order for Stoicism to become popular. A person may be famous and prosperous, and yet it often happens that the things for which he or she is envied by others turn to ashes; the things sought and worked for become meaningless once they are attained. In that case, happiness will be sought in emotional divorce from all such things, and only then will peace be found.

Several criticisms could be offered of the Stoic view. It could be charged that the Stoics have a formula, not for achieving happiness, but for *avoiding unhappiness*—that their whole conception is a negative rather than a positive one. To this the Stoics would probably assent, saying that the most we can attain in this world is peace of mind, which is only possible if we do not depend on what is outside our control. Under certain conditions, this may well be true.

The notion that we should depend only on what is within our control, however, is an extreme view. It goes "contrary to human nature," which is imbued with constant and unending desires. The Stoics would doubtless admit that their view is contrary to human nature in the sense that it is difficult to achieve and not "natural" to us, but they would maintain nevertheless that it represents our only hope of enduring happiness. The Stoics would also admit that not many people really attain such a state, but that, they would say, is why most people are unhappy.

It is not clear how far the Stoics would carry this. Can a person be happy while being tortured on the rack? If only Stoic *apatheia* counts, the answer would have to be yes. Being tortured is not in itself bad, but one's response to it (if one is made unhappy by it) is. But isn't this too much to ask of anyone? Indeed, is it possible at all?

The Stoics could also be challenged on the desirability of emotional withdrawal from the world. Perhaps the life of desire, which does sometimes grant some fulfillment, is more satisfying than if we never indulged desire at all but tried to suppress it. Parents who have had sons killed in war often say that it was better to have had the children, even if it meant losing them, than never to have had the experience of having them at all—and that indeed they would do it all over again, even knowing what would happen. If they are truly happier in depending on the outside world for their happiness even in the knowledge that the source of their happiness could be taken away from them at any moment, on what grounds could the Stoics say they are mistaken?

Anyway, the world isn't always so hostile to the fulfillment of desires as the Stoics claims. This is an empirical contention, and doubtless it is not always true. Much depends on what the world is like in the era in which one lives, but also, perhaps even more, on individual native temperament. When nothing in the outside world is rewarding, people are inclined to "be Stoic" about it and turn inward. But does this show that everyone should always eschew the external world as a source of happiness, even when (as surely happens sometimes) it fulfills people's desires most of the time, or more often than not?

The charge is sometimes made against the Stoics that they are emotionally sick, disturbed, maladjusted, abnormal. As one writer put it:

> The Stoic, though he seems strong and brave and imperturbable, is really an emotional weakling who cannot stand to get hurt and so takes out insurance against failure in advance by toning down his desires and hopes to the point where he knows they can be fulfilled. He is afraid to gamble lustily and play for great stakes. . . . In his fear of suffering the death of great disappointment, he chooses to live half-dead rather than taste the full joy of living, with all its possibilities of tragic ending. . . .
>
> From a diagnostic and therapeutic standpoint, any philosophy like Stoicism, which is able to transmute evil into good and call submission to defeat "happiness," plays into the hands of an unconscious will-to-failure. This prevents shy and retiring persons especially from coming to grips with the real problems of their unhappiness. . . . It is more wholesome . . . to admit to themselves that they are unhappy so that they will be stimulated to find the source of their frustration and correct it, instead of running away from it into the easy pseudo-happiness of resignation, humility, and inner peace.[8]

The author of this quote makes some emotionally loaded charges, and it is not obvious exactly what they come to as criticisms. When people's attitudes clash sharply, each is inclined to call the other abnormal or sick. But is this more than mere name-calling?

By the term "normal" we can mean statistically normal; what is normal is what is usual. It is normal for people to have two eyes, two ears, and so on. But in a different sense, "normal" means conforming to or fulfilling some norm, or standard. In this sense it doesn't matter whether most people fulfill it or not. Vision of 20-20 is considered normal eyesight, but most people

[8]Millard S. Everett, *Ideals of Life* (New York: Wiley, 1954), pp. 107–108.

don't see that well. Nevertheless it is a norm used by the navy and other organizations to screen out candidates. Abnormal psychology in no way assumes that the majority of people are normal; the majority might well be mentally ill or maladjusted in some ways.

Sometimes when people (or their views or practices) are called abnormal, we mean they don't like what most people like or do what most people do. Someone might retort, "So what's so wonderful about being like the majority? Geniuses are abnormal, since most persons aren't geniuses; does that make them in some way bad or undesirable? Or, if we are criticizing a person's views or failure to live up to a norm, we could ask *what* norm, and why should everyone live up to it? The norm that a father sets for his son's behavior may not be the kind of norm the son wants to live up to; it may not even be suited to the son's development. 'Not being adjusted to one's environment' is considered abnormal by many educators, but what if the environment encourages conformity or stupidity? Might it not be better to try to ignore it, change it, or leave it, rather than adapt to it? Beethoven and Van Gogh didn't live up to most of society's norms—they acted in ways that were considered wild, peculiar, eccentric, or crazy—and yet we are all better off because they lived. Would we really want them to have conformed to society's norms?"

The Stoics may be, in several senses, "abnormal," but in whichever sense we take it, this is hardly a damaging criticism. Are the Stoics, then, subject to another part of the last charge against them—that they are emotional weaklings, who can't stand to get hurt? Calling them weaklings is more a subjective evaluation than a description. In any case, if a person has the high degree of self-discipline necessary to develop *apatheia* and really become indifferent to "the slings and arrows of outrageous fortune," that is hardly the kind of achievement that should be characterized as weak.

Nor is the Stoic attitude aptly described as one of "resignation," except to *external* misfortune. And is "inner peace" really a "pseudo-happiness"? It seems rather that that would be a very considerable achievement, not attained by most people. The Stoics may go too far in the direction of indifference to the world; but is the critic in a position to condemn things like "inner peace," by whatever route it is reached? Doubtless the Stoic route is not the only route, but if it does succeed, and people are happier that way than they could be any other way, it is difficult to see how it can be condemned, at least on egoistic grounds. If some people have succeeded in reaching *apatheia* and can truly say that they have all they want, are they not more to be envied than criticized?

C. Aristotle

We have already considered Aristotle's conception of *eudaimonia* as an ideal toward which all human beings should strive, and as a distinctively human *arete* (see pp. 46–48). But how should human beings attain this ideal? What kinds of actions should they perform?

Aristotle was not, at least not entirely, an ethical egoist, but most of his *Nicomachean Ethics* is concerned with how individuals should find their own well-being. Aristotle's view is a much more common-sensical one than the extreme view of the Stoics and the somewhat less extreme view of the Epicureans. Many conditions, and not just the exercise of the rational faculty which is peculiar to humans, are required for happiness, according to Aristotle. None of them is sufficient to guarantee happiness, but each one is necessary. To be happy, people must not be dominated by any strong emotion, such as anger, hatred, or resentment, which tends to obscure the exercise of their rational faculties. Neither must they suffer from paralysis of the will: they must be able to act as well as think. They must be at peace with themselves, not torn by conflicting emotions; they must think well enough of themselves (in modern terms they must have enough self-esteem) so that they are not constantly doubting their self-worth.

There are physical conditions also: they must have a certain amount of financial security and material possessions, that is, they must know where their next meal is coming from, for they cannot be expected to be happy when hungry. They must have a congenial domestic life as well as congenial friends: without friends (not just acquaintances, people whom one knows but with whom one is not intimate) happiness is impossible. People also must have a considerable amount of personal freedom to do as they choose. They must even have a certain amount of good looks (at least not be repulsive in appearance), and it is desirable as well to come from a good family. Such things as good looks alone do not make for happiness, but not having them can make for unhappiness. A social position in the community is helpful, too. So is freedom from pain: Aristotle would have found the Stoic contention that a person can be happy while being tortured on the rack quite ridiculous.

Clearly not everyone can be happy, for some of these conditions are genetic and beyond change. Aristotle believed that slaves cannot be happy, for they do not have the freedom required to act in accordance with their choices (even though slaves in Greek society were better off then in most, even possessing the right to own property). He also believed that women cannot be happy—and perhaps, in ancient Greek society, with its male chauvinism, this may have been true. But since slaves and women can certainly exercise their rational faculties, it is clear that rationality, although the distinctive endowment of humans in contrast to the animals, is far from being the only thing required for happiness.

Aristotle's prescriptions for human action can be summarized in his *doctrine of the mean*. A good life is a mean between extremes. For example, we should be confident of our abilities rather than insecure, but, on the other hand, we should not be so smug as not to be able to take criticism from others. Courage is a virtue, and it is preferable to cowardice, yet courage is to be distinguished from the extreme of rashness. The rash man who dashes into battle even with little chance of success is wasting his life and is no more to be admired than the cowardly man who is always afraid to act. Generosity is a virtue, but it too is a mean between extremes: at one extreme is niggardliness, for example, the person who never gives anything to anybody; at the other extreme lies prodigality, exemplified in the person who gives to any cause indiscriminately. A person who indulges in pleasures all the time, "always out on the town," is not leading a good life, but neither is the person who never relaxes or seeks pleasurable outlets. Temperance is called for, but temperance is not total abstinence on the one hand nor constant self-indulgence on the other. To temper our desires is not to expunge them, but only to control them. (This is a very different meaning of "temperance" from the one found in, for example, the Women's Christian Temperance Union, in which temperance is made synonymous with total abstinence, in this case, from alcohol.)

Aristotle's notion is simply the Greek ideal of "moderation in all things," neither too much nor too little. But how much is too much and how little is too little? For this, Aristotle contended, there is no general prescription: it differs from case to case. What is too much for one person may be just right for another. There are vague guidelines, but in order to be more specific knowledge of the individual person would be needed. For a person who has a tendency toward timidity, a degree of self-confidence would be desirable that would not be recommended for a person who is already overly self-assertive. Aristotle did tell us that the desirable point, "the mean," is not necessarily to be found midway between the extremes. Courage is nearer to rashness than it is to cowardice; generosity is nearer to prodigality than it is to niggardliness. But to be generous in the right degree, to the right person, at the right time—*that* is what is difficult, and no exact specifications for this can be given that will cover all cases. We simply make mistakes and then learn from experience. Virtue (the Golden Mean) can be attained by practicing virtuous actions until skill in their performance is derived, just as swimming can be learned only by getting in the water and trying, not by reading manuals on how to swim.

Some virtues, Aristotle added, are not a mean between extremes at all, but are extremes "by their very definition." It should not be argued, "I'll be moderate in all things, including the number of murders I commit—not more than three per month." Some acts, such as murder, theft, betrayal of confidence (and adultery, according to Aristotle), are bad whenever they occur and are always the mark of the unvirtuous person.

Aristotle's account leaves some questions, however.

1. Are the qualities Aristotle recommended really situated between extremes? Cowardice may be lack of courage, but is rashness too much courage? It would seem that rashness is more like courage without the use of intelligence, which places it on a different continuum. Prodigality isn't just being too generous, but is rather being generous without using rational judgment.

2. If the desirable state is a mean between extremes, how are we to know when we have found the satisfactory mean in our own case? Do we just introspect and see? And *what* do we see? If the mean is at a different place for different individuals, how do we know when we have reached the right point?

3. Moreover, if virtue is not always a mean between extremes, how are we to tell in which category a particular kind of action belongs?

Despite the questions raised, Aristotle's view is an interesting contrast to the ethics of self-denial. The latter arises in a world which is felt to be hostile to the fulfillment of people's desires, and Aristotle did not picture humans as inhabiting a world in which all or most of their desires are doomed to frustration. Happiness is possible by a life of moderation and by the development of human beings' distinctive feature, reason, which controls the other aspects of human nature.

Some critics would suggest, however, that instead of laying down so many conditions as necessary for happiness, it would have been preferable to make them a matter of degree. For example, people *can* be happy while poor or even somewhat hungry, but they are more likely to be happy when these conditions are removed. People doubtless are happier with friends on whom they can rely, but this is not to say that without friends they can't be happy at all.

And surely there are enormous individual differences with respect to the conditions for happiness. Most people like to be recognized and respected by others, but a person who by his own preference becomes a hermit in the woods is thereby showing that he isn't attaching much importance to such things. Some people would be unbearably unhappy if they couldn't pursue knowledge in some way; others would hardly miss it. One person can be amazingly happy even in the face of loss of money and friends and family, even of health or eyesight; whereas another person may be permanently shattered by the loss of any one of these. Happiness seems to be more a matter of temperament than of external circumstances: some people seem "naturally happy," and when ill-fortune strikes them or the loss of loved ones, they rise above it quickly and go on living with courage and tenacity; other people, no matter how much good fortune they have, manage always to turn it into a source of unhappiness, and misery seems to be their constant state no matter how much good luck they have or how much they achieve. Some people can survive mountains of adversity intact, while others are knocked out by things that would scarcely affect the first group.

There is so much individual difference that people are probably often ill-advised to tell others how to be happy: each must find a road which belongs to no other. A person who advises others, with every good intention, on what to do to make them happy may be telling them merely what would make the adviser happy; for others the advice may be the perfect formula for misery. Concerning the sources of happiness, the only generalization that would appear to be safe is that no generalizations are safe.

D. Self-realization Theories

A view closely related to Aristotle's is that the life which each person should pursue is a life tending toward his or her *self-realization*. The word "realization" is not used here in the customary sense of "becoming aware," as in "Don't you realize what you are doing?" It is used, rather, in the literal sense of "making real." *Self-realization theories* assert that we should strive to realize, or make real, our own capacities, or *potentialities*. If we have, for example, an unusual talent for mathematics, we would do well to realize (actualize) this potentiality; most people don't have it, and this special ability is like a gift which, if unused, is simply wasted.

Thus far, telling people to "realize their potentialities" doesn't come to much. Are we to try to actualize *all* our potentialities? But this would be impossible. We all have potentialities which we don't even know about, and if we were to try to develop all of them, it would take thousands of lifetimes. Most of us probably have the capacity to raise weasels, yet few or none of us will ever realize this capacity. We could spend time realizing diverse potentialities by painting over windows, preparing sandwiches containing sawdust, counting all the dandelions within a mile of us, barking like a dog for ten minutes each morning, and drinking through a straw while doodling and thinking about Paris. But what point would there be in actualizing all these potentialities? Whenever we actualize some, we necessarily forgo others; life is too short to realize them all. So which potentialities should we work on? There are different views about this.

There is what we might call the *smorgasbord* pattern of self-realization, which requires development of a wide *range* of potentialities. Those who recommend this pattern would say, "Don't stick to just one thing; be a well-rounded personality: go in for some sports (don't try all of them, of course), some intellectual activities but not too much, some social interests, and so on." Some people apparently enjoy living their lives in this way and believe that everyone should do as they do. Still, it tends to create jacks of all trades and masters of none, and many would be most dissatisfied living in this way. It would be rather like designing a cathedral in such a way as to include just a little of all the various architectural styles.

The *dominant theme* pattern of self-realization, in contrast, is one in which a person concentrates on one thing, the one that he or she has the most talent for or takes the greatest interest in, and develops that to a high degree, with everything else built around it. To many people this pattern is much more satisfying. If someone had told Albert Einstein in his youth that he was doing far too much math and physics and that he should diversify by playing some soccer, doing some road building, taking up falconry, and doing a few other things, his unsatisfied curiosity about the problems of physics would have made him miserable doing the other things. His all-consuming interest was in one area, and it had to be "catch as catch can" for all the other things.

And surely he was better off that way. (And the human race, too, on the receiving end of his genius was probably better off.)

But *why* should we live our lives by the first pattern or the second, or something in between the two? One obvious answer is: so as to achieve maximum happiness; you must find whatever combination makes you the happiest. But the ethics of self-realization is much more often recommended in a different context, that of *maximum fulfillment of desires.* The two are not the same: we may fulfill all or most of our desires and yet not be happy (that depends on what things are desired); sometimes we may be happier frustrating many of our desires, depending again on what our desires are. The ideal is one of maximum possible *fulfillment.*

It is at this point that an important distinction must be introduced. There are some desires which if fulfilled (and some capacities which if realized) tend to *cooperate with,* or to *be harmonious with,* the fulfillment of other ones. And there are also some desires (and capacities) which get in the way of, or are *obstructive of,* some or most of the others. Thus, alcoholism and drug addiction do fulfill the desires of many people; but if they are gratified as much as possible, they would soon find that *other* desires must be frustrated. For example, if besides regular heroin shots someone also wanted financial security, a harmonious family life, a good standing in a profession, the respect and admiration of friends or neighbors, or a long and healthful life, he couldn't have them all: the fulfillment of the one desire gets in the way of (obstructs) the realization of all the others. Therefore, fulfilling this desire to any great degree correspondingly inhibits fulfilling other desires, with the result that fewer desires are fulfilled (and fewer capacities realized) than if a lid had been put on this particular desire in order to make possible the realization of others.

On the other hand, cultivating health by exercising and eating nutritious foods is likely to be harmonious with the fulfillment of other desires, since (as a rule) people can get on with these other things better if they are in good health and free from pain. Similarly, satisfying intellectual curiosity about one subject by studying it intensively is likely to be harmonious with studying other things, for the habits of mind and intellectual self-discipline required to master the first will probably make it easier to cultivate the second and third (what psychologists call "transfer of learning").

Suppose you desire the actualization of two of your potentialities about equally. If one of them is exercising an hour each day and the other is painting the town red an hour each night, it is likely that the realization of the first will be more harmonious with the development of your other capacities than the realization of the second. Consider another example. Mr. Doe desires an intimate affair with Miss Smith about as much on the whole as with Miss Jones. If Miss Smith will give him affection and concern and at the same time encourage him in his studies, while Miss Jones will so resent all time not spent with her that she will have a jealous fit if he doesn't do just what she wants when she wants it, he will do better with Miss Smith, since being with her is harmonious with the realization of his other desires while Miss Jones's company will be obstructive of them. In general, if the ideal is to maximize fulfillments, you can do this better by fulfilling those desires which harmonize with others rather than by fulfilling those which are obstructive of others.

The ideal of self-realization is to have a *maximally coherent system of mutually harmonious fulfillments,* whether these fall into a smorgasbord pattern (the jack-of-all-trades case) or a dominant theme pattern (the Einstein case), or some compromise between them. It's not always easy to reach maximum self-realization, of course: if you are a student who is a mathematical genius but you don't particularly like math and much prefer to write music (at which you aren't very good), should you do what you like or what you're best at? Doing what you're best at will bring you recognition, perhaps renown, and almost certainly a comfortable living; doing what you have a consuming passion for will satisfy one very strong desire but may often leave you wondering where your next meal is coming from. In such a case it is far from easy to figure out which would be a life of maximum fulfillment for you, because each of the two main potentialities for development tends to get in the way of the other. (Sometimes it is possible to compromise by doing the one for a living and the other for a hobby.)

Besides such practical problems in achieving maximum self-realization, there are some questions that can be asked concerning this rather attractive-sounding idea. First, we have assumed so far that even heroin addicts have *other* interests which their addiction gets in the way of. But what if this is not so? What if everything in the life of a certain addict is centered on this one all-consuming desire, and he or she really has no interest in the realization of any other capacities? Shall we say that since that individual's range of desires is rather narrow, he or she should continue to fulfill the pronounced desire for heroin since there are no others?

If we want to avoid this conclusion, we shall have to speak not of the desires that the addict actually has but the desires (or potentialities) that he or she *could* have, or *might* have had. Although the individual no longer cares about anything but the addiction, he or she has the *potentiality* for intellectual, social, and other types of development which now remains unrealized. But, of course, the other side of this coin is that the person who is a whiz at organic chemistry and is making breakthroughs in DNA research *might* have, and *could* have, developed some abilities as a salesperson. But that, we say, wouldn't have been as *worthwhile* as what the individual is now doing. But worthwhileness is something else again. It is at least partly a social concept and not judged entirely by how happy something makes people or whether it provides *them* a set of mutually harmonious fulfillments.

Once we start on what desires people *might* have had which they didn't have, or could have had but didn't, we are faced with the question of why they *should* have had these, even if by having them they would have had a larger range of desires which could be integrated harmoniously. Why have an integrated system if one dominant desire will do? If we condemn or pity people for living certain kinds of lives, is it because they're not "realizing themselves" or because they aren't leading *socially useful* lives? But life that is useful to others is not the same as a life that maximally fulfills an individual's desires.

Besides the question of how to deal with potential desires, there is a second question of the limits of *self*-realization. Suppose the dominant theme around which all your interests center is safecracking: not only are you more interested in this pursuit than in anything else, you are also better at it than at anything else, so there is no conflict. Safecracking is the potentiality you wish to develop, and you are also highly motivated to do it, since nothing else really interests you very much. Robbing banks and wealthy homes to meet the challenge of locked safes and vaults is what gives you your zest for living. (The money doesn't much matter, only the challenge.) Suppose you are very successful in these endeavors, and the money enables you to have an attractive home and family, belong to exclusive clubs, and travel abroad every summer. Your working hours are short, so you can develop cultural pursuits in your spare time much more than you could if you worked eight hours a day hauling rubbish for a living and came home every evening too tired to do anything but sleep. Can anyone deny that such a life is more fulfilling for you, and enables you to realize more of your potentialities, than an ordinary nine-to-five life? Haven't more of your capacities been tapped, and don't your desires together with fulfillments form a mutually coherent system—much more so, at any rate, than many ways of making an honest living?

As long as we are talking about *self*-realization, it would be very difficult to fault such a mode of life as lacking fulfillment. If we consider only your level of self-realization as a safecracker, it seems to be pretty high. But it just so happens that you would be engaged in what is called an "antisocial activity": by realizing yourself in this way you are harming others (owners of valuables, depositors, insurance companies, etc.). By realizing yourself, you are doing your bit to keep *them* from realizing themselves. But if it is *individual* self-realization we are concerned with, it would seem that such considerations are irrelevant.

Defenders of the theory could, of course, extend the self-realization theory to include a whole group together and thus say that your activity as a safecracker isn't *socially* self-realizing. But this seems to be double talk: it *is* very fulfilling personally, although it is not so for other members of society. Safecracking is harmful to others, but that doesn't keep it from being extremely fulfilling for anyone who engages in it. "Social realization" is not *self*-realization, and to speak of them in one breath as if they were the same thing, or as if they always went together, is to ignore the fact that they may collide with each other.

Consider a person who gives up her life for a cause in which she believes. Suppose this cause is of great value to society as a whole and that people are greatly indebted to her for her sacrifice. Although her heroism may help many other people to realize *their* potentialities (e.g., by enabling them to live in freedom again after she has helped assassinate a dictator and has been shot for it), how has it helped her to realize *hers?* How is getting yourself killed a means of realizing yourself? The sacrifice may be worthwhile from the point of view of others, but how can it be called *self*-realization? Can you have achieved self-realization when you are not even alive to do any realizing? The realization of self doesn't seem to be compatible with the extinction of the self. "Social realization" of some kind it may be, but *self*-realization it is not. To put the two together and speak of "social self-realization" appears to be only consoling double talk. Self-realization as an ideal of *personal* fulfillment has been replaced by something that is not personal fulfillment at all: the loss of life is the loss of any possibility of fulfilling anything.

E. Following Nature

One final ethical theory of well-being counsels people to live according to nature. "Be natural"; "do what comes naturally"; "let nature be your guide"—all these are popular watchwords meant to serve as guides to living. But as they stand they are not very clear; it would be difficult to extract any specific directions for action from them. Our first task, then, is to make these vague precepts more manageable by trying to make clear what they mean. Here are some ways in which they might be construed:

1. "Follow nature" could mean the same as "obey the laws of nature." But this fails not only as moral advice, but as any kind of advice at all. It would be quite pointless to advise people to do what they can't help doing anyway. How could we help "obeying" the law of gravitation? If we fall out of a window, we can't help going downward. Besides, we do not really *obey* laws of nature: laws of nature are simply generalized descriptions of the way nature works, not prescriptions as to how nature ought to behave (in the way that laws of a legislature are prescriptive). It would be more accurate to say that everything we do is an *instance* of some law (or laws) of nature. If we eat, the process of assimilation and digestion is an instance of certain biochemical laws. If we fall off a roof, our fall is an instance of laws of physics. If we free-associate, our action is an instance of certain laws of psychology.

But many people who talk about "obeying nature's laws" mean something more than this. They mean that the laws of nature are such that if we do certain things, we shall enjoy or suffer certain consequences. If we don't observe certain elementary rules of health, we shall suffer from malnutrition and disease. In this sense, the laws of nature don't say that we must or ought to follow certain rules of health, but only that *if* we don't, certain things will happen to us in consequence. Few people would be likely to recommend that we "disobey" those laws of nature that have to do with matters of life or death. But it all depends on which consequences will follow from which actions: if you know that drinking three martinis will get you drunk, you may drink them just the same; indeed this may be the purpose you have in mind in drinking them.

2. "Do what's natural" may mean the same as "go primitive." In the Romantic movement, philosophers often expressed a yearning to return to the primitive, to be "natural"; for example, French philosopher Jean Jacques Rousseau considered the state of "the noble savage" to be the ideal state of the human race. In a life dominated as our own is by such irritations as buses and subways, strikes and shortages, freeways and factory smoke, it is "natural" to rebel and cry out for a return to nature. City dwellers feel this urge more strongly than rural dwellers, who for their part often crave more nearness to people, more big stores, nightclubs and other things that cities afford. But should the whole of our lives be dominated either by city or by nature? To enjoy the pleasures of the city while living in the country seems to most people to be more desirable than either extreme taken alone, and many of those who cry out most loudly for a return to "life in the raw" would not wish to do so without medicine, electric lights, plumbing, and means of quick transportation.

If you share this ideal of "going primitive," how far would you take it? Is it enough to go for a picnic in the woods every other Sunday afternoon? Critics of this ideal like to follow this line of argument to its *reductio ad absurdum:*

> Where shall such Sabbath forays into nature's jungle end? How aboriginal should one get? Shall one play Indian and creep through the woods in a loincloth? Or should one identify oneself with more primitive natural species and go about barking, growling, or chirping? But why stop here? Why not go the limit in the direction of biological simplicity and like Diogenes bask in the sun, quietly thermotropic? Or if this is still too complicated, give oneself up like a stone to the eternal forces of gravitation?[9]

3. "Follow nature" often carries the meaning of "do what's natural" in the sense in which "natural" is the opposite of "artificial." What is artificial is, it would seem, any human artifice. It is not clear why anything that is crafted should be avoided. Paintings, cities, sewage systems, power plants, hearing aids, and manufactured drugs are all artificial. Should we then refrain from making things, devising new inventions and curing diseases, or using our intelligence to employ the materials present in nature in order to make new things to satisfy our needs and desires?

Although the chemical elements are to be found in nature, is there any reason why we should use them only in the form in which they are found in

---

[9]Lucius Garvin, *A Modern Introduction to Ethics* (Boston: Houghton Mifflin, 1952), p. 374.

nature? Why should we limit ourselves in this way? Why should herbs be permitted in cures but not the results of medical research? Finding the right herbs for the right disorders is itself medical research. Some may say that herbs are better for us in their natural form, and sometimes this is true (or at any rate, there is some controversy in the case of "natural" versus synthesized vitamins). But what about penicillin, anesthetics, surgery, and countless other medical advances which have saved thousands of lives? The "nature lover" must condemn all these things because they are not found in nature and are therefore not "natural." But should we refrain from using products from medical laboratories simply because they are not "natural"? Medical research is required partly because of the fact that what we find in nature, at least in the form in which we usually find it, is ineffective or insufficient. If all people had good eyesight, they would not need glasses; but because some do not, a clearly artificial product, eyeglasses, has been devised to remedy this deficiency of nature. Most people who need them and have them would be very reluctant to do without them, "natural" or not.

4. Sometimes "follow nature" is taken to mean the same as "follow *your* nature." But what does that mean? A person's nature can be identified roughly with his or her predominant personality traits—the person's strongest tendencies, as exhibited in what he or she most regularly does and seems most highly motivated to do. But in this sense, should we encourage a person to "follow his or her nature" no matter what that is? If an individual's strongest tendency is to commit ax murders or rob banks, shall we say that this is what he ought to do to be true to his nature? The assumption here is that whatever your nature is, it's good, and therefore you should follow it. This assumption is surely questionable. If that is what "behaving naturally" is, we might at this point write a few paragraphs in praise of artificiality.

5. In nature there is an endless variety of species of animal life. "Follow nature" can be taken to mean, "Do as the animals do. Live by your instincts. The lion follows its natural instincts and kills in order to eat. Human beings should be 'natural' by behaving as the animals do." The problem is that different animals live in different ways. The lion and the cougar live by catching live prey and eating them, as do other carnivores; but the deer and the antelope live on herbs and grasses, as do other herbivores. Which are we supposed to follow?

As for "following our natural instincts," it's not clear why we are supposed to do this instead of following models of behavior which are learned rather than instinctive. Anyway, as long as the topic is "natural instincts" (tendencies to behave in ways which don't have to be learned), don't human beings at least have a "natural instinct" to be intellectually curious and to pursue knowledge?

It is said that all animals behave selfishly, each animal acting so as to ensure its own survival; and it is true that animals tend to be indifferent to the suffering and death of other animals. But it is also true that animals often act so as to protect, not their own individual lives, but the lives of other members of the group: for example, at the outskirts of the nightly resting grounds a hyena will sacrifice its life to warn others of the approach of a lion, even if in so doing it is caught and eaten by the lion. (For other examples of this instinct, see Chapter 4 of Charles Darwin's *The Descent of Man* and Robert Ardrey's books *African Genesis* and *The Territorial Imperative.*) Animals, acting on their instincts, behave in a great many ways. Which of these then, are human beings supposed to emulate? And why should humans spend their lives "following their natural instincts" at all?

Each species of living thing survives in its own distinctive ways. Some survive through physical strength, others by sheer weight of numbers. If human beings had to survive by pitting their strength against other animals, they would find themselves quite helpless in comparison with charging buffaloes. It is not through strength that *homo sapiens* has mastered the earth and conquered virtually the entire animal kingdom (eliminating much of it in the process). Human beings have triumphed over nature through the use of their distinctive faculty, their intelligence. They have more brain power than any other species, and to the extent that they have used it they have succeeded in the struggle for existence. They cannot survive long through the unaided use of whatever "natural instincts" they have: a puppy or kitten is programmed to survive on its own after a few months, but a human baby or child cannot. Unlike the other animals, humans must *figure out* what to do in order to survive and prosper:

> For man, the basic means of survival is *reason*. Man cannot survive, as animals do, by the guidance of mere percepts. A sensation of hunger will tell him that he needs food (if he has learned to identify it as "hunger"), but it will not tell him how to obtain his food and it will not tell him what food is good for him or poisonous. He cannot provide for his simplest physical needs without a process of thought. He needs a process of thought to discover how to plant and grow his food or how to make weapons for hunting. His percepts [senses] might lead him to a cave, if one is available—but to build the simplest shelter, he needs a process of thought. No percepts and no "instincts" will tell him how to light a fire, how to weave cloth, how to forge tools, how to make a wheel, how to make an airplane, how to perform an appendectomy, how to produce an electric light bulb or an electronic tube or a cyclotron or a box of matches. Yet his life depends on such knowledge—and only a volitional act of his consciousness, a process of thought, can provide it.[10]

If wolves and tigers tried to survive as human beings do, they would fail, for they lack the capacity; in precisely the same way, if human beings tried to

---

[10] Ayn Rand, "The Objectivist Ethics," in *The Virtue of Selfishness* (New York: New American Library, 1964), p. 21.

survive as wolves and tigers do, they would also fail, for they are not "programmed to behave" as other animals are, to survive without the exercise of their intellectual powers.

6. Sometimes it is not the behavior of animals but the manner in which laws of nature operate in relation to living things on this planet that is the main thrust of the precept "Follow nature." Following nature then becomes the way human beings use nature's processes as *models for imitation*.

But what sorts of things does "nature" do? Or, if we do not want to personify nature, what sort of events and processes occur in the world apart from human participation? Nature provides moisture, warmth, and nutrients for the crops to grow; but nature also provides a limitless supply of destructive forces: droughts, floods, famines, earthquakes, volcanic eruptions, freezing cold, and blistering heat—all of which kill organisms by the millions. John Stuart Mill commented on just such a destructive tendency in nature:

> In sober truth, nearly all the things which men are hanged or imprisoned for doing to one another, are Nature's every day performances. Killing, the most criminal act recognized by human nature, Nature does once to every being that lives, and in a large proportion of cases, after protracted tortures such as only the greatest monsters whom we read of ever purposely inflicted on their living fellow-creatures. . . . Nature impales men, breaks them as if on the wheel, casts them to be devoured by wild beasts, burns them to death, crushes them with stones like the first Christian martyr, starves them with hunger, freezes them with cold, poisons them by the quick or slow venom of her exhalations, and has hundreds of other hideous deaths in reserve, such as the ingenious cruelty of a Nabis or a Domitian never surpassed. All this, Nature does with the most supercilious disregard both of mercy and of justice, emptying her shafts upon the best and noblest indifferently with the meanest and worst; upon those who are engaged in the highest and worthiest enterprises, and often as the direct consequence of the noblest acts; and it might almost be imagined as a punishment for them. She mows down those on whose existence hangs the well-being of a whole people, perhaps the prospects of the human race for generations to come, with as little compunction as those whose death is a relief to themselves, or a blessing to those under their noxious influence.
>
> Such are Nature's dealings with life. Even when she does not intend to kill, she inflicts the same tortures in apparent wantonness. In the clumsy provision which she has made for that perpetual renewal of animal life, rendered necessary by the prompt termination she puts to it in every individual instance, no human being ever comes into the world but another human being is literally stretched on the rack for hours or days, not unfrequently issuing in death. Next to taking life (equal to it according to a high authority) is taking the means by which we live; and Nature does this too on the largest scale and with the most callous in-

difference. A single hurricane destroys the hopes of a season; a flight of locusts, or an inundation, desolates a district; a trifling chemical change in an edible root, starves a million of people. The waves of the sea, like banditti seize and appropriate the wealth of the rich and the little all of the poor with the same accompaniments of stripping, wounding, and killing as their human antitypes. Everything, in short, which the worst men commit either against life or property is perpetrated on a larger scale by natural agents. . . . [Nature's] explosions of fire damp are as destructive as human artillery; her plague and cholera far surpass the poison cups of the Borgias. Even the love of "order" which is thought to be a following of the ways of Nature, is in fact a contradiction of them. All which people are accustomed to deprecate as "disorder" and its consequences, is precisely a counterpart of Nature's ways. Anarchy and the Reign of Terror are overmatched in injustice, ruin, and death, by a hurricane and a pestilence.[11]

Almost everything we consider worthwhile in human life, Mill argued in this classic essay, consists not in "following nature" but in transcending and improving upon nature. If we wish to improve the quality of our lives, live longer and more healthfully and happily, and decrease suffering, we can't take nature as a model for imitation but should rather seek to improve on it. Most people are "naturally" lazy in that they do not undertake any great efforts unless extinction stares them in the face; yet the survival and continuation of any kind of civilized life depend on unremitting labor and the cultivation of "unnatural" habits of work. If we want human life to be secure, we should not "kill as nature kills," and certainly not *because* nature does it. What nature does gives us no direction as to what *we* should do. That nature behaves in certain ways is one thing; how human beings should behave is quite another.

4. OBJECTIONS TO ETHICAL EGOISM

The views we have considered are predominantly egoistic—in some cases, entirely so; but all have been primarily concerned with how individuals can ensure their own happiness or fulfillment, and any attention paid to doing good deeds for others has been fairly incidental.

There are a number of objections, however, that have been made to impersonal ethical egoism in all its forms and manifestations. Let us now consider four of the most important of these.

1. Many attempts have been made to show that ethical egoism contradicts itself (is self-contradictory) in some way. The thrust of such attempts is to

---

[11]John Stuart Mill, "Nature," in *Three Essays on Religion* (1873). Reprinted in *Nature and the Utility of Religion,* ed. George Nakhnikian (New York: Liberal Arts Press, 1958), pp. 20–22.

show that the theory allows one and the same act to be both right and wrong.

If every person is to pursue his or her own interest exclusively, then, it is charged, person *A,* if it is in his or her interest, should kill or injure *B* in some way, and *B* should attempt to kill or injure *A.* In other words, it would be right for *A* to do (preserve *A*'s life) what would be wrong for *B* to do (preserve *A*'s life). If *A* and *B* both want the same woman, and she won't have both, and *A* and *B* both feel strongly enough about it to kill in order to get her, then (assuming that the winner would be happy with her and that nothing else could make him as happy) *A* should kill *B* to get her, and *B* should kill *A* to get her.

But, objectionable as some of us might find this situation, there is no contradiction here. It might well be right for *A* to resist whatever moves *B* might make, and right for *B* to resist whatever moves *A* might make. What would be right for *A* to do (pursue *A*'s interests) would not be what would be right for *B* to do (preserve *B*'s interests). After all, *A* killing *B* and *B* killing *A* are not one act, but two different acts: for *A* to kill *B* is one act, for *B* to kill *A* (even to resist *A*'s attempts to kill him) is a different act; so it is not true that the same act would be, according to ethical egoism, both right and wrong.

Whether it really *is* in the interests of *A* and *B* to kill each other could also be denied. Wouldn't it be more in the interests of each to ask the lady whom she prefers and then abide by her decision? If she prefers *A* and *B* gets her, *B* wouldn't be getting what he wanted anyway (namely, the woman who prefers him to everyone else). In this case, as in most others, some mutual arrangement, some agreed-upon *modus vivendi,* even some scheme of cooperation, is likely to be more in the interest of each one than mutual destruction. Suppose *B* loses out and later meets a woman he likes even better; surely it would be more in his interest to stay alive than to run a 50-50 chance of being killed by *A,* and not staying alive to meet her. To present ethical egoism as if it recommended mutual destruction is to make of it a gross caricature.

Similarly, if *A* and *B* are business competitors, it is in *A*'s interest to compete successfully with *B,* even perhaps (sometimes) to do so well that *B* is forced into bankruptcy; and the same with *B.* Or perhaps it is in the interest of each just to run a successful and prosperous business without knocking the other out at all. (Business competitors do often cooperate with one another to their mutual advantage—for example against objectionable government regulations that affect both of them.) But as egoists each should try to succeed as much as possible. Is there anything wrong with this?

Consider another example. It is often considered the duty of one person or group to resist attempts by another person or group. In a wartime situation the duty of every prisoner of war is to try to escape; but the duty of every prison camp official is to foil or prevent all such attempts to escape. Each is trying to prevent a certain action by the other (imprisonment or escape).

This kind of situation may be unfortunate, but there is no contradiction in conceiving of it, or even in practicing it.

Most of the time, however, it is in the interest of both parties to work out some kind of *modus vivendi;* both cooperation and competition are preferable (for both parties) to killing or running the risk of being killed or injured by the other. Many apparent conflicts of interest can be resolved in this way. Assume, for example, that two egoists do piecework in a factory, and the boss makes them keep the factory floor clean to avoid fire department violations. If the floor is not cleaned, it is a fire hazard, and the building will be closed down, resulting in job loss. The egoists use most of the floor, but they don't want to clean it because they don't want to lose money while they could be turning out pieces of work for money. According to egoism, each one should act so as to maximize her own interest. Does egoism, then, direct each worker to clean the floor and also *not* to clean the floor—for if one worker does clean, the other will be making money meanwhile, and if she doesn't she will lose her job? This dilemma is again only an apparent one for the egoist. Why do something that will cause one to lose a job? Wouldn't it be preferable for the first worker to make an agreement with the second, saying, "Let's each clean half the floor each day; that way we'll keep our jobs, and neither of us will be losing paid work to the other." Not only would this be a sensible solution, but it would be in the interest of each worker to make such an agreement and stick by it.

2. Another objection to ethical egoism is that the egoist is committed to giving *inconsistent advice.* Suppose that A, an ethical egoist, is asked by B what he, B, should do. A replies, "Promote your own interest exclusively, even if that means harming C and D." Then C asks A what she, C, should do, and A replies, "Promote your own interest exclusively, even if it means harming B and D." The same advice is then given to each questioner. It certainly seems as if A is offering inconsistent advice. Doesn't the advice to B conflict with that to C, and the advice to each person (to promote his or her own interest exclusively) contradict the advice to every other person? Or perhaps A is pathologically addicted to changing his mind—perhaps he favors B over C when he talks to B, and favors C over B when he talks to C. Or perhaps he is just a hypocrite, who praises people to their face and then betrays them behind their back. Whatever his reason, it appears that what he tells one person is inconsistent with what he tells another.

But this objection, too, is ill-founded. He needn't be constantly changing his mind, nor need he be a hypocrite. He might collect B, C, and D together before him and say to each one, "I believe that you should each try to promote your own interest exclusively." In doing this he would not be acting differently from a person attending a ball game who gives a pep talk to both teams to try to get each to win, so as to make the game a more exciting one to watch. There is surely nothing hypocritical in this.

If what A is saying to B is, "I *hope* you come out ahead of everyone else," and if what he is saying to C is, "I *hope* you come out ahead of everyone else," then indeed he is either vacillating rapidly in his allegiances or being hypocritical. But he need not be *hoping* for each one to come out on top. (Can he hope for each team to win the game?) He might only be saying to each one, "Try your best to come out on top." If a good contest is what he wants, this might be just what he would say.

He might say all of these things if none of the actions of *B*, *C*, or *D* in any way adversely affected *him*. But what if they did? Suppose that as an ethical egoist he is committed to the view that he, *A*, should try to promote his own interests, but that *B*, *C*, and *D* should also try to promote their own interests individually. But suppose that *A* owns the only drugstore in a small town and that *B* is thinking about opening up a competing drugstore in the same town. *B* might hurt *A*'s business; if he is very aggressive in his sales-manship, he might even put *A* out of business, if the town isn't big enough to support two drugstores. What, then, will *A* advise *B* to do? Will he advise *B* to compete with him, knowing that if *B* does this it will hurt *A*?

Surely he will not do this, for if he does, he will be doing something that is detrimental to *his own* interests, and as an ethical egoist he is committed to furthering those interests. In this case he will advise *B* *not* to open the drug-store. Even if it would advance *B*'s interests to open one, he will, as an egoist, advise *B* not to. In short, when advising people what to do, *A* will not advise them to do anything that will harm his own interests, even if this means giving *B* false advice. Indeed, *B*, if he is thinking about opening a competing drugstore, would be well-advised not to seek advice from *A*, knowing him to be an egoist and a competitor; in this situation *A* would be about the last person from whom *B* would ask for advice.

In fact, *A* as an ethical egoist needn't be in the business of advising other people at all. When advising people isn't in his own interest, he won't give them any advice. After all, what's in it for him? Why should he advise other people when doing so might hurt him? If he is interested in seeing an exciting game, he might advise each side to try to win; but if he doesn't care, why should he bother? His ethical egoism commits him only to holding to a certain moral theory; it doesn't also commit him to telling other people what they should do. He might believe that they should try to advance their own interests individually, but it doesn't follow that he should *tell* them that that's what they ought to do; in many cases he would be well-advised, as an egoist, to keep his advice to himself.

If you are playing chess with someone and you look at the board and see some move that your opponent could make to defeat you, should you tell her about it? This is the move your opponent *should* make—at least she should if she wants to win the game. (Participants in a game can be assumed to be egoists, at least for purposes of the game.) But it surely isn't the move that you should *tell* her to make. Rather, you will keep silent, hoping that she isn't smart enough to think of the move that would defeat you. The egoist is committed only to following a certain course of action (promoting his or her own interests); he or she is not committed, in addition, to advising other people that they should also follow that course of action (thus promoting their own interests), even if he or she believes that they should do so.

This would mean, in many cases at least, that *A,* an egoist, should advise others to be altruistic, because if they are, *A* will benefit; and *B* ought to advise others to be altruistic, so that *B* will benefit; and so on. Each egoist would then end up advising others to be altruistic, whereas in fact (according to the egoist) no one *ought* to be altruistic. Isn't this a contradiction of a sort? It certainly would be a disparity between what an egoist *believes* and what he or she *advises.* And in the end the result would be that no one would believe in an egoist's advice. This might, for many purposes, be an unfortunate consequence; but it would simply be a matter of failed tactics. The egoist could no longer give advice that would be trusted by anyone else; but he or she would still *believe* that everyone ought to be egoistic.

Besides, it wouldn't necessarily be the case that an egoist would always advise other people to be altruistic; the advice to be egoistic would be offered only when the egoist's own interests weren't affected, and the advice to be altruistic would be offered only when doing so would promote the egoist's own interests—and that would certainly not be all of the time, nor even perhaps very much of the time. Most of the time people's interests don't conflict; it is only occasionally that they do. If *A* wants to support herself and *B* wants to support himself, their interests don't conflict; but if *B* wants to be supported by *A* and *A* doesn't fancy this arrangement, but it is nevertheless forced on her, their interests do conflict, for *A* must now work to support both *A* and *B*.

3. But isn't there still an inconsistency, not in what the egoist *advises,* but in what he or she *believes* or professes? If *A* believes that he should promote his own interests exclusively and believes too that *B* should promote *B*'s own interests exclusively, does he really believe—not advise, just believe—that *B* should promote *B*'s interests when those interests conflict with his own? Does he really believe *B* ought to harm him? True, he won't *advise B* to start the other drugstore; but will he even *believe* that *B* should, when *B*'s doing so might ruin *A?* One might say no, since, as an egoist, he can't believe his interests should be harmed. But one might also say yes, he does believe it, just as he believes as a chess player that his opponent should make the move that will destroy him. But can *A,* an egoist, consistently believe that *B* ought to do something that would harm *A*'s interests? Isn't the whole point that *A*'s interests ought to be promoted?

No, the point is that *A*'s interests ought to be promoted *by A.* And *B*'s interests ought to be promoted *by B. A* might really think that *B* would be a fool not to further *B*'s interests, even if doing so harms *A;* only of course he isn't going to tell *B* this, any more than the chess player will reveal the possible brilliant move to his opponent. *A* might say to himself, "If I were *B,* I would do *X*—even if it harms me. *B* would be a fool not to do *X.*" Why can't he sincerely believe this? Were all the ethical egoists of history, from Epicurus on, being inconsistent when they told each person to think of himself or herself first, to tend to personal affairs and let other people look after theirs? One could condemn the position as self-interested (but the egoist wouldn't view that as condemnation, of course); one might disagree with it, but that's not the same as refuting the theory by showing it to be inconsistent.

4. There is, however, a fundamental objection that has been made to ethical egoism—that it is incapable of settling interpersonal disputes in which one action or policy is in one person's interest and a quite different action or policy is in another person's interest. There are certain interpersonal decisions that have to be made that, it is said, transcend the egoist's point of view. A certain legislative act would be to the advantage of A and B but not to that of C and D. Yet the act has either to be passed or not. If the legislature decides to enact it because the number of people it will help exceeds the number of people it will hinder, or because the total amount of satisfaction if it is passed will exceed the total amount of dissatisfaction if it isn't, then it is being enacted for reasons that take each individual's interests into consideration, but not because it works to this or that individual's advantage. It can't be to the advantage of each one, because the very act of enacting it into law will work to the advantage of some but not of others. Consider this example, provided by Kurt Baier:

> Suppose the problem under discussion is whether or not a certain traffic roundabout [traffic circle] should be erected at a certain intersection. I can look at this from various points of view, that of a pedestrian or a motorist, a local politician or a manufacturer of roundabouts, and so on. In cases such as these, we have in mind the point of view of self-interest as applied to certain special positions or jobs or functions in a society. To look at our problem from the point of view of a motorist is to ask whether the erection of a roundabout at this intersection is in the interest of a motorist. For different points of view there may, of course, be different, even opposing, answers to the same practical questions. The roundabout may be in the interest of a motorist but not of a pedestrian, in the interest of a manufacturer of roundabouts but not of a local politician who depends for his votes on the poorer section (the pedestrians) of the population.[12]

If each person involved in this dispute were an ethical egoist, what would be the result? If all agreed to put the matter to a vote, the side with the most votes would win. If they didn't agree to vote on the matter, they might fight it out, but this might well turn out to be to no one's advantage. More probably the defeated minority would shrug off the defeat and say, "You win some, you lose some." In the present example the decision would probably be made by the city planners without taking a vote at all, but what would

[12]Kurt Baier, *The Moral Point of View* (Ithaca, N.Y.: Cornell University Press, 1958), pp. 184–85. Reprinted by permission of the publisher.

determine *their* decision? They might personally get no advantage out of the outcome either way. If they were egoists, how would they decide? They might decide on the basis of which policy would be more likely to get them reelected or reappointed to their jobs, and this would indeed be an egoistic reason. But they might also decide on the basis of whether all or most of those concerned were better off with or without the traffic circle. Such a decision would be impersonal, in the sense of not being based on any considerations of personal advantage to themselves.

A husband in divorce court finds it in his interest to have exclusive custody of the child; the same is true for the wife. Thus, their egoistic interests conflict. A judge has to decide between their conflicting claims. She might decide on the basis of what the child preferred, or where she thought the child would be happiest whether that's what the child preferred or not. But presumably the judge's decision would not be based on what she thought was advantageous to herself: indeed, a decision one way would be no more so than the other way, since she will probably never see the couple again and thus will have nothing to gain or lose personally by the decision. But if she decides *impartially,* she will take the interests of all parties into account, showing bias in favor of none of them (nor against them either), but sorting out all the considerations and trying to adjudicate the dispute in a way that is best for all concerned. That may not be possible; if both husband and wife would be worse off without the child, and she cannot satisfy them both, she will have to choose—perhaps using the child's preferences as her final basis for judgment. But the point is that she would consider the interests of all the parties, while herself remaining *dis*interested (i.e., impartial as between the conflicting interests of the parties, but not *un*interested).

When there is a conflict of interests and not all egoistic interests can be satisfied, there must be some mechanism, such as the judiciary, for deciding among them. The judge takes what is sometimes called the moral, or "God's-eye," point of view—that of an impartial authority who cannot satisfy all parties in all respects but does the best that can be done in considering the interests of each one. Such a point of view transcends the egoistic point of view. The question that the egoist must then answer is: Don't many decisions require this?

The judge and the city planners, we say, should be impartial in judging conflicting interests. That has a nice sound, but it also is somewhat vague. Suppose the husband would be less lonely without the child and is also able to be a better role model for the child, who is a boy; suppose the wife would miss the child more than the husband would if she didn't have him and might provide better meals for him but would also be engaged part time in husband hunting, in which enterprise the presence of the child might be an annoyance or embarrassment. How is a judge, however impartial, to weigh these considerations against one another? What should determine whether she should attach more importance to the wife's being with the child or to the husband's helpfulness as an ego ideal for the child? (And if she should become a judge in criminal court, should she give as much consideration to the interests of the convicted rapist as to those of the rapist's victim? Does impartiality require that too?) Once we try to get behind the noble-sounding word "impartiality," it is less than clear what kinds of actions it requires.

Should the impartial judge be warmhearted, empathizing in agony over the sufferings of all those before her? Or should she be more of a no-nonsense type, leaving people to sort out their emotions for themselves ("That's their problem") and just doing what she considers "sensible"? Should she consider the child more than the parents? Is the health of the child more important than the child's emotional well-being, or vice versa? Is giving the child a fairly high standard of living more important than giving the child what he wants? Should the judge's sympathetic emotions dominate her good judgment, or should the reverse be the case? Should she be guided more by love or by knowledge? There is a whole array of such questions to which no answer is obvious when one asks what is involved in the concept of impartiality.

Moreover, special relations which we also find important seem to preclude impartiality. Most people, at any rate, believe they are not acting wrongly when they help their own children but not the neighbors' children, or when they support their own parents but not other people's parents. Are they supposed to be impartial as between their own parents and somebody else's? Does impartiality demand that they not consider the fact that this is their own mother and not somebody else's? Is it wrong to be partial to relatives? Or does the idea of impartiality already include within it a preference for those who are related in a special way, such as parents and children and friends? Most people would find it quite odd to be told that they must be impartial as between friends and strangers when they are giving out invitations for a dinner party.

That some impartial interpersonal decisions have to be made, however, seems clear enough. To say that they should be made egoistically, on the basis of the self-interest of the person doing the deciding, is (to say the least) strange: the person doing the deciding may have no personal stake in the decision at all. (If the judge does have a personal stake—for example, if she is the wife's sister—she is not supposed to try that case, precisely because she does have a personal stake in it.) When ethical egoists tell us that we should always act so as to maximize our own interest, it would be interesting to know how this advice is supposed to help the judge in making a decision in which she has no personal interest. This is one rather solid objection to ethical egoism as a universal principle of human conduct. Whether other moral principles are more satisfactory remains to be seen.

5. FINAL COMMENTS ON ETHICAL EGOISM

Whatever may be said of these objections (and each one of them is a subject matter of continuing controversy), the picture presented of a practicing ethical egoist is likely to be somewhat distorted by the typical examples that are given. The stereotype of the egoist as someone who would rather kill than cooperate is inaccurate, since it is seldom in anyone's interest to risk being killed for failure to achieve some desire. Nor is life necessarily conceived by the egoist as a *contest* between conflicting groups, as the analogy with games suggests. Sometimes it is indeed a contest, but more often it is simply a challenge. In light of the criticisms just discussed, then, what conclusions can be reached about ethical egoism?

1. In defense of ethical egoism, it must be noted that there are many activities which are engaged in constantly with self-interest in mind but which nevertheless benefit others. This situation occurs far more frequently than the conflicts of interest which critics repeatedly emphasize. A man decides to start a business enterprise, partly as a challenge, partly to make profits for himself; thus far, he is entirely egoistic. But if he is to produce a product that people will buy, he must build stores or factories, purchase supplies (or produce them himself), and hire employees. All of this activity provides work for many who would otherwise be unemployed, or who leave their previous jobs for his because he pays them more or provides better working conditions. Not only does he thereby create work for others, but he creates an additional product or service, thus giving consumers more choices than they had before; nor can he force them to buy the product or service, which must be either better or cheaper than that of competitors for the business to stay afloat. He does not start the business for others' benefit, yet by undertaking it, and assuming the risks of loss or bankruptcy, he benefits a large number of other persons. He is often criticized for being selfish in his motivation, but at any rate the effects of his enterprise are widely beneficial to others: he may be a pillar of society or a Boy Scout leader in his spare time, but none of these activities do nearly as much good for others as his being in a business that keeps employees on the payroll and provides consumer goods for large numbers of people at competitive prices.

2. There are many more occasions than it may seem at first, in which it is to one's interest to care what happens to others. If something isn't going to affect the egoist one way or the other, he or she will be indifferent to it; but there are many more things that affect us than at first appear to do so. We may be indifferent to the existence of a dictatorship in a nearby country. "It's nothing to me," we might say, but we might be mistaken. After conquering armies have squelched all opposition in the nearby country, the dictator tries to take over the next one. How many people in Europe were indifferent to the rise of Hitler and Stalin until they were killed or enslaved by their forces? Or again, we sometimes fail to care about who is mayor of our town or who is the county commissioner or how big government bureaucracies become, until we are penalized in some way by one of them—something that might have been prevented with a little more civic mindedness and attention to what was happening in government. It is true, at least to some degree, that no man is an island: if one person is arrested by the secret police or railroaded by means of a mock trial, it is more likely to happen to other people, includ-

ing perhaps the egoist who didn't care. It *is* in our interest, as a rule, to care about such things. Epicurus said that you shouldn't get involved in the political process, because it is like knocking your head against a stone wall—and very often this is maddeningly true; but if most people took this attitude, their country would be ripe for totalitarian takeover. In a world in which there are so many subtle connections between what affects your life and what affects others, it is wise to look again at what seems not to affect it. Very often you may conclude that it does after all.

Besides learning to spot what truly affects self-interest, it is wise to keep in mind the distinction between what is of interest in the long and short run. Many activities that provide an immediate egoistic payoff do not do so in the long run, and there are many things you might be tempted to do if you considered only the short run rather than the long haul. Consider a big-time American farmer who has successfully agitated in Congress for larger agricultural subsidies. He gets, say, $100,000 a year for growing certain crops (or for not growing them, and letting his land lie fallow). He doesn't deny that this is simply a piece of pork-barrel legislation, in which money is taken from other taxpayers to pay him. Yet he's getting richer and couldn't really care less as an egoist how much other people are penalized for his prosperity.

But is he really practicing his egoism consistently? For the long term, he may not be. For the more money that is collected from people in taxes to pay for these things, the less incentive they will have to work and make profit for themselves, since it will only be drained away in taxes. And the less productivity there is, the less the tax revenue that will be collected from which to appropriate amounts for special interests like the farmer's. The government can run off more printing-press money to pay for such projects, but this will mean inflation: then everybody's dollar will be worth less than before, including his. Either way, the result will be the ruination of the entire national economy, which really *will* affect him. If he says, "I'll take my payments, and *après moi le déluge,*" the deluge will come down on him too, sooner or later. So in the long run it will be in the farmer's self-interest *not* to agitate for such special subsidies, but rather to help keep the economy free and productive. He will have to *earn* his money rather than *take* it, but as long as everyone is in the same position, he (as well as the rest of the country) will be better off, and he will be, egoistically, the gainer.

3. There is yet another point that is easily overlooked by critics of ethical egoism. It is true that ethical egoists are committed to acting in their own personal interest, but they cannot do this unless they are free to choose among alternatives. A certain degree of personal freedom must be theirs in order for them to be in a position to practice egoism. What this comes to, as we shall see in Chapter 7 on rights, is that others must leave certain aspects of the egoist's life free from interference; egoists must possess certain rights which are not violated by others in order to be capable of genuine voluntary action. If one egoist admits this to be true, he or she must admit it to be *true for all*. In universal ethical egoism, *every* person must be free to pursue his or her

own interests, not just one person. And if this proviso is accepted, there need be no more talk about ethical egoists enslaving or killing other persons, for a stricture on the ethical egoist's actions is that he or she must respect the rights of others just as they must respect the egoist's. The egoistic position would then be that each person should pursue personal interests within the limits fixed by the imperative not to violate others' rights. (Many people who would not otherwise accept ethical egoism would do so with this express proviso.)

4. There is a further way to conceive of ethical egoism if we take it to apply not to individual actions but to rules of human conduct. It is then called *rule egoism*.

According to rule egoism, there are certain rules of conduct which it is in the interest of *everyone*, not just a single individual, to observe. Sometimes you may get so angry, you may want to kill someone, and if you didn't fear being caught you might do it. You might then wish there was no law prohibiting such conduct. But without such a law, you yourself would be in much greater danger, for other people might not refrain from killing you if there was no such law. Weighing the pros and cons, you become convinced that it is in your interest to have such a law: it keeps you from doing some things you might want to do to others, but it also keeps others from doing what they might want to do to you. You have to restrain some impulses you have, but others will also have to restrain theirs. And in all probability you will gain by having the restriction: it is more to your interest to not kill and not be killed than it is to be able to kill but also risk being killed. In some cases it might even be in your interest to kill someone—for example, if someone is frustrating your interests and you are not likely to get caught. But rule egoism commits you, not to believing that you should do every *act* which is in your own interest, but to following (and trying to get others to follow) those *rules* whose adoption within the society would be in your interest.

There are many such rules. Laws enforcing contracts are an example; they force you to keep a contract when you don't feel like it, but they also force others to keep theirs and not cheat you when they otherwise might. And again, you gain more on balance from such a rule than you lose; in fact, without such a rule no contracts would be worth the paper they're printed on. A will is a kind of contract, and it's in your interest to leave your worldly goods to whomever you choose in your will; that the conditions of a will be followed, as the laws enforcing wills provide, is in your interest, as it is in most other people's interests. Laws against theft are another example. For theft to be legally prohibited means you will be arrested for stealing from someone else, but also that they will be arrested for stealing from you; once more, in all probability you will gain more than you will lose by such a rule.

Of course, not everyone may agree on all the rules. There may be rules which are in some people's interest to have on the books, but not in the interest of others. We shall have a lot more to say about rules and their enforcement in coming chapters. Suffice it to say here that this form of ethical egoism (some would say it is a very diluted form) enjoins the following of certain rules, particularly those that make civilized life possible, for such rules are preconditions for the well-being of each person.

Thus far, ethical egoism has been presented as if all life was a game and the only question was who was going to win. But life need not be pictured as a contest, and rule egoism provides an alternate model, one that would avoid criticism of ethical egoism as based on conflict and cutthroat competition. Life can be compared, instead, to a *highway* along which everyone is traveling. You are driving, and everyone else is driving, along this highway. You may not care about the other drivers; perhaps you are interested only in arriving at *your* destination safely. But you know that if this is to occur, there must be certain rules of the road which everyone is required to observe. For example, people can't drive on whatever side of the road they feel like. They shouldn't drive while intoxicated or in other ways dangerous to fellow drivers. They shouldn't drive in cars without brakes or headlights. They shouldn't pass cars while going up hills or around turns. As an ethical egoist, you profit from the existence of such rules: to the extent that there are such rules and they are enforced, *you* benefit. True, the rules restrict your activities somewhat: you can't go through stoplights when you feel like it. In return for such minor restrictions, however, you can travel much more safely. Even if you don't care whether the other drivers get to their destinations safely, you care whether you do, and you know you are less likely to do that if there are no rules of the road. It is in *your* interest, then, as it is in every other driver's interest, to have rules of the road which are generally observed. You needn't observe them out of any particular love for others (though you may); it is enough if you (and the others) obey them, seeing that such rules are in your own (and their) interest. They enhance your life more than they take away from it. From an egoistic point of view, you want them around.

Some rules might be doubtful. For example, would you, as an egoist, pick up pieces of glass or other sharp objects from the road, so that the next motorist wouldn't get a flat tire? If you have already passed the spot safely, would it be in your self-interest to stop and do this? Some people might say, "I'll do it for the next guy; perhaps someone will do it for me sometime." But it is extremely unlikely that you yourself would be the beneficiary of this action of yours: the next motorist might be benefited by your action, but the chances that *your* tires would be saved on some future occasion because of your doing this for some unknown motorist now are infinitesimal. But it *might* be to everyone's interest to have a rule, with the force of law, requiring every motorist to do this; in that case you would have to do it when someone else is the beneficiary, and they would also have to do it for others, of whom you might be a beneficiary. (But "might" is the word, not "would," for it could be argued that stopping on a highway to pick up glass might be dangerous—another car might hit you from behind, for example—

and would also delay people's trips so much that it might be preferable to let each motorist take a chance with an occasional pile of broken glass.)

Consider another example, this time off the highway and in the air. As an egoist you might want to lean back as far as possible in order to rest while riding on an airplane, and the fact that doing so would inconvenience the passenger sitting behind you might not bother you. But since the designing of airplanes is not something that can be done just for one person, the rule (how far back a seat should be designed to go) must be the same for everyone. If you wanted to push the seat far back, you would then have to face the consequence that the passenger in front of you might do the same to you. Not everyone would agree on what the maximum degree of inclination of a seat should be; but very likely it would be in everyone's interest that seats should go back somewhat but not so much as to prevent the passenger behind from stepping out of his or her seat. The point is that it would be impractical to have one rule for you and another one for everybody else. As an egoist you would want the rule adopted which would be most in your interest, and you might write letters to airplane manufacturers indicating your wishes in the matter; but at the same time you could be assured that whatever the final design, it would be the same for everyone, and you would not be a special case. If in the interests of luxury you preferred to have a seat that goes far back, you would have to weigh that advantage against the possible disadvantage that the passenger in front of you would be able to do to you what you have done to the one behind you. This consideration might influence you considerably in deciding what rule to favor.

EXERCISES

1. Assess the following dialogue:
   A: A person always acts so as to satisfy himself.
   B: What of the husband whose first thought is to please his wife and who is more interested in her happiness than in his own?
   A: All that means is that it satisfies him to satisfy her. It's still egoistic.
   B: Isn't there a difference between the husband who likes to satisfy himself sexually and doesn't care about his wife, and the one who tries to make sure that his wife is satisfied also?
   A: Yes, but they're both egoistic: in both cases the husband is interested in his own pleasure, but the source of the pleasure is different in the two cases.
2. Can the following be accounted for on the basis of psychological egoism? Explain.
   a. A man wants his children to be happy and successful in life after he is dead.
   b. A woman wants to have payments taken out of her paycheck for welfare purposes, even though she herself (who doesn't need welfare) will lose financially by having such an arrangement.
   c. A man would give up everything he has earned for many years if he could be sure the world would be at peace after his death.
3. Do you consider the following examples to be favorable to psychological egoism (in any of its forms), unfavorable to it, or neither? Why?

a. A man picks up a nail from the highway and says, "Maybe someone will do the same for me some day, before my car comes along."

b. A man picks up a nail from the highway to prevent other cars from getting flat tires. He is not driving that day and has no plans to return to the vicinity in the future. He has no hopes or thoughts about someone doing the same for him. He does it simply out of habit.

c. The same as *b,* except that he does it not out of habit but because he believes it to be his duty.

d. The driver asks the hitchhiker riding with her, "Which is the way to town *A?"* The hitchhiker gives her a truthful answer, although he himself is going to town *B,* and if he had given the driver the directions to town *B* instead (saying it was the way to town *A*) the driver would have gone toward town *B,* where the hitchhiker wanted to go. The driver would, of course, have discovered the lie, but not until the hitchhiker had been taken to where he wanted to go.

e. The driver at night stops her car to replace a sawhorse marked "Open Trench" which has toppled over in the wind. Asked why she did it, she replies, "It's a kind of unwritten rule of the road."

f. The driver stops to pick up an injured dog on the road, saying, "It hurts me to see an animal just lie there and suffer."

4. Try to resolve the following controversy. Can you detect any shift in the way in which the term "selfish" is being used?

A: Cats are selfish. They want you only for the meal ticket which you supply. But dogs will really sacrifice for you—they will starve at your feet rather than leave you, and they will travel a thousand miles, undergoing great hardship, just to be with you again.

B: I disagree with you. Even dogs are selfish. They won't do anything for you unless there's something in it for *them.* They want your love and affection more than they want food, and they fear insecurity more than hunger.

A: In the Arctic some time ago an explorer was found who had been dead for three weeks. His dog lay starving at his feet, while his cat was eating his eyes out. Don't you consider that evidence for my position?

B: No. Both the dog and the cat were selfish, but in different ways. And the same for human beings. They are always selfish too, but their selfishness more often includes a concern (selfish concern, of course) for the welfare of others.

A: I disagree once again. Dogs are less selfish than cats, and human beings *can* be more unselfish than either. Neither dogs nor cats act contrary to their own interests from principles of duty, but people do. Perhaps the dog finds it easier or less unpleasant to be with its master even if it is starving, but people often do the more difficult thing and the thing that they *don't* want. You have commanded the dog not to go outside; although it wants to go out, perhaps it stays indoors because it fears punishment or loss of affection. But people sometimes do things for others without expecting anything in return—not even the satisfaction or security which the dog expects.

B: I think all three species are equally selfish, always. I grant that people may act from a sense of duty, unlike the dog, but I don't believe they would do so if they didn't think they would derive more satisfaction (or avoid dissatisfaction) by so doing.

5. In which of the following circumstances would *you* behave egoistically?
   a. You know that you will sell your car in a year or two anyway and that by "breaking it in hard" you will probably not be hurting the car during the time that *you* own it but that the person who buys it from you will have many extra repairs because of your earlier treatment of the car. (Assume also that the results of your mistreatment will not be obvious at the time to the buyer, to prevent that person from buying it.)
   b. Would you, if you were a car manufacturer, put together a car cheaply and without necessary safety devices, if you had considerable statistical evidence to prove that many more people would be attracted to your product because of its lower price than would refrain from buying it because of its shoddy construction?
   c. If you had a ring (like the Ring of Gyges in Plato's *Republic*) which would make you invisible, would you steal articles from stores rather than buy them outright, knowing that you could never be detected?
6. If one always behaves selfishly, is one the loser in the end? Consider the following cases pro or con:
   a. During a New York power failure, there was a sudden demand for flashlight batteries. Supplies were running low, so many merchants, knowing that they could sell their product for any price, sold countless ten-cent batteries for five dollars each, thus making a killing. Someone wrote a letter to the editor after the incident commenting that it would have been much more in their own long-run interest if they had given the batteries away free. They would have generated good will and thereby could have cultivated many prospective customers.
   b. During a New York subway strike, there was a terrible drain on taxis. Thousands of people couldn't cross from Manhattan to Brooklyn, since busses don't run across the bridge. So taxis drove people the half mile from the Manhattan end of the bridge to the Brooklyn end, each taxi full of passengers and charging them each five dollars. This was just as much of a holdup as charging five dollars for a flashlight battery. If the taxi drivers had made the trips for nothing, they might have received thanks and good will, but other than that *they* wouldn't have received anything for their work. For when you hail a taxi in New York, there isn't one chance in ten thousand that you will have the same taxi driver whom you have had before. If *everyone* in the taxi company had given free rides, if it had been company policy, then the company would have cultivated good will and won many customers. But that would not have been the result if only certain individual taxi drivers had been beneficent. In this case, an unselfish policy would not have paid off for the taxi drivers.
   c. Should a garageman be honest in the repairs he makes? Perhaps he doesn't particularly want to make thorough repairs on the cars he handles, for many of the customers won't know the difference anyway for a while; but in the long run, it might be argued, if he wants to keep his business, he had better be honest and thorough; otherwise he won't keep his business for long.
      But someone might argue in opposition that this is not necessarily the case. In a small town where the garageman is known to everyone, if he makes bad repairs, the word will soon be around and he will soon be without any business. But in a large metropolitan city there are many dishonest

repairmen who do very well fleecing their customers. By the time the customer knows he has been rooked, he may be a thousand miles away and can no longer retaliate. The local people won't come back after once being cheated, but for every such person that stays away, there may be two new ones coming in (to be cheated in turn). Since the people in a large city very seldom know one another, they can't tell the newcomers to stay away. Many such dishonest garagemen in large cities seem to do a more lucrative business than the honest ones do.

7. Is ethical egoism a tenable theory? Discuss in light of the following dialogue:

    A: When people stand in line—for example, while waiting for a bus—the best way to ensure order is to follow the principle "First come, first served." People stand in line in the order in which they arrive, and newcomers take their place at the back of the line.

    B: But not if you're an egoist; then, if you can get by with it, you'll go right to the head of the line, since that way you can advance your interests by getting on the bus first. As an egoist, none of the other people in line matters to you in the least. You see how impossible a society of egoists would be: each would be crowding the other to get to the head of the line, and the result would be sheer chaos.

    A: No. Assume that I'm an egoist. I will reason that I prefer order to chaos, and besides, everyone—not just myself—has an equal right to be egoistic. So I will opt for the arrangement that makes things best for me (and incidentally for everyone else in the line). All this is perfectly compatible with ethical egoism.

8. Which of the following points about pleasure would you agree with? Why?

    a. We should never pay attention to what pleases other people.

    b. Sardanapalus, the Assyrian King: "Eat, drink, and play; for nothing else would I give a snap of the fingers. The dinners I have eaten, the wanton acts I have exulted in, the delights of love I have enjoyed—all these things still belong to me, although my blessings have now disappeared."

    c. Edward Fitzgerald, *The Rubaiyat of Omar Khayyam:*

    > Ah, my Beloved, fill the cup that clears
    > Today of past regret and future fears.
    >   Tomorrow!—why, tomorrow I may be
    > Myself with yesterday's sev'n thousand years.

    d. Old man: Have your fling while you're young, my boy; I can't any more and am glad I did when I was young. The other pleasures you can always have later.

9. Do you think that the following excerpt from Alexander Pope's *Essay on Man* contains a just evaluation of Stoicism? Explain your answer.

    > In lazy apathy let Stoics boast
    > Their virtue fix'd; 'tis fix'd as in a frost;
    > Contracted all, retiring to the breast;
    > But strength of mind is Exercise, not Rest;
    > The rising tempest puts in act the soul;
    > Parts it may ravage, but preserves the whole.

10. To what extent, and in what respects, do you think that the following readings reflect the basic attitude of Stoicism? Justify your answer.
    a. The Book of Job.
    b. The Book of Ecclesiastes.
    c. B. de Spinoza. *Ethics,* Books 4 and 5.
    d. B. Russell. *Mysticism and Logic.*
    e. William James, "The Sick Soul," in *The Varieties of Religious Experience* (Gifford lectures, 1901–1902 [London: Longmans, Green, 1952], pp. 127–65).
    f. Marcel Proust's theory of love, as contained in his *Remembrance of Things Past.*
    g. A. E. Housman. "When I Was One and Twenty." (From *Complete Poems of A. E. Housman,* published by Holt, Rinehart and Winston, Inc. Copyright 1959 by Holt, Rinehart and Winston, Inc. Also reprinted by permission of The Society of Authors as the Literary Representative of the estate of the late A. E. Housman, and Messrs. Jonathan Cape, Ltd., publishers of A. E. Housman's *Collected Poems.*)

When I was one-and-twenty
  I heard a wise man say,
'Give crowns and pounds and guineas
  But not your heart away;
Give pearls away and rubies
  But keep your fancy free.'
But I was one-and-twenty,
  No use to talk to me.

When I was one-and-twenty
  I heard him say again,
'The heart out of the bosom
  Was never given in vain;
'Tis paid with sighs aplenty
  And sold for endless rue.'
And I am two-and-twenty,
  And oh, 'tis true, 'tis true.

    h. Kurt Baier, *The Meaning of Life* (Canberra: Australian University Press), Section 3.

11. Evaluate the following sonnet by Matthew Arnold, "To an Independent Preacher Who Preached That We Should Be in Harmony with Nature" (1888):

> "In harmony with nature?" Restless fool,
> Who with such heat dost preach what were to thee,
> When true, the last impossibility—
> To be like Nature strong, like Nature cool!
> Know, man hath all which Nature hath, but more,
> And in that *more* lies all his hopes of good.
> Nature is cruel, man is sick of blood;
> Nature is stubborn, man would fain adore;
> Nature is fickle, man hath need of rest;
> Nature forgives no debt, and fears no grave;
> Man would be mild, and with safe conscience blest.
> Man must begin, know this, where Nature ends;
> Nature and man can never be fast friends.
> Fool, if thou canst not pass her, rest her slave!

12. Evaluate the following passage from G. L. Dickinson, *The Meaning of Good,* p. 46:

I'm not much impressed by the argument you attribute to Nature, that if we don't agree with her we shall be knocked on the head. I, for instance, happen to object strongly to her whole procedure: I don't believe much in the harmony of the final consummation . . . and I am sensibly aware of the horrible discomfort of the intermediate stages, the pushing, kicking, trampling of the host, and the wounded and dead left behind on the march. Of all this I venture to disapprove; then comes Nature and says, "but you ought to approve!" I ask why, and she says, "Because the procedure is mine." I still demur, and she comes down on me with a threat—"Very good, approve or not, as you like; but if you don't approve you will be eliminated!" "By all means," I say, and cling to my old opinion with the more affection that I feel myself invested with something of the glory of a martyr. . . . In my humble opinion it's Nature, not I, that cuts a poor figure!

13. Distinguish the following positions carefully from one another and comment on each of them.
    a. Only my happiness is intrinsically good.
    b. My happiness is intrinsically good for me, and yours for you.
    c. The statement that my happiness is intrinsically good is true for me but not true for you.
    d. My happiness is the only happiness that ought to concern me.
14. "It isn't necessarily true that an ethical egoist will refrain from advising someone, even if the taking of the advice means that the other person will adversely affect the egoist's interests. For one of the ethical egoist's interests may be to give people advice—it makes him or her feel good or important to do this—and this propensity may outweigh whatever harm the competitor who seeks advice may cause." Discuss.
15. James J. Walker, in *The Philosophy of Egoism*, p. 13, writes:

    What are the causes of the evils in society, if these can be generalized, and what is the nature of an efficient remedy? Is it egoism? Remember that all animals except man live in accordance with that principle. Do we hear of fanaticism among them, or of fighting within the species except in defense of their persons or property or on a matter of rivalry among males? But what do we read in the history of mankind except wars, woes, persecutions, and catastrophes beggaring description, and all related in some way to the determination of mankind to *interfere with each other's actions* . . . for the purpose of making people think better or behave better as conceived by the aggressor?

    Speculate on which of the following types of interference in other people's affairs is most prevalent, and which has caused the most suffering:
    a. *A* interferes with *B* in order to increase *A*'s well-being (e.g., *A* steals from *B*).
    b. *A* interferes with *B* in order to do what (in *A*'s opinion) is *good for B* (e.g., to promote *A*'s ideal, which *B* does not share, but which *A* thinks it is very important for *B* to have, for *B*'s own good).
16. Discuss the following passage:

    After every economic crisis, new millionaires are created. It isn't that they profit from others' misery; it is that they're the individuals of foresight. *They* are the true benefactors of society, the ones who have conserved some wealth and kept it from the destructive hands of the bureaucrats. They have it available to build a new society from the ashes of the old one, the society that was destroyed by the insatiable appetites of governments.

. . . Your patriotism will be appealed to: "Buy bonds"; "Save the banks"; "Don't rock the boat"; "Don't undermine confidence"; "Invest in America." But you should react by saving *yourself,* not the government.

Be careful how the word "we" is thrown around. When people say to me, "Isn't it terrible what we've done to the value of the dollar?" I feel like replying, "I didn't know *you* were a party to the crime. But please don't include me in that 'we'—I didn't have anything to do with it."

You aren't responsible for what's happened; it is the government that's destroyed the currency. . . . The mistakes have been made by power-hungry individuals who wanted to play God with the lives and resources of the American people. Their schemes are coming to an inevitably tragic end. And as that end nears, they'll appeal to that "we" for help. They'll appeal to unity, to patriotism, to anything they can—hoping that *you* will pay the price of their mistakes. But *I hope you won't do it.*

You have no commitment to throw your wealth into the fire along with all the rest that is being destroyed.

If you're determined to be altruistic about it, the only way you can be of any good to others is for *you* to be *self-sufficient.* The biggest burdens in a crisis are those who were so concerned about the welfare of everyone else that they never provided for themselves. (From Harry Browne, *How You Can Profit from the Coming Devaluation,* pp. 199–200. Reprinted by permission of Arlington House Publishers, Westport, Connecticut.)

SELECTED READINGS

Psychological Egoism

Broad, C. D. "Egoism as a Theory of Human Motives." In his *Ethics and the History of Philosophy.* London: Routledge & Kegan Paul, 1952.
Brown, Norman J. "Psychological Egoism Revisited." *Philosophy* 54 (1979): 293–309.
Ronald Milo, ed. *Egoism and Altruism.* Belmont, Calif.: Wadsworth Publishing, 1973.
Slote, Michael A. "An Empirical Basis for Psychological Egoism." *Journal of Philosophy* 61 (October 1, 1964): 530–37.

Historical Readings on Egoistic Ideals

Aristotle. *Nicomachean Ethics.* Many editions. See especially Books 1, 2, and 10.
Campbell, Charles A. "Moral and Non-Moral Values" (1935).* In Wilfrid Sellars and John Hospers, eds. *Readings in Ethical Theory.* Englewood Cliffs, N.J.: Prentice-Hall, 1970.
———. "Moral Intuition and the Principle of Self-Realization." *Proceedings of the British Academy* 34 (1948): 23–56.
Epicurus. *Writings.* In Whitney J. Oates, ed. *The Stoic and Epicurean Philosophers.* New York: Random House, 1940.

*Dates in parentheses are dates of first publication.

Epictetus. *Discourses*. Many editions.

Flew, Antony. *Evolutionary Ethics*. London: Macmillan, 1967.

Huxley, Thomas Henry. "Evolution and Ethics" (1894). In Albury Castell, ed. *Selections from the Essays of T. H. Huxley*. New York: Appleton-Century-Crofts, 1948.

————, and Julian Huxley. *Touchstone for Ethics*. New York: Harper & Row, 1947.

Marcus Aurelius. *Meditations*. Many editions.

Mill, John Stuart. "Nature." In his *Three Essays on Religion* (1873). Reprinted in George Nakhnikian, ed. *Nature and the Utility of Religion*. New York: Liberal Arts Press, 1958.

Pater, Walter. *Marius the Epicurean*. Many editions.

Schopenhauer, Arthur. "On the Sufferings of the World" and "On the Vanity of Existence" (1856). In his *Studies in Pessimism*. New York: Modern Library, n.d.

Contemporary Readings on Ethical Egoism

Baumer, W. H. "Indefensible Impersonal Egoism." *Philosophical Studies* 18 (1967).

Benditt, Theodore. "Egoism's Inconsistencies." *Personalist* 57 (1976): 43–50.

Brandt, Richard. "Rationality, Egoism, and Morality." *Journal of Philosophy* 69 (1972): 681–97.

Brunton, J. A. "The Devil Is Not a Fool, or Egoism Revisited." *American Philosophical Quarterly* 12 (1975): 321–30.

————. "Egoism and Morality." *Philosophical Quarterly* 6 (1956): 289–303.

Dwyer, William. "Criticisms of Egoism." *Personalist* 56 (1975): 214–27.

Emmons, Donald. "Refuting the Egoist." *Personalist* 50 (1969): 301–19.

Gauthier, David P., ed. *Morality and Rational Self-Interest*. Englewood Cliffs, N.J.: Prentice-Hall, 1970.

Glasgow, W. D. "The Contradiction in Ethical Egoism." *Philosophical Studies* 19 (1968): 81–85.

Hospers, John. "Baier and Medlin on Ethical Egoism." *Philosophical Studies* 12 (1961): 10–16.

————. "Rule-Egoism." *Personalist* 54 (1973): 391–95.

Kalin, Jesse. "In Defense of Egoism." In David Gauthier, ed. *Morality and Rational Self-Interest*. Englewood Cliffs, N.J.: Prentice-Hall, 1973.

Machan, Tibor. "Recent Work in Ethical Egoism." *American Philosophical Quarterly* 16 (1979): 1–15.

MacIntyre, Alasdair. *A Short History of Ethics*. New York: Macmillan, 1966.

Milo, Ronald D., ed. *Egoism and Altruism*. Belmont, Calif.: Wadsworth Publishing, 1973.

Nagel, Thomas. *The Possibility of Altruism*. Oxford, Eng.: Clarendon Press, 1970.

Olson, Robert G. *The Morality of Self-Interest*. New York: Harcourt Brace Jovanovich, 1965.

Quinn, Warren. "Egoism as an Ethical System." *Journal of Philosophy* 71 (1974): 456–72.

Rachels, James. "Two Arguments Against Ethical Egoism." *Philosophia* 4 (1974): 297–314.

Rand, Ayn. *The Virtue of Selfishness*. New York: New American Library, 1964.

Regis, Edward, Jr. "What is Ethical Egoism?" *Ethics* 91 (October 1980): 50–62.

Sanders, Steven. "Egoism's Conception of Self." *Personalist* 58 (1977): 59–67.

Sidgwick, Henry. *The Methods of Ethics*. 7th ed. New York: Macmillan, 1874. See Book 2.

4

The General Good

Most people are egoistic in their actions to a large degree; if they are to preserve and sustain their own lives, they have to be. Yet they are not entirely so: they often act on behalf of others even when there is nothing in it for themselves. People have "limited benevolence," the tendency to act at times quite unself-interestedly. Most people probably consider their own happiness or well-being to be the main purpose of their lives, but to varying degrees they are also generous and genuinely care for the well-being of others. They are seldom the "pure egoists" depicted in many current controversies about ethical egoism.

But even less are they pure *altruists*. Ethical egoists consider only their own interests; ethical altruists consider only the interests of others, ignoring their own. A pure altruist, if there was one, would lack any concern for his or her own interests and would live only to promote the interests of others: such a person would simply be a doormat for other people, disregarding self in order to serve others.

A consistent altruist would not be likely to stay alive for long. When hungry, an altruist would give up food in order that others might have it, since only the interests of others count. An altruist might eat just enough to stay alive, in order that his or her efforts to further the interests of others would not be cut short by death. There would be no concern with self-interested pleasures or satisfactions: when given a ticket to a concert, an altruist would be duty-bound to give the ticket to someone else, even if that person enjoyed it less: if the altruist enjoyed it +5, and the other person only +2, the +5 would count for nothing, since that enjoyment would be self-interested. If offered the tiniest luxury, an altruist would give it up in favor of someone else: the only consideration would be "Will my action promote the welfare of others?" If total misery were the result of such servitude, the altruist would feel duty-bound not to be concerned about such unhappiness, because after all it is only his or her own unhappiness, which counts for nothing.

Pure altruism could flourish only in a world that was largely not altruistic. Life would be a kind of series of curtsies and retreats. "You take the food"; "No, you take it" and so on. Who would end up taking the food? If everyone were an altruist, wouldn't each person be committed to giving it to someone else? And then what would happen in the end? If there are to be *givers,* there also have to be *takers;* there would be no point in giving—indeed there would *be* no giving—without others to take what is given. (And what is given must first be produced.) Then what of the morality of the takers who are so necessary for the altruist's continued functioning? If they are also altruists, they are also committed to giving, since, after all, their own needs don't count; only those of others do. "Whatever it is, it should go to somebody else"—but there have to be others on the receiving end of the beneficence who are that somebody else. And if "emptying oneself" by giving is moral and taking from others is immoral, can giving to the takers be moral? Wouldn't such giving encourage taking and thus promote wrong actions rather than right ones?

What is often described as altruism is actually *universalism,* the view that people should promote their own interests as well as those of others: everyone counts, not just you and not just others, but everyone, yourself included. Such a view goes by the traditional name of utilitarianism, which we shall now consider.

1. THE UTILITARIAN THEORY

Some people live for themselves only. Other people live for themselves *and* their families; they will give up things themselves, including their lives, if doing so will increase the happiness, or decrease the unhappiness, of members of their families. Some may say this is still egoistic, since they will be unhappy if their families are unhappy. But this isn't always so, as we saw in discussing psychological egoism in Chapter 3. Sometimes parents will make themselves *less* happy in order to provide *greater* happiness for their children. A person often will go through much suffering for other members of the family, and it is not obvious that this will always make him or her happier; it is *for them* that the sacrifice is made, not for *his or her own* happiness. If parents had to choose between their own happiness and that of their children, more often then not they would choose the children's.

But most people will not go much farther than this. They will do things for members of their family or close friends that they wouldn't do for strangers or acquaintances. Still, there are some who will go farther and do things for inhabitants of their own country that they would never do for people from other countries, and some who will go still farther and do things to benefit humanity in general, regardless of family, race, or nation. They consider all humans equal in being worthy of consideration and being the beneficiaries of possible actions. The suffering of an unknown peasant in Bengal is just as bad, and just as worth alleviating, as the suffering of one who happens to be within sight and close by, even though for various reasons it may be less easy to alleviate the suffering 10,000 miles away than next door.

The position just described goes by the name of *utilitarianism*. If happiness is intrinsically good, why shouldn't it be good *no matter who has it?* If happiness is a good, why should I try to increase only my own, or my family's, or my community's? Why not try to grant it to the largest community of all—the human race?

As between your good and the good of other people, which should you choose if faced with a choice between them? According to utilitarianism, you should choose whichever alternative will result in the *greatest total good,* no matter whether yours or that of others predominates. John Stuart Mill wrote in his classic work *Utilitarianism:* "The happiness which forms the utilitarian standard of what is right in conduct, is not the agent's own happiness, but that of all concerned. As between his own happiness and that of others, utilitarianism requires him to be as strictly impartial as a disinterested and benevolent spectator."[1] Thus, if choice *A* would result in 5 units of good for you and 15 for others, and choice *B* would result in 8 units of good for you and 3 for others, you should choose *A,* because the amount of total good is greater, even though there is less for you. On the other hand, if choice *A* results in 10 units of good for you and 2 for others, and choice *B* results in 5 units of good for you and 5 for others, you should choose *A,* not because more good goes to you in that alternative, but again because the total amount of good produced is greater.

Ethical egoism says that it is only the total good coming to *you* that should be considered in deciding which actions to pursue. Its opposite, ethical altruism, says that it is only the total good of *others* that should be considered: your own good doesn't count at all. Utilitarianism is neither of these: it is a form of ethical universalism that considers everyone's good, your own included as one of many. It is irrelevant whether the alternative resulting in the greatest good has a preponderance of the good coming your way or whether most of it goes to others; it is the greatest total good that counts, not to whom it goes.

Though all utilitarians agree that we should act so as to maximize intrinsic good for all, not all utilitarians agree on what things are intrinsically good. The main historical proponents of utilitarianism, Jeremy Bentham and John Stuart Mill, were, as we have seen, hedonistic utilitarians: they considered pleasure, enjoyment, satisfaction, and happiness intrinsically good and their opposites intrinsically bad. But a pluralist about intrinsic good (such as the contemporary philosopher G. E. Moore) could also be a utilitarian: when a

---

[1]John Stuart Mill, *Utilitarianism* (1863), Chapter 2.

pluralist says that we should act so as to maximize intrinsic good, he or she means not just happiness but such other things as those we considered in Chapter 2 (knowledge, moral qualities, and the like). Though some of our examples will deal with happiness only, our formulation of the utilitarian theory is neutral with respect to these two theories of intrinsic good. Utilitarianism is a theory of the right and not of the good, and it can be formulated as the view that all persons should always act so as to maximize intrinsic good, leaving open the question of what things can be called intrinsically good. "The maximization of good" is, then, the only formula that we will use to describe the utilitarian theory.

According to both ethical egoism and utilitarianism, right action is a means to achieve good. But whereas in egoism it is only the agent's own good that is sought, in utilitarianism it is everyone's good, or the "general good." Should everyone in the human race be considered? Yes, though few if any of your or my actions are ever going to affect everyone in the human race. In practice, our range of influence is far smaller than that. Most of your actions affect you primarily, sometimes you and your family, or at most you and part of a small circle of friends or acquaintances. If you break a promise to someone who has relied on your keeping it, the bad effects of breaking it will be felt largely by the person on the receiving end of the broken promise; the effects may be confined to that person plus yourself and will certainly not include the entire human race or even all the people in your community. If you become president of the United States, some of your actions may affect people in the entire world, but short of that, the consequences of your actions have a far smaller range. Some of them perhaps *should* have a larger range than they do (e.g., when you ought to help others but choose to help only yourself), but even in their widest range most of your actions will affect only a comparatively small number of people. Most of your actions, in fact, will affect primarily yourself: it is generally better for you to take care of yourself than for others to take care of you; also, since you know your own needs better than you know the needs of others, you know what is likely to make you happy much better than you know the requirements of strangers or even acquaintances. Often when you try to help them, you do more harm than good, because you don't know their interests and needs as you know your own. It isn't that you are more important than they are, but that you are more likely to maximize total good by tending to your own interests (and others by tending to theirs) than by adopting a busybody policy of trying to tend to others' needs while they try to tend to yours. This policy rests not on ethical egoism (the view that each should act solely to maximize his or her own good), but on the fact (when it is a fact) that total good for both parties can usually be maximized by this arrangement; but the moment you can produce more total good by helping others, then that is what you should do.

The utilitarian thesis is very simple. If happiness (or fulfillment of desires or well-being) is good, why is it good only if I have it? If it is good, isn't it better if everyone has it? If I am happy in situation *A* and both you and I are happy in situation *B,* isn't situation *B* better than situation *A?* And if situation *B* is better, isn't it the one which we should try to attain? Or to put it another way, if something is intrinsically good, isn't it good no matter *who* has it? But then shouldn't we each try to work toward everyone having the good, and not just ourselves?

The utilitarian view was formulated by Bentham as "the greatest happiness for the greatest number." But this phrase is somewhat misleading: it sounds as if only the "greatest number" are to be considered, whereas *everyone* affected by the action is to be considered. It is more accurate to describe utilitarianism as saying that we should attempt to *maximize* good—that is, to create by our actions as much good as possible. But even this has to be clarified. Consider these points:

1. If you are faced by one alternative which in its total consequences will produce 5 units of good and another alternative which in its total consequences will produce 4 units of good, you should, of course, prefer the first. Would the act that produces 5 necessarily be the right thing for you to do? No, not if there were *another alternative* open to you that produced 6. You are to choose whatever alternative is open to you that will produce the *maximum* amount of good, in its total consequences, for all concerned.

2. But we must distinguish between *gross* and *net* good. If act *A* will produce 5 units of good and 3 of bad, and act *B* will produce 3 units of good and no bad, act *B* is to be preferred. Although *A* produces more good, it also produces some bad consequences, and you should consider the *net* good (the good that remains after the bad has been subtracted). *A* has 2 units of net good, and *B* has 3, so *B* is what should be done, assuming that it produces more net good than anything else you could have done instead.

(Don't say that if an act produces more good than bad consequences, it is therefore the right thing to do. Both *A* and *B* produce more good than bad consequences, but since *B* produces *more* net good than *A* does, *B* is the right act, not *A*.)

3. Should we then say that the right act is the one that produces a greater *surplus* of net good over bad than any you could have done instead? No, for sometimes the only acts possible are those in which there is a surplus of bad consequences over good ones: you must sometimes choose "the lesser of two evils." If one course of treatment will lead to the patient's pain followed by death and another course will be followed by a period of distress and pain with a 50 percent chance of survival, you might select the second as the lesser of two evils, but the second alternative still involves a surplus of pain over pleasure; under the circumstances, however, there is no alternative that is better than these two. Although the second alternative still contains a surplus of bad consequences over good, it should still be preferred to the first, which has even worse consequences. So the utilitarian theory should be formulated more accurately to read that each person should endeavor to maximize good consequences *and* minimize bad consequences.

4. Should you consider *long-term* consequences or *short-term* consequences? You should consider *all* consequences, whenever they occur. If act *A* will produce 5 units of net good today and none later, and act *B* will produce no good today but 50 units of net good next year, act *B* is to be preferred because it will result in greater net good, although that good is not as immediate as the good resulting from *A*. Often much is to be gained by giving up a smaller good today for a greater good later (e.g., saving money you might have spent today in order to have it when you need it in the future; giving up pleasures available to you today in order to study so that you can pass the bar examination and be assured of a good livelihood later; or not giving your child what she wants every time she wants it, in order that when she faces the world on her own she will not expect it to provide her whatever she wants just for the asking).

The future good, then, is just as much to be considered as the present good. (Of course, the preference will not always go to the future good. Between 5 units of good in the future and 10 units in the present, the 10 is to be preferred.) But the assumption here is that the future and present goods are equally certain to occur. In general, however, this is not the case. "A bird in the hand is worth two in the bush." Today's good may be smaller, but at least it's more nearly certain than next year's. What would you rather have, $100 today or $150 a year from now? Many people would prefer the $100 today, for good reason: the promiser might be dead by next year, or not in a position to give the $150; you yourself might not be around next year either; you might need it badly today and not need the greater amount next year; and at a considerable rate of inflation the $150 would not buy you as much next year as the $100 would today. You might prefer the $150 next year *if* you could be certain that it would be forthcoming; but as a rule you can't be as certain of what will happen a year hence as you can of today.

How, then, are we to decide between a future and a present good? Assuming that there are only two alternatives, you first consider the total good to be produced by each (e.g., 10 units today vs. 30 units later) and then consider the *probability* that each will occur (100 percent probability today vs. 50 percent probability of the later event). In this case you get 10 versus 15 units, so it will be preferable to wait till next year. Of course you must consider the total situation—not just the probability that the $150 will be forthcoming next year, but the probability that it will bring you happiness (or some other intrinsic good) if it is forthcoming. If you need money today but probably won't next year, you will be wise to take the $100 now, since doing this will make you happier than taking the 50-50 chance on the large amount later. If you are a perennial worrier, you should take the smaller amount now, since at least you'll have it and will spare yourself the worry you would have endured if you had waited, wondering if you would really get it.

It all sounds easy, but in actual practice, of course, such calculations are very difficult to perform with any reliability. We have spoken of 4 versus 5 units of good as if moral consequences were easily quantifiable. Even if we are talking about a specific kind of good such as pleasure, and not a more intangible one such as knowledge or moral qualities as in value pluralism, we still have tremendous problems: if I can't even say with any great confidence that I enjoyed my breakfast this morning 2.5 times as much as I did yesterday morning, how can I possibly engage in interpersonal comparisons of the amount of pleasure I have on a certain occasion and the amount that you experience? I can say, "I enjoy this more than that," or "I enjoy this *much* more than that." Sometimes I can say, "I enjoy this more than you do"—for example, if I am an opera fan and you go along to a performance but walk out at the end of Act 1. But an exact calculation of interpersonal comparisons is just impossible. Many people have rejected utilitarianism for the sole reason that it requires us, in estimating the rightness or wrongness of actions, to do something that no human being can possibly do. Utilitarians can reply that this is not their fault but the world's. The consequences of actions are so complex and far-flung that they cannot easily be calculated; people can't be as sure of others' experiences as of their own, and even their own can't be quantified. So our calculations, especially when they involve the far future, can't be very accurate—but that's the way things are, and we just have to do the best we can with what we have. The alternative, according to the utilitarians, would be not to consider the consequences of our actions at all, which is surely still worse.

But it's not only that we can't quantify states of consciousness; we also can't estimate the future with any great reliability. The farther into the future the consequences of our actions reach, the less reliable our estimate of them becomes. When the Monroe Doctrine was proclaimed in 1823, could President Monroe and his advisers have had any clear idea of what the consequences of it would be a century or two centuries later? All they could do was estimate the consequences as far as they could, weighing the alternative of announcing versus not announcing it, thinking more of the immediate future because that was clearer than the distant future, and being quite unable to peer far into the future to determine whether in the very long run the net consequences would be good to all who were affected by it. It's perfectly reasonable not to worry too much about the consequences of even important actions a hundred years from now, since it is impossible to envisage what they might be. When it *is* possible to predict them with any probability, then, of course, we should do so. If the far future is less to be considered than the present, that isn't because it's the future, but because the probability of our calculations about it being right is less. Many people are concerned about the world having an adequate supply of oil a century hence; but there seems to be some probability that technology will have made oil obsolete by that time, so that our present sacrifices to conserve it would be for nothing. But again, say the utilitarians, the fact that the future is less predictable than the present is the fault of nature (or human nature, for not being omniscient), and again we have to do the best we can with what we have.

The problem of estimation of probabilities is well illustrated by the question: "Does the end justify the means?" Let's see how this question applies to utilitarianism.

We can't give any general answer to the question: sometimes the end is so important that we are right to seek means to achieve it, and sometimes not. If the end is getting rid of a toothache and the means is going to the dentist, most of us would find it worthwhile for a sufferer to go to the dentist, in spite of some temporary pain, in order to get rid of the pain permanently. On the other hand, we would not be justified in killing the sufferer to get rid of the toothache. True, that person would never have a toothache again—but the price (the means) is too high.

How do we determine whether the end justifies the means in a particular case? By calculating the total good and bad (to everyone concerned) of the means as well as the end. If the total good exceeds the total bad, should we then take the means to achieve the end? No, only if the good exceeds the bad by *more* than any other alternative we could have chosen instead. Admittedly, it is often difficult to figure out which alternative that is.

The difficulty is made ever so much greater by the problem of calculating future probabilities. As a rule we can be much more sure of the means than of the end: the means is some action to be undertaken now; the end is something in the future that may never happen, since the means we use may not achieve the end at all. We may spend thousands of hours trying to get on intimate terms with someone, and yet the hoped-for intimacy may never eventuate.

The problem of calculating probabilities is particularly troublesome when large-scale social movements are involved. Revolutionaries often believe that if only they had their way, the world would be a better place, and there would be no more hunger, no more injustice, and so on. Of course they first have to kill and imprison a few thousand people who might oppose them; but what's a few thousand when millions are going to be benefited? Fired up by this thought, they do undertake the means: some people are killed, others imprisoned, and a police state is formed ("only temporarily, of course") to get the Great Plan into action. But the glorious end that is envisioned never comes to pass (indeed, the planners usually have only the haziest idea of what it will be like). The evil has been done, but the good never comes from it; people have been sacrificed in vain. Since so many have been killed already, the revolutionaries think they must determinedly go ahead with their plan so that their loss will not be in vain. Consequently, more are sacrificed, but the realization of the end gets lost somewhere in the process; the result is more terror and more injustice than there was to begin with. What has happened? (1) The means was considered a sure path to the end—but though the means were undertaken, the end never came about. (2) Even if the end had been achieved, it might not have been as good as those who strove for it imagined; it may have been good according to *their* vision of it, but what if other people didn't share their taste for the ideal that was to be imposed upon them? (3)

In any case, the end was realized at tremendous expense; considering the means taken, was the end worth it? (4) In fact, as more and more people were killed, the end became impossible to achieve because the very people who were to achieve it became different: the evil involved in the means they undertook changed them so that they would be incapable of fulfilling the end they had envisaged originally.

2. OBJECTIVE VERSUS SUBJECTIVE DUTY

Suppose you volunteer to drive your grandmother home to another part of the city (as your good deed for the day), and on the way a drunken driver strikes your car and injures your grandmother, who ends up in a hospital with a broken hip. Did you do wrong by driving her home? It is doubtful that anyone would say you acted wrongly; after all, you had no way of predicting that through no fault of your own such an accident would occur. Yet the consequences of your taking her home were quite catastrophic; if an act was judged by its actual consequences, you would surely have committed a wrong act. Any number of alternatives, such as her staying at your house overnight, would have been preferable, as things turned out.

There seems to be something wrong, then, with judging the rightness or wrongness of an act by its actual consequences. The actual consequences of an act are largely outside your control: you can initiate a train of events by your action, but many of the results are quite unpredictable. In view of all this, how can you be accused of committing a wrongful act? (We might say that the drunken driver caused her injury, and it is true that if that car hadn't hit your car the accident wouldn't have occurred; but it is also true that if you hadn't been driving at that place at that moment, it wouldn't have occurred either.)

In Nicholas Monsarrat's World War II novel, *The Cruel Sea,* the captain of a British vessel in the Atlantic sees many British sailors afloat on the ocean, survivors of a Nazi U-boat attack. He gives orders to rescue them; but just then his radar operator tells him that there is an undersea object, presumably a submarine, below the very spot where the men are struggling in the water. The captain is willing to take some chances with the lives of his men to rescue the others; but in view of the great probability of an enemy submarine lurking below, it seems virtually certain that if he attempts a rescue, his ship, together with all the men, will be blown to bits. So, with enormous reluctance, he orders the ship to proceed on its course, away from the submarine lying in ambush, to save his own ship and crew, even though he thereby leaves the men to drown. Later it turns out that the immersed object was not a submarine at all, and he could have rescued the men quite safely. He feels enormous guilt over this. But did he act wrongly?

Your *objective duty,* according to utilitarianism, is to produce the best possible consequences for all concerned. Let us assume that the best possible consequences in this case would have occurred if he had rescued the men.

The trouble with making "objective duty" your actual duty is that you have no way of foreseeing all the consequences. You would have to be omniscient, particularly with regard to foreseeing the future, and no human being is; it would be asking the impossible. If your act turns out to have the best possible consequences for all concerned, this is as much a matter of luck as of merit. Bertrand Russell called doing your objective duty the "most fortunate act"—indicating thereby that if the act has the best possible results, good fortune had its part.

Shall we say, then, that what you ought to do is not what *actually* has the best consequences, but what you *think* (at the time of acting) will have the best consequences (i.e., will maximize good)? The trouble with this imperative is that people can think ignorantly, foolishly, even maliciously. Suppose people sincerely think, as some primitive tribesmen do, that children should be beaten unmercifully and burned with hot irons in order to purge the devils from their bodies. They are doing what they think will have the best consequences, but does that make their acts right? Suppose a physician who hasn't read a medical book since World War II thinks that an operation should be performed in a certain way, although the way has been shown to be extremely dangerous and is now long since outmoded. Is he to be excused because he didn't know any better? If he hadn't read a medical book for forty years, shouldn't he at least have refrained from performing the operation?

What people *think* will produce the best consequences (i.e., their *putative duty*) is unsatisfactory as a criterion of what's right, because people can sincerely think all kinds of weird and foolish things. If someone believes something ignorantly or foolishly, acting on that belief is not necessarily right. We can't expect people to be omniscient, but on the other hand, to say that people should do whatever they think at the time will have the best consequences is to encourage ignorance of probable consequences with the excuse, "Well, they thought they were doing what was best."

There is a third conception of duty, sometimes called *subjective duty*, which instead of being the "most fortunate act" (objective duty), is the *wisest act.* What you should do is not what actually *will* have the best consequences (you can't foresee these), nor what you happen to *think* will have the best consequences (you may think ignorantly or foolishly), but what in fact *will probably* have the best consequences—what looks now as if it will have the best possible consequences, on the basis of the best evidence available at the time. On the basis of the best evidence then available, there was a submarine under the spot where the rescue was contemplated, so the captain did the right thing by ordering the ship to proceed, even though the consequences turned out to be highly unfortunate. On the basis of the best evidence then available, you were doing a good deed by taking your grandmother home; the probability of an accident occurring was very small, and you had no more evidence that would lead you to refrain from the trip than you would have had at any other time: if that small probability of an accident, always present, had stopped you then, it should have stopped you from ever driving at all.

What, then, is it people's utilitarian duty to do? The answer is, they must do their subjective duty (the wisest act, in light of the evidence available at the time). Action has to be taken *prospectively,* that is, before the consequences are fully known. The actual consequences can only be known *retrospectively,* after the evidence is in and long after the action is over. An omniscient God may be blamed for not doing his objective duty, since he can foresee all the consequences, but a human being can't be.

Suppose you arrive at an intersection where there is a stoplight which is red at the moment; bushes block sight of whether or not any vehicles are traveling on the street you want to cross. Suppose, too, that you go through the stoplight, since you are in a hurry, and it turns out that there were no vehicles traversing the cross-street. Did you act rightly? (After all, everything turned out all right.) No, you didn't act rightly, because you had no way of knowing whether or not there were cars on the cross-street; you were just lucky. For all you knew, you might have caused a serious accident. You did what actually had the best consequences (you got to your destination earlier, and nobody was hurt), but you had no way of foreseeing that your act would produce the best consequences. The wisest act would have been to wait at the stoplight for the thirty seconds it would have taken the light to change. If you had been carrying a wounded passenger to the emergency room of a hospital, the assessment of the act might have been different—but not necessarily, since you still would have been taking the chance of injuring or killing other persons by going through the stoplight and also thereby delaying your passenger's arrival at the hospital. For an ambulance to go through the stoplight would not be wrong if the ambulance had its siren on, thereby warning all possible travelers in the cross-street.

Consider one more case. Mr. *A* decides to kill Mr. *B* by shooting him as he passes on the street, but the gun doesn't go off and the attempt on *B*'s life is unsuccessful. But at that moment a stranger, Mr. *C,* is experimenting with his gun nearby, thinking it isn't loaded (although it is), and quite unexpectedly the gun goes off, killing Mr. *B.* Though *A* pulled the trigger of his gun, his act had no effect on Mr. *B,* since the gun didn't go off; thus, he didn't do an objectively wrong act. But *A* did do a subjectively wrong act, since it was probable on the basis of the evidence available to him (the gun having been loaded and in working order) that firing the gun would bring about *B*'s death. *A* was guilty of attempted murder. *C,* whose act actually caused the death, was not, though he might be found guilty of criminal negligence for playing with a gun in a place where a passer-by might be hit.

3. UTILITARIANISM AND MORAL RULES

We have all been on the receiving end of moral rules since early childhood. We have been told that it is wrong to kill, wrong to steal, wrong to cheat, wrong to break promises, and so on. What does a morality based on the utilitarian principle have to say about these rules?

The utilitarian morality has only one fundamental principle: "Act so as to maximize intrinsic good" (or more accurately, net expectable intrinsic good—net as opposed to gross, and expectable to indicate subjective duty as opposed to objective duty). The observance of moral rules—at least some moral rules—does tend to maximize happiness: a society in which people go about killing and plundering one another without restraint would certainly contain less happiness (as well as knowledge and other pluralist goods) than one in which people observed prohibitions against such practices; any kind of civilized life would be virtually impossible without moral rules.

But would the observance of such rules *always* tend to maximize good? It certainly seems as if it would not, since rules tend to have exceptions. In general, telling lies creates mistrust; the expectations generated in those who believe you are telling the truth will be frustrated, and if you constantly lie to people, finally they will no longer believe you (even when you are telling the truth). But if the secret police are searching for a friend of yours (who has voiced dissent against the dictatorship and become an "enemy of the State"), and they demand that you tell them where she is, are you obliged to tell them the truth, when telling the truth would mean that your friend will be tortured or shot?

Most rules aren't very clear as to exactly what kinds of acts they cover. Does "Thou shalt not kill" include a prohibition against killing in self-defense? That is what pacifists say: they will not take the life of any person. But what if terrorists burn down a man's home, rape and mutilate his wife, and kill his children? Is he supposed to stand idly by through all this? And what about killing in wartime? What about abortion? What about unintentional killing, as in an accident? What about killing an armed robber who has forcibly entered your house and threatens your life although no one has yet been killed?

You are not supposed to cheat, but does this include "forgetting" about a few items on your income tax form? You are not supposed to break a promise, but what if the promise you have made is rather trivial, something very important comes up, and you can't reach the person to whom you have made the promise? You are supposed to be honest, but if you find a hundred dollars lying in the street, are you supposed to try to find the owner? (And if yes, how hard?)

Utilitarians say, "Maximize good," and they would advocate following a moral rule only when we have reason to believe that doing so will maximize good. All moral rules, according to utilitarianism, are rules of thumb: following them may maximize good most of the time, but not all the time, and when they do not, they should not be followed.

It is often impossible to know whether following a rule will indeed maximize happiness. Actions have long-term consequences as well as short-term ones, subtle consequences as well as obvious ones. Even coming to a reasonable assessment often requires much thought and investigation. We are told that it's wrong to lie. Very well, but suppose a physician has a patient with incurable cancer. Should she lie or tell the truth to the patient? It seems as if concealing the truth would make the patient happier, and many physicians conceal the truth in order to spare the patient misery. Still, there are other consequences of lying in such a case which may not occur to the physician immediately:

1. Has the physician sufficient reason to believe that the patient would be happier not knowing the truth? Perhaps the patient would be happier, or at least less unhappy, knowing the truth: he would be distressed at the news, of course, but he would be able to set his affairs in order and prepare for death in his own way. Shouldn't the patient at least have the opportunity to do this? (And if knowledge is an intrinsic value as well as happiness, then this is an additional reason that the patient ought to be told.)

2. Should the physician take it upon herself to deprive her patient of vital information? Why should she take such a decision out of the patient's hands? If you lie to people, aren't you assuming that the people you lie to are not strong enough to withstand the information that is withheld from them? Most people, when asked whether they would rather be told in case they ever had such a disease, respond that they would like to be told. Shouldn't this consideration count rather heavily? Why should the physician play God with the patient's life? (Most patients, if they are terminally ill, suspect it anyway and would rather not have to play games with relatives and physicians. They would have much more peace of mind knowing the truth.)

3. Might it not cause more harm to lie, since lies have a tendency to spread? If the physician tells her patient that "everything will be all right," knowing all the time that the patient is incurably ill, the patient's relatives will know that the physician lied. Suppose one of the relatives later comes under the physician's care, and the physician says (truthfully this time), "Everything will be all right." The patient now may not believe her; the physician lied before, and quite possibly she may be lying again. Such a patient will then feel tense, depressed, insecure, wondering if he is being lied to. In this case such worry is needless, but there is no avoiding it after the physician has lied once. Even if other physicians assure him that all will be well, he may still be suspicious: physicians tend not to contradict each other, especially not in each other's presence.

4. The physician may be conscientious and lie only in extreme circumstances, but does she know that she is so much a master of herself that she will not break her truth-telling habit a second or third time? It's usually easier to lie a second time, once you've broken the habit by doing it once.

None of this, of course, shows that we should *always* tell the truth, which depends on circumstances unique to the individual case. What it does show is that, contrary to what a superficial examination of the situation may seem to indicate, the moral rule "Tell the truth" is the best one after all. That's probably why such rules have survived; they have stood the test of time. When we flout them, we go against the cumulative experience of the human race.

You may *think* that a case you may be facing at present is so different from previous ones that you can break the rule in this instance; and you may be correct. But the odds are against you. If you think that perhaps an innocent man should be railroaded just *this* time (to set the populace at rest), or that you should take by force what belongs to one person to give it to someone else who needs it more, more likely than not you are mistaken. You are faced with such considerations as these:

1. Is your knowledge of all the consequences great enough to entitle you to say that the situation before you is a genuine exception to the rule? If in a large majority of cases the observance of a certain rule is useful, then the probability is great that breaking the rule would be wrong in any particular case; and uncertainty about both the effects and their value in particular cases is so great that it seems doubtful whether your individual judgment that the effects will probably be good in this case can ever be set against the general probability that that kind of action is wrong.[2]

2. In addition, all of us are inclined to be biased by the fact that we strongly desire one of the results, which we hope to obtain by breaking the rule. In short, we *rationalize.* Thus, the fact that you want to break the rule will tend to make you rig your estimate of the probable consequences in such a way as to justify the action you want to do anyway. What this *tends* to show is that the chance that a rule should always be observed on grounds of utility is greater than the chance of your being likely to decide rightly that you are involved in an exception to the rule. As G. E. Moore noted, "Though we may be sure that there *are* cases where the rule should be broken, we can never know *which* those cases are, and ought, therefore, never to break it."[3]

3. Even if you *can* clearly recognize (which is usually not possible) that the present situation is one in which the violation of the rule is justified, and even if you are so studiously impartial as not to be prejudiced in your own favor (and rig your calculation of the consequences accordingly), you set an *example* to others by breaking the rule; thus by breaking the rule this time, even if you are justified in doing so, you thereby tend to encourage other violations of the rule which are *not* justified. When your example has any influence, the effect of a right action that is an exception is to encourage many wrong ones.

4. Finally, making an exception not only sets an example for others but sets a precedent for your own future actions. If you have violated the rule in a situation in which the violation is justified, the *habit* of making exceptions will be reinforced, and you will be all the more likely to violate the rule in cases where the violation is *not* justified. "It is impossible," Moore concluded, "for anyone to keep his intellect and sentiments so clear, but that, if he has once approved of a generally wrong action, he will be more likely to

[2] See G. E. Moore, *Principia Ethica* (Cambridge, Eng.: Cambridge University Press, 1903), p. 162.
[3] Ibid., pp. 162–63.

approve of it also under other circumstances than those which justified it in the first instance."[4]

Even with these considerations, the theme of utilitarianism remains the same: it is the utilitarian principle that is the ultimate criterion of rightness, not the rules. Moreover, there are situations which are *not covered* by general rules at all or which are so extreme that no rules seem to fit. It is probably a good utilitarian rule not to permit torture of prisoners; pain is an intrinsic evil, and the good that ensues, if any, seldom outweighs the pain caused, as well as the terror that would be produced every time someone was called into the police station, fearing that torture would be used. (The level of happiness in communist and fascist dictatorships in which torture is regularly used is surely lower than in those countries where the use of torture is outlawed.) Still, suppose that someone has planted an atomic device set to go off at a certain hour somewhere in your city, that you are the police chief and find the culprit, and that the only way you can get the information out of him (as to where he placed the bomb) is through the use of torture. Wouldn't you use it to save the entire city? Most rules are not intended for such extraordinary situations, and those situations were not thought of when the rules were devised and promulgated.

There are also situations in which rules *conflict*. If one rule tells you not to lie and another tells you not to sacrifice a human life if it is in your power to save it, what of situations in which telling the truth will cause a life to be lost? In such cases the best utilitarian consequences usually will ensue from not telling the truth. But the situation is not always so clear. If you see someone cheating on an exam and the teacher asks you whether the student cheated, are you to tell the truth, even if your answer may cause the student to be expelled and lose all chance of going on to medical school? What if there is only a 10 percent chance of the consequences happening? Should you still tell the truth?

Exact calculations of consequences are often impossible to make, yet important decisions may depend on making them. So important is the *calculation* of the probable effects of your actions in utilitarianism that the question may be raised as to how much time should be devoted to it. It could almost be said that any time you have to choose between two alternatives, *A* and *B,* you actually have a third alternative, *C*—namely, calculating whether you should do *A* or *B*.

Admittedly, there are times when very little calculation has to be done: you see a child falling from the stepladder and you rush to catch her before she hits the floor. But at other times, when your actions are likely to have long-term or subtle consequences, much more calculation is called for. The amount of time varies, however, with the case at hand. If you are offered a scholarship by five different universities, considerable thought and investigation are called for; your whole future is at stake. But other decisions, even

[4]Ibid., p. 163.

very important ones, call for quick action: you have to choose between rescuing a drowning person (thus risking your own life) and not rescuing him (leaving him to drown). This is a decision of great importance both to you and to the drowning person. Yet if you spend the next fifteen minutes calculating the probable results of each alternative, the occasion for choice will have passed. You will be like the donkey standing midway between two bales of hay that starved to death trying to decide which pile to take.

Still, it seems safe to say that most people act with too little thought rather than too much. Some don't think at all—they just act; or more usually, they think of one consequence only and ignore the rest, or they have some end in mind which is very important to them and don't spend enough time reflecting on the alternative means available for reaching the end. They "dive into action" at once, and later they see that they could have done better, or reached the end in such a way as to produce fewer bad consequences. Spurred by the passions of the moment, they launch into action, "consequences be damned," and later they (and sometimes others) have to suffer the ill effects of their thoughtless actions.

Does this mean that we should use our head but never our heart in planning actions? "The heart," said French philosopher Blaise Pascal, "has its reasons that the head does not know." This enigmatic statement may refer to a rather obvious truth, namely, that the "life of feeling" is involved in every action: you rush to a doctor to save your child's life, which you would not do if you did not *care* about the child's survival and *want* the child to live. At the same time, many bad consequences befall people who do *not* use their heads sufficiently. An employer, sympathetic with the plight of people in mental institutions and aware that they have a tough time getting jobs when they come out, hires a number of them. But he hasn't investigated their individual quirks and tendencies, and soon one of them, who was placid enough in the artificial environment of the institution, is insulted or ridiculed by one of the other workers and suddenly takes out a knife and stabs him and several other persons close by. Had the employer used his head and investigated the former patients' psychological histories a bit, he might have been aware of this danger in time to prevent the catastrophe. But he was so strongly motivated by sympathy for these people that his lack of judgment helped cause the death or injury of some of his workers.

The head, too, has its reasons that the heart does not know. Benevolence can often be combined with thoughtlessness as well as with stupidity; consequences may ensue that are quite catastrophic and that could reasonably have been foreseen. Benevolence and intelligence are both required in order to perform actions which maximize good. Intelligence without benevolence produces cold husbands and wives as well as merciless tyrants; benevolence without intelligence produces sentimentalists, bumblers, and idiots. Neither group acts to produce as much good as when intelligence and benevolence are combined in the same person.

4. UTILITARIANISM AND ANIMALS

Thus far we have restricted the scope of our discussion to the actions and interactions of human beings. But why, one may ask, should it be limited in this way? Shouldn't dogs and cats, horses and cows, rabbits and guinea pigs, and the rest of the animal kingdom also be considered? They are conscious beings too: we don't know how far down the scale of life consciousness ends, but we do know that mammals, reptiles, and some others have nerves and nerve endings and that those animals certainly give every behavioral indication of feeling pain. It doesn't seem likely that a dog is pretending to feel pain when its foot is cut off in a buzz saw. Thus animals, we may say, do experience at least pain and probably also pleasure. If Aristotle is right, they aren't capable of happiness or unhappiness, but, like human beings, they do exhibit contentment, agitation, and other qualities.

Whether or not you could describe their state as happy, it is clear that there are many things they aren't capable of, such as the delights of knowledge, aesthetic experience, discussion, and so on. Thus the range of their hedonic possibilities is much more limited than ours, in both directions: they can't appreciate art or converse with us, but neither can they commit suicide or become bored. They can't project themselves into the future (at least beyond a very short time) nor conceptualize what is absent. Thus their range of interests and possibilities is limited; but at least they do have sensations and some feelings. They are *sentient beings* like us, so there is every reason to consider them too when we are considering various possibilities of action.

Utilitarians would certainly consider it wrong to be cruel to other people (e.g., children). Would it not also be wrong to be cruel to animals—to inflict needless pain on them, for example? We may object to such cruelty not just because a person who is cruel to animals is likely also to be cruel to other people, but because the cruelty to animals itself is wrong: it is the infliction of pain, and pain is an intrinsic evil whenever it occurs. (We might inflict pain on an animal, as on a person, in order to cure it of a disease or set a broken limb, but here the worth of the end far outweighs the temporary pain of the means.) A person who whips a horse, at least beyond what is absolutely necessary for training it; a person who beats seal cubs to death to get their hide; a person who catches sparrows and hangs them by a string and beats them for sport; a person who hunts animals with a gun and then leaves them wounded to die—such a person is as surely doing wrong as a person who sadistically beats children.

Human beings inflict a tremendous amount of *unnecessary* suffering and death on animals. Conditions in slaughterhouses, where animals are supposed to be put to death painlessly but often aren't, and conditions surrounding their raising, which are often extremely crowded and uncomfortable, attest to this fact. Chickens like to root in the dirt—at least that's what they do when given a chance—but now they are grown on wire netting and never see the ground. Pigs are raised in such crowded pens that they can barely move. Consider what is done to goose to make its liver tasty to eat: its webbed feet are nailed down so that it can never move, and then it is force-fed by mouth to make it fat as quickly as possible, all so that consumers can enjoy the gourmet delicacy pâté de fois gras. All this is avoidable, yet people do it. But now some disagreements emerge:

A: I agree that to inflict unnecessary suffering is wrong. But when an animal is an ever-present danger to people, when it's a choice between a person and an animal, I'd say it's right to kill the animal. I'd say the man did wrong by *not* killing the cobra (see p. 8) when he had the chance. The child is of greater value than the snake, because, among other things, he has specifically human faculties and potentialities, and is also capable of terrors animals can't feel, such as dread of death and fear of pain before it occurs. Also the child can grow into an Isaac Newton or a Beethoven, which the snake never can, so the child's death would be the greater loss. But even if he doesn't become an outstanding person, the range of his possible experience is still far greater; as far as intrinsic good is concerned, the loss of the child is inestimably greater to the world. (And not just to the world: the child's parents and siblings will grieve, unlike those of the snake.)

In addition to cases where an animal must die so that a person can live, there are many cases in which animals are killed or made to suffer for a good and worthy purpose. Many medical experiments (e.g., testing new vaccines) have to be conducted on animals first before they can be judged safe and effective for human beings. Making animals suffer or die unnecessarily, I would admit, is wrong, but not when they die so that human beings may live.

B: Just because we consider ourselves more important than the animals, should we then consider them expendable and let them suffer—for example, by stuffing them with carcinogenic substances and watching them suffer and die, recording the times and conditions?

A: When it's unnecessary, I agree it's wrong; but sometimes it's necessary. For example, sometimes the only choice is between conducting an experiment on animals and conducting it on human beings. Would you rather have your child or a rat die? It would be wrong to run over a dog on the road deliberately, but suppose it was necessary to run over the dog in order to keep from running over a child? When the choice is between people and animals, animals must go so that people can be saved.

B: You say "when it's necessary." But necessary for *what*? Necessary for saving the child's life—O.K., you kill the cobra. But if killing animals is necessary to get the hide, is that also all right because it's necessary? Force-feeding the goose is necessary *if* you want to get the most delicious pâté de fois gras; but isn't the end trivial compared with the terrible means used to obtain it? If beating pigs to death was necessary to get tender pork, would that justify us in beating the pigs? What if it *is* necessary for that end? That doesn't make it right. What if we hunt down or torture animals just to amuse ourselves: that's for an end too, but surely that end doesn't justify the means. Now let's take a really controversial case: I hold that it's wrong to consume the flesh of animals for meat. We can live on vegetable matter, which doesn't involve the suffering of sentient beings; so the deliberate infliction of death, even painless death, on animals just so we can eat them is wrong.

A: On that we disagree. I agree that hunting them for sport and then leaving them wounded or dying is wrong, since it serves no purpose; but to kill them in order to eat them is not useless. Yes, it *is* possible to live without animal flesh, particularly if you don't exclude eggs and dairy products. But humans need protein, and most high-grade protein comes from animals (including fish). You have to eat an awful lot of nuts and other things to make up for the loss of animal protein. If this is so, it's like the cobra—a matter of either them or us. When it comes to a choice, I vote for human beings. Now you may deny what I say about the necessity of eating animal flesh, on empirical (in this case nutritional) grounds, and I don't want to get bogged down in an empirical discussion at this point. Rather, I'll ask you: if you grant that it is necessary for human beings to have high-grade protein, that their digestive systems are adapted to it, since human beings lived on meat for thousands of years before they ever grew any crops, would you say that we are justified in eating meat, for our own healthful survival?

B: Would animals, if they needed human flesh to survive, be justified in eating human beings?

A: That's a meaningless question. Animals aren't moral agents, and moral choice is impossible for them. So you can't say that they're morally justified or that they aren't: they would just eat people when they could get them, or they would starve. But human beings are capable of choice; and what I want to learn from you is, assuming that what I say about the need for meat to sustain human life is true, aren't we justified in eating the flesh of animals?

B: If I saw a pig fatally run over by a vehicle, I would be justified in cooking and eating it, for I wouldn't be harming the pig. But I would not be justified in killing it. Even if the death were painless, I would be bringing an end to a life that could have been continued and, in its own way, enjoyed.

A: I think you're living in Fantasyland. The whole order of nature is, as Tennyson said, "red in tooth and claw." All living things devour other living things so that they themselves may stay alive. Life feeds off other life and can continue in no other way. Typically, many times more young are born or hatched than ever can live to maturity; the rest die of starvation or exposure, or are devoured by other animals. Other than pets (animals adopted by people), how many animals live to a ripe old age? Only a minority of them reach maturity, and the weak and crippled die at once. Each species is vulnerable to predators and is attacked and eaten by other species (or other members of the same species). And if a species had no predators, it soon would overrun the earth. This is simply the way of all life. Children who see their pet cat coming home with a mouse between its teeth or watch nature programs on television showing snakes killing birds and mammals, strangling or poisoning them and then engorging them, are horrified that animals are so "cruel" and exist in such an un-Disneylike manner; but this is reality, and we can't change it. It's just as true in the sea, with fish living on other fish, as on land. The amount of animal pain and suffering is absolutely stupendous, and just unimaginable to us. As far as the infliction of pain is concerned, nature is the cruelest system that could be devised. But life is sustained on this planet within that system. It is a scene of universal carnage and destruction.

B: I grant that this is how life exists on earth. But the question is what *we* human beings should do. My point is that we should prevent animal suffering and death whenever possible.

A: I know an old lady who feeds the birds outside her window every day all winter long, so that the birds can survive the winter. But, of course, she is barely scratching the surface of all the death and starvation that countless birds encounter every winter. It's such a futile gesture on her part.

B: But a fine one. And not quite futile: she does save some birds. If everyone did as she does, lots of birds would be saved.

A: Yes, and you would soon upset the balance of nature. If you let too many birds survive, their numbers would quickly multiply, and soon there wouldn't be enough food for all of them to eat. Vast numbers of them would starve, because by feeding them people would have upset the balance of nature. By enabling some to survive, people would have caused the death by starvation of many times more of them. If you kill the snakes, the rodent population gets out of hand. In the Middle Ages it was thought that cats were instruments of the devil, and they were killed; as a result the rat population exploded, causing the Black Death.

B: That may be. But even if it's true, I'm not responsible for the way nature works. I only know that if I can prevent some animal suffering and death, and fail to do so, I am doing wrong, because I am causing suffering or death that by my action I could have avoided.

A: Don't you realize that the deer you refuse to kill will soon starve to death the next winter, be killed by animal predators, or in some other way die a lingering death? Compared with that, instant death by a gun is merciful.

B: Perhaps. But again, I am not responsible for the suffering that nature inflicts. I am only responsible for the suffering that *I* inflict. And that suffering I can help to prevent by not killing the animal. That it would soon die anyway is, in any event, something that I do not know of this animal; I just do what I can.

A: That's a cop-out. By insisting on what you're responsible for, you try to excuse yourself for a worse consequence, which you could have prevented by thinning the herd. You are thus bringing about more suffering than was necessary. By the way, I suppose that if you're opposed to killing animals for food, you are also opposed to killing them for obtaining their hides?

B: Of course. Animal hides are no more necessary to human life than is the eating of animal flesh.

A: In northern climates, where people's only protection against the elements may be clothing made from animal hides, that's not true. Many would have died of cold were it not for this clothing. In such cases, survival depends on killing animals; and in my opinion the survival of a person is more important than that of the animal killed to make it possible. Let me repeat: I don't approve of wanton cruelty to animals, but when it comes to a choice between the survival of a human being and the survival of an animal, I vote for the former. Nor is this choice irrational, for human beings have greater value than any species of animal does. Can you honestly deny that? If you had to choose between killing an animal and killing a child, do you mean to tell me that you'd hesitate for a moment to kill the wolf in order to save the child?

B: I'd probably kill the wolf, but then I'm a human being. The question is not what I *would* do but what I *ought* to do. And as a utilitarian, I must consider *all* sentient beings, not just those of my own species. Within the human community some people are guilty of racism; given a choice between human beings and animals, many people are guilty of species-ism. I don't want to be guilty of favoring the human species just because I belong to it. The effect of human actions on *all* sentient beings must be considered. I should consider the pain and death of animals just as much as I should consider the pain and death of a human being.

A: But as I said, human beings are of greater value. They can gain knowledge, be inspired by the starry heavens, and cure diseases, including those of animals. No other animals can. This is simply an objective fact. And *that* is why you ought to save the human being. Even among different species in the animal kingdom, I think you would be selective. You would save the life of a horse before you would that of a rat, and the life of a dog before that of a snail. And quite rightly. The dog is of greater value (and not just to humans) than the snail.

B: Insofar as the dog is capable of greater pain and pleasure, that is probably correct. I limit my remarks solely to beings capable of pain and pleasure, and I don't know whether the snail, or at any rate the worm or the amoeba, is capable of these things. But if any of them is, I *shouldn't* (whether or not I actually would) prefer one to the other; my *liking* one more than the other isn't a good reason.

A: I would let a hundred dogs die rather than one child. If I killed animals wantonly, that would be a minus (pain). But if I kill animals only to enable people to survive, the death of a hundred animals doesn't weigh as heavily on the scales of evil as the death of one child. If that's species-ism, so be it, but I submit that it's a weighing of lesser value against the greater, and the greater rightly wins: the child lives. Tell me, would it make a difference to you if the death of the animal was painless?

B: Of course. To kill an animal *and* inflict pain first is worse than to kill it painlessly. But to kill it at all is worse than to let it live. I do wrong if I kill it, even painlessly, when I could have let it live (even if nature kills it later through no fault of mine).

A: But now I think you have a problem. If you kill the animal (at least one that has lived to full maturity) painlessly you may be doing it a favor: it will never suffer any more pain, and the kind of death that nature usually inflicts on it—through slow starvation or being torn limb from limb by a predator—is something that it will never have to suffer.

B: But I don't know *that* when I kill it. All I know for sure is that *I* have killed it; I have taken away its life by my action.

A: Yes, but in utilitarianism you have to go by probabilities; and you have to admit that it's overwhelmingly probable that the animal will meet the kind of death I described. You are sparing it that extremely probable fate by killing it painlessly.

B: By the same argument, you could justify killing practically any human being over eighty years old, if you did it painlessly, saying that most of the person's happiness is over, and from now on there will be regrets at lost youth, the aches and pains of old age, and usually a very slow process of dying. I don't *know* this will be so for the old person I kill. Often it isn't. But I know what the probabilities are. Would you say that more likely than not you'd be doing the aged a favor too?

A: I would say that it should be up to the old to decide whether they want to continue living, it is not for me to decide that by killing them. An animal cannot make such a decision.

But with that consideration, we are introducing a new element into the argument—something to do with human rights—which isn't utilitarian, and goes quite beyond utilitarianism. Animal rights will be discussed later in Chapter 7, where the subject of human rights is discussed.

5. UTILITARIANISM AND RELIGION

Utilitarianism commits you to assessing the total probable consequences of your actions. It does not try to indicate what items are to be included in the total. Believers in life after death, for example, will insist that the consequences of your actions will keep going even after your bodily death has taken place. And if this is so, then all those posthumous consequences will have to be considered too. If you commit a murder, even if you are not found out in this life, you will be punished in the next one, and this consequence may deter you (for egoistic reasons, even if not utilitarian ones) from committing the crime. At least such consequences will have to enter your calculations.

There is no new principle involved in "religious utilitarianism." You are still to consider all the consequences of your actions, to yourself and to others. It's just that a belief in life after death requires you to extend the range of those consequences enormously. (If the punishment is "for all eternity," then the consequences extend to infinity.) And if you believe that those who die unconverted must suffer in an afterlife, then it would be your utilitarian duty to try to convert them, since without such conversion they would suffer forever.

Such a belief, then, makes an enormous difference in calculating the total consequences; indeed, the few years spent in this world will pale into nothing compared with the happiness or misery experienced throughout eternity in the next. Many people whose lot in this life is primarily one of misery or pain are consoled by the thought that after this life is over they will experience, perhaps as a reward for their labors, an infinity of perfect happiness. Only this prospect enables them to endure the pain.

Whether Christianity or any other religious belief is *true* is, of course, not within the province of ethics to discuss, even though its truth or falsity will make an enormous difference to conduct. But it is relevant at this point to discuss, not the truth, but the *utility* of religious belief. What are the consequences of having such belief, as opposed to not having it? Five are worth mentioning.

1. There are many people who would not do anything for others if they were not told that God had commanded them to do so and that they would get eternal rewards for doing so (and perhaps eternal punishment for not doing so). Many people would love their neighbor without the promises of reward or threats of punishment that religion holds forth. But there are others who require more motivation than simply benefiting others. They want to know, "What's in it for me?" And what's in it for them is heavenly rewards. Thus motivated, they may be led to do good deeds which they would otherwise fail to do.

Yet this motivation in most people is not as strong as it might seem, even in those who sincerely believe that divine rewards and punishments will be granted. It doesn't seem possible that anything could motivate people more strongly than the promise of eternal happiness or the threat of eternal torture. Yet though they believe in it, there are two great psychological deterrents. First, the threat of punishment, though very great, is also remote. Death always seems remote, and before that time people think they can disobey the commands, be forgiven, and still come in under the wire. Second, the threats are not very vivid in people's minds because they have never actually *seen* anyone suffering torments in hell. If they had witnessed just one or two sample cases, it might strike their imagination. But what has never been observed isn't nearly as likely to motivate as something that is personally experienced. Seeing people die in a car accident may motivate some to drive more safely, simply because they have seen for themselves what can happen if they don't.

Considering the immensity of the promised rewards and threatened punishments, which if taken seriously ought to outweigh all other considerations for those who believe in them, it is perhaps surprising that in general they have so little effect. For every one dedicated Christian who practices his or her belief, there are perhaps a hundred who, as far as their moral behavior is concerned, are difficult or impossible to distinguish from unbelievers: they will quarrel with their spouses or cheat on business deals as much as any unbeliever. Still, there are many devout Christians, Jews, Buddhists, and so on who, because of their beliefs, are more likely to try to promote the well-being of others more than many nonbelievers.

2. In addition to this consequence, there are certain qualities inculcated by religions which are, or may be, somewhat less likely to occur when people are not inspired by religious beliefs. Humility is an example. There is humility and humility, of course: sometimes what passes for humility is masochistic self-abasement: "Please trample on me" and "Why don't you spit on me?" are the signals unconsciously given out by masochistic personalities, and there probably isn't much utilitarian value in such a "virtue." Much that passes for humility is a vacillation between dramatic self-abasement on the one hand and strident egotism on the other, with sporadic delusions of grandeur. But humility of a steady and constant sort, which is not entirely self-abnegating but is quietly sustained, is a personality characteristic which often is apparent in religiously oriented persons. Patience in dealing with other people is another: Who can match the patience of dedicated nuns who tend the crippled and sick for years on end without complaint?

But there is another side to the coin of humility, and that is spiritual pride. It is difficult to be completely self-effacing for long, and "the old ego" tends to come out in one way or another: "If I've done all this for you, the least you can do is believe as I believe." "If you don't come to me in sackcloth and ashes, after all I've done for you, you are ungrateful." People who empty themselves for others often exact a high price for the gift in the end.

One of the manifestations of this false humility is intolerance. Religions are particularly liable to this danger, for each religion professes to have the truth (which means that those religions that conflict with it don't). In the past those who dissented from the accepted religious orthodoxy were broken on the rack or burned at the stake. Anyone who asked an honest question or exhibited intellectual curiosity—for example, "How do I know that what you tell me about God is true?"—was reminded that the most unforgivable sin of all is doubt, doubt of the truth of revelation. People may thus be cowed into submission, their inquiring minds imprisoned, with irreparable effects on their personality and thirst for knowledge.

And *if* the beliefs of those who held to the "one true religion" were true, their actions (however immoral they may seem to us) might have been justified. After all, by torturing people for just a few hours you might "bring them round" and save their souls (see pp. 14–15). There is no lack of basis for such beliefs in the Bible; it all depends on what passages you emphasize. This aspect is not emphasized today because most people don't take religious belief that seriously any more. Today preachers, priests, and rabbis discuss the issues between them in televised conferences as though they were friends "agreeing to disagree." But each of them in past ages would have viewed the others as lost souls who faced the most horrible of punishments unless they came round to the "true belief," which it would have been a primary duty to instill in them.

3. Some say that it is of great importance that children be brought up in religious belief, not only for their eternal salvation, but because only if moral rules are taught them in the name of religion will they have a solid basis throughout life on which to act and from which they will never depart.

But religion as an inculcator of morality is a mixed bag. For one thing, it depends on what moral rules the religion enjoins. Baal worship required all parents to sacrifice their firstborn children; some modern versions of devil worship make similar demands. Followers of Reverend Sun Yung Moon of the Unification Church were once told that to initiate violence is wrong unless it is in the service of Reverend Moon, and then violence is all right. There are all kinds of moral rules inculcated in the name of religion—some good, some bad.

It is also true that, although early moral training done in the name of religion may indeed be highly effective throughout the person's life, moral training can be done without religion. For example, the Spartans of ancient Greece imposed a severe moral code. In addition, when morality is tied to religion, then if religion goes, the morality may go too. People who have been told that there is no reason to behave honorably to others beyond the fact that God commands it and later lose their belief in God have (in their view) no reason left to behave honorably.

The great influence that early religious training seems to have is due more to its being *early* than to its being *religious*. Small children don't really understand the specifically religious character of the command; it is, in effect, the command of parents or parent surrogates, and if they disobey the command parents will punish them—which looms much larger in their eyes than the threat that God will (after they are dead) punish them.

As Mill pointed out in his classic essay "The Utility of Religion," not only are moral rules most effective in later life when they are inculcated repeatedly and early (whether in the name of religion or not), but they are most likely to be retained and practiced when they are reinforced by *public opinion*. Religious belief alone, without the backing of public opinion (at least within the community), has but little effect on the majority of people. Dueling was long practiced without many qualms of conscience, although it was always forbidden by the religious commandment against killing. Illicit sexual intercourse has almost always been more frowned upon for women than for men, although the biblical injunction against fornication and adultery applies equally to both sexes. "Without the sanctions superadded by public opinion," Mill claimed, the sanctions of religion "have never, save in exceptional characters or in peculiar moods of mind, exercised a very potent influence."[5]

[5]John Stuart Mill, "The Utility of Religion," in *Three Essays on Religion* (London: Longmans Green, 1874), p. 88. Reprinted in Mill, *Nature and the Utility of Religion* (New York: Liberal Arts Press, 1958).

4. Though the effect of religious belief in encouraging moral behavior is disputable, there is one consequence that utilitarians claim is absolutely undesirable. In any religion there are duties to God as well as duties to human beings, and of the two, the duties to God take first place. "Believe in the Lord thy God," the Bible says; "this is the first and greatest commandment; and the second . . . is, Love thy neighbor as thyself." Thus, along with belief in God come things like Sabbath observance and the attempt to convert others. From the viewpoint of secular utilitarianism all this is a waste: with so many unmet human needs, people who discharge their duties to God take valuable time and effort away from what most needs doing, problems of this world. People may observe the Sabbath, go to confession regularly, and so on, all of which may (if their religious belief is true) help them to get to heaven, but such duties take away much needed time from tending to the problems of other human beings.

But of course if the religious belief is true, then it *is* necessary to have both kinds of duties and to put the duty to God ahead of the duty to fellow human beings. It is only from the standpoint of the person who does not share the religious belief that the time spent on the first kind of duty appears to be a waste.

5. For the believer the utility or disutility of religion is really a side issue. The important thing is its *truth*. If someone was to say, "Believe in Christianity because it is useful" or "Believe in it because doing so has good moral effects," the recipient of this information would not be particularly motivated to believe that the doctrine were true. If a religious belief is taught, it must be taught as the truth: without that, religious belief would be missing its vital center. It is in the truth of a religion that people believe, and its utility or moral effects are by-products. As one writer notes:

> Suppose that we could prove that adherence to a certain religion does tend to encourage good behavior, would it then follow that the religion should be given a privileged position in the social structure, taught to children and maintained as the orthodox creed? Is it not rather the case that religious truths, if such exist, must be maintained and propagated on the ground that they are *true* and not merely that they are *useful*? If religion is true *and can be shown to be so* then it should be taught, whether or not its effects are fortunate. And if it cannot be shown to be true then it ought not to be propagated officially, even though its social consequences are excellent.[6]

There is, of course, a problem in showing a religion to be true. Champions of each religious belief assert that their belief is true and the others mistaken (at least in some respects). In the attempt to *defend* their belief against all others, champions often appeal to arguments which, if valid, would prove

[6]D. J. O'Connor, *An Introduction to the Philosophy of Education* (London: Routledge & Kegan Paul, 1957), p. 135.

their opponents' views also. For example, they point to certain miraculous events as proof of their belief; but members of other groups deny these and claim miraculous events of their own. Each side is then placed in a position of defending its belief denying those of the competition. Each tends to minimize and distort the claims of the others, presenting them in an oversimplified form and in an unfavorable light to reduce their plausibility, and tries to find whatever arguments it can, however farfetched, to support its own. This tendency toward what Mill called "the subornation of the understanding" is particularly apparent to intelligent and sensitive minds, who are intellectually repelled by the whole procedure. Moreover, it tends to spread: once people become accustomed to defending their views by questionable means, the tendency easily extends to other areas; finally, as Bertrand Russell noted, they develop the habit of defending views to which they are already committed rather than searching honestly for the truth wherever that search may lead:

> If you think that your belief is based upon reason, you will support it by argument rather than by persecution, and will abandon it if the argument goes against you. But if your belief is based on faith, you will realize that argument is useless, and will therefore resort to force, either in the form of persecution or by stunting and distorting the minds of the young in what is called "education." [7]

An especially cynical form of this tendency of religion to distort is to be found in Pascal's famous "wager," which can be paraphrased as follows: Religious belief, with its promise of heavenly rewards, may be true or it may not. If it is, you will be made to suffer for not having believed it; whereas if it is false, it won't make any difference anyway after you're dead. Therefore, it is advisable for you to believe it.

There are several problems with this argument. First, can people sincerely or genuinely believe (rather than just pretend to) on the basis of such a wager? And second, doesn't belief, in fact, make a difference in the here and now? If you sacrifice many things you want and do many things you don't like to do, just in the hope of reward or out of fear of punishment, and the belief you based it all on turns out not to be true, then you have sacrificed much of the only life you will ever have for no purpose.

Indeed, the wager could be extended. "It's safer to be Catholic than Protestant," someone might say, "since Protestants say that both Catholics and Protestants can go to heaven, whereas Catholics (at least traditionally) have said that only Catholics can enter heaven. So, if Catholicism turns out to be right, you'll be safe either way." To which Bertrand Russell once replied, "How do you know there isn't a God who respects sincerity and intellectual honesty and basing one's opinions on evidence rather than faith, so much

---

[7] Bertrand Russell, *Human Society in Ethics and Politics* (New York: Simon & Schuster, 1954), p. 220.

that he will punish forever anyone who adheres to a religion just to be on the winning side?"[8]

From the point of view of the believer, then, religious belief (at least the one believed in by the adherent) is not only true but extremely useful, both to the individual and to everyone else. From the point of the skeptic or the non-believer, however, the utilitarian merits of religious belief are dubious.

6. OBJECTIONS TO UTILITARIANISM

The utilitarian principle is simple, neat, and tidy. In practice, as we have seen, the maximization of net expectable intrinsic good is fraught with complexities. But the complexity of application to specific cases is the result of the far-flung consequences of human actions and the difficulty of calculating them. A utilitarian might apply the following syllogism:

1. Acts which maximize net expectable intrinsic good are right.
2. This act maximizes net expectable intrinsic good (maximizes utility).
3. Therefore, this act is right.

The practical difficulty lies with the second premise, not the first.

But there have been many objections made to the utilitarian principle itself. Some of them will be developed in coming chapters, when we consider justice and rights. Here are some of the principal ones:

1. The rightness of all acts can't be judged by their utility alone, according to critics. I hire someone to type a paper for me. When the work is done and the time comes for me to pay, should I pay the typist only if there is no other act in the world that I could have done which had no better consequences? Would it be right to refuse to pay him and give the money to charity instead? When I make a promise, should it be with the understanding that I should keep it only if there is no other action I could take instead which would maximize utility? Most of us certainly do not think so.

Or again, if my car collides with yours, and the accident is my fault, should I decline to pay if I discover that you are pretty well off and can afford the expense of repair more easily than I can? Our ordinary moral consciousness seems to deliver a different verdict: the person who is at fault should pay, without regard to who will be happier as a result. Should the calculation of happiness and unhappiness for each alternative (either you pay, or I pay) even be considered in a case of this kind? (Courts certainly do not think so.) It has seemed to many people that utilitarianism is mistaken in the view that our only duty is to maximize utility.

2. There are factors that determine pleasure and displeasure, happiness and unhappiness, which, it may be said, *shouldn't*. Suppose your baby cries or

---

[8] Quoted in Millard S. Everett, *Ideals of Life* (New York: Wiley, 1954), p. 30.

your dog howls in a particularly irritating way, so that it "sends you up the wall" to hear it and that it affects everyone else in the household the same way. The amount of displeasure created by such noise (which irritates many people, keeps them from being able to do their work, etc.) is much greater than the pleasure the baby or dog experiences by making it. Suppose that in the utilitarian calculation the suffering of the hearers turns out to be the most important factor. Since the baby or dog can't help making the noise and there is no other way short of muzzling the noisemaker to stop the irritation, is it justifiable to use that method? Many will say no, because we should not feel as irritated as we do; yet we can't seem to help it, though we may feel guilty for being so annoyed.

Consider another example. Many people are not only deeply distressed but strongly repelled at the sight of a disfigured face or a withered limb. Yet those afflicted are in no way responsible for their disfigurement. If the repulsion of a hundred people at such a sight was so great as to outweigh the pleasure a disfigured person takes in having human company, is the group justified in excluding that person from its company (and for all people to exclude such people from their company), just because of this intense repulsion?

One more case: if you succeed in obtaining some worthy goal, there will be others who are bitter with envy; they will hate you for your success and may try to destroy you. In a utilitarian calculus such negative feelings will count as minuses. They might be so strong and so widespread that they would constitute more of a minus than your happiness (and that of your friends) at your success would constitute a plus. But should you count the envy of others into your calculations? If you believe that it's something they shouldn't feel, shouldn't you ignore such negative feelings in your calculation of consequences?

3. Many critics of utilitarianism have contended, in addition, that it is simply *too demanding*. According to utilitarianism, whatever has the best consequences possible for everyone is what ought to be done. Nothing less will suffice; everything else, even what does a little bit less good, is wrong. Ordinarily we make more subtle distinctions. We say, "It would be wonderful if you did that" or "It would be nice if you did"—expressing degrees of merit. But such distinctions do not exist in utilitarianism: if you fail to do the act that is *optimific* (one that maximizes net expectable utility), the act is wrong, no matter how worthy it may be. If you do one fine deed when you could have done a finer, it is wrong because nothing but the best is right. It seems plain to many people that when a man comes home from a long day's work and sits down and reads a detective novel or watches television for relaxation, he is *not* doing wrong, even though there are all kinds of things he might do instead which would have better consequences for more people.

In ordinary discourse we make a distinction between what you *ought* to do and what is *right* to do. To say you "ought" to do it is to say that it would be *wrong not* to do it; to say it is "right" is to say that it would *not be wrong* to do it. Right has more the meaning of "O.K.," "all right," or "permissible." But in utilitarianism the only time that more than one act could be right occurs in those special cases when there is more than one act you could perform at a certain time which would have the best expectable consequences; then if each act had a net expectable utility of, say, +50, and no other had as much, then any of them you did would be right, because any one of them would maximize good. But still, this doesn't allow much elasticity: the act with +49 would still be wrong, even though it was just slightly less good (in its consequences) than the best.

In utilitarianism there is no room for *supererogatory acts,* that is, acts over and above the call of duty. If you do more than you need to, more than anyone expects of you, if you do something especially noteworthy or heroic, there is no category in utilitarianism to cover such an act. If it is something that you *can* do and if it is the very best thing that could be done (has the best expectable consequences), then it is what you *ought* to do, and anything less would be a wrongful act. Is utilitarianism correct in blurring the distinction ordinarily made between duties and supererogatory acts?

4. As we have seen, utilitarianism is a universalistic moral principle and not an altruistic one; you are to consider yourself as one among many. But you are only one person and others *are* many, so when your act affects a large number of people, the difference between considering 10,000 people (utilitarianism) and considering 9,999 (all except yourself—altruism) becomes very small indeed. And thus, if it is your duty to maximize good *wherever* it may occur, your life could, in fact, be mortgaged to every needy and hungry person around the globe. No matter how hard you work and save, no matter how many hungry people you help across the globe, no matter how many of their lives you may save by sacrificing everything you earn working fifteen hours a day, there are always millions more of the needy and hungry, waiting for help. Shouldn't you feel guilty for every luxury you have, every bit of toothpaste or shampoo you use, as long as there are people anywhere doing without necessities? Couldn't you do more good by helping them instead of buying those extra books or records for yourself? You are only one, they are millions. The help you can give in a lifetime is limited, but as long as you can, isn't it your utilitarian duty to do so? It is true that utilitarianism isn't altruism, but doesn't it almost come to the same thing? Your own satisfactions are a small thing in comparison with the satisfactions others could have if their hunger and want were alleviated. True, you should think of yourself insofar as guarding your health so that you can live to help for more years, but your welfare must be weighed against that of millions, and thus your main effort should go to help the millions.

Utilitarians may suggest a reply to all this, however. They may argue that when you help someone who is hungry with charity, you drain yourself in order to help, and that person will be hungry again tomorrow. Such temporary help is useless; what is needed is to get at the root causes of this massive poverty. Millions of people are unnecessarily in a state of want.

Many people are able and willing to work, but can't find work or can't find it at sufficient pay to stay alive. Much of the reason for this is that their rulers retain such tight control over them that they are like serfs or slaves, allowed only enough for their labor to survive. Power-hungry rulers and cynical bureaucrats consume the fruits of their labors. Governments which provide them no incentive to work and no reward for working more productively stifle their efforts. Relax those tight controls over their lives, and much of the problem would be solved. Christianity, for example, extols charity while often condemning employers because they earn profits; yet they have to do so to stay in business and keep workers employed. Employers are doing the needy much more good by offering them jobs than charitable organizations are by offering them food. Employers restore people's self-respect, put them back on the production line. Perhaps the industrialist John Paul Getty was a better utilitarian than the charitable organizations ever were when he wrote:

> If I were convinced that by giving away my fortune I could make a real contribution toward solving the problem of world poverty, I would give away 99.5% of all I have immediately. But a hard-eyed appraisal of the situation convinces me that this is not the case. The best form of charity I know is the act of meeting a payroll. If I turned over my entire fortune to a charitable foundation, would it do any more good than I can do with it? The answer is no. However admirable the work of the best charitable foundation, it would accustom people to the passive acceptance of money, and incidentally deprive of their jobs thousands of hard-working people who are associated with me.[9]

As an account of how poverty can be alleviated, this argument has much to recommend it. But it doesn't really solve the problem for utilitarianism. The question still remains: Is it true that your life should be devoted primarily to the needs of others—that if 10 million need your assistance in order to be even minimally happy, and you can help to provide it, you should give most of your life over to helping them (including trying to change their politico-economic system so that there will be less want)? Should the main goal of your life be to minister to the needs of others? (It's true that most of your acts usually affect only you, your family, and your friends; but if by doing other things, such as helping poor people overseas, you *could* affect more lives, wouldn't it be your utilitarian duty to do so?) Should you really be "as impartial as a disinterested and benevolent spectator" in choosing between satisfying your requirements for happiness and satisfying those of utter strangers? If you could keep two children in India from starving by letting your own child starve, should you do so because it's two against one? Should you even give something less than your life? If you could save a Cambodian's life by burning half your body in hot flames for ten minutes (and spend half

[9] Quoted in *The Saturday Evening Post,* May 22, 1965, p. 10.

a year in the hospital in great pain), would it be your duty to do so? Not only don't most people act on such a belief, but they don't even believe that such a tremendous sacrifice is their duty. Most people aren't totally egoistic: they do serve the needs of others, often at a cost to themselves. But they aren't full-fledged utilitarians either, considering the happiness of an unknown peasant just as important as their own or that of their family. Is their special concern for their own family a moral error on their part?

5. Besides the overall problem of the difficulty of living up to the ideal, there is a special problem in utilitarianism about taking life. Consider a person who is old, sick, and alone in the world; it seems overwhelmingly probable (though we would need more facts than just these to make it so) that her life from this point on will contain much more pain, misery, and sadness than pleasure, joy, and gladness. If you can kill her painlessly—say, by giving her a quick-acting poison just before she goes to sleep, thus ensuring that she will never wake up—wouldn't you be doing her a favor? You would be decreasing the amount of suffering in the world. Yet we don't view the matter in this way at all. "No normal person," according to one writer, "would try to justify a murder by saying, 'It wasn't really a painful death,' or 'His soul went to the good place,' or 'He won't be missed,' or 'He wouldn't really have been happy if he had lived.' " [10] Isn't killing a person, even painlessly, simply wrong, even when we know that the remainder of his or her life would be unhappy?

What if a group of people would experience far more satisfaction than the victim would experience dissatisfaction (including pain) at being killed? Would the murder be justified? Several objections may be raised:

a. You may say, no, the group shouldn't do it, because the members might get caught, which would mean quite a bit of unhappiness for all of them while they are in prison. But suppose there's practically no chance of being caught. If the law is lax or corrupt, does that fact make the murder any more permissible? (Many would say it isn't even relevant to the matter of whether the killing is wrong. But in utilitarianism, which is based on a calculation of all the states of pain and pleasure, happiness and unhappiness, this would indeed be a relevant consideration.)

b. You may say, no, they shouldn't do it, because the victim will experience pain and distress on being killed. But this isn't so: it is easy to kill people painlessly.

c. You may say, no, they shouldn't do it, because even if the killing is painless, the victim will experience horror in the knowledge that she is about to die, a tremendously intense mental pain. But that consideration doesn't apply if she is suddenly and unexpectedly hit over the head: she'll feel nothing after that—not dread or anything else.

d. You may say, no, because the killing will cut off whatever chances of happiness she would have had if she had been permitted to live. But suppose

[10] Richard Hensen, "Utilitarianism and the Wrongness of Killing," in *Understanding Moral Philosophy,* ed. James Rachels (Belmong, Calif.: Dickenson Publishing, 1976), p. 153.

that the victim's chances of having an unrelievedly miserable time for the rest of her life, given her condition, are at least 99.9 percent. Also she has no family to grieve for her, and nobody would even miss her. Wouldn't they actually be doing her a favor by killing her? Think of the pain and distress they would spare her by putting her painlessly out of the way!

e. You may say, no, because once word gets out that this sort of thing is happening to people and that the perpetrators are getting away with it, the community will live in dread and terror; everyone will wonder whether he or she will be the next victim of someone's "favor." The sick, the aged, the lonely, will feel special dread. This, indeed, is a very real consequence *if* the fact that the deed has happened becomes known. But suppose there is only one killing and that it's done in secret, so that nobody ever knows about it. The person killed is without a family and will never be missed, and nobody will dread the same fate because nobody will ever learn that this secret murder was committed. (Utilitarianism would consider the consequences of the act worse if other people knew about it and thus experienced constant dread than if it were done in secret. But would the act be any the less wrong for being done in secret, so that these bad consequences didn't occur?)

f. You may say, no, the act shouldn't be done because it will set a bad example for others. But this isn't so; no one else will know. It may be bad for the perpetrators themselves, since *they* will have to live with the fact that they did it. But they may not mind; they may even be happy at having brought the act off successfully. Nor is it always the case that they will be more inclined to do it again later. (Even if they did, again in secret and again to someone who would not be missed, would this second act of killing be any less wrong than the first one?) In fact they may not ever want to do it again: many killers never kill a second time.

It would certainly seem that a pretty good case has been made for the rightness of killing this person, according to utilitarianism. The scenario has been written in such a way that the usual objections do not apply. And yet in all this, haven't we avoided the main issue—whether it is right to take a person's life against that person's will? If the old woman we have used in the example wants to die, there are various ways in which she can arrange it. If she is tired of life and wants someone else to put her painlessly out of the way, perhaps it should be permissible for that other person to do so. (We shall discuss that separately when we treat the problem of euthanasia in Chapter 9.) But if the person wants to live, whether or not she will be happy, whether or not she will be in pain, then who has the *right* to take her life? Have we the right to play God with life and say, "You're life isn't going to be very happy from now on, so we're going to eliminate that unhappiness by killing you"? Will any amount of such utilitarian calculation, however correct it may be, make it right to take her life?

But if we should preserve life even if there is a resultant increase of unhappiness, aren't we going contrary to what utilitarianism prescribes? We consider it wrong to kill the woman, not because letting her live would maximize happiness (it wouldn't, under the circumstances described), but because she has a *right to life*—a subject we shall take up when we discuss human rights in Chapter 7.

But we can carry the objection to utilitarianism still further. Consider the large number of people who spend their lives consuming (and robbing others to obtain) hard drugs and the perhaps equally large number of petty thieves who are disinclined to work and whose principal aim in life is to rob and defraud others. Consider, too, those people who, instead of trying to obtain happiness for themselves, do their best to make all those around them unhappy, planting seeds of jealousy here and revenge there, souring all ongoing human relations in their vicinity. Wouldn't the world be better off without these people in it? Wouldn't the sum total of happiness in the world be greater without these and other obnoxious sorts? Suppose they could all be killed painlessly; the world would be a better and happier place to live in. Why, then, according to utilitarianism, shouldn't this be done? Some years ago, speaking of persons who are both stupid and malicious, the popular iconoclastic moralist Philip Wylie wrote:

> They have no aptitude for learning, make no use of what they do manage to be taught, and are a waste of tax money. A group of that group, the least stable and reasonable, should be politically disenfranchised. No one in the entire multitude should ever be permitted to hold public office. And a certain small percentage of this dreadful offal, much of which regularly accumulates in the bleachers of our ball parks, should be quietly put to sleep.[11]

Assuming that the happiness in the world would be increased by their absence, the main utilitarian consideration against killing them would seem to be that other people would learn about it and live in fear and dread lest they be the next on the hit list. But even if the killings could be done in such a way that others never found out, would it still be right to do such a thing? And why would it *not* be right according to utilitarianism?

6. It seems, from the preceding discussion of killing, that people, as individuals, don't really count in utilitarianism. What counts is the total amount of good produced. As moral philosopher W. D. Ross noted:

> For a utilitarian it is morally indifferent whether by your act you produce x units of pleasure for A and inflict y units of pain on B, confer $x - y$ units of pleasure on one of them, since in each case you produce a net increment of $x - y$ units of pleasure. . . . But we think the principle 'do evil to no one' more pressing than the principle 'do good to everyone.'[12]

---

[11]Philip Wylie, *Generation of Vipers* (New York: Holt, Rinehart & Winston, 1942), pp. 92–93.
[12]W. D. Ross, *Foundations of Ethics* (London: Oxford University Press, 1939), p. 75.

Isn't it more important not to harm people than to help them? If you could give 10 units of pleasure to A by inflicting 9 units of pain on B, would this be the right thing to do (assuming the only alternative to be *not* doing it)? Are you justified in harming one person just to give pleasure or happiness to another? You can choose 10 units of pain for yourself in order to spare another person 12 units of pain; but are you justified in choosing 8 units of pain for Jones in preference to 10 units of pain for yourself, just because the total amount of pain is less when Jones has it?

As a result of this "impersonality," each individual's goals, no matter how precious to him or her, are subject to veto if working for someone else's goal has greater utility. Suppose you have a research project which interests you and which you want very much to pursue. But if someone else's project is more important or would increase general utility more than yours, utilitarianism might well require you to abandon your own and assist in the other person's. Your own ideas would be at the mercy of anyone else who could demonstrate the superior utility of his or her own. The impersonality of utilitarianism is captured in the following analysis of it:

> [The Utilitarian] has no defenses against utility black holes that suck up aid at prodigious rates. Therefore he must eschew serious commitment to any end other than the attainment of utility in any guise it may take. A world populated by utilitarians would be one in which everything matters somewhat and nothing very much. This, of course, is the world he recommends. It is one in which individuality is neither present nor missed. It is a world thoroughly unlivable for beings such as ourselves. . . .
>
> . . . Ends are perfectly socialized. No matter who produced them, they belong to all equally, and all have an equal stake in advancing them. The fact that E is crucial to some deeply held project of *mine* creates no reason for its promotion by me. But then, in what sense can E still significantly be said to be *my* end? True, I brought it into being, but that gives me no proprietary rights. I am called upon to maximize utility in whatever way I am most able. If that involves pursuing E, it is no more than an accident. . . . [A utilitarian] can represent a person only as a convenient locus at which utility can be produced and as the instrument for producing utility at yet other loci. It is not persons as such that really matter, but rather the utility they can realize.[13]

7. There is still another objection to utilitarianism, closely related to the previous one. The aim of utilitarianism is to maximize happiness (or intrinsic good). But doesn't it matter *to whom* it goes? As Ross noted, according to utilitarianism, if you can make two people happier

> it ought to be quite indifferent how an 'extra dose' of happiness should be distributed among the population, provided the total amount of the

---

[13] Loran Lomasky, "A Refutation of Utilitarianism." Forthcoming in *Canadian Journal of Philosophy*.

dose is unaltered. It would be morally just the same whether A is made very happy and B only very slightly happy, or whether A and B are both made rather happy, provided that the net gain in happiness for A and B taken together were equal in both cases.[14]

But does it really not matter who you make happy (or happier)? Suppose that *A* is a father who is sadistically cruel to his children, and *B* is a kind, gentle, and understanding father; or that *A* has made other people's lives miserable and *B* has made their lives happier; or that *A* has made lots of money cheating people and *B* is trying to raise a family but is having a hard time making ends meet. Does it still not matter which one you are helpful to? Surely *B deserves* your help more than *A* does.

A utilitarian might reply that if you help bad people you encourage their bad deeds and thus cause more harm in the world, whereas if you help good people you will be helping to create more good (and indirectly, happiness); thus, if you consider the *total* happiness created, you would really be doing more by helping *B*. That, of course, would change the estimate of total consequences with which the example began. But suppose this *is* the total: by aiding *A* you are increasing total happiness by a certain amount, and by aiding *B* you are increasing it by the same amount. Isn't it still the case that you would do better to increase *B's* happiness, simply because *he deserves it,* and not because of any good consequences that might occur later? We shall pursue this issue further when we discuss justice in Chapter 8.

8. The principle of maximizing happiness can be shown to give rise to still another problem for utilitarianism. If you could choose between creating a society with 10,000 people, each with 100 net units of happiness, and a society with 20,000 people, each with 100 net units of happiness, you would choose the second, since the amount of total happiness would be double that in the first case. But suppose the choice was between 10,000 people, each with 100 units of happiness, and 20,000 people, each with 50 units of happiness. The total amount of happiness in the two cases would be the same, so for the utilitarian it would be a matter of indifference which society you would bring into being. But this seems to many people to be mistaken. Each of the people in the second society would have only half the happiness of the people in the first society. If you had to choose, wouldn't you do better to choose the first society, since it would consist of happier people, even though they were fewer in number?

People often encounter this kind of choice in family planning. If the parents are of limited means, should they have a small family which they can easily support, or a large family which they can't easily support and in which all the children will be deprived of many happiness-producing things? Almost everyone would say the parents should have a small family; it has fewer members, but those that do exist are much better off than the one in the large family (though, of course, "financially better off" doesn't always trans-

---

[14] Ross, *Foundations of Ethics,* p. 71.

late into "happier"). Even if the *total amount* of net happiness is the same in both cases, isn't it better for *each individual* to be happier, rather than spreading resources so thin that there's very little opportunity for the large family to be happy? For the same reason, you would probably consider it preferable to have a world populated by 2 billion fairly happy individuals than by 10 billion less happy individuals, even though the total quantity of (net) happiness was somewhat greater in the second world.

These and many other objections have been made to the utilitarian theory. Some of them may strike you as having greater weight than others. At any rate, several other views of right and wrong action to which the same objections do not apply must be considered. These are the subjects of the next few chapters.

EXERCISES

1. The following excerpt from R. C. Mortimer, *Christian Ethics,* pp. 8–10, contains numerous mistakes in its description of utilitarianism. Find as many as you can.

> Utilitarianism distinguishes between right and wrong solely by reference to pleasure or expediency. That is right which tends to make me happy. The rightness of an action is to be judged by whether its consequences will bring more pleasure than pain, either to me or to society. By that, and that alone. When a man judges by reference to his own pleasure only, he is called a hedonist. Such a man is essentially selfish; for even though he may perform actions which give pleasure to others, his reason for doing so is that he himself derives pleasure from giving pleasure. That is why he thinks the action right.
>
> Utilitarians, properly so called, are those who think that right conduct consists not in pursuing their own pleasure but in promoting "the greatest happiness of the greatest number." In either case the decisive objection is that there is no means of distinguishing between one pleasure and another, except by its intensity. It is as right, perhaps more right, to indulge a passion for another man's wife than to listen to a classical concert. Moreover, any action may be justified by its end: if, on balance, it causes more happiness than pain, it is right. Thus it would be right to murder an irritating mother-in-law and so restore peace and harmony to a whole family.

2. Concerning objective versus subjective duty, give your considered judgment on the following examples:
    a. An experienced driver may sometimes actually reduce traffic hazards by violating a speed law or some other traffic ordinance. Is doing so justified every time it does reduce the hazard?
    b. You see a suspicious-looking person hanging around the gunpowder plant. No one else is in the vicinity, and there is no time to report his presence to anyone. He lights a match; should you wait to see whether he uses it to light the fuse which may set the entire plant on fire? Or should you take the law into your own hands and try to stop him forcibly now, on the assumption that his intentions are evil?

c. A physician is driving her car on an emergency call. She isn't sure it is a life-and-death case until she arrives at her destination, but the telephone call reported it to be crucial and she dares not assume that it is less serious than it seems to be. On the way she witnesses an automobile accident in which she may be of service to the victims, and indeed a bystander sees the M.D. sign on her car and waves for her to stop. What should she do? Assume that she is the only physician in the vicinity.

d. As a physician, you can save the life of a man who is *almost* certain to kill again if he lives. Or you can give him a drug that will painlessly put him out of the way now. Assume that no one would ever find out, or if they did, would not prosecute. What should you do?

e. OFFICER: Don't you realize that by taking that boat without permission and rescuing your brother (who had been left behind on the island when the troopship moved out) you were endangering not only your own life but that of all the troops on board, by informing the enemy of our presence?
ENLISTED MAN: Yes, I know, but I took the chance and nothing happened, and everything turned out all right, didn't it?"
Did the enlisted man do wrong? Should he be punished?

3. Assume that you are a utilitarian and consider the following problems:

a. In Fyodor Dostoyevsky's novel *Crime and Punishment,* the main character, Raskolnikov, plots and carries out the murder of an old woman who has a considerable amount of money in her apartment. After killing her, he steals the money. He argues that (1) she is a malicious old woman, petty, cantankerous, and scheming, useless to herself and to society (which happens to be true), and her life causes no happiness to herself or to others; and (2) her money, if found after her death, would only fall into the hands of chiselers anyway, whereas he, Raskolnikov, would use it for his education. Would you, as a utilitarian, justify his action?

b. In Sinclair Lewis's novel *Arrowsmith,* Dr. Arrowsmith has perfected a new vaccine which, if used, will end an outbreak of the plague in the West Indies. If he uses the vaccine on everyone, most or all will be cured. But his vaccine will not be accepted in scientific circles (and thus used to prevent later outbreaks) unless he divides the population into two parts, giving vaccine to one half and not to the other half. If he gives vaccine only to some, he will needlessly cause the death of many people; yet must he not do this to prove to others that it was the vaccine which saved their lives?

c. You are contemplating stealing a large sum of money from a secret hiding place of a friend who is now lying on her deathbed. No one else knows of the hiding place or of the existence of the money. Access to it is easy, and let us assume that there is no chance of being caught. You are not the kind of person whose conscience bothers you. The usual consequences of stealing—effects on society, effects on general respect for law, effects on your conscience—do not exist in this situation. Moreover, you will make excellent use of the money. Would the theft be justified?

d. Would it be justifiable to whip pigs to death if more succulent pork resulted from this process, giving the consumers of the pork more pleasure than the pigs received pain from being flogged?

e. Your neighbor's family belongs to a religious cult which teaches that all nonmembers of the cult will be punished eternally in hellfire. Your neigh-

bor's children tell this belief to your children, and your children ask you
whether it is true. You do not believe it; but if you deny it, your children
will tell the neighbor's children, who in turn will tell their parents, creating
mistrust and hostility. At the same time, you do not want to tell your
children anything that is not only extremely disturbing to them but that is
also, you honestly believe, untrue. What should you do?

f. Queen Elizabeth held Mary Queen of Scots prisoner in the Tower of London and finally had her executed on charges of conspiracy against the
crown. Elizabeth knew that her specific charges against Mary were groundless, but she also felt that the execution would restore order in the kingdom
and set an example to would-be plotters, thus increasing national security
at a time when the very existence of the nation was threatened by Spain.
Was Elizabeth justified in putting Mary to death?

g. Before the Bolshevik Revolution of 1917 there was a provisional government led by Alexander Kerensky. Kerensky was a less fanatical, more le-
nient, and more democratic man than Lenin or Stalin, and the history of
the Soviet Union in the last half-century would almost certainly have been
far less bloodthirsty if he had remained in power. But during the brief period that he was head of the government, he decided to show the Russian
people that he was earnest and sincere in his claims of tolerance and his
opposition to tyranny; so he declared an amnesty for all political prisoners.
The result was that his political enemies were released from prison and they
took advantage of his leniency to overthrow his government. Would it have
been better if Kerensky had ordered all political prisoners shot?

h. You are driving a trolley whose brakes give out at the top of the hill. If it
continues on the track, it will kill four people at the bottom. But if you
pull a lever and switch it to another track, it will kill only two people.
Should you switch it to another track?

    A: Yes, of course, fewer lives would be lost that way.

    B: No, for you are now interfering with the "course of nature" to
       kill, by your deliberate act, the two people at the end of the other track.

i. You are alone in a boat, and nearby are two large rocks filled with persons
waiting to be rescued; there are five people on one rock and four on the
other. Assume that you cannot rescue both groups. Does utilitarianism
commit you to rowing to the rock that contains the larger number of people?

4. According to utilitarianism, you should choose 2 units of pain for yourself as
opposed to 4 units of pain for someone else (the lesser of two evils), if these are
the only choices. You should also, if these are the only choices, choose 2 units of
pain for Jones in preference to 4 units of pain for Smith. Is the latter case morally
different from the former one? Have you the right to choose pain for someone
else without that person's consent?

5. "We do not have a duty to do good to others or to ourselves, or to others and/or
to ourselves in a judicious mixture such that it produces the greatest possible
amount of good in the world. We are morally required to do good only to those
who are actually in need of our assistance." (From Kurt Baier, *The Moral Point of
View* [Ithaca, N.Y.: Cornell University Press, 1958], p. 203. Reprinted by permission.)

    Do we have a duty to those in need of our assistance whom we happen to come across? Or should we seek them out? And is there any end to them? Assistance in what way? Alleviation of hunger? Psychological problems? Company for loneliness?

6. Discuss the view called "negative utilitarianism": you don't have a duty to help other people, but you do have a duty to refrain from harming them.

7. Many people consider it wrong to pull the plug on an unconscious person even when there is no chance that the person will ever regain consciousness. But if we can put animals out of their suffering, why can't we do the same with a human being? (The main consideration that operates with other human beings—that they can anticipate death and would dread being on the receiving end of a "pull-the-plug" policy by other people—does not operate in the case of the unconscious any more than in the case of animals.)

8. Evaluate the following comment from A. C. Ewing, *Ethics,* pp. 40–41, on utilitarianism:

> It seems to me pretty clear that utilitarian principles, logically carried out, would result in far more cheating, lying, and unfair action than any good man would tolerate. . . .
>
> In any actual instance of a kind that could provide a ground for dispute the effects will be very complicated and uncertain, so that it will always leave a loophole for the utilitarian to argue that I am wrong in my view as to their bearing on the general happiness and that the act which seems right to common sense is really after all on a long view that most productive of happiness. And even if there are some instances where this is very unplausible (as indeed I think there are), he may reply by amending common-sense ethics here and saying that the act we ordinarily think right in this case is not really so.

9. Keeping in mind the utilitarian attitude toward animals, what would be the utilitarian attitude toward intelligent beings on other planets? (If we had to choose, should we sacrifice our happiness to theirs if it were proved to us that they had a greater potential for happiness than we and were also more likely to actualize this potential?)

10. "Why do people go to such lengths to save one member of an endangered species, such as the whooping crane or the California condor? Isn't one human being many times more important than one animal?" Comment.

11. If you feel justified in killing an animal (for food or hide or other purpose useful to human beings) but not a child (because the child has a human potential), what about killing people in advanced stages of senility (since they have no more rational potential, their rationality is gone, and the memory cells in their brain are dead)?

12. Do you consider the following as "useful purposes" for taking the life of an animal?
    a. Its noise bothers me at night.
    b. The wolf is killing my sheep.
    c. Its meat makes a tasty dish.
    d. I enjoy seeing it squirm.
    e. The gophers are destroying my vegetable garden.
    f. I hate snakes. (Assume it's a useful nonpoisonous snake.)
    g. The coyotes don't bother me but they kill my puppies.
    h. The condor (an endangered species) swoops down and kills my chickens.

13. "People have no duties to animals, just as animals have no duties to us. But if I am cruel to animals, I am more likely to be cruel to people; it creates bad habits. Behavior toward animals is thus a training ground for good behavior toward people." Comment.
14. How much difference do the following considerations make, in your view, as to whether animals should be eaten by human beings for food?
    a. We don't know how much pain certain creatures suffer, if any. Does the fish experience pain when harpooned or only exhibit avoidance behavior?
    b. Animals don't have any terror in anticipation of death: cattle chew grass in the pasture quite contentedly even an hour before they are killed by the farmer.
    c. Wild animals would probably die anyway, a more lingering death than we administer by shooting them.
    d. By killing excess wild animals we help to restore the balance of nature.
15. Which of these treatments of animals do you find most objectionable, and why?
    a. Raising and killing rabbits for food
    b. Clubbing baby seals over the head and killing them for their skins
    c. Raising chickens under crowded conditions on wire netting
    d. Slitting open the bodies of cattle in slaughterhouses before they are unconscious
16. What would you do, and what do you think you *should* do, in each of the following choice situations?
    a. Choosing between running over a convicted murderer and running over a dog
    b. Choosing between running over a stranger and running over *your* dog
    c. Choosing between running over a dog and running over a skunk or weasel
    d. Choosing between walking outdoors and staying in (remembering that every step you take on the ground results in the death of thousands of tiny organisms)

SELECTED READINGS

Utilitarian Theory

Ayer, Alfred J. "The Principle of Utility." In his *Philosophical Essays*. New York: St. Martin's Press, 1955.
Bayles, Michael D., ed. *Contemporary Utilitarianism*. New York: Anchor/Doubleday, 1968.
Bentham, Jeremy. *An Introduction to the Principles of Morals and Legislation* (1789).★ Many editions.
Brandt, Richard. *A Theory of the Good and the Right*. London: Oxford University Press, 1979.
Brody, Baruch A., ed. *Moral Rules and Particular Circumstances*. Englewood Cliffs, N.J.: Prentice-Hall, 1970.
Ewing, Alfred C. *Ethics*. New York: Macmillan, 1953. See Chapter 5.
Glover, Jonathan. *Causing Death and Saving Lives*. Baltimore: Penguin Books, 1977.

★Dates in parentheses are dates of first publication.

Gorovitz, Samuel, ed. *Mill: Utilitarianism, Text and Critical Essays*. Indianapolis: Bobbs-Merrill, 1971.

Hearn, Thomas K., Jr., ed. *Studies in Utilitarianism*. New York: Appleton-Century-Crofts, 1971.

Henson, Richard G. "Utilitarianism and the Wrongness of Killing." *Philosophical Review* 80 (1971): 320–37.

Hodgson, D. H. *Consequences of Utilitarianism: A Study in Normative Ethics and Legal Theory*. London: Oxford University Press, 1967.

Hume, David. *An Inquiry Concerning the Principles of Morals* (1751). Many editions.

Lyons, David. *Forms and Limits of Utilitarianism*. London: Oxford University Press, 1965.

Mill, John Stuart. *Utilitarianism* (1863). Many editions.

Moore, G. E. *Ethics*. London: Oxford University Press, 1912.

——— *Principia Ethica*. Cambridge: Cambridge University Press, 1903.

Narveson, Jan. *Morality and Utility*. Baltimore: Johns Hopkins Press, 1967.

Rashdall, Hastings. *Theory of Good and Evil*. 2nd ed. 2 vols. New York: Oxford University Press, 1924. See Volume I, Book 1, Chapter 7.

Schneewind, J. B., ed. *Mill's Ethical Writings*. New York: Collier Books, 1965.

Sidgwick, Henry. *The Methods of Ethics*. 7th ed. London: Macmillan, 1874.

Smart, J. J. C., and Bernard Williams. *Utilitarianism: For and Against*. Cambridge: Cambridge University Press, 1973.

Smith, James M., and Ernest Sosa, eds. *Mill's Utilitarianism: Text and Criticism*. Belmont, Calif.: Wadsworth Publishing, 1969.

The Treatment of Animals

Clark, Stephen R. L. *The Moral Status of Animals*. Oxford, Eng.: Clarendon Press, 1977.

Regan, Tom, and Peter Singer, eds. *Animal Rights and Human Obligations*. Englewood Cliffs, N.J.: Prentice-Hall, 1976.

Singer, Peter. *Animal Liberation*. New York: Avon Books, 1975.

Utility and Religion

Huxley, Thomas H. "Agnosticism and Christianity" (1889). In Alburey Castell, ed. *Selections from the Essays of T. H. Huxley*. New York: Appleton-Century-Crofts, 1948.

Mill, John Stuart. "The Utility of Religion." In his *Three Essays on Religion*. London: Longmans, Green, 1874. Reprinted in J. S. Mill. *The Nature and Utility of Religion*. New York: Liberal Arts Press, 1958.

Niebuhr, Reinhold. *An Interpretation of Christian Ethics*. New York: Harper & Row, 1935.

Rashdall, Hastings. *Theory of Good and Evil*. 2nd ed. 2 vols. New York: Oxford University Press, 1924. See Volume I, Book 3, Chapter 2.

Russell, Bertrand. "Will Religious Faith Solve Our Troubles?" In his *Human Society in Ethics and Politics*. New York: Simon & Schuster, 1954.

5

Kantian Ethics

1. MORALS AND MOTIVES

Utilitarianism is a theory about right action; it has very little to say about motives. But motives are what move people to act; and we would do well to stop and ask which of the motives people have are best.

According to utilitarianism, the goal of right action is the maximum production of good. But various motives can inspire right action. I may pay my debt to you because after all I owe it to you, and I want to do the right thing; or I may repay you out of fear of a lawsuit if I don't. A woman may give to charity out of the goodness of her heart, because she sympathizes with the lot of suffering people; on the other hand, she may give in order to be thought of by others as a charitable and generous person. You may help me out of a jam because you really want to, or you may hate it but do it from a sense of duty. An eighteen-year-old may enlist in the Marines in order to escape an unhappy home life, to have a decent wage, to be thought a man, or to help save the world.

A. Utilitarianism and Motives

Does it matter for the utilitarian what motivates people to do the right thing, as long as they do it? Yes, it matters for their *future* actions. If I pay my debts only from fear of a lawsuit, I am not likely to pay them the next time if there is no threat of a lawsuit. If a woman gives to charity only in order to be considered charitable, she will not give anonymously or under any circumstances in which her giving is not conspicuous to others. The best motives, according to utilitarianism, are those which are the *most likely to cause people to perform right acts.* Thus, giving out of the goodness of one's heart is better than giving in order to impress friends, since in the latter case no giving would occur (assuming this to be the right thing to do) if others were not present to see how nobly the giver was behaving. Paying my debts from the conviction that I ought to is preferable to doing so from fear of the law, since in the latter case, if there was no fear of the law I would decline to pay them. Utilitarians judge motives by the degree of their tendency to produce right acts.

There is a distinction to be drawn between acts which are *morally good* and those which are *right*. Moral goodness has to do with the motive from which the act is done, and rightness (according to utilitarianism) has to do with the probable consequences of the act. We can praise agents for their motives ("They meant well") while withholding any praise for the act ("How did they ever think they could succeed in such a silly plan?").

A motive is not as directly under a person's control as is an action. If I am a coldhearted, nonbenevolent person, you can expect me to pay my debt to you, but you cannot expect me to pay it out of good will or kindly feeling. To say that people ought to do something implies that they can do it; I can pay my debt (assuming I have the money) but I cannot do it from a kindly motive if I am incapable of acting from such a motive. Sociopaths may refrain from committing theft or murder out of fear of the law, but we can't expect them to refrain out of any moral sense, for they have no sense of right and wrong which can be tapped to cause them to behave from that motive.

Over a long period of time some motives can be changed. Good will and benevolence can be gradually instilled in people (though not all people), through training and imaginative identification with the situations of others. A person may not have much kindness in her, but what there is can be encouraged and rewarded, so that in the course of years she may actually perform acts from benevolent motives.

The utilitarian judges traits of character in much the same way as motives. Which character traits are desirable (virtuous) and which are undesirable (vicious) depends on what kinds of acts they are most likely to generate. If I have a benevolent disposition toward other persons, I am more likely to try to promote their welfare than if I am hostile, indifferent, or coldly calculating. Thus benevolence is considered a desirable trait of character—not intrinsically, but instrumentally, because it achieves more right actions. If I have a lot of human sympathy and feel distress at the sufferings of others, I am more likely to help them than if I lack such sympathy, and therefore sympathy is considered a desirable character trait.

Concerning most character traits, however, the utilitarian would say, "It all depends." Is loyalty a desirable character trait? That depends on what one is loyal to. Loyalty to the Soviet KGB, the Mafia, or some other criminal organization is likely to produce more evil in the world than if there were no loyalty to such organizations. Self-denial is desirable if it serves a worthwhile purpose; otherwise it is pointless. Humility is sometimes to be considered a virtue, but if it causes people to deny utterly their own desires and to serve the interests of people who are foolish or evil, it is worse (in its effects) than if people did not have it. Even benevolence is not always a virtue: it must be accompanied by intelligence, for the uncritical use of benevolence may cause it to be wasted on silly causes or frittered away on worthless objects.

B. Kant's Theory of Human Motives

The eighteenth-century German philosopher Immanuel Kant (1724–1804) had a special view of moral goodness, which it is important to consider before we take up his theory of right and wrong action. Most of the things that we consider good, said Kant, are not good without qualification. (Kant did not use these terms, but we can read "good without qualification" as meaning roughly the same as those already used—"good in itself" or "intrinsically good.") Happiness, he said, is not good without qualification: whether we are happy depends on a large variety of circumstances, many of which we cannot control, such as a pleasant disposition, intelligence, a favorable early environment, or a measure of good luck. We may be happy but not deserve it, and we may deserve happiness but not have it. The only thing, Kant said, that is more repellent to contemplate than someone enjoying undeserved happiness is someone suffering undeserved unhappiness.

Kant also mentions "moderations in the affections and passions, self-control, and calm deliberation"[1] as admirable human qualities. Yet these too are not good without qualification. They may even sometimes be thoroughly bad. The coolness of villains and their complete self-control in planning and perpetrating crimes make them more abominable than they would have been without these qualities. All other traits of character are similarly double-edged. The only thing that is good without qualification is what Kant called a *good will:*

> A good will is good not because of what it performs or effects, not by its aptness for the attainment of some proposed end, but simply by virtue of the volition—that is, it is good in itself, and considered by itself is to be esteemed much higher than all that can be brought about by it.

> Even if it should happen that, owing to a special disfavor of fortune, or to the niggardly provision of a step-motherly nature, this will should wholly lack power to accomplish its purpose, if with its greatest efforts it should yet achieve nothing, and there should remain only the good will . . . then, like a jewel, it would still shine by its own light, as a thing which has its whole value in itself. Its usefulness or fruitlessness can neither add to nor take away anything from its value.[2]

[1] Immanuel Kant, *Fundamental Principles of the Metaphysics of Morals,* trans. Thomas K. Abbott (Chicago: Henry Regnery, 1945), Section 1, p. 10.
[2] Ibid., pp. 10–11.

But exactly what is a good will? When Kant used the term, he did not mean by it what we so often mean in everyday life, namely, good intentions. "The road to hell is paved with good intentions." People who always intend to do their duty and never do so, people who are full of kind and benevolent feelings but somehow never put their noble intentions into practice, are not at all what Kant had in mind. A good will, according to Kant, is "not a mere wish, but the summoning of all the means in our power"[3] to do our duty.

According to Kant, agents are morally good with respect to certain acts if they do them entirely *from motives of duty,* simply because they believe them to be what they ought to do, and for no other reason. But here a distinction must be made at once: to do something *from* duty is one thing; to do it merely *in accordance with* duty is another. Suppose that as you are playing chess with someone and contemplating your next move, a small child comes along takes hold of one of the chessmen and moves it to another position on the board. Suppose too that the move the child makes is in accordance with the rules of the game—a permitted though perhaps not a brilliant move. Yet the move, though in accordance with the rules of chess, is not made from any knowledge of the moves of chess. The child has no idea what the permitted moves are, for he has no conception of the rules of the game. Let us now apply this example to the moral realm. Suppose it is your duty to be benevolent toward others, helping them when they are in need. Suppose also that because you are by nature a kind and benevolent human being who is always distressed at seeing those around you unhappy or in want, you help them out. You can't be happy unless they are happy, so by satisfying them you are satisfying yourself also. You don't help others because it is your duty—you don't even think about duty—but just because you want to, because it makes you feel good. If it didn't make you feel good, you wouldn't provide the help.

Whether such actions are *right* is a matter we shall consider in the next section in discussing Kant's theory of rightness. But according to Kant, such acts are not *morally good;* more precisely, you are not morally good with respect to such acts, and you cannot be accorded any moral merit for doing them. It is just good luck that you happen to be benevolently inclined toward others by temperament. You are just "doing what comes naturally," and if doing something entirely different came more naturally to you, you would do that instead. You will help others only as long as it pleases you to do so, and when it doesn't, you won't be moved to help them by considerations of duty. What you do may be *in accordance with* duty, but it is not done *from* the motive of duty; that is, it is not performed *because* of the conviction that it is your duty. You are acting not from duty but from inclination—in this case, a benevolent inclination.

Sometimes what is our duty coincides with what we are inclined to do anyway. For example, Kant said it is our duty to preserve our own lives,

[3] Ibid., p. 11.

and it would be wrong to commit suicide only to avoid pain or because we are tired of living. But most people are inclined to preserve their own lives anyway, so there is no special merit in their acts of self-preservation. In such a situation, duty and inclination propel us in the same direction, and we do not need the sense of duty to make us do the right thing. But there are other, probably more frequent, occasions when duty and inclination conflict. Let's say that it is your duty to keep a certain promise you have made, but you don't particularly desire to keep it; your inclination is to forget about the promise, especially since keeping it would cause you considerable inconvenience. Here is a test of whether you are acting from duty or inclination: if you keep your promise anyway, in spite of your inclination to the contrary and simply because you believe it is your duty to do so, then you are acting from duty and your action is morally meritorious. Many characteristically moral situations are like this: your sense of duty pulls you one way and your inclination pulls you the other way, and the test of your moral character is whether you are strong enough to follow duty in spite of your inclination not to.

The picture presented by Kant seems clear enough when duty and inclination impel us in opposite directions. But when inclination and duty impel us in the same direction, must we say that we always act from inclination and never from duty? Not necessarily. It is possible that we sometimes act from duty even though we are already inclined to perform the act. For example, it is our duty not to steal from our friends, but most of us are not inclined to do so anyway, and it never even occurs to us to do so. We usually do not need a sense of duty to back up our inclinations in such a situation. Even so, it is possible that we may be acting from duty just the same, at least to some extent, but whether we are or are not is very difficult to discover. The test would be: *If your inclination were the other way, would you still do the act anyway out of a sense of duty?* The trouble is that we cannot really carry out this test, for by the very nature of the situation, duty and inclination *do* pull us in the same direction. About all you could do in such a situation would be to ask yourself, *"If at this moment my inclinations turned the opposite way, would I still refrain from stealing out of a sense of duty?"* It would then be necessary to be as honest with yourself as you possibly could in answering this question. Even if you tried to be very honest in answering it, you might well rationalize, convincing yourself that you *would* have acted from duty anyway. Such introspective tests are dangerous and inconclusive; it is extremely easy to say that you are doing something out of a sense of duty when actually you are inclined to do it anyway and are camouflaging your inclinations by talking about duty to make the act seem more respectable. At any rate, it is certainly possible that you are acting from duty even on occasions when your natural inclinations propel you in the same direction.

Many readers of Kant have been somewhat shocked at Kant's account. "Do you really mean," they ask, "that there is no moral goodness belonging to an act if the act is done from inclination? Do you mean that if you are *inclined* to do something, you deserve no moral credit for doing it, but that if you are not inclined to do it and have to fight against your inclinations every step of the way, then and only then is your action morally good? Why should an act be morally good when it is done solely from duty, and not when it is done from inclinations or desires which achieve the same result?"

Kant's reply was that actions done from inclination may achieve the same result—they may indeed be equally *right*—but that the people who do them deserve moral credit if they do them solely out of a conviction that it's their duty rather than from "natural inclination." Even if what they do is wrong, the fact that they did it because they *believed* it to be their duty is to their credit. If you do something merely from "natural inclination," you really deserve no more credit for it than water does for flowing downhill; you're just "doing what comes naturally."

People with a naturally friendly and benevolent disposition just *like* to do things for others. "The drinks are on me!" such a person might say as he enters the bar. But benevolent people are not acting from a sense of duty; they may not even have a sense of duty—may never succeed in doing the difficult thing (or even try) in the face of temptations, or strong inclinations in the other direction. They just do what they enjoy doing, and their benevolent disposition may lead them often to do the right thing—just as the child who knows nothing about chess may place the chess piece in the right square during a game—but they deserve no more credit for their actions than the child does for his deed. Their benevolence is a kind of lucky accident; they follow their benevolent inclinations "naturally," just as, if they had a malevolent nature, they would perform malevolent actions "naturally." Your pet dog probably *always* acts from its natural inclinations; even when it wants to climb on the sofa but doesn't because it fears punishment, it is still acting from inclination, since it is not inclined to do what will bring punishment. Animals are incapable of acting any other way; they have no conception of moral duty and cannot act from that motive. But human beings differ from animals in that they have a moral sense, and a moral sense is what leads people to act from duty, to do things because they believe it their duty as moral agents to do so. Two things were to Kant the most awe-inspiring in the universe: "the starry heavens above and the moral law within." When we act solely from the motive of duty, without regard to the inconvenience or sacrifice that may require, we are giving expression to the "moral law within."

Kant's view on human motives in acting morally has not gone without criticism. In the first place, is it true that when people act from benevolent impulses they are necessarily acting from "natural inclinations"? It depends on what is meant by "natural." Perhaps some benevolent inclinations are indeed innate; but for the most part they are learned. Benevolence is encouraged through childhood training and upbringing, as well as in social interaction with other people in adulthood. It is an oversimplification to say that when people act from benevolent motives they are just "doing what comes naturally," as a river flows downhill; the proper analogy is to the way a garden looks after it has been carefully cultivated rather than the way it is "naturally," that is, untended and full of weeds. Some people encourage and cultivate their benevolent impulses and some people don't. And if we do, and thus act benevolently as a result, shouldn't we get moral credit for that?

In the second place many philosophers, from Aristotle to John Dewey, have argued that "acting from duty" is only a stage—and should not be the final stage—in people's moral development. If you are constantly tempted to steal and are only dissuaded from doing so by a strong sense of duty, is that really better, morally better, than if you aren't tempted to steal at all, and the thought of stealing from someone else never even occurs to you? At an early stage of moral development you may have to fight off temptations to do all kinds of things; but if you discipline yourself and get yourself into the right habits, finally you won't even think about stealing anymore—the prospect won't even tempt you—and then you will be honest from inclination rather than from the motive of duty. Isn't it morally better not to have to go through paroxysms of temptation and conflict every time before you act, with duty winning over inclination after a severe inner struggle? Before becoming morally developed, people may have to go through such agonies, but after the elapse of some time they enter a new stage when second nature becomes first nature: they are no longer tempted to do the wrong thing. What is better: a person with a tendency toward pyromania who has a severe inner struggle every day in which he triumphs each time over his urge to set fires, or a person who has finally got to the point where the prospect of arson doesn't even tempt him any more?

Perhaps there is something noble about acting from duty even in the face of great personal sacrifice, the critic will say, but isn't there something even nobler about having overcome a tendency to do evil, and not having to fight it anymore? The moral life is surely more serene and untroubled in the second case than in the first. And isn't moral behavior more reliable after people are no longer tempted? Which person would you rather live next door to— a neighbor who had no inclination to burn your house down and never thought about such things, or a neighbor who had a tremendous urge to burn your house down and only refrained from doing so because of a strong sense of duty? Probably the first, for, you would suspect, sooner or later the second person's inclinations would be likely to get the better of him and he would do what he had a strong impulse to do: there would always come that day when he could no longer keep his inclinations in check. If your neighbor has no inclination to harm you, you don't have to worry about him the way you do if he has such an inclination but keeps it in check with a strong sense of duty. A sense of duty would be a valuable *accessory,* a kind of second line of defense, in case his inclinations didn't carry him through; but it would surely be better if he had no inner battles to fight over the matter at all.

In most people, at any rate, the sense of duty is not regular enough to be reliable; it operates by fits and starts, while inclinations are with them all the time. The sense of duty usually has to be pushed and probed. But, as eighteenth-century philosopher David Hume noted, compared with the sense of duty,

> a man's natural inclination works incessantly upon him; it is forever present to the mind, and mingles itself with every view and consideration. . . . It is certain, from experience, that the smallest grain of natural honesty and benevolence has more effect on men's conduct, than the most pompous views suggested by theological theories and systems.[4]

Besides the danger of raising duty to a plane above that of natural inclination, is it even accurate to describe our moral nature as a battleground between our sense of duty on the one hand and our inclination on the other? After all, perhaps acting from duty is just acting from *another* inclination, namely, the inclination to do what we ought? This inclination is very strong in many people, but isn't it just another inclination? The battle would then be not between people's sense of duty and inclination, but between one kind of inclination (the inclination to do their duty) and others.

A Kantian could reply, however, that moral conflicts are not *experienced* in that way: they are experienced as genuine conflicts between desire on the one hand and duty on the other. Describing it in the second way seems to give a better account of the way the conflict is felt. As we remarked in discussing psychological egoism, we can conclude that when duty wins over desire this is really only a case of one *desire* (the desire to do our duty) winning over another desire only if we *assume* that "the strongest desire always wins" (the one that wins being automatically labeled the strongest). But isn't it preferable, after all, to say that our sense of duty has won out even over our strongest desires? Not only does this seem to be a more accurate account, but it also gives credit to us for overcoming a tremendously strong desire in order to do what we believe we ought.

One further observation must be made before concluding this section. We should remember that acting from duty—doing what we believe to be our duty—may not be doing what actually *is* our duty. We may be mistaken in our estimate of what we should do. We may act from duty and still act wrongly—just as we may act rightly (in accordance with duty) and do so from bad motives. For example, parents may act from duty as members of a religious group which refuses to allow a child to have a blood transfusion necessary to save the child's life. Such parents don't *want* their child to die, so they are certainly not acting from "natural inclinations"; but they believe

---

[4]David Hume, *Dialogues Concerning Natural Religion,* 2nd ed. ed. Norman Kemp Smith (New York: Social Sciences, 1948), Part 12, p. 221.

that permitting the transfusions would be a mortal sin and that their duty is to refuse permission for the transfusion. We may believe they are mistaken in this belief, but they are acting from a strong sense of duty, which triumphs over the desire to save the child. We may admire them in a way, for having such a strong sense of duty that they follow it no matter at what cost, but at the same time we may condemn as wrong what their sense of duty leads them to do. There are two kinds of moral condemnation—of motives as bad and of acts as wrong—and the two do not always go together.

What then is more important—to act rightly or to act from duty? Is a right act done from inclination preferable to a wrong act done from a sense of duty? This question can be meaningful only to an outside observer from the vantage point of a different moral standard. You may think a woman you know acted wrongly, but when that person acts from duty, she thinks she is acting rightly: if she did not believe she was acting rightly, she would not be acting from a sense of duty at all. You can never ask *yourself*, "Should I do my duty or what *I think* is my duty?" You can deliberate carefully as to what your duty is, and you can be charged with acting hastily if you don't deliberate about it; but once you have decided, you can only do what is, to the very best of your knowledge and belief, your duty. You cannot say, "Act *A* is right because it is my duty, but act *B* is morally good because *I think* it is my duty." The moment you say, and mean, that act *A* is your duty, you are by that very statement implying that you *believe* that act *A* is your duty. If you didn't believe it, you couldn't sincerely say that it was your duty; and if you believe that act *A* is your duty, you cannot turn about and say that something different, act *B,* is what you *believe* to be your duty. To say sincerely that something is your duty is already to commit yourself to saying that you believe that it is. At the time of your action, therefore, this conflict cannot arise for you. It can arise only in a different context—for someone else who is judging your act or for you yourself judging it at a later time; then and then only can you ask, "I did what I did out of a conviction that it was my duty, but *was* it my duty?" (What would it mean to say, "I *am doing* this act from the conviction that it is my duty, yet I am not convinced that it *is* my duty"?)

According to at least one contemporary writer, the conflict arises from a failure to distinguish different questions from one another. The question "Ought a person to do his duty or what he sincerely believes to be his duty?" is a question which

can perplex us only because we have no more than a confused understanding of its sense. As soon as we make clear to ourselves the various things it can mean, the problem vanishes. If we mean (1) "Does thinking that something is one's duty make it so?" the answer is obviously "No." If we mean (2) "Does the moral man do what after careful consideration he has worked out to be what he ought to do?" the answer is, of course, "Yes." If it means (3) "Should a person who has worked out what he ought to do as carefully and conscientiously as can be expected be rebuked for acting on his results?" the answer is plainly "No." If it means (4) "Is a man ever to be rebuked for doing what he thought he ought to do?" the answer is, of course, "Yes, sometimes, for he may culpably have failed in his theoretical task" (of figuring out carefully, impartially, and free from rationalization, where his duty lies).[5]

2. KANT'S THEORY OF DUTY

Animals always act from inclination, Kant maintained, and are incapable of acting from the motive of duty. They never act in recognition of a moral principle, but only from inclination. Only rational beings are capable of acting on principle. But what is the moral principle on which their actions should be based?

It is not a utilitarian-style principle of maximizing happiness. Human beings' proper end is the development of their rational nature, not the cultivation of happiness. According to Kant, if our purpose in life were to achieve happiness

> then nature would have hit upon a very bad arrangement in selecting the reason of the creature to carry out this purpose. For all the actions which the creature has to perform with a view to this purpose, and the whole rule of its conduct, would be far more surely prescribed to it by instinct, and that end would have been attained thereby much more certainly than it ever can be by reason.[6]

Feelings, attitudes, temperaments vary enormously from person to person; but the dictates of reason, if they are correctly employed, are universal. The concept of universality is central to Kant's ethics. The principle of human conduct that Kant sought had to be one that is universal in the sense that it applies to all rational beings. As we shall see shortly, moral rules and principles are also universal in the sense that they contain within themselves no exceptions.

A principle of human conduct must not only be universal, but also unconditional, not depending on conditions and circumstances that vary with a person's inclinations, desires, and situation in life. We are constantly bombarded by conditional rules: "If you want to be healthy, you should eat nutritious foods." "If you want this, you should do that." "If you want happiness, you should do so and so." Conditional rules make what you should do depend on what you happen to want. They are *hypothetical imperatives*—hypothetical in the sense that all sentences of the form "If . . . then

[5] Kurt Baier, *The Moral Point of View* (Ithaca, N.Y.: Cornell University Press, 1958), pp. 146–47. Reprinted by permission of the publisher.
[6] Kant, *Fundamental Principles of the Metaphysics of Morals,* Section 1, p. 12.

. . ." are. The principle Kant sought is, rather, *categorical:* "Do so and so
. . ." with no ifs, ands, or buts.

There is a rule of this kind with which we are already familiar and which
is a kind of first cousin of Kant's principle. If we see why Kant rejected it,
we shall better understand Kant's own principle. It is the Golden Rule of the
New Testament: "Do unto others as you would have them do unto you."
(The Confucian rule is negative in form: "Don't do to others what you
would not have them do to you.") We should treat others the way we would
wish to be treated. If little Billy hits little Johnny over the head with a baseball bat, his parents, besides punishing him, may try to reason with him:
"You know what it feels like to be hit over the head. Well, that's the way
little Johnny feels. If you don't want people to do that to you, why then you
shouldn't do it to them either." This helps (sometimes) to enable Billy to put
himself imaginatively in Johnny's place and may suffice (sometimes) to keep
him from acting in this way toward Johnny the next time. Putting yourself
imaginatively in the position of others is an important aspect of moral training which does not come naturally: some people never learn it at all. But if
they do, it enables them to treat others as they themselves would wish to be
treated.

But what you should do to, or for, others depends on what you *wish*
others to do to, or for, you. And what you wish depends on who you are.
Some people wish others to treat them with kindness and love; but others
are more standoffish, even hostile, preferring to be treated with contempt
and disdain. Should such people therefore treat others with contempt and
disdain, because that is the way they want to be treated? "Don't do to others
as you would have them do to you," said British playwright George Bernard
Shaw; "their tastes might be different."

Suppose I would like other people to join me in my criminal activities.
Should I therefore join them in their criminal activities? Wouldn't that be
doing for others what I would wish them to do for me? It all depends on
what I wish—and a person can wish almost anything. If masochists wish
others to beat them to a pulp, should they do as they would be done to and
beat others to a pulp?

It is because of the variability of what people wish that Kant rejected the
Golden Rule as a universal principle of human conduct. Kant's *Categorical
Imperative,* by contrast, says, "Act as if the maxim of thy action were to
become by thy will a Universal Law of Nature."[7]

A maxim is a directive for a particular kind of action: "Do this," "Don't
do that." When you universalize a maxim (extend it to include everyone),
you get a *rule* of conduct ("Everyone should do *X*"). Kant said that everyone
should act as though his or her every action were about to become a universal rule of human conduct.

Some rules of conduct are thus acceptable, and others not. The rules of

[7] Ibid., Section 2, p. 43.

conduct that are acceptable are those that can be universalized, or in some formulations, those that a rational moral agent could *wish* universalized—though the latter formulation leaves the question as to what an entirely rational person would be and like and do.

At least some instances of rules of conduct can be eliminated without considering anyone's wishes, simply on the ground of inconsistency. Very few maxims are inconsistent in themselves (commanding "Do X but don't do X"), but some are inconsistent because they cannot be made into universal rules. A newspaper ad may say, "Be the first to answer this ad and win first prize," but not everybody can win first prize, nor be the first one to answer the ad. There is a saying in New York, "Don't buy a newspaper when you go on the subway; read a paper over someone else's shoulder; everyone else does." But not everyone can do this: at least one person has to obtain a paper so that others can read it. You can advise a person not to work for a living but rather to live by panhandling or begging or stealing from those who do. But not everyone can live in this way; if some people depend on others for their daily bread, those others will have to work to obtain what others will take.

It is possible for others to help you even though you never help them; but it is not possible for everyone to act on this maxim, since there have to be some persons who at some time help others. "I may do what I like to hurt or offend other people, but they may not act that way toward me" could not (logically) be universalized, for the moment the maxim is universalized, everyone will be hurting and offending people, and there will be no one left to *not* act in that way. "It's all right for you to steal from others, but they may never steal from you" can't be universalized, for the universalization of it will mean that everyone steals, and there can be no "others" left to refrain from doing so.

Some people constantly gossip about others, while some never do; some don't mind, and some do. Let us examine the possible rules about this:

1. I may gossip as much as I like about others, but others may not do the same about me.
2. Others may gossip as much as they like about me, but I may not do the same about them.
3. No one may gossip about me, and I may not gossip about others. (All parties' privacy is protected.)
4. I may gossip as much as I like about others, and they may gossip as much as they like about me. (No one's privacy is protected.)

Maxims 1 and 2 are both inconsistent when universalized; each person reading them is the "I," and there can be no one left to be the "others." Some people do act as if 1 was true: they gossip endlessly, but if anyone does it about them they are indignant. No one is likely to embrace 2.

But maxims 3 and 4 can both be universalized. As far as universal applicability is concerned, there is nothing to choose between them. They simply represent two different kinds of rules of behavior. We could give arguments preferring one to the other of them on utilitarian grounds, but not on the ground of their universalizability.

It is impossible to universalize a maxim which directs you to do something while others do not, for a universal rule prescribes that everyone should do it. As long as universalization is required, the maxims you can act on are limited, though many people do act on maxims which cannot possibly be universalized into rules of human conduct. Some people hurt the feelings of others, though they are indignant when others do it to them. They fail to respect the privacy of others, though they fully expect others to respect theirs. They act *inconsistently:* that is, if they were to generalize the maxim of their action into a universal rule, they would arrive at a rule on which it is logically impossible for everyone to act.

We have considered the maxim of action of a particular person, A, universalized so that it applies to everyone (B, C, D, E, F, etc.). But if we consider the small-scale case of only two people, A and B, we get the same result. Here the concept involved is called *reversibility.* A cheats B, but she objects if B cheats her. But how, in the same circumstances, can it be right for A to cheat B but not right for B to cheat A? To pass the consistency test, a maxim must be reversible: if it is not reversible when only two people are involved, it cannot be universalized into a rule of human conduct applicable not only to A and B but to everybody else as well.

The Golden Rule can be (and has been) interpreted as a statement of the reversibility test. The rule may "really" mean that if a certain act is wrong for others to do, then it is (in the same circumstances at least) wrong for you to do; and if it is right for you to do it, it is also right for others to do it. "Morality is no respecter of persons." If you follow the rule thus interpreted, you can't rationalize, as people so often do, saying it's all right for you but not for others. If you are righteously indignant when someone picks a fight with you, you cannot turn around and pick a fight with him under the guise that you're just "teaching him a lesson." You may rationalize yourself into thinking it's all right for you to take (borrow with no real intent to return) something that doesn't belong to you, but you cannot legitimately condemn someone else who does it to you. If the rule applies to one case, it also applies to another. Whether this is the "real" meaning of the Golden Rule is an open question.

A. What Can Be Universalized?

Thus far we have considered a few maxims that could be candidates for universalization. Let us now examine a few maxims, universalized into rules, which could not become universal rules of human conduct.

1. "Always tell a lie, never the truth." Every time a statement is true,

substitute one that you know is not true. When the true statement would be "The wall is blue," say, "The wall is not blue"; and when it's not true that it's raining, say, "It's raining." Never utter a statement that is true.

Universal lying may be possible for a while, but not for long. People would soon catch on. If anyone said it's raining, you would immediately conclude that it's not raining, and if anyone said it was, you would conclude it wasn't. You would learn to take the word "not" out of a sentence and thus get a true statement; or you would put the word "not" in if it wasn't there, and again get a true statement. In fact, the word "not" would have changed its meaning from a negative to an affirmative, and with the meaning it would then have, the sentences would all be true.

If people *always* uttered false statements, you could often conclude what *a* true one was, though not always what *the* true one was. For example, if they said, "It is blue," you could conclude that it is not blue, but not what specific color it was. In a way, the situation would be preferable to the one we have now: you could always infer from people's utterances a statement that was true, whereas now you can't be sure whether they are telling the truth or not, because the present situation is that people *sometimes* lie, and the problem is to discover when they're lying and when they're not.

2. "Always break promises." Is this a possible universal rule of conduct? As things are, people sometimes break their promises, but could they always do so? Yes, but then the effect would be that there would *be* no promises. After all, what would be the point of having promises if they were never kept? Breaking them is contrary to the nature of promises, namely, the intention to keep them. This, of course, doesn't keep some people from breaking them: but if everyone *always* broke them, or even did so 80 percent of the time, promises either would cease to be made or, if made, would cease to be trusted.

3. What about the rule "Always break contracts"? That too cannot be universalized. If a contract could be broken at the whim of either party, no matter what the contract said, it would in effect contain as its final clause, "Notwithstanding the above provisions, they shall have no force." And this would not only be contrary to the very nature of contract, but it would stop all contracts from being made. There would, in fact, no longer *be* such a thing as a contract. The following example from Kant attempts to show this:

> [A man] finds himself driven to borrowing money because of need. He well knows that he will not be able to pay it back; but he sees too that he will get no loan unless he gives a firm promise to pay it back within a fixed time. He is inclined to make such a promise; but he has still enough conscience to ask "Is it not unlawful and contrary to duty to get out of difficulties in this way?" Supposing, however, he did resolve to do so; the maxim of his action would run thus: "Whenever I believe myself short of money, I will borrow money and promise to pay it back, though I know that this will never be done." Now this principle

of self-love or personal advantage is perhaps quite compatible with my own entire future welfare; only there remains the question "Is it right?" I therefore transform the demand of self-love into a universal law and frame my question thus: "How would things stand if my maxim can never rank as a universal law?" I then see straight away that this maxim can never rank as a universal law of nature and be self-consistent, but must necessarily contradict itself. For the universality of a law that everyone believing himself to be in need can make any promise he pleases with the intention not to keep it would make promising, and the very purpose of promising, itself impossible, since no one would believe he was being promised anything, but would laugh at utterances of this kind as empty shams.[8]

Such a maxim, if universalized, would indeed go contrary to the meaning of the promise contained in a lending agreement. Soon no such agreements would be made or taken seriously. It has not been shown that promises of this sort are desirable, only that if everyone acted in the way described in Kant's example, such promises would cease. Some persons might even believe that it would be a good thing.

Thus far, the question has been: Is it possible to universalize this maxim? But in Kant's later examples, the question shifted to: Can one *wish* this maxim to be universalized? (Can different people wish to universalize different but opposite though internally consistent things?) Kant apparently thought this was not possible, as the following example indicates:

[A man] finds in himself a talent which could, by means of some cultivation, make him in many respects a useful man. But he finds himself in comfortable circumstances and prefers indulgence in pleasure to troubling himself with broadening and improving his fortunate natural gifts. Now, however, let him ask whether his maxim of neglecting his gifts, besides agreeing with his propensity to idle amusement, agrees also with what is called duty. He sees that a system of nature could indeed exist in accordance with such a law, even though man (like the inhabitants of the South Sea Islands) should let his talents rust and resolve to devote his life merely to idleness, indulgence, and propagation—in a word, to pleasure. But he cannot possibly will that this should become a universal law of nature or that it should be implanted in us by a natural instinct. For, as a rational being, he necessarily wills that all his faculties should be developed, inasmuch as they are given him for all sorts of possible purposes.[9]

[8] Ibid., Section 2, p. 44.
[9] Ibid., Section 2, p. 45.

But why can't he will it? One person wishes industry and thrift to be universalized: as a result of this, we get modern civilization, technology, medicine, a high standard of living. Another person, more indolent and easygoing by disposition, prefers idleness and relaxation to be universalized. In many parts of the world, such as deserts and arctic regions, the result would be death for everyone, but in some parts, such as the South Pacific, people could get by with it. Of course, the standard of living wouldn't be very high, and if they needed penicillin to save their lives there wouldn't be any. (If Sir Alexander Fleming had adopted indolence as a maxim, he wouldn't have discovered penicillin.) But to the indolent person, this might be a price worth paying. Which of the two maxims—"Always be industrious" or "Always be indolent"—is it preferable to universalize? Both are certainly *possible* to universalize, since there is no inconsistency in universalizing either of them. The first ideal may be more *desirable* to universalize—it may have better consequences—but Kant's ethics is not a consequentialist ethics, and from his ethical works it seems that no appeal to consequences is to be invoked at all.

Kant's next example is as follows:

[Another] man, for whom things are going well, sees that others (whom he could help) have to struggle with great hardships, and he asks, "What concern of mine is it? Let each one be as happy as heaven wills, or as he can make himself; I will not take anything from him or even envy him; but to his welfare or to his assistance in time of need I have no desire to contribute." If such a way of thinking were a universal law of nature, certainly the human race could exist, and without doubt even better than in a state where everyone talks of sympathy and good will or even exerts himself occasionally to practice them while, on the other hand, he cheats when he can and betrays or otherwise violates the rights of man. Now although it is possible that a universal law of nature according to that maxim could exist, it is nevertheless impossible to will that such a principle should hold everywhere as a law of nature.

For a will which resolved this would conflict with itself, since instances can often arise in which he would need the love and sympathy of others, and in which he would have robbed himself, by such a law of nature springing from his own will, of all hope of the aid he desires.[10]

But again, different people will wish to universalize different things. Of course, there are some people who never help others in need but always expect help from others when they are in need. We have considered such people already; their maxims cannot be universalized. But now consider two other types of people. In the first category are those who are willing to help others and who appreciate (or expect?) help themselves when they are in

[10] Ibid., Section 2, pp. 45–46.

need. In the second category are people who do not help others but do not expect, or even want, assistance themselves. One can call them standoffish or selfish or lone individualists, but their stand *is* consistent: they leave others alone and they want to be left alone themselves.

Consider someone who steals for a living. It is not possible for everyone to live only by stealing, for things have to be produced by some before others can steal them. But would it be possible for everyone to practice the maxim "Steal sometimes" or "Steal when you can get by with it"? Apparently it would. True, most thieves don't like to be stolen from: the maxim "Steal when you can get by with it" is one they are unwilling to extend to others. But couldn't a thief adopt a rule such as "Everyone is free to steal from others without penalty for it unless caught in the act, in which case the owner can take measures against him"? A thief might gain more than he lost that way; if he was clever, he might lose some things through theft by others but would gain more by stealing from them. And even if he did lose more than he gained financially from such a scheme, he might well be the gainer emotionally, since he wants life to be exciting and chancy, and this sort of arrangement would gain him more in kicks and thrills than he would lose in money.

What mode of action, what style of life, people wish universalized depends largely on temperament. The effects of a life style that one person wishes to be universalized would certainly be unwelcome to others, but there seems little doubt that different people can wish different patterns of actions to become universal and that they can do this with perfect consistency. "Everyone should behave self-interestedly" is just as capable of being universalized as "Everyone should behave with primary concern for others." The effects of each may be different, but although the one may (if universalized) produce more happiness than the other as far as utilitarian consequences are concerned, each one can be universalized quite consistently.

The argument may be carried one step further, however. We might say to the man who wants theft universalized, "You're clever, but if you weren't that good a thief, and lots of others could get the better of you in the game of thievery, would you still want theft universalized?"

To this the thief might reply, "I might not prefer theft universalized if I wasn't such a good thief myself, but so what? The same is true of the middle-class businessman who hates theft above almost everything else, and whose motives and habits are geared to the accumulation and retention of personal possessions. It's by cherishing those values that he excels. If he was stupid or inept in economic competition and would always be the loser, he might not want his middle-class values universalized either. Isn't he in the same position that you say I am?"

We might respond, "You happen to have an adventurous temperament and like to play the game of life for high stakes at high risks. But suppose you had a different temperament? Would you still want theft universalized?"

To which he might answer, "It is probably true that if I had a different temperament I would want different policies and a different life style universalized. But so would the person with a cautious temperament. That's just the way it is. What does that prove?"

"Suppose," we persist, "that you were in the situation of the disembodied souls pictured by Plato at the end of *The Republic,* who drew lots to see which bodies they were going to inhabit while on earth, and consequently which temperaments they would have. Would you wish to see theft or other forms of high-risk living made into a universal policy *before you drew a lot?* You might come off well with such a policy, if you happened to draw an adventurous temperament, but you certainly would not do well if you didn't. It would depend on whether you drew the temperament of a pirate or the temperament of a shopkeeper. Before you knew what kind of temperament you would inherit, would you approve or would you not approve the rule that permits universal theft or depredation?"

"The problem with this argument," one could then respond, "is that it presents an impossible situation. A disembodied soul, if such a thing can be conceived of at all, would not even *have* a temperament of any kind to begin with. And if I didn't have some kind of temperament—either cautious or adventurous, given to reasoning or given to acting on impulse, mercurial or phlegmatic, full of high spirits or low-keyed, intense or easygoing, workaholic or indolent—how could I possibly *be* anyone at all? What would I be, prior to having some kind of temperamental predisposition or other? No vessel of 'pure reason' could do or choose anything at all. In order to make any choice at all, I would have to have some predispositions to behave in one way or another. I would have to *have* some kind of temperament in order to make the choice of what kind of temperament I would want to have once embodied. A being without some temperamental predispositions (even toward survival as against nonsurvival) wouldn't do anything at all, including making any decisions, or preferring one thing over another. So the last question, of what I would choose *before* I knew what kind of temperament I was going to have, appears to be meaningless."

If the rightness of an action, then, depends on whether an individual can wish the maxim of that action universalized into a rule of human conduct, it must be admitted that different people can quite consistently wish very different things, not only for themselves but as universal rules of conduct.

There is, however, one maxim which it is quite plausible to say that all human beings can wish universalized. "Rational beings," said Kant, "all stand under the law that each of them should treat himself and all others, never merely as a means, but always at the same time as an end in himself." [11] It is always wrong, according to Kant, for one person to use other persons merely as a means to his or her own ends. Much controversy

[11] Ibid., Section 2, p. 53.

surrounds the interpretation of this rule. When a woman buys something at a store, isn't she using the merchant as a means to her end (getting the merchandise) and isn't the merchant using her as a means to his end (getting the money)? No, each one is entering into an arrangement mutually satisfactory to both: the merchant would rather have the money than the merchandise, else he wouldn't part with it, and the customer would rather have the merchandise than the money, else she wouldn't surrender the money. An example of what the rule clearly *would* prohibit is slavery: in this situation slave owners use slaves simply as means to their own ends, without considering whatever ends the slaves might desire for themselves.

Perhaps there are people who are so passive that they want someone else to make all their decisions for them and not take responsibility themselves, but even such individuals will presumably want to *choose* to be enslaved, not to have this fate forced upon them from birth by another. The same may be said for masochists, who want to be used as means to fulfill the sadistic ends of others: they want to *choose* to whom they are to be subservient and what the "rules of the game" will be. (Perhaps being beaten is pleasing to them, but not being given a pain-inducing drug.) It is, indeed, difficult to conceive of people who do not wish to decide upon their own ends, rather than being the passive vessels of other human beings who use them for their own purposes. This rule is actually an assertion of a principle of human rights, which we shall consider in Chapter 7.

B. Rules and Universalizability

Kant believed that any maxim that could not be generalized into a universal rule of human conduct was wrong and apparently also that any maxim that could be generalized into a universal rule of human conduct was right. Many more commentators agree with Kant about the first part than about the second. Maxims like "Get out of bed on the left side" and "Place the fork at the left side of the dinner plate" can certainly be universalized, as can "Always behave first and foremost with your own welfare in mind," and yet many people would say that these aren't satisfactory moral rules or even (in some cases) rules of morality at all.

Certain maxims which Kant believed could never be made into universal rules of human conduct, such as "Always tell lies," Kant regarded as pointing to actions which were wrong in all circumstances: telling a lie (a deliberate untruth) is thus always wrong. But what if the secret police come to your door demanding to know the whereabouts of your friend, and you know where he is? Is it your duty to tell the truth? No, according to Kant, you may remain silent: you may say nothing, but if you do say something you must tell the truth. Still, there are situations in which silence is tantamount to admission or consent. If you are captain of a ship transporting Jewish refugees from Nazi death camps and a Nazi inspector boards your ship and asks whether there are Jews on board, aren't you entitled to say no? No, Kant would say, you are entitled only to be silent. But wouldn't this give the truth away as much as if you had said, "Yes, there are"?

If you are going by rules, an important point to remember is that *qualified* rules are just as universal as unqualified ones. "Never tell a lie" is a universal rule, stated with no qualifying clauses, but "Never tell a lie except to save life" is also a universal rule: it tells you always to say the truth other than in one specific type of situation. "Do not kill" is an unqualified rule, accepted by pacifists, but "Do not kill except in self-defense" is a qualified rule that is just as universal as the first: it restricts the scope of the rule somewhat by saying, "Never commit killings that aren't in self-defense," but it still applies to all members of the class described. In general, then, a rule may be universal and still contain within itself certain classes of exceptions. These are not to be considered exceptions *to* the rule stated; rather, they are simply certain qualifications, *built into the rule,* so that the rule now applies to a somewhat smaller class of actions. If a rule says, "Always do *X* other than in circumstance *C*" and you are in circumstance *C,* your action does not fall under the rule. Once this fact is recognized, there is no longer any need to state rules in a simple and unqualified manner: a qualified rule may indeed be preferable to a simple unqualified one.

Amending a simple rule by putting in such qualifications does not in any way take away the universality of the rule. But one way of qualifying rules which Kant and almost everyone else would condemn is inserting proper names, that is, the names of specific individuals or things. "Never tell a lie unless you are Stuart Smith, in which case lying is all right" would be a rule containing a proper name; so would "All ships and planes should be inspected by customs at the border, unless I happen to be one of the passengers." (For the personal pronoun "I" the name of the speaker can be substituted.) Putting in proper names is playing favorites. In fact, when a rule contains a personal pronoun such as "I," the insertion of the pronoun defeats the entire rule, since everyone who reads it can take the "I" to refer to himself or herself: everyone is the exception, and if everyone is an exception to the rule, the rule is inoperative.

The prohibition against proper names, however, is not enough to rule out a great many discriminatory rules. "All persons other than blacks may eat in public places" is one such rule; it mentions no individual, only a class of individuals. In fact, you may make the qualifications and specifications within the rule so detailed that although the rule contains no proper names, the only exception to a rule is yourself. "All persons are prohibited from cheating, unless they are . . ." can thus be qualified by inserting your exact height, weight, and other characteristics, such as your fingerprints and the moles on your cheek that distinguish you from everybody else in the world. Such a rule, in effect, substitutes a definite description for a proper name. If the New York State legislature proposes that "All communities of less than 5 million population shall be exempt from this tax," it is perfectly clear that the measure is directed against New York City, since it is the only city in that state with over 5 million population; the law has exactly the same effect as if New York City had been referred to by name.

Even if proper names are excluded, then, there is no guarantee that rules which don't contain them, however highly qualified they may be, are better (or worse) rules than simpler unqualified ones. There are ever so many mutually contradictory maxims that can all be generalized into rules—"Always behave selfishly," "Always behave unselfishly"; "Always give to the poor," "Never give to the poor"—and it still remains to be seen whether we can discover a criterion for preferring some such rules to others.

In stating specific rules as applications of his Categorical Imperative, Kant pitched the rules at a certain level of generality, and there is no apparent reason why they cannot be pitched at a different level. Just as a mink can be classified as a a mammal, a fur bearer, or a quadruped, depending on what features of the animal we are taking as the basis for a classification, so lies also can be classified as those told out of spite, those told with intent to deceive, those told to save a life, those told out of mercy, and so on. Moreover, lies themselves can be classified more generally as statements, as emissions from the human vocal cords, and so on. For example, of a given lie which someone tells, we can say of it that it is (1) a lie told to save a life, (2) a deliberate falsehood (a lie, plain and simple), and (3) a statement. The second is more specific (less general) than the third, and the first more specific than the second. At which level of generality should the act be placed? Kant chose to place it at the second by calling it a lie, and he concluded that all telling of lies is wrong. Why can't we make it more general, calling it a statement, and say perhaps that it is right to make a statement? Or why can't we place it at a less general level, calling it a lie told to save a life, and then say that lies told under such a condition are right? (Kant said that the purpose of language is communication and that the purpose of communication is to convey the truth, but there are many sentences which do communicate something between speakers and listeners and which are neither true nor false, such as "What time is it?" "Shut the door!" "Let's get out of here," and so on. Comments, suggestions, and questions communicate something, but they are neither true nor false.)

Since lies are told in a great variety of circumstances, may not some of those circumstances justify the telling of the lie? Must all deliberately uttered false statements be lumped together as lies and condemned as wrong in all cases? Why not make the distinction more subtle by differentiating the circumstances under which lies are told and thus qualifying the original rule against lying? Disagreement may arise on some kinds of lies—such as "white lies" told to save a person's feelings—but considering more specific classifications may be more fruitful than calling all deliberate untruths lies. Isn't someone who says "This is an act of divorce; therefore it's wrong" insensitive to the differences among individual cases? Wouldn't he or she do better to admit that some acts of divorce are right (e.g., when the two married people are constantly quarreling and irreconcilable) and some are wrong (e.g., when they could patch it up if they tried, but don't try very hard)? By ignoring such differences, aren't people being unfair by pasting the same label on all of the acts because of *one* feature they have in common and then calling all of them wrong?

Similarly, if one act in a certain category is right, it is not necessarily the case that every other in that same category is, for each act may be different in important respects. The fact that a woman's husband has been gone for ten years seems to justify her remarrying, though the fact that in ten years together she had only one quarrel with him does not. The fact that a member of the family must be rushed to a hospital may justify a man driving while intoxicated; the fact that he wants to go on a joy ride does not. Between every act and every other act there are countless differences, which may or may not be relevant to an evaluation of those acts as right or wrong.

Sometimes the circumstances that differentiate one act from another act within the same class are facts about the *external* circumstances: for example, it's not wrong to be late for an important appointment if you were delayed on the way by an automobile accident. But sometimes the facts may be *internal* ones about one of the agents. There may be two identical car accidents, both describable as acts of going through a red traffic light at rush hour at a certain busy intersection, resulting in a collision with another vehicle; but even though the two acts are externally as nearly identical as you please, there may be internal differences: for example, one act may be deliberate (done purposely to create damage), another wholly accidental. A judge may even penalize the driver in one accident but not the driver in the other because one person is accident-prone (as shown by numerous previous traffic violations) whereas the other is a first offender. There can always be *some* difference between two acts of the same kind that may make one of them right but the other wrong, though, of course, some differences—such as whether the car is red or blue—are irrelevant to judgments of right and wrong.

What can we safely say, then, about two acts falling in the same category? Only this, it would seem: for two acts identical in both their external and internal circumstances, if one of them is right then the other is, and if one of them is wrong the other is. (Compare: if two paintings are identical, one of them can't be good and the other bad.) If one is right and the other not, some relevant difference must exist between them to constitute a basis for the difference in judgment. Only if two acts are exactly alike must they both be right or both wrong.

But if this is true, of what use is it? The Categorical Imperative doesn't apply any longer to actual situations in the real world, for in the real world there is always some difference between two acts (other than the fact, that is, that they are numerically distinct—two acts and not one). Saying that if two acts are identical, the judgments on them must be identical is useless, since no two acts, in all of their circumstances, are ever identical. Nevertheless, when all is said and done, this may be all that can be inferred safely from Kant's Categorical Imperative—not even that any specific acts are right or wrong, but only that *if* one of two identical acts is right, then the other one must be right also. As Sir David Ross has noted, this falls short of what Kant claimed for the Categorical Imperative.

> The only safe way of applying Kant's test of universalizability is to envisage the act in its whole concrete particularity, and then ask "Could I wish that everyone, when in exactly similar circumstances, should tell a lie exactly similar to that which I am thinking of telling?" But then universalizability, as a short cut to knowing what is right, has failed us. For it is just as hard to see whether a similar act by someone else, with all its concrete particularity, would be right, as it is to see whether our own proposed act would be right.[12]

In spite of this failure, the universalizability criterion may have considerable value, although, as Ross notes, not the value Kant claimed for it:

> *Logically* we gain nothing by posing the question as a question for everyone rather than for oneself; for it is the same question. But *psychologically* we gain much. So long as I consider the act as one which I may or may not do, it is easy to suppose that I see it to be right when I merely see it to be convenient. But let me ask myself whether it would be right for everyone else; their advantage does not appeal to me or cloud my mind as my own does. If the act is wrong, it will be easier to see that it would be wrong for them; and then I cannot reasonably resist the conclusion that it is wrong for me. Other writers before Kant had for this reason advocated the adoption of the attitude of the impartial spectator.[13]

Both the Golden Rule and the Kantian Categorical Imperative require us to perform acts of imaginative identification—to put ourselves in someone else's place and try to imagine how a situation appears from that person's vantage point. But there are limits beyond which no one can do this and still remain the same person. Consider the following case:

> [Suppose there was] a white man who said "Africans who have been brought up in a tribal society, whose moral outlook is consequently quite different from ours, who don't accept European standards of culture, education, etc., are not worth the slightest moral consideration, but should be treated simply as chattels by their white masters." There is no point in saying to this man, suppose him to be a South African farmer of Dutch descent, moderate means, secondary school education,

---

[12]From Sir William David Ross, *Kant's Ethical Theory* (New York: Oxford University Press, 1954), p. 34.
[13]Ibid. Italics mine.

and rigid Calvinist principles, "What do you, Heinrick Potgeiter, say of
a hypothetical situation in which *you*, Heinrick Potgeiter, are in the situation of such an African?" For what can count as being in the situation
of such an African other than having not only the physical characteristics
but also the upbringing, outlook, sympathies, and interests of such an
African? And what is this other than actually being such an African? But
what is the sense of the supposition that a white farmer of Dutch descent
etc. might in certain circumstances be an African of a totally different
educational level and moral and social outlook? Surely the only sense is
that the farmer has come to *be another person.* But the whole force of the
argument depended on the assumption that the person in the hypothetical situation and the person required to legislate for that situation should
be *the same* person.[14]

One final problem about universal rules: not all moral directives are universal. The directives "Do this!" and "Don't do that!" can be applied specifically to you and to no one else. Someone might object that they should be
universalizable: if you should do *X*, anyone in the same position should also
do *X*. But is this necessarily so? Someone could say sincerely, "This is what
I ought to do. Whether others should do it also, I do not presume to say.
Even if they were in exactly the same situation as I, it is not necessarily true
that they ought to do what I believe I should do." When Martin Luther said,
"Here I stand, I can do no other," he was speaking of himself only; he was
convinced that he, in his particular situation, should take on the Church of
Rome. Whether others, even in the same situation, should have done the
same as he is something to which he did not claim to be committing
himself. "God commands me to do this" does not imply that God commands everyone else in the same situation to do the same thing. Similarly,
the statement "The demands of morality require that I do this" may not
apply to everyone else in the same situation. Many persons would accept a
command in the singular—when it concerns what they ought to do—without
necessarily committing themselves to its being accepted by others. If this is
so, then moral precepts are, contrary to what Kant believed, not even implicitly universal.

EXERCISES

1. Consider the ethics, not of doing one's duty, but of doing *more than* one's duty
   ("over and above the call of duty"). Read on this point the very interesting essay
   by J. Urmson, "Saints and Heroes," in *Essays in Moral Philosophy,* ed., A. I. Melden (Seattle: University of Washington Press, 1958), pp. 198–216.
2. Consider the following examples in the light of the concept of conscientious action
   (acting from duty):

[14] C. C. W. Taylor, Review of Hare's *Freedom and Reason. Mind,* 14 (1965): 287.

a. STUDENT A: When he has made up his mind what's right, he goes ahead and
will not swerve or deviate from it; he will not be bribed, he will not compromise, nothing can bend him. Threats and torture would not make him
reveal something if he thought it would be wrong to reveal it. That's the
kind of man I admire—one who acts on principle and who will not compromise the principles he acts on.

STUDENT B: And suppose his principles are all wrong?

A: That's unfortunate, but it makes no difference to my admiration. I don't
want to deal with a man who acts on his desires or inclinations, I want him
to act on principle. Then, if I know what his principles are, I have a more
reliable criterion of his behavior.

B: Perhaps. But I find there is nothing more worthy of suspicion than these
"men of principle." They are righteous people who pride themselves on always doing their duty. They can always do what they want to do and call it
duty. They fool themselves, consciously or unconsciously, into thinking that
something is their duty, and they make you try to swallow *their* convictions
and live up to *their* standards of duty. If you don't, they will excoriate you
and take revenge on you without mercy. Having, they think, a moral warrant for their actions and Right behind them, they can now indulge in
aggression without guilt. No, I'd rather have a man follow his inclinations
every time, especially if they are benevolent inclinations, than have to deal
with a "man of principle."

A: Would you rather have your friend, who acts on his inclinations, let
you down in a pinch because he "just didn't feel like helping you"? Remember, if he acts on principle, he will help you even if it means self-sacrifice;
your man of inclination won't do this. With him it just depends on what his
inclinations are.

B: No, the "man of principle" will always trim or interpret his principles
so that he can still do what he wants. He will hedge and amend and make
exceptions, saying "The present case is unique in that . . ." or "Under the
circumstances, I feel it is my duty to follow my wife's advice and . . ."
They "put on the armor of God" and ram their convictions down your
throat.

b. "Even if you *did* go around saving guys' lives and all, how would you know
if you did it because you really *wanted* to save guys' lives, or whether you
did it because what you *really* wanted to do was be a terrific lawyer, with
everybody slapping you on the back and congratulating you in a court when
the goddam trial was over, the reporters and everybody . . . ? How would
you know you weren't being a phony? The trouble is, you *wouldn't.*" (From
J. D. Salinger, *The Catcher in the Rye,* p. 155.)

c. "If you wish to save the last of your dignity, do not call your best actions a
'sacrifice': that term brands you as immoral. If a mother buys food for her
hungry child rather than a hat for herself, it is *not* a sacrifice: she values the
child higher than the hat; but it is a sacrifice to the kind of mother whose
higher value is the hat, who would prefer her child to starve and feeds him
only from a sense of duty." (From *Atlas Shrugged* by Ayn Rand. © Copyright 1957 by Ayn Rand. Reprinted by permission of Random House, Inc.,
p. 1029.)

3. Do you think that the following criticisms of Kant are justified? Give reasons for your answer.
   a. When Kant talks about happiness not being the end, or purpose, of human-kind, he is using teleological language to which he is not entitled without a specific supernatural theory. For a purpose implies a purposer. If human beings were designed for some end, someone, presumably God, must have designed them so. But Kant has not begun, or even tried, to show that human beings were designed by a Divine Being to fulfill some end. So all this teleological talk is without foundation.
   b. Besides (continuing the above), it isn't true that instinct would be sufficient if our true end were happiness. We would still need reason to tell us which actions are most likely to lead to happiness (either our own or others').
   c. In saying that a good will alone is good without qualification—and assuming that "good without qualification" means the same as "intrinsically good"— Kant was confusing instrumental good with intrinsic good. Good will usually leads to intrinsic good, but how can it be intrinsically good itself?
   d. How can Kant speak of actions as being consistent or inconsistent? It is only propositions which can be consistent or inconsistent with each other.
   e. Kant's universalizability rule can't be applied to matters of feeling, like whom a person should marry. In the first place, Kant's whole emphasis was on reason, which is at the opposite pole from feelings. In the second place, if I love Mr. *X* and want to marry him, I certainly couldn't wish this universalized, for I certainly don't want *everybody* to marry Mr. *X*.!
   f. "Kant seems to have held that all particular rules of duty can be deduced from the one fundamental rule 'Act as if the maxim of thy action were to become by thy will a universal law of nature.' But this appears to me an error analogous to that of supposing that formal logic supplies a complete criterion of truth. I should agree that a volition which does not stand this test is to be condemned; but I hold that a volition which does stand it may after all be wrong. For I conceive that all (or almost all) persons who act conscientiously could sincerely will the maxims on which they act to be universally adopted: while at the same time we continually find such persons in thoroughly conscientious disagreement as to what each ought to do in a given set of circumstances." (Henry Sidgwick, *The Methods of Ethics,* 7th ed., pp. 209–10).
4. What do you think of the following as examples of the application of Kant's universalizability rule? Explain your reasons.
   a. Since I enjoy playing tennis, I like to be invited by others to play tennis. Since I should do as I would be done by, I should invite others to play tennis with me on all possible occasions, regardless of whether they enjoy the game.
   b. For the sake of my health I take liver pills every day. If it is right for me to do this, it is right for everyone to do it; therefore it would be right for everybody to take liver pills every day.
   c. I could not wish everyone to become a professional philosopher; the human race would starve if that happened. But no act, according to Kant, is right unless it can be universalized into a general rule. Therefore nobody ought to become a professional philosopher.

d. If I prefer blondes, I should wish everyone else to prefer blondes.

e. Suicide is always wrong, for if universalized, it would be inconsistent with the continuance of life.

f. Lying is always wrong, for if universalized, it would be inconsistent with the function of language, which is to tell the truth.

g. It cannot be your duty to love your enemies, for if everyone loved his or her enemies there would be no enemies left to love.

h. It cannot be your duty to give to the poor, since if everyone did so, the recipients would be poor no longer, and there would be no poor left to whom to give.

i. Kant himself was inconsistent: he was a bachelor and he had no children. If everyone had followed his example, the race would have died out. If suicide is always wrong (as Kant believed it was), why not celibacy, which would have the same result?

j. A teacher says, as he lights a pipe at the opening of a test period, "Since the maxim of my action should be universalizable, you may smoke during this test."

A student replies, "I was wondering whether you might not be universalizing a different maxim: 'All teachers may smoke during test periods.' "

5. Are the following maxims universalizable? Would they pass Kant's criteria? Why?

a. Everybody except me is bound by moral rules.

b. Don't stand in line; force yourself in at the head of the line so that you won't have to wait for everyone else to be served first.

c. Hurry now, get your tickets today so that you will have them later when everyone else is clamoring to get them.

d. Write the best essay and win First Prize!

e. Be the exception—be there on time.

f. If two trains meet at a crossing, each should wait till the other has passed.

g. Be ruthless to everyone.

h. Be more charitable than anyone else.

i. Whoever disagrees with me should be shot.

j. Never speak until you are first spoken to.

k. Wait for the hostess to begin eating.

6. In Victor Hugo's *Les Miserables,* the hero, Jean Valjean, is an ex-convict living under an assumed name. He has built up a successful business in which he employs most of his fellow townspeople; he becomes mayor and a public benefactor. Then he learns that another man, a feebleminded old beggar, has been arrested as Jean Valjean and will be sent to the galleys. The real Jean Valjean then decides that it is his moral duty to reveal who he is, even at the price of being sent back to the galleys.

a. What do you think Kant would say about Jean Valjean's decision? Why?

b. What do you think the utilitarians would say? Why?

c. What would you say? Give your reasons.

7. Evaluate the following examples, using the concept of *reversibility*.

a. *A* throws an orange at *B*'s face; *B* becomes angry; *A* resents *B*'s anger. *B* says, "I bet *you'd* be angry if I did it to you." *A* replies, "Maybe I would, but I'm me, I'm not you."

b. The mother of a juvenile delinquent who has murdered another boy weeps and says her son is not really bad; she asks that he be released in a short time into her care. She is horrified when the judge gives him a thirty-year sentence. How do you think she would feel—or how do you think you would feel—about the situation if you were, not the mother of the aggressor, but the mother of the murdered boy?

8. Evaluate this statement by R. M. Hare, *Freedom and Reason,* p. 32: "Offenses against the thesis of universalizability are logical, not moral. If a person says 'I ought to act in a certain way, but nobody else ought to act in that way in relevantly similar circumstances,' then, on my thesis, he is abusing the word 'ought.' "

9. According to Kant, certain maxims, such as "Make your living by stealing," are unacceptable because they cannot be made into universal rules of human conduct.

   a. Which of the following do you consider the most plausible reason for this? (1) Stealing is inconsistent with respect for property, just as universal contract-breaking is inconsistent with "the nature of contract." (But so what? you might ask. If *A* is inconsistent with *B,* what's bad about this unless *B* can be shown to be desirable? And isn't everything inconsistent with something else, such as its own opposite?) (2) Stealing is impossible as a universal policy, because someone first has to produce a book or a television set before someone else can steal it. (3) Stealing could not be considered desirable as a universal policy—just as, in Kant's view, "Don't help others and don't expect help from them" is less desirable than a policy of each person helping others when they are in need.

   b. What would count as stealing? (1) If you take from someone an article that he has stolen from you, is that "stealing it back"? (2) Is taxation stealing, since it's taking from you without your consent? Is all taxation theft, or is it just "rendering unto Caesar"? (3) What would you say, with regard to classifying it as theft, of an example much more complex than Kant apparently had in mind in his prohibition against stealing, such as the following: The Federal Reserve Bank extends credit through its member banks, thus lowering the interest rates (because of the plentiful supply of credit) but increasing inflation (because of the expansion of the money supply). As a result, business is stimulated, businessmen borrow from the banks to finance new enterprises or expand old ones, and workers are employed in the new projects, which helps them in spite of the increased inflation that raises their cost of living. Then the Fed, to slow down the inflation, creates a "credit crunch," refusing (at least for a time) to expand the money supply. The result is that interest rates go up (because of intense competition for loans with the limited supply of available money), and thousands of businesses go bankrupt because they cannot afford to borrow at the new high interest rates. The banks then foreclose on the businesses that cannot repay their loans, taking possession of the enterprises that are caught in the squeeze. What would you say to the remark, "It's just a big con game—it's outright theft of those businesses by the Fed—first dangling the loans in front of them to get them to expand and put them in debt, then tightening the screws and calling in the debt"? (See H. S. Kenan, *The Federal Reserve Bank;* Silas W. Adams, *The Legalized Crime of Banking;* and John Pugsley, *The Alpha Strategy.*)

SELECTED READINGS

Kant

Acton, H. B. *Kant's Moral Philosophy*. London: Macmillan, 1970.

Aune, Bruce. *Kant's Theory of Morals*. Princeton, N.J.: Princeton University Press, 1979.

Beck, Lewis White. *A Commentary on Kant's Critique of Practical Reason*. Chicago: Phoenix Books/University of Chicago Press, 1960.

Brandt, Richard. *Ethical Theory*. Englewood Cliffs, N.J.: Prentice-Hall, 1959. See Chapter 2.

Broad, C. D. "Conscience and Conscientious Action." In his *Ethics and the History of Philosophy*. New York: Humanities Press, 1952.

Harrison, Jonathan. "Kant's Four Examples of the First Formulation of the Categorical Imperative." *Philosophical Quarterly* 7 (1957): 50–62.

Kant, Immanuel. *Critique of Practical Reason* (1788).★ Translated by Lewis White Beck. Indianapolis: Bobbs-Merrill, 1956.

————. *Fundamental Principles of the Metaphysics of Morals* (1785). Translated by Thomas K. Abbott. Chicago: Henry Regnery, 1949.

Paton, H. J. *The Categorical Imperative: A Study of Kant's Moral Philosophy*. New York: Harper Torchbooks/Harper & Row, 1967.

Ross, Sir William David. *Kant's Ethical Theory: A Commentary on the Grundlegung zur Metaphysik der Sitten*. London: Oxford University Press, 1954.

Silber, John R. "The Contents of Kant's Ethical Thought." Pts. 1 and 2. *Philosophical Quarterly* 9 (1959): 193–207, 309–18.

Contemporary Works in the Kantian Tradition

Baier, Kurt. *The Moral Point of View*. Ithaca, N.Y.: Cornell University Press, 1958.

Donagan, Alan. *The Theory of Morality*. Chicago: University of Chicago Press, 1979.

Foot, Philippa. "Morality as a System of Hypothetical Imperatives." *Philosophical Review* 81 (1972): 305–16.

Gert, Bernard. *The Moral Rules: A New Rational Foundation for Morality*. New York: Harper Torchbooks/Harper & Row, 1973.

Gewirth, Alan. *Reason and Morality*. Chicago: University of Chicago Press, 1979.

Hare, R. M. *Freedom and Reason*. London: Oxford University Press, 1963.

Harrison, Jonathan. *Our Knowledge of Right and Wrong*. London: Allen & Unwin, 1971.

Locke, Don. "The Trivializability of Universalizability." In Wilfrid Sellars and John Hospers, eds. *Readings in Ethical Theory*. Englewood Cliffs, N.J.: Prentice-Hall, 1970.

Singer, Marcus. *Generalization in Ethics*. New York: Random House, 1961.

★Dates in parentheses are dates of first publication.

6

Contemporary Theories
of Right

1. MULTIPLE SOURCES OF OBLIGATION

Two men are trapped inside a burning building, and you are the only person nearby; there is time to rescue (at most) one of them. One of them is your father, and the other one is a great scientist who is well on the way to finding a cure for arthritis. Which one should you rescue? The utilitarian would not hesitate: far more good will be done by rescuing the scientist. And yet, your father is the one you know and love, to whom you owe an enormous debt of gratitude for all he has done for you, sacrificing so that you could go to college, doing without things so that you could have them. The scientist, on the other hand, is a stranger to you. Is it really obvious that you should rescue him and let your father die? Most people in this situation wouldn't hesitate to try to rescue their father first; would they really be committing a moral wrong by doing so?

Suppose that two explorers in the Arctic have only enough food to keep one alive till he can reach the base, and one offers to die if the other will promise to educate his children. No other person can know that such a promise was made, and the breaking or keeping of it cannot influence the future keeping of promises. According to the utilitarian theory, it is the duty of the returned traveler to act precisely as he ought to have acted if no bargain had been made: to consider how he can spend his money most expediently for the happiness of the human race, and, if he thinks his own child is a genius, to spend it on him.[1]

Let us assume that the returned explorer is financially unable to provide higher education for both his own children and that of the dead explorer and

[1] This example is presented in E. F. Carritt, *Ethical and Political Thinking* (Oxford: Clarendon Press, 1946), p. 64.

that more total good can be achieved by educating his own and never revealing his promise to the dead man. Most of us would still feel inclined to
question whether he had done the right thing. He almost certainly *would* have
done the right thing according to utilitarianism (since his act produced the
most good), but we would still be bothered by it. A man laid down his life
in the belief that the promise would be kept. True, no one except the returned explorer ever knew that such a promise was made, and if he says
nothing about it, no one will ever know about the promise having been
made, but does that make the promise any less binding? Are promises made
in secret any different, as far as the obligation to keep them is concerned,
from those that are not? Isn't the man's first obligation to keep the promise
he made to the man who sacrificed his life?

Still, that people should *never* break their word—the Kantian position—
seems too stringent. If it's a promise that should never have been made in
the first place, or if some enormous good such as saving a city from destruction could be achieved by breaking a promise, then, let us grant, it should
be broken. But neither would most people be content with saying that people should keep a promise only if they believe, even with good evidence,
that more net good will come about from keeping it than from breaking it.

It is situations like these that have prompted some moral philosophers to
try to find a middle ground between the Kantian and utilitarian views. Such
a theory was worked out by Richard Price in the eighteenth century, but its
best-known exponent in our own day is the British philosopher Sir David
Ross (1877–1971). According to Ross, there are a number of distinct sources
of obligation, which cannot be reduced either to a set of unbreakable rules or
to the duty to promote the maximum good. If you asked an ordinary citizen,
uncorrupted by any study of ethics, why she is keeping a certain promise,
she would probably reply simply "Because I made it." This wouldn't commit her to keeping all promises under all conditions, but it tells us that the
fact that the promise was made is at least as good a reason for keeping it as
that keeping it would produce the most good for the most people. If the
woman has replied to our question by saying, "Because I thought that keeping it would produce more good than breaking it," we might be somewhat
suspicious of her: we would probably conclude that on another occasion she
would break her promise if she thought that breaking it would do more
good. We would be less likely to trust her promises in the future.

Most people believe that they have more of an obligation in time of need
to their own children than they do to their neighbor's children. Their own
children are persons they have brought into the world by their own actions,
and isn't their primary responsibility to them, and not to just anybody and
everybody? Nor would they consider this a moral weakness on their part, a
partiality for their own when they ought to be impartial, but rather a moral
duty: they *ought* to provide for their own children first. Far from its being a
breach of duty to take thought for their own children first, they would consider it a breach of duty if they did *not* do so. If we could achieve 10 units of

net good by helping our own children and 12 units by helping our neighbor's children, we would probably think it quite right and proper to do the good for our own children, not only because we love them but because they are our own special responsibility. If it were between our own children and our cousin's children, we would still give preference to our own children, though the fact of our cousin's children being in need might strike more of a responsive chord in us than the fact of a stranger's children being in need somewhere in the world. Maybe blood shouldn't be thicker than water, but still, is the attitude "She's one of our own, after all" entirely unjustified?

In the same vein, if a perfect stranger (who happened to pick your number out of a telephone book) phoned you at three o'clock in the morning and asked you to help him out of a jam, you might feel no obligation at all; you might hang up on him. But if a close friend phoned you, particularly if he had done things for you in the past, you would probably feel obliged to help him even though you might feel disinclined to do so. Certainly you would feel guilty if you didn't, whereas you would probably feel no guilt at failing to help the stranger who called. Doesn't the fact that it's a friend make a difference? But if utilitarianism is correct, you should distribute your beneficence wherever it can be maximized: if you can confer more good on the stranger than on your friend, you should help the stranger. Not only *would* most people *not* help the stranger (at least not at first, if the choice were between a stranger and a friend), but they would sincerely believe that they *should not*—that "friends come first, and that's what friendship is all about." Are those (and this surely includes all of us) who place friends first and strangers second guilty of a breach of moral duty?

Duty, said Ross, has a much more *personal* character than the utilitarian account permits. Ross does not deny that we should attempt to maximize good and minimize evil, but this is not our only duty. We also have special duties for special reasons to special people. We have duties to our parents, our children, our benefactors, and those to whom we have made commitments which we do not have to those outside these special relationships. And such duties are not just (as utilitarianism would have it) instances of the general duty to maximize good. Our utilitarian duty is to produce by our actions the best consequences possible; that is, we act *in order to* produce maximum good in the future. But some of our duties, at least, are not future-looking duties of this kind but past-looking ones: they are not *in order to* but *because of*. I should keep a promise not only in order to produce good by keeping it, but *because* (in the past) I made it. I should help a benefactor not only in order to do good to her, but *because* in the past the benefactor has helped me. I should try to recompense someone for harm I have caused not merely in order to do him good, but *because* in the past I harmed him and should try to make up for the harm.

Suppose that I have a choice between two acts, A and B. By doing A, I would be keeping a promise and producing a total of 1,000 net units of good; by doing B, I would be breaking a promise and producing a net total of

1,001 units of good. According to utilitarianism, I should do *B*. But Ross says this is mistaken: I should consider not only how much good I can do, but also the fact that I have made a promise in the past, the keeping of which is not merely a matter of producing the most good.

I can't escape this conclusion by saying, "But *A* will produce the most good after all, because you've forgotten that keeping the promise will also have a favorable effect (through example) on the future keeping of promises; so keeping the promise, in addition to producing the 1,000 units of good, will produce (let's say) 100 units *more* good because of the example it sets to others as well as to myself. So Ross and the utilitarians agree on this example after all." This ploy won't work: in the example 1,000 units is the *total* net good that will be achieved, and the effect on the future keeping of promises is already considered in the total. To be sure, the amount of good produced is not irrelevant to the case: if by breaking a not terribly important promise I could cause $1 million to be donated to the muscular dystrophy fund, then I would probably be justified in breaking the promise. But no *small* edge of good in *B* over *A* would be sufficient to justify me in breaking the promise.

My duty to keep the promise is not, then, just a special case of my duty to maximize good. But neither is my duty to keep a promise inflexible. On that point, said Ross, Kant was mistaken; he considered certain kinds of acts, such as lying, breaking one's word, and killing, to be wrong under all circumstances. He erected certain prohibitions into unconditional rules, when actually they have perfectly legitimate exceptions. And this brought him to an impasse in cases of conflict of duty, as when someone has to tell a lie to save a life; in such cases Kant faced the problem of an irresistible force confronting an immovable object. All such duties, such as telling the truth and saving lives, said Ross, are *prima facie duties,* not absolute or unconditional duties. The term "prima facie" means "at first sight," or "prior to further inspection." I have a prima facie duty to keep a promise I've made, and this is an absolute duty *if* no other prima facie duty, such as to maximize good, interferes with it; if it does, then I must attempt to mediate between these two prima facie duties, and such conflicts of prima facie duties present us with our most difficult moral decisions. But if one prima facie duty does not get in the way of another prima facie duty, then there is no problem: with no conflicting duty in its way, the prima facie duty (that which is my duty unless some other duty intervenes) becomes an absolute duty (that which I should do). That we do have some prima facie duties seemed to Ross far more certain than what specifically we ought to do when two or more prima facie duties conflict with one another. Ross mentioned several sorts of prima facie duties:

1. There are prima facie duties which arise because of *my previous acts.* There are, first of all, duties of *fidelity,* to keep promises, contracts, or other commitments which I have voluntarily undertaken to make. It is probably true that keeping them usually results in the most good and that the institution of promising is worth having because it yields good results that would not occur without it; but the obligation to keep a promise is not merely a

special case of the obligation to maximize good: it is a distinct prima facie duty of its own. There are, in addition, duties of *reparation* for previous wrongful acts I have done to others. If I have inadvertently backed my car through my neighbor's fence, I at least owe him a new fence. If I said to him, "Instead of fixing your fence I think I'll give the money to the Salvation Army, because I could accomplish more total good that way," he would undoubtedly treat my suggestion with some coolness—and shouldn't he? It was after all *his* fence which was destroyed, and moreover it was destroyed *by me*. If I give the money to someone else, this is no recompense to him, since he is still without the fence he had before. I may or may not be able to produce the best consequences by making this reparation to him; but whether it produces the best possible consequences or not, I still owe him the fence.

2. There are also prima facie duties which rest, not on previous acts of mine, but on *previous acts of others.* If others have helped me when I needed it, even if they did not expect a return and did not do so to get a return, I still owe them a special debt of *gratitude.* My parents have done more for me than strangers have, and I owe them something in return. If I could achieve 1,000 units of good by conferring a benefit on strangers, my duty would still be to my parents, not because I would be producing the greatest total of good that way (I might not), but because of the special duty of gratitude owed to my benefactors.

The prima facie duties described thus far have been past-looking, and they are duties to special people for special reasons. But there are future-looking prima facie duties also.

3. There is the duty of *beneficence,* that is, of promoting the maximum good possible by my action (utilitarian duty). In Ross, this is only one among many prima facie duties. Beneficence is not the same as benevolence: the word "beneficence" (from the Latin *bene* and *facio*) means "doing good deeds," whereas "benevolence" (*bene* and *volo*) means "having a good will," or "being benevolently inclined." It is the doing of acts, not the having of a certain kind of disposition, which is a prima facie duty. In its utilitarian meaning it usually includes the next duty, which Ross distinguishes from it.

4. There is the duty of *non-maleficence,* that is, the duty of refraining from harming others. Ross considers the duty of non-maleficence, or not harming others, as a stronger prima facie duty than that of beneficence, or helping them. I may not have a duty to help everyone I meet on the sidewalk, but I do have a duty to refrain from harming them. It would be wrong to do X amount of harm to one person in order to do $X + Y$ amount of good to somebody else. I may not rob Peter to pay Paul, even though doing so helps Paul more than it harms Peter. As Ross said, "We should not in general consider it justifiable to kill one person in order to keep another alive, or to steal from one in order to give alms to another."[2]

5. There is also the prima facie duty of *justice.* Justice is the subject of

[2] W. D. Ross, *The Right and the Good* (London: Oxford University Press, 1930), p. 22.

Chapter 8, and we shall consider it in more detail there. As Ross uses the term, it has to do not with the total *amount* of good produced but its *distribution*. If *A* is a saint and *B* is a villain, it is better for me to make *A* happy than to make *B* happy, even if I could make *B* happier than I could make *A*. If *C* is a nephew who is careful of his money and will use it to further his education or start a career and *D* is a niece who is a spendthrift, it is better for me to give it to *C* than to *D*—not only because my doing this will have better consequences, but because *C* *deserves* it more. But whether or not *C* is more deserving of it is a matter of his past record; I cannot determine it merely by calculating probable future consequences, but by examining the person's performance. Thus this prima facie duty is also past-looking.

6. There is, finally, the prima facie duty of *self-improvement.* "You owe it to yourself to take a rest after all that hard work" and "You owe it to yourself to make use of your talents and not be a drifter all your life" are examples of this duty. You owe such things to yourself not merely because you will make the *world* better or happier, thereby, but because you will make *yourself* better or happier. There are "self-regarding" duties as well as "other-regarding" duties, and this last prima facie duty listed by Ross gives recognition to this fact.

Ross's view will seem to many rather like enlightened common sense, or an account of our duties as we actually view them but had never quite articulated them. Nevertheless, questions come to mind with regard to it. For example: Where do you draw the line? It was difficult enough, as we saw, to make interpersonal calculations of happiness and of many other things. But utilitarian calculation was simple compared with what we encounter in Ross, for here we have to weigh good maximization against a whole array of other things, such as the value of promises, gratitude, and so on. And how do we do this? We might agree with Ross that *if* you could say with confidence that alternative *A* involves 1,000 net units of good and the keeping of a promise and alternative *B* involves 1,001 net units of good and the breaking of a promise, we should do *A*. We might also grant that if *A* involves 1,000 net units of good and the keeping of a promise and *B* involves 10,000 units of good and the breaking of a promise, we should do *B*. But where do we draw the line? At 5,000? At 2,000? At 3,579? How much good must be produced before we are justified in breaking our word to produce it? If you were *sure* that the scientist in the burning building was going to find a cure for arthritis, would that justify you in leaving your father to burn? How do you put gratitude on a scale and weigh it against the production of good to discover which weighs more?

Ross gave no definite answer to such questions. Obviously you cannot weigh these things on any scale. Even if you said, "I draw the line at 3,978 units," such information would be useless until a criterion was provided whereby you could know when that number of units had been reached. Still, in spite of its vagueness, Ross's account is not useless in estimating our duties. We do have to take all the factors he mentioned into consideration; the simple utilitarian criterion of good maximization won't do, and most people already assent to this. What to do when one kind of prima facie duty conflicts with another is always a problem, and it is in this area—at the junctions of our moral concepts—where the most agonizing moral conflicts occur. Ross is concerned primarily to "do justice to all the data," which he believed utilitarianism fails to do. Admittedly his account makes moral decision making more complex, but that is something we have to live with; his account of several duties is also conceptually messier than if we had just a single kind of duty such as the utilitarian, but so be it. "I didn't invent all this," he might say. "Don't you agree that fidelity, gratitude, and so on are duties which are not reducible to the duty of good maximization? And if that's so, then you have to live with it too. If vagueness results, and cases become undecidable, that's regrettable, but that's the way it is. As Aristotle said, let's not demand more precision of a subject matter than that subject matter permits."

Although there are some undecidable cases and some cloudy ones, there are many others where the result is quite clear: you don't break your word to someone *just* because you think, even with reason, that a bit more good may result from doing so; you don't ignore the fact that this man is your father; you don't ignore a friend as you might a stranger; and so on. What Ross considered morally certain is that we do have specific prima facie duties; what is not certain, and is often undeterminable, is what we should do in specific cases in which these prima facie duties conflict.

In any case, utilitarians are not in a position to press this charge, since they have enough undecidable cases of their own, in which the amount of net good produced by the various alternatives is quite impossible to ascertain. Kantians, of course, *can* press the charge: they may say that the moment you knowingly break your word or turn your back on a benefactor, morally speaking the game is already up, you have already compromised your principles, and the rest is just a matter of how much more compromise you would accept. "Would you go to bed with a man who isn't your husband for a million dollars?" a man asks a woman. "Well," the woman replies, "a million dollars is a lot of money." "Well, I'm offering you ten dollars." "Ten dollars! What do you think I am?" "We've already determined what you are," he says, "we're just disputing the price." Breaking your word for any reason, Kantians would say, already shows that there's a price for which you will do it.

But then, *shouldn't* you break your word to save a life? Kant is still stuck with the problem of what to do in a case of conflict of duties. Ross at least offers us some clues.

Still, Ross can be criticized on other grounds. He presented us with a rather heterogeneous collection of prima facie duties, without any unifying principle underlying them. This presumably would not disturb him: "That is just what, on careful introspection, I believe my duties to be," he might reply. But why is it just this list and not a somewhat different one? Ross, for example, included a duty of gratitude, the duty to return good for good; but he included no duty of revenge, the duty to return evil for evil. Presumably he believed as do most persons in a Christian culture, that we have no such duty. But probably most people the world around believe and have believed that we do have such a duty and that it is at least as important as any other. One reason for not believing it a duty may be the well-grounded conviction that revenge is counterproductive, that if you start with revenge it just keeps going, with no end to bloodshed. But that is a utilitarian reason, concerning the consequences of acts of vengeance. Besides, most of us do believe in punishment for criminals, and that is, in a way, returning evil for evil. But all this belongs under the heading of duties of justice, which we shall discuss more thoroughly in Chapter 8.

2. UTILITARIAN GENERALIZATION

Faced with the criticism we have just considered, utilitarians have merged to defend their views, though in a different form. They are still consequential-ists—still judging the rightness or wrongness of actions by considering the consequences to everyone—but they now consider, not the consequences of each individual action, but the consequences of everyone doing likewise. In this endeavor they have seized upon the concept of universalizability, already developed in connection with Kantian ethics, and have used it to formulate their revised view. Consider the following conversation:

A: Look at all those apples on the tree. They're nice and ripe. Why don't we pick some of them?

B: But it's not our orchard, and they're not our apples. We'd be stealing.

A: But the owner isn't at home. And he has so many trees full of apples that he'd never miss the few that we'd take. He might not even pick them.

B: That may be. But what if everyone who felt like it came along and took whatever apples they wanted to? Soon the orchard would be stripped bare, and the man who cultivated the orchard and grew the apples would be left without anything.[3]

Let's assume that if *A* and *B* picked up a few dozen apples the effect on the whole orchard full of apples would be very slight, perhaps not even no-ticed. The consequences of *this* particular act of taking apples, considered by itself, would be negligible. The takers would dearly enjoy them, and the owner might not even miss them. Utilitarians traditionally might have said, "Go ahead and take some." But the new consideration is not "What will be the consequences of *my* taking some?" but rather "What if my action was universalized? What if everyone—or even lots of people—did what I am about to do?" The effects of *that* would be considerable. And if you include

[3] This example is adapted from David Lyons, *Forms and Limits of Utilitarianism* (Oxford: Clarendon Press, 1964), p. 2.

not only this orchard, but every other orchard, and if people were permitted to take fruit from the trees whenever they felt like it, nobody would bother to grow fruit trees anymore, knowing that they'd probably be vandalized anyway.

Consider the matter of voting. What are the chances that your vote is going to make any difference in a national election in which millions of people go to the polls? The chances are almost infinitesimally small. In view of the small probability of your vote making a difference in the election, you might well decide to stay at home; there are doubtless many things you could do that would be fruitful and constructive and have good results, better results at any rate than going to the polls.

Why is it, then, that many people nevertheless believe they have a duty to vote? Do they really believe their vote is likely to swing the election? No, their conviction rests on the consideration that if everybody said, "I'll stay home, since my vote won't make any difference," nobody would vote, and that would be the end of democratic government. It's not each person's own vote that's going to determine the outcome of the election, but all the votes together. The consequences of one person not voting are negligible; the consequences of everyone's not voting would be tremendous. (Even the consequences of most people staying away from the polls would be considerable.) It is the actions of a great many people, rather than that of one person, whose consequences make the difference.

The principle that emerges from such examples is the principle of *utilitarian generalization:* "If the consequences of everybody doing X are better than any alternative, then you should do X." And "If the consequences of everybody failing to do X are better than those of doing X, then you should refrain from doing X." Thus, you should vote, at least *if* everyone doing so has the best consequences, but you shouldn't pick the apples from someone else's orchard.

The case is not entirely open and shut, even in the two comparatively simple examples we examined. Suppose you were approaching the apple orchard and you were starving; you might then make a good utilitarian case for taking some apples, and perhaps even making restitution later to the owner as you were able. But then you would be going by the utilitarian consequences of this *one* action (stealing a few apples), not by the consequences of *everyone* doing it. (Should you then use utilitarian generalization sometimes but not always?) And similarly with the voting example: Is it clear, using considerations of utilitarian generalization, that everyone ought to vote? Should people who know nothing about the issues, and care less, vote, just to increase the vote totals? A case could be made for saying that only those who know something about the issues involved in the election should go to the polls, because then the results would be better.

There are even more difficult cases which the principle of utilitarian generalization runs up against. "I shouldn't cheat on exams, because think what would happen if everyone cheated." Well, if everyone cheated, the purpose of exams would be defeated, and they would be eliminated or proctors would be assigned or some other way would be found to test mastery of material (such as oral exams).

But a question remains: If everyone else cheats (or even if most students do), are you sure you are doing the right thing by saying, "No, no matter what, I'm not going to do as the rest do; I'm not going to cheat"? What if the result is that others get higher grades than you by cheating? What if the cheaters (by virtue of their grades) get to professional school (which they don't deserve because they had to cheat to pass the tests) whereas you don't because you were honest? Beyond a certain point, wouldn't you say, "I may as well do as the others do, if I'm going to get admitted to graduate school"? Wouldn't you then be considering the effects of *your* action alone, not those of everyone else? Wouldn't you be estimating what to do on the basis of the consequences of *your* act, considered *in the light of* what other people were doing?

Or consider an analogous case. Suppose I wish to preserve certain standards in grading students. I don't give A's and B's unless I believe that students really deserve them. But studies have shown that in comparison with previous generations, members of the television generation have suffered a sharp decline in the ability to read and write, particularly in the ability to master abstract thought and argument from the printed page. "All the same," I say, "I'm going to keep my standards up." So I give lower grades than before. But I find that other teachers are subject to "grade inflation": they give high grades for work to which they would not have assigned such grades a few years before. I become one of the few holdouts. Students come to me and say, "I'd like to take your course, but you're known as a low grader, and I have to keep my grade average high in order to get into graduate school, so I have to take the courses in which the instructor gives practically nothing but A's and B's." Now I'm out of sync with the relaxed grading standards of the other teachers. I could, of course, stick to my principle and become the lone holdout. I could say to myself, "If everyone did as I did, the standards would be retained." On the other hand, I could bend with the wind, and admit that an A doesn't indicate the degree of mastery that it used to. The fact is that most teachers are not doing as I do—and doesn't this make a difference? Why chase students away from courses from which (in my opinion, at least) they might profit, when by compromising my standards somewhat I could have lots of enthusiastic students, whose subsequent lives might (once in a while) be changed because of my courses? Is my tenacity worth this price? Is it perhaps just stubbornness?

Again, I consider what I should do in terms of the probable consequences of either sticking with the old standards or relaxing and following new ones. But then it looks as if I am deciding on the basis of good old-fashioned utilitarian considerations. What would it profit me (would it even be right?) to say, "I'll stick to the old standards, because if everyone did so, high grades would mean more than they do now"? I must balance "grades meaning something" against other considerations such as keeping students (and possibly even doing them some good).

Or consider the following case. You are the owner of a factory in a community in which racial feelings run high and racism is rampant. You would like to employ qualified workers of all races: what race a person belongs to makes no difference to you, as long as the person can do the job. But you have discovered after many unpleasant experiences that the workers don't feel the same way. Every time you have a crew of racially mixed workers, fights break out, machinery is demolished, people get hurt, and at the end of it racial antipathies are more intense than ever. To top it all, your insurance company won't cover you anymore unless you change your hiring practices. You have given lectures and pep talks and had discussions with your workers, but nothing seems to help; the feelings are too deep-seated. And so you decide either to hire people of one race only or to have people of different races in different parts of the factory having no contact with each other.

But if you used the utilitarian generalization argument, you would say, "If every factory and store owner who had people of different races available for jobs was to do as I did originally, racial barriers would in time break down, and people would see how irrational their hatreds were. Since it would have good consequences if *everybody* did it, therefore *I* ought to continue to do it." The trouble is that *your* doing it without a lot of cooperation from others would not only do no good but actually increase the harm.

Nor are you saying that your good deed would set an example to others: you've tried that and it didn't work. The argument has nothing to do with any good effects of your individual action; it has to do only with the good effects that *would* occur *if* everybody acted like you. The problem is that most other people haven't acted like you in the past, and there is no evidence that they are about to do so in the future. Is it still clear that you should act on the basis of utilitarian generalization, perhaps having your entire factory destroyed and numerous people killed in riots in the process? (And if your company is partly owned by stockholders, don't you have a duty to them, too, to protect the factory and keep it safe from uninsured vandalism? They have expressed their confidence in you by investing money in your company. Have you no obligation to make sure they don't lose everything on that investment?)

You might say, all the same, "In every worthy cause there have to be some pioneers, some trailblazers. To correct a bad situation, I shall be one of those trailblazers." But now you are not appealing to utilitarian generalization; you are appealing to the *example* which you set by *your* action (not the actions of everyone). And if you do not succeed in setting an example—if riots continue and if the incidents don't hit the papers, with the result that others never hear of your heroic resolve—it won't make any difference to the rest of the world; you won't correct the situation you wanted to and may even make it worse. Whether you should set an example depends on the good or bad consequences of doing so; if you don't succeed in influencing others' actions by your example, your martyrdom is pointless. In any case, you are no longer using utilitarian generalization, but the original utilitarian principle, which assesses the rightness or wrongness of your action by *its* consequences, not by the consequences of everyone else doing likewise.

Consider one more example. Suppose you argue, "If nobody engaged in violent behavior against anyone else, there would be no wars, nor even ordinary street fights. What a fine and peaceful world that would be! Therefore, I shall not use violence of any kind myself, even if attacked." It's not that by doing so you would be setting an example for others; that would be the old utilitarian consideration, having to do with the consequence of *this* act. Rather, the reasoning is that you should refrain because if everyone refrained, the consequences would be highly desirable. It's the consequences of everyone refraining from violence that guides you, not the consequences of your solo act of nonviolence.

This seems to be what at least some pacifists say. They will not take up arms against anyone, even in self-defense. What is the result? People attack them and kill or maim them, and rob and loot them of their belongings. In fact, when such a policy of nonviolence is announced in advance (as pacifists often do), the pacifists are "sitting ducks" for any aggressor who comes along and robs them, burns down their houses, and hurts their families. Pacifists can say with their dying breath, "If everyone was as peaceful as we are, there would be no wars," but meanwhile they are eliminated while the aggressors inherit the earth.

When people do succeed in setting an effective example, as Gandhi did in India with his policy of passive resistance, this can be justified on traditional utilitarian grounds: it had the best consequences. But can it be justified by arguing, "I'll do it because if *everyone* did, the results would be excellent"? The unfortunate fact is that not everyone is going to refrain from violence. And if even a few people don't refrain, the remainder will be their victims. Not everyone *will* behave peacefully; and in view of this fact, isn't it better to be prepared for possible aggression from them than to say, "I shall do *X*, because if everyone did *X* the world would be a wonderful place"? Not everyone *is* going to do *X*, and doesn't this make a difference? You may say, as at least one writer has, "It is simply irrelevant to reply, 'Not everyone *will* do it,' "[4] But is it irrelevant? What good is it to be pledged to nonaggression as long as other people are engaging in aggression? You may ignore them as long as they don't attack you, but when they do, and when they kill your family before your eyes, are you still going to say—indeed, *should* you say— "I remain peaceful because if everyone remained peaceful this would be a wonderful world"? Aren't you making the world somewhat less wonderful by letting the aggressors get by with it?

[4] See Marcus Singer, *Generalization in Ethics* (New York: Random House, 1961), Chapter 4, Section 7.

3. RULE-UTILITARIANISM

Our discussion of utilitarian generalization leads us into the most extensively discussed form of utilitarianism today, *rule-utilitarianism*. Instead of trying to find what *act* will have the best consequences (maximum net expectable intrinsic good), rule-utilitarians try to find the *rule* which will have the best consequences. Their goal is to discover and formulate the best rule appropriate to each type of action, and the test of the rule is its consequences in practice.

Two things must be kept in mind about the theory, however. First, sometimes the consequences will be best if the rule has the force of law, requiring everyone to follow it on pain of penalty, as in the case of rules prohibiting murder; but sometimes the consequences will be best if the rule does not have the force of law, and compliance is voluntary and not legally mandatory, as with rules about keeping promises to friends and taking care of indigent parents. Second, which rules are best can vary from society to society, because of conditions in one society that are not present in another. In a desert society, it might be a good rule to prohibit the wasting of water (see p. 18); but in societies where water is plentiful, such a rule would have no good effects. Rules penalizing lack of punctuality might be desirable in an industrial society (since much time is lost if a worker is a half-hour late from lunch and thereby holds up all the other workers on the assembly line); but in an agrarian society there is much less need to be punctual. With these clarifications in mind, let's consider a few examples from the perspective of rule-utilitarianism.

Example 1. David Hume, one of the first proponents of rule-utilitarianism, constantly emphasized the importance of following general rules, even though not every case falling under the rule would have the best consequences. He gave the following example. A wealthy man leaves his fortune to his spendthrift son, whereas you and others believe (with good reason) that he would have done more good by leaving it to charity instead, and you and they would like to "break the will." Let's admit that far better consequences would have occurred if the man had left his fortune to charity rather than to his son. Still, said Hume, the rule (in this case embodied in law) that people should be free to leave their money to whomever they designate as their heirs is a good one: the money is the father's, and it is for him to decide to whom it should be left. Besides, the knowledge that his business and other assets will be left to his son on his death provides an incentive to the man to keep on working so that the son can carry on the family business. It's not that the son deserves it but rather that the father, since it's his money, should be free to leave it to whomever he chooses. (If, as others claim, the son has no right to it, since the father earned it and not he, do those who criticize the father's decision, who didn't earn it either, have a right to determine where it should go after the father's death?) Now, said Hume, even though applying the rule in this case may cause more harm than good, it is more important not to tamper with the rule. The rule is a good one, the best general rule that could be adopted with regard to wills. This being the case, the rule should be followed in spite of its not having the best results in every single case. Having a rule to cover all cases of a certain kind, and keeping the rule inviolable, will also provide an important element of predictability: the father can rest quite secure in the knowledge that the will won't be broken and that the money will go to whomever he designates. When you have a good rule, you shouldn't tamper with it unless you can think of a better one and show that it *is* better.

Example 2. Is "Always keep your promises" a good rule? At once we can think of exceptions. Not if the promise was made under duress, like the promise to give a burglar the contents of your wallet. Not if it was a bad promise to begin with, such as the promise to be a Mafia hit man. Not if by breaking the promise you could achieve some very great good, such as saving someone's life. A rule-utilitarian would try to qualify the original rule "Always keep your promises" in such a way as to improve it, that is, to make it a better rule (one whose adoption would have better consequences than the unamended one). Each proposed amendment would be viewed with an eye to whether it would thus improve the rule. Not every proposed amendment would, of course: if someone suggested, the amendment "Promises should be kept unless they were made in secret," this addition would not improve the rule, for though there may be considerable utility in breaking such promises—the promise made in the Arctic, promises made to your dying father, and so on—the world would be somewhat worse off if people could not rely on the keeping of such promises. For traditional *act-utilitarians,* the fact that the promise was secret (and thus could not set a bad example to others and have other bad consequences) would make breaking such a promise more excusable than breaking a publicized one; but for rule-utilitarians this would make no difference at all. They would consider only the consequences of the general *practice* of following the original rule, as opposed to the consequences of the general practice of following one or another of the amended rules.

How much should a rule be amended? As much as it takes to improve it. If a proposed amendment to a rule makes it worse, it can be discarded, and if it leaves the consequences unchanged, it can be ignored. If someone proposed the amendment "People should keep their promises except on Tuesdays," rule-utilitarians could reject such an amendment because it wouldn't improve the rule: as far as anyone knows, the consequences of promise keeping on Tuesdays are the same as the consequences of promise keeping on any other day of the week. If the world were different, so that promises kept on Tuesdays always resulted in catastrophe, the proposed amendment would increase the utility of the rule. But since its being a Tuesday makes no difference, rule-utilitarians would reject this irrelevant amendment and adopt only those which if adopted would make the rule better.

Example 3.   What is the best rule concerning the use of force against other persons? "Never use physical force against others against their will" would be one possible rule. (The provision "against their will" would take care of cases in which people want a masseur to slap them, as well as cases of masochists who want to be whipped; in these instances there is no *unwilling* use of force.) But if someone pulls a gun on you, shouldn't you be free to defend yourself, even though the aggressor doesn't *want* you to use retaliatory force against him? We have already seen what happens if you accept the simple utilitarian generalization "Don't use unwilling force against anyone, because if no one did, we would have a peaceful world": nonpeaceful persons would use the rule to get rid of peaceful persons. A better rule would be "Don't engage in the use of physical force (against the other person's wishes) except in self-defense"—that is, unless the other person has initiated force against you. This rule prohibits you from injuring, maiming, and killing other people, unless they initiate such action against you, and in that case you may respond in kind. It doesn't have the disastrous consequences that complete pacifism would. If nobody raises a hand against you, there is no reason for violence on your part, but if someone does, the rule permits you to respond in order to protect yourself. Indeed, this rule accords well with the laws prevailing in most nations: when fights break out, the first question a court asks is, "Who started it?" If you can prove that you were only defending yourself against someone else's aggressive act, you are not guilty before the law, even though you did use force against the aggressor.

Note that the rule applies not to some ideal world but to this world, with all its imperfections. It doesn't say that you should never use force because universal peace would result if nobody did; such a rule ignores the facts of the actual world in which we live. The present rule takes account of the fact that there are aggressors in the world and provides for that contingency by permitting you to defend yourself against them.

What rule-utilitarians desire is not just a good rule but the *best* one for the kind of behavior in question (in this case, the use of force against others). It may be that the rule "Don't use force against others except in self-defense," although an improvement over the previous one that permits no self-defense, is still not the best one. What further qualifications or amendments to the rule might improve it? There are several possibilities. (1) Why does an act of force have to be in *self*-defense? Why can't it be in defense of family, friends, strangers, or anyone who is the victim of aggression? If you see someone being held up or mugged on a dark street, shouldn't you be permitted to use force on the aggressor to save the victim? Doesn't any such act of aggression make it morally permissible for a would-be rescuer to come to the victim's aid? (2) Is it necessarily the case that only the use of *force* entitles you to respond with force? Suppose someone is trying to bait you and repeatedly calls your wife a whore and your mother even less complimentary names. Are you supposed to keep quiet and do nothing until the individual actually pulls a knife or a gun? (3) It may be that not the actual use of force but the *threat* of use of force entitles you to respond. Anticipatory response is a dangerous business, because you may shoot someone thinking that he or she is about to shoot you, which may not be the case: perhaps it's all a bluff, or the aggressor has a change of mind. Yet if you wait till you've actually been shot, it's a bit too late. There must, then, be good evidence, perhaps overwhelming evidence, or evidence "beyond a reasonable doubt," that someone is about to shoot you. (The code of the West was that if a man reached for his gun, you could shoot him first to prevent him from shooting you.) (4) What *degree* of force is permissible? In most states you may not shoot a trespasser on your property, but after someone has broken into your house you may shoot in order to stop the intruder, since by that time it's clear what the purpose is. But suppose the intruder is unarmed; may you use a gun then? Or suppose the housebreaker has a toy pistol which you mistake for a real one? The law prescribes that you use "the minimum force necessary" to neutralize an act of aggression: if you shoot a person in the leg you are legally in the clear, whereas if you hit him in the head you may not be. But it is very difficult to know, on a moment's notice and in the dark of night, how much force an intruder is prepared to use and what means he has to wield it. This is a "gray area" in the law which has not been worked out to everyone's satisfaction. The answer seems to vary so much with the circumstances of the individual case that it is practically impossible to state in advance any general rules—rules that aren't so vague as to be subject to widely varying interpretations.

Nevertheless, in all this the attempt is to find the *best rule*. We have seen how difficult it is to find it: no matter what formulation is decided on, there is always the possibility of finding a better one by qualifying the rule further. The rule finally hit on as the best may be extremely complex, with many qualifying clauses. But this complexity is a price that must be paid for finding the best possible rule.

But now another question is pressing: What is meant by the "consequences of the rule"? A rule itself doesn't have consequences; only the *adoption* of it does. We are inclined to add that it is the adoption of it by everybody that matters. But who is "everybody"? In the case of a law, the "everybody" is quite clear: if it's a federal law, everybody in the nation is required (under penalty) to obey it, and if it's a state law, everybody in the state, and so on. In these cases whether a rule should be adopted depends on whether a law should be passed. When we ask whether a law is good or bad, according to rule-utilitarianism, we answer by determining what are the probable consequences of passing a certain law for that geographical area.

But in the case of a rule of conduct that does not have the force of law, such as the keeping of promises, voluntary adoption of a rule of conduct is involved. We may ask what the consequences of everyone adopting a rule of conduct would be, but here the "everyone" is more vague. It varies from case to case: sometimes "everyone" could be just the community in which we live, sometimes any area in which we travel (outside of which the rule of conduct might not affect us), sometimes the entire nation or even the world. Nor need it be quite "everyone": if a small percentage of people broke a rule of conduct, the consequences of it might not be so serious as to make the rule ineffective, but if a very large number of people (say, 75 percent) broke it, that might cast some doubt on whether, under the circumstances, you should also break it (as in the case of cheating on exams).

And so we have two distinct issues: (1) the consequences of the adoption of a rule, if *everybody* (in the society, the community, or wherever) observes it, and (2) the consequences of the adoption of a rule if *some* or *most* people fail to observe it. What you or I should do seems to depend on whether other people, and how many of them, will break the rule. If the rule is a good one—that is, if it would have the best possible consequences if everyone observed it—should it still be followed if *not* everyone observes it or if a large number of people fail to observe it? Let's consider a few examples.

Example 1. Suppose you are habitually prompt in keeping your appointments: if someone wants to see you at two o'clock, you don't keep her waiting fifteen minutes. But suppose that most people of your acquaintance (*not* necessarily everyone in the world) are usually late and that finally your promptness strikes them as a bit strange: when, having been asked to a party at eight, you arrive then but nobody is there yet and the hostess isn't ready, you are actually believed to have arrived early. In such a case should you keep on being prompt? Maybe it would be a good rule for everyone to be prompt; but most people aren't. Doesn't that make a difference?

Example 5. A sign says, "Do not walk on the grass." Many people ignore the sign and cut across the grass anyway. Should you obey the sign or take the shortcut? The example seems trivial, but it illustrates the problem we are examining very neatly, for the answer seems to depend on how many people have already violated the rule. (If there was a considerable chance of being fined for walking on the grass, you would have a reason not to do so regardless of other people's violations; but let us assume that the chance of being fined for this is negligible.) If no one else has violated the rule, you have no reason to violate it either (except perhaps in emergency cases). If the grass has been walked over so much that it's already dead, you have no reason to make the detour: you won't save the grass by making the detour. (At most, you may set an example to others who see you do it.) The difficult question is: What if many people have obviously broken the rule already and the grass is trampled over to a considerable degree, but not yet beyond recovery? Should you observe the rule then?

There is a case to be made for saying that *if* the rule is a good one, you should observe it even if many other people have not. The reasoning is as follows: if it was right for *me* to violate a good rule, then it would be right for *other* people also to violate the same rule; yet if *all* of us violated the rule, the consequences would be bad. In other words, if it was all right for me to break the rule, then it was equally all right for *A, B, C, D,* and so on to break it (assuming that I had no more justification for breaking it than they did), yet if we all broke it, a good rule would have gone down the tubes.

What if the rule is a good one, but I don't know whether others will violate it or not? Then I should not violate it. For suppose *A* violates it, saying, *"B, C, D,* and others are going to violate it anyway." And *B* says to himself, "I might as well violate the rule, because A, C, D, and still others are going to violate it anyway." And so it goes for all the others. A good rule thus would be violated by everyone, with ensuing bad consequences, just because each person thought that the others were going to violate it. It is only when I know that others have violated a rule to such a degree that nothing is any longer achieved by my observing it that I am entitled to violate it myself. One commentator summarizes the point this way:

> When a [rule] utilitarian asks himself what others would probably do in his circumstances, consistency does not demand that he shall assume . . . that they will be asking the same question and will be guided by the degree of their assurance about the answer to it. The question for him is rather: "What ought *any* man to do in a world in which not all men do as they ought?"[5]

Example 6. "Why should I pay my taxes? I owe $500 for this year, and if I don't pay it, the government won't miss the money. It wastes more than that every second. But the $500 means a lot to me, and I could put it to excellent use." Here, it is true that the consequences of *your* not paying would not be catastrophic, but a catastrophe might result if *nobody* paid. If you were an act-utilitarian you could well argue that the consequences of your not paying would be negligible and therefore you need not pay, while still admitting that the consequences of everyone not paying would be catastrophic. (Tax rebels and advocates of the privatization of all public services would not grant the bad consequences if no one paid. But in this example let us assume that there would be such consequences.) The contention is not, "The consequences of *my* failure to pay would be bad," but rather, "The consequences of *everyone* failing to pay would be bad." What should *you* do? Rule-utilitarians reply: "If *you* are entitled to break the rule, then *others* are entitled to break the rule. Yet if everyone (or even a large percentage of the population) was permitted to break the rule, the consequences would be bad. So you are not entitled to break it either."

[5] A. K. Stout, "But Suppose Everyone Did the Same?" *Australian Journal of Philosophy* 32 (1954): 22.

Is it really true that the consequences would be catastrophic if not everyone observed the rule—if even one person violated it? Certainly not; far more than one person violates it and the country still staggers on. As in the voting case, the "everybody" doesn't really mean everybody. Still, the more people violate the rule, the more the treasury will be wanting, and, in order to make up for the deficits caused by the nonpayers, the higher the taxes are likely to be on those who pay. Assuming that we all get benefits from the services of government (a large assumption, since many would say we get more burdens than benefits), everyone should contribute to the receiving of those services by paying his or her share into the fund that provides the benefits. (There are, as usual, special circumstances. Perhaps some are paying entirely too much in relation to others, but that would be an argument for reducing your tax, not for eliminating it. Other considerations connected with this example, such as fairness, have not been raised in this example either.)

Example 7. I give a certain student a C in a course, believing this to be the grade she deserves. After the term is over the student comes to me and pleads to have it changed to a B. I look over her written work again and am all the more convinced that she deserves no more than a C. She then confesses that she was lazy during the course and didn't deserve a B but requests a change of grade on an entirely different basis: she has to retain a certain grade average to get into medical school, and a C in my course will put her just below that average. "You don't want to block my whole professional career, do you?" she asks and then adds, "I'll be happier if you change the grade. You may be unhappy for a little while but you'll soon forget about it. Nobody else will know, so there will be no effect on others, like students who did a little better than I did and still got C's. So from a utilitarian point of view you ought to give me the B."

I assent to all this, but I still believe it would be wrong to change the grade. After all, if she doesn't get into medical school, another person will be admitted in her place who didn't have to cheat to preserve his grade average. Also, I would feel guilty about the change, and I might be tempted to do the same thing another time, which will probably be easier to do then since I have the present case as a precedent. But the most important consideration is this: the purpose of the grading system is to represent the student's actual achievement in each course. If I give her a B, the graduate school or her future employer and anybody else who examines her record will believe, falsely, that she has achieved a certain level of competence in my course. It's not that I believe the consequences of this one act would be so bad (especially if nobody found out and no one examined her record), but that if every teacher engaged in this practice, or even if a great many teachers did it, the entire grading system would be undermined.

It could be argued that the grading system we have isn't so great, so the undermining of it would be no tragedy. But thus far any attempts to change it have proved less satisfactory than the present system: if you are graded

Pass or Fail, graduate schools have no idea whether you have just barely passed or passed with distinction (and the latter students might be overlooked in the granting of scholarships); and grading on the degree of improvement leads some students to pretend to be very stupid at the beginning of a course so that they can exhibit lots of improvement between the beginning and the end of the course. So, it appears that having a system of grades, based on achievement in courses, is a good thing to have and that abiding by it has on the whole better consequences than any alternative. Therefore I should stick with that system, not because it produces consequences that are the best in every individual case, but because the rule (grade according to achievement) is on the whole a good one, better than any alternative, and I should not do anything to compromise the effectiveness of the rule.

The student might retort that I'm really not compromising the rule very much by making an exception in this case, especially if nobody else knows about it. But I am trying to protect the rule, not the individual case: I argue that if I can make an exception to the rule in this case, I can do so in another case, and so can other instructors. If I have a right to falsify the true grade, so do all the others on the instructional staff. And the result of this would be to make the whole system unworkable, which *would* be a considerable consequence. If I were an act-utilitarian, I might well change the grade; but as a rule-utilitarian, I would not. (There are other considerations involved here as well, such as fairness and justice, but these will not be taken up until Chapter 8.) If it was clear that most, or even a large percentage of instructors, were falsifying grades, then I might be tempted to do so myself (though even then I might do better to work for the abandonment of the present grading system); but since I have no such knowledge, I ask instead, "What ought any person to do (in these circumstances) in a world in which not all people do as they ought?"

Objections to Rule-Utilitarianism

Contrasted with act-utilitarianism, rule-utilitarianism appears to provide a satisfactory solution to many moral problems which people confront with act-utilitarianism. Still, there are some objections which have been made to rule-utilitarianism as well.

1. If we are to go by the consequences of (adopting) rules rather than the consequences of acts, we must have rules to guide us in every situation. But what happens when new or unique situations arise, not covered by any known rules of conduct? Consider just one situation: a spaceship lands nearby, obviously not from earth, and we wait for whatever creatures are inside to come out. Are they friendly? Are they hostile? Perhaps we should wait and see. They may satisfy our astronomical curiosity about outer space and our biological curiosity about other forms of life; indeed, they may be

more technologically and morally advanced than we are and be able to tell us much to help in solving our own problems. What an opportunity! On the other hand, what if they wish to take over the earth, and the moment the door opens they will release a poison which will instantly exterminate all earthly life? If we assume they are benevolent, we may all be killed immediately; but if we assume they are malevolent, we may, by "nuking" them, lose our only opportunity to make contact with other forms of life. There is simply no evidence either way. Have we any rules covering this kind of situation? We could try to make one up on the spot, of course. But how do we know it would be a good one? Very likely we would wonder, not what *rule* to devise, but what *particular act* to perform under these unusual circumstances.

2. There are, furthermore, situations in which rules, even good rules, conflict. "Never knowingly punish innocent persons" and "Take all due steps to stop the rapid spread of a plague" are two good rules. But what if the only way to stop the plague is to kill instantly suspected carriers of it? We would probably end up killing the carriers (who can't help being carriers) in order to stop the plague, but then what happens to our first rule? Of course we could qualify the rule by saying, "Never kill innocent persons except . . . "; but how are we then going to be able to state in advance all the possible exceptions? And if any rule seems to demand no exceptions and, indeed seems to be the paradigm case of a good rule, it is the one prohibiting the killing of the innocent. Once that rule goes, what rule is safe?

We could say that in case of conflict of rules there are second-order rules to indicate which of the first-order rules takes priority. But how do we determine such second-order rules? And what happens in the case of a clash of second-order rules? Can we keep going to infinity?

3. The act-utilitarian, for one, will consider rule utilitarianism a kind of "rule worship." If I know in a particular case which act *will* have the best consequences, why should I turn my back on that and discover which rule *would,* if adopted, have the best consequences, especially when that rule may not have the best consequences *in this case?* If I follow the rule even in such a case, I would knowingly be doing an act which has something *less* than the best consequences. In other words, I would be producing less good by following the optimific rule than I would by doing the optimific act. To the act-utilitarian it seems silly to say, "Following the rule has the best consequences most of the time, so therefore you should follow it this time as well, even knowing that this time it does *not* have the best consequences." By adhering to the rule instead of the act, we would be making the world somewhat worse than we would if we had done the optimific act itself.

4. Some critics have voiced the suspicion that rule-utilitarians first consider certain acts to be right or wrong, and then tailor the rule so as to fit those acts. Consider one of the numerous cases discussed by moral philosopher Richard Taylor:

A man of military age decides to resist a summons to serve; he will go to jail first, or perhaps flee the country. Why? "Because killing is wrong" (the appeal to a principle). Does he mean *all* killing is wrong—for that is what the principle seems to assert—such that one may not innocently swat a mosquito that is biting him, for example? This he dismisses as pettifogging. Obviously, what he is talking about is killing *people*. This is what is wrong, and because serving in war might oblige him to do it, he will, in obedience to his conscience, resist serving. (Here, it will be noted, "conscience" comes into the picture and plainly means nothing more than allegiance to a principle.)

So the principle—and it is a slightly new one—is that it is always, without exception, wrong to kill any *man*. Then one may not drive a car, even with due care, over any considerable distance on crowded highways, or build great bridges or tunnels for human convenience, or fly in airplanes, because all such activities clearly risk life, and in fact take great tolls of it each day? This he again dismisses as pettifogging—he was not talking of that sort of thing. What he meant was the *deliberate* taking of human life—shooting at people, and that sort of thing. That is what is morally wrong, and is always so. So the principle, it must not be overlooked, has been changed still again.

At this point the discussion can go in either of two directions, each of which will, in its own way, get us a bit further from the question at hand. First, one can seek a definition of "deliberate," which will conveniently serve to rule out what the man wants to rule out while preserving what he wants to preserve—a definition, for example, that will enable one to say that driving down crowded highways is not deliberate, whereas marching off to boot camp, the alternative being jail, is.

Or secondly, one can skip all that and look at the new principle here. Suppose we go in the second direction. Here someone will say, "What if a madman is approaching your wife and children with a knife, bent on cutting them to pieces, and you can only stop him by shooting at him?" Or, perhaps, "What if your wife were pregnant, but in such a way that her life could only be preserved by an abortion?" Or other cases of that sort that are, of course, proposed as the *deliberate* taking of human life.

Now the challenge is to modify the principle still once more, thus producing what is really a new principle—and so on and on. But here is the thing to note: At every stage of this attempted justification, a moral principle, already enunciated, is modified for the obvious purpose of *ruling out* those cases to which it *does not apply*. And why does it "not apply" to these? Not, obviously, because they do not in fact fall under it, for they do. If killing is wrong (period), then killing a mosquito is wrong. The principle is thought not to apply to these cases because they are *not* considered morally wrong. It is thought to be no sin to kill a mosquito, drive a car with due care, or (perhaps) even permit an abortion in some circumstance. The principle was not *meant* to cover things of this sort. What it was *meant* to cover is the thing with which we began: going off to war.

But now look at what has happened. It is assumed that we already know, without appealing to any principle, that certain things are *not wrong*. Moreover, someone seems to be assuming, before he even has any principle to justify it, that something *is* wrong, and the only job then is to tailor some principle to show why it is wrong. This is the whole course of the discussion. Something is just assumed to be wrong and other things not wrong, quite independently of any principles of right and wrong, and then the whole discussion is aimed at finding some principle that will *fit* what is thus already assumed. This is not the justification of anything. It is at best a game of definition, and at worst, pure rationalization.[6]

5. Perhaps the problem of special pleading can be overcome; perhaps rules can be formulated without rationalization or *ad hoc* definitions. Even so, the prospect of finding a rule to cover every kind of situation is one of dizzying complexity. Suppose you are a member of a family in which everyone regularly tells the truth to every other member, in a firm but friendly manner, sparing nothing if the remark is believed to be true. The members of the family become accustomed to this practice and expect it. Even though "the truth may hurt" at the time, in the end they are all happier for it; each person knows where he or she stands and knows too that no one else in the family is going to lie or "pull something" on him or her.

Now suppose that you, as a member of this family, come to move about in families and other circles in which this practice of truth telling is not adopted. People tell "white lies"—deliberate untruths told to spare others' feelings—and even though they have the best of intentions, they often succeed only in making others wonder whether they are being told the truth. Some people in these families even court lies if they are flattering. ("Tell me something nice about me; I want to hear it, even if it's not true.") You wonder how they can derive satisfaction from this practice, but apparently they do, and for them it fills a genuine need.

Suppose that you sincerely believe that truth telling is the best policy and would be the best rule of behavior. Now, do you want to elevate this policy, so successful in your own family, to the status of a general rule covering all cases and circumstances? Would you move into those other circles and have all members tell the truth unsparingly? Might you not be disturbing and upsetting them without benefiting them? Wouldn't you at least believe it better to introduce your total-truth policy gradually? How, then, would you formulate a rule about such a situation? Would the rule be "Always tell the

---

[6] Richard Taylor, *Good and Evil* (New York: Macmillan, 1970), pp. 164–65. Reprinted by permission of The Macmillan Co.

truth, except when people aren't accustomed to it, in which case do it gradually, until they are"? Such a rule is certainly vague: How fast is "gradually"? Might not the pace of implementing a total-truth policy differ from case to case? Besides, some people never would get used to the new policy. They might be "so far gone" that they would always feel more disturbed than happy, even more harmed than benefited, from such unsparing revelations. Considering all these individual differences from person to person, family to family, society to society, is there any way you can possibly encapsulate your "best rule about truth telling" into a statable general rule, even a very complex one? Isn't the whole situation so fluid that you have to "play it by ear" for every case, without being able to give any specific rule in advance? And in that event, what happens to the rule-utilitarian ideal of the general rule whose adoption will have the best consequences?

6. A different kind of attack on moral rules comes from the *existentialists*. Existentialism is not primarily a theory of ethics at all: its main ethical tenet is that the main characteristic of human life is the omnipresence of choice. All actions imply choices; even when I do not consciously choose, my action is what it is because of previous choices, or, sometimes "implicit choices" (though it is difficult to say just what this phrase means). Certain criteria may govern my choices, but they are themselves chosen, and, says the existentialist, no rational grounds exist for these choices: we simply "commit" ourselves to them without the possibility of justification. No one general rule of action has more validity than any other.

But there is another reason why rules are useless as guides to action: each decision must be made in the context of the particular situation in which we find ourselves, and every situation is different: yours is different from mine, and mine is different at time t_1 from what it is at t_2. Any moral rule would have to have the form "In circumstances C_1, do A," and "in circumstances C_2, do B," but the precise concatenation of events in circumstances C_1 and C_2 never recur, so the rule would apply to only one case. French existentialist writer Jean-Paul Sartre (1905–1980) gave the example of the Frenchman during World War II who felt an obligation to join others in fighting for the Free French against the Nazis, but who also felt an obligation to stay at home as the sole support of his indigent mother.[7] His situation was not exactly like anyone else's, not even that of another male civilian of military age who was also the sole support of his indigent mother. *He* had to decide what to do in his unique case, and no general rule would have been of any help to him. Whichever way he decided, he would not be entitled to universalize his decision by saying, "And anyone in my situation should do as I do." Each situation is unique, as is each person, and no general rules of conduct can be forthcoming in view of this double uniqueness.

Not everyone, however, would respond favorably to this skepticism about

[7]Jean-Paul Sartre, *L'Existentialisme est un Humanisme* (Paris: n. p., 1946), p. 39; translated by Walter Kaufmann in his *Existentialism from Dostoyevsky to Sartre* (New York: Meridian Books, 1956), p. 295.

general rules. Difficult though they may be to formulate, especially in conflict situations, once an individual has decided what should be done, many, including British philosopher R. M. Hare, would say with Kant that he or she must believe that *if* there was someone else in exactly the same situation, that person should act likewise.

> I should not expect him to produce quickly some simple maxim; he would, no doubt, find it extremely hard to formulate in words any universal proposition to cover the case. But I should be sure that he would consider the particular case carefully and sympathetically in all its details, and after doing that try to find a solution to which I could commit, not only myself, but, as Sartre puts it, "the whole of humanity."[8]

7. Though many disagree with the existentialist critique, they still believe rule-utilitarianism is flawed. A frequently heard criticism is that rule-utilitarianism, far from being contrasted with act-utilitarianism, actually collapses into it. The two are "extensionally equivalent": though formulated differently, the verdicts of both theories on any actual question turn out to be the same.

Rules, if they are to have the best consequences possible if adopted and if they are to be made to cover all situations, must be qualified over and over again. Let's begin with "Stop at a red traffic light." The qualifications that would improve the rule might include "unless the car is an ambulance" (or rather "unless it's an ambulance with the siren going," since if it weren't it could collide with many cars at an intersection) and also "unless it's a fire truck or police car" (again, with siren on).

But these are only the obvious qualifications. Suppose that in an ordinary civilian car, you are transporting someone to the emergency ward of a hospital; the person is losing blood fast and his life is at stake. May you go through the light then? No, we may say, because you may hit other cars. But suppose you keep your horn blowing. And suppose you can see in both directions, and there is no car coming either way. That might be all right. But now suppose it's not quite such a dire emergency, but you are in a great hurry to get to an important engagement; it's three in the morning, you know the area well, the road is always deserted at that time, and you can see well in both directions. Again, the rule becomes questionable.

The problem is, aren't there a myriad of possible situations, most of which you might never think of till the occasion arises, in which it might be all right to go through the light—and thus qualify still more the rule that says you shouldn't? Even the color and visibility of your vehicle and the driving habits of the driver could turn out to be relevant. All such qualifications would be too complicated to put in an actual law of the land, of course. But our problem is to find the rule that if adopted would have the best conse-

---

[8] R. M. Hare, *Freedom and Reason* (Oxford, Eng.: Clarendon Press, 1963), p. 48.

quences. And might not such a rule be infinitely, or at least indefinitely, complex, with thousands of "if's" and "unless's" in it?

What would be the point of trying to find such a rule? Couldn't we shorten the whole search and simply say, "Do not go through a stoplight, except in those cases where doing so would result in maximum net expectable utility"? Then whatever unanticipated situation arose, it would already be taken care of in advance by the except clause. That ploy would save a lot of trouble, and we would have all the contingencies already embodied in the rule. But such a rule would be an act-utilitarian formula over again. The ideal rule would be the rule that maximizes good, and that is already given by the act-utilitarian formula. In practice, then, rule-utilitarianism, adding one qualification upon another, has become equivalent to act-utilitarianism.

In fact, we could formulate every rule as follows:

Don't take human life, except when doing so will maximize good.
Don't break promises, except when doing so will maximize good.
Don't take what belongs to others, except when doing so will maximize good.
Don't annoy your neighbors, except when doing so will maximize good.

But all such rules can easily be generalized into "Don't do anything that doesn't maximize good," which is the act-utilitarian principle over again.

It is doubtful, however, whether all rule-utilitarian cases can be reduced as easily to act-utilitarian ones. The voting case and others in which the consequences of a single act are negligible but those of everyone doing the same act are considerable (i.e., cases in which the single act has a value of almost zero, say X, but the consequences of 1,000 people doing it are more than 1,000X) don't seem to be touched by this criticism. But even in such cases, we saw some reason for not following the rule always: the fact that many people will not follow the rule will make a difference as to whether I should because of the consequences (not of the rule, but of *my* following or violating the rule).

We can also reformulate rule-utilitarianism to escape the objection. We can say, with good reason, that rules of great complexity cannot be learned by most people; also even if a highly complex rule occupying three pages would be the best possible rule if everyone (or most people) followed it, it would not be followed because it could not be remembered or perhaps even comprehended. That is why primitive tribes have to have a small number of simple and easily understandable rules; these would have the best consequences *given the mentality of tribal members,* even though, *if* they could understand and remember more complex rules, the complex ones would yield better results. The same applies to children. To a lesser degree, it also applies to the average adult. Even fairly complex legal rules are less effective than they might be, since most people cannot understand or remember them. And so we can stop the endless array of qualifications to rules (each designed to improve it) by specifying that a set of rules must be *learnable in a reasonable period of time* by the average person of the society in question. Thus, the highly complex rule that would be the best one if everyone followed it would not turn out to be the best in practice, because most people would be unable to follow it. If we allow only rules that are not overly complex, rule-utilitarianism would not have to collapse into act-utilitarianism.

To be sure, the act-utilitarian's rule "Do what maximizes good" *is* brief and simple. The trouble with it is not that it is too complex to understand, but that it is too difficult to apply in practice. Suppose that you taught your children only the rule "Do whatever produces the most good." What would happen? They wouldn't know where to begin in applying it to specific kinds of behavior. They wouldn't know how it would apply to stealing, to cheating, to beating up on little brother, and so on. Children need instruction on what to do in specific kinds of situations—what to do, what not to do, what not to do except in circumstance *C,* and other simple kinds of rules. If they were given the act-utilitarian principle and nothing else, they would usually end up rationalizing: they would calculate that whatever they happened to want to do (such as ride a bicycle very fast or not study until next month) would be what *really* would produce the maximum good. They would be adrift in a stormy sea without any compass.

8. There remain objections to rule-utilitarianism of a much more general kind, however. Act-utilitarians consider our only obligation to be to do acts that produce the best consequences; rule-utilitarians consider our only duty to be to act in accordance with rules that produce the best consequences. But is duty limited to the production of the best consequences? Have we really overcome Ross's objection that because some duties are past-looking and not future-looking, there are special duties to special people for special reasons, other than the single duty to produce the best consequences all round? Most of us persist in believing that we have special duties to our children that we do not have to others, because we brought the children into the world. Has rule-utilitarianism really shown itself to be an improvement on act-utilitarianism in this respect?

Perhaps it has. Rule-utilitarians might suggest that the best rule is "Take care of your own children first, and others only as you are able," and that this rule would have the best consequences if everyone adopted it. The rule may well be a good one, but is the reason for adopting it the one given by rule-utilitarians, namely that such a rule has the highest possible *utility?* If adopting the rule didn't have the highest utility, wouldn't we still have special obligations to (for example) the children we have brought into the world?

It may also be that the practice of keeping promises is the best one (with the usual qualifications about duress and so on), but is the reason why we should keep promises the fact (if it is a fact) that the general practice of promise keeping has the highest utility, or is it just possibly, in addition, the fact that we *made* the promise? But no such past-looking duty can be admitted into utilitarianism without destroying the theory. Utilitarianism is a consequentialist theory or it is nothing.

9. We have not yet discussed the issue of rights and justice, but criticisms have come from those concerned with such issues as well. Suppose that there was a rule whose adoption would produce as much utility as any other and also that there was a second rule whose adoption would produce an equal amount of utility, and that no other rule would produce as much. But now suppose that the first rule permitted the commission of injustices (e.g., one person having to assume burdens for many others although all reaped equal benefits) or that it involved the violation of some fundamental human right (e.g., the killing of a few people in order to make others better off), and suppose that the second rule, whose adoption had equally good consequences, involved no such injustice or right violation. Wouldn't the adoption of the second rule be preferable to the adoption of the first rule? It would certainly seem to most people that it would, though not because of its greater utility, since the utility of the two, according to our assumption, are the same. The superiority of the second rule would rest on different grounds—that it involved no injustice and no violation of rights. These are matters to which we must now turn.

EXERCISES

1. After reading the following list of moral situations, try to determine what solution a utilitarian would recommend. Then try to determine what solution a disciple of Ross would recommend and why. (Do any of these examples impel you to add to Ross's list of prima facie duties?)

   a. "I did you lots of favors, didn't I? Besides, I am your brother, and so you owe me something. And you also promised me that if I ever wanted you to do something for me, you would. Well, I'm asking you now. I want you to help me get even with this guy. You engage him in conversation during his walk through the park, and I'll come up from behind, knock him out, and then rob him."

   b. Ordinarily you would not hesitate to tell the authorities where an escaped murderer is hiding. But he once saved your life, when he could just as easily have ignored you; in fact, by saving yours, he risked losing his own. You feel that you should not do anything to cause him now to lose his. Should you reveal his location to the authorities?

   c. A capable young actress who for years has been trying to get a break, is offered a part in a play which may bring her fame and fortune. But she strongly disapproves of the idea she is called upon to express in her lines, and she believes the entire play is evil and immoral. She knows that if she turns down the part, other actresses are ready to step into her place and perhaps handle the part less capably than she. The play is going to be performed anyway, regardless of what she does. Should she nevertheless turn down the part?

d. A man who made his fortune from Mafia activities and houses of prostitution makes a gift of $500,000 to a church, offering to keep his name (together with the source of funds) a secret. Church committee members try to decide whether to accept the gift. By accepting it they can do a great deal of good; at the same time they feel that "it's dirty money" and that it will never be blessed coming from such a source.

e. "I can't understand why you are leaving so much money in your will to foreign organizations. Your first prima facie duty is to your own country."

f. You know who murdered your uncle; you saw it happen. But if you testify in court, the gang who killed him will hunt you down and kill you too. The police have offered you protection, but they can't do it for a lifetime, and anyway they can't be foolproof in their protection so you are still in danger. Should you testify, or should you save your skin by refusing, thereby allowing murderers to run loose?

g. An old woman lives with her grandchildren and depends on them for support. She is a Christian, but they are not. As a Christian she feels it her duty to try to convert as many people as possible to Christianity, and she devotes all her spare time to this end. She attends meetings and rallies, is active in church groups and the Salvation Army; but she asks herself what kind of a Christian she can call herself if she doesn't even pay attention to those in her own family. At the same time, she hesitates to try to influence her granddaughter and the granddaughter's husband, because she is beholden to them financially and depends on them for a roof over her head. Should she be less concerned for their souls because she depends on them for money?

h. A Catholic priest in Italy worked with the Allied underground, and one day bombed a supply train. As a result, the Nazis shot twenty hostages per day and promised to continue to do so until the culprit was found. But he did not give himself up to the authorities. When asked whether he failed to do so because of future deeds of valor which he would yet perform, he replied, "No. I am the only priest in this remote region, and the people depend on me for the sacraments. What dies is only the physical bodies of twenty hostages a day; we hope their immortal souls will be saved. But until there is another priest in this region to replace me, I must remain alive, for without me many souls cannot be saved; they depend upon me for absolution."

i. PERSON A: But it was only because I owed you the money and had to get it back to you somehow—that is why I resorted to bribery and illegal manipulations.

PERSON B: And am I expected to praise you for doing that? It's only because you took the money from me in the first place without my consent that you had to go to such lengths to return it; if you hadn't performed that initial act, all that followed would have been unnecessary. If you do something wrong, should I praise you for doing other things, no matter what, to redress the wrong, to restore the balance you destroyed? It's not as if you had done anything to *increase* the balance in my favor by performing those acts.

j. In a story taken from life (made famous in the motion picture *Call Northside 777*), an aged mother scrubs floors for almost twenty years to earn the money required to get lawyers to reopen the case for her son, who has been sentenced to life imprisonment for a murder he did not commit. Would she have been entitled (or had she a duty?) to gain the money by illegal means if she had been unable to do so in any other way?

k. The owner of a grocery store refuses to extend credit to any customer. His helper, nevertheless, extends credit to a poor family who, because of the husband's invalidism and the wife's illness, would otherwise go hungry. Would you say that the helper has a prima facie duty to obey his employer's orders? Does he also have a duty to produce good? Which should be paramount in this instance? (If there were no danger of the helper's being caught and losing his job, would it make any difference?)

l. One of Caesar's trusted servants came to him when Pompey, who was threatening Caesar's rule, and his fellow conspirators were guests on board Caesar's ship, and said, "I can put something into their drinks and get rid of them all at once" (or words to this effect). Caesar looked at him and said, "Alas, if you had done this without my knowledge, and come to me afterward, I would have praised you. But now that you have mentioned it to me beforehand, it is my duty to condemn you for it and take whatever measures I can to prevent you from realizing your plan."

2. Do you think that the duty of non-maleficence would prohibit you from ever inflicting harm on people in order that good may come out of it?

3. Assume that we have a prima facie duty of showing gratitude to our parents because of the things they have done for us. Now suppose our parents are shiftless good-for-nothings who have caused us much harm and no good (other than bringing us into the world in the first place). Is it still our duty to benefit them—more than other people—just because they are our parents? (If your father were a drunken scoundrel, would you arrive at a different conclusion in the burning building example?)

4. If we have prima facie duties to our parents for things they have done for us, do we have duties to our young children, who have as yet done nothing for us? (On what principle might you base the belief in a prima facie duty to your children?)

5. Does the duty of fidelity—for instance, to the wishes of the dead—require that we always abide by the terms of our parents' will? What if your father willed his entire estate to his cat?

6. Is your first duty to your family? Suppose you could be an excellent president of the United States but it would mean not being a good father to your family. Should you try to be elected?

7. Discuss the following exchanges:

a. PERSON A: I believe we have special duties of gratitude to those who have benefited us.

PERSON B: What a merry-go-round that would cause: A helps B, B helps A back, A helps B again, and so on. Life would become a series of curtsies and retreats. And meanwhile other people would stand in the background needing help much more. One wealthy snob introduces another one to a person he wanted to know; the second would later return the favor, and so on back and forth *ad nauseam*. (This is like the Kentucky feuds that never end, only with favors instead of harm.) Each person would think he or she had a special duty to the other because of past favors and would do it even though the other hadn't the slightest utilitarian *need* for it. Meanwhile others, who hadn't been caught up in this stupid merry-go-round of favors, would need the favors badly and never get them.

b. PERSON A: Except in direst extremity, promises should be kept. Making a promise commits you to keeping it.

PERSON B: Well, I should think it is more important to be sure you make the right promises in the first place. If you make a rash promise or a hasty one or an unreasonable one, you are less guilty for breaking it than you are for making such a promise in the first place. Suppose you promise someone you won't tell anyone what she is about to tell you, and she then confides in you that she is about to blow up the bank or kill her husband. Promises to keep a secret no matter what it is, are always unwise. What if you have promised to keep a secret that injures another or violates his or her rights? Then, it would seem, you've put yourself in the position of violating some rule no matter what you do—breaking your promise or standing by and seeing a great injustice done. It is less important to keep promises once made than to be very careful about what promises we make to begin with.

8. Do you feel that you have a stronger prima facie duty to your mother than to your father? To your children than to either parent? To your stepchildren than to your parents? To a neighbor than to an uncle you barely know? To your aunt than to your cousin? Do you have a duty to the brother of a friend? To a stranger recommended by a friend? To a third cousin you have never seen? To someone you knew in childhood but haven't seen for years? In short, does blood relationship make any difference, over and above the fact that you know and care for the person or that he or she has done things for you in the past?

9. To the question "Why did you do this?" each of the following answers refers to the past or present, not to the future. Evaluate each of them.

   a. Because Grandfather would have wanted me to.
   b. Because I said I would.
   c. Because it's the law (not because obeying the law will have good results).
   d. I used my influence to get theater tickets for him because he's a friend; I wouldn't do it for just anyone.
   e. I didn't cheat her because—well, one just doesn't do such things.
   f. Because that's the way I was brought up.
   g. Because it's not as bad stealing from a stranger as from a friend.

10. Is an Englishman who says, "I should do X because it would improve Britain's balance of payments" thereby committed by the generalization test to saying that he should do X if it would improve the balance of payments of some other country? That *anyone* should, if it's his own country? (See Don Locke, "The Trivializability of Universalizability," in *Readings in Ethical Theory,* ed. Wilfrid Sellars and John Hospers.)

11. If I believe I should eat dinner between six and seven in the evening, am I committed to saying that everyone ought to eat dinner then? If I believe that I should do farming for a living, am I committed to saying that everyone should farm for a living? (See Marcus Singer, *Generalization in Ethics,* Chapter 4.)

12. Department stores will sometimes spend $100 to collect a bill of $10. Is there any rule-utilitarian justification for their adoption of such a rule of conduct?

13. How would a rule-utilitarian handle the following situations? Pay special attention to the consideration, "But suppose everyone did the same."

   a. "If I do a bit of small pilfering from the office in which I work, the loss will be negligible. The few things I take mean more to me on my limited income than they would to the multimillionaire management."

b. "Why sell it legally? You can get much more for it on the black market."

c. "But it does make a difference whether everyone else does it too. I probably won't try to bribe a police officer on a traffic charge if no one else does, but if it's an accepted custom (however illegal) I shall be more inclined to do the same and to feel justified in doing it—especially if the money would only go for graft anyway if I paid it to the city and if my right action in refusing to bribe would not deter anyone else from doing it."

d. "Sure I stole the money out of the pockets of the man who was lying drunk in the gutter. If I hadn't done it, the next person would have, and I might as well get it as he. Besides, I probably needed it more."

e. "What do I care what my apartment looks like after I've moved out of it? I don't know the next tenant from a hole in the ground."

f. PERSON A: I'm going to stop eating beef and pork, on account of the inhumane way in which the animals are killed in slaughterhouses.
PERSON B: But how will *your* ceasing to eat meat cause more humane methods to be instituted?
PERSON A: It won't; but if everybody stopped until such time as humane methods were introduced, they would be introduced soon enough.

g. Labor union *A* demands a 25 percent pay-increase for its members (for doing no more work than they did before). Union *B* then demands similar increases for its members; union *C* and union *D* do the same. The producer of product *A* proportionately increases the cost of the product to the consumer, and so do the producers of *B, C,* and *D.* (See Henry Hazlitt, *Economics in One Lesson* [New York: Harper & Row, 1946], Chapter 19. This book contains much excellent illustrative material for rule-utilitarianism.)

h. "If everyone were celibate all his life mankind would soon die out. . . . If everyone suddenly stopped smoking, drinking, gambling, and going to the pictures, some states might go bankrupt." (From Kurt Baier, *The Moral Point of View* [Ithaca, N.Y.: Cornell University Press, 1958], p. 210. Reprinted by permission.)
Is abstinence from these things therefore wrong?

i. "Of course I'm not going to invest with them this year, because I don't think anyone else will either, and so they will go bankrupt. Why should I put my money into a sinking ship?"

14. Consider the following situations from the point of view of rule-utilitarianism. In which of them do you think the rule-utilitarian answer would be different from that of the act-utilitarian?

a. In Tennessee Williams's play *Suddenly, Last Summer,* a wealthy widow promises a large amount of money to support a much needed hospital, on condition that a certain female patient (who is quite sane) be committed as insane and have a lobotomy performed on her so that she will never make any trouble by revealing facts embarrassing to the wealthy widow. One life would be ruined, but many others, through the new hospital, would be saved.

b. Your neighbor refuses to put a yard light in his backyard even though the yard is considerably used and the terrain is treacherous in the dark. Should you, a neighbor, do it for him even though you do not use the yard?

    c. The miners, to be safe, take small quantities of condensed food with them into the mines each morning, to keep them going in case there should be a cave-in. A few of them, however, refuse, saying that this practice only serves to remind them that every day may be their last. One day there is a cave-in, and some of those entombed have no food with them. Should those who do share with those who don't, even though sharing might mean starvation for all of them before help comes, if it comes?

    d. Should the airlines institute a policy that pilots over sixty years of age may not pilot commercial planes? True, most of them are experts by the time they have flown that long, and the regulation would do them an injustice. On the other hand, a small number of them beyond that age have had heart attacks during flight, thus endangering all the passengers in the plane.

15. Evaluate the following interpretations of, or comments on, rule utilitarianism.

    a. According to rule-utilitarianism we really need only one rule: don't do the act in question unless performing it will (to the best of present available knowledge) result in the maximum intrinsic good. (Would the rule "Don't do *X*—steal, kill, etc.—except when *X* will do the most good" be the one whose adoption would produce the most good? Why?)

    b. Rule-utilitarianism turns out to be the same as act-utilitarianism in the end; for each class of actions (e.g., breaking promises, breaking promises to save a life, breaking promises to save a life when another life will be lost by so doing, breaking promises in this special circumstance *A, B, C* . . .—including just those particular circumstances I am in) can be so specified— relevantly specified—as to include *only that act* which I am performing or am about to perform. And thus rule-utilitarianism reduces to act-utilitarianism after all. All I have to do is circumscribe the rule sufficiently.

    c. PERSON A: If I accept utilitarian generalization, I should not use water during the prohibited hours (in a time of water shortage), because if everyone did so, the water supply would be dangerously depleted.
    PERSON B: But what if everyone else uses the water during prohibited hours?
    PERSON A: This makes no difference to me as a rule-utilitarian; I only reason, "*If* they did, the city would run out of water." And that is why I refrain.
    PERSON B: On the contrary, according to rule-utilitarianism you *should* take into account what others will probably do, for if the water supply is already depleted, the little bit that you use won't make any difference anyway. Why make a useless sacrifice?

    d. Rule-utilitarianism suffers from an infinite regress (or from what A. K. Stout calls an "infinite shuttle"); for when I consider what to do (whether I should vote, whether I should use the water, whether I should walk on the grass, etc.), I must include among my deliberations the consideration of whether or not others will do the same; and they, for their part, must equally include a consideration of whether others will do the same, and for them "others" *includes me*. In deciding how they will act, I must judge how I believe they will act; and they in their turn, in deciding how they will act, must have a belief about how I will probably act; and so I must have a belief about how they believe I will act, and so on. But how can they have a true belief about what my belief is, when my belief in turn depends on what their belief is? Their belief includes a belief about how I will act, but how can my belief include a belief about their-belief-about-how-I-will-act?

16. No matter how strongly most Americans may disapprove of the performance of a president, and however strongly they believe that his replacement would be for the good of the country, they seldom condone assassinating him. Could this position be justified by (a) act-utilitarianism? (b) rule-utilitarianism?

SELECTED READINGS

Multiple Sources of Obligation

Blanshard, Brand. "The Impasse in Ethics and a Way Out." *University of California Publications in Philosophy* 28 (1954): 93–112.
Brandt, Richard. *Ethical Theory.* Englewood Cliffs, N.J.: Prentice-Hall, 1959.
Price, Richard. *A Review of the Principal Questions in Morals* (1758).★ New York: Oxford University Press, 1949.
Prichard, Harold Arthur. "Moral Obligation" and "The Obligation to Keep a Promise." In his *Moral Obligation.* New York: Oxford University Press, 1949.
———. *The Right and the Good.* New York: Oxford University Press, 1930.
Raphael, David Daiches. *Moral Judgment.* New York: Macmillan, 1955.
Ewing, Alfred C. *Ethics.* New York: Macmillan, 1953. See Chapter 5.
Rashdall, Hastings. *The Theory of Good and Evil.* 2 vols. London: Oxford University Press, 1924.
Ross, William D. *Foundations of Ethics.* London: Oxford University Press, 1939.
———. *The Right and the Good.* London: Oxford University Press, 1930.

Utilitarian Generalization

Locke, Don. "The Trivializability of Universalizability." *Philosophical Review* 78 (January 1968): 25–44. Reprinted in Wilfrid Sellars and John Hospers, eds. *Readings in Ethical Theory.* Englewood Cliffs, N.J.: Prentice-Hall, 1970.
Lyons, David. *Forms and Limits of Utilitarianism.* Oxford, Eng.: Clarendon Press, 1964.
Singer, Marcus. "Generalization in Ethics." *Mind* 64 (1956): 361–75.
———. *Generalization in Ethics.* New York: Random House, 1961.
Sobel, Howard. "Generalization Arguments." *Theoria* 31 (1965): 32–60.

Rule-Utilitarianism

Brandt, Richard. *Ethical Theory.* Englewood Cliffs, N.J.: Prentice-Hall, 1959.
———. "In Search of a Credible Form of Rule-utilitarianism." In George Nakhnikian and Hector-Neri Castenedu, eds. *Morality and the Language of Conduct.* Detroit: Wayne State University Press, 1961.
———. *A Theory of the Good and the Right.* London: Oxford University Press, 1979.
Ewing, Alfred C. "What Would Happen if Everybody Acted Like Me?" *Philosophy* 28 (1953): 16–29.
Fletcher, Joseph. *Situation Ethics.* Philadelphia: Westminster Press, 1966.
Harrison, Jonathan. "Utilitarianism, Universalization and Our Duty to Be Just." *Aristotelian Society Proceedings* 53 (1952–1953): 105–34.

★Dates in parentheses are dates of first publication.

Harrod, R. F. "Utilitarianism Revised." *Mind* 45 (1936): 137–56.

Hazlitt, Henry. *The Foundations of Morality*. New York: Van Nostrand, 1964.

Mabbott, J. D. "Interpretations of Mill's *Utilitarianism.*" *Philosophical Quarterly* 6 (1956): 115–20.

McCloskey, H. J. "An Examination of Restricted Utilitarianism." *Philosophical Review* 66 (1957): 466–85.

Rawls, John. "Two Concepts of Rules." *Philosophical Review* 64 (1955): 3–32.

Smart, J. J. C. "Extreme and Restricted Utilitarianism." *Philosophical Quarterly* 6 (1956).

Smart, J. J. C., and Bernard Williams. *Utilitarianism: For and Against*. Cambridge, Eng.: Cambridge University Press, 1973.

Stout, A. K. "But Suppose Everyone Did the Same?" *Australasian Journal of Philosophy* 32 (1954): 1–29.

Strang, Colin. "What If Everyone Did That?" *Durham University Journal* 53 (1960): 5–10.

Urmson, J. O. "The Interpretation of the Moral Philosophy of J. S. Mill." *Philosophical Quarterly* 3 (1953): 33–39.

7

Human Rights

Among the many atrocities of twentieth-century dictatorships, one of the least known is what the Soviet government once did to obtain gold. After the Russian Revolution, among the arrests made for countless other things, people were arrested in order for the government to obtain any gold that was in private hands. Russian author Aleksandr Solzhenitsyn gives this account of the episode:

Who was arrested in the "gold" wave? All those who, at one time or another . . . had had a private "business," had been involved in retail trade, had earned wages at a craft, and *could have,* according to the GUP [the Soviet secret police] deductions, hoarded gold. But it so happened that they often had no gold. They had put their money into real estate or securities, which had melted away in the Revolution, and nothing remained. They had high hopes, of course, in arresting dental technicians, jewelers, and watch repairmen. Through denunciations, one could learn about gold in the most unexpected places. . . . Whether or not [a person owned gold] could be discovered only inside prison walls. Nothing—neither proletarian origin nor revolutionary services—served as a defense against a gold denunciation. All were arrested, all were crammed into GPU cells in numbers no one had considered possible up to then— but that was all to the good: they would cough it up all the sooner. . . . Only one thing was important: Give up your gold, viper! The state needs gold and you don't. The interrogators . . . had one universal method: feed the prisoners nothing but salty food and give them no water. One gold piece for a cup of fresh water!

. . .

If you in fact had no gold, then your situation was hopeless. You would be beaten, burned, tortured, and steamed to the point of death or

240

until they finally came to believe you. But if you had gold, you could determine the extent of your torture. . . . Anyone who had already mastered the rules of the institution would yield and give up his gold— that was easier. But it was a mistake to give it up too readily. They would refuse to believe you had coughed it all up, and they would continue to hold you. But you'd be wrong, too, to wait too long before yielding: you'd end up dying, or they'd paste a term on you out of meanness. One of the Tatar draymen endured all the tortures: he had no gold! They imprisoned his wife, too, and tortured her, but the Tatar stuck to his story: no gold! Then they arrested his daughter: the Tatar couldn't take it any more. He coughed up 100,000 rubles. At this point they let his family go, but slapped a prison term on him. The crudest detective stories and operas about brigands were played out in real life on a vast national scale. . . . In this wave they burned out whole nests, whole families; and they watched jealously to be sure that none of the children—fourteen, ten, even six years old—got away; to the last scrapings, all had to go down the same road, to the same common destruction.[1]

Shortly after this persecution vast quantities of gold were discovered in eastern Siberia, in the Kolyma district, next to the Arctic, the most inhospitable climate on the earth. But because of climate, the inaccessibility of the region, and the total lack of transport, the problem was to obtain it. According to historians of the period:

There were two possible solutions. One was to allow unrestricted initiative to pioneer prospectors, who would have obtained the gold in the same way as prospectors in California and Alaska had done before them. The other was to invest a large amount of capital, which was needed . . . to build roads and other means of communications in the region. The policy of the Soviet Government ruled out the first method, since those were the years when private trading and manufacturing of any kind were being relentlessly suppressed throughout the country. As for investing capital, there was none to invest, for the government . . . lacked the cash to pay for the huge orders of foreign-built machinery under the construction program of the first Five-Year Plan. . . .

The solution was found in an entirely different direction. While the Soviet Government had no free capital in the old "bourgeois" meaning of the term, it had a plentiful supply of a different kind of capital— human lives. . . . Stalin was carrying out "complete collectivization" of farms and banishing to Siberia . . . the peasants who refused to join.

[1] From *The Gulag Archipelago 1918–1956: An Experiment in Literary Investigation I–II,* Volume One, by Aleksandr I. Solzhenitsyn, pp. 53–55. Copyright © 1973 by Aleksandr I. Solzhenitsyn. English translation © 1973, 1974 by Harper & Row, Publishers, Inc. Reprinted by permission of the publisher.

These numbered millions, almost all of them good workers, strong and hardy and accustomed to the heavy labor of peasant life. Exiled with them were also hundreds of scientists and engineers who only a short time before had held responsible posts but for one reason or another had come under suspicion of having a critical attitude toward the government. Here, therefore, was a mass of people able to supply both manpower and expert leadership for large projects. Strictly speaking, in the eyes of the government they were all condemned to slow death as "socially hostile elements" who would never reconcile themselves to the Soviet system. The only question was how, by what means, the government could squeeze out of them the remainder of their working power, and how this remainder could best be utilized for the purposes of government.[2]

And so millions of prisoners were shipped to the region, which often registered temperatures of 60° below zero, and while there they were provided with no clothes but what they wore in prison and no shelter from the elements. Almost half died of cold, starvation, and malnutrition the first season, but more were shipped to replace them: with enormous casualties they built a harbor (now the city of Magadan), roads through the taiga (frozen in winter, swampy in summer), and communications lines to the Kolyma gold fields 300 miles away. About half a million slave colonists were shipped there each year. According to Robert Conquest, one researcher on the subject, of the 70 million dead in Soviet labor camps, 3 million died in the Kolyma camps alone.[3] (Kolyma was one of about 130 complexes of slave labor camps, many of which are still in operation today.) Human lives were cheap, and those shipped there were an embarrassment to the Soviet rulers and had to be dealt with somehow; why not dispose of them by making them serve a useful purpose before they died? According to historians, the Soviets paid a high price in human life for the gold:

> Every metric ton of Kolyma gold cost the lives of 700 to 1,000 human beings. One human life for every kilogram of gold—such is the price on the slave market of Magadan. . . . "When we achieve victory on a world scale," [Lenin] said, "we will use gold to build public toilets in the streets . . ." The "realist" communists of our own days are filling the swamps of the taiga with human bones in order to get as much of this very gold as they can lay their hands on. Much has changed since those early days of the Revolution. Much water has flowed under the bridges. Alas, not only water.[4]

[2] Reprinted by permission of Yale University Press, from *Forced Labor in Soviet Russia* by David Dallin and Boris Nicolaevsky, 1947, pp. 114–15.

[3] Robert Conquest, *Kolyma: The Arctic Death Camp* (New York: Viking Press, 1978), pp. 227–28. See also his *The Great Terror* (New York: Viking Press, 1966). The figure of 70 million is an estimate made by several scholars, and is quoted by Aleksandr Solzhenitsyn in *From Under the Rubble* (Boston: Little, Brown, 1975), p. 119.

[4] Dallin and Nicolaevsky, *Forced Labor,* p. 146.

What is it that we find so shocking, so repellent, in these and countless other instances of man's inhumanity to man? Is it not primarily the constant and ceaseless violation of what we believe to be the *rights* of the individuals who are victimized? We might, indeed, object to the system on utilitarian grounds as well: it certainly doesn't maximize happiness in the Soviet Union. But this does not really go to the heart of the objection. Even if X number of people were made happy by it, at the expense of Y number of people whose lives and liberties were sacrificed, if the good to the X group outweighed the sacrifices of the Y group, and no other alternative yielded better net results (which is, of course, most unlikely), then it might be possible to give utilitarian sanction to such a system. We are more sure that it is wrong at its very inception than that it could not be justified on utilitarian grounds. Even if some great good were ultimately to come of it, instead of more cruelty and death (as usually happens), what we find wrong is the nonvoluntary use of human beings by others. We must never, said Kant in his second formulation of the Categorical Imperative, treat human beings, ourselves or others, merely as means to other persons' ends. It is the treatment of persons as means to forward the ends of others that we find so objectionable in these examples.

True, we use physicians as means to achieve our ends when we consult them concerning our health. We use merchants as means to our ends when we purchase items from their stores, and they use us as means to their ends (increased income) when they sell to us. But this is a voluntary exchange of money for goods; we would be using them *merely* as means (as things, rather than human beings) if we made them slaves or forced them to give us the merchandise or be killed. The objection to using entire human lives to serve the purposes of others is voiced by Ivan Karamazov in Fyodor Dostoyevsky's novel *The Brothers Karamazov* when he says, "Surely I haven't suffered, simply that I . . . may manure the soil of the future harmony for somebody else."[5]

The basic flaw in utilitarianism, as many persons see it, is that it has no respect for the *individual:* individuals count as part of a total, an aggregate; but as units of that aggregate their liberties and rights can be sacrificed and their very lives snuffed out on the altar of "social betterment." Utilitarians may find some purpose, even in these official instructions to the KGB (the current initials of the Soviet secret police):

You must think of all humanity—past, present, and future—as one great body that requires surgery. You cannot perform surgery without severing membranes, destroying tissue, spilling blood. Similarly, in intelligence we sometimes destroy individuals who are expendable tissues on the body of humanity. Occasionally we must perform unpleasant acts,

[5] Fyodor Dostoyevsky, *The Brothers Karamazov* (New York: Modern Library, 1937; originally published in 1882), p. 253.

even kidnapping and liquidation. But none of this is immoral. All acts that further socialism are moral acts.[6]

But regardless of the utility of such instructions, they exhibit utter disregard for the value of individual human lives, which are used as mere vehicles for the achievement of other people's ends. That such use of human beings by other human beings, without their voluntary consent, is wrong is the contention of any view that supports the concept of *human rights*.

1. THE CONCEPT OF RIGHTS

Why shouldn't one person be killed if a hundred people would thereby be happier? If the killing is painless, the utilitarian calculus might countenance such a killing. Yet, many of us would argue that to do so would be wrong. Why? One answer that we could give is, "Because I have a *right* to life." Similarly, no matter how much "social good" torturing might accomplish, a person has a right not to be tortured.

Why shouldn't your wealth be distributed to others if their happiness exceeded your unhappiness in consequence of the act? Because, we might say, if you've earned it, you have a right to what you've earned. A thief may have more use for your television set than you do, yet you bought it, you are the owner of it, and you have a right to keep it. Where your rights are concerned, other people may not trespass. Rights are like a no-trespassing sign beyond which people may not go in their treatment of other people.

It is sometimes held that a right is a *claim*. But, of course, not any claim can be a right: I may claim that your television set is mine, but that doesn't give me the right to it. A right is a *justified* claim, or a *valid* claim. Whatever "valid" means here, can't people *have* a right without claiming it? A woman may have a right to an inheritance which she doesn't yet know exists, or you may be entitled to a TV set stolen from you and since recovered without your claiming it.

Perhaps it is preferable simply to say that a right is an *entitlement*. If someone gives me his car, I am entitled to the car (whether I claim it or not). This, while true, is not very helpful; it gives us only a synonym for the term "right." It is much more helpful to trace the connection between *rights* and *duties*.

1. *If A has a right, other people* (B, C, D . . .) *have a duty*. This is always and necessarily so. How could you have a right to your life if I and others didn't have a duty to refrain from killing you? If someone said, "You have a right to your life, but I have no duty not to kill you," we might say, understating the case, that your right to life doesn't amount to much. If you have a right (both legal and moral) to your television set, others have a duty

[6] Quoted in *John Barron, KGB* (New York: Reader's Digest Press, 1974), p. 366.

to refrain from stealing it. (If they didn't, what would have happened to your right?)

2. *A right of A does not imply a duty of A.* You can have rights without your having duties. Infants have a right to be cared for until they can take care of themselves; that means that other people (parents) have a duty to take care of them, but it does not mean that the infant has duties. The infant doesn't yet have the concept of a duty, much less the ability to carry it out.

There is also a theory of the "divine right of kings," whereby a king is said to have all the rights and his subjects have all the duties. His rights imply others' duties, but since the others have no rights, he has no duties. This is no longer an accepted view, but it is a possible view, whereas the view that the king (or anyone else) has rights but no one else has duties corresponding to those rights is not.

3. *A duty of B does not necessarily imply a right of A.* If you have a duty, others may not have a corresponding right. You may have a duty to feed your dog, but does the dog have a right to be fed? (Not everyone agrees that animals have rights, as we shall see below.) Perhaps you ought to help out a friend in need; but does the friend have a claim on you? Can she claim your help as her right? As a driver, you have a duty to stop at a red traffic light, but who has the right that corresponds to this duty (especially at an intersection where there are no pedestrians in sight)?

A. Classification of Rights

It is also important to distinguish various kinds of rights. The kinds of rights discussed below overlap, so that an instance of one kind of right can also be an instance of another, though not for the same reason.

1. We often speak of *legal rights,* as opposed to *moral* or *human rights.* If you are in Nevada, you have a legal right to gamble; in most other states you do not. What you have a legal right to do depends on the city, county, state, and nation in which you live. But moral rights have to do with what you are morally entitled to: if you live in a totalitarian nation you have no legal right to say anything against the government, and yet, we could say, you have a moral right to do so; you *ought* to have the legal right even if you don't. One of your rights as a human being is being denied by the government under which you live.

2. We also speak of *general rights* as opposed to *specific rights.* If I have promised to return you $100 on a certain day, you have a right to the money as of that day. But your neighbor, to whom I did not make the promise, has no such right. *A*'s children have a right to parental care (*A*'s support), but the neighbor's children (*B*'s children) do not have the same right to *A*'s support. If *A* helps to support *B*'s children anyway, such support is a beneficence, but it cannot be claimed by *B*'s children as their right. Specific rights are claimed by specific people for specific reasons. General rights, however,

are those which all human beings possess: the traditional examples are the rights to life, liberty, and the pursuit of happiness. We shall try to show shortly what these rights come to; but if we have them, it is simply because we are human beings, not because we stand in some special relation to another person.

3. We distinguish between *positive* and *negative rights*. If *A* has a positive right, others have a duty to *do* something to fulfill it. If *A* has a right to the $100 *B* borrowed from him, *B* has a positive duty to return it to him. But if *A* has a right not to be killed (a negative right), *B* has only the negative duty of *noninterference*: she doesn't have to *do* anything; she simply has a duty *not* to kill *A*. If *A* has a right to marry whom he chooses, then others have the duty not to interfere in the choice. If someone else has a negative right, no action of yours is called for except to sit back and do nothing; all you are obliged to do is *not to interfere,* that is, to exhibit *forbearance* and let the other person exercise his or her right. (As we shall see, some contend that all general rights are negative rights.)

4. Finally, we can distinguish between *active* and *passive rights*. Active rights are rights you can *exercise:* they are rights to *do* something. The right to paint your house purple, to marry whom you like, to walk on the sidewalk, to give away something that belongs to you—all are rights to *do* something; and, of course, if you have these rights, other people have the (negative) duty of noninterference with your exercise of these rights. But we also speak of rights when we are on the receiving end: you have a right not to be killed, not to be tortured, not to be vandalized, and so on. These are not rights you can exercise (for how would you exercise your right not to be killed?); they have to do with what others may not do—with ways in which you should or should not be treated by others—and thus are called "passive rights." Some philosophers hold that speaking of passive rights is just another way of speaking of other people's duties—that it is the duty of others not to do certain things against you that is primary, and that speaking of your right not to have these things done is just a way of saying the same thing in the passive voice: the duty generates the right, not the other way round. In any case, an active right is the right to *do* something with which others have a duty not to interfere; a passive right is the right not to have something done to you by others.

B. The Basis of Rights

Any number of people who would agree that human beings have certain rights, and that they should be respected, might nevertheless disagree on why we have them.

1. It has often been declared that rights are "god-given," that is, that God has endowed human beings with certain "inalienable rights." Whether or not this is so is outside the scope of ethics. But it is worth asking whether people

who allege a divine origin of rights really mean to say that if they were to lose their belief in God, they would also conclude that no human beings possess rights.

The theological view might be reformulated to say that God has created human beings with certain characteristics or features which make them possessors of rights. But in that case, it is the *having* of those features and not how they *got* there that matters in saying that human beings have rights.

2. Others have alleged that rights have their basis in the capacity to experience pain and suffering, and that without this capacity there would be no rights. But several objections may be raised to this allegation: (a) Human beings have this capacity to varying degrees; does this mean that they have rights in varying degrees, depending on their capacity for suffering? (b) Animals too have this capacity, so it would follow that they have rights also. To many people this is a perfectly satisfactory conclusion, but there are others who deny that animals have rights and maintain only that human beings have duties to them. (c) If a person is killed painlessly, there is no suffering, so it is difficult to see how this account of rights would cover a most important right, the right not to be killed. (d) If someone has gone into a permanent coma, say because of some disease, would he or she then have no rights? (e) Sometimes the infliction of pain or suffering is the only way to achieve some necessary purpose, such as curing a disease. Would such infliction then be a violation of rights?

3. Another account of rights connects rights with *rationality*. Human beings, Aristotle said, are rational animals, that is, all have rational capacities even though they do not always develop them, and in that special capacity lies the basis of human rights. There are objections, however, to this position as well. (a) Some people are more rational than others; is there a corresponding variation in the degree to which they possess rights? (b) Some people are simply "human vegetables," through genetic defects or brain surgery; have they on this account no rights at all? (c) If animals other than human beings are not rational, they have no rights; this would be a welcome conclusion to some but not to others. (d) In any case many psychologists would say that the difference between human beings and anthropoids with respect to rationality is a difference of degree, not a difference of kind. Can there be a corresponding difference of degree with respect to rights? (It is true, of course, that only rational beings can act on principle—for example, refrain from acting on desires because those desires would violate someone's rights. But this is only a special case of moral action in general: whether dealing with rights or not, only human beings can act from a belief that something is right or wrong, since only human beings, on this planet at least, have any concept of right or wrong.)

4. Rights are often thought to derive from the fact that all human beings have a certain intrinsic *worth,* and that in view of this worth all human beings should be treated in certain ways and not in other ways. But it is difficult to see what this "intrinsic worth" is. Certainly not all persons are equally wor-

thy: some people are conniving, villainous, outright despicable, and the world would be better off had they not been born. What, then, is this worth which all human beings possess? One author, Gregory Vlastos, describes it this way:

> To be sincere, reliable, fair, kind, tolerant, unintrusive, modest in my relations with my fellows is not due them because they have made brilliant or even passing moral grades, but simply because they happen to be members of the moral community. It is not necessary to add "members in good standing": the moral community is not a club from which members may be dropped for delinquency. Our morality does not provide for moral outcasts or half-castes.
>
> It does provide for punishment. But this takes place *within* the moral community and under its rules. It is for this reason that, for example, one has no right to be cruel to a cruel person. His offense against the moral law has not put him outside the law. He is still protected by its prohibition of cruelty—as much so as are kind persons. The pain inflicted on him as punishment for his offense does not close out the great reserve of good will on the part of others which is his birthright as a human being; it is a limited withdrawal from it. Capital punishment even is no exception. The fact that a man has been condemned to death does not license his jailors to beat him or virtuous citizens to lynch him.[7]

5. Instead of saying that rights are tied to human worth, it has been suggested that rights are tied to the concept of human *dignity*. Human beings have (to varying degrees) the capacity for full human development—not only reason but will and emotion as well; and if I interfere coercively with your attempt to fulfill your human potential, then I am (to the extent that I do this) dehumanizing you, treating you as something other than a human being with a mind and will of your own. If, for example, I use physical force (instead of reasoning or persuasion) against you to make you do something against your will, I am not treating you as a human being, and thus I am violating your rights as a human being.

6. It may be that our attribution of rights to human beings is simply the result of our viewing people from the "human point of view." We can think of our fellow human beings in a number of ways—as foolish, or dangerous, as lawyers or street cleaners. But, according to some moral philosophers, when we view them from the human point of view, we mean that:

> They are all capable of being viewed by others imaginatively from their own point of view. They "have shoes" into which we can always try to put ourselves; this is not true of mere things. It may follow (causally,

[7] Gregory Vlastos, "Justice and Equality," in *Social Justice,* ed. Richard Brandt (Englewood Cliffs, N.J.: Prentice-Hall, 1963), p. 47.

not logically) from this way of so regarding them that we come to *respect* them in the sense tied to the idea of "human worth." But "human worth" itself is best understood to name no property in the way that "strength" names strength and "redness" redness. In attributing human worth to everyone we may be ascribing no property or set of qualities, but rather expressing an attribute—an attitude of respect—toward the humanity in each man's person.[8]

In whatever way human rights are conceived, their importance in the arsenal of moral concepts is great:

> Rights are not mere gifts or favors, motivated by love or pity, for which gratitude is the sole fitting response. A right is something a man can *stand* on, something that can be demanded or insisted upon without embarrassment or shame. When that to which one has a right is not forthcoming, the appropriate reaction is indignation; when it is duly given there is no reason for gratitude, since it is simply one's own or one's due that one received. A world with claim-rights is one in which all persons, as actual or potential claimants, are dignified objects of respect, both in their own eyes and in the view of others. No amount of love and compassion, or obedience to higher authority, or noblesse oblige, can substitute for those values.[9]

2. BASIC RIGHTS

Let us now consider the rights of human beings that have been held to be the most basic—how they can be formulated and what can be said for or against them. Following this, we shall consider some special problems in applying the concept of rights, specifically to children and to animals.

A. The Right to Life

Let us consider the first of the traditional rights, the right to life. But it is not clear just what the phrase means. At a minimum it means the right not to be killed—a negative right and a passive right, negative because it requires of others only that they not kill you, and passive because you can't exercise it, though others can (by not killing you). But if this is all the right to life comes to, it doesn't amount to much. A slave master can keep slaves alive in order to get more work out of them and can mistreat them and malnourish them, but as long as they stay alive he has respected their right to life. Respecting

[8]Joel Feinberg, *Social Philosophy* (Englewood Cliffs, N.J.: Prentice-Hall, 1973), pp. 93–94.
[9]Ibid., 58–59.

people's right to life in this limited sense is certainly a *necessary* part of what is usually called the right to life, but it is not the whole of it. It is only what we may call the *minimal* interpretation of the right to life.

To make the right a little less minimal, we could identify the right to life as the right not to be killed or injured. Then it would include a right not to be assaulted, maimed, beaten up, raped, or have other kinds of bodily harm inflicted. This too is a negative right: others need do nothing, merely not interfere; and it is also a passive right, since only persons other than yourself can exercise it by not doing these things to you. Others can, without violating your right, do such things to you *with* your consent. If you are a masochist who enjoys being beaten, others can beat you up without violating your rights. Or in the case of a religious sect that accepts the practice of wife beating, if the wives accept this treatment as a sacred duty, the husbands would not be violating their right. (When such cases come before the law, however, the state usually considers them violations of rights anyway and initiates an assault and battery charge against the husbands, even though the wives made no complaint and indeed consented to be treated in this way.) It is not the use of force against you *per se,* but the use of it against your will, to inflict on you bodily injury, that constitutes the violation of the right. The crucial point is not only what is done to you but whether you consent to its being done. Sexual intercourse is not rape, no matter how violent, as long as a woman consents.

If we choose to interpret the rights to life still more broadly, to include the right not to have your possessions stolen from you, it becomes the right to property, which is usually classified as a distinct right (which we shall consider below). But we may pursue the right to life in another direction. Doesn't it include, besides the right not to *be* treated in certain ways, the right to *do* certain things (with no interference from others)? Doesn't the traditional right to life include the right to perform certain activities with impunity? Indeed, the traditional right to life is a kind of vague mixture of active and passive rights, but it also includes certain liberties, certain freedoms to act, which entail the negative duty of others not to interfere with the actions.

And so we come to what we may call the *maximal* interpretation of the right to life—the right to *live your life according to your own choices,* except the choice to interfere coercively with the choices of others. If I have the right to marry whom I please, others have the duty not to interfere with that choice. (They may advise me, if I choose to listen, but they have no right to force me.) I have the right to choose the occupation I wish, and again others may advise me but not force their choice upon me.

Some other examples of the right to life, in this maximal interpretation, include the following:

1. *Suicide.* Though others have no right to kill you, you have the right to take your own life if you so choose. Since you are the owner of your own body, it is for you and no one else to say how it shall be used. If, however

unwisely, you decide to end it, no one has the right to force you to preserve it. The permissibility of suicide is not based on the utility either of the individual act or of the general rule (permitting suicide); it is based on the fact that nobody else owns you, and therefore it is your right and your decision to use your life in whatever way you choose and preserve it or not preserve it as you choose. The Stoic philosopher Marcus Aurelius said, "The room is smoky, so I leave it," and in this maximal interpretation of the right to life, no one has the right to say him nay. The law, of course, does not customarily recognize this right, but we are speaking of moral, not legal, rights.

2. *Medical experimentation.* You have a right to volunteer yourself for a medical experiment, even a very risky one, if you choose to do so. Perhaps you are ill with a certain disease yourself, and you think (perhaps contrary to prevailing medical opinion) that you have the best chance with a new experimental drug. The reason that you have a right to try the drug is that it's your body, and nobody but you owns it; permissibility of the action is based not on the *utility* of your doing it, but on your *right* to do it. Nor does the government have any right to prohibit you from using it if you choose to. What rights do others have over the use of *your* body?

Or perhaps you are not ill yourself but choose to have a certain drug injected into your veins as a part of an experimental test of a new medication, since you believe that your participation in the experiment will be of value to medical science. Again, you have a right to do this if you choose. Perhaps you are mistaken in your belief; perhaps the experiment will be useless. You may die or suffer harmful aftereffects from the new drug, and it may turn out to have no utility whatsoever. Still, you have a right to volunteer yourself; since you have the right of free choice, it's up to you.

What others do *not* have a right to do is to force you to be a guinea pig for one of their experiments. Even if the results to science would be very useful, even if they need a thousand people to participate and can't get enough people to volunteer, they have no right to use you. In Nazi camps, if physicians wanted to conduct an experiment on pain tolerance or inject people with drugs in order to note their reactions, they did so, and the same thing is done constantly on prisoners in Soviet labor camps. But this nonvoluntary use of human beings as a means to others' ends is a violation of their right to life. The practice may have some utility, and some scientific breakthrough might possibly occur as a result of it; but the fact of utility does not keep the practice from being a violation of individuals' rights to use their own bodies as they see fit rather than as others see fit. If a person in a position of high authority who was going blind could prove that he had a better use for your eyes than you do, that by having them he could do more good than you could, and if such an operation was feasible, would he have a right to forcibly take your eyes from you so that he could use them himself?

3. *The draft.* Given the maximal interpretation of the right to life, it is up to you whether or not you want to serve in your country's armed forces. If

you believe in the cause, you may volunteer; but if you don't believe in the cause and believe you will be uselessly sacrificed, or even if you do believe in it and for one reason or another choose not to defend it, that is your decision and no one has a right to force you. It is even possible that if neither you nor some thousands of others volunteer, your country will be conquered, and you too will be killed or enslaved. If you believe this, it is to your advantage to volunteer your services in order to help save the country, or at least yourself and your family, not to mention the political-economic system which you prefer to the totalitarianism which is threatening; but the battle cry "The cause I believe in is so important that I am even willing to sacrifice your life for it" is not a very heroic one. It indicates other people's willingness to use your life, which no one else has a right to do, neither any individual person nor a collection of persons called the State. Your life is not the property of other human beings to use as they see fit.

But if you decide even so not to do so, no one has a right to force you. You are not a means to other people's ends. Some may object, "But it's *your* ends, too. *You* may be enslaved if you don't enlist." Perhaps that's true, but if you don't believe it, or even if it's true and you don't see it, others have no right to force you to risk or give up your life because *they* believe (even if they believe correctly) that using you would preserve the system, and you along with it.

Are there no limits, no qualifications, to the right to life, maximally interpreted? Here are some that have been suggested:

1. Infants and children cannot always be permitted to live by their own choices; they have no idea of the probable consequences of their actions, and until they have reached maturity (which varies troublesomely from one individual to another), others must make certain decisions for them, sometimes coercively, but always with a view toward helping them to make their decisions for themselves later. For example, we pull children out from a street full of cars, since they have no idea that they may be fatally injured. We prohibit children, on pain of force, from doing certain things, such as injuring others, to protect those others, and from swallowing whatever is in the medicine bottle, to protect themselves. We do this also with other people who are unable to make their own decisions, such as the insane and the senile. We shall discuss this issue further in Chapter 9 under the heading of legal paternalism. For the moment at least, we restrict the right of free choice to persons who are in possession of their mental faculties and can anticipate the probable consequences of their actions.

2. What of those who have violated the rights of others—for example, convicted murderers? Have they the right to live by their own choices, even if they choose to kill some more? No, though they had the same right as others to live by their choices prior to committing murder, once they violated the rights of others, they forfeited their right to choice: they cannot be permitted to continue denying others their rights. (They have rights, but so do the victims, and it is the victims' rights that they are jeopardizing.)

Thus far, all that this calls for is the criminals' incarceration; whether capital punishment is also called for, or even permissible, is more controversial. It may be argued that in our society we try to live by certain societal rules, the minimum required to have a peaceful society; murderers have violated those rules, so by administering capital punishment, we are simply treating them by the same rules by which they treated others. They believed that killing others was permissible, and we are only dealing with them the way they dealt with others. By assigning the death penalty we are only adopting with respect to them the same maxim they adopted toward their victims. This was Kant's position; we shall consider the subject of punishment further in Chapter 8.

There are other actions, of course, besides killing, which forcibly interfere with others' voluntary choices. Mugging, raping, kidnaping, and maiming are a few. Theft (a crime against property rather than a crime against the person) may also constitute forcible interference, because a holdup interferes with a person's voluntary choice of how to use his money.

If people do violate your rights, what kind of action is called for? The criminal law has punishments for theft and embezzlement as well as for kidnaping and murder, though these punishments are not always fair (nor fairly administered); we shall consider this topic in Chapter 8, when we discuss punishment. At the moment the point is merely that, just as in the case of murder, if you have violated the rights of others you have also compromised your own. (But not all your own: even convicted murderers have rights. They are tried, convicted, and punished according to certain legal procedures; participants in lynchings violate murderers' rights and are answerable to a charge of murder for their acts.)

3. Some people suggest that the maximal interpretation of the right to life is unfairly limited by people's varying situations in life. One person has a small range of choices, *A* through *C*, while another has a larger range of choices, *A* through *N*. The second person is better off than the first, at least with respect to available options. Doesn't the person with the smaller range of choices have a *right* to the larger range? If an individual has to choose between being a dishwasher and being a short-order cook, just to make ends meet, and no other job is offered, is his or her right to life being honored as much as the person who can choose among lots of other things, such as spending the winter in the south of France?

If not being able to vacation in France is a violation of rights, it would be hard to say what is not. If a father is poor and can't provide his son with as much as a neighbor provides his son, that's too bad, but there isn't any violation of anyone's rights in that situation. The first son just has fewer choices, but he is still free to choose among the alternatives he does have—including working for a sociopolitical system which will allow more people more options.

If a tornado devastated my house and land, I can cry in vain, "But I have a right to it!" But if I have a right, others must necessarily have duties, and what duties can they possibly have to me because a storm destroyed my house? It is only when the actions of others have deprived me of what is mine that my right has been violated. If robbers have burglarized my house, I have a right to the things stolen because, after all, they are mine.

4. Some have suggested that all rights, including the right to life, are prima facie. Just as (in Ross) there are prima facie duties, so there are also prima facie rights. You have a prima facie right to life, but it can be counterbalanced by a prima facie right of the government to, for example, commandeer your services, regulate your business, or force you to do jury duty.

The problem with the notion of prima facie rights, however, is that it places all rights on a shaky foundation. What value is a right if others can be justified in violating it? It is the absoluteness of rights that makes us secure in claiming them, as we would not be if they were only prima facie. However, as we shall see in the next section, conflicts of rights do occur, and the adjudication of such conflicts can be very troublesome.

B. The Right to Property

A claim to the right to life is often accompanied by the claim to ownership of material possessions, called "property." Your property is anything to which you have the right to use and dispose of: your clothes, your books, your car, your typewriter, your house. (Your children are not your property: they are human beings with rights of their own. The same can be said of animals you take as pets. We shall discuss these below in the sections on children's rights and animals' rights.) Over nonsentient things you can have exclusive rights; anyone who takes them from you without your consent is robbing you of what is yours by right.

The *right to property* is a special case of the right to life in its maximal sense: you have the right to live by your voluntary choices, and among those decisions are the ones to earn and buy things you can call your own. The importance of the right to own things can hardly be overestimated. If human beings were incorporeal spirits, they would not need possessions; but since humans live in the material world, they need food and shelter in order to survive. Moreover, they can prosper only if they can plan their lives long-range—for example, by working and saving for the future—and they can't do this if there is nothing they can rely on as their own. If you are a slave, the slave master can take away from you anything he chooses. If you live in a communist nation in which you receive wages from the State but the State owns the land you are on and the dwelling you live in (everything except the clothes on your back), and can take them away from you the moment anyone reports you as saying anything against the State, you can't plan for the future, or if you do, your plans can be laid low by the desire of any government official to arrest you. To have even a modicum of predictability of action, you must have exclusive use and control of at least some things.

But what makes something your property? Ordinarily, you buy it from someone else; the right of property is not the right to steal it from someone who already owns it. But what entitled the seller to own it? Probably he or she bought it from someone else or made it. In the case of land, what determines who owns it? Let's say your father left it to you in his will, so you own it; it is yours by reason of inheritance. But what enabled him to own it? If we go back far enough, we find someone who did not buy it from someone else but rather worked it in some way—felled trees, built a house, or raised plants and animals on it. That individual "mixed his labor with the land," and the labor conferred ownership. As English philosopher John Locke (1632–1704) put it:

> Though the Earth, and all inferior Creatures be common to all Men, yet every Man has a *Property* in his own *Person*. This no Body has any Right to but himself. The *Labour* of his Body, and the *Work* of his Hands, we may say, are properly his. Whatsoever then he removes out of the State that Nature hath provided, and left it in, he hath mixed his *Labour* with, and joyned to it something that is his own, and thereby makes it his *Property*. It being by him removed from the common state Nature placed it in, hath by this *Labour* something annexed to it, that excludes the common right of other Men. For this *Labour* being the unquestionable Property of the Labourer, no Man but he can have a right to what that is once joyned to, at least where there is enough, and as good left in common for others.
>
> He that is nourished by the Acorns he pickt up under an Oak, or the Apples he gathered from the Trees in the Wood, has certainly appropriated them to himself. No Body can deny but the nourishment is his. I ask then, When did they begin to be his? When he digested? Or when he ate? Or when he boiled? Or when he brought them home? Or when he pickt them up? And 'tis plain, if the first gathering made them not his, nothing else could. That *labour* put a distinction between them and common. That added something to them more than Nature, the common Mother of all, had done; and so they became his private right. And will any one say he had no right to those Acorns or Apples he thus appropriated, because he had not the consent of all Mankind to make them his? Was it a Robbery thus to assume to himself what belonged to all in Common? If such a consent as that was necessary, Man had starved, notwithstanding the Plenty God had given him. We see in *Commons,* which remain so by Compact, that 'tis the taking any part of what is common, and removing it out of the state Nature leaves it in, which *begins the Property;* without which the Common is of no use. And the taking of this or that part, does not depend on the express consent of all the Commoners. Thus the Grass my Horse has bit; the Turfs my Servant has cut; and the Ore I have digg'd in any place where I have a right to them in common with others, become my *Property,* without the as-

signation or consent of any body. The *labour* that was mine, removing them out of that common state they were in, hath *fixed* my *Property* in them.[10]

Before anyone worked the land, *no* one owned it; labor made it someone's. If you see a wild tree growing fruit in the wilderness, you are entitled to pluck the fruit. But if you come across an orchard cultivated by someone, you have no right to it: the one who raised the trees and cultivated the land has property rights to it.

Locke had certain qualifications to this rule, for example, that people should use only as much as they had need of and should not waste any. But the main point that emerges from his discussion is that labor is the origin of property. A person who created a farm out of the wilderness can lay claim to that farm, because he or she, and not others, labored for it.

Many questions arise, however, even concerning this simple and seemingly obvious account. First, why does the fact that a person has "mixed his labor with the land" give that individual title to it? Tilling the soil and growing crops may give someone title to the crops, but does that entitle him or her to the land on which they grow? True, without the land the crops can't be grown; but how does clearing the land and growing the crops entitle someone to *own* land? The most obvious answer is a negative one: How does it entitle anyone else to the land? The *farmer* has done the work; if others (or a government) come in and claim the land, they are expropriating the fruits of another's labor. What have the expropriators done to earn it? If the one who worked the land doesn't deserve it, who does? This answer is framed in terms of the concept of *deserts,* or deservingness, which is central to the concept of justice and will be discussed in the next chapter.

A utilitarian answer could also be given: a system of property ownership based on labor is the best one from the point of view of consequences. If people cannot own the land on which they work, they are less motivated to work and less productive too; if the land isn't theirs, they also are less likely to make necessary improvements on it. In the Soviet Union, most of the land is owned by the State, but a few private plots are permitted, on which farmers may grow their own crops and sell the proceeds for profit. Although less than 3 percent of the land in the Soviet Union is involved, it produces about one-third of the total crops.[11] Apparently people are more motivated to work when they can do so for themselves. If a particularly industrious person works twice as hard but must share the proceeds from her toil with a thousand others, who all benefit from her hard work as much as she does, she becomes less inclined to work hard for the one-thousandth of the added income she would receive for her extra work.

Even granted that labor entitles a person to the fruits thereof, including the

[10]John Locke, *Second Treatise of Civil Government* (1690), Chapter 5.
[11]Dr. S. Pejovich, *Report Card on Socialism* (Dallas, Tex.: Fisher Institute, 1979), p. 94.

land, a second question must be raised: what gives that person the right to transmit the property thus earned to heirs on his or her death? Well, something has to be done with it; it can't just lie unused forever, and since the person owns it, doesn't he or she have a right to say to whom it will go? Again, if others (or a government) came in and said, "No, it's ours," what would entitle them to it? What did *they* do to deserve it? It's not that the heir necessarily deserves it—he or she may be quite undeserving—but that the person who owns it, whether it is land or television sets or money, has the right, as the owner, to say to whom it will go. Without that right, in what way would it be *personal* property? (As an added utilitarian point, knowing that relatives will inherit the estate will also motivate the original owner to work. No such motivation will occur—especially as the owner approaches retirement age—if the State, or a group of strangers, will inherit what someone has labored to produce and sustain.)

If property is stolen from you, it belongs not to the thief but to you, even though it is in the former's possession. And if the thief sells it, it still belongs to you: there is no more right to sell stolen property than to steal in the first place. If the stolen material is found, it still belongs to you, not to the person who illegally bought it, even if he or she didn't know it was stolen property.

Very difficult practical problems arise, however, in connection with transmission of property confiscated from the owners. In World War II Jewish homeowners in Germany were evicted from their homes and sent to concentration camps; their homes were confiscated by the Nazi government and sold to Germans who wished to buy houses. In the course of years they improved the property, often quadrupling its value. Then descendants of the victims came to demand their property back: it had belonged to their parents, who presumably would have (had they lived) willed it to their children. But those houses were already occupied by German families who had presumably bought them in good faith; moreover, they had added to them many nondetachable improvements. What is the solution in such cases? The German government could either (1) evict the present occupants and restore the homes to the children of the rightful owners (now dead); or (2) allow the present occupants to remain but pay the rightful inheritors in money for the value of the house. (In most cases the inheritors had no great desire to reside in Germany, and the second policy was adopted.)

But why should property be owned by individuals? Why not have it communally owned? Many primitive tribes own property in common, and this is also the case with some collective farms. Sometimes people organize a commune and buy property, which is owned jointly by all members. When this is the decision of each member, no violation of rights is involved. But unless the members share the same ideals and are extremely tolerant, difficulties usually arise. Suppose that a few people do all the work, and the rest do little or nothing; they all get an equal share of the proceeds, the lazy as much as the industrious. Often the industrious persons get tired of sustaining the freeloaders and leave, and when the most industrious or imaginative persons are gone the commune breaks up. Nevertheless, this arrangement was the one they had all agreed upon to begin with, so there is no violation of property rights.

But when the communal arrangement is not voluntarily entered into by all its members, as with state farms in the Soviet Union and China, no individual's right to ownership is granted. He may plow the land and harvest the crops, but the land does not belong to him, and its use is controlled not by him but by government officials. People are told, to be sure, that they all "really own it together," that it "belongs to all the people." But none of the people (save the state officials) have a legal right to its use and disposal save what the officials grant them, and this is not a right but a permission, a permission that can be revoked at any time. The peasant does the work, while others retain control of the conditions of his work and the fruits of his labor.

Property rights, the right to possess things in the world to add to your own security, are of tremendous importance. Yet many questions have arisen which make many persons believe that property rights are prima facie rather than absolute. Let us suppose that you have a house and yard; what rights do you have with regard to their use?

1. The city council votes to build an art museum on the spot where your property is (or to convert your house into one). It condems the house, gives you what it considers "fair compensation," and tears it down (or starts the conversion). This is not quite the same as confiscation, for compensation is given (though often not for the property's market value). But suppose you don't want to sell it? Suppose you like living where you are and say the house is not for sale? Many people say that your property rights are only prima facie and can be abrogated in case of "public need": but many others of course, deny this, reminding us of the example of giving up your eyes in deference to an official who is considered more important than you are.

2. If you had an absolute right of domain on your own property, you could torture people in the basement and bury them in the yard, and no one would discover the deed if no one was permitted in to investigate. Of course, you would be violating others' right to life, but the point remains that you may not violate the rights of others, even on your own property.

3. You work until twelve and enjoy giving parties, which keep the neighbors awake, after that time. They complain, but you respond that it's your property and not theirs. Nevertheless, sound waves emanate from your property onto theirs and may make life unlivable for them. And your neighbors have rights too, not only to own their property but to enjoy it in peace. This is a difficult case, for if your neighbors are particularly astute of hearing, even a very small noise may keep them awake. The law usually specifies that "creating a disturbance" involves more than a "reasonable" amount of noise, leaving it vague what "reasonable" is. (It also depends on the hour: more

noise is permitted by day; but this, of course, makes it difficult for a person who sleeps by day and works at night.)

4. You allow animals to graze in your yard, offending your neighbors' sense of smell; or you leave your garbage out, collecting flies and rats. In both cases there may be a health hazard. Some people insist on a very high standard of cleanliness and others do not; this may be a matter of taste. But health hazards are not a matter of taste. Uses of your property which harm your neighbors would seem to constitute a violation of *their* right not to be harmed. You would undoubtedly believe they had violated your right not to be harmed if they did the same to you.

5. Potential hazards may also limit property rights. A neighbor raises poisonous snakes in his back yard. You haven't been bitten yet, but one of these days a snake may get loose and strike you. What is appropriate on a snake farm isn't necessarily so in the city. Again, depending on context, you are not entitled to just *any* use of your property. It isn't the ownership of it that is in question here, but the use of it, which may be a hazard to others.

6. To protect your property against marauders, you build a fence around it and electrify the fence to deter trespassers. Or you construct a moat around the house, filling the water in it with piranhas. Is this a violation of the rights of others? No, you may say, since they shouldn't be trespassing on your property. Still, to be zapped to death or eaten alive seems quite an extraordinary punishment for trespassing. The trespasser has violated your property rights, but haven't you violated his or her right to life? Again the situation is tricky, because a violation of your property rights is involved, and just as in the case of the murderer, hasn't the rights violator given up certain rights? Some kind of proportionality between the violation and the punishment is usually insisted on by the law: if you catch the neighbor boy stealing one of your watermelons, you are entitled to stop him, but not to shoot him dead on the spot.

Do these examples show that property rights are only prima facie? Only the person who believes (as in the first example) that others have a right to take your property from you will be inclined to believe this. The other examples do not deny your property rights but insist that there are uses of your property which are a threat to others and should be denied to you because, while you do have a right of ownership, others also have a right not to be harmed. Thus certain qualifications have to be built into the rule (law) entitling you to possession of your property.

Most people receive compensation for labor in the form of wages. Money can be used to buy possessions, including real estate. The form of property you elect to have is thus a matter of personal choice, within the limits of your income.

Special forms of property rights are conferred by *patents* and *copyrights*. If you have written a book, perhaps a labor of years, the fruits of your labor are in the completed manuscript, just as the fruits of your gardening labors are in the harvest. You cannot copyright the ideas contained in the book but only the series of words; that is, if someone issued that same series of, for example, 100,000 words which may have taken you two years to write, under his or her own name, this action would be theft as much as if the person had stolen the furniture or art objects that took you two years to construct. (Indeed, even if only a few hundred of your words are stolen, that is a violation of copyright law.) In the same way, if you have created an invention, the work of your brain, you can patent it, which means that others cannot use it without your consent.

Both forms of property, however, are legally limited in time. A copyright on a book expires fifty years after the author's death (by the International Copyright Agreement); in this way the author's heirs can also profit from his or her labors, but only immediate descendants (children); remote descendants cannot profit from it, for the work then goes into the public domain and can be reprinted by anyone. The children are a part of the family the author was laboring to support, but the more remote descendants would not be, nor would they be deprived of the author's time while he or she was creating. Similarly, a patent expires after a limited period, since it is believed (usually with good reason) that someone else would have had the same idea in the course of time; but the time of expiration, often ten years, is fairly arbitrary.

Laws of nature are discovered, not invented; they are no one's private domain, and their discovery cannot be patented. The *use* of them, however, can be, for a limited period. Recipes cannot be copyrighted at all, however ingenious. Nor can ideas, such as Plato's theory of universals, be copyrighted; only (had he lived in an era of copyright) the succession of words in which the ideas were set forth can be. One reason sometimes given for this law is that just as no one owns laws of nature, there is no individual ownership of ideas. (If Plato had been able to copyright his theory, many subsequent philosophers who published variations on it would have been out of business.) Another reason is simply a consideration of utility: it is desirable to disseminate knowledge as widely as possible, and the author is already sufficiently protected in the succession of words he or she has created, even if the ideas embodied in those words are in the domain of everyone.

C. The Right to Freedom of Expression

If we interpret the right to life in its maximal way, then the *right to freedom of expression* is already part of it: if you have a right to live by your own choices as long as you do not violate the rights of others in so doing, you have the right to speak and write what you wish.

The right to enjoy freedom of speech and the press is of special importance because of the great value attached to knowledge and its communication. We may disagree publicly with our neighbors, with our church or school, and with the government. Because governments have tried to keep people from expressing their own ideas when they conflict with official government views, they have been the principal violators of this right, by censoring whatever was unwelcome to them. It is with this realization that the Founding Fathers of the United States incorporated into the Constitution the First Amendment: "Congress shall make no law . . . abridging the freedom of speech, or of the press."

In Chapter 2 of his classic book *On Liberty,* Mill argued for virtually unlimited freedom of speech and the press. It makes no difference, said Mill, if your views are opposed to the official ones, nor if you are in a small minority (and thus easily suppressed); the smallest minority, a minority of one, has the same right to express an opinion publicly, as does the majority. "If all mankind minus one," said Mill, "were of one opinion, and only one person were of the contrary opinion, mankind would be no more justified in silencing that one person, than he, if he had the power, would be justified in silencing mankind." [12]

Suppose, conjectured Mill, that the opinion people are attempting to suppress is *true.* (1) By assuming it to be true, without permitting it to be discussed, they are assuming their own infallibility. (2) If they do not fear the opposing view, why suppress it? Why not let it be discussed publicly so that everyone can come to see its falsehood? (3) It is only by testing a view in the marketplace of ideas that we can come to know that it is true; if it is suppressed, without the presentation of contrary evidence, we can only *assume* it to be true. (4) Almost every important idea has at some time been suppressed; such suppressions have often set back human progress for centuries and kept all but the most courageous from putting forth their ideas at all. This is a tremendous loss to the human race, besides being an ignoble way to treat humankind's most original minds. (5) If it is objected that certain things, such as religion, should be instilled in everyone, for utility's sake, in order to "hold together the moral fabric of society," Mill responded that the usefulness of an opinion is itself a matter of opinion, as disputable (and as open to discussion) as the opinion itself.

Suppose that the opinion the authorities are attempting to suppress is *false.* Again, they cannot know it to be false unless they submit it to open and free discussion. Besides, false opinions are needed to keep the truth vivid in people's minds. A view, even if true, must be challenged constantly, else it will become a dead dogma, an inherited prejudice, taken for granted rather than passing through the crucible of criticism.

Mill presented many other arguments. But what all were designed to show is the great *utility* of having freedom of expression. If there was no such utility, would the authorities then be justified in suppressing freedom of speech? Mill's answer is not clear, but Mill certainly did not put any emphasis upon it as a right.

[12] John Stuart Mill, *On Liberty,* (1859), Chapter 2.

To what, then, are you entitled by right of the freedom of speech? A number of troublesome cases quickly come to mind.

1. There is a stock question used almost every time freedom of speech is discussed: Do you have a right to yell "Fire!" without cause in a crowded theater? (The "without cause" is important; if there really is a fire, you may save lives by detecting it, although even so you probably are better advised to tell the manager so that the patrons can exit in an orderly manner.) If people can say what they like any time, why can't you do this?

The answer is that the right to freedom of expression does not entitle you to say anything you want at any time. In this case, the right is restricted by the property rights of others. The owner or manager permits moviegoers to enter the theater for one reason—to see the picture and to do so quietly enough so that other patrons are not disturbed. Playing a trick on them by yelling "Fire!" is not one of the things a member of the audience is permitted to do, by the terms of the implicit contract between patron and owner. Indeed, you are not even permitted to disturb the other patrons, and the owner has a right to evict any individual who does. The owner permits you, on payment of admission, to enter the theater and see the film in a way that does not disturb the rest of the audience; and you have the right to remain and watch the film only so long as this condition is met.

2. For the same reason, you have no right to enter a church and shout obscenities there. It is not that you have no right to express your opinion, but that you can't do it *there,* on someone else's property, under conditions to which the owners of that property would not consent. On your own property you have certain rights that others do not have: just as you can plant flowers in your own yard as you choose, although your neighbors cannot (without your permission), so you can say and do things in your own house (subject to the usual conditions of not disturbing your neighbors unduly) that others cannot. If you are a guest, you are there by your host's sufferance, and if you act so as to annoy him, you may be told to leave. (Of course, as with any other active right, the host may not choose to exercise it.)

3. If you own a newspaper or magazine, you have a right to publish what you like in it (subject to certain conditions, as the discussion of the First Amendment below makes clear). But if someone else comes in and demands that you publish a certain item in your paper, you have the right to say no; indeed, you have the right to refuse even if the person offers to pay for an ad, if you consider it in some way objectionable. You have property rights with respect to your own paper, and no one else has the right to put what he or she wants in it; if you publish the piece anyway, for free or even paying the author for it, that is a privilege you extend to him or her but not a right. Others may then boycott the paper if they find its coverage one-sided, or they may start one of their own, distribute mimeographed handbills criticizing you, or publish something critical of you in another newspaper or magazine. You have no right to stop them from doing any of these things, but,

as novelist Ayn Rand contends, you do have property rights over your own paper:

> The right to property means that a man has the right to take the economic actions necessary to earn property, to use it and dispose of it; it does *not* mean that others must provide him with property.
>
> The right of *free speech* means that a man has the right to express his ideas without danger of suppression, interference, or punitive action by the government. It does *not* mean that others must provide him with a lecture hall, a radio station, or a printing press through which to express his ideas.
>
> Any undertaking that involves more than one man requires the *voluntary* consent of every participant. Every one of them has the *right* to make his own decision; but none has the right to force his decision on the others.[13]

4. Suppose that a large billboard on top of a building contains words or pictures which many people find offensive. They can criticize and boycott the merchants who caused or permitted the sign to be erected above their premises. But what if the billboard is on public property? What of the sex magazine racks along the sidewalk, also on public property, which contain words or pictures which many people consider offensive?

If the sidewalks were privately owned, it would be up to the owner to decide whether to risk loss of some profit resulting from a boycott of the store. If the risk was serious enough, the offending material would probably be removed; if not, it would stay, and some shoppers would go elsewhere instead. But there is a problem with "public property," namely, *who* owns it? "The people," comes the reply, or, "Everyone." But we have already seen the trouble with this concept: everyone who pays taxes helps to pay for it, but only a few people (say, in city hall) control it: it is for them to decide whether such material should or should not be available for public scrutiny. But in matters involving "collective ownership," usually a large number of people are never satisfied, no matter what the decision is. Some people, who have paid taxes for the upkeep of streets and sidewalks, want the offending material there, or they would not buy it; and others are equally vehement in not wanting it there, and they have paid taxes too. In such a case the question of why people should help to pay for something they don't want and wouldn't voluntarily consent to is not answerable to everyone's satisfaction.

Whether public or private, however, there are some uses of words (written or spoken) that the courts have come, rightly or wrongly, to construe as not covered by (or implicitly contained in) the First Amendment. The main categories are:

---

[13] Ayn Rand, "Man's Rights," in *The Virtue of Selfishness* (New York: Signet, 1964), p. 97.

1. *Threats to national security.* If you reveal where some American atomic submarines are, or if you publish the location of ICBM's so that enemy missiles can destroy them, you are endangering the lives of other persons. Such "exercise of free speech" is therefore prohibited, not because it is speech but because it is a threat to the lives and liberties of other human beings (yourself included). It is true that much material that should not be (or should no longer be) kept under wraps is still listed as "classified" by the government; but if your divulging it really is a threat to the lives of others—or could reasonably be construed to be—your decision to publish or circulate it could well conflict with the right of other people to their lives.

2. *Obscenity.* Much material, both words and pictures, is considered obscene. Standards of obscenity have relaxed considerably since the ban on James Joyce's *Ulysses* (because of a few four-letter words in it). In 1924 that ban was lifted, but still some material that contains such words and has no "redeeming social value" (however that phrase may be construed) is subject to government censorship (federal, state, or local).

Whether the government should be able to censor material remains a subject of hot dispute. If people want to read "trash" or see X-rated films, shouldn't they be free to do so? The late Supreme Court Justice Hugo Black observed that the First Amendment contains no if's, and's, or but's—that constitutionally anything that anyone wants to say should be permitted under the First Amendment. But perhaps, others say, such conditions were implicit (though there is no trace of them, and Black certainly seems to have a point). Whether or not censorship of pornography is constitutional, the question remains whether it *should* be available. The most prevalent view on this point is that adults should be permitted to go to "adult" bookstores and see X-rated movies but that children should not. (Children's rights are discussed below.) Perhaps such offending material should not be displayed to children, on street-corner bookstands, and they should be prohibited from entering "adult" bookstores or X-rated movie theaters.

What then of adults? Some adults find this material so offensive that they demand that all such bookstores and theaters be closed by law. But there is one fairly powerful objection to their view: if they don't like them, they don't have to go in. Nobody forces anyone to enter them. Isn't demanding that others be stopped from doing so the equivalent of moral busybodyism? Would they like it if a law was passed stopping *them* from entering bookstores that sold things they wanted to buy (e.g., tracts of certain offbeat religious cults)? After all, the claim can't be made, as in national security cases, that lives are jeopardized by the display or purchase of such material. Objectors may complain that their morals are in jeopardy, but then, one might ask, shouldn't their morals be their own affair? In any case, what seems immoral to one person may seem innocent or highly moral to others. Seeing X-rated movies may even discharge, through "substitute gratification," impulses which, left to build up without release, would result in great frustration and perhaps rape. Isn't it possible that having such movies available is a kind of "moral safety valve"? [14]

A few years ago a young man paraded through the halls of a Los Angeles courthouse wearing a leather jacket on the back of which was inscribed, in large letters, the words "Fuck the draft." Such words, it was argued, were permissible in books available in certain bookstores (although not everyone agreed even to this); however, they should not be permitted when paraded about in a public place, where even those people who sought to avoid them could not easily do so. There was no breach of national security here, only the expression of a view; he should have been entitled to express the view, opponents claimed, but not to use obscene language in doing so. Should he have been protected under the First Amendment? (In fact, he was, for the case was dismissed.) The issues intertwined here were (a) whether the use of "offensive language" rather than more neutral language was permissible; (b) whether using such language in a public place was legal; and (c) whether the young man was engaged in "free speech" or something else, such as incitement to illegal actions.

3. *Libel and slander.* You cannot ruin another person's *character* by attacking him or her verbally, but you may ruin his or her *reputation*. (Character is what you are, reputation is what others think of you.) To what extent this use of words should be prohibited is a matter of continuing controversy. When you write words attacking another person falsely, it is *libel;* when you speak the words orally, it is *slander*. (Originally libel was considered the worse offense because the offending words were available to many more people than words spoken orally. But with the invention of radio and television, the spoken word can be communicated to a much larger audience than can be reached by the written word.) In the case of both libel and slander, you can inflict damage on others through the use of words, and damage to people's reputation can be as serious and lasting as injury to their body. Usually charges of libel or slander can be made to stick only if the plaintiff can prove specific damage, such as loss of a job or ability to make a living, loss of business, or, sometimes, wounded feelings and bodily suffering.

As usual, there are many borderline cases. (a) A woman believes that, though all names in a movie are supposed to be fictitious, the film audience will recognize a certain characterization as an unflattering portrait of her; so she sues the studio for libel. (b) A newspaper ad for yo-yos uses a far-out imaginary name for the proud owner of a yo-yo, "Mr. Blenerhasset"; whereupon a man actually named Blenerhassett who works on Wall Street sues the advertiser for libel, alleging that he has been held up to ridicule by the ad. (c) A pharmacist whose name has been omitted inadvertently from a directory of American pharmacists sues the company issuing the directory,

---

[14] See John Hospers, *Understanding the Arts* (Englewood Cliffs, N.J.: Prentice-Hall, 1981), Chapter 6.

saying that he has been damaged in his profession by the omission. (In most cases malicious intent is required, but was not in this case.) (d) A picture of a man is shown in a magazine in such a way as to make him look ridiculous; he sues the magazine. (In this case only the picture appears, but no words.) (e) A Mississippi newspaper carries a local news item about a certain lady who was consorting with a "cultured gentleman," but the newspaper misprinted "cultured" as "colored," which, she says in her suit against the newspaper, has damaged her reputation in the community. (f) A man trains his parrot to say nasty things about a business colleague of his, and on cue the parrot repeats those remarks at a dinner party at which the colleague is present. He sues, but the defendant alleges that it was the parrot who made the remarks, not he. Cases like these appear all the time in the courts.[15]

That individuals can damage one another by words as well as by violent acts is surely true. Most people agree that malicious remarks made falsely about someone in public should be subject to legal penalties. Some would say, however, that if everyone was permitted to say anything he or she wished about anyone else, eventually no one would believe what was being said, whereas now it is likely to be believed unless the person institutes a defamation (libel or slander) lawsuit against the accuser. In any case, many of the attempts to show that someone has been "wounded in mind" by false allegations are somewhat ridiculous; but doubtless they will continue as long as there are lawyers who accept such cases and juries who will convict.

4. *Speech inciting to riot.* When the American Nazi party requested permission to parade along the streets of Skokie, Illinois, with anti-Jewish banners and slogans, they defended their request as freedom of speech under the First Amendment. It was objected that the choice of Skokie, a large percentage of whose population were survivors of the Nazi death camps, was not coincidental; thus under the banner of free speech their march was actually an incitement to riot, since the would-be marchers knew full well that their Nazi slogans would foment a violent reaction among the people of Skokie. And so the march was banned. Should it have been? Was the denial a violation of the right of free speech?

The issue hinges on the distinction between speech and action. The Nazi marchers were not prevented from expressing their views in their publications, which were available in their bookstores and carried through the mails. Words can be used not only for informational purposes and propaganda, but also as an incitement to riot and civil commotion. And when they are so used, human lives may be endangered. The fact that *words* were used does not prove that the words were intended for an informational purpose (which was the sole purpose Mill considered in *On Liberty*); if they were in fact intended as incitement to violence, then perhaps it was right for the march to be banned.

---

[15] For a discussion of such cases, see the chapter on defamation in Charles Gregory, Harry Kalven, and Richard Epstein, eds., *Cases and Materials in Torts* (Boston: Little, Brown, 1978).

Some would object that even so the march should not have been banned: there was only a chance that violence would occur, and the chance of violence is not yet the *fact* of violence; until the march occurred no one knew whether violence would materialize. Involved in this dispute is the delicate question of *how much* risk of life there was. If people were certain to be killed or injured, then perhaps it was right to ban the march; but what if the chances were only 10 percent or 1 percent? Wasn't the importance of free speech worth the danger?

5. *Speech inciting to criminal action.* Suppose I say to someone, "That jewelry store at the corner is a perfect setup for robbery," but I let it go at that and say no more; so far, there is only speech, no action. Suppose that later I say, "I wonder what it would take to rob the place?" Still no action. Suppose I start to draw up plans concerning how to pick locks, and I purchase various supplies such as material that can neutralize burglar alarms. Still no action. Then I say to the other person, "I have the material and the plans. Let's hit the place tonight at midnight." Should that be protected under the heading of freedom of speech? After all, I'm only talking, not robbing the store. In general, the law says no; the activity described is no longer merely speech protected by the First Amendment, but a conspiracy, and conspiracy is subject to criminal sanctions (since it is a felony). This is not an example merely of speech. Just as the Nazi marchers were an example of incitement to riot, so this is an example of incitement to robbery.

As the examples discussed above show, the limits of freedom of speech are a matter of considerable and continuing controversy. The limits of the right to free speech are reached when they collide with *other* rights. Under the circumstances either we can say that all the rights are prima facie and that in the conflicts of rights we investigated, one or the other must be sacrificed; or we can say (although this is more difficult) that all the rights are absolute and, provided they are stated carefully at the outset with the required qualifications (such as by distinguishing speech from incitement to riot), no conflict need occur. But whether all the relevant qualifying conditions can be laid down in advance is a thorny problem (one we have already touched upon in discussing the objections to rule-utilitarianism on pp. 224–32).

D. Welfare Rights

Many other rights besides those already discussed have been claimed. "I have a right to two weeks of paid vacation per year." "I have a right to free textbooks at school." "I have a right to $500,000 a year plus a yacht." Almost everything that people want for any reason whatever tends to be claimed by them as a right. The California Welfare Rights Organization recently claimed the right to "jobs at the executive level" before its members would consent to do without welfare payments.

In some contexts a person does indeed have a right to such things as money and vacations as a *special* right, not as a *general* right owed to all human beings. If you have a contractual agreement with your employer to receive a certain wage for a certain period of time plus a paid vacation every year, then you have a right to that wage plus the paid vacation. (It may not even be a *just* wage. As we shall see in our examination of justice in the next chapter, there are many instances of injustice which involve no violation of rights.) Of course, the employer has a right to your labor for a specified period in return; in other words, you are contractually obliged to provide the work, and he or she is contractually obliged to provide the compensation. The question is: Other than special rights, what general rights of this kind (if any) do all human beings have, simply as human beings?

There is a difference between the rights we will now discuss and all the previous examples of rights: the previous ones were all *negative* rights, and these are *positive* rights. Respecting others' rights to life, property, and liberty requires only that you forbear to interfere with their exercise of them. But if welfare rights exist, then others must not only forbear to interfere, they also must positively *do* something. If you have a right to food and shelter from me, then I have an obligation to supply that food and shelter. And your right may involve a considerable compromise of my right to live by *my* choices.

All *welfare rights* involve a positive obligation to assist in providing for other persons' welfare. The claimant to welfare rights does not say merely, "It would be a fine thing if you would help me out" or "It would be wonderful of you" or "I shall be forever grateful if you help me" but "You are obliged to help me; I have a right to your assistance."

To what kind of assistance do people claim to be entitled by right? Few would go so far as to claim "jobs at the executive level," particularly if dishwashers and janitors have to pay in taxes to sustain those claimants. What is usually claimed under the heading of welfare rights is the "right to a minimum standard of living," or a "right to whatever is necessary."

The meaning of the term "necessary" is elastic, for it does not sufficiently describe anything very definite. For a kingship, royal blood is necessary; for a boxing match, an arena is necessary. "Necessary for sustaining life" may be what is meant. But, as Epicurus said, only water and a few simple foods are necessary for sustaining life; shelter in colder climates is also necessary. Is medicine necessary? Yes, often, to cure diseases which would otherwise cause death. Penicillin may be necessary; so may kidney machines, artificial lungs, oxygen tents, and all manner of medical paraphernalia, depending on the circumstances. Moreover, in some cases a car may be considered a necessity for getting around, a telephone for keeping in contact with job opportunities, a television set for keeping up with the news, and so on. Countless things may be counted as necessary for special purposes involving people's economic well-being, even their economic survival in the face of competition (at least for certain kinds of jobs). In an American city indoor toilets and baths may be considered a necessity, although in a jungle village on the Amazon they may not be so. What is considered "minimal" is variable in the same way. Moreover, as one need after another is fulfilled, there is an almost irresistible tendency to include others as also "minimal."

In what does the right to welfare consist, then? Is it a right at all? There are two contrasting views on these questions, as the following dialogue illustrates:

A: I believe that everyone in the world has a right to at least a minimum standard of living, a floor below which no one should be permitted to fall. People cannot pursue their distinctively human activities if they are in constant fear of starvation or death from cold. They must have at least the minimum, though admittedly this minimum varies from place to place on the earth's surface.

B: But there are places in which even this minimum cannot be supplied. There are nations so poverty-stricken that there is no way in which the hundreds of millions of people who live there could all receive what we would call a decent standard of living. In time the givers soon would become poverty-stricken themselves and in need of the same welfare as they were trying to supply to others.

A: In some cases that might be true. But my contention is that those in need have a right to welfare, even though at some particular times or places there is no way of implementing the right by supplying that need.

B: But what can we say of a right that can't be implemented? If a person says, "I have a right to X" but there's no way to supply X, such a right surely isn't worth much.

A: It means that those in need still have a moral *claim* on those who are not, even if in certain circumstances that need cannot be fully met. It serves to remind those who are not in need that they have a duty to fulfill that need.

B: I agree that it would be highly desirable if no one faced poverty or want. But given the world situation—burgeoning population, governments that confiscate the fruits of people's labor, fertile lands turning into deserts, and other climatic changes—poverty is simply a fact of life now, nor is it likely to go away in the foreseeable future. What I challenge is not the desirability of everyone having enough, but the claim that this is a *right*. If help is freely given, it may be freely and gratefully received; but no one can claim a portion of the earned income of others as a right. Remember, a right of A implies a duty of B, C, D, and so on; and in the case of welfare, it is not a negative right—which requires only the duty of noninterference from others—but a positive right, one that requires positive action from others (their giving up some of their income).

A: But you grant this in other cases, don't you? If Smith buys a car from Jones and has agreed to pay for it in six monthly installments, Jones, who has surrendered the car to Smith, has a right to those promised payments. That's a contractual right.

B: Of course; this is a case of a special right, which exists by virtue of a contract voluntarily drawn up between Smith and Jones. But I don't remember being a party to any contract between me and all the rest of my countrymen, or the whole human race. Those that are in poverty I shall help to the limited extent that I can. But I am not the cause of their poverty; I sympathize with them, but I did not bring about their condition. I shall be benevolent to as many of them as I can, but since I am not responsible for their plight, I don't see how they can claim my benevolence as their right. Remember again that a positive right is a claim on the resources of other persons. If they have a right to a portion of my earnings, then I (and others) have the duty to give it to them; and if it is their right, they can claim a portion of what I have earned as theirs; without so much as a thank you: even if they scoff and sneer at me, even if they spend my earnings on foolish things, if theirs is the right to receive, mine is the duty to give.

A: And don't you have such a duty—and I too? We are all here together on spaceship Earth, and the least we can do is try to help one another.

B: I am not arguing that we should not; I am saying only that others cannot claim your or my beneficence as their right. If people who live in my vicinity, especially relatives and friends, are in need, I shall help if I can. But 2 million Cambodians in recent memory were killed under Pol Pot's regime in an act of systematic genocide,[16] and there is little or nothing you or I could have done about that. As long as I did not cause their condition, and did not owe them any recompense, I don't see how they could have claimed my beneficence as their right—or how it would have helped them even if they could have.

A: But don't you owe them something, just because they are human beings like yourself? If you were to exchange places with them, wouldn't you desire their beneficence?

B: Desire it, yes; but even so I would not believe that I was *entitled* to it. I would be entitled to it only if they were responsible for my being in a condition of need.

A: I would say that your attitude in the matter is not very humanitarian.

B: I would be humanitarian with my own money, on behalf of those people or causes I felt needed the help and deserved it. I would try to make sure that the money I earned and gave to them was well spent. Under those conditions, I would do it voluntarily, of my own free will. But I would oppose being forced to do it by the political route, through taxation; for when governments take it from me and it goes to whatever causes those in power

[16] See John Barron and Anthony Paul, *Murder of a Gentle Land* (New York: Reader's Digest Press, 1977).

decide to embrace, I can usually be pretty certain that it will *not* always go to worthy causes and that it will *not* be well spent. Consider the $150 billion that the U.S. government—that is, the U.S. taxpayer—has poured into foreign aid since World War II; very little of it alleviated the world's poverty, and most of it lined the pockets of politicians and kept alive petty dictatorships that oppressed the very people they were supposed to help. Or consider the nearly $300 billion of the American federal budget that goes to transfer payments—welfare, food stamps, subsidized housing, and the like. Some of it does get to the deserving poor, but much of it pays for the army of thousands of bureaucrats who administer those programs and who don't want to see them diminished because then they would lose their influence and power. (And let's not forget the politicians who promise more programs in order to get reelected.) Much of the money also goes to those who are poor but needn't be—who could have jobs if small businesses weren't so hamstrung by high taxes that they go bankrupt or have to lay off employees, adding still further to the lists of the needy. And much of the money goes to such poor as buy drugs or cases of Scotch with their welfare payments and let their children starve, or who waste it on foolish things that taxpayers who provide this income can't afford themselves. Would you voluntarily give in light of such massive waste and corruption? Let me read you just two examples (there are thousands) from writers who have investigated the subject.

> Between 1960 and 1971, the total level of expenditure on social welfare programs increased from $50 billion in 1960 to $171 billion in 1971—about a $120 billion dollar increase.
>
> It so happens that, according to the Bureau of Census, there are about 25 million poor people in the United States. . . . If we take those 25 million poor people and divide them into the $120 billion increase, *not* the whole thing, *just* the increase—we discover that if we had simply taken the money and given it to the poor people, we would have given each of them an annual stipend of $4,800, which means an income for a family of four of $19,200. That is, we could have made every poor person a relatively rich person. But we didn't. . . .
>
> What happened to the money? It went to social workers and counselors and planners and social engineers and urban renewal experts and the assistant administrators to the administrative assistants.[17]

> If you divided the budget of the Bureau of Indian Affairs by the number of Indians in the country, the average Indian family would receive over $30,000 a year. You could cut the budget in half, fire all the bureaucrats, and still give each Indian family $15,000+. But . . . there are certain individuals who have a vested interest in ridiculing this idea: employees of the Bureau of Indian Affairs.

---

[17]Irving Kristol, "Where Has All the Money Gone?" *Conservative Digest*, February 1977, p. 39.

[How to get rid of poverty?] Hold a meeting of all the leading experts on poverty somewhere in the middle of the Pacific and not let them go home for ten years. When they came back, they would discover there was no more poverty.[18]

In fact, the dislocations of the economy, caused by the very taxes and regulations that are supposed to end poverty, will actually increase it, depriving people of jobs and unnecessarily keeping them as permanent dependents in the welfare system.[19] And so, through the years, taxes, the national debt, and inflation have reached such proportions that they are crippling the economy and limiting the opportunities to rise that have always been the hope of the poor in America. Taxation can't possibly raise all the money spent on these programs, so the government simply prints more money to cover the deficit (inflation), thus reducing the value of each unit (dollar) and destroying the savings of the thrifty. When economic catastrophe finally occurs and the poor (unemployed because of the ball and chain on private enterprise) appeal for more funds, there will no longer be any way to provide for them; the cry "We did it for you" will not help them. Our misplaced humanitarianism, which led more people to feed out of the public trough than could possibly be sustained, will have destroyed us as a nation, rich and poor alike.

A: All that, even if true, is an indictment of the methods used, not of the humanitarian goal itself.

B: The methods are part of "the nature of the beast": whenever you have lots of money to spend which isn't your own, and know that if you waste it there's more where that came from (by raising taxes or inflating the money supply), it's simply inevitable that you won't spend it as wisely as you would if you had earned the money yourself. Trusting government with your money is like trusting the fox to guard the chickenhouse. What's more, voluntary charity languishes when government decides for us (through taxation) to what causes we must contribute.

A: What then do you suggest, since apparently you don't disapprove of helping the poor?

B: Take the shackles off the small businesses that would employ most of

---

[18] The first paragraph is quoted from Gary North, *Remnant Review,* August 15, 1980. The second paragraph is quoted from an interview with economist Thomas Sowell in *Reason,* December 1980, p. 5.

[19] See, for example, Henry Hazlitt, *The Conquest of Poverty* (Westport, Conn.: Arlington House, 1973); Clarence B. Carson, *The War on the Poor* (Westport, Conn.: Arlington House, 1969); Isabel Paterson, *The God in the Machine* (Caldwell, Idaho: Caxton Press, 1943), especially the chapter "The Humanitarian and the Guillotine"; John Hospers, *Libertarianism* (New York: Laissez Faire Books, 1971), especially Chapter 7; George Reisman, *The Government against the Economy* (Ottawa, Ill.: Caroline House, 1979); and George Gilder, *Wealth and Poverty* (New York: Basic Books, 1981). For statistics and other empirical data, see, for example, Donald Lambro, *Fat City* (South Bend, Ind.: Regnery/Gateway, 1980); Shirley Scheibla, *Poverty Is Where the Money Is* (Westport, Conn.: Arlington House, 1968); and Frances F. Piven and Richard A. Cloward, *Regulating the Poor* (New York: Random House, 1971).

the poor. If you feed the hungry, they will be hungry again tomorrow; but if you start a business and give them a job, they will soon be self-sufficient and won't need your charity. In a thriving economy only a comparatively small number—the physically and mentally incapacitated—will need your charity. Virtually everyone else could be employed if the economy weren't hobbled by taxes and regulations. The U.S. government has poured billions of dollars into India, for example, without alleviating its poverty; the nation has a strangling bureaucracy which makes it almost impossible for people to rise on their own, no matter how great their ability. Indians who emigrated to other countries, such as Fiji, are among the most industrious and prosperous of the inhabitants; it's just that back home they can't make it, not for lack of industry but for lack of an incentive: the government keeps them down. If you transformed the economy of even that overpopulated nation into one in which people had incentives to rise to the top of the economic ladder, it wouldn't be long before the need for charity would be eliminated. Trying to attack poverty directly is like bailing water out of a leaky boat: it can be done in dire emergencies, but it isn't the answer. The real answer lies in eliminating the *causes* of poverty, by leaving people economically free and getting the governments of the world off their backs. A rising tide raises all boats.

A: Please remind me not to rely on *you* when I am in need!

B: If your need is unavoidable and not the result of your own foolishness, and if I am able, you can indeed rely on me. Being generous to others is a fine thing; but being generous with other people's money, which is what governments do, is not. You may think so highly of a "humanitarian" program that you entreat me to assist you in your cause; and if I consider it a worthy cause, I shall do so. But if you say, "The cause I believe in is so important that I not only consent to help it, I also consent for *you* to help it," I will have to draw the line: you cannot consent on my behalf, for *my* consent can be given only by me. Yet this is just what governments do: they consent, on my behalf, to take my tax dollars and pour them into enterprises so unworthy to begin with, and so full of waste and corruption besides, that I would never even in a moment of craziness voluntarily consent to support them. Yet I am forced to support them because those in government can imprison me for not paying the taxes that support the programs.

A: But if the proposals you recommend don't work, I still say that those in need have a right to our assistance.

B: "Right" is a very precious word, one that I would reserve for very special contexts. If someone helps me, I don't claim to have a right to his help; I am simply grateful for a gift freely given. It has become customary to take anything people happen to *desire* and call it a *right:* if they want an apartment at rates so low that they have to be subsidized by every other taxpayer, they just get off the hook by saying they have a *right* to it. Not everything people want, or even need, can be a right, or else there would be no end to the corresponding duties of others. There would be a bottomless pit of unending needs. Let me leave you with two quotes that summarize what I'm trying to say:

Jobs, food, clothing, recreation, homes, and medical care, education, etc., do not grow in nature. These are manmade values—goods and services produced by men. *Who* is to provide them?

If some men are entitled *by right* to the products of the work of others, it means that those others are deprived of rights and condemned to slave labor.

Any alleged "right" of one man, which necessitates the violation of the rights of another, is not and cannot be right.

No one can have a right to impose an unchosen obligation, an unrewarded duty or an involuntary servitude on another man. There can be no such thing as *"the right to enslave."*

A right does not include the material implementation of that right by others; it includes only the freedom to earn that implementation by one's own effort.[20]

Anyone who says that economic security is a human right has been too much babied. While he babbles, other men are risking and losing their lives to protect him. They are fighting the sea, fighting the land, fighting diseases and insects and weather and space and time, for him, while he chatters that all men have a right to security and that the State must give it to them. Let the fighting men stop fighting this inhuman earth for one hour, and he will learn how much security there is.

Let him get out on the front lines. Let him bring one slow freight through a snowstorm in the Rockies. Let him drive one rivet to hold his apartment roof over his head. Let him keep his own electric light burning through one quiet cozy winter evening when the mist is freezing to the wires. Let him make, from seed to table, just one slice of bread, and we will hear no more about the human right to security.

No man's security is greater than his own self-reliance. If every man and woman worth living did not stand up to the job of living, did not take risk and danger and exhaustion and go on fighting for one thin hope of victory in the certainty of death, there would not be a human being alive today.[21]

---

[20] Rand, "Man's Rights," pp. 96–97.
[21] Rose Wilder Lane, *The Discovery of Freedom: Man's Struggle against Authority* (New York: Arno Press, 1943), p. 60.

E. The Rights of Children

Just as the greatest philosophical perplexities occur at the joints of concepts, so the most difficult moral questions occur at the juncture of rules. One rule we have concerning children is "Since children are not always able to make decisions for themselves, parents should make them on the children's behalf"; another is "Since children are human beings, they have the right to make their own decisions." Clearly, these two rules can come into conflict.

Your chair is your property; you have the right to the use and disposal of it, and you can hack it to pieces and burn it if you so choose. Your children are not your property in this way. You do not own your children; children are human beings, with rights and privileges of their own. What makes children different is that (to varying degrees with different children) they are not fully capable of exercising those rights: an infant can make no decisions, a child can make some, and a teen-ager can make many more. The boundary lines are not sharp, and within each group there is enormous variation.

With increasing maturity children can come to exercise free choice to an even greater extent. Some indications of maturity are: (1) the ability to respond to reasoning and to recognize the possible consequences of actions, (2) the willpower to act in accordance with these considerations, (3) the ability to look ahead to the remoter consequences and plan actions accordingly, and (4) the ability to give up present pleasures if in the long run they will cause grief and misery.

Since children are not their parents' property, parents have no right to abandon, mistreat, or in any way be cruel to them. Parents are *guardians* of the children's rights until they are able to exercise them independently. But such guardianship should continue only as long as the parents *do* fulfill the obligations incumbent on them in guarding the children's rights. Many parents do not even begin to prepare their children for the assumption of their rights. There are parents who keep children in locked closets for months, put lighted cigarettes on their skins, beat them mercilessly, tie them hand and foot, even bake them in ovens; sometimes neighbors hearing cries call the police and enable the children to be rescued, and sometimes the children die, with no one outside knowing what has happened to them. Such parents, of course, have violated the rights of their children and demonstrated their unfitness for guardianship over them.

But if children are not parents' property, neither are they the State's. In Plato's *Republic* and other works describing utopias, communes of men and women held children in common, so that no child would know who his or her parents were; in totalitarian societies, the State takes children away from their parents at an early age and trains them, so that the children will not be under the "corrupting" influence of parents. The State can thus condition the children to accept its propaganda while they are in their formative years and not easily able to question what they are told. A society of obedient slaves is thereby brought into being.

In the Soviet Union children are taught to spy on their parents and to turn them in if they say or do anything against the Soviet State. In one village in the Ukraine a farmer gave refuge to some who were fleeing from the secret police. His twelve-year-old son, having learned at school that it was his sacred duty to report all such things, informed on his father. The father was shot the same day. The enraged peasants lynched the boy. Today the Soviet Union maintains the house where the son betrayed the father as a sacred shrine; *Pravda* wrote, "In this timbered house was held the court at which Pavlik unmasked his father who had sheltered the kulaks. Here are the reliquaries dear to the heart of every inhabitant of this village." [22]

Before children are taken to state orphanages, which often happens if their parents become dissidents or church members, they must sign a statement: "As from today's date I ask not to be considered the son, or the daughter, of such-and-such parents. I renounce them as socially harmful elements and I promise in the future to have nothing whatever to do with them and to maintain no communication with them." [23]

When parents are thought to be, or in some cases actually have proven themselves to be, incapable guardians of children's rights, a tremendously difficult problem arises. If the State places the children into foster homes, the results may be worse than in all but the worst of parental environments. Even if the attention they receive from their own parents is not benevolent—indeed is quite hostile—at least they know that they are receiving personal attention; in foster homes, usually nobody really cares about them, and although they receive their bed and board, the cold impersonality of the situation is worse for them than even a certain amount of mistreatment by parents. They know well enough that foster parents are caring for them because of the monthly check. Before the era of State intervention, an unwanted child, or a child who didn't want to stay with parents who mistreated him or her, often went to live with a benevolent uncle and his family, or with a grandmother or maiden aunt—a practice which appears to have had a better batting average than today's practice of putting a child into a foster home. If no relative wants the abused child, the best resolution is often adoption by a couple who desire children of their own but who cannot have them.

In a 1972 case a child was placed in a foster home after his parents abused him. Then his parents changed their minds, and although the child expressed great fear of his father, social workers forced the boy to return to his parents against his will. Four months later the father beat the boy to death, crushing his skull. In this case the child would have been better off in the foster home. But in other cases, the State forces children to leave their parents even though they want to stay and places them in foster homes because it considers the parental environment "unsuitable" or because the parents do not go along

---

[22] Barron, *KGB*, p. 12.
[23] Aleksandr Solzhenitsyn, *Cancer Ward* (New York: Farrar, Straus & Giroux, 1969), p. 481.

with the government's current theories of educational psychology. (Is there any *general rule* that rule-utilitarians would prescribe for such cases?)

Yet parents too have rights. Do they not have the right to bring up their children in their own chosen religion? Do they not have the right, if their little boy keeps injuring his newborn sister (jealous because there is a newcomer in the family), to inflict corporal punishment if all reasoning and persuasion have failed? Do they not have a right to require children to do certain things, such as brush their teeth, for their own good? The twelve-year-old girl may happily *consent* to a sexual encounter, but aren't the parents within their rights to forbid this? If a twelve-year-old wants to try out PCP or some other harmful drug, or place himself in a situation full of dangers which he doesn't appreciate, again haven't the parents the right (indeed, the obligation) to deny such a request? Shouldn't parents prevent children, by force if necessary, from playing with their father's gun? In many cases, parents should be expected to exercise more, not less, control.

As children grow older, the rights they can exercise increase and the rights of parents over them diminish. In most states children become legally adults at the age of eighteen. They can then incur debts, have a bank account, sign contracts, drive cars, and drink in bars (There is considerable variation from one state to another on all these matters.) Admittedly this age is arbitrary, though any other age would be equally so. Some children are quite capable of handling their own affairs before they are eighteen, and some are incapable of doing so after it. More confusing still, a teen-ager may be perfectly capable in one sector of his or her life but quite incapable in others.

The burden of proof is surely on the parents to show that their child is *not* capable of making his or her own decisions: if a sixteen-year old can hold down a job, as proved by the fact that she does so, why shouldn't she be permitted to leave her parents' home and rent an apartment, being in all ways on her own? Many teen-agers are capable of doing so and are only prevented by state laws which make them a ward of their parents until they are eighteen. The other side of this coin is, of course, that while exercising their rights as adults, they also should have adult responsibilities: they must be liable for paying their own debts and damage suits and should no longer be able to shift this financial responsibility to parents, as most state laws now require until the child reaches eighteen. (Sometimes the parent cannot keep the child at home, yet is financially responsible for whatever scrapes the child may get into prior to the age of eighteen.)

The difficulty of properly adjudicating between the rights of parents as guardians and the rights of children as developing voluntary agents is shown by the following imaginary dialogue:

A: Surely the Amish have a right to raise their children in their own chosen religion. This involves devotion to the Amish beliefs, and they perceive higher education as a threat to those beliefs. They think their children need only learn to read and write, and the rest of their education can be completed outside of school. That's why they refuse to send their children beyond the eighth grade, and they even won a court case in Wisconsin over this matter (*Wisconsin* v. *Yoder*).

B: Let's grant that they have the right to bring up a child in their own religious beliefs. But do they have the right to *stunt* the child's opportunities?

A: *They* don't think they are stunting them. They think they are doing them a favor by protecting them against evil outside influences. Maybe they're mistaken, but don't they have this right?

B: Well, suppose they believed that they shouldn't send their children to *any* schools at all, that even elementary schools are wicked and pernicious influences. Would they have the right to keep their children illiterate?

A: They could educate them at home.

B: And keep them confined in their narrow viewpoint for life? They surely have no right to do this to their children. It would stunt their later opportunities. In fact, not letting their children go to high school and college might do that too. And just remaining in that authoritarian atmosphere is stultifying and unfair to children.

A: You call it deprivation, but *they* call it fulfillment. You call it stultifying; they would call it sacred and ennobling. *Given* their theological premises, their behavior is justified: they are in the right and the rest of the world is cruelly mistaken. Don't they have the right to hold (and teach) these theological premises?

B: They should teach them in such a way that the children, once they grow up, will have various options and will be able to choose for themselves whether or not they want to accept their parents' beliefs.

A: That seems clear to you; but from their point of view doing so would be giving in to the sinful temptations of the outside world. *You* want all children to be educated for maximum freedom to choose; *they* consider such freedom to be an evil. By restricting their children, they are only doing what they believe is best for them, just as you, by making your children brush their teeth, are doing what you believe is best for them.

B: But the parents are behaving so as to severely limit their children's choices.

A: What parents don't, by indoctrinating them in one way or another? In any case, by doing so, they believe they are exercising their right to train their children to walk the straight and narrow path. They don't want your kind of freedom. By training them as they do, they are acting as they think best; and if the children, by the time they reach sixteen, want nothing more than to remain with the Amish and share their beliefs, they too are doing what they believe is best. They are not aware of any restriction on freedom as *they* conceive it.

B: But in fact such training constricts them throughout their lives. True, they may be a dedicated Amish by the time they're sixteen, never having been permitted to come in contact with any other views. But then they are no different from the fanatical followers of Hitler who loved Hitler and could think of no better life than following him slavishly.

A: And you can think of no better alternative than having all options open and choosing among them. That satisfies you, but it would be rejected by the Amish, both parents and children. You are simply being a moral busy-body with regard to them, wanting to force on them ideals they themselves would reject.

B: I don't want to force anything on them. I simply want to have alternate ideas available to them, so that they can choose freely among them.

A: A wide range of choices is your conception of what's best for them; it is not theirs. What right have you to tamper with their ideals and tell them what to do? You think they are restricting their children's rights; I say it is you who are violating *their* rights by preventing them from acting on the choices that they believe to be best, however incorrect you may believe those choices to be. Once you follow that path, some day government officials will be restricting *your* choices because, from *their* point of view, your choice is mistaken and they consider it their duty to set you straight.

F. The Rights of Animals

Do animals have **rights**? Let us assume, taking up where we left off in our discussion of the treatment of animals (pp. 150–55), that human beings have certain duties to animals, such as not to be cruel to them or mistreat them. Do animals also have rights corresponding to these duties?

It is difficult to see how animals could have *active* rights—rights they can claim and exercise. They have no conception of rights or claims, and they can't act in recognition of rights, any more than a chair or a tree can. If this is so, neither animals nor infants can possess active rights.

It is more plausible to contend that animals have *passive* rights—the rights not to *be* mistreated, abused, or made to suffer unnecessarily. (People disagree on what "unnecessarily" means here: some say that medical experiments on animals are necessary in order for human diseases to be cured.) Unlike a chair an animal is a sentient being and has interests which should be protected by human beings. Can't we then say that an animal has a (passive) right to be treated in certain ways? When the law makes it a crime to steal a dog, doesn't it recognize this right and give the dog certain legal protections?

Isn't it the dog's owner, however, who has the rights? The law protects not the dog, but the dog's *owner*, the human being, against theft of the dog; the law considers the animal to be someone's possession, and compensation for loss is made to the owner. In the case of an unowned dog, there is no one to whom to make compensation. It is the owner who has the rights, not the dog.

But if the law makes it a misdemeanor for you to abuse a dog, even your own, doesn't this recognize the passive right of the dog not to be abused? But even if this is conceded, it does not mean that the law really protects any rights of animals; what it does is *confer certain duties* on human beings. If we grant that human beings have certain duties to animals (see p. 154), need we really say more? Isn't anything said about animal *rights* just a roundabout way of talking about *human duties?* When we say that the animal has a right, we are actually adding nothing to the statement, already agreed on, that we have duties to animals. The primary concept here is the duty, and the right is consequent upon that. Just as the passive right of A not to be robbed can be said to be just another way of saying that others (B, C, D, etc.) have a duty not to rob A, to speak of the passive rights of animals not to be mistreated is just another way of saying that we have an obligation not to mistreat animals. Perhaps, then, this says all we need to say. Those writers who have made the strongest case for animals, even to the point of vegetarianism, have framed their thesis on the basis of human duties to animals, not of animals' rights.

3. RIGHTS AND THE LAW

The principal function of the law has often been said to be the protection of human rights. If people did not violate one another's rights, police and courts would have little to do. The law itself is an instrument of coercion and (in theory at least) exercises the same coercive restraints on everyone. The law exists to deter persons from violating others' rights and to penalize violators after the violations have occurred.

A. Laws Concerning Physical Harm

In law the duty of non-maleficence is more important than that of beneficence: though there are laws, as we shall see, requiring people to help one another, the greater part of the legal system is concerned with trying to keep people from harming one another. But there is a difference between harms *intentionally* inflicted and those which occur *unintentionally*. (Most people feel more anger at a small hurt inflicted intentionally than at a much greater hurt inflicted accidentally.)

When is the infliction of a harm, or for that matter the commission of any act, intentional? In general, if an agent *desires* that certain consequences shall follow from his or her act, then the act is intentional with respect to that consequence. If you desire to drive fast and do so but don't desire to kill a pedestrian, your act is intentional with regard to speeding but not intentional with regard to killing the pedestrian. (Murder is intentional killing; manslaughter is unintentional killing.) A consequence may be desired, and thus be intentional, even if it is not expected as probable: even if you are a bad shot, if you aim a gun at someone and kill him, the act is intentional.

If the consequence is not itself desired, it is still considered intentional if it is known to be a *regular or inevitable consequence* of what is desired; thus, if a sadistic surgeon removed a patient's heart, not to kill the patient but to perform an experiment, the doctor could be charged with homicide because he knew that death must be a consequence of the act (removing the heart) which he intentionally committed. In a British case after World War II, a British broadcaster who was in Germany at the outbreak of the war was commanded to do radio broadcasts for the Nazis, or else his family would be killed. It was his intention to save his family, not to assist the Nazis. Yet by doing the broadcasts he did assist them, and he knew at the time that by broadcasting he would be assisting them. Thus his act was intentional, although there might have been reason in this case to plead extreme duress as a defense.[24]

The most difficult cases are those of harms unintentionally inflicted. Often people intend no harm but are merely *negligent*. Negligence is conduct in which an agent does not take what the law calls "reasonable care"—a vague phrase, but one whose application varies so much from one context to another that it seems impossible to make it more precise. For example, if you forget to bring your bicycle in and instead leave it on the sidewalk when you come home, and a blind person stumbles over it and is injured, your conduct is negligent: you did not take reasonable care. If you have reason to suspect that a glass contains poison but neglect to warn the person who is about to drink it, you are negligent, though you would not be if you had no reason to suspect that the glass contained anything but water.

There are many cases of negligence in which both parties are somewhat at fault, but it is difficult to assign any amount to each. A drives her car into B's, but B has placed an obstruction in A's right of way. A forgets to dim her headlights, blinding B and causing him to collide with A's car. A is intoxicated and cannot stop her car in time to avoid colliding with B's, but B was driving at ninety miles per hour, and if he had not been speeding, A could have stopped in time.

Negligence is conduct which exposes other persons to an "unreasonable" degree of risk. But when is conduct "reasonable"? The following statement has become a classic:

> The test of reasonableness is what would be [the] conduct or judgment of what may be called a standard man in the situation of the person whose conduct is in question. A standard man does not mean an ideal or perfect man, but an ordinary member of the community. He is usually spoken of as an ordinarily reasonable, careful, and prudent man. That definition is not exactly correct, because in certain cases other qualities than reasonableness, carefulness, or prudence, e.g. courage, may be important; but it will do for our present purpose. It is because the jury is supposed to consist of standard men, and therefore to know of their own knowledge how such a man would act in a given situation, that

---

[24]See Glanville Williams, *Criminal Law: The General Part,* (London: Stevens, 1953), p. 30.

questions of reasonableness and negligence are usually left to the jury.

Every man, whether he is a standard man or not, is required to act as a standard man would. If by chance he is not such a man, he may, as has been said, make a mistake and act so as to be guilty of legal negligence, though he has used all such care and forethought as he was capable of. In the case of contributory negligence there is an exception to this rule in the case of abnormal persons, such as children and persons of unsound mind. They are not required to act like a standard man, but only to use such judgment as they are capable of. But as to negligence which is not merely contributory, as to negligent wrongs against others, the standard man test applies to their conduct also. . . .

Anything that a standard man would do is reasonable. If there are several different courses which he might take, any one of them is reasonable, even though one would be more reasonable than another. All that the law requires of a man is reasonable conduct, not the most reasonable nor even the more reasonable. Also even a standard man, being human and therefore fallible, may err in his judgment.[25]

Should persons who are of below average intelligence have lower standards of negligent behavior applied to them? Justice Oliver Wendell Holmes wrote:

When men live in society, a certain average of conduct, a sacrifice of individual peculiarities going beyond a certain point, is necessary to the general welfare. If, for instance, a man is born hasty or awkward, is always having accidents and hurting himself or his neighbors, no doubt his congenital defects will be allowed for in the courts of Heaven, but his slips are no less troublesome for his neighbors than if they sprang from guilty neglect. His neighbors accordingly require him, at his proper peril, to come up to their standard, and the courts which they establish decline to take his personal equation into account.[26]

As far as precision is concerned, all such definitions leave much to be desired. Yet is there any way of defining "negligent conduct" and "reasonable man" so that when a judge and jury are confronted by a particular case they will be able to determine when conduct is negligent or a person reasonable? The "standard man" is clearly a legal fiction, and the effect of such pronouncements is to let each individual judge and jury decide, when confronted by the facts of the case before them, whether the conduct was negligent or the defendant reasonable.

Let us consider a few sample legal cases in which the defendant faced a charge of negligence.

1. In an 1856 case, a waterworks company had installed water mains, with

[25] Henry Terry, "Negligence," *Harvard Law Review* 40 (1915). Reprinted by permission.
[26] Oliver W. Holmes, *The Common Law* (Boston: Little, Brown, 1923), p. 108.

fire hydrants in various places, according to legal requirements. But because of an unprecedented cold wave, some water from the hydrants leaked through the earth and into someone's house, causing damage. The apparatus had worked well for twenty-five years. But the homeowner sued the water-works company for negligence. In this case he did not win: the court decided that the hydrants had been laid down "with reasonable care," taking into account all ordinary weather, and that it would have been unreasonable to require them to work in such unusual and unexpected circumstances as a cold wave.[27]

2. A woman boarded a train at 1 A.M. on a cold winter night. At 4 A.M. she felt sick and went into the rest room. The coach was heated by steam going through pipes along the floor. She fainted, and when she came to, her head was on the floor under the water cooler with her face against a hot steam pipe. She had been severely burned, and she sued the railway company for negligence. The lower court found in her favor; the higher court reversed the verdict, arguing that the part of the room where the steam pipes were located was not intended for the use of passengers and that with the exercise of reasonable care there was no reason to anticipate a passenger coming into contact with the pipes.[28]

3. An oil company sent a high-school chemistry teacher a display kit marked "For Teachers Only" and consisting of six bottles; each bottle had a label indicating its contents. The teacher opened the bottle marked "kerosene" without smelling it or otherwise testing it and poured its contents onto some sodium. (Sodium is preserved in kerosene but is highly explosive when exposed to water.) There was an explosion, and he received several injuries, including severe burns and the loss of one eye. The bottle had been filled with water, to make the kit mailable. The oil company contended that the bottles were "for display only." The court found the oil company guilty of negligence and the company was required to pay full damages to the teacher, for medical expenses, pain and suffering, and the loss of the eye.[29]

4. Children from a certain neighborhood enjoyed spending Saturdays playing in the railroad yard. Since the gate was closed and locked they had to enter by climbing a high fence containing an array of "No trespassing" signs as well as "Danger" signs. The watchman repeatedly told the children to leave, but they did not. Finally, as they were playing at a railroad turntable, a boy got his foot caught in the mechanism and the foot was severed. The mother sued the railroad company for negligence and won.[30]

5. The absentee owner of a vacant lot in a small Kansas town was unaware that a small pool of liquid has collected at a low spot in the lot. A family of itinerant laborers parked nearby in their truck. The children saw the pool and jumped in. They were badly burned because the water contained sulfuric

---

[27] Blyth v. Birmingham (England) Waterworks Co. (1856).
[28] Hauser v. Chicago Rock Island and Pacific Railway, 205 Iowa 940, 219 N.W. 60 (1928).
[29] Pease v. Sinclair Refining Co., 104 F.2d 183 (1939).
[30] Railway v. Stout, 17 Wallace 657 (1873).

acid. They sued the owner for negligence with regard to his property and won.[31]

The cases cited here are but a few of those handled by attorneys, some of whom specialize in such cases. Different cases are decided on the basis of quite different considerations: in the last one, for example, it was decided that the stagnant pool was an "attractive nuisance," and the owner should either have removed it or put up a fence. But in the preceding case it could hardly be claimed that the railroad company was negligent, since the company took every reasonable precaution and more. When companies are involved, the deciding factor often is not "Who's at fault?" but "Who's able to pay?" It is felt that since the victim has already suffered pain and injury, someone, however tenuously connected with the case and however little at fault, should pay damages.

In situations where negligence is provable, the injured party can collect damages. But what about cases in which there is no negligence, but another person is nevertheless harmed? Doesn't that person deserve compensation too? The need for compensating the victim has led to a gradual shift from negligence to a different standard, *strict liability*. Under this standard, the person who caused the damage, however inadvertently, is liable for damages whether he or she was negligent or not. In a famous 1865 case in England, a man built a reservoir on his land to collect water which would not have escaped from the reservoir but for the fact that there were long-abandoned coal mines under the property, unknown to anyone then alive in the region. The weight of the reservoir caused the land to sink, which in turn caused the reservoir to burst into the abandoned shafts below; the shafts then led to the collapse of a neighbor's land and the house that was situated on it. Here there was no suspicion of negligence. No one knew of the abandoned mines, and the reservoir had been constructed by competent engineers according to the highest standards. Nevertheless a court decided that the plaintiff (the neighbor) had a right to recover and that the defendant was *strictly liable* for the damage caused.[32]

In our own day there are many situations covered by strict liability in which negligence does not have to be shown. For example: (1) If a bar owner serves an underage customer, it does not matter whether he has taken reasonable care, nor even if the person has shown an impeccably forged birth certificate. The owner can have his bar closed down if he *in fact* serves someone under the legal drinking age; he doesn't have to be negligent by failing to demand identification. (2) People engaged in a hazardous occupation, such as dynamiting or fumigating, are strictly liable for all damage and injury caused, although they may have taken all "reasonable care" and even extraordinary care to prevent such damage. (3) If factory workers are injured or maimed by factory machinery, it doesn't matter whether they have been careless, or even if they have not been using required safeguards; the factory

---

[31] United Zinc and Chemical v. Britt, 258 U.S. 268 (1922).
[32] Fletcher v. Rylands, 3 H. & C. 774 (Exch. 1865).

owner is strictly liable for all injuries. (4) If a man elopes with an underage girl whom he believes to be of age, what he reasonably believes is of no legal consequence; all that counts is that she is in fact under age, and for the act of eloping with someone under age he is strictly liable. (5) If you think you are on your own property but have actually crossed the boundary to your neighbor's, and are in fact taking some of her apples although you think they are your own, you are strictly liable.

Desirable as strict liability may be from the point of view of claimants, it seems to be unfair to the people who inadvertently cause the damage. They may take reasonable care, perhaps even extraordinary precautions, yet some fluke accident occurs which makes them liable. (Often they are insured for such things, but this only adds to the cost of their overhead, if they are in business, and consequently of their services.) But in situations of this kind something has to give: if negligence has to be proved, this is fair to the defendant but may deny recovery to the plaintiff; if strict liability is used, the plaintiff is more likely to get recovery, but from a faultless defendant.

B. Laws Concerning Nonphysical Harm

Harm can be caused by other things than personal injury and damage to property. We have already examined the case of defamation (libel and slander). Still another kind of nonphysical harm that has become the subject of litigation is *invasion of privacy*. A child prodigy, who is now thirty-five years old and whose life has been utterly undistinguished, wants merely to be left alone, but a newspaper reporter dredges up his past and writes about him in an article. He makes no false statements, nor does he attempt to damage the person, so there is no defamation; but he can be sued for invasion of privacy. A movie star's past life is spilled all over the newspapers; no false statements are made, so no defamation occurs, but her privacy has been invaded.

Sometimes the "right to privacy" is added to the list of rights. But where does this right end? Can nothing be said about you of which you don't approve in advance? The law, in fact, makes several exceptions. If a person, such as a politician, has courted publicity, and if it is believed that his or her history is relevant to whether people should vote for the candidate, those who bring up his or her past can't be sued: by running for office the politician has forgone the right to privacy. Also, if something is news, no invasion of privacy is actionable; "news comes first." A man who tried to keep pictures of his daughter's near brush with death in a car accident out of the papers did not succeed, because it was "news"; but some years later when those same pictures were used in a magazine article, "They Ask to Be Killed," he sued the magazine and won.[33] It is considered an invasion of your privacy if someone takes your picture and a newspaper publishes it

[33]Leverton v. Curtis Publishing Co., 192 F.2d 974 (1951).

without your consent; but if you are one of many people in a crowd scene, there is held to be no invasion of privacy, and your consent is not required.

Sometimes the reasons given are highly peculiar: the deeds of one Sergeant Stryker, who raised the American flag on Iwo Jima, were celebrated in a movie called *The Sands of Iwo Jima*. The movie included some incidents from his past, and he sued for invasion of privacy, which was not granted. According to the court, "Men who are called to the colors subject their activities in that particular field to the public gaze and may not contend that in the discharge of such activities their actions may not be publicized."[34] Most people believe that certain sectors of a person's life should remain private if the person wants them to remain so. Usually such sectors are those which if publicized would offend him or her, but what each individual finds offensive varies enormously from person to person. This fact goes far to explain the disagreements about the limits of the right of privacy.

There are certain other privacies which, it is felt, should be protected, but there are others equally important which are not. For example:

1. Organizations that compile your credit record can run a credit check on you and grant or deny you credit, often on the basis of facts unknown to you, and often on the basis of what are not facts at all but computer errors. Errors are not always committed but the fact remains that they can learn virtually your entire financial history without your consent. It could be said, of course, that you consented to all this when you asked for credit in the first place. You can't expect to be granted credit without their knowing whether you are financially reliable. Still, there are many cases of such knowledge being abused—never more so than as a result of the Bank Secrecy Act (which should have been called the Bank Prying Act), which requires the bank to microfilm all your checks for the Internal Revenue Service and to make a report of all checks over a certain amount. (This entire government operation could be called an invasion of privacy.[35])

2. What a person reveals to a priest in confession is legally privileged: someone can confess to committing murder and still the priest's lips are sealed. The same holds true for the relation between an attorney and client: the defendant may confess to his or her lawyer the commission of a murder, but the lawyer may say nothing about it. What about the relationship of a physician and patient? Isn't the nature of the patient's illness a matter to which only a physician should be privy? In thirty-four of the fifty states all communications between physician and patient are privileged: the physician may not reveal in court what he or she learned from a patient concerning the patient's maladies. But in the other sixteen states there is no such privileged relation, and a physician is required to tell a judge and jury what a patient revealed in confidence. Surely, the preferable arrangement is to protect the patient's privacy. But this too can have curious consequences:

---

[34] Stryker v. Republic Pictures Corp., 108 Calif. App. 2nd 191, 238 p.2d 670 (1951).
[35] See Henry Hohenstein, *The I.R.S. Conspiracy* (Los Angeles: Nash Publishing, 1974).

You've been treating a patient for sciatica over a two-year period. Last month, he slipped and fell while getting out of a taxi. Now, alleging he never had a backache in his life before the accident, he has sued the cab driver for injuries. One sentence from you on the witness stand—"I've treated this man's sciatica for two years"—would prove him a liar. But the law in your state holds that your treatment of his sciatica is "privileged." So you can't say a word about it in court. As a result, the verdict goes to your patient, and the luckless cabbie loses out.[36]

Similarly, if a surgeon wanted to sue to collect for an operation, he would be unable to do so if he could not prove his services without revealing key facts about the patient's condition.

What is and is not "privileged," who is covered and who is not, varies so much from state to state that, as one author contends, a great deal of confusion has resulted:

> In New York, dentists as well as physicians are privileged. Nurses are privileged in Arkansas. Physicians (unprivileged) must answer court questions in New Jersey, but newspaper reporters (privileged) need not. And in Georgia and Tennessee, where physicians must tell all about their patients in court, psychologists cannot.
>
> An Indiana doctor was once forbidden to testify about the cause of a patient's death, although such testimony was essential in settling a claim. Yet the death certificate, which listed the cause, was a matter of public record. Everyone but the jury was entitled to the facts. In a similar case, a Michigan court ruled that "although the death certificate is admissible, the physician who made it is prohibited from testifying as to the facts therein stated." An Arkansas court once decided that a notary public who had typed and notarized a patient's history for a doctor could talk about it, but the doctor couldn't.[37]

3. Even more personal is the relationship between patient and psychiatrist (or psychological counselor). Patients would not bare their souls to their psychiatrist if they thought he or she would turn around and divulge to others the contents of their conversations. Yet there have been cases in which such things were revealed. A student once informed his counselor that he was homosexual, and this information was recorded in the counselor's data book. A potential future employer, who was considering hiring the student for a sensitive national security job, demanded to see the counselor's records. The counselor refused, claiming that they contained privileged information. But the court decided that since the college was a municipal one, the city and not the student or the counselor was the owner of the data book. As a result the

[36]Henry A. Davidson, "Professional Secrecy," in *Ethical Issues in Medicine,* ed. E. Fuller Torrey (Boston: Little, Brown, 1968). Reprinted by permission of Little, Brown.
[37]Ibid. Reprinted by permission of Little, Brown.

student didn't get the job. (But, many would say, such information was necessary for the future employer, lest the employee be blackmailed into giving up security secrets under threat of having his personal secrets revealed.)

In a famous case, *Tarasoff* v. *Regents of the University of California*,[38] a student was in psychotherapy with the student health service. He told his therapist that he wanted to kill a certain unmarried girl who lived in Berkeley but was at the moment away on a summer trip. The psychologist reported the matter orally to the campus police and sent them a letter requesting that the student be detained and committed for observation to a mental hospital. The campus police questioned the student but "found him rational" and let him go after he promised to stay away from the girl, Miss Tarasoff. The police reported back to the director of psychiatry. Two months later, Miss Tarasoff returned, whereupon the student went to her home and killed her.

The parents of the girl sued the university, the campus police, and the psychologist. The police were protected by law from such suits, but those in psychiatry were not. The Supreme Court of California declared that the psychologist had a duty to warn Miss Tarasoff, which he had neglected, though he was protected by legal immunity against most damage suits. However, the case seems to indicate that whether or not to breach physician–patient confidentiality is up to psychiatrists and psychologists: they may do so but don't have to (in California).

In any case, a number of questions are raised: Must psychiatrists always warn potential victims of death threats, but exercise discretion regarding less dangerous threats? Every time a patient makes a threat against an unnamed person, must the therapist try to find out who it is and warn him or her, and suffer damages if the threat is carried out? After all, patients (not to mention people in general) are constantly making threats, which they seldom carry out; when one is carried out, should the psychiatrist be held responsible? And why should a psychiatrist be made guarantor of the safety of a person (on the basis of a threat which might never be carried out), especially when that person is not even a patient? When the probability of a threat being carried out is less than 1 percent, should a psychiatrist break faith with a patient (thus losing the patient's confidence and throwing away the opportunity to help him or her) in order to warn all possible victims?

Still another threat to privacy is posed by wiretapping and other means of electronic surveillance. Your telephone is tapped without your knowledge or consent. With advanced technology, the phone doesn't have to be off the hook: it is necessary only that someone be talking in the same room, and listeners far away can hear it. Or, a little device that looks like a button can be clamped on the outside wall of your house or a window sill so that the conversations going on inside can be heard. Is this not an invasion of privacy?

---

[38] Discussed in William J. Curran, "Confidentiality and the Prediction of Dangerousness in Psychiatry: The Tarasoff Case," *New England Journal of Medicine* 293 (August 7, 1975): 285–86.

When the Constitution was adopted, John Marshall, who later became Chief Justice, remarked:

> Force and violence were [once] the only means known to man by which a government could directly effect self-incrimination. It could compel the individual to testify—a compulsion effected, if need be, by torture. It could secure possession of his papers and other articles incident to his private life—a seizure effected, if need be, by breaking and entry. Protection against such invasion of "the sanctities of a man's home and the privacies of life" was provided by the Fourth and Fifth Amendments. . . . But . . . subtler and more far-reaching means of invading privacy have become available to the Government. . . . Ways may some day be developed by which the Government, without removing papers from secret drawers, can reproduce them in court, and by which it will be enabled to expose to a jury the most intimate occurrences of the home. Advances in the psychic and related sciences may bring means of exploring unexpressed beliefs, thoughts, and emotions. . . . Can it be that the Constitution affords no protection against such invasion of individual security?[39]

Marshall foresaw the danger, but where is one to draw the line? Justice Robert Jackson commented:

> The use of bifocals, field glasses, or the telescope to magnify the object of a witness' vision is not a forbidden search or seizure, even if they focus without his knowledge or consent upon what one supposes to be private indiscretions. It would be a dubious service to the genuine liberties protected by the Fourth Amendment to make them bedfellows with spurious liberties improvised by far-fetched analogies which would liken eavesdropping on a conversation with the connivance of one of the parties, to an unreasonable search or seizure.[40]

There are thus instances in which eavesdropping seems to be permissible. Justice George Sutherland concurred in this conclusion in a discussion of police surveillance techniques:

> My abhorrence of the odious practices of the town gossip, the Peeping Tom, and the private eavesdropper is quite as strong as that of any of my brethren. But to put the sworn offices of the law, engaged in the detection and apprehension of organized gangs of criminals, in the same category is to lose all sense of proportion. In view of the safeguards

[39] Quoted in Conrad Paulsen and Sanford Kadish, eds., *Criminal Law and Its Processes* (Boston: Little, Brown, 1962), p. 873.
[40] Quoted in ibid., p. 876.

against abuse of power furnished by the order of the Attorney General, and in the light of the deadly conflict constantly being waged between the forces of law and order and the desperate criminals who infest the land, we well may pause to consider whether the application of the rule which forbids an invasion of the privacy of telephone communication is not being carried . . . to a point where the necessity of public protection against crime is being submerged by an overflow of sentimentality.[41]

If the only way the police can catch a murderer is by evidence from wire-tapping or other forms of surveillance, isn't the invasion of privacy worth it, particularly if the murderer is about to strike again? In such a case we have a conflict of rights—the right of privacy against the right of others to life. The trouble is that once invasion of privacy occurs in one case, what is to prevent law-enforcement officials from invading privacy in all manner of other cases in which there is nothing but a slender suspicion as a basis or in which the crime is not a serious one or the police are out to get someone in whatever way they can? How many of our lives, if we include all the conversations we have with others, would withstand such scrutiny and still escape free of any violations of law? "Give them an inch and they'll take a mile"—wasn't that the lesson of Watergate?

C. Harm versus Offense

One can harm a person by killing, maiming, or injuring, by causing the person to suffer, by defamation (libel and slander), and (though the limits of this one are much more controversial) by invasion of privacy. But what about mental or spiritual harm? Fundamentalist parents allege that teachers who acquaint their child with heretical and "pagan" ideas have harmed the child far more than they could by injuring the child's physical body. Yet the parents will not be able to recover if they try to sue, for the courts have held that the dissemination of ideas, true or false, is desirable; the parents are entitled to shelter their child if they can until he or she becomes an adult, but not to recover damages if the child absorbs ideas which are unwelcome to them. Most educated persons would use many of the arguments from Mill's *On Liberty* to show that the exposure to new ideas is a part of growing up and, far from harming the children, actually helps them (whether they accept the new ideas or not) by expanding their conceptions of alternatives. If most people came to believe that young people were really harmed by religious toleration, they would attempt (as some have done) to rewrite the First Amendment.

But can't ideas *really* harm people, particularly the impressionable young? It certainly seems that ideas can harm children more than bodily wounds;

---

[41] Quoted in ibid., p. 883.

instilling in impressionable young people ideas that may incite them to violence against others for the rest of their lives may indeed be extremely harmful. But even if such harm can be shown, there is a vast difference between physical and mental harm: physical harm is something that is *inflicted* on people, usually against their wishes, but new ideas, however evil, cannot be instilled without the recipients' cooperation. Ideas cannot be effective in their lives by being inflicted like wounds. Freedom of choice is involved in accepting and acting on ideas, but not in the case of receiving bodily wounds.

The law is written largely to prevent people from inflicting harm on others and to penalize them when they do so. But some laws are not concerned with harming others but with *offending* them. In most cities people are not permitted to lie naked in public parks or in their own front yard to get a suntan if they can be seen by the public or neighbors. It would be difficult to show that having such a view is *harming* others; it only offends (some of) them, and so "for decency's sake" exposure is not permitted. Can such laws be defended? Is there a "right not to be offended" alongside the right not to be harmed? During your lifetime you are bound to be offended by many things; why should the law select some of those things and make them illegal?

In fact, behavior which is offensive to most people, to a majority of people, or even to a large number of people—from advertising that is considered obscene to films that show behavior that is considered obscene—is often made illegal. It could be argued plausibly that people *shouldn't* find the sight of nude bodies, even engaged in copulation, offensive, and that they would be much better off if they weren't offended by such things. (Why is violence, which destroys life, not considered as offensive on television as sex, which creates it?) Nevertheless, the fact is that they are offended, and hence legislation has been passed in response. Those who argue that such laws should be passed because the *majority* of people are offended by it should consider the minority that wants it legalized. Doesn't the law infringe on *their* freedom?

What offends one person often does not offend another. Some people are offended not only by people copulating in a public park but by the *thought* that they are doing so in their own bedrooms. Must such delicate sensibilities be catered to by declaring all sex illegal, simply because the thought of it is offensive to these persons? And what if some others are offended by the thought of people *not* engaging in sex? "X is offensive" is never a complete statement; what is offensive to A is not necessarily offensive to B.

If you know that something is going to be offensive to others, you can try to withhold any sight of it from them *or* try to moderate their appetite for being offended. Passing laws to prohibit behavior which does not harm but only offends (some people) is an extremely dubious and tricky business which smacks of moral busybodyism. ("I am offended by it, and if you aren't you should be.") Still, if many people find certain types of behavior offensive or disturbing to them, it may be desirable, at least from a utilitarian point of view, for the remainder to make certain (hopefully minor) sacrifices to their sensibilities. But this is at best a somewhat uneasy compromise and can hardly be elevated to the status of a right. If it is, do we then have to add a right not to be shocked or embarrassed or coldly or contemptuously treated? What about a right to be preferred to one's rival or a right not to have foods which are offensive to sight or smell eaten in public places? If all these were rights, there would be no end to the list, and human life would be so hedged about with prohibitions and restrictions as to be virtually unlivable. Such an accumulation of prohibitions would defeat the very purpose of invoking human rights—to promote life and make it safe and more enjoyable, or at any rate more tolerable, than it would have been without them.

D. The Law and the Duty to Help

You are standing on a bridge, and you see someone struggling in the swirling waters below. You wonder how much risk there would be to you if you tried to rescue the person, and whether you could get there in time, or whether you might be drowned yourself. So you do nothing, and the person drowns. According to the long tradition of British and American law, there is no legal duty to help (though there may be a moral duty). You are not responsible, for the person's condition and fate would have been the same if you hadn't been around. But the moment there is a suspicion that you threw the individual in or were in any way the *cause* of the drowning, the legal picture abruptly changes: you are now legally responsible for whatever happens to him or her.

There is a difference between doing something that *harms* someone and failing to do anything to *help*. But it isn't merely the difference between acting and not acting: you are sometimes legally responsible for omissions as well as commissions. If you're a parent and fail to feed your children, you are as responsible for their death as if you had killed them; having brought the children into the world, you have a legal duty to support them. If you've agreed to tend your neighbor's plants while she is away and you fail to do so, you may be charged with breach of contract. If you say, "But I didn't *do* anything; I committed no act," the court will respond, "An omission counts as an act if what you omit to do is something you have a legal duty to perform." In the drowning case, however, your omission is not legally actionable, for you had no legal duty to help in the first place. Not only have you committed no act, you have omitted to do nothing that you had a legal duty to do.

But *should* you have a legal duty to help in such situations? Should there be *Good Samaritan laws,* which require you to help and impose penalties on you if you do not? Many people contend we all have a duty to help those in distress, not merely through welfare (to which we all contribute through taxation) but by acts of assistance to individuals whose lives are imperiled.

Such laws are operative in many states and nations. What should be said about them?

Suppose that the Cadillac on the turnpike just in front of you suddenly swerves and hits a small convertible sports car, whose driver is thrown onto the shoulder of the road, where his face is covered with blood and he lies still. It's all over before what has happened really sinks in, and by that time you are half a mile down the road. Should you go back and try to be of assistance? You are already late. Your thoughts might go something like this:

> If I did go back, what could I do? I'm not a doctor. He needs a doctor. Maybe it would be most helpful if, as soon as I get home, I phoned for a doctor and ambulance. But the state police patrol every twenty minutes. By the time I get home they would certainly have found him and radioed for help. By now a couple of dozen cars have passed him. One of them may be a doctor and has stopped to heal him. Anyone who drives a sports car on this death trap is asking for it. And that guy in the big car, what could he have been doing? He was going steadily just ahead of me. And look at all those cars going in both direction, I'm not doing anything out of the ordinary. Everybody seems to be going on his way. That must mean that somebody is helping. It would be a hell of a thing if everybody stopped anyhow. If would block traffic. The ambulance couldn't get through and he'd be worse off—just because of morbid curiosity. We have a very efficient state patrol. Seems to me I read somewhere that amateur first aiders do far more harm than good. By now there are probably several police cars rerouting traffic and seeing to it that he gets all the care he needs.[42]

Is this a rationalization, or are your reasons sound? Consider another case, this time an actual one. A man and his cousin boarded a railway car at Niagara Falls. It was dark, and the man fell off the car as it lurched over a precipice and fell to his death below. His cousin saw only that he was missing and insisted that the train be stopped so that he could go and look for the missing man. The conductor declined, and the cousin got off the car anyway; he was then injured on the rocks during his search. He sued the railway company for injuries. The company was willing to pay damages for the man who fell off but not for the injuries of the "Good Samaritan" searcher. However, Court of Appeals Justice Benjamin Cardozo decided that the railroad company should pay for both, saying that a plea for help is an invitation to respond and that all possible assistance should be rendered to those in distress, whatever the circumstances:

> Danger invites rescue. The cry of distress is the summons to relief. The law does not ignore these reactions of the mind in tracing conduct to its

---

[42]Lawrence Z. Freedman, "No Response to the Cry for Help," in *The Good Samaritan and the Law,* ed. James Ratcliffe (Garden City, N.Y.: Doubleday/Anchor Books, 1966), p. 174.

consequences. It recognizes them as normal. It places their effects within the range of the natural and probable. The wrong that imperils life is a wrong to the imperilled victim; it is a wrong also to his rescuer."[43]

A considerable amount of Good Samaritan legislation has been passed since Cardozo's influential opinion in this case. What shall we say of laws not designed to prevent or punish harm, but to require people to be of help to one another?

There are times when a person's life is saved because of such Good Samaritan laws. A motorist who but for the law might not have stopped at the scene of an accident, stops, gives aid, or calls an ambulance, and thereby saves the life of the accident victim. On the other hand, as with any rule of conduct that has the force of law behind it, such laws can also have unfortunate consequences. Consider these cases: (1) A man, in response to a law requiring people to stop at the scene of an accident and render assistance, got out of his car but was mugged and robbed by those in the car who enacted the scene to set up a passer-by for just such crimes. Should anyone be required to stop on a lonely street or road at night, where most people wouldn't even go walking by day if they could help it? (2) A man rushed to the assistance of a young grade-school boy who looked as though he were being beaten up by two adults. The two men turned out to be policemen (not in uniform) and the rescuer was prosecuted for assault. Though the conviction was quashed in a lower court because the man reasonably believed they were street hoodlums, a higher court reinstituted the conviction, holding him strictly liable and saying that freeing the man "would not be conducive to an orderly society."[44] (3) Members of the medical profession who have stopped to give assistance have later been sued for malpractice because the accident victims claimed the doctors did the wrong thing in their treatment at the scene.

There are two lines of thought concerning Good Samaritan laws. On the one hand, there is the *utilitarian* line, which concludes that in spite of certain risks it is preferable to require people to help others, thus (hopefully) maximizing utility. On the other hand, there is the line of reasoning based on the concept of individual *rights:* as long as a person has not violated the rights of others, he or she should have the right to decide what to do in emergency situations. (The person who takes this line may add that the act has moral worth only if it is voluntarily undertaken.) Since he or she did not cause the victim's condition, and hence has not harmed anyone or violated any rights, it should be up to the individual whether to rescue the person in distress. A choice not to do so does no wrong to the victim; the would-be rescuer has not violated the victim's rights, for the victim has no right to the services of others who had no connection with the misfortune and only happened to be in the vicinity at the time. (The victim, however, may claim a positive rather

43 Wagner v. International Railway Co., 232 N.Y. 176 (1922).
44 People v. Young, New York State, 210 N.Y.S. 2d 358 (1961).

than a negative right to be helped, which imposes on others the positive duty to be of assistance.)

If, for whatever reason, we decide that there should be Good Samaritan laws, another problem arises: Should the Good Samaritans who are required to provide the help be legally protected against lawsuits by the people they try to help? Some nations do have laws protecting Good Samaritans; for example, in some countries a physician is protected against those who would sue him or her for injuries while moving them from the scene of an accident.

If this second set of laws is needed to protect the Good Samaritan, what about a third to protect people *from* Good Samaritans? "Anti-Don Quixote" legislation may sometimes be needed. In Miguel de Cervantes' novel, Don Quixote rushes out to help all apparent victims of violence. He assaults official guards who are conducting a chain gang of convicts to the galleys; the convicts break loose, beat up Don Quixote, and then roam the countryside robbing and terrorizing people. Some Good Samaritans are inept, clumsy, and stupid; often the victim of misfortune would be better off without their ministrations. Shouldn't the victims be protected against such well-meaning Don Quixotes?

One clear way to stop a chain of legislation of this sort is to return to the time-honored legal tradition of having no Good Samaritan laws at all. It seems quite legitimate to hold that though a bystander may have a moral duty to help, there should be no legal duty, provided that he or she did not contribute to the victim's predicament.

EXERCISES

1. Evaluate the following dialogue:
    A. No one should use others—including pets—as means to a personal end. A dog may turn out to be useless but extremely devoted to its master. Every time the master is gone, the dog waits disconsolately for him to return. But the dog is a lover, not a fighter: it doesn't defend the premises—the reason the man got the dog in the first place. The man knows that if he gave the dog away, it would spend most or all of its life waiting for him to return. So he keeps the dog.
    B. You're crazy. Get rid of it! A dog is only a tool.
    A. But many persons treat not only pets but other people the same way—as tools. If friends are no longer useful to them, they get rid of them, cut them off. Isn't this "treating people as means," which Kant condemned?
    B. But everybody treats others as tools, just different kinds. People get attached to other people—husbands and wives, girlfriends and boyfriends—but then they drop each other in time if they no longer feel any mutual attraction. They're using each other as emotional tools. Everyone treats others as means to his or her own personal ends, only sometimes in very subtle ways.
2. In the film *Circle of Deception,* based on an actual incident, British Intelligence in World War II send a man out to be an unwitting decoy for the Nazis. They drop

him by parachute into occupied France, knowing that the chances are high that he will be captured. If captured, he will be tortured, and on the basis of previous psychological tests they know (that's why they selected him) that if tortured he will talk. They give him *false* information, which he sincerely believes to be true, so that under torture he can't reveal anything else (since he knows nothing else). The ploy works: he is captured and tortured, and on the basis of his remarks under torture the Nazis conclude that the D-Day invasion will be at a certain spot, many miles distant from Normandy, where it actually will occur. In this case the British used the man—who was a psychological wreck forever afterward—totally as a means to their end; and he was an unwilling means, since if he had known what they were going to use him to do, he would never have volunteered for the job. At the same time, by successfully deceiving the Nazis, hundreds, probably thousands, of Allied lives were saved. Countless individuals could return home to their families afterward, which they wouldn't have been able to do if this man had not (unknown to himself) deceived the Nazis:

Should utility take precedence over rights in this case? Or have no rights been violated? (See William Stephenson, *A Man Called Intrepid.*)

3. If someone violates your rights, are you entitled to violate that individual's rights in return?

4. If a man is engaged in espionage in a foreign country and is captured, no attempt will be made to rescue him; he is considered a nonperson, nonexistent. Does this practice go contrary to Kant's requirement that a person be treated as an end and never merely as a means?

5. A family that discovers oil or gold on its property hasn't worked for it (though there is subsequent expense involved in digging for it). Because the family members did not labor to produce it, should they be denied the mineral rights to what lies under their property? If you think they shouldn't have it, who should?

6. If you believe public nudity should be banned, what reasons would you give for doing so?

7. Which of the following do you consider to be rights, and which are privileges which can be revoked?
   a. A driver's license
   b. A license to practice medicine
   c. Walking on the sidewalks of a town or city
   d. Swimming at a public beach at any hour of the day or night

8. Evaluate:
   a. "Our descendants have a right to be left an unplundered planet; they do not have a right to new miracle cures. We have sinned against them if by our doing we have destroyed their inheritance—which we are doing at full blast; we have not sinned against them if by the time they come around arthritis has not yet been conquered (unless by sheer neglect)." (From Hans Jonas, "Philosophical Reflections on Experimenting with Human Subjects," *Daedalus,* Spring 1969, pp. 230–31.)
   b. "Experimental physicians never have the right to select martyrs for society. Every human being has the right to be treated with decency, and that right must always supersede every consideration of what may benefit mankind, what may advance medical science, what may contribute to public welfare. No doctor is ever justified in placing society or science first and his obligation to patients second. Any claim to act for the good of society should

be regarded with distaste because it may be merely a highflown expression to cloak outrageous acts." (From "The Willowbrook Letters," *The Lancet*, April–July 1971.)

   c. "[According to the totalitarian view] each human life is not an end in and of itself, but rather a means to another end, which is the good society. . . . Experiments can be performed on a member of this generation in order to assist members of future generations. A small injustice to this pre-viable infant may result in great benefits to mankind. . . . Lives which grossly lack 'quality' should be terminated early for their own and society's good." (From Eugene F. Diamond, "Redefining the Issues in Fetal Exper-imentation," *Journal of the American Medical Association* 236, no. 3 [July 19, 1976].)

9. What should be the legal limitations on property rights? "A man's home is his castle," yet he is not permitted to commit murder in it. Which of the following acts, if any, should the law also prohibit people from doing on their property?
    a. Mistreating animals
    b. Shooting the boy who's stealing watermelons out of the garden
    c. Shooting an intruder in the yard, after giving fair warning
    d. Shooting a burglar after the burglar has broken into the house
    e. Surrounding the yard with an electrified fence
    f. Playing music so loudly that neighbors are disturbed
    g. Nude sunbathing in the yard although the neighbors object
    h. Raising mountain lions in the back yard
    i. Leaving the garbage out, causing a stench and attracting flies and rats
    j. Keeping their property although the city wants to make it a public park
    k. Keeping their property free from city condemnation although a hill above is liable to produce mud-slides which will enter the house
    l. Placing solar heating panels in the yard although the neighbors complain that they're an eyesore
    m. Retaining the overhang of a living room, although if there's an earthquake it will fall on a neighbor's house below
    n. Building a reservoir, although it will lower water pressure in the neigh-borhood
    o. Retaining a cherished memento though the police want to use it as evi-dence
    p. Polluting the neighbor's yard with smoke
    q. Throwing garbage into the river, thus polluting it for neighbors down-stream (Does it make any difference who settled there first?)

10. Do the following in your view constitute invasion of privacy—legally, so that the person or organization doing it should be subject to legal action?
    a. Someone bursts uninvited into your living room when you already have guests, but you don't want this person's company.
    b. Someone watches you in your living room (through the open curtains) from across the street.
    c. The university psychiatrist holds onto your records, which contain much intimate information about you, claiming that the records belong to the university and not to you.
    d. The police department taps your telephone to discover whether you are dealing drugs.

e. A private organization (e.g., the Pinkerton Detective Agency) taps your telephone.

f. Police officers place an instrument on the outside wall of your house which enables them to eavesdrop on every conversation going on inside.

g. Someone tapes his conversation with you without your consent.

h. Someone places a tape recorder in your bedroom and plays it while you are asleep (without your knowledge or consent), in order to induce you to act in accordance with the recorded suggestions.

i. A credit corporation gives your entire credit history to an organization (e.g., Master Charge) that wants to see it.

j. Someone keeps telephoning you constantly, although the calls are unwelcome to you and you've let the person know this.

k. A magazine to which you subscribe sells its mailing list to another company, with the result that you get piles of junk mail in your mailbox after that.

l. Your neighbor watches you with binoculars from her window.

m. A columnist reveals intimate details of a Congressman's married life, all of which are true. (Would your opinion be different if the person were not a politician but a film star, businessman, or housewife?)

n. A policeman frisks you on the street, demanding details about your source of income and your sex life.

11. In the case of *Kerby* v. *Hal Roach Studios* (53 Calif. App. 207 [1942]), studio representatives devised a stunt to advertise the movie *Topper:* they sent 1,000 copies of a letter in a feminine hand in pink envelopes to male homeowners in Los Angeles. The letter read: "Dearest: Don't breathe it to a soul, but I'm back in Los Angeles and more curious than ever to see you. Remember how I cut up about a year ago? Well, I'm raring to go again, and believe me I'm in the mood for fun. Let's renew our acquaintanceship and I promise you an evening you won't forget. Meet me in front of Warners Downtown Theatre at 7th and Hill on Thursday. Just look for a girl with a gleam in her eye, a smile on her lips, and mischief on her mind! Fondly, your ectoplasmic playmate, Marion Kerby." Marion Kerby was the name of a principal character in the movie and in the novel on which it was based. But a woman in the Los Angeles telephone directory had the same name, and she suffered considerable harassment because of telephone calls from both men and irate wives. She sued the studio for invasion of privacy. How would you have disposed of the case?

(The court decreed that although the harm was unintentional and not malicious, "the letter did, in fact, refer to the plaintiff in clear and definite fashion, and would reasonably have been so understood by anyone who knew of her existence. The wrong complained of is the invasion of the plaintiff's right to privacy, and such an invasion is no less real or damaging because the invader supposed he was in other territory.")

12. In *U.S.* v. *Payner* (1980), Payner was accused of income tax violations but said the evidence obtained to convict him was made possible through the theft of materials from a bank vice-president's briefcase. The government did not deny this but said that "the Government affirmatively counsels its agents that the Fourth Amendment standing limitation permits them to purposefully conduct an unconstitutional search and seizure." The federal district court agreed with the

government and the restricted the right of privacy in such cases. Do you agree with the court's ruling?

13. In light of the following dialogue between a young man and his psychiatrist, determine how you would act if you were in the psychiatrist's place:

"Sometimes I think that what I really want to do is to kill people and drink their blood."

Dr. Allen Wolfe looked at the young man in the chair across from him. The face was round and soft and innocent looking, like that of a large baby. But the body had the powerful shoulders of a college wrestler. There was no doubt that Hal Crane had the strength to carry out his fantasies.

"Any people in particular?" Dr. Wolfe asked.

"Women. Girls about my age. Maybe their early twenties."

"But no one you're personally acquainted with."

"That's right. Just girls I see walking down the street or getting off a bus. I have a tremendous urge to stick a knife into their stomachs and feel the blood come out on my hands."

"But you've never done anything like that?"

Crane shook his head. "No, but I'm afraid I might."

Dr. Wolfe considered Crane a paranoid schizophrenic with compulsive tendencies, someone who might possibly act out his fantasies. He was a potentially dangerous person.

"Would you be willing to take my advice and put yourself in a hospital under my care for a while?"

"I don't want to do that," Crane said. "I don't want to be locked up like an animal."

"But you don't really want to hurt other people, do you?"

"I guess not," Crane said. "But I haven't done anything yet."

"But you might," Dr. Wolfe said. "I'm afraid you might let yourself go and kill someone."

Crane smiled. "That's just the chance the world will have to take, isn't it? I told you I'm not going to let myself be locked up." (From *Intervention and Reflection: Basic Issues in Medical Ethics* by Ronald Munson, ed. © 1979 by Wadsworth Publishing Company, Inc. Reprinted by permission of Wadsworth Publishing Company, Belmont, California 94002.)

14. Should a psychiatrist be required to inform the authorities of a patient's intent to commit a felony, regardless of the seriousness of it? One psychiatrist is reported to have said that it depends on the nature of the crime. "If a patient says he's going to forge a check, it wouldn't disturb me. If he says he is going to commit serious bodily injury, it *would* disturb me; my action would depend on whether I felt he was likely to do it." (Quoted in Henry Davidson, "Professional Secrecy," in *Ethical Issues in Medicine,* ed. E. Fuller Torrey [Boston: Little, Brown, 1968]. Reprinted by permission of Little, Brown.)

15. What would you do in this case?

A victim of an automobile accident lay severely injured in the emergency room. Dr. X was preparing to administer the Babinski test when out of one sock fell a packet of heroin. Dr. X faced this dilemma: how to resolve the conflict between his desire to respect the confidentiality of the physician-patient relationship and his duty to preserve the law? If he failed to report the incident to the police, he might face a charge of concealing a wrongful act. On the other hand, if he permitted the law to take its course, he would risk a lawsuit for violating the physician-patient relationship. (From ibid. Reprinted by permission of Little, Brown.)

16. A doctor refuses to prescribe a drug, claiming it will do physical harm. Consider the following responses by a patient. Indicate what your reaction to each one would be and also whether the law should be invoked in any of the cases.
    a. "You're mistaken. It won't cause me harm."
    b. "But that's just what I want. I want to harm myself."
    c. "I don't care if it harms me. I'll enjoy myself so much taking the drug that I don't mind whatever harm it does me." (Adapted from Joel Feinberg, *Social Philosophy,* pp. 50–51.)

17. Sometimes patients do not consent to electric shock, drug therapy, aversion therapy, and other devises and techniques used to change their behavior. In such cases, according to Seymour Halleck (in his article "Legal and Ethical Aspects of Behavior Control," *American Journal of Psychiatry* 131 [1974]:381–85), physicians have the right to force patients to submit to such treatment if the following conditions are met: (*a*) the patients must be judged to be dangerous to themselves or others; (*b*) those who are providing treatment must believe there is a reasonable probability that treatment will be of benefit to the patients as well as those around them; and (*c*) the patients must be judged to be incompetent to evaluate the necessity for treatment. Discuss this position. Can you see any loopholes in the conditions as stated? (Judged by whom?)

18. What should count as harm? In criminal law all the following things count as harm:
    (*a*) actual physical injury or death; (*b*) assault without battery (threat of violence, without the violence occurring); (*c*) an attempt to commit a crime (taking a "substantial step" toward committing it); (*d*) soliciting someone or conspiring with someone to commit a crime; (*e*) an attempt to aid a suffering person (when the person doing the aiding is not competent to extend it); and (*f*) injury to oneself. Should all of these be considered harmful, in your opinion? Should people be subject to criminal prosecution for each of them?

19. Who, if anyone, is harmed by (*a*) trampling on the flag; (*b*) committing perjury; (*c*) failing to stop at a red light when there is no traffic; (*d*) walking naked down the street; (*e*) mutilating a corpse? Should any or all of these be against the law, and if so what kind of penalty should they carry?

20. Give your opinion on each of the following questions concerning children's rights:
    a. Do parents have the right to prevent their children forcibly from using playgrounds in dangerous neighborhoods?
    b. Does the State have the right to force children to continue their education through a certain age? If so, through what age, or to what degree of education?
    c. To what extent do parents have the right to use force or the threat of force to make children do useful things such as sweeping the floor, mowing the lawn, and washing windows? To make them go out and earn money by

doing things like taking on a paper route? To keep the money the children
earn themselves?

d. Do parents have the right to bring up their children in a certain religion?
To keep their children away from playmates whose families profess a different religion?

e. Should homosexual teachers be excluded from elementary and high schools
on the ground that they may influence the child's choice of life styles?

f. May parents forcibly prevent their children from reading certain books or
looking at pictures in *Playboy* and other magazines?

g. Do teen-agers have a right to try LSD if they choose to do so?

h. Does a girl of fourteen who becomes pregnant have the right to decide
whether she will have an abortion, or do her parents have that right?

i. Do children have a right to decide whether they will accept the offer of
being nude models for magazines (i.e., pose for "kiddie porn")? Do parents
have the right to prevent them forcibly?

j. Should a twelve-year-old boy be permitted to remain in the United States, as
he desires, or be required to return to the Soviet Union along with his parents?

21. Evaluate this proposed rule by James Barr Ames in 1908, concerning Good Samaritan laws: One who fails to interfere to save another from impending death
or great bodily harm with little or no inconvenience to himself, when death or
harm follows as a consequence of his inaction, shall be punished criminally and
make compensation to the party injured or his family. Specifically: a person has
a duty to act whenever (*a*) the harm or loss is imminent and there is apparently
no other practical alternative to avoid the threatened harm or loss except his own
action; (*b*) failure to act would result in substantial harm or damage to another
person or his property, and the effort, risk, or cost of action is disproportionately
less than the harm or damage avoided; and (*c*) the circumstances placing the person in a position to act are purely fortuitous.

22. On most social issues, such as gun control, there are numerous utilitarian arguments that can be marshaled on both sides of the question. In favor of gun control
one might argue that (1) if there were no guns available, fewer people would be
killed in family quarrels, fewer children would suffer accidental injury by guns,
etc.; (2) many householders who own guns become the victims of those same
guns at the hands of intruders; (3) if guns were confiscated and the law enforced,
they would gradually disappear from circulation. Against gun control one might
argue that (1) the guns would only go underground—criminals and the Mafia
would always get hold of them anyway, and the question would be whether a
householder would be permitted to have the means to defend himself against
armed intruders; (2) when it is known that people have guns (as in Switzerland),
there are far fewer robberies; (3) guns are one's ultimate defense against government itself when it violates citizens' rights: it would not have been possible for
millions of people in the Soviet Union to be taken from their homes and shot or
sent to the Gulag if they had not first been made disarmed victims, with the
police having a monopoly of the guns.

   Is the issue less inconclusive if you supplement utilitarian arguments with arguments concerning human rights? Assume that a person has the right of self-
defense against aggression. First, what form should that right take? Owning a
Saturday night special complete with silencer? Owning a butcher knife? Taking

lessons in karate? What exactly should each person be entitled to in order to im-
plement this right? Second, what should an individual be entitled to do by virtue
of possessing this right? To retaliate only after the other person has pulled the
trigger? To retaliate against threats (any threats?)? To shoot trespassers? To set
spring-guns for burglars?

23. How far should constitutional guarantees of the right to freedom of religion extend? Should the following be prohibited by law?
    a. Believing that God commands you to kill every tenth person you meet
    b. Killing every tenth person you meet, in the belief that this is God's com-
       mand
    c. Sacrificing your firstborn child to the god Baal
    d. Practicing polygamy in the name of religion (as was done by the Mormons
       in the United States prior to the Supreme Court prohibition of it in 1892)
    e. Holding religious revivals with live rattlesnakes, in the belief that God will
       not permit them to bite
    f. Faith healing (as a cure for diseases)

24. Should all the land in North and South America be returned to the Indians as the
original owners? Why or why not? (Does it make any difference whether they
were agricultural or nomadic?)

    Blacks were (as far as we know) the first to settle central Africa; whites were
the first to settle what is now South Africa. Does this make any difference to the
issue of present property rights in those areas?

25. About 60 percent of the inhabitants of Northern Ireland are Protestants who wish
to remain united with Britain, and about 40 percent are Catholics who desire
political union with Ireland. Can you think of any peaceable way to solve this
"Irish problem"?

SELECTED READINGS

The Concept of Rights

Andelson, Robert V. *Imputed Rights*. Athens, Ga.: University of Georgia Press, 1971.

Becker, Laurence. *Property Rights*. London: Routledge & Kegan Paul, 1977.

Blake, Ralph M. "On Natural Rights." *Ethics* 36 (1925): 86–96.

Brandt, Richard. *Ethical Theory*. Englewood Cliffs, N.J.: Prentice-Hall, 1959. See
Chapter 17.

Brody, Baruch, ed. *Abortion and the Sanctity of Human Life*. Cambridge, Mass.: M.I.T.
Press, 1975.

Carritt, Edgar F. *Ethical and Political Thinking*. New York: Oxford University Press,
1947. See Chapters 6 and 15.

Feinberg, Joel. "Duties, Rights, and Claims." *American Philosophical Quarterly* 3
(1966). Reprinted in E. Kent, ed. *Law and Philosophy*. New York: Appleton-Century-Crofts, 1970.

————. "Human Duties and Animal Rights." In M. K. Morris and M. W. Fox, eds.
On the Fifth Day. Washington, D.C.: Acropolis Books, 1978.

————, ed. *The Problem of Abortion*. Belmont, Calif.: Wadsworth Publishing, 1973.

————. *Social Philosophy*. Englewood Cliffs, N.J.: Prentice-Hall, 1973. See Chapters
4–6.

Hart, H. L. A., "Are There Any Natural Rights?" Stuart M. Brown, Jr., "Inalienable Rights"; William K. Frankena, "Natural and Inalienable Rights." *Philosophical Review* 64 (1955): 212–32.

Kordig, Karl. "A Theory of Rights." *Pacific Philosophical Quarterly,* Vol. 62, No. 2 (April 1981): 170–83.

Locke, John. *First and Second Treatises on Civil Government* (1690).* Many editions. See Book 2.

Lyons, David, ed. *Rights*. Belmont, Calif.: Wadsworth Publishing, 1979.

Macdonald, Margaret. "Natural Rights." *Aristotelian Society Proceedings* 47 (1947–1948): 225–50.

Machan, Tibor. *Human Rights and Human Liberties*. Chicago: Nelson Hall, 1975.

———. "Some Recent Works in Human Rights Theory." *American Philosophical Quarterly* 17 (Spring 1980): 103–15.

McCloskey, Herbert J. "Rights." *Philosophical Quarterly* 15 (1965).

Melden, A. I. *Rights and Persons*. Berkeley: University of California Press, 1977.

———. *Rights and Right Conduct*. Oxford, Eng.: Blackwell, 1959.

O'Neill, Onora, and William Ruddick, eds. *Having Children*. New York: Oxford University Press, 1980.

Pollock, Lansing. *The Freedom Principle*. Buffalo, N.Y.: Prometheus Books, 1981.

Rand, Ayn. "Man's Rights." Included in her works *The Virtue of Selfishness*. New York: Signet, 1964. And *Capitalism, the Unknown Ideal*. New York: Signet, 1966.

Raphael, D. D. *Political Theory and the Rights of Man*. Bloomington, Ind.: Indiana University Press, 1967.

Rollin, Bernard E. *Animal Rights and Human Morality*. Buffalo, N.Y.: Prometheus Books, 1981.

Ross, Sir William David. "Rights." In his *The Right and the Good* (1930). Reprinted in Wilfrid Sellars and John Hospers, eds. *Readings in Ethical Theory*. Englewood Cliffs, N.J.: Prentice-Hall, 1970.

Steinbock, Bonnie, ed. *Killing and Letting Die*. Englewood Cliffs, N.J.: Prentice-Hall, 1980.

Rights and the Law

Bentham, Jeremy. *Introduction to the Principles of Morals and Legislation* (1789). 2 vols. Partially reprinted in E. A. Burtt, ed. *English Philosophers from Bacon to Mill*. New York: Random House/Modern Library, n.d.

Berger, Fred, ed. *Freedom of Expression*. Belmont, Calif.: Wadsworth Publishing, 1980.

Cahn, Edmond, ed. *The Great Rights*. New York: Macmillan, 1963.

———. *The Moral Decision*. Bloomington, Ind.: Indiana University Press, 1956.

Devlin, Patrick. *The Enforcement of Morals*. London: Oxford University Press, 1965.

Donnelly, Richard, Joseph Goldstein, and Richard Schwartz, eds. *Criminal Law*. New York: Free Press, 1962.

Dworkin, Ronald. *Taking Rights Seriously*. London: Duckworth, 1978.

Feinberg, Joel. "Duties, Rights, and Claims"; "The Nature and Value of Rights"; "The Rights of Animals and Unborn Generations"; and "Human Duties and Animal Rights." In Joel Feinberg, ed. *Rights, Justice, and the Bounds of Liberty*. Princeton, N.J.: Princeton University Press, 1980.

*Dates in parentheses are dates of first publication.

————. *Social Philosophy*. Englewood Cliffs, N.J.: Prentice-Hall, 1973. See Chapters 2–5.

Feinberg, Joel, and Hyman Gross, eds. *Philosophy of Law,* 2nd ed., Part 4. Belmont, Calif.: Wadsworth Publishing, 1980.

Fletcher, Joseph. *Humanhood: Essays in Biomedical Ethics*. Buffalo, N.Y.: Prometheus Books, 1978.

Gregory, Charles, Harry Kalven, and Richard Epstein, eds. *Cases and Materials in Torts*. Boston: Little, Brown, 1968.

Hall, Jerome. *General Principles of Criminal Law*. 2nd ed. Indianapolis: Bobbs-Merrill, 1960. The sections on ignorance and mistake are reprinted in Herbert Morris, ed. *Freedom and Responsibility: Readings in Philosophy and Law*. Palo Alto, Calif.: Stanford University Press, 1961.

Hart, H. L. A. *Law, Liberty, and Morality*. Palo Alto, Calif.: Stanford University Press, 1963.

Hayek, F. A. *The Constitution of Liberty*. Chicago: University of Chicago Press, 1972.

Houlgate, Laurence. *The Child and the State*. Baltimore: Johns Hopkins University Press, 1981.

Kohl, Marvin, ed. *Infanticide and the Value of Life*. Buffalo, N.Y.: Prometheus Books, 1976.

Mill, John Stuart. *On Liberty* (1859). Many editions.

————. *Principles of Political Economy* (1848). Many editions.

Morris, Herbert, ed. *Freedom and Responsibility: Readings in Philosophy and Law*. Palo Alto, Calif.: Stanford University Press, 1961.

Munson, Ronald, ed. *Intervention and Reflection: Basic Issues in Medical Ethics*. Belmont, Calif.: Wadsworth Publishing, 1979.

Partridge, Ernest, ed. *Responsibilities to Future Generations: Environmental Ethics*. Buffalo, N.Y.: Prometheus Books, 1981.

Paulsen, Konrad, and Sanford Kadish. *Criminal Law and Its Processes*. Boston: Little, Brown, 1952.

Rachels, James. "Active and Passive Euthanasia." *New England Journal of Medicine* 292 (1975). Reprinted in James Rachels, ed. *Moral Problems*. New York: Harper & Row, 1979.

Radcliffe, Peter, ed. *The Limits of Liberty: Essays on John Stuart Mill's On Liberty*. Belmont, Calif.: Wadsworth Publishing, 1966.

Ratcliffe, James, ed. *The Good Samaritan and the Law*. Garden City, N.Y.: Anchor Books, 1966.

Reiser, Stanley, et al. *Ethics in Medicine*. Cambridge, Mass.: M.I.T. Press, 1978.

Visscher, Maurice B., ed. *Humanistic Perspectives in Medical Ethics*. Buffalo, N.Y.: Prometheus Books, 1976.

Williams, Glanville. *The Criminal Law*. London: Stevens & Sons, 1953.

————. *The Sanctity of Life and the Criminal Law*. New York: Alfred A. Knopf, 1957.

8

Justice

The concept of justice and that of rights overlap somewhat. Mill listed violation of rights as one of the senses of "injustice." Yet the general thrust of justice is different, and together the two concepts of justice and rights constitute the principal challenge to utilitarian ethics.

In a *general* sense, a rough synonym for "justice" is *fairness*. In this sense, to be justly treated is to be fairly treated; a just distribution is a fair distribution, a just procedure is a fair procedure. But the more *specific* sense of "justice" has to do with *getting what you deserve*. If you get the grade you deserve in a course, you have been justly treated (as far as that grade is concerned); if you get a lower grade than you deserve, you have been unjustly treated, and also if you get a higher one (though fewer students complain about this). The wage you deserve is a just wage, and if offenders get the punishment they deserve their treatment is just.

But aren't the two senses the same? Not quite. If pirates have agreed to share the loot equally, a fair distribution would be an equal share for each. But they don't *deserve* any of it, since they have gained it by robbery and it doesn't belong to them in the first place. Or, if the job of digging a ditch is given to a platoon of army men, all of whom are about equally qualified though only about five are needed to get the job done efficiently, a fair procedure would be to choose the five by lot. But this wouldn't necessarily result in justice, for, assuming that all get equal benefits out of having a ditch and that the job is an onerous one for whoever has to do it, each of the men chosen could say, "What did I do to deserve this nasty job, when those guys over there are being let off without doing anything?" Their deserts are, let's say, equal, but the burdens they are required to assume are not.

In 1840 a ship sank off the Labrador coast. There were not enough lifeboats to hold the survivors. Almost forty people crowded into a lifeboat intended for less than a dozen persons. There were not enough provisions for everyone, and there seemed to be no way in which everyone could survive even a few days until a ship might come by. Then storm clouds began to appear, and it seemed certain that the lifeboat could not survive the coming storm, at least not with so many people in it: the only chance was to lighten the lifeboat. A few left voluntarily, and then the captain decided that the only way to save some of them was to force others to go over the side. He could have chosen them by lot; instead, knowing that only the hardiest were likely to survive in any case, he chose for survival the strongest and ablest persons, and those who were weak or ill and would not be likely to survive anyway were put overboard. (After the storm, when a ship did appear, the survivors were rescued and the captain was tried and convicted of manslaughter. If he had let them all remain aboard all would have died, but this would have been an "act of God" and no one's fault; according to the court, the captain was playing God with the lives of others, which he had no right to do.) [1]

The fate meted out to each of the passengers by the captain was not just, for none of them deserved to die; but the arrangement by which they were chosen could nevertheless be deemed a fair arrangement. If not, what would have been fairer in these circumstances?

Besides this general distinction concerning the meaning of the term, several other distinctions must be made about the concept of justice:

1. Justice involves the treatment of human beings by other human beings. Racial prejudice is unjust, since it involves treating some persons not in accord with their deserts. But being born crippled or diseased, however unfortunate, is not unjust, since injustice requires that there be someone to inflict the injustice, and hereditary malformations are misfortunes of nature not inflicted by anyone. (Some would say that God inflicted them, and that God was unjust for doing so. But most believers do not wish to say that God was unjust; hence they sometimes find another way out, saying perhaps that in some unknown way the person deserved to be born that way. But then there would be no injustice, since no one, not even God, would be guilty for inflicting it.)

2. Justice, unlike utility, is past-looking, not future-looking. Justice requires that people be treated in accord with their deserts, and their deserts depend on their past record. If someone deserves punishment for committing murder, it is because in the past he or she committed the murder. If someone deserves a reward for extraordinary merit, it is because he or she has earned it in the past. Sometimes it is said that a person deserves a job, not just because of past accomplishment, but because of the potential for the future the individual shows; but even so, the potential must be evident in the pres-

[1] United States v. Holmes, 26 Fed. Cas. 360 (Pa. 1842).

ent. It need not come out in the entrance exams, but in some talent, enthusiasm, or other personality feature exhibited in the present.

3. Justice is individualistic. One person may deserve one thing (e.g., grade, compensation, or punishment), while another may deserve something else. It is individuals who deserve good or ill, not groups. We may say that a gang of terrorists deserves a certain punishment, but if so that is because we believe that each member deserves that punishment. If some students in a class got A's, some B's, some C's, some D's and F's, and the teacher was to average all the grades and assign everyone in the class that grade, each student would not be treated according to his or her individual deserts; such a practice would ignore individual deserts and treat the class as a collection, with no individual differences. This would be *collectivism* in the assigning of grades, the opposite of individualism. Such collectivism would of course be unjust, since the good students would be pulled down to the average and the bad students would be pulled up to it.

Collectivistic thinking is probably the main source of injustice. Someone in a tribe has been murdered, and other members of that tribe take revenge on every member of the clan to which the murderer belongs; but most of the people in the clan had nothing to do with it, didn't even know about it, so that punishing them is unjust (i.e., they don't deserve such treatment). During World War I the music of Richard Wagner was banned in the United States, because he was a German. But since Wagner had nothing to do with World War I (having been dead long since), banning his music was a particularly crude kind of collectivism: he was a German, and "Germans were bad," so he was condemned along with the rest.

Primitive people, and many "civilized" people as well, tend to bunch large numbers of other people together and slap the same label on them, then condemn all simply on the basis of the label. In our own day ethnic groups are treated as a collective. People lump together all blacks, Hispanics, Jews, Chinese, and so on. But within each of these groups are countless individual differences: some are moral, some immoral; some are intelligent, some stupid; some are friendly, some hostile; some deserve a certain reward or punishment, while some do not. Justice commits us to look at each person's *individual* merits or demerits, not the average of the group as a whole, nor the behavior of some of its members. (The fact that some are bad doesn't mean that all are bad.) Even if it was true that, say, the average intelligence of one group is lower than that of another, this fact would be totally irrelevant to the intelligence of a given individual: a person may be a genius even if he or she belongs to a group whose average intelligence (or average honesty, etc.) is lower than the average of another group. Not to give a job to a certain individual simply because one has found *other* members of his or her ethnic group untrustworthy is a flagrant case of injustice.

Sometimes, instead of taking revenge on the whole tribe, members of a second tribe will select one individual from the first tribe at random for murder; it can be anyone, as long as the individual belongs to that tribe. This isn't exactly collectivism (or at least it is a variation on collectivism), for no action is being taken against everyone in the group: the whole group is not being tarred with the same brush. But still it is unjust, for the person killed is innocent of the crime.

4. We do sometimes speak of *comparative* justice or injustice. This is not collectivistic justice, for there is no such thing; it has to do with the way one person is treated *in relation to* another. If one person commits a crime and gets the penalty she deserves, whatever that is, and a second person commits the same crime and is let off because he has bribed a judge or attorney, the first person cannot complain of injustice as far as her individual treatment is concerned, for she got what she deserved. The treatment of the second person was unjust, however; for the second person to be let off for the same offense for which the first was put in jail is a comparative injustice. (Many criminals do not object so much to their punishment, if they believe they deserve it, as to seeing someone else who has committed an equally serious crime get off scot-free or with a very light sentence.)

Individual justice may miscarry for many reasons. Most often the law is unjustly administered, as when one person gets a light sentence while another gets a heavy one for the same offense. But it is also possible for the law to be written so that all people accused of a certain offense get a worse punishment than they deserve; for example, poachers and pickpockets were hanged in the nineteenth century. This was not a case of comparative injustice, for they all got the same punishment; it was a case of all the punishments for that crime being out of proportion to the gravity of the offense, and thus being undeserved.

1. JUSTICE AS EQUAL TREATMENT

Justice requires that everybody be treated equally. However, there is a problem about the use of "equal." Strictly speaking, the word applies to mathematical quantities: $2 + 2 = 4$. But two identical tables are not equal to each other; they only have the same properties—same size, same color, same weight. Rather than "equal," they should be described as "qualitatively identical" (as opposed to "numerically identical," which they are not, since they are two tables and not one).

If we speak of the grades on two students' papers as equal—both receiving an 89, for example—this doesn't mean that the two papers have the same characteristics, but only that they have the same *rating;* one may be long, one short; one clear but thin, the other less clear but more detailed. Two dogs may be rated the same in a dog show without having the same features.

What, then is meant by justice as equal treatment? "It means," someone may volunteer, "that everyone should be treated *the same.*" But this clearly will not do. Felons are sent to jail and non-felons are not; this is unequal treatment—that is, they are not treated the same. Those who win the competition get a prize or award, while those who don't do not. Those who work get wages, whereas those who don't do not. If justice is treatment in accord with deserts, nothing is more obvious than that human deserts are unequal (i.e., not the same); and since deserts are unequal, rewards, prizes, compensations, and punishments are also administered unequally. "Justice," said Aristotle, "is treating equals equally and unequals unequally."[2]

"What I mean is that nobody should get any *special treatment*," the person may persist. But this isn't accurate either. The winning team gets special treatment that the losing team doesn't get. The president of the United States has bodyguards to keep him from danger of assassination, and the rest of us don't. Do we all deserve to have bodyguards just because the president does? Don't the responsibilities and dangers of his office entitle him to this bit of special treatment? The head of a corporation has an office to himself or herself; a secretary in the same corporation may not. Is that unjust? Should one complain of this special treatment for the corporation head?

"No," the individual may pursue the argument, "what I mean is rather that in life situations, from the assignment of grades to job opportunities, nobody should be *discriminated against*." But to discriminate is simply to choose one above another; a discriminating taste is one that is able to distinguish a well-prepared meal from a poor one or to distinguish genuine works of art from trash. Whenever we choose one thing over another, we discriminate against the second—that is, we choose one in preference to another. Is that unjust? Should we "select" everyone indiscriminately, that is, without discriminating?

"Let me try again, then. When I say that two people should be treated equally what I mean is that no one person should be preferred to another or chosen above another for *irrelevant reasons*." At last, we seem to be getting somewhere. The problem is to determine which reasons are irrelevant. In some cases this is quite easy. If two students in the same class get the same grade, it should be because their performance in the course is roughly the same (not having the qualities, but the same rating). If the teacher assigns a higher grade to one girl because he finds her sexually attractive, this is a comparative injustice because the characteristic in question, sexual attractiveness, is not one that is relevant to the assigning of grades for a course.

If you invite a bunch of friends and acquaintances to a party, is this an injustice to all those whom you do not invite? Granted that their rights haven't been violated—they had no right to be invited—but have they nevertheless been unjustly treated? No, we are inclined to say, because the purpose of a party is to invite whomever you wish to, for whatever reason you like or for no reason at all. It is the fact that you want these people together on this occasion that counts. You may not observe any racial or ethnic quotas, but that is your privilege; it's your party. If you have repeatedly gone to

---

[2] Aristotle, *Nicomachean Ethics*, Book 5.

Jones's parties and you don't invite Jones to yours, Jones may feel left out—may even feel unjustly treated—but *has* there been an injustice? If this is an injustice, then all those not invited are also the victims of unjust discrimination.

"Not every kind of activity involves justice or injustice," it may be said: "who you invite to your party is strictly up to you. But who you hire for a job is not; you should observe justice in your hiring practices." Employers may question even this, saying that as long as it's their money they're risking, they should be entitled to hire whomever they choose; it's their business enterprises, they're taking the risks, so it's for them and no one else to say who is hired. Perhaps there is higher utility in doing it this way, and whether there is or is not, they may claim it as their right. (*If* they hire incapable people, they themselves take the economic loss.)

But our question now is, Where does justice lie? What would *just* hiring practices be? If justice has to do with deserts, what kinds of consideration are relevant to judgments of deserts in job hiring?

Suppose someone says that A deserves a job more than B does because of skin color. This, we are inclined to say, is an irrelevant consideration; whatever qualifies a person for a job, skin color has nothing to do with it. But if we are told that the applicant should be disqualified because of membership in the Association of American Terrorists, we are inclined to agree, since no one would feel safe in the office with someone like that around. Since in both cases it is membership in a certain group that we use as a basis for our judgment, what is the difference between them? Is it that A has no power over the physical characteristics with which he was born (such as skin color), but that membership in organizations is something he does voluntarily and therefore reflects his character and predilections?

This, though important, is not exactly the distinction we need. Voluntary membership in some organizations has nothing to do with qualifications for a job; a person can be a good bank manager whether she is a church member or not. But, sometimes characteristics over which people have no control *are* quite relevant. That a man has a large build may help to qualify him for a football team or as a bouncer in a bar; that a woman is graceful in motion may help qualify her as a dancer. Even skin color may be relevant for certain jobs: if you need someone to play the part of Kunta Kinte, the person must be black, and if you need someone to try out a new bronzer to simulate a suntan, he or she cannot be. Almost any characteristic could be relevant or irrelevant, depending on what kind of job is in question.

An employer doesn't hire women as stevedores because, he says, they are not physically up to the job, and this is surely a relevant consideration for that kind of work. But now some women turn up who are just as physically qualified for the job as men, so he hires them. Two weeks later, however, he dismisses them because, he says, not as much work gets done when members of both sexes are on the same job, and some of the men don't like the situation since they can't talk in the way they usually do. Also, according to the boss, there is only one dressing room for employees, and he can't afford to install another. Are these relevant considerations? Should they be ignored, even if they hurt the employer in the pocketbook? Is the firing or refusal to hire women in such cases an injustice? Or is it, though an injustice, one which should nevertheless be tolerated on utilitarian grounds?

Should we say that any hiring of people for jobs on any basis *other* than their qualifications for the job is an injustice? If two persons are equally qualified, and no other applicant is more qualified, must both be hired? What if there is only one opening? Is an employer being unjust no matter which applicant is hired? "No," it might be replied, "but you shouldn't hire one and not the other because of race, for example." But what if they are of different races? How is a decision to be made between two equally qualified persons of different races? Isn't a consideration like the probability of other employees getting along with the new person in the office relevant? What about the idea that in hiring teachers attention must be paid to providing role models for children who do not already have them to imitate? Still, these considerations don't seem to be relevant to the job applicant's qualifications but rather to other people's needs. Should such considerations be dismissed then in deciding whether to hire a certain person?

The simplest view to take in this matter is that the only thing relevant in hiring is the applicant's qualifications for the job: if *A* is better qualified for the job than *B* is, then *A* should be hired, regardless of race, color, or sex. To hire a less qualified person, thereby passing over a more qualified applicant is always unjust (as it is always unjust to give the better student the lower grade). There may be special reasons for ignoring qualifications on some occasions—utilitarian reasons such as the expense of installing another dressing room in a small plant—but justice is done only when the most qualified person is hired. (Sometimes the qualifications would include membership in a certain race, as in our Kunta Kinte example.)

Still, aren't there good reasons for sometimes hiring the less qualified applicant—not in the interests of utility but of justice? A number of such reasons have been advanced. Let's consider some of them.

1. Some say members of a minority deserve preference in job applications because *other* members of that group have been discriminated against in the past. This argument by itself is not very plausible, however. Indeed, it is sheer collectivism. How, for example, does the fact that *other* persons with black skin have been discriminated against in the past count as a reason for discriminating against a person with white skin now (assuming that the white applicant has the superior qualifications)? Prior to the Civil War blacks were unjustly held as slaves; but how does discriminating against a white person now "make it up" to those persons? Besides, what if the white applicant had nothing to do with past discrimination? Should he or she be turned down for the job today because other white persons (long since dead) discriminated against some black persons in the past? Is "reverse discrimination" any less unjust than the original discrimination was?

Would it even be doing a service to a minority person to hire him or her because of race rather than because he or she is highly qualified for the job? If a teacher is hired because of compulsory racial quotas and students know it, and know that they will be taught by a person of less ability when they could have had one of greater, won't they resent the person being hired (not because the teacher is from that minority, but because he or she is less qualified)? If you went to a symphony concert and a few of the players played out of tune and made constant mistakes, and you were told, "You have to forgive them; we could have obtained better players, but we were required to include a quota of Falkland Islanders in the orchestra," would you agree that the right thing had been done? If not, is it any more right to hire less qualified teachers and foist them on students? The results may be less visible to the public and take longer to become manifest, but is this case really different from that of the orchestra? And while we are speaking of justice, what about justice to the students, who could have had a better teacher but didn't?

2. A more plausible reason for giving preference to one person, *A,* because of race or minority status is that *this person* has suffered from past discrimination; perhaps other present members of the same group (*B, C, D,* etc.) have also suffered in the same way, so they too should be given preference, again because of past injustices to the individuals concerned. Preferring those applicants now would be performing the duty of *reparation.* It has been suggested that all or most blacks and women today

> have suffered the consequences of the down-grading of other blacks and women: lack of self-confidence, and lack of self-respect. For where a community accepts that a person's being black, or being a woman, is right and proper grounds for denying that person full membership in the community, it can hardly be supposed that any but the most extraordinarily independent black or woman will escape self-doubt. All but the most extraordinarily independent of them have had to work harder—if only against self-doubt—than all but the more deprived white males, in the competition for a place amongst the best qualified.[3])

Here the fact that someone has endured past injustice is given as a reason for being given preference now. The same could be said not only of victims of racial and sexual discrimination, but of those who have rendered special services in the past, such as war veterans. They have made a considerable sacrifice, and whether or not one approves of the war in which they engaged, the sacrifice has been made; shouldn't they too be given preference as partial reparation for their past? Those who make this argument do not contend that blacks, women, or veterans are necessarily more *qualified,* but only that they are more *deserving* of the job because of past injustices or past services. Maybe

[3]Judith Jarvis Thomson, "Preferential Hiring," in *Equality and Preferential Treatment,* eds. Marshall Cohen, Thomas Nagel, and Thomas Scanlon (Princeton, N.J.: Princeton University Press, 1977), p. 36.

the orchestra won't be quite as good as it might have been if qualifications were the only basis for hiring, but (it would be argued) the price is well worth paying in order to fulfill our duties of reparation.

Another way in which people have suffered in the past is not to have received the kind of education or training required to qualify for the job. "They can't help it—they weren't given a chance." We usually feel that for persons not given the chance, a special effort should be made to make up for the past. (Sometimes, of course, their failure was their own fault or brought on by sheer laziness; many prominent intellectuals were raised in the slums, educated in vastly inferior school systems, and lived in hellish home environments. But we are considering now only those cases in which present failure to qualify for a job is the result of factors not of the person's own making.) This situation is still another variant of giving people a special break as a duty of reparation.

How far should this line of reasoning be carried? What if it's not an employer's fault that the applicant had insufficient training? Should the burden of reparation be placed on him or her? Wouldn't following such a policy be courting disaster? You can't hire as a flutist someone who has never played a flute until today, just because she never had a chance to own or practice a flute; you'd wreck the orchestra. You can't hire as an accountant a person who can't add, even if his inability to add is the result of the failure of teachers to do their job. (Even if doing so were just to the ill-prepared applicant, how about justice to the clients?) Any employer who did such things would soon go broke, and then all the firm's employees would be out of jobs. Reparations made to unqualified applicants (at least those unqualified through no fault of their own) can best be made by giving them better training, not by giving them jobs for which they aren't qualified.

The fact that people have unjustly suffered in the past or have rendered extraordinary service or haven't been given a chance does tend to make us go out of our way to be especially considerate of them now; we bend over backward to right past wrongs. Such cases strongly appeal to our sense of justice. Superior qualifications for the job count, but past sufferings or services also count. We may end up trying to get the best orchestra regardless of these considerations, but if we are aiming at not merely the best orchestra possible but doing justice to each individual in the selection of its members, we can hardly count these considerations as irrelevant.

Nor can we ignore the problem of how to render justice to those who have been unjustly treated in the past without being unjust to other persons in the present. What do we say to the superior trombonist whom we turn down in preference to one who can't play very fast and hits some sour notes but is a disabled war veteran? The main problem with discrimination, including reverse discrimination, is that it tends to perpetuate discrimination in the future. Suppose that last year *A* was hired for a job in preference to *B*, because of some kind of discrimination. And suppose that today, when a similar job is again open, *B,* who was passed over, is in competition with a new applicant, *C*. Because *B* was passed over before, we give *B* the job now; but what of the equally qualified or more qualified applicant, *C*, who is passed over today? We are now discriminating against *C* in order to rectify past discrimination against *B*. Shall we say to *C*, "That's the breaks, but the next time we'll give *you* preference"? And if we do, may we not thereby be discriminating against *D*, whom we then reject in order to rectify our discrimination against *C*? The pattern will go on and on, with no end in sight, each act of discrimination breeding the next one. Is this really justice? In view of the tendency of acts of discrimination to lead to other similar acts, many would suggest that the only solution is to stop discrimination now, hiring persons solely on their merits, even if this means that past injustices cannot always be rectified.

Equality Before the Law

Whatever may be said about hiring practices, one important area of justice—the one in which "equal justice for all" looms most important—is that of "equal consideration before the law." But again there is a problem of how this phrase is to be construed. It is possible for a law itself to be unjust: for example, a law that prescribes an extremely harsh penalty for a minor offense punishes *all* offenders more harshly than they deserve.

More frequently, however, it is the *administration* of the law that is unjust. If two persons are both convicted of, say, armed robbery, it would be unjust if one received a long prison sentence and the other no penalty at all because he had bribed an attorney or a judge or was the judge's cousin. Being related to or bribing a judge has nothing to do with the nature of the offense, and that is the source of the injustice. If offenses are the same, the punishments should be the same, we say, whether the defendant is rich or poor, black or white, blue-collar, white-collar, or bowery bum. (It doesn't always work out that way, of course; being poor or black often leads to *un*equal treatment. But this, at any rate, is what is meant by "equal treatment before the law.")

Even so, the formula is vague. If two motorists are guilty of speeding and one of them is caught and the other isn't, is that injustice? Can the one who is caught say, "This is unjust! The other driver was speeding and you should have caught her too"? There does seem to be an injustice in "selective enforcement" of the law; the uncaught motorist deserves a fine as much as the one who was apprehended. Still, the one who was caught does deserve the fine, so at least individual justice, even if not comparative justice, has been served. Given the limitations of personnel, the police can't be expected to catch everyone who speeds; but if a deserved penalty is assigned those who are caught, at least justice has been done in their case.

Suppose now that *A* and *B* are both guilty of going through a stoplight, under the same conditions (busy street, same hour of day, and so on), but they get unequal fines. Is this unjust? Not necessarily. One may have been taking a bleeding patient to an emergency hospital, and the other may have sped through the light just for kicks. Well, then, one of them did it under conditions C_1 and the other under conditions C_2; the two cases are different because some of the surrounding circumstances are different.

But suppose that the conditions were exactly the same, with no extenuating circumstances in either case, and they still get different fines. Is that unjust? Again, not necessarily. Even if the *external* conditions are the same, the *internal* conditions may not be; one may be a reckless driver who needs to be taught a lesson, the other a careful driver who never had a violation before and couldn't see the light from the place where she was supposed to stop. Might this not be a relevant difference?

What, then, is the result? We appear to be saying that when two acts of the same kind (such as going through a stoplight) are performed under *identical* conditions (both internal and external), it is unjust (because undeserved) to levy a certain fine on one of them and a smaller one or no fine at all on the other. Identical deserts demand identical punishments. But isn't this rule useless? We never do get identical conditions, both internal and external. Any two acts always differ, either in the nature of the action itself or in some of the circumstances surrounding it.

Suppose that we broaden this principle to make it useful. Let's say that any two acts of the same kind should be treated the same if they are (not identical, but) *similar* in *relevant* respects. But how are we to determine what respects are relevant? That is the problem.

It seems clear enough that being the judge's cousin is an irrelevant consideration as far as the proper penalty for the offense is concerned; so too is skin color. But is it equally clear that *age* is irrelevant? If not in a traffic court, at least in a criminal court, an extremely youthful offender might receive a lighter sentence by reason of his or her youth. A young offender might not fully comprehend the consequences of his or her actions, and there could be other such considerations. In the disposition of a case, should the fact that a person has a previous record for the same kind of offense be considered relevant? Some say no, neither judge nor jury should have such information: each case must be tried on *its* merits, not in relation to possible previous offenses. Others, however, are just as insistent that the past history of an offender is a relevant consideration in determining the severity of the punishment: it is just for second or third offenders to be dealt with more harshly than first offenders.

That there is disagreement on what is *relevant* is one problem; another is that different *criteria* seem to be appropriate to different kinds of situations. What determines whether or not you deserve a prize, whether or not an instructor deserves to be promoted, whether or not a law violator deserves a certain punishment, or what wages a worker deserves for work performed? We should not assume that whatever the criteria of desert are for one kind of case are also applicable to all other types. Even in one category, such as hiring, we have seen that seemingly irrelevant considerations such as skin

color can be relevant in some contexts. Let us, then, consider the main suggested criteria in two highly important areas: first, compensation for work
performed, and second, punishment for crimes committed.

2. CRITERIA OF DESERT

A. Equal Distribution

If all students received the same grade no matter what their performance was
like, the grading system would be quite pointless. Let us consider, then, one
ideal of justice in the economic area—equality of income. According to this
criterion of desert, everyone should receive the same income, no matter how
skilled or unskilled the job, no matter how long or short the hours of work.
Whatever people earn, they should all share equally.

This is a policy that sometimes works well in small groups such as communes, where everyone shares the same ideals and is willing to work for
them. It is much less likely to succeed in very large and diverse groups in
which people do not know one another and are not particularly sympathetic
to others' life styles. Many communes were formed in the United States by
dissidents from overseas in the nineteenth century. In one of them, for example, many different trades and professions were followed to make the
group self-sufficient, and some went outside to be trained and later returned
to the group. But tensions began to appear: some people worked harder than
others and still received the same uniform stipend from the central committee. Some of the doctors among them were much abler than other doctors,
and everyone wanted to go to the best doctors, with the result that their
schedules were overloaded and those of the less able ones were not, though
all received the same wage. In the course of time there was a "brain drain,"
in which the ablest people left. Finally the communal style was discontinued,
and each person received his share of the communal pot and from then on
was on his own. Today the members of that community are making lots of
money producing Amana freezers.

When a group comprises several hundred million people an equal-income
policy cannot be made to last except by a tremendous exercise of police
power, and even then those in charge vote themselves a disproportionately
large share of the income. Let's imagine, though, a society in which at the
outset everyone has received an equal income; perhaps the government has
confiscated everyone's earnings and is now doling out an equal amount to
each person of, say, $1,000 apiece.

How long would this equality last? Some people would spend all of their
money the same day and be penniless by nightfall. Others would spend it in
a week or two. Still others would bank or invest most of it. The most adventurous ones would put it all into some new enterprise and borrow from
others, so that they would have enough to start the venture; with this they

would buy a store or factory and materials, and put other people to work for wages. The workers would then be able to save much of their original $1,000 and spend only what they had earned. At the end of a month, some would have nothing, some would have part of the original sum, others would have increased the amount, and still others would be on the way to becoming wealthy.

Suppose now that the government intervened once more to make them all equal again. Those who had nothing left would get $1,000. Those who had $400 left would get $600. Those who had more than $1,000 would give up their surplus to provide the others with what they'd spent. What would happen next?

Those who had spent it before would doubtless spend it again, believing that they would get another $1,000 to spend. Those who had spent only part of it would now spend all, knowing they'd get a full $1,000 at month's end, and the more they'd spend the more they'd get. And what of those who had worked and increased their assets? They would be very cautious about doing so again, believing that it would only be taken away from them once more. So they might end up spending it too. But if everyone spent rather than saved, where would the money come from to distribute the next time? In the end there would be equality, but it would be equality of zero—"splendidly equalized destitution."

Many people talk of equality of income as an ideal, but few would be able to live with it in practice once its consequences came home to them. If an acquaintance of yours has $10,000 and wants to spend it all on some hairbrained scheme which you know will cause him to lose it all, and you repeatedly warn him and he doesn't take your advice, will you still be just as willing, after he has lost the money, to share yours equally with him as part of a scheme of general equality? Or if Robinson Crusoe works hard and Friday declines to work at all, yet claims half of Crusoe's harvest as his right, should Crusoe be willing to share with him 50-50 in the name of justice? People do not identify that kind of equality with justice: equal wages for equal work perhaps, but not equal income no matter what you do, and certainly not when you do nothing at all.

What many egalitarians desire is not so much equal income for all as equal happiness. But such an ideal is even more unattainable: if all had equal money, they would be far from being equally happy. Some would be unhappy no matter how much money they had, and others would be happy with little. In view of the diversity of temperaments and sources of happiness, there is no way to supply people with equal amounts of happiness. Even if there were, would this be justice? Don't some people *deserve* more than others? Doesn't a person who by the tenor of his or her life makes others happy deserve happiness more than the person who makes everyone miserable? Would you be willing to make a Hitler or a Stalin happy in the name of justice?

B. Effort

Perhaps, then, all workers should get the same wage if they put forth the same effort. This need not mean that two people who each put in eight hours a day should get the same pay, for one person may work very hard during the whole eight hours and another may work at half-capacity, punctuating the day with coffee breaks and phone calls to friends on company time. It is the degree to which individuals fulfill their potential, not the amount of time spent, that counts.

The idea that those who do their best—no matter in what line of work and no matter how long or short the period of training required to perform the job—should receive equal pay was put forth in the nineteenth century by Edward Bellamy. In his "futuristic" novel, *Looking Backward,* he described the idea this way:

> "Some men do twice the work of others!" I exclaimed. "Are the clever workmen content with a plan that ranks them with the indifferent?"
>
> "We leave no possible ground for any complaint of injustice," replied Dr. Leete, "by requiring precisely the same measure of service from all."
>
> "How can you do that, I should like to know, when no two men's powers are the same?"
>
> "Nothing could be simpler," was Dr. Leete's reply. "We require of each that he shall make the same effort, that is, we demand of him the best service it is in his power to give."
>
> "And supposing all do the best they can," I answered, "the amount of the product resulting is twice greater from one man than from another."
>
> "Very true," replied Dr. Leete; "but the amount of the resulting product has nothing whatever to do with the question, which is one of desert. Desert is a moral question, and the amount of the product a material quantity. It would be an extraordinary sort of logic which should try to determine a moral question by a material standard. The amount of the effort alone is pertinent to the question of desert. All men who do their best, do the same. A man's endowments, however godlike, merely fix the measure of his duty. The man of great endowments who does not do all he might, though he may do more than a man of small endowments who does his best, is deemed a less deserving worker than the latter, and dies a debtor to his fellows. The Creator sets men's tasks for them by the faculties he gives them; we simply exact their fulfillment."
>
> "No doubt that is very fine philosophy," I said; "nevertheless it seems hard that the man who produces twice as much as another, even if both do their best, should have only the same share."

"Does it, indeed, seem to you?" responded Dr. Leete. "Now, do you know, that seems very curious to me? The way it strikes people nowadays is, that a man who can produce twice as much as another with the same effort, instead of being rewarded for doing so, ought to be punished if he does not do so. In the nineteenth century, when a horse pulled a heavier load than a goat, I suppose you rewarded him. Now, we should have whipped him soundly if he had not, on the ground that, being much stronger, he ought to. It is singular how ethical standards change."[4]

Unfortunately, effort is very difficult to gauge. How do you tell whether a person is working at full capacity? Some people who work hard could work much harder, given proper incentive; and some prefer to get by with just average output, even though they could easily do more. Accordingly, in some lines of work (such as contracting) people are typically paid by the job rather than by the hour. When this is done, people are not being paid for the amount of effort they put in (or the proportion of the effort they put in that they could have put in) but for the work actually completed.

Suppose that a dull person puts in eight hours at full capacity, and a bright person puts in eight hours at full capacity. If it is a policy of the employer to give both the same wage, and if companies are free to compete for employees, then another company, which doesn't have this policy, is very likely to offer the bright employee a job at a higher wage. As soon as that happens, that person will be paid a higher wage for the same effort as the person who remains at the first place of employment. Such a practice can be stopped only by forcibly preventing the person from taking the offered job, by preventing the competing company from offering it, or by not permitting individual companies to exist at all, but having the government own all business enterprises and assign a uniform wage to everyone, based on personal effort. Who determines how much effort each worker has put in? Presumably the commissar in charge. Thus, not the objective quantity of a person's output, but the *assessment* of his or her effort by a superior becomes the criterion for the wage received. An enormous emphasis is thereby placed on someone's estimation of people's efforts, with all the possibilities of favoritism and bribery that this entails. Such a system also requires almost total control of the economy by government to prevent other employers from offering a capable worker a higher wage; indeed, the government must prevent such employers from existing by controlling the entire economy itself, thus unleashing still further opportunities for political favoritism and corruption.

---

[4] Edward Bellamy, *Looking Backward* (1888). Passage quoted is in Millard S. Everett, *Ideals of Life* (New York: Wiley, 1954), p. 513.

C. Achievement

Whether for grades in courses or work done for an employer, the usual criterion employed is not effort expended but actual achievement. Students are supposed to be assigned grades for courses on the basis of their actual achievement in the course—how much material they mastered and how well they mastered it. For students who receive an A in elementary logic, their graduate schools or future employers are thereby put on notice that they mastered elementary logic to a high degree—not that they tried to, but that they did; not that they put forth lots of time (they may not have had to, if it came easily to them), but that whatever time they put in, they succeeded well, compared with the rest of the class, in learning what they were supposed to. If the instructor had given grades on the basis of amount of effort expended, some means of determining how many hours each student put in studying for the course and how thoroughly each student concentrated during those hours, would have been needed; but such a means would have been of little value in determining achievement, for some students can grasp a great deal very quickly and others grasp very little even after many hours of effort.

Occasionally attempts have been made to make student grades depend on the degree of *improvement* between the beginning of the course and the end. But if one student starts from zero and goes up to 75 percent, the degree of improvement for that student is greater than that of another who starts from 75 percent and works up to 95 percent. Still, doesn't the second deserve the better grade? Also students can pretend to be very stupid at the beginning so that they can exhibit a high degree of improvement. Moreover, it is not their improvement which employees are likely to desire information about, but their mastery of subject matter.

It might be argued, with some plausibility, that there should be no grading system at all, because of numerous abuses of it; but if there is one, what employers and graduate schools expect of it is an indication of the students' mastery of the material in various courses. If it does not do that, it misleads the people who desire such indicators. Some colleges use a pass-fail system, but thereby penalize their students, because graduate schools, not knowing whether the pass is an A or a D, overlook such students in granting scholarships.

Usually in an employment situation the person who hires pays for work actually delivered—not what the employee *intended* to deliver but what he or she *did* deliver; this is true no matter whether the job is piecework in a factory or generating new ideas in aeronautical engineering in an airplane manufacturing plant. If a person works hard but can't deliver the goods, he or she may deserve an A for effort but no salary increase at raise time. If one store or factory hired on the basis of effort and the other on the basis of achievement, the second would soon get all the best employees and would be able to pay them higher wages because of higher productivity.

There are, of course, different ways of estimating achievement. Employers can consider quantity—how many pieces a seamstress can sew in an hour—or quality—one good creative idea generally being more useful to the company than a dozen unoriginal ones. Depending on the type of work and the nature of the employer, the emphasis placed on each of these may vary; ideally, employers desire a maximum of both. Sometimes the criteria involved are a mix of the two: some teachers achieve a great deal in the way of communicating knowledge or skills and spend much time with students, whereas others spend less time but are much better at research and creativity. The criteria that should be used to determine which teachers should be promoted depends on the kind of institution (small college versus large research university) as well as on the expectations of those in charge of hiring.

In contest-type activities, such as a track meet, achievement is measured by who comes in first: the runner who crosses the finish line first gets first place. Is this just? Suppose a second runner is better but had a twisted ankle that morning and therefore came in second. Did he deserve the first prize? He may deserve an A for effort, but by the rules of the contest, the one who came in first deserves the first place in the meet.

Perhaps, though, the man who came in first doesn't really deserve it. Perhaps he wasn't running at his best and only came in first because the others did even worse. Perhaps we should say that, since he came in first, he is *entitled* to first place, but that he doesn't really *deserve* it. (There are contests such as essay competitions in which all the contestants are so bad that nobody deserves a prize, and none are awarded.) In that case, however, might it not also happen that four or five people all deserve to have first place, because they are all so good? What then happens to what is called *"the* first place"? If five people get first place, is it really first place, or first-through-fifth? In any case, if the runner who came in first doesn't deserve first prize, who does? The one who would have come in first except for the twisted ankle? The one who had greater athletic ability and *would* have come in first if he had trained a little harder? The one who *would* have come in first if he'd bothered to go out for track, but in spite of great ability did not because he was too lazy or undisciplined? Once we start speculating about who could have come in first if circumstances had been different, we may soon end up giving all first prize—and then what would happen to that special distinction, first place, reserved for one person only? Whatever the conditions, the runner who comes in first is *entitled* to first prize whether or not he has performed well enough to *deserve* it. A defeated presidential candidate may *deserve* to have won the election, but the winner, whatever his deserts, is entitled to it by "the rules of the game."

D. Need

"The ones who deserve it the most are those who need it the most," some might say. This criterion is sometimes used as a supplement to others, but it could hardly be used as the sole criterion of desert. The person who needs a job the most is usually the one who has no employable skills: that's why he or she needs a job. Should that person then be hired and given a skilled worker's wages, simply because of need? And what effect will this have on other workers who need the job less because they have been thrifty and saved more money in the past, and those who are excellent at their jobs because they have learned them thoroughly (perhaps sacrificing to go to night school), are industrious, and add greatly to the firm's production? The degree of a person's need is likely to be in inverse proportion to his or her skill; those with a marketable skill are much less likely to be in need.

In some situations, such as caring for the poor, need is indeed a criterion: you don't dole out money for the poor in Beverly Hills (only the federal government does that). But what would be the effects if hiring was based solely on need? The unskilled, the lazy, those unable to fulfill the simplest tasks would rush to get such jobs, not because they could perform them, but because they needed them. The fact that a person needed a job is no guarantee that he or she would be any good at it or would even put forth any effort once on the job. A person with a somewhat besmirched work record, say, for kicking the boss downstairs and getting fired a number of times, has a very great need for a job, but should he or she be hired just because of that need?

Sometimes need is considered as an ancillary criterion. Two assistant professors are up for promotion, and only one of them can receive it. If one of them needs the promotion but is poorly qualified, she will probably not receive the promotion no matter how great her need. But if the two are about equally qualified, then the promotion often goes to the one who needs it more—the one who is the sole support of a large family rather than the one who is fairly independent financially. The question to be asked, however, is whether such a decision is based entirely on grounds of desert or deservingness. Does the one person *deserve* the promotion (with its higher salary) more because she *needs* it more? Is it not more plausible to say that the two are equally deserving, but that the promotion went to one rather than the other not because of greater deservingness but because of greater need?

E. Ability

Ability, too, is sometimes used as a criterion of deservingness. Employees may be hired on the basis of ability but are seldom retained in their jobs just because they have it; ability must be expressed in actual achievement. An ability which remains forever dormant is of no use to anyone. If I have greater ability at math but I prefer to sit and doodle, it can hardly be alleged that I deserve a high wage just for the ability I have in my head. Native ability is not something a person can take credit for; acquired ability (such as the ability to take shorthand) is a different matter, since it requires training.

Even so if the ability is not reflected in actual achievement, it hardly deserves a compensation.

A particularly insidious (but often fatally attractive) combination of criteria occurs in the Marxist slogan "From each according to his ability, to each according to his need."

Suppose that an automobile factory is operated in accordance with this criterion. What will happen? Assume that workers in the factory are paid not by how much they produce, or even by how much effort they put forth, but by how much income they *need*. Able and industrious people may need less than dullards (since the dullards are probably less employable and need the income more); if no correlation exists between productivity and wages, the industrious workers thus may get less if their need is less. If an intelligent and imaginative employee sees ways of improving production and suggests them, he is made to work harder as a result ("from each according to his ability"), but he is not rewarded for it ("to each according to his need"). Instead, the shiftless, the indolent, those who can corral a dozen needy relatives and put them on the payroll as their dependents, are attracted to this factory, since after all they are paid not by the work they do but by the amount of their need, and predictably they see to it that their needs constantly increase. The industrious workers, seeing their wages go to the shiftless to buy drink and bring in more shiftless relatives, conclude that they are being penalized for the very qualities that would make the factory successful, and gradually they come to resent and hate the employees who benefit from the labor of the industrious. And so the flow of innovation stops, the quality of production declines, and the reputation of the factory, whose work force is increasingly peopled by the needy, also declines. The quality of its products goes down until customers no longer care to buy them. Orders trickle down to almost nothing, and the only customers who finally remain are those who do not pay for the product and do not intend to.

In a factory operated in such a manner, honest and able workers who see what is happening soon get out, and only the shiftless and needy remain, until the factory goes bankrupt. But if an entire nation adopts Marx's criterion, there is no place for them to go (and as a rule they are not permitted to emigrate elsewhere). An entire nation run in this way soon finds its economy grinding to a halt.[5]

It would appear, then, that some incentive system is required in order to keep an individual enterprise, or a nation's economy, running. Even the Soviet Union, which officially operates on this Marxist slogan, finds it necessary to provide some incentive, usually in the form of higher wages for those who do dangerous or difficult work, for those who engage in military production, and for those whom it desires to lure into work in inhospitable

---

[5] The dramatic story of one such factory that puts the slogan "From each according to his ability, to each according to his need" into practice, and the consequences thereof, is told in Ayn Rand, *Atlas Shrugged* (New York: Random House, 1957), pp. 660–70.

regions such as the Arctic. (Those who are prisoners, of course, do not have to be lured: they are compelled.)

F. Justice and the Market

How is justice related to the free market, the uncoerced exchange of goods and services? Of the *utility* of allowing the unhampered operation of the market there is little doubt; of its justice there is much more doubt. When people are free to invent, free to produce goods and services and sell them to others, their ingenuity in producing things that other people want to buy is limited only by the possibility of producing what others want, the ability of others to buy them, and the profitability of producing them. (If only a few customers want a certain product, the item may not be worth producing.) Competition for customers tends to keep the price down, and labor-saving machinery plus mass production of goods makes the cost per item low. In a market economy there is a profusion of goods available at prices that most people can afford, such as never exists in highly regulated economies. The reason is that there is an incentive to produce more or better products in a market economy that simply does not exist when government plays a large role in solving a nation's economic and social problems:

> Suppose you had lived in 1900 and somehow were confronted with the problem of seeking a solution to any *one* of the following problems:
> 1. To maintain an efficient system of [mail delivery].
> 2. To increase the average span of life by 30 years.
> 3. To convey instantly the sound of a voice speaking at one place to any other point or any number of points in the world.
> 4. To convey instantly the visual replica of an action, such as a presidential inauguration, to men and women in their living rooms all over America.
> 5. To develop a medical preventive against death from pneumonia.
> 6. To transport physically a person from Los Angeles to New York in less than four hours.
> 7. To build a horseless carriage of the qualities and capabilities described in the latest advertising folder of any automobile manufacturer.
>
> Without much doubt you would have selected the first problem as the one easiest of solution. In fact, the other problems would have seemed fantastic and quite likely would have been rejected as the figments of someone's wild imagination.
> Now, let us see which of these problems has been solved. Has the easiest problem been solved? No. Have the seemingly fantastic problems been solved? Yes, and we hardly give them a second thought.[6]

[6] John C. Sparks, in *Cliches of Socialism* (Irvington-on-Hudson, N.Y.: Foundation for Economic Education, 1970), pp. 180–81. The first example has been changed from roads to mail.

The market does tend to correct many injustices:

1. We believe that if a person has a dirty or dangerous job, he or she should receive higher pay for doing it; and this is usually the way it works out, since higher wages are an inducement to get people to take those jobs. If the man who walks daily on a catwalk a hundred feet above the river to inspect a bridge received no higher wages than a filing clerk, he would not be likely to take such a job except in dire emergency. (When the pay is not subject to market constraints, such as a soldier risking his life in the infantry, then the "higher pay" principle doesn't work, for his wages are set not by the market but by act of Congress.)

2. Most people also believe that if a person has put years of arduous work into preparing for a profession, and given up many of the delights of youth in order to make that preparation, he or she deserves higher pay when the goal is achieved. Therefore physicians, psychiatrists, and high-level executives who have to make important decisions for thousands of employees deserve more when they reach that position. The market does indeed reward them in that way: if a physician received no higher income than a janitor, he or she might find it much less taxing to be a janitor. "But nobody deserves $500,000 a year, not even for being head of General Motors!" some may exclaim. But what if the executive saves the company $10 million a year in overhead or gains it that much in new creative ideas? (Public school teachers often receive less in proportion to the work they do, but their wages are determined not by the market but by school boards; low wages may not produce a shortage of teachers, but a shortage of *good* teachers.)

3. It is also true that people often will not go into enterprises that are risky unless they can make a very considerable amount of money if the risk pays off. If you go into debt to start a business and bear the whole risk (losing everything if it fails), you are not likely to take such a risk unless the payoff is considerable in the event that you succeed. Once such a business enterprise has succeeded, many people resent the entrepreneur who started it and say, "He's getting too much money"; but would they have had the ability and the will to take those same risks themselves?

But there are aspects of the market which, many persons would insist, require intervention by legislation in order to prevent or correct injustices. For example, suppose the community is afflicted with racial prejudice and that several employers refuse to hire blacks or Hispanics. In that case legislation prohibiting discrimination in jobs on grounds of race would help to correct the situation. The market *might* (though it would not always) take care of the situation without legislation, however. Suppose that half the qualified applicants belong to the groups discriminated against; by refusing to hire them employers are then failing to avail themselves of half their (potentially) best workers. This is an economic loss to them, as they will discover if owners of other stores or factories exhibit no racial discrimination and hire these applicants themselves, outdoing the discriminatory firms in productivity.

Another area that may seem to require government intervention is worker safety. High standards of safety in factories are vitally important to workers, but some of the precautions that have to be taken are expensive and cut into employers' earnings. Again, the market might (though not necessarily would) take care of the situation. If factories are known to have effective safety equipment, better workers will be attracted to them. It will also usually pay the employer to install such equipment rather than risk expensive lawsuits (or expensive insurance policies). However, laws concerning safety are often called for, along with the threat of court action.

If the kind of "justice" demanded is equal pay for all types of work, or even equal pay for all those employed in one type of work (regardless of the amount of effort, ability, productive capacity a worker shows), then stores or factories operating on this ideal would attract primarily workers without industry or ability (since the able ones would be lured into higher-paying jobs elsewhere). This would lead to a decline in production, and with it a decline in profits for the firms involved, to the point where the enterprises would have to close down; such an arrangement would have great disutility, and it would really not be just either. (Doesn't the eager beaver deserve more?) Here is a brief description of factory conditions in the Soviet Union, where no one can own a business enterprise (since ownership is considered "exploitation") and everyone in a certain work category receives the same wage. (It also explains why productivity, and the standard of living along with it, is so low there.) The Russian Vladimir Bukofsky writes:

> Nobody in the bus factory was in a hurry to work; the workers preferred to sit in the smoking room until the foreman appeared, when they all dashed to their places. "Why should we hurry for the money they pay us?" said the workmen. "Work's not a wolf, it won't run into the forest!" In the mornings they were almost all drunk or hung over, and throughout the working day people would be regularly detailed to slip over the fence for some vodka. Only one man put in a full day's work. The rest hated him, and when pointing him out would rotate one finger meaningfully by the temple. They were always looking for chances to do him dirt, either by surreptitiously damaging his machine or by stealing his tools. "Want to be a champion and raise the targets?" they said spitefully. It turned out that if one man exceeded the target, the target would be raised for all of them the following month, and they would have to work twice as hard for exactly the same money.[7]

It is quite clear that in a free-market economy there will be great inequalities of wealth. Utilitarian reasons can be given justifying such inequality. For example, if people know that they can keep all or most of the money they make from their business, they will have an incentive to keep on work-

---

[7] Vladimir Bukofsky, *To Build a Castle: My Life as a Dissenter* (New York: Viking Press, 1977), p. 123.

ing and producing. However, if they know it will be only taken away from them, they are more likely to stop and to work less diligently while on the job. If this tendency becomes widespread, it may have a marked effect on the productivity of the entire nation. There will be fewer goods and services available, since people who produce them can't retain the fruits of their labor. Thus in a market economy total productivity is enormously greater, which is another justification for allowing inequalities to exist. Free traders on a free market will be able to put their ideas for new or improved goods and services into practice, and with increasing mechanization more and more goods will be available at even lower prices. When machinery was first introduced into the British stocking factories, workers destroyed the machines, thinking they would lose their jobs; yet in the century between 1800 and 1900 the price of stockings was less than 10 percent of what it had been, and instead of a luxury for the few they had become virtual necessities in all strata of society.[8] There are, of course, thousands of other examples. Those who grow up in the midst of this plenty take it for granted, not realizing that the freedom to produce and trade is the source of their bounty. In an egalitarian society, the income distribution is relatively equal, whereas in a free-market society, there are extremes of wealth and poverty, with the bulk of the people being neither poor nor rich. But in the free-market society, goods formerly available only to kings and princes (and often not even to them) are available to virtually everyone. Yesterday's rare luxuries become today's necessities.

But there is another argument favoring the free market, based on the concept of rights. If I have earned the money, it is mine to dispose of as I wish; it does not belong to those who have not earned it. If I bought a television set, it belongs to me, and if someone takes it from me without my consent that person is guilty of theft. If I earn $100 a week, that also is mine to spend as I wish, and anyone who takes it from me without my consent is just as guilty of theft as in the first case, whether it was stolen by an individual, an organization, or a government. People tend to assume that we all contribute to some "national wealth pie" and that it is for the politicians in power to divide it up and say who may have what; but if what I have earned is mine by right, my part of the pie is not theirs to divide. Many people admit that "the removal of incentives to effort may diminish the total stock of goods to be divided up,"[9] but the point that is lost in such statements is a much more important one: no one has the right to divide up other people's earnings in the first place, in the interest of egalitarianism or anything else. There are no "national assets," only the assets earned by individuals.

It is morally obscene to regard wealth as an anonymous tribal product and to talk about "redistributing" it. The view that wealth is the result of some undifferentiated collective process—that we all did something

[8]Henry Hazlitt, *Economics in One Lesson* (Westport, Conn.: Arlington House, 1979), p. 50.
[9]R. M. Hare, "Justice and Equality," in *Justice: Alternative Political Perspectives,* ed. James Sterba (Belmont, Calif.: Wadsworth Publishing, 1980), p. 114.

and it's impossible to tell who did what, therefore some sort of equalitarian "distribution" is necessary—might have been appropriate in a primordial jungle with a savage horde moving boulders by physical labor (though even there someone had to initiate and organize the moving). To hold that view in an industrial society—where individual achievements are a matter of public record—is so crass an evasion that even to give it the benefit of the doubt is an obscenity.

Anyone who has ever been an employer or an employee or has observed men working, or has done an honest day's work himself, knows the crucial role of ability, of intelligence, of a focused, competent mind—in any and all lines of work, from the lowest to the highest. He knows that ability or the lack of it . . . makes a difference of life or death in any productive process. The evidence is so overwhelming . . .—in the events of history and in anyone's own daily grind—that no one can claim ignorance of it. Mistakes of this size are not made innocently. When great industrialists made fortunes on a *free* market (i.e., without the use of force, without government assistance or interference) they *created* new wealth—they did not take it from those who had *not* created it. If you doubt it, take a look at the "total social product"—and the standard of living—of those countries where such men are not permitted to exist.[10]

3. JUSTICE AND PUNISHMENT

To punish someone is not simply to inflict unpleasantness (pain or discomfort) on someone else. We use the word "punishment" somewhat loosely in ordinary speech. We say, for example, that a boxer took a lot of punishment in the ring, meaning that one boxer inflicted a considerable amount of pain or discomfort on another one. But not all pain and suffering are punishment. One boxer wasn't punishing the other one for something he did; pain and discomfort are simply the price the boxer pays for being involved in the match, which both boxers engaged in voluntarily. Again, a person who is sick may suffer a great deal, but unless you believe that this suffering is a punishment from God, the suffering is just that—suffering, not punishment.

Punishment must, indeed, involve unpleasantness of some kind; if it was a pleasant experience, you would tend to seek it and not avoid it, and it wouldn't be punishment. Punishment must also be *for* something, some offense that a person has committed. ("I'm punishing you." "What for?" "Nothing." This would be a contradiction in terms; but a person could inflict *pain* on someone else for no reason.) Furthermore, punishing can't be done by just anybody; it must be done by some person or group that has some special authority to do it, and it must be done according to certain rules

---

[10] Ayn Rand, "What Is Capitalism?" in *Capitalism the Unknown Ideal* (New York: New American Library, 1967), p. 30.

(normally, laws) which have been violated through the committing of the offense.

Parents (or parent-surrogates) are in a position of authority to bring up children and on occasion to punish them for offenses committed. Leaving aside the question of whether they should actually do it, they have the authority to punish, whereas strangers do not. But the principal context in which we speak of punishing is a *legal* context: through the authority of the State and its laws, people are punished for disobeying those laws. Whether the law itself is a good or bad one or whether the person accused is actually guilty of the violation of the law, punishment can be meted out to violators only in the context of legal rules and legal procedures (arrest, trial by judge or jury, prescribed rules of evidence). Without that context such treatment is not properly called punishment at all.

Punishment is thus an *institutional* concept, and as such it should be carefully distinguished from *vengeance*. If a prisoner is in jail awaiting sentence, and the man whom he injured, unable to wait for the law to take its course, abducts the prisoner himself from the jail, takes him out on a lonely road, and shoots him, this is not punishment. In spite of the fact that it was *for* something (having injured the man who seeks the vengeance), it was not done according to the prescribed procedural rules and by the "duly constituted authority." Perhaps the prisoner was about to receive the death penalty from the court anyway, but even so the man who "takes the law into his own hands" and shoots the prisoner himself becomes guilty of murder.

Why should the court try the man and administer sentence, rather than the aggrieved party, who, after all, was the victim of the crime? There are several reasons:

1. Punishment according to law is supposed to end the matter once and for all: a person is found guilty and punished, and that finishes the affair. An aggrieved party who seeks vengeance after that would then be guilty of violating the law. By contrast, acts of vengeance can go on indefinitely. Some Kentucky mountain feuds (the Hatfields and the McCoys) have gone on for generations, with a member of one clan killing a member of the other, a member of the second then killing one of the first, and so on indefinitely.

2. It is also true that punishment administered by a court, with a judge or jury who do not know the defendant personally, can be done without bias. If the judge or a member of the jury knows the defendant personally, he or she is eliminated from judgment on the case. By contrast, if the settlement of the dispute was left to the aggrieved parties, they would almost always exaggerate the severity of the offense aginst them. A woman with a delicate ego might well shoot a man to death for the crime of accidentally stepping on her toe; a man who stole a few apples from someone's orchard might well, if the owner of the orchard were irate enough, find himself shot in the head by the owner of the orchard.

3. A final advantage of legal punishment is that, unlike the person who "takes the law into his own hands," the law administers punishment accord-

ing to prescribed rules (laws) which are written and can be known in advance. No matter how indignant an aggrieved party may feel, the penalty for the offense cannot exceed what is permitted by law. The fact that the punishment must be administered according to prescribed rules known or knowable in advance gives to people's actions a certain *predictability:* if there is a range of punishment stipulated by law for armed robbery, and if you go in for armed robbery, then you know in advance what kind of penalty you can expect if you are caught. The punishment, in other words, is not left to just anyone's whim, especially not the whim of the aggrieved party.

The law also contains the machinery for exonerating persons from their allotted punishment. This can be done (depending on the jurisdiction) by the president, the governor, or the mayor. But *pardoning* is a legal act, not to be confused with *forgiving*. If the injured party says, "I forgive you," the statement means that he or she will no longer hold it against the offender, but the offender may still have to serve time for the offense. The governor may pardon, but only the aggrieved party can forgive. If the offender asked the injured person, "Will you forgive me?" and the person said "No," it would be possible for a stranger to enter the room at that moment and say, "That's all right, *I* forgive you." But the stranger could only utter the words, not actually offer forgiveness: only the aggrieved party can do that. No one can assume the responsibility of forgiving an act not done to him or her. "I don't want the mother to embrace the oppressor who threw her son to the dogs!" wrote the Russian novelist Fyodor Dostoyevsky. "She dare not forgive him! Let her forgive him for herself, if she will, let her forgive the torturer for the immeasurable suffering of her mother's heart. But the sufferings of her tortured child she has no right to forgive." [11]

Punishing, because it involves the deliberate infliction of pain or other unpleasantness on other human beings, demands a special justification. What gives one person or group of people the right to inflict such things on other people? Is not deliberate infliction of harm on someone a violation of that person's rights?

Indeed, it is, and it is only justified by the fact that the offender has already, in his or her actions, violated the rights of others. The lawbreaker has acted by the rule "I can injure others if I want to," and by exacting punishment we are only applying the same rule that he or she applied to other people. But does the fact that A violated B's rights give B the right to violate A's in turn? (Does the fact that someone lied to you entitle you to tell lies in return?) Do two wrongs make a right? Moreover, the reasoning that justifies punishment does not cover the entire corpus of legal crimes. What about victimless crimes such as prostitution (concerning which many people believe there should be no laws at all), in which both parties voluntarily enter, and consequently there is no victim? And what about crimes against "the system" such as overparking and perjury?

[11] Fyodor Dostoyevsky, *The Brothers Karamazov* (New York: Modern Library, 1937; originally published in 1882), p. 254.

Whatever justification of punishment is offered, in actual practice the rationale for punishing is that if no one was ever punished, there would be such an outbreak of crimes that a peaceful and orderly society would be impossible, and no one would be safe. It is undoubtedly preferable to try to *prevent* crimes before they occur, so that no harm is done: you can put safety devices and burglar alarms in your house to prevent people from robbing you. But the fact remains that in spite of such preventive devices crimes do occur, and then the question about what should be done about them must be faced. If we simply ignore them, they will multiply; so the only alternative seems to be to punish in some way those who commit them. But the reasons given for punishing—the justification of punishing—are still subject to endless controversy despite many years of rethinking them. We shall now consider the main theories of the justification of punishment.

A. The Utilitarian Theory of Punishment

Jeremy Bentham set forth in his *Principles of Morals and Legislation* (1789) the first clear statement of the utilitarian theory of punishment. The punishment of offenders against the law, said Bentham, should always have as its aim the good of society. But Bentham was also a psychological egoist, believing that people always act to promote their own interests. How, then, were people thus motivated to be made through egoistic motives to do what was good for society in general? To make self-interest serve the general interest, Bentham proposed sanctions for criminal behavior. First, there are *internal sanctions*—the development of conscience in children, mobilizing feelings of guilt and shame at the thought of performing antisocial acts. And in case these were not successful, *external sanctions,* specifically laws providing penalties for such actions, should be imposed. Thus, even if a person was highly motivated to commit a crime, he or she would be deterred from doing it by the thought of the punishment that would follow.

Every utilitarian judges an act (or a rule) by whether it promotes maximum expectable utility, and the same applies to the act of punishing someone (or a rule prescribing punishment). Punishing someone is justified, then, only if it does more good or prevents more harm than not punishing or doing something else to the accused. No matter how serious the crime, there is no point in punishing a criminal if the punishment doesn't produce good consequences or, when that is not possible, prevent harmful consequences.

But in what, specifically, does the "good for society" consist? There are several ways in which punishing someone can produce good consequences and avoid bad ones. Let us first distinguish these effects clearly from one another.

1. *Effects on the offender: rehabilitation or reformation.* It is one of the intended aims of punishing someone for a crime that the person who has committed it shall never again repeat the act, because he or she will have been purged

and cleansed by the healing process of "paying" for the crime. To anyone who has served even a moderate sentence, however, this official justification is at best a bad joke. Very few prisoners are rehabilitated by serving a sentence. On the contrary, by associating with habitual criminals, whose principal topic of discussion is crime and how to get away with it, even a person who was not inclined to criminal activities before incarceration will be strongly inclined in that direction after imprisonment. If rehabilitation was the sole aim of punishment, prisons might as well close up shop at once.

Since prison sentences by themselves seldom improve the character of the offender, psychiatric treatment is often suggested instead. But treatment under prison circumstances seldom achieves its effect either and is undesirable for several reasons. (a) If the treatment is compulsory, prisoners resent it, so that such treatment seldom helps. (b) It is not always clear by what standards the treatment is to be conducted: different therapists have different standards for what constitutes cure. (c) If great pressure is brought to bear on prisoners, such as solitary confinement for months, for refusal to participate in "treatment," this gives the reigning psychiatrist an enormous power over the life of prisoners. (d) Not only has the psychiatrist power over the life of prisoners while in jail, he or she can pretty much determine the release dates of prisoners. If a psychiatrist does not pronounce them "cured," they can be kept even beyond the limits of their sentences, or for years on end if their sentences are indeterminate. They become, in effect, the therapist's prisoners, and if they don't respond in the desired way, their fate can be far worse than that of ordinary prisoners who simply have to do their time before being released. There are prisons in which the magic word is treatment, not punishment, and all commitments are for an indeterminate sentence (or "life top," as prisoners call it). At one such prison, Patuxent, which psychiatrists once praised as a model of progressive prison reform, prisoners used to begin their term by spending thirty to sixty days in solitary, where they were held incommunicado in a 9-by-6-foot cell, with no books, letters, or visitors; their promotion to higher levels was entirely at the pleasure of the treatment staff. Journalist Jessica Mitford detailed the plight of prisoners who would not conform to the expectations of those who ran the facility:

> Patuxent picked for commitment those it thought it could break. Then came a flood of politicized and radical prisoners, mostly black, who weren't going to be broken and weren't going to suck up to white middle-class orthodox psychiatry in order to wheedle their way out. . . .
>
> [One of them,] Edward Lee McNeil, a black youth described . . . as "highly intelligent, steadfast, iron-willed" . . . then aged nineteen, was convicted without a jury trial of assault on a police officer and assault with intent to rape, charges he consistently denied. He had no prior criminal record. He was a high school graduate, employed at the time, and living with his parents. No evidence of insanity, drug addiction, or

drunkenness was offered at his trial. The judge sentenced him to imprisonment for "not more than five years" . . . [He] declined to be "evaluated" or "treated" after his first few experiences with the social worker assigned to his case. . . . Consequently he was locked up on the bottom tier for *six years.*[12]

McNeil could have remained there for the rest of his years but for the fact that through a long and tortuous chain of appeals, his case went to the Supreme Court, where Justice William O. Douglas wrote: "The state indeed intends to keep him there indefinitely, as long as he refuses to submit to psychiatric or psychological examinations. [But] McNeil's refusal to submit to questioning is not quixotic; it is based on his Fifth Amendment right to be silent."[13]

But psychiatric treatment at many such institutions is compulsory. Some types of "treatment," in fact, are more nonvoluntary than others. What is called "behavior modification therapy," for example, is usually undertaken against the prisoner's wishes and attempts to transform an inmate against his or her will into a different type of person. In the book and film *A Clockwork Orange,* a prisoner, who has strong aggressive impulses, is treated with electric shock until the very idea of violence makes him retch, and after his release he is unable to defend himself even when attacked. Such possibilities are no mere science fiction fantasies. In an article entitled "Criminals Can Be Brainwashed—Now," Dr. James McConnell wrote that "the day has come when we can combine sensory deprivation with drugs, hypnosis, and astute manipulation of reward and punishment to gain almost absolute control over an individual's behavior."[14] Sensory deprivation is a behavior modification technique that involves confinement for months or years in an adjustment center. Besides this technique, therapists can use chemotherapy (chemical behavior modifiers that make a subject ineffectual), aversion therapy (which uses pain and fear to bring about behavioral changes), and neurosurgery (which involves cutting or burning out portions of the brain believed to cause aggressive behavior). Such "treatment" is carried out in secret, and even outside physicians are not permitted to witness it.

In countries such as the Soviet Union, many political dissenters are taken to psychiatric "treatment centers," where they are pumped full of painful chemical agents until they recant their views or die.

2. *Effects on potential offenders: deterrence.* A much more pervasive effect of punishing, it is hoped, is to deter others from committing similar crimes. When one person is imprisoned for armed robbery, friends and others who may hear of the punishment may be deterred from committing such a crime

[12] Jessica Mitford, *Kind and Usual Punishment* (New York: Knopf, 1973), pp. 111–12. See also Bruce Ennis, *Prisoners of Psychiatry* (New York: Harcourt Brace Jovanovich, 1972).
[13] Quoted in ibid., p. 112.
[14] James McConnell, "Criminals Can Be Brainwashed—Now," *Psychology Today,* April 1970; quoted in ibid., p. 125.

themselves, knowing that there is a good chance that they will be caught and imprisoned if they do. This intended consequence of punishment is so important that sometimes the utilitarian theory of punishment is simply called the "deterrence theory" (which is a mistake, since there are other hoped-for utilitarian consequences of punishing besides deterrence).

Deterrence, however, operates very unevenly. Some people are indeed deterred from committing crimes by the fact that other people have been punished for doing so, but many other people are not deterred at all. They may not think about or even know of the punishment, they may not care, or they may think that they can get by with the crime, unlike the stupid fool who has been caught. Crimes of passion, committed in the heat of the moment, are not subject to deterrence at all, since by definition such crimes are committed in a fit of rage, with no thought at all of any consequences. The deterrent effect of punishing is strongest in minor offenses, such as parking in a no parking zone: if your car is repeatedly tagged in a no parking zone, it isn't worth the effort to go to court and pay the fine every time, and you soon learn to park somewhere else. This is ordinary "commonsense" deterrence, but for major crimes such as murder, deterrence is often far less effective because commonsense considerations are less present in motivating them.

Deterring others is not an effect of the punishment being administered, but of other people *knowing* that it has been administered. If the fact that someone has been punished doesn't make headlines, not many people know about it and can therefore be deterred by it.

The effectiveness of deterrence, however, is not the result of any one offender being punished, or even any series of them. If it is effective at all, it is so because there is a *pervasive system of law* in the entire society: at all times the police, the courts, and the jails are in operation, and there is always a good chance that they will catch violators of the law. The fact of this omnipresent legal system—except when it is so inefficient or corrupt that it catches very few offenders or when offenders can bribe their way out if caught—is probably what deters potential lawbreakers more than anything else.

3. *Effects on society at large: protection.* If a person who has committed a crime is likely to do it again, then one effect of punishing him or her with a prison sentence is to isolate the individual from the rest of society and thus to protect innocent persons. If there is a dangerous criminal on the loose, the dread and fear most people in the area experience are extremely great; even locking their doors and windows, they feel, won't be enough, and they can be robbed, kidnapped, or killed unawares at any time. The solution is to imprison criminals, place them on a work farm, or in some other way isolate them from the rest of society; they may then be a danger to each other, but unless they escape they will not be a threat to the people outside. Even if there was no rehabilitation, and if deterrence was utterly ineffective, this utilitarian reason for imprisoning criminals would remain.

Important though protection is, though, there is one interesting problem about it. Many of the perpetrators of the most serious crimes are one-timers who have no propensity to repeat their acts and would never commit them again. A peaceful man comes home from the office and finds his wife in bed with another man; he shoots first and thinks afterward. As far as protecting others against him is concerned, people need no such protection, for he is not the slightest danger to anyone else. Perhaps by being in prison he is deterring others, but others are not being protected against him, for no protection is needed.

These three hoped for consequences of punishment do not always occur together. Sometimes the deterrent effect may be considerable (e.g., if the crime and its punishment are prominently featured in newspapers), while the protection afforded to society is nil (for the murderer is a model prisoner and not dangerous to anyone else). Sometimes the opposite is true: the deterrence afforded is negligible (because no one is deterred by the offender's incarceration), while the protection afforded is great (if the offender is dangerous to others). It is difficult to know what a utilitarian would recommend in any individual case regarding punishment, for it is extremely hard to assign comparative weights to these three factors in specific cases: How do we know how much of a danger a prisoner is to others at any given moment? If an inmate has served the sentence mandated, shouldn't he or she be released whether dangerous or not? Indeed aren't most of the people who threaten the safety of others already loose on the street because they have never been convicted of anything or because they have already been released?

There are other utilitarian considerations which would be relevant to whether utilitarians would imprison someone, or release him or her early if already imprisoned, which have nothing to do with the gravity of the offense. For one thing, if prisons are already crowded, there will be a tendency not to convict (to avoid making crowded conditions even worse) or to release a prisoner prematurely. For another, if there is a wave of a certain kind of crime, such as house burglaries, there is a tendency to make the sentences for that offense more severe in order to deter others from committing such burglaries in the future, although burglary as such is no more or less serious a crime in that particular year than ten years before when the incidence of it was less frequent. One other consideration is that if a certain kind of crime is more difficult to detect than others, there is a tendency to make the punishment for it more severe, simply to deter people from committing it in spite of the slim chance of their being caught. This consideration applies to many crimes, from robbing someone on a deserted road to driving with bright headbeams on, thus temporarily blinding oncoming drivers and causing more accidents. Utilitarians would contend that punishments *should* be more severe when these conditions are present, though such considerations have nothing to do with the gravity of the offense committed.

The utilitarian theory of punishment has not gone without criticism. The main criticisms are:

1. To punish a person severely simply to deter others from committing

similar crimes is to use that individual as a means to other people's (or society's) ends. For example, if the death penalty was given for speeding, it would deter speeders, but however great the deterrence it would be unjust to the offender.

2. If it is only the utility of the punishment that is important, it is not even necessary that the person punished be the one who committed the crime. You can deter people from crime by punishing the wrong person as well as the right one, as long as the secret doesn't get out. If it does, of course, then public distrust of the forces of law and order becomes so great that the punishment of the wrong person (as in the Dreyfuss case in France in the last century) has the opposite of the desired effect. But suppose the fact that the authorities arrested and convicted the wrong person could never become known: perhaps the person convicted was a drifter without family ties and anyone to stand up for him; perhaps, too, the person who committed the crime has died, a crime wave was stopped by the fact that the innocent man was arrested, and the community's confidence in the police and judicial system was restored. From a utilitarian point of view, would it not be right to convict the innocent man?

Perhaps it would be right according to act-utilitarianism, but what about rule-utilitarianism? Those who believe that rule-utilitarianism collapses into act-utilitarianism would say that the rule-utilitarians' verdict on the case would be the same. But if they are considered distinct, could rule-utilitarians consistently say, *"Never* convict a person known to be innocent of the crime of which he or she is accused"? What about those (hopefully rare) cases in which some great good would come of arresting someone and the facts will never come out? Wouldn't rule-utilitarians have to amend their rule at least to say, "Do not convict a person known to be innocent *unless* a great good will come of it," or "Do not convict an innocent person except in exceptional circumstances (such as described in this example) *and other cases similar to it"?* It would seem that they must, for if in one case punishing an innocent person would have the best consequences, then *in all cases like it* punishing an innocent person would also have the best consequences.

3. Finally, the utilitarian theory of punishment says not a word about the *justice* of a punishment. It speaks only of its utility. But a punishment that is useful (to the offender or to society, or both) may not be just, and a just punishment may not be useful. It may be socially useful to keep petty thieves in jail year after year, especially if their condition is unchangeable and they will keep on committing crimes whenever they are out of jail; but if their crimes are minor, it wouldn't be just to keep them incarcerated indefinitely. At the opposite end of the scale, there may be little utility in punishing some murderers severely, especially if they have no inclination to repeat their crime; still, it could be argued that they deserve severe punishment for a major crime like murder and that the utility of punishing them isn't, to say the least, the only factor that should be considered.

Non-utilitarians will be less concerned about the utility of the punishment than about the justice of the punishment. It may be that in most cases the just punishment also has the greater utility, but what of those cases in which it does not? Let us imagine two possible cases: (a) A woman is punished for a particularly serious crime, but the punishment did not improve her, no one was deterred by her imprisonment, and no one was protected because of her isolation from them. Does this show that the punishment was unjust? Non-utilitarians will reply no. (b) Suppose, now, that a man is punished and emerges changed and better, that many others have been deterred from crime by his detention, and that many more have felt protected (and perhaps really were protected) because he was incarcerated—but that in fact he never committed the crime for which he was convicted. Would any or all of these social benefits show, or tend to show, that punishing him was just? Non-utilitarians will again answer no. They will say that the utilitarians are not really concerned with justice at all but simply with "social engineering." And the utilitarians may, in turn, reply that they are indeed concerned with social engineering and that when good results are afoot the appeal to an old-fashioned concept like justice is simply mistaken.

B. The Retributive Theory of Punishment

The non-utilitarian referred to is usually a champion of a theory opposite to that of the utilitarian, the *retributive theory*. The utilitarian theory of punishment is sometimes called the "results theory," and the retributive is called the "deserts theory." According to the retributive theory, punishment should be administered *only* when it is deserved, and then only to the extent that it *is* deserved. Punishment is not, as the utilitarians say, *in order to*, but *because of*: to produce good results may be a happy result of punishing, but it does not provide the justification for punishing, which is that a person who has committed a crime *deserves* to be punished for it. The nineteenth-century philosopher F. H. Bradley put the matter succinctly:

> Punishment is punishment, only when it is deserved. We pay the penalty because we owe it, and for no other reason; and if punishment is inflicted for any other reason whatever than because it is merited by wrong, it is a gross immorality, a crying injustice, an abominable crime, and not what it pretends to be. We may have regard for whatever considerations we please—our own convenience, the good of society, the benefit of the offender; we are fools, and worse, if we fail to do so. Having once the right to punish, we may modify the punishment according to the useful and the pleasant; but these are external to the matter; they cannot give us a right to punish, and nothing can do that but criminal desert.[15]

[15] Francis Herbert Bradley, *Ethical Studies* (London: Oxford University Press, 1876), pp. 26–27.

A contemporary philosopher, C. S. Lewis, objected to both the substitution of "treatment" for punishment and to punishing simply in order to deter others:

> They [the psychiatrists] are not punishing, not inflicting, only healing. But do not let us be deceived by a name. To be taken without consent from my home and friends; to lose my liberty; to undergo all those assaults on my personality which modern psychotherapy knows how to deliver; to be re-made after some pattern of "normality" hatched in a Viennese laboratory to which I never professed allegiance; to know that this process will never end until either my captors have succeeded or I [have] grown wise enough to cheat them with apparent success—who cares whether this is called punishment or not? That it includes most of the elements for which any punishment is feared—shame, exile, bondage, and years eaten by the locust—is obvious. Only enormous ill-desert could justify it; but ill-desert is the very conception which the "humanitarian" theory has thrown overboard.
>
> If we turn from the curative to the deterrent justification of punishment we shall find the new theory even more alarming. When you punish a man *in terrorem,* make of him an "example" to others, you are admittedly using him as a means to an end, someone else's end. This, in itself, would be a very wicked thing to do. On the classical theory of punishment it was of course justified on the ground that the man deserved it. That was assumed to be established before any question of "making him an example" arose. You then, as the saying is, killed two birds with one stone; in the process of giving him what he deserved you set an example to others. But take away desert and the whole morality of the punishment disappears. Why, in Heaven's name, am I to be sacrificed to the good of society in this way?—unless, of course, I deserve it.[16]

Why "crime demands punishment" is something to which not all advocates of retributivism give the same answer. According to one account whose history goes back to Babylonian and Hebrew law, justice is like a scale which must be kept in balance. When everyone is respecting the rights of others, there is a "moral balance" in society, which is disturbed when someone violates these rights. Then a "moral imbalance" arises, the scales of justice are tipped, and the balance has to be restored by means of punishing the offender. Kant wrote:

> What is the mode and measure of punishment which public justice takes as its principle and standard? It is just the principle of equality, by which the pointer of the scale of justice is made to incline no more to the one

---

[16] C. S. Lewis, "The Humanitarian Theory of Punishment," in *Res Judicatae* (1953), p. 225.

side than the other. It may be rendered by saying that the undeserved evil which anyone commits on another, is to be regarded as perpetrated on himself. Hence it may be said: "If you slander another, you slander yourself; if you steal from another, you steal from yourself; if you strike another, you strike yourself; if you kill another, you kill yourself." This is the Right of Retaliation (*jus talionis*).[17]

Others have contended, however, that such a "moral ledger," in which all the debits and credits are listed and balanced, is nothing but an interesting pictorial analogy. A more modern version of retributivism is that in any society there have to be laws prohibiting violence and deception. Compliance with those laws is to the benefit of everyone. The benefits are that when such laws are obeyed people's lives and bodily security, as well as other things such as contracts voluntarily entered upon, are protected. With laws, there is a sphere in each person's life which is immune from interference by others. But corresponding to these great benefits there is a great burden:

> The burden consists in the exercise of *self-restraint* by individuals over inclinations that would, if satisfied, directly interfere or create a substantial risk of interference with others in proscribed ways. If a person fails to exercise self-restraint even though he might have and gives in to such inclinations, he renounces a burden which others have voluntarily assumed and thus gains an advantage which others, who *have* restrained themselves, do not possess. . . .

> . . . A person who violates the rules has something others have—the benefits of the system—but by renouncing what others have assumed, the burdens of self-restraint, he has acquired an unfair advantage. Matters are not even until this advantage is in some way erased. . . . He owes something to others, for he has something that does not rightfully belong to him. Justice—that is, punishing such individuals—restores the equilibrium of benefits and burdens by taking from the individual what he owes, that is, exacting the debt.[18]

"Punishment should be in accord with desert": this is the standard formula of retributive theory. Whatever a person deserves, that should be his or her punishment, no more and no less. However, as it stands this formula is too inflexible even for most supporters. What if an offender has committed a crime just as deserving of punishment as any other of the same kind, but the man is old and sick and has been given only a few months to live? Clearly he shouldn't be found innocent; but shouldn't he be given, perhaps, a sus-

[17] Immanuel Kant, *The Philosophy of Law,* trans. W. Hastie (Edinburgh: T. & T. Clark, 1887), p. 196.
[18] Herbert Morris, "Persons and Punishment," in *Human Rights,* ed. A. I. Melden (Belmont, Calif.: Wadsworth Publishing, 1970), pp. 113–14.

pended sentence? The punishment that should be given him might be different from the punishment that he *deserves;* that is, there are situations in which
the punishment should be less, but never more, than a person deserves.

Suppose that a Nazi war criminal was found in South America and that
for many years he has been leading a useful and productive life. It has now
been forty years since his crimes were committed, and during those years his
character has improved enormously. He is a changed person, and no good
purpose would now be served by sentencing him. Should he still be arrested,
tried, and imprisoned for the rest of his life? Many retributivists would say
that he should: the crimes he committed are as heinous as they were when
he committed them; the mere passage of time has not altered either the
wickedness of his acts or the fact that he deserves punishment. True, *he* has
changed since then, but so might a large number of other war criminals who
were caught and imprisoned, if they had not been caught. If he had been
caught in 1945, should the fact that he *would* have become a worthy citizen,
assuming that could have been known in advance, have mitigated his sentence? Many retributivists would balk at this, saying that his crimes demand
punishment as much in the 1980s as they would have in 1945. They maintain
not only that he deserves to be sentenced, but that he ought to be. To say
otherwise would be to dilute considerations of justice with considerations of
utility.

Whether or not justice should be tempered with utility, shouldn't justice
be tempered with *mercy?* Mercy in the present context would presumably
mean giving a criminal a *lesser* penalty than he or she deserves. This would
clearly be an injustice—an individual injustice, for the person wouldn't be
getting what is deserved, and a comparative injustice, for if others convicted
of similar crimes were getting their deserved punishment, while someone
else was let off, they would certainly complain of unfair discrimination
against them. But isn't that the very point of mercy? Mercy isn't justice but
something other than justice, and some would say it is greater than justice.

Still, there are problems with mercy. Mercy is selective. Of several equally
guilty defendants, convicted of the same crime, some are sentenced, and one
is "mercifully treated" and let go. This is welcome to the one who is let go,
but what of those who are not treated with mercy? Don't they have as much
right to be treated mercifully (if that is a right) than the one who was? Isn't
this unfair? If each one gets what he or she deserves, no more and no less,
this, say the retributive theorists, is justice; and justice is enough. Any tamp-
ering with it makes for both individual and comparative injustice.

To avoid such discrimination, why not universalize the practice of mercy?
Why not be merciful to everyone and let every criminal go free? That would
really be mercy! But what would be the result of such a universal practice?
Supporters of retributivism would object to it because no one would be receiving the punishment that was deserved. And utilitarians would object to
it because the results would be disastrous: if no one was punished for killing
and assaulting other people, there would be a crime wave. People would

know they wouldn't be punished for doing such things, and so they would loot and kill as they liked. Universal mercy to criminals would be most unmerciful to innocent victims.

None of this, however, solves the main problem that attends retributive theory: What, specifically, does an offender deserve for a certain offense? Historically, the most influential view is that the punishment should in some way "equal" the crime. The Old Testament formula was "an eye for an eye, and a tooth for a tooth." There are two views about this, however, which are often confused with each other.

The first view is that the punishment should be of the same degree of severity as the crime, and moreover it should be *like* the crime itself. In the case of murder, the killer should be killed. (That is, if a person really has killed another, he or she deserves to be killed for it. Society might refrain from doing so because there is still some chance that the accused person didn't do it, and if it should turn out that way, he or she can be released from prison, which, of course, execution eliminates the possibility of.) We may call this the "mirror image" theory: the punishment must be a kind of mirror image of the crime itself. In the case of homicide, the theory is easy to apply, but what of theft? If the punishment for stealing $100 is to have $100 taken back from the thief, this isn't much of a punishment: only if the thief is caught does he or she have to return the money, which could be profitable for anyone who escapes detection. That is why medieval Anglo-Saxon law prescribed a penalty of treble damages for such crimes ("three teeth for a tooth"). And if being killed is the proper punishment for killing, what is the proper punishment for rape?

The second view of punishment equaling the crime is that it must be, if not a mirror image, in some way suited to or *appropriate* to the kind of crime that was committed. After the Italian dictator Benito Mussolini had been killed by Italian patriots at the end of World War II, he was hanged by his toes in the public square. This wasn't exactly punishment, since he was already dead, but it was felt to be peculiarly appropriate nevertheless, since it was the fate to which he had condemned so many others. Among the punishments gleefully suggested by the Mikado, or emperor, in Gilbert and Sullivan's operetta, all have some kind of special appropriateness to the nature of the crime committed:

> All prosy dull society sinners
> Who chatter and bleat and bore,
>   Are sent to hear sermons
>   By mystical Germans
> Who preach from ten to four.
>
> The advertising quack who wearies
> With tales of countless cures,

His teeth, I've enacted,
Shall all be extracted
By terrified amateurs.

. . .

The billiard sharp whom anyone catches,
His doom's extremely hard—
He's made to dwell
In a dungeon cell
On a spot that's always barred.

And there he plays extravagant matches
In fitless finger-stalls,
On a cloth untrue
With a twisted cue
And elliptical billiard balls.

Still, when it comes to most punishments for most crimes, there is little to be found by way of "appropriateness." In some states robbery carries a mandatory sentence of one year in jail, and armed robbery five years. What relation has each of these sentences to each crime? About the only general rule it seems possible to come up with is "The more serious the crime, the more severe the punishment"; to have a more severe punishment for a less serious offense would be unjust. But this raises other questions: Which offenses are the most serious, and which punishments are the most severe?

There seems to be no doubt that murder, which takes away a person's life, is a worse crime than injury, which at least leaves the victim alive and usually capable of recovery; also injury to the body is worse than taking away someone's possessions. But there are exceptions even to this very general rule. Some persons would rather be dead than be blinded, and some would also rather lose an ear lobe or a little toe than the rare coins it took them years to acquire. It all depends on what kind of injury and how great the loss of possessions. Loss of bodily parts is generally (but not always) irreplaceable, whereas property is replaceable; yet some property (e.g., an original painting or a family heirloom which has a special meaning to the possessor but not to anyone else) is not. When a judge awards $20,000 for the loss of the tip of the little finger in an accident, some (e.g., pianists) would prefer to have the finger tip than the $20,000, and others (e.g., filing clerks) would gladly give up the finger tip in return for $20,000.

As to the severity of the punishment, there is no doubt that five years in prison is a less severe punishment than ten years. But some prisoners would prefer the death penalty to life imprisonment, and some would not. Some would prefer ten years in a well-ordered and uncrowded prison to five years in an old and crowded one. Some would rather do thirty days in jail than pay a fine of $1,000, but to others the fine means nothing and the jail sentence a great deal. To some extent the punishment is adapted to the way the offender conceives the severity of the punishment: a millionaire who has been fined heavily for reckless driving repeatedly is "taught a lesson" by being made to serve thirty days in jail, though most municipalities would rather have the income from the fine than to pay board and room for an extra prisoner. To some prisoners the very fact of incarceration is devastating: even if they were incarcerated in the Waldorf-Astoria for a year, they would dread it almost as much as confinement in the county jail, simply because they could not go where they chose. But others would not particularly mind confinement in the Waldorf-Astoria: they might even commit a burglary or two in order to live there for a while without cost to themselves.

Retributivists would attempt to match the seriousness of the offense (on which there is no unanimity of opinion) with the severity of the punishment (on which there is no agreement either). Admittedly they could not assign definite values to certain crimes, such as saying that a burglar deserves one year in prison and an armed robber five years; but they could try to assign indefinite values, saying that if crime A is more serious than crime B, and B more serious than C, the punishment for A should be more severe than for B, and for B more severe than for C. At least that way there would no such thing as a more severe punishment for a less serious crime. Even if indefinite values could be worked out, however, problems would still arise: A might be much more serious than B and B only slightly more serious than C, and it would certainly be difficult to fine-tune the punishment to the seriousness of the offense, particularly since every offender has a somewhat different conception of which punishments are most severe. Moreover, when the legal punishments for certain crimes are practically automatic and made so by law (e.g., thirty days for this, a year for that), the amount of fine-tuning to individual cases that can be done is extremely limited.

It is tempting, in view of such difficulties, to try to seek some combination of retributive and utilitarian theory. We could incorporate from retributivism the important tenet that, in the name of justice, no one should be convicted for something he or she hasn't done, no matter how useful the punishment might be and no matter how beneficial to society or how deterring to would-be lawbreakers. Nor would punishment ever be excessive, no matter how useful it might be in certain cases to make it so. We could also incorporate the retributive tenet that in general more serious crimes call for more severe punishments, again in the name of justice, but we would have to make numerous adjustments and modifications in individual cases, depending on the utility of the punishment in each case. Retributivism would exercise a kind of negative constraint on the punishments we could allot: certain things we could not do, no matter how great their utility. We would always punish *because of,* and if there was no "because of" (no crime) there would be no grounds for punishing. With this principle accepted, we could then go on to modify punishments, or even suspend sentences, depending on utility: model prisoners could be released early even if they had committed serious crimes, and others could be isolated from society for a longer period if they continued to be dangers to society in the event of their release. (Yet if they had served their term and were still dangerous, they would have to be released anyway.) Much more fine-tuning to individual cases could be done in adjudicating the conflicting demands of retributivism and utilitarianism than could be done within the confines of retributivism itself.

That, at any rate, is one possible compromise. But there is yet another possibility we have not yet explored, which calls for an entirely different way of conceiving of punishment.

C. The Restitution Theory

There is one party to the affair who has scarcely yet been mentioned—the victim. He or she is the one whose rights have been violated, who has been injured or whose possessions have been stolen, who has been forced to surrender something of value. If the crime was a mugging or robbery, it may be a consolation to that individual if the culprit is caught and put away for a while, but none of this restores what was lost; in fact, the victim may have to pay higher taxes for the upkeep of the assailant in a county jail or state prison and may even be in danger when the angry assailant is released. The victim is very much the one who is forgotten in the arena of crime. We have speculated on what punishments the criminal deserves; but the *victim* deserves at least compensation for losses or injuries sustained, and this is usually something not granted.

In America prior to the American Revolution, criminals were required to pay back their victims. Defendants convicted of larceny were required to pay treble damages. If they could not pay, they were given to their victims in servitude for the length of time in which they could earn the amount owed. Crime was conceived of as primarily an injury to the individual victim, not as an "attack against society."

> Today, the situation is reversed. Crime is regarded as an offense against the state. The damage to the individual victim is incidental, and its redress is no longer regarded as a function of the criminal justice process. The victim is told that if he wants to recover his losses he should hire a lawyer and sue in civil court. The criminal justice system is not for his benefit but for the community's. Its purposes are to deter crime, rehabilitate criminals, punish criminals, and do justice, but not to restore victims to their wholeness or to vindicate them. . . .
>
> In contemporary America, the victim's well-being and fair treatment are not the concern of the criminal justice system or any other institution. The victim has to fend for himself every step of the way. When there is a rash of burglaries in his neighborhood, for example, he will have to form a neighborhood vigilante system if he wants any real pro-

tection. The "increased police patrols" that the local police will provide amount to nothing more than a few extra passes of a squad car through the general vicinity. The victim might even try to concoct a trap in his house to catch an intruder. He may make a false arrest; or he may be charged with murder if a burglar breaks in and manages to get himself killed by the trap. But, in either case, he runs serious risks of violating the law himself.[19]

To correct all this, the *restitution theory* is suggested. The victim is the principal party who has been wronged, and it is the victim who should be compensated by the offender, not according to the victim's whims (since he or she is likely to overestimate the damage) but according to the judicial process. Any defendant found guilty must pay for the cost of the trial plus damages to the plaintiff. Those unable to do this must be made to "work out their debt," either on the plaintiff's property if the plaintiff is willling and needs work done there or at a place of work (work farm, factory, or store), where a considerable fraction of the offender's wages will be withheld until the debt is paid off. (To some extent the restitution theory is already applied in civil cases, but in criminal cases the debt is considered discharged when the defendant has done time in prison, with no compensation going to the victim.)

There are certain advantages to this conception of punishment. It satisfies the retributive theory's requirement of punishment by requiring labor of the offender, often for a long period of time. But it does so in a more useful way than letting the offender spend time in prison, rotting away or making license plates: he or she is doing productive labor for the person wronged and is in repeated touch with the victim, as a continuing reminder of the wrong done by the crime, which enables the offender to imaginatively put himself or herself in the victim's place (an unlikely outcome for anyone who is jailed). Thus, there is also a utility in the punishment which there is not likely to be in imprisonment.

One further point: almost all talk about justice in the criminal process centers around the desert of the offender—the punishment he or she deserves. But the restitution theory is also concerned with the desert of the victim: Doesn't the victim deserve something too, namely, compensation? True, there is really no way to compensate the rape victim for the dread, the terror, the nightmares afterward, the fear of walking in the streets; but insofar as the victim can be compensated at all, something is better than nothing, for at least the victim will be able to do things she could not have done without the monetary compensation. And if the offender refuses to work or is unable to gain employment, confinement to some employment project, such as a factory producing goods or service, could be substituted.

[19] William F. McDonald, "The Role of the Victim in America," in *Assessing the Criminal,* eds. Randy Barnett and John Hagel (Boston: Ballinger Publishing, 1978), pp. 295–96, 298.

Nevertheless, some problems arise in connection with the restitution theory, and opinions differ on how they can be solved.

1. No restitution is possible for the crime of murder: you can't make restitution to the victim's family and dependents, so that the loss of the family breadwinner, for example, would be somewhat less severe in financial terms. If it is thought that even such a punishment is not severe enough for murder, it could be made to last a very long time. Besides, in anticipation of possible murder, a person could decide in advance who would have the legal right to any restitution. It has even been suggested that some form of insurance policy could be taken out against the possibility of murder:

> The natural owner of an unenforced death claim would be an insurance company that had insured the deceased. The suggestion has been made that a person might thus increase his personal safety by insuring with a company well known for tracking down those who injure its policy-holders. In fact, the partial purpose of some insurance schemes might be to provide the funds with which to track down the malefactor. The insurance company, having paid the beneficiaries, would "stand in their shoes."[20]

2. A rich person would find it easy to make monetary restitution, but a poor person would not. Since the damage is the same whether a crime was done by a rich person or a poor one, this is always a problem. But crime would turn out to be pretty expensive, even to a wealthy person; and in spite of the person's wealth a judge might well prescribe factory or farm work as an essential part of the restitution to be paid.

3. If the guilty person was disabled or very old or sick, he or she would not be able to do the compensating; the same thing would result if a criminal died a week after the restitution process had begun. The family of the offender might also suffer as a result of the offender's prolonged restitution.

4. Perhaps the greatest difficulty with the restitution theory is that the difference between intentional and unintentional injury or damage does not figure in this punishment; the damage is the same, whether inflicted by design or by accident. A person who kills someone through an unlucky accident surely doesn't deserve the punishment that another person does who killed with premeditation. A person may, with no malicious intent and without negligence, experience brake failure while driving and seriously injure a pedestrian. The amount payable for this unintentional injury could be enormous—months of expensive hospitalization, plus compensation for pain and suffering. All for a stroke of bad luck! On the other hand, a person may intend to murder but be a bad shot and miss, so that no actual damage results; should he or she get off scot-free? (Or would the intended victim de-

---

[20] Randy Barnett, "Restitution: A New Paradigm of Criminal Justice," in ibid., p. 367.

serve restitution for an *attempt,* even if the attempt was a failure and no harm resulted?)

The fact is that many of the actual consequences of our actions are largely the result of chance factors outside our control at the time. An arsonist deliberately starts a fire but the wind dies out and it doesn't catch. On the other hand, a woman who has a candle lighted in the dark to see the cow she's milking finds that a sudden gust of wind spreads the flame to a pile of combustible material in the corner, and the building burns down; and since the direction of the wind is just right, the entire city of Chicago is set in flames (if we are to believe the story of Mrs. O'Leary's cow). The poor woman would have to spend the rest of her lifetime, and a dozen others if she had them, working off such an enormous debt, because of the tremendous damage done by a chance and unintended event.

Damages that occur from natural causes, such as storms and floods, are not punishable because no human being committed them; in the law these are called "acts of God," for which no one can be sued (at least, no one can collect unless insured for such things). But damages that occur from human causes can be laid on the person or persons who caused them (unless the perpetrators are children, in which case their parents are legally responsible). Sometimes they are intentionally caused, sometimes unintentionally caused through negligence or recklessness, and sometimes inadvertently caused, even though there is neither negligence nor recklessness but just bad luck. The last are the most difficult cases, for damage or injury has occurred for which the victim deserves compensation, yet it may not really be the *fault* of the person who is causally, but not morally, responsible.

The rock on which *any* theory of punishment (not just restitution) may break is a class of cases in which harm occurs but the person causing it is without fault. Early in this century there were "Typhoid Mary" cases: the women were not sick with typhoid themselves, but they were carriers of it; whenever they came in contact with other persons, they would spread the disease to others, and before the advent of vaccine the fatality rate was very high. Should the Typhoid Marys then be quarantined (somewhere away from contact with other people) for the rest of their lives? If we consider only the danger of their contact with others, the answer would seem to be yes, since they are as dangerous to the lives of others as knife-wielding psychotics. But surely this is unjust; they have performed no criminal acts—indeed, they have *done* nothing at all—but just happen to be the unfortunate carriers of a dread disease. Should they then be free to move about in society? But if that is permitted, many people will catch the plague and die of it. The hazard to others is at a maximum, but the guilt is zero.

As far as criminal desert is concerned, there in none; as far as utility is concerned, isolating such people would be useful to others, though not to the carriers; as far as restitution is concerned, why should they have to make restitution to others for a condition for which they are in no way to blame?

Ordinarily the unpleasantness that goes with punishment is the penalty for blameworthy actions; but in this case there are no such actions, and even if they are isolated, is that punishment? (If so, what for?) But the fact that they're "not really being punished" is no comfort to those that are quarantined. "We're not punishing you; we're only keeping you in the house for the rest of your life" is not a particularly consoling reflection. Utilitarian consideration would appear to justify it; deserts would not.

If we see some merit in each of the theories of punishment and would like to combine them in some way, we confront here an example in which they cannot be combined: What utilitarian theory would justify, retribution and restitution theory could not. Such an example is intellectually humbling, leading us to realize that no theory of punishment has yet been devised which is satisfactory in dealing with all cases.

4. PRAISE AND BLAME

Persons are not only punished and rewarded, they are blamed and praised. Though blame and praise are only verbal, they can have enormous effects, sometimes more than physical punishment. A child who throughout years of growing up is constantly blamed for doing certain things often will either continue to feel guilty at doing them for years thereafter or will rebel against parental authority and make a point of doing those things for which he or she was blamed.

When is it right to blame or praise someone? There are two main answers to this question, depending on whether blame and praise are considered to be past-looking or future-looking. The *utilitarian theory* is future-looking, the *deserts theory* past-looking.

The utilitarian theory is extremely simple in outline. Smith does act *A;* then Jones blames Smith for doing act *A;* let us call Jones's act of blaming Smith *B.* Just as the rightness of Smith's act *A* is judged by its consequences (maximum net expectable utility), so the rightness of Jones's act *B* is judged in exactly the same way. If the consequences of blaming Smith are bad, she should not blame Smith. We should not blame people if blaming them won't do any good. Often we may feel very much like blaming someone in very severe terms, but we should refrain from doing so if it would accomplish no good purpose. Sometimes, depending on our manner and tone of voice, blaming can be counterproductive, only making the person blamed resentful or angry. Even so it may be worth doing that if the person henceforth refrained from repeating the act, but often blame doesn't do that either. A psychiatrist seldom blames patients for what they do but is usually much more effective in altering people's behavior than those parents or spouses who are perennial blamers.

When a person is constantly blamed, even for a serious offense, he or she tends to become immunized to the accusation and pays no further attention, except perhaps to become annoyed at the person who keeps doing it. A calm, quiet talk often accomplishes far more good than repeated acts of blaming. Blaming is often an effective means of "letting off steam" for the person who *does* the blaming and is thus therapeutic for the blamer even if it does no good whatever for the blamee; it also gives the blamer a feeling of righteous accomplishment: "Well, at least I've done my duty; now if she does it again it's her responsibility. At least I've done what I could." Talk is cheap, and blaming others often relieves pressures and makes blamers feel good. This is, of course, to be considered in estimating the total utilitarian effects, but such good effects are often outweighed by the highly unfavorable effects on the person at the receiving end of the blame.

Particularly unhelpful is the act of blaming someone when the person really couldn't help it. Old people are very often blamed for being forgetful: "I told you three times and you still forgot!" But blaming is clearly ineffective when the act for which the person is blamed cannot be *altered* by the blaming. A person on the brink of senility may feel guilty for being forgetful, without being able to help it; he does the best he can but can't remember things the way he used to. To blame people for what can't be helped would be an immoral act, even if it is therapeutic for the blamer. Of course, it is often difficult to know whether people could have altered their behavior by trying a little harder. Sometimes blaming people does make them try harder and even succeeds occasionally. But even so the value of blaming people when they have almost, though perhaps not entirely, done their best is questionable; its negative effects—guilt, anger, resentment, self-doubt—will almost surely occur while its positive effects—altering the behavior of the person blamed—are dubious at best.

Similar considerations apply to praise. Praise boosts a person's self-image, and for someone never to be praised for anything can be a desolating experience, creating enormous self-doubt. Even if what a child has achieved is a small thing, it may be desirable to offer praise, even rather extravagantly, particularly if doing so will spur the child to new efforts or make the child more confident. The other side of the coin, however, is that being praised constantly for what doesn't amount to much may give the child an inflated conception of his or her accomplishments; out in the world people will not offer such praise for small accomplishments, and hurt and disappointment may result because of the unrealistic expectations engendered by the praise.

The deserts theorist will respond to all this that everything has been discussed except the main issue—whether the person does or does not *deserve* the blame or the praise. The act of blaming or praising someone must have as an anchor the past deeds for which the blame or praise is conferred. Parents may praise extravagantly in order to give their child self-confidence, but they must at least be sure that there is an act for which the child deserves praise. Praising for nothing at all, or for doing something wrong, might in some circumstances have good effects, but still it should not be offered because such praise is totally undeserved. Similarly, blaming someone for what he or she hasn't done might also in some circumstances have good effects (it might take the individual's inflated ego down a notch), and yet to be blamed for that, or for something that isn't one's fault, is always unjust.

To be sure, "It would be *right* to blame A" doesn't mean the same as "It would be *just* to blame A." There are times when blaming someone would be just—that is, when the person deserves blame—and yet it would be right to withhold it for some special reason, such as that the person has recently undergone a shattering personal experience or is about to leave on a life-threatening mission. Justice may be tempered with utility, but justice must not be forgotten in the process. To blame unjustly, for what the person blamed does not deserve, is always wrong, even if by some quirk it turns out to have good effects. That, at any rate, is the view of anyone who bases blame or praise on deserts and not merely on utility.

EXERCISES

1. Do the following, in your opinion, count as examples of injustice? Why?
   a. Some people are born crippled; others are not.
   b. The supervisor receives a higher hourly wage than the other workers.
   c. A farmer receives a higher income in some years than in others because of varying weather conditions and the market demand for grain.
   d. A third offense receives a stiffer penalty than a first offense.
   e. Some criminals don't get caught.
   f. Some people can buy caviar, and others can afford only bread.
   g. Some children are loved by their parents, and others are not.
   h. A person may often receive more income on welfare than by working.
   i. A handicapped child receives more in his father's will than the other children do.
   j. The child who happens to be "daddy's favorite" receives more in her father's will than the other children do.
   k. One driver repeatedly gets arrested for speeding, whereas another who speeds just as much never gets caught.
   l. The law provides a severer penalty for trampling on the flag than for bloodying someone else's nose.
   m. A housewife borrows a dozen eggs from a neighbor, promising to return them the next week. But the next week the price of eggs has gone down by half. "A dozen are only worth half as much now," the neighbor objects, "so you owe me two dozen!"
   n. A man has two dogs but treats one better than he treats the other.
   o. A woman who knows somebody on the hospital staff uses her influence to obtain preferential treatment for her brother, a patient in the hospital. Another patient, who lacks such influence, cannot obtain this treatment.
   p. Some people volunteer for a dangerous medical experiment and some do not.
   q. Two men, out of a whole platoon, are selected to go out on a dangerous mission with a 50 percent chance of returning alive. They are selected (1) by the lieutenant because he holds a personal grudge against them; (2) by

lot; (3) because they possess qualifications for the job which the other men in the platoon do not possess.

r. Ten men must die in order to hold off the enemy in a position that cannot be defended for long, in order that thereby one hundred men may escape to safety.

s. A rich widow leaves in her will $1,000 to every citizen of her community who is more than six feet tall.

t. A national television and radio network gives equal free time to the Republican and Democratic parties but refuses it to seven or eight minor political parties.

u. A Board of Education rejects a rich donor's offer to build a new public high school in his neighborhood, on the ground that all the neighborhoods in the city are entitled to equal treatment, and thus the acceptance of any offer which gave one neighborhood advantages not possessed by another would be an injustice.

v. "If a poor man were to leave one tradesman and deal with another because the first had turned Quaker, we should hardly call it an act of injustice, however unreasonable we might think it; but if a rich country gentleman were to act similarly towards a poor neighbor, many persons would say that it was unjust persecution." (Henry Sidgwick, *The Methods of Ethics,* 7th ed., p. 270.)

w. You are driving on a turnpike which has a speed limit of 65 miles per hour. You are driving at 70, and another driver passes you at 80. The turnpike policeman arrests you. You say, "That's unjust! He was driving 80!" The policeman replies, "I know it, but you were both violating the speed limit. So you can't claim injustice. Besides, you were easier to catch."

x. A merchant charges a single price for an item, whether the customer is rich or poor.

y. You marry the girl you just met and not the one you've gone out with for two years.

z. You decline to invite a racially mixed group to your party.

2. In which of the situations below do you think the persons in question are giving good arguments for justified inequality and in which situations are they not? Why?

"I should get more than he or she does (or I should get it and he or she shouldn't) because

a. I'm rich and she's poor. (in appealing a case to a higher court)

b. I'm white and he's black. (in marrying a white girl)

c. I'm poor and she's rich. (in regard to getting the same merchandise for less money)

d. I'm an officer and he's an enlisted man. (in regard to getting better food)

e. I'm a professor and she's an instructor. (in regard to teaching fewer hours)

f. I'm intelligent and he's stupid. (in regard to having the right to vote)

g. I'm a property owner and she isn't. (in regard to eligibility for public office)

h. I'm a native American and he isn't. (in regard to becoming president of the United States)

i. I'm a writer and she's a hack. (in regard to receiving the Nobel Prize for literature)

    j. I'm a man and she's a woman. (in regard to getting higher pay for equal work)

    k. I'm a man and she's a woman. (in regard to obtaining a job as a truck driver)

    l. I'm an adult and he's an adolescent. (in regard to obtaining a job as camp counselor)

    m. I work harder than she does. (in regard to getting more pay for the same job)

    n. I need more, since I have five dependents and he has none. (in regard to getting more pay for the same job)

3. Which of the following arguments for inequality of wages do you think are justified and why? Assume that each statement is made by the owners or managers of a factory to employees, in response to a request for less inequality between management's income and theirs.

    a. We top executives bear a greater load of responsibility.

    b. We have to take more risks.

    c. We are more indispensable than you are; you need us more than we need you.

    d. We deserve more than you do because there are fewer people with a talent for doing our job than there are for doing yours.

    e. We have more training for our jobs than you do, so we deserve more money.

    f. We have more ability than you; if we didn't we wouldn't be where we are now.

4. Evaluate: "What a person deserves for his work should depend not on what he has accomplished nor on how much effort he has put into it but on what he *would* have accomplished if he had been given a chance." (See Mark Twain's story "Captain Stormfield's Visit to Heaven.")

5. Evaluate the following assertions about justice:

    a. "It's unjust for anyone to have caviar as long as anyone lacks bread."

    b. "It's unjust for a person to be permitted to inherit wealth instead of earning it personally."

    c. "From each according to his abilities, to each according to his needs."

    d. "The income tax is unjust. I am taxed 80 percent of my annual income just because I earn a great deal, whereas a poorer person is taxed 15 percent or less. What could be more unjust?"

    e. "You Americans have a much higher income than we do, in terms of what your wages will buy. Since you work no more hours than we do, and no harder, we deserve just as much as you do. You are lucky; your nation has space and natural resources; it rewards private enterprise; and it has escaped wartime privations. But is it just for rewards to be dependent on luck? Of course not. Therefore, it is just that you should give us a portion of your income—as much as is required to make other nations your equal in buying power."

6. There are three main theories of taxation: (*a*) each person should pay an equal amount, on the theory that each gets equal protection from the law; (*b*) each person should pay a fixed proportion of his or her income; (*c*) the higher the income, the higher the proportion of income that should be taxed (graduated income tax). Which of these in your opinion is the most just (or least unjust)?

7. Make a decision in the following case and justify your decision: You are in charge of an institution which gives free psychiatric help to those who can't afford to pay for it. Faced by a large group of candidates who all have an equal right to treatment and who all need it badly, you have to choose which of two policies to pursue: (*a*) providing infrequent sessions (say one every two weeks) for each of the 1,000 people who desire and need help, although such a procedure will not provide enough treatment to cause any substantial improvement in the conditions of any except possibly a very few of them; (*b*) providing really effective psychiatric help for 100 patients (at least several months of treatment, at least three sessions a week) and letting the remainder go untreated.

8. The instructor gives the class a test containing ten questions. Some students can finish all ten in the allotted time; but as the period progresses, the instructor sees that most of them probably cannot, so she says, "Please omit question 10." Some students answer it anyway, though the instructor has told them that it won't count; for if she counts the answer for some, she must do so for all. Some students object that
    a. it's all right to count the tenth question for those who have answered it and not to count it for those who haven't.
    b. it is unjust to include the question, because to do so puts a premium on speed and this isn't just a speed test.
    c. it is unjust to exclude the question, because some students are able to answer it and so should get credit for doing so; if some students are slow, the fast students shouldn't be penalized for it.

    Evaluate these objections in the light of justice as equal treatment.

9. Discuss whether the market provides justice as well as utility, in light of the following quote:

    The market is an enormous computer, far superior to any electronic computer ever devised. . . . Data from all over the world, of the most varied and complex nature, are automatically and quickly processed, answers coming out as prices. These prices are stop-and-go signals which clearly say to all would-be enterprises: "Go into this activity at once, the supply is short and the demand is heavy" or "Get out of this activity now, the supply is bountiful and the demand small." . . . Tomatoes, let's say, are suddenly "in short supply." Millions of people like tomatoes, so the demand continues high. The few growers who have escaped the destructive blight discover that they can sell their small supply for $2 a pound, and they do. Salad lovers who can't afford this "exorbitant" price are inclined to say: "They're robbers." Yet they are only adhering to the computer's instructions, and behaving exactly as you and I act when we accept an increase in our wages. . . .

    In a free market, what would happen? Several corrective forces would immediately go to work. First, the high price, with promises of profit, would entice others to grow tomatoes: more important, it would lead to the development of blight resistant strains. In a short time, there would be tomatoes galore, perhaps at a dollar a bushel—within the reach of all.

    For contrast, imagine the other extreme: a law to keep the price at its old level. What would be the probable effects? At that price there would be little incentive for new tomato growers to enter the field. And thus, *favoritism* instead of prices would necessarily determine the allocation of the reduced supply of tomatoes. (From *Cliches of Socialism* [Irvington, N.Y.: Foundation for Economic Education, 1970], p. 165.)

10. Insurance companies are collectivistic when they charge all males under twenty-five years of age more per year for insurance than other clients. Some males under twenty-five are safer drivers than any others, and the rates surely constitute an injustice to them.

    Is such collectivism ever justified in the name of cost efficiency? Suppose that it took so much company time to investigate the individual records of each male under twenty-five that everyone's rates would go up somewhat as a result. Would this be a satisfactory price to pay for justice?

    If a bonus of $10 were to be distributed among ten workers, should you spend $5 trying to discover their deserts in terms of their work, or just divide it equally among them regardless of individual desert?

11. Indicate whether you would agree or disagree with the court in the following decisions and discuss why:

    a. Richard Reed, a minor, died, and his adoptive parents, who had separated before his death, were in conflict with each other as to which of them should be in charge of the son's estate. Idaho law required that "of several persons claiming and equally entitled to administer, males must be preferred to females." The mother contested this law as being inconsistent with the "equal protection" clause of the Fourteenth Amendment of the Constitution. The U.S. Supreme Court sustained her claim, reversing the judgment of the Idaho Supreme Court, and required that the matter be settled in such a way as not to give preference to either party on grounds of sex. (Reed v. Reed, U.S. Supreme Court, 404 U.S. 71 [1971].)

    b. Allan Bakke, a white male, applied for admission to the medical school of the University of California and was rejected in spite of being qualified. The university had two admissions programs for the entering class of one hundred students: under the regular admissions program, candidates whose grade-point average fell below 2.5 were rejected, and those above 2.5 were given an interview which determined who would be admitted; under the special admissions program, which was only for members of minority groups (blacks, Chicanos, Asians, and American Indians), the sixteen applicants with the highest averages were admitted even though some of them had grade-point averages of less than 2.5. Bakke contested this procedure as a violation of the "equal protection" clause of the Fourteenth Amendment, claiming "reverse discrimination" against him because he was white. The Supreme Court decided in favor of Bakke's claim. (University of California v. Allan Bakke, U.S. Supreme Court, 98 S. Ct. 2733 [1978].)

12. Should traffic fines be adjusted for the individuals' ability to pay? If the standard fine for parking in a no-parking zone is $20, should the rich person be required to pay more and the poor person little or nothing?

13. If I am innocent and running away from police officers, am I entitled to shoot them in self-defense? And if I'm in a crowd, may I shoot whatever innocent bystanders are in my way (aiming for my pursuers but missing)?

14. A man is convicted of a felony which he didn't commit. He serves a two-year prison term. When he comes out, someone "frames" him for another crime. The

person who does it is a friend of the police department and knows that his own word will be accepted in preference to that of a convicted felon. The man swears to "get even" with the one who framed him. Is he justified in circumventing the legal system when the legal system has only done him injustices?

15. From the point of view of justice, is underpunishing someone as bad as overpunishing?

16. In the courts of Scotland three verdicts are possible—(a) guilty, (b) not guilty, and (c) not proven. Do you consider this system preferable to our own?

17. Someone has stolen some of your belongings and hidden them in his house. The police would need a search warrant to recover the goods, which they either cannot obtain or do not consider worth the trouble to obtain. So you decide to recover your property yourself by breaking into the thief's house. Would the owner be justified in forcibly preventing you from entering the house to recover your belongings?

18. "The utilitarian theory of punishment is mistaken, for according to it crime is no different from disease, and imprisonment no different from quarantine." What do you think of this objection? In what way or ways do you consider imprisonment to be like quarantine, and in what ways unlike it? (Does it serve the same functions as quarantine? How, and how not?)

19. If you knew that your nation had just been destroyed in a nuclear war and you were able to deliver a mortal blow to the aggressor nation which would destroy it completely, would you feel justified in doing so—not in order to produce good (which you would not) but simply because that nation had destroyed yours?

20. Consider the following biblical and religious punishments in the light of justice:
    a. "He that killeth a beast shall make it good; and he that killeth a man shall be put to death." (Leviticus XXIV:21.)
    b. "Ye shall take no ransom for the life of a manslayer which is guilty of death, but he shall surely be put to death." (Numbers XXXV:31.)
    c. Uzzah touches the Ark of the Covenant, and he and all his fellow townsmen are put to death.
    d. Eve ate the forbidden fruit, and as a result all humankind forever after are condemned to live in sin.
    e. Eve sinned, and in consequence another life must be taken, through death by crucifixion, in order to atone for this. One being must die for the sins of another, to restore the moral balance.
    f. Justice requires that each person get what he deserves. But there is another and greater dispensation than that of Justice, and that is Grace. If God were *only* just, He would send us all to eternal damnation. But by Grace, a certain selected number of those who are justly damned, are saved by Grace— a salvation which none of them deserves.

21. Adolf Eichmann, charged with the extermination of 5 million Jews in Hitler's concentration camps, claimed, "I will leap into my grave laughing because the feeling that I have five million human beings on my conscience is for me a source of extraordinary satisfaction." He was found in Argentina in June 1960 by Israeli government officials and taken to Israel for trial. An American news magazine remarked:

   Remembering the stinking holes of Poland's Auschwitz, the smoking crematoriums of Germany, the boneyards and mass graves of the Ukraine, vengeful

Israelis are not disposed to argue the fine points of the law. Instead, they debate what punishment could possibly fit the crime. Hanging, most agree, is too easy. Said one survivor of Eichmann's camps: "He should be made to live under the very same conditions that we lived in the camps, eat the same crumbs of dried bread, work the same, smell the same putrid odors from the furnaces. Let's see how long he would last." (From *Time*, 75 [June 6, 1960], p. 29)

Would retributive punishment be justified in this case?

22. The following examples of punishment in the Soviet Union are all taken from Aleksandr Solzhenitsyn's *The Gulag Archipelago*. Assess the punishments in each case from both the retributive and the utilitarian points of view.

    a. A man turns off Stalin's speech on the radio before it is over. A neighbor reports him. His punishment is ten years in a labor camp.

    b. Under his breath a man makes a remark critical of the government. He is overheard and arrested. His punishment is twenty-five years in a labor camp.

    c. Engineers on the Balmoral Canal were required to use wood since no concrete was available, and were nevertheless held responsible for the result. When the edifice collapsed, they were charged with sabotaging a state project. All were punished with death.

    d. "How long a sentence did they give you?" "Twenty-five years." "What was your offense?" "Nothing." "But that's impossible—the sentence for nothing at all is ten years."

    e. A boy of twelve was sentenced to death for getting drunk and taking a ride around the block on an officer's horse.

    f. A group of juveniles was given a twenty-five-year sentence in the Gulag for putting objects on railroad tracks.

    g. When a thirteen-year-old, having worked on the state farm the entire day, took some wheat from alongside the road for the use of his own family, he was caught and sentenced to twenty-five years for stealing state property. (Children who filled their pockets with potatoes from the state farm, to keep themselves from being hungry, were given eight years.)

    h. Children who ran away from factory apprenticeship training were sentenced and made to dump excrement from the latrines. The children were hitched up like horses to carts containing barrels of this sludge, while the guards urged them on with clubs.

23. "Legal systems fix a more severe punishment for the completed crime than for the mere attempt. How is this to be justified? Here a retributive theory in which severity of punishment is proportioned to the allegedly evil intentions of the criminal is in grave difficulty; for there seems to be no difference in wickedness, though there may be in skill, between the successful and the unsuccessful attempt." (From H. L. A. Hart, "Intention and Punishment," in his *Punishment and Responsibility*, p. 129.)

24. Which is more important—to ensure that the guilty be punished or that the innocent remain free? Anglo-American law considers the latter more important and would presumably rather have the "ninety and nine guilty" go free than have one innocent person unjustly punished. For this reason in criminal cases we have

(typically) a jury of twelve citizens whose vote must be unanimous before a conviction is possible.

But if we wanted to be more nearly certain that no innocent person was found guilty, why not have a jury of fifty or a hundred people and require them to be unanimous? Many more guilty persons would thus remain unconvicted (perhaps few would be convicted at all), but there also would be much less chance that an innocent person would be sentenced. We apparently don't consider that price worth paying. By contrast, in some nations such as France, a 7 to 5 vote by the jury can convict. (See the French film *Justice*.) And this seems to us not nearly as conducive to the freedom of the innocent as it should be.

Where would *you* draw the line, and why? How high a price would your suggested system be willing to pay to ensure that the innocent were not convicted?

25. Even when the case against a defendant is very strong, the case is likely to be thrown out if any illegal methods (such as entering a home without a search warrant) were used in obtaining evidence. In many other nations evidence illegally obtained would be admitted, on the assumption that anything relevant to the case is important, but the arresting officer might then be dismissed for his or her illegal actions. Which do you think is the preferable procedure?

26. Is it preferable to try to *prevent* the crime, or take the violator to court afterward? Consider these cases:

   a. A person is arrested for drunk driving (not for being drunk but for driving while drunk), although no accident has yet occurred, because of the high *risk* of accident when a person drives in that condition.

   b. A person has not yet committed a robbery or murder, but has planned one and discussed it with others; if the case can be proved, he or she is subject to arrest and trial for *conspiracy* to commit a felony.

   c. Some psychologists claim that they can detect with 95 percent accuracy, by means of psychological tests, which children of eight will become juvenile delinquents at fifteen or so. It has been suggested that these children be removed from their home environments at eight and placed elsewhere (where?), so as to *prevent* the crimes that, it is alleged, they *would* commit at the age of fifteen if they remained in their home environments.

   d. A crazed neighbor in the apartment upstairs from you comes down the fire escape with a knife and threatens to kill you and your family in their sleep. You call the police and an officer says, "We can't do anything until a crime has actually been committed; most threats are never carried out." (How many times has a person said in the heat of a family quarrel, "I'll kill you!" and never done it?) Should the person be interned before the threat is carried out or punished afterward?

   e. People are subject to fines and sometimes worse penalties if they (knowingly or unknowingly) build a house that is not "up to code"—that is, does not conform in every detail to the city regulations; the penalty also is imposed if the electrical wiring, plumbing, and the like do not in every way meet the specifications listed in the code. What is preferable, having a code and enforcing it, or having no code and no regulatory agencies but penalizing a person in civil court after a violation if damage (e.g., a collapsed house, flood, or fire) occurs as a result?

f. Should there be an Occupational Safety and Health Administration (OSHA) to make unexpected, on-the-spot inspections of factories and warehouses and stores in order to check compliance with safety and health regulations? Or, should there be no regulatory agency, but damage suits against those whose stores or factories contain "demonstrable hazards" to the health and safety of occupants? Should someone be able to sue before, or only after, the damage has occurred? (For details on OSHA, see Dan Smoot, *The Business End of Government.*)

27. A robber who threatens a victim by using a toy pistol that looks like a real one is usually subjected to the same punishment as someone who threatens with a real gun. Is this just?

28. If a juvenile commits a robbery, he does not usually receive the same punishment as an adult ("he didn't know the full consequences of his actions"). Is it just to distinguish juveniles from adults in such matters? Sometimes an adult hires a juvenile to commit a robbery, knowing that if the juvenile is caught his punishment will be comparatively light, and that it will probably be stricken from his record when he becomes eighteen. Should robberies committed under such conditions be followed by the full adult punishment for the juvenile?

SELECTED READINGS

Justice, Desert, and Equality

Aristotle. *Nicomachean Ethics.* Many editions. See Book 5.

Barry, Brian. *The Liberal Theory of Justice.* London: Oxford University Press, 1973.

Bayles, Michael. *Principles of Legislation.* Detroit: Wayne State University Press, 1978.

Bedau, Hugo. "Radical Egalitarianism." In Hugo Bedau, ed. *Justice and Equality.* Englewood Cliffs, N.J.: Prentice-Hall, 1971.

Bird, Otto. *The Idea of Justice.* New York: Praeger Publishers, 1967.

Bowie, Norman. *Toward a New Theory of Distributive Justice.* Amherst: University of Massachusetts Press, 1971.

Cohen, Marshall, Stuart Nagel, and Thomas Scanlon, eds. *Equality and Preferential Treatment.* Princeton, N.J.: Princeton University Press, 1977.

De George, Richard, and Joseph Pichler, eds. *Ethics, Free Enterprise, and Public Policy.* New York: Oxford University Press, 1978.

Dworkin, Ronald. "What Is Equality?" *Philosophy and Public Affairs,* 10, nos. 3 and 4 (1981).

Feinberg, Joel. *Doing and Deserving.* Princeton, N.J.: Princeton University Press, 1970.

―――. "Noncomparative Justice." In his *Rights, Justice, and the Bounds of Liberty.* Princeton, N.J.: Princeton University Press, 1980.

Flew, Antony. "Justice *or* Equality?" *Midwest Studies in Philosophy, Studies in Ethical Theory,* Vol. 3. Morris: University of Minnesota, 1978.

―――. *The Politics of Procrustes: Contradictions of Enforced Equality.* Buffalo, N.Y.: Prometheus Books, 1981.

Gross, Barry. *Reverse Discrimination.* Buffalo, N.Y.: Prometheus Books, 1980.

Hardin, Garrett. "Lifeboat Ethics: The Case against Helping the Poor." *Psychology Today,* 8 (1974): 36–43, 123–26. Reprinted in Vincent Barry, ed. *Applying Ethics.* Belmont, Calif.: Wadsworth Publishing, 1982.

Hare, R. M., "Review of Rawls' *A Theory of Justice*." Pts. 1 and 2. *Philosophical Quarterly* (1975).

Held, Virginia, ed. *Property, Profits, and Economic Justice*. Belmont, Calif.: Wadsworth Publishing, 1980.

Hospers, John. "Socialism and Liberty." In *Libertarianism*. New York: Laissez Faire Books, 1971. Reprinted in James Sterba, ed. *Justice: Alternative Approaches*. Belmont, Calif.: Dickenson Publishing, 1980.

Hume, David. *Treatise of Human Nature* (1739).★ Many editions. See Book 3, Part 2.

Kristol, Irving. "Capitalism and Justice." In Richard De George and Joseph Pichler, eds. *Ethics, Free Enterprise, and Public Policy*. New York: Oxford University Press, 1978.

Lucas, J. R. "Against Equality." *Philosophy* 40 (1965). Reprinted in Hugo Bedau, ed. *Justice and Equality*. Englewood Cliffs, N.J.: Prentice-Hall, 1971.

———. "Against Equality Again." *Philosophy* 52 (1977): 255–80.

Matson, Wallace I. "What Rawls Calls Justice." *The Occasional Review* 8–9 (Autumn 1978): 45–58.

Mill, John Stuart. *Utilitarianism* (1963). Many editions. See Chapter 5.

Pincoffs, Edmund. "Are Questions of Desert Decidable?" In J. B. Cederblom and William Blizek, eds. *Justice and Punishment*. Cambridge, Mass.: Ballinger, 1977.

———. *The Rationale of Legal Punishment*. New York: Humanities Press, 1966.

Rashdall, Hastings. *Theory of Good and Evil*. 2nd ed. 2 vols. New York: Oxford University Press, 1924. See Volume 1, Book 1, Chapter 8.

Rawls, John. *A Theory of Justice*. Cambridge, Mass.: Harvard University Press, 1971.

Rescher, Nicholas. *Distributive Justice*. Indianapolis: Bobbs-Merrill, 1966.

———. *Welfare*. Pittsburgh: University of Pittsburgh Press, 1972.

Sidgwick, Henry. *The Methods of Ethics*. 7th ed. New York: Macmillan, 1874. See Book 3, Chapters 5 and 13.

Sterba, James. *The Demands of Justice*. Notre Dame, Ind.: University of Notre Dame Press, 1980.

———, ed. *Justice: Alternative Political Perspectives*. Belmont, Calif.: Wadsworth Publishing, 1980.

Vlastos, Gregory. "Justice and Equality." In Richard Brandt, ed. *Social Justice*. Englewood Cliffs, N.J.: Prentice-Hall, 1962. Also in Joel Feinberg, ed. *Moral Concepts*. New York: Oxford University Press, 1970.

Williams, Bernard. "The Idea of Equality." In Hugo Bedau, ed. *Justice and Equality*. Englewood Cliffs, N.J.: Prentice-Hall, 1971. Also in Peter Laslett and W. G. Runciman, eds. *Philosophy, Politics, and Society*. Oxford, Eng.: Basil Blackwell, 1964. And in Joel Feinberg, ed. *Moral Concepts*. London: Oxford University Press, 1970.

Wilson, John. *Equality*. London: Hutchinson University Library, 1966.

Wollheim, Richard, and Isaiah Berlin. "Equality." *Aristotelian Society Proceedings* 56 (1955–1956): 281–326.

Punishment

Barnett, Randy. "Restitution: a New Paradigm of Criminal Justice." In Randy Barnett and John Hagel, eds. *Assessing the Criminal*. Boston: Ballinger Publishing, 1978.

Bentham, Jeremy. *Principles of Morals and Legislation* (1789). Many editions. See Chapters 12–15.

★Dates in parentheses are dates of first publication.

Cederblom, Jerry, and William Blizek, eds. *Justice and Punishment*. Cambridge, Mass.: Ballinger, 1977.

Ewing, Alfred C. *The Morality of Punishment*. London: Routledge & Kegan Paul, 1929.

Feinberg, Joel, and Hyman Gross, eds. *Philosophy of Law*. 2nd ed. Belmont, Calif.: Wadsworth Publishing, 1980. Part 5.

Flew, Antony. *Crime or Disease?* London: Macmillan, 1973.

Gross, Hyman. *A Theory of Criminal Justice*. New York: Oxford University Press, 1979.

Grupp, Stanley E., ed. *Theories of Punishment*. Bloomington, Ind.: Indiana University Press, 1971.

Hart, H. L. A. *Punishment and Responsibility*. London: Oxford University Press, 1968.

Kleinig, John. *Punishment and Desert*. The Hague: Martinus Nijhoff, 1973.

Lewis, C. S. "The Humanitarian Theory of Punishment." *Res Judicatae* 6 (1953): 224–3. Reprinted in Wilfred Sellars and John Hospers, eds. *Readings in Ethical Theory*. Englewood Cliffs, N.J.: Prentice-Hall, 1970.

Mabbott, J. D. "Punishment." *Mind* 48 (1939). Reprinted in Joel Feinberg, ed. *Moral Concepts*. New York: Oxford University Press, 1969.

Madden, E. H., Rollo Handy, and Marvin Farber, eds. *Philosophical Perspectives on Punishment*. Springfield, Ill.: Charles C. Thomas, 1968.

McCloskey, H. J., "A Non-utilitarian Approach to Punishment." *Inquiry* 8 (1965): 249–63. Reprinted in James Rachels, ed. *Understanding Moral Philosophy*. Belmont, Calif.: Dickenson Publishing, 1976.

Morris, Herbert. "Persons and Punishment." *The Monist* 52 (1968): 475–501. Reprinted in James Rachels, ed. *Understanding Moral Philosophy*. Belmont, Calif.: Dickenson Publishing, 1976.

Mundle, C. W. K. "Punishment and Desert." *Philosophical Quarterly* 4 (1954): 216–28.

Murphy, Jeffrie. "Marxism and Retribution." *Philosophy and Public Affairs* 2 (1973): 218–43. Reprinted in Joel Feinberg and Hyman Gross, eds., *Philosophy of Law*. Belmont, Calif.: Dickenson Publishing, 1980.

Ross, Alf. *On Guilt, Responsibility, and Punishment*. London: Stevens, 1975.

Ross, Sir William David. *The Right and the Good* (1930). See Chapter 2 and Appendix. In Wilfrid Sellars and John Hospers, eds. *Readings in Ethical Theory*. Englewood Cliffs, N.J.: Prentice-Hall, 1970.

Schoeman, Ferdinand. "On Incapacitating the Dangerous." *American Philosophical Quarterly* 16 (1979): 27–35. Reprinted in Joel Feinberg and Hyman Gross, eds. *Philosophy of Law*. Belmont, Calif.: Dickenson Publishing, 1980.

Szasz, Thomas. *The Manufacture of Madness*. New York: Harper & Row, 1977.

Von Hirsch, Andrew. *Doing Justice: The Choice of Punishment*. New York: Farrar, Straus & Giroux, 1976.

Waelder, Robert. "Psychiatry and the Problem of Criminal Responsibility." In Richard Donnelly, Joseph Goldstein, and Richard Schwartz, eds. *Criminal Law*. New York: Free Press, 1961.

9

Moral Responsibility

1. RESPONSIBILITY AND EXCUSE

People are said to be *legally* responsible for their actions when they are liable to legal consequences (such as fines and jail sentences) for doing (or not doing) them. They are said to be *morally* responsible for their actions when they can rightly be praised or blamed for doing them, though when it is or is not right to praise and blame them for action is a matter of some disagreement. (Sometimes, of course, a person's action is not the subject for either praise or blame, as when an individual decides to take a brief walk in the garden.) In a very general sense, we say that people are responsible for their acts when they have the ability to control what they do, and their responsibility (ability to control) may then become a reason for holding them liable for legal consequences or moral censure.

Yet there are many actions for which we do not hold others, or ourselves, responsible. People may not deny that they did certain acts, but they may claim (1) that the acts were not wrong (or illegal) and therefore do not *need* to be excused, or (2) that while the acts were wrong (or illegal) there were *excusing conditions* which kept them from bearing responsibility for the act.

Under what conditions are people's actions excusable, or, more precisely, under what conditions are people excusable with respect to certain actions? Aristotle in his *Nicomachean Ethics* discussed the two kinds of conditions which he believed to be excusing—*ignorance* and *compulsion*. But by casting our net somewhat wider, we may find excusing conditions that cannot be subsumed under either of these two concepts. (In any case the modern concept of compulsion is somewhat broader than Aristotle's.)

A. Ignorance

"I didn't warn her," says the husband, "that her drink had been poisoned, because I didn't know that someone had slipped poison into the drink." "I didn't know," says the housemaid, "that he wanted me to save every scrap of paper that he'd thrown into the wastebasket." "I didn't know she was allergic to feathers when I gave her the pillow; I thought I was doing her a favor." "I didn't know when I operated on this patient that there had been advances in open-heart surgery during the last twenty years. I'm sorry she's dead, but I beg to be excused." We shall undoubtedly not respond the same way to each of these examples, but why?

One useful distinction can be made at the outset between *avoidable* and *unavoidable* ignorance. If the ignorance was unavoidable—that is, there was no way that the person in the circumstances could have avoided it—then the person cannot be held responsible for not knowing what he or she was ignorant of: "ought implies can." To be ignorant of the existence of the rings of Saturn prior to the invention of the telescope was unavoidable, for no one could have known about them. The first Indians to drink the Europeans' alcohol could not have known that it would make them drunk. Unavoidable ignorance is excusable, or else a person would be held responsible for what he or she could not possibly have known.

But it does not follow that people should always be held responsible for avoidable ignorance. We could all avoid much ignorance by going to encyclopedias and libraries and spending all our time there, but should we be expected to do so? I am ignorant of certain facts of organic chemistry, but am I to blame for not knowing such facts? It would seem to depend on what the context of the situation is: if I am a teacher of organic chemistry and through ignorance I misinform my class, I should be held responsible because, by the nature of my profession, that is something I ought to know. On the other hand, if I am a mere philosophy professor I should not be held responsible for not having all this recondite information: a mistake in philosophy would be more serious in my case than a mistake in chemistry.

The maid *could* have asked her employer whether he wanted every scrap of paper in the wastebasket saved and thus could have avoided her ignorance of the matter. But was it her responsibility to do so? If something is in the wastebasket, it's a fair assumption that the employer wants it thrown away (what are wastebaskets for?), unless he gives instructions to the contrary. Thus her ignorance was quite *reasonable*. In legal cases, even when ignorance is avoidable, people are not held responsible for the ignorance if, in the situation, the ignorance is considered reasonable by the court.

A railroad conductor, said a Missouri court in 1879, "is justified in forcibly ejecting (a passenger) from the car, because he, the conductor, honestly believes that the passenger has not paid his fare, but persistently refuses to do so." If you reasonably believe your life is in danger, you are (usually) excused for protecting yourself against an intruder in your house, even if the intruder is armed only with a toy pistol.

Many people have very little idea what goes on under the hood of their cars. If a man has car trouble on the way to an important meeting and misses it as a result, should he be excused by pleading ignorance of automotive mechanics? "But it was such a simple thing, he could have fixed it himself," someone might object. But what if the individual didn't know it was a simple thing? Should he then be responsible for this ignorance? "Well, if he didn't know, he could have started out earlier and still been on time for the meeting." But he didn't know he was going to have car trouble. True, he knew that he always *might;* but is it therefore his duty to start out two hours early for every meeting just on the chance that he might have car trouble on the way?

I arrive at a room on the campus where I am scheduled to speak, and there is already another meeting in progress there. "I didn't know," pleads the student who invited me, "that the room scheduling office had already assigned that room to another group for the same hour." But shouldn't she have remedied this bit of ignorance? "But I didn't know that the rooms for all visiting lectures have to be cleared through the room scheduling office." Still, wasn't it her business to know? Perhaps the incoming freshman need not know this, but shouldn't the head of a student organization who invites visiting speakers to the campus know it? Should she be excused for her ignorance?

Different standards of reasonableness are required of different individuals. In law, everyone is held responsible for knowing (not being ignorant of) certain "elementary truths of natural science," but it is far from clear how far such ignorance may go. What if a person claimed that he did not know when he jumped off the ledge that he would go downward but thought that he would rise upward to heaven like Elijah? If he honestly thought this, we might consider him mentally deranged and thus he would fall under a different category, mental illness, which we shall discuss shortly. Or we might consider his statement to be a lie: How do *we* know that he honestly believed this, particularly if it is someone else he pushed off the ledge who happened to be his favorite enemy? Still, if an ordinary layperson claimed that while she knew that water puts out fires she didn't know that water should not be used to put out gasoline fires, is this not a case of reasonable ignorance? It might be a good idea for her to know such things, but should she be held legally responsible for not knowing if she is dragged into court by a plaintiff who says she should have known this before she used water to put out the fire?

All the examples given have to do with ignorance of general laws or ignorance of the specific facts of the case. But in legal contexts there is also *ignorance of law.* "But your honor, I didn't know that there was a speed limit of 25 miles per hour in this town." "I've just moved out here, and I didn't know that there was a law against gambling in this county." Sometimes, of course, the very existence of a particular law is unfortunate, but that is another matter. The point here is that the law does not grant ignorance of the law as an excuse. It refuses to grant this, in spite of the fact that the codes of law of the state as well as the nation contain hundreds of volumes which it would take anyone many years to read. If you run afoul of the law and plead ignorance of even one small bit of fine print in it, you are not excused. But what if a pharmacist, for example, was on the high seas when the law on prescriptions was revised, and immediately after his return he prescribed a substance to a patient which had just been made illegal? Wasn't his ignorance reasonable under the circumstances? Isn't it the law's refusal to grant ignorance as an excuse that is unreasonable?

Yet there are reasons for this intransigence. In the first place, if a court, in addition to determining whether the defendant was innocent or guilty, was required to determine whether a defendant's plea of ignorance was true, it would have to subpoena witnesses and use lie-detector tests and other means to try to determine sincerity; this would make the machinery of the law even more cumbersome than it now is. In the second place, the effect of such a plea on the law would be suicidal for the law itself. If someone could plead, "But your honor, I didn't know there was a law against murder in this state," he might be let off if his statement was true. If ignorance of the law was made excusable, there would be a widespread cultivation of ignorance in order to circumvent the law. "It is no doubt true," wrote Supreme Court Justice Oliver Wendell Holmes, Jr., "that there are many cases in which the criminal could not have known that he was breaking the law, but to admit the excuse at all would be to encourage ignorance where the lawmaker has determined to make men know and obey." [1]

Just as ignorance of the law is not excused by the law, so too *disagreement* with the law, however sincere, is not accepted as an excuse. The plea "Your honor, I really feel that laws against burglary are a bad thing" would not get a defendant far in a burglary case. Neither would "I disagree with the law about conscription" in a draft-evasion case, even if the defendant was right and the law was wrong. To admit disagreement with the law as an excuse would, for the law, be tantamount to having no law at all; anyone could get out of obeying a law by claiming disagreement. "The following law will be enforced, except against those who don't agree with it" would invite disagreement by everyone who chose to disobey it. The law's position is, rather, that we may indeed disagree with a law, but while disagreeing with it, we must nevertheless obey it or pay the penalty. (The law may provide for disagreement in such cases as conscientious objection to the draft, but in that case, a rule about conscientious objectors, and the conditions they must meet, such as doing nonmilitary service, is itself written into the law, so that conscientious objectors do not necessarily become violators of the law.)

---

[1] Oliver Wendell Holmes, Jr., *The Common Law* (Boston: Little, Brown, 1923), p. 48.

In a similar vein, ignorance of a court's *interpretation* of the law is not considered excusing. Many laws, such as tax laws, are written in such obscure and vague language that it is difficult or impossible to know what they mean. Suppose you take one of them to mean one thing, which seems to you the plain and obvious meaning, but the Internal Revenue Service interprets it in a different sense. The matter goes to court, and the court decides for the government. Then the law means whatever the majority of the highest court that decides on it says that it means, and disagreement with the court's interpretation is futile: even though you could not have known what the court would decide, even though your interpretation seems reasonable and even obvious to you, you are still guilty of ignorance of law. As one writer comments:

> Knowledge of the law . . . means coincidence with the subsequent interpretation of the authorized law-declaring official. If there is coincidence, the defendant knew the law, and his action is legal. If there is not coincidence, it can avail nothing that the defendant thought his conduct was legal. This is the special meaning of *ignorantia,* which distinguishes it from the ordinary meaning of ignorance, expressed, e.g., in *ignorantia facti* [ignorance of fact].
>
> . . .
>
> So far as *ignorantia juris* [ignorance of law] is concerned, . . . the defendant and his lawyer, in effect, are setting their interpretation of the word defining a penal law against that of the authorized officials. From a theoretical viewpoint, this is precisely what a legal order cannot consistently admit.[2]

B. Mistake

Suppose you intend to steal someone's umbrella, but you take your own from the rack by mistake. Morally, you are guilty of intent to steal; legally, you are guilty of nothing, for you only took what was yours, whatever your intention may have been. The law does consider intentions, but only when they are accompanied or followed by the acts which you intend. In law there must be an act; once there is, the severity of the punishment is sometimes determined by whether or not the act was intentional.

Suppose you intend to take your own umbrella, but you take someone else's by mistake. Morally, you are guilty of nothing, except perhaps negligence (and even that would hardly apply if the other person's umbrella looks just like yours). By law you are guilty of taking what is not yours, that is, theft; however, since the theft was unintentional (and in this case trivial), nothing would be likely to happen. If you had gone off with someone else's

[2]Jerome Hall, *General Principles of Criminal Law,* 2nd ed. (Indianapolis, Ind: Bobbs-Merrill, 1960), pp. 389, 407.

car, even one that looked exactly like yours, the legal consequences might be more serious.

Again, the concept of reasonableness is invoked in the case of mistake. "I reasonably thought the substance was oil," someone might say, only it was water and was poured on sodium.

> We had a little Willie.
> Now Willie is no more.
> For what he thought was H_2O
> Was H_2SO_4.

In a 1638 case "the defendant was awakened in the night by strange noises in the house; thinking he was attacking a burglar, he ran his sword through a cabinet where the intruder was hiding and killed a friend of his servant, present by the latter's invitation."[3] But he was not held guilty of manslaughter, because he did it without intention to hurt the person who was killed. Hamlet thought he was killing his uncle, but by mistake he killed Polonius instead. Nevertheless, sometimes a mistake, however reasonable, is not excused because it is one of the offenses for which strict liability is invoked. If a man mistakenly believes that the girl with whom he elopes is over eighteen (to him and to everyone else she looks over eighteen), his mistake is not legally excusable. Such a mistake may be quite reasonable—a faked birth certificate may even be involved—but if it comes under the range of cases covered by strict liability legislation, the mistake is not excused in law.

It is for just this reason that strict liability legislation has been criticized on moral grounds. "If you do all you reasonably can and still make a mistake, how is it your fault? What more can you expect of people than their best?" What strict liability holds people responsible for is not "the facts as they reasonably seem to them" but "the facts as they *are,*" however difficult (or even impossible in the circumstances) it may be to discover what they are. But how can people be expected to know that when even many experts do not? Isn't that expecting the impossible?

Yet strict liability does guarantee settlement to injured parties: a man may have been killed by mistake, but he is no less dead for all that, and presumably his widow deserves compensation in either case. Still, although she deserves compensation and should presumably receive it from the one who killed her husband, if the killer killed by mistake, thinking reasonably that it was a burglar, does he deserve the punishment? Once again we are caught in the same dilemma that confronted us in the Typhoid Mary case.

Morally rather than legally, however, mistake is often excusing, provided that in the circumstances the mistake is *reasonable.* If I offer to lend you a certain book but lend you by mistake a different one with the same title, you will probably excuse me for my mistake. If a bottle is labeled "soy sauce"

---

[3] Ibid., p. 365.

and it looks like soy sauce, I may reasonably pour it on the chow mein; what I do not know, and could not reasonably have known at the time, is that the hostess was a compulsive saver and once the bottle was empty of soy sauce she had filled it with ink, and later, having forgotten that she had done this, she put it on the kitchen shelf thinking it to be soy sauce. Was *her* mistake reasonable? It would seem that her putting something into the bottle that wasn't soy sauce was unreasonable—or, certainly, doing that *and* putting it on the kitchen shelf.

Consider now a man who drives home late at night quite intoxicated. All the tract houses look alike, especially at night. He tiptoes into the house through the unlocked door and goes into the darkened bedroom, but since he entered the wrong house by mistake, the woman he makes advances to is not his wife. She presses charges against him for attempted rape. But under the circumstances, was the mistake not quite reasonable? Thinking himself to be at home, he naturally assumed that the woman in the bed was his wife. Was he then to blame for *getting* himself into the circumstances, namely, getting drunk? Yet if he had merely gotten drunk and not made this mistake, nothing would have happened. Exactly what then is he guilty of morally?

C. Unintentional Acts

Many acts are unintentionally rather than intentionally performed. For example, in the process of passing you the sugar I may inadvertently upset your teacup. Philosopher J. L. Austin describes inadvertent acts as follows:

> I do an act A-1 (say, crush a snail) *inadvertently* if, in the course of executing by means of movements of my bodily parts some other act A-2 (say, in walking down the public path), I fail to exercise such meticulous supervision over the courses of those movements as would have been needed to ensure that they did not bring about the untoward event (here, the impact on the snail). By claiming that A-1 was inadvertent we place it, where we imply it belongs, on this special level, in a class of incidental happenings which must occur in the doing of any physical act.[4]

We can also plead that "I did it *accidentally*," as in, I accidentally tripped and fell, breaking the vase in so doing." Neither the falling nor the breaking of the vase was intentional. But whether it is excusable depends on the context: What if I was drunk at the time? What if I was simply negligent or careless and didn't look where I was going? What if I was in a hostile frame of mind and unconsciously was determined to break my wife's favorite vase? Many acts are "purposely accidental," that is, they appear to be accidental

[4]J. L. Austin, "A Plea for Excuses," *Aristotelian Society Proceedings* 57 (1956–1957): 16.

but a psychoanalyst could convince me (or a court) that "down deep" they were purposeful.

In addition, countless cases of acts have consequences which occur "by accident." "I didn't intend to hit the child; I intended only to get the stray dog off the yard." "I didn't intend to kill him; I only intended to bloody his nose. How was I to know that he was a hemophiliac and would bleed to death?" "It's true that I was holding a box of explosives in my hand, but it fell by accident. I was just getting out of the train when the train gave a lurch." In many such cases the circumstances which led to the accident couldn't have been foreseen, and the person is totally excused. But when an act was intentional with regard to one consequence, *A,* though unintentional with regard to another, *B,* a person might also be held responsible for *B,* even if *B* was not a probable consequence and could not reasonably have been foreseen. If a woman is target practicing and accidentally shoots someone, she is guilty of manslaughter, even though she is practicing in an area where people seldom pass, and even if she is a bad shot and couldn't intentionally hit a target if she tried. Few people are hemophiliacs, but if a man did pick a fight with one, he would not be excused in spite of the great statistical improbability of this specific victim being a hemophiliac. The reason is that though he did not kill intentionally, he did something else intentionally, namely, punch the man in the nose. A person who initiates aggressive actions against another person is, as a rule, legally liable for the consequences of such aggression, whether those consequences could have been foreseen or not. Still, if the court decided that this consequence was not reasonably foreseeable, it might hold him guilty of assault and battery rather than manslaughter.

It is not always clear whether the court's reason for upholding the general principle is that the individual aggressor deserves it or that some such measure is desirable in order to deter aggression. But in the case of the Felony-Murder Act, which is law in some states, the clear purpose seems to be to deter aggression. The act provides that any death that occurs during the commission of a felony automatically makes all the participants in the felony chargeable with murder. If during a bank robbery one of robbers holds a toy pistol to the cashier's head, and the cashier has a heart attack and dies, all the robbers are guilty of murder in the first degree, in spite of the fact that the death of the cashier was not intentional. Without doubt the act was passed in order to deter bank robberies and similar felonies. (Interestingly, however, the same law would not be applied if the causation was more indirect: if the cashier's wife, looking through the bank window and seeing her husband being held up with what appeared to be a real pistol, suddenly had a heart attack and died, the robber would not be guilty of murder.)

Cases where aggression leads to a death that was unintended always offer a challenge to the legal system. Consider the following case. A woman jealous of a rival who had supplanted her in a man's affections, went to her rival's house, poured gasoline in the mailbox, then stuffed newspapers through it, and lit it. The house caught fire and two children sleeping there were burned to death. She pleaded that her act was unintentional and that she only intended to frighten her rival. Though the court agreed that she had not intended to burn down the house or kill the children, she was convicted on the charge of murder (intentional homicide). Her act was not intentional with respect to the consequence which brought her to court (the death of the two children), but the fact that she had intentionally poured the gasoline and lit the newspapers was considered sufficient. Is a person responsible for all the consequences of his or her acts, even if they were not foreseen? One judge thought that there must be a direct intention of murder (which was not present in this case), but that it was enough that there was an intention to expose a victim to a serious risk of death or grievous bodily harm without actually intending to cause death. Another thought that foresight of a likelihood (or even a possibility) of death was sufficient to convict for murder.[5]

D. Compulsion

There are situations in which no one tried to force us to do anything, but in which, as we say, "we were compelled by *circumstances*" to do something. "A storm was coming up, so we were compelled to throw the cargo overboard." "I fell into a crevasse and was compelled to remain there until help arrived." These are not really cases of compulsion, because there was nobody to do the compelling. In the second case I got myself into circumstances in which there was nothing else I could do but wait in the crevasse. In the first case, because of the impending storm, we had to throw the cargo overboard in order to save our own lives; here there was a choice, but it was between two "bad" alternatives, one of which (death) was so undesirable that for all practical purposes we had no choice but to jettison the cargo. But none of this is compulsion. Talk of compulsion when nobody is there to do the compelling is an understandable but misleading figure of speech.

Let us turn, then, to cases of genuine compulsion. Acts done under *compulsion* are intentional acts, but they are performed under pressure by other human agents.

When a man's fingers are held to the trigger by another man who is stronger than he is, and from whose clutches he tries in vain to escape, the act is that of the second man, not the first. This is simply a case of someone being forced to do something and becoming not the agent but the patient. In genuine cases of compulsion by other persons, however, the agent was, as we say, "forced against his or her will" to *do* something; he or she did the act but under compulsion. When the robber says, "Your money or your life!" with a gun in your back, you give up the money rather than your life (or, sometimes, your life and your money besides). But were you *forced*?

[5] This case is described in Anthony Kenny, *Freewill and Responsibility* (London: Routledge & Kegan Paul, 1978), pp. 54–55.

Unlike the man whose fingers were pressed onto the trigger, you *had* a choice, though admittedly not a very pleasant one: you could surrender your money or refuse to. Why, then, is this called a case of compulsion? Because you were made to exercise your choice on the basis of a threat; except for the threat, you would not have surrendered the money. There are various kinds of, or degrees of, compulsion.

1. *Torture* is the most extreme means by which one person can use compulsion on another. The victim still can choose whether or not to divulge the secrets that captors desire but believes that not divulging the secrets will lead to more torture. Different persons have different thresholds of pain. Some can withstand torture for days without revealing what they know. But for most people withholding information becomes progressively more difficult, and finally a point is reached (which differs from person to person) at which anything seems preferable to enduring more torture. It may be (though it is very difficult to say) that a point is reached at which it is impossible (for that person, in these specific circumstances) to withstand more torture and that whatever is said or done by the victim under torture is excusable.

To many people whatever is said or done under torture seems excusable. Yet the armed forces of most countries do not consider torture an excuse for divulging anything beyond one's name, rank, and serial number. Nor is torture deemed excusable for those in underground movements: "If you thought you were going to succumb under torture, you should never have joined us in the first place, because you would be a danger to our cause."

2. *Threats* are less extreme than torture but may still constitute compulsion. The robber threatens you with death if you don't surrender the contents of your wallet. A kidnapper threatens to kill your child if you don't deliver the ransom. A hijacker threatens to blow up the plane if the pilot doesn't take the plane to wherever the hijacker commands. Typically, compulsion consists of a threat by one person to do something to another person (or a loved one of the other person) if the victim does not give in to the aggressor's demands. Ordinarily, we excuse the threatened person for doing what he or she does and place the entire blame on the person who does the threatening. Yet in law it is not always so: if a man forces you at gunpoint to kill someone else, the law holds that you should permit yourself to be killed rather than to escape by causing the death of an innocent person; the fact that you were compelled at gunpoint doesn't legally excuse you.

In a 1975 case, a man was forced by gunmen of the Irish Republican Army to drive them to a place where they shot a policeman. The man was charged with murder, but the House of Lords sustained his claim that since he was not the actual killer, but was compelled at gunpoint only to drive the others, he was innocent of the murder of the policeman. However, in a 1976 case a man participated in killing a woman at the command of the head of a commune where he lived; his life and his mother's had been threatened. But he was not excused for the murder of the woman. To allow such a defense to killers would set a precedent for terrorists, gang leaders, and kidnappers, said Lord Salmon in his opinion on the case:

> A terrorist of notorious violence might, e.g., threaten death to A and his family unless A obeys his instructions to put a bomb with a time fuse set by A in a certain aircraft, or in a thronged market, railway station or the like. A, under duress, obeys his instructions and as a result, hundreds of men, women and children are killed or mangled. Should the contentions made on behalf of the appellant be correct, A would have a complete defense, and, if charged, would be bound to be acquitted and set at liberty. Having now gained some real experience and expertise, he might again be approached by the terrorist who would make the same threats and exercise the same duress under which A would then give a repeat performance, killing even more men, women, and children. Is there any limit to the number of people you may kill to save your own life and that of your family?[6]

Our humane impulses lead us to excuse actions performed under threats of death. Yet, if killings performed under such threats are excused, terrorists, by threatening various people, can confer immunity on those upon whom they use compulsion to further their ends. They can't with impunity kill them themselves, but if those whom they threaten can, there will surely be more murders.

Threats can vary in degree. Threats of death and dismemberment (of oneself or one's family or loved ones) are as a rule the most serious; threats of bodily harm and injury are next; then come threats of loss of money or possessions, as in the threat to firebomb an unoccupied store. But there are also threats of exposure (blackmail) and threats of economic loss, such as loss of a job. If the boss said, "Unless you sleep with me on the weekend, I'll fire you" a woman would normally acquiesce to loss of the job and seek another. How serious the threat of loss of a job is depends on such factors as a person's present economic condition, the availability of jobs in the field, and how far the individual would have to go to get a job comparable to the old one. During an economic depression the threat of loss of a job would be an extremely serious one, as it would be to a person whose skills are no longer in demand: workers in the last buggy plant before the advent of automobiles would find the loss of their jobs quite devastating, though they could still learn new skills (something they would probably have to do in any case) and get into other trades or professions. And then there are threats that are of no serious consequence at all. "If you don't do what I want, I'll jump out of the window" might invite the response, "Go ahead and jump!" And sometimes the threat turns into an inducement ("Is that a threat or a promise?"), as when the mother-in-law says, "If you don't do what I want, I'll move out!"

To be effective, not only must the threat pose a serious loss to the person being threatened, but the threatener must be in a position to carry it out—or, at any rate, the person threatened must believe this to be the case. The victim must also believe that the threat is sincere, that the threatener is not joking. If these conditions were not met, actions performed as a result of threats would not be excusable.

3. *Influence* or *pressure* is sometimes thought to constitute compulsion. "As a result of watching countless television ads, I was compelled to buy this product." In this case, however, the person still could conceivably exercise judgment as to whether to buy the product or not; perhaps the individual was so weak-willed that the ads were irresistible, but at least he or she had the option of turning off the television set. What about the case of a tape recorder playing the message "Eat Wheaties" while someone is asleep, whereupon the person wakes in the morning with a tremendous desire for Wheaties? In such a case, much depends on whether the individual had previously consented to this experiment: if she has, she is hardly in a position to complain of her morning desire; if she has not, she has been used against her will for other people's ends. In the latter case, it was not *her* mind that made the decision but the minds of others using her as a means to their own ends.

There are various kinds of *pressure* that one person can put on another that do not exactly count as compulsion, yet they can direct the person's decision in a certain way. Shy people are easily intimidated by others, especially those with a loud voice, an authoritative manner, or a "strong" personality. Juveniles are constantly confronted by peer pressure to experiment with dangerous drugs, even against their better judgment. By similar pressures people constantly seek advancement in their positions, and fighters always feel compelled to take on a dare. Such influences can often be as effective in getting their intended result as torture in prying loose state secrets.

Yet people are not being compelled by these influences; if they *choose* to act in accordance with them, they are hardly being *compelled* to act in accordance with them. And indeed such influences are often resisted in spite of the pressure. If a man finds it difficult to escape the influence of con-artists, he can steel his resolve, lock the door, or perhaps consult a therapist to work on his weakness of will.

Since children and juveniles are often extremely impressionable and are not fully capable of appreciating the probable consequences of their own actions, they are often at least partially excused by the courts, as having what is called "diminished responsibility," resulting in diminished punishment. But diminished responsibility is an extremely slippery concept. Does the fourteen-year-old girl who obtains a pistol and shoots both her parents not know the consequences of her actions? Should a hypoglycemic adolescent be permitted to claim that he couldn't help getting into a gang fight because after eating lots of Twinkies his blood sugar was low? (If he knew this, couldn't he have refrained from consuming Twinkies?) When a girl disobeyed her parents' orders by staying out all night, they decided to teach her a lesson by forcing her to shoot her pet dog; instead she took the pistol and shot herself in the head. (The police said that no charges could be filed against the parents except possibly cruelty to animals.[7]) Didn't she know exactly what she was doing?

Still, isn't it plausible to claim diminished responsibility in many such cases? If an impressionable thirteen-year-old boy commits a robbery identical to one he has seen on television, perhaps he shouldn't be let off entirely, but should a judge give him as severe a punishment as would have been given the boy's father if he had committed such a robbery? Should a juvenile, craving acceptance by his peers, who accepts a challenge to run his motorcycle off a cliff with himself and a passenger on it, be charged (if he lives) with murder or manslaughter as an adult would? This is an extremely "gray area" of the law; some judges charge juveniles with murder like adults, while others let them off completely under the excuse of diminished responsibility. But if a juvenile can be let off lightly because of diminished responsibility, why not also many adults who have grown older chronologically but not rationally or emotionally? Once this excuse is admitted, where is the line to be drawn? The fear is probably well founded that the plea of diminished responsibility, once admitted, will be used as an escape-hatch for exonerating a person from liability for whatever crime he desires to commit.

E. Unconscious States

Shortly after the Civil War a veteran arrived late at a hotel in Kentucky, sat down in the lobby, and went to sleep. The veteran's companion paid for a room for the night for both of them, and to get his friend to go to the room he tried to wake him by shaking him. Not succeeding in this, he asked the porter to try to wake him, but he too failed, and at first he believed the man was dead. He then shook him harder until the veteran looked up and asked, "What do you want?" "Go to your bed," said the porter. "Go away and leave me alone," the veteran muttered sleepily. But the porter persisted, saying, "It's getting late, I want to close up." Holding the veteran by the coat, the porter then raised him up, at which point the veteran threw his hand to his side, drew a pistol, and shot the porter. He was indicted for murder.

The veteran had never seen the porter before, nor was there any motive for killing him. It developed that the veteran had been a sleepwalker from early childhood. Others testified that in his sleep he had often walked, talked, even answered questions, yet was unconscious of what he was doing; that with him, as with many others, there was a period between sleeping and waking in which he was unconscious, though he seemed to be somewhat awake; and that because of his war experience his instinct was to defend

[7]*New York Times,* February 7, 1968.

himself first and investigate afterward. The judge ruled that *if* the man was asleep or unconscious at the time of the shooting, the defendant should be released since, he said, no one can be responsible for acts performed during sleep:

> If the appellant was unconscious when he fired the first shot, it cannot be imputed to him as a crime. Nor is he guilty if partially conscious, if, upon being partially awakened, and finding the deceased had hold of him and was shaking him, he imagined he was being attacked, and believing himself in danger of losing his life or of sustaining great bodily injury at the hands of his assailant, he shot in good faith, believing it necessary to preserve his life or his person from great harm. In such circumstances, it does not matter whether he had reasonable grounds for his belief or not. He had been asleep, and could know nothing of the surrounding circumstances. In his condition he may have supposed he was assailed for a deadly purpose, and if he did, he is not to be punished because his half-awakened consciousness deceived him as to the real facts, any more than if, being awake, the deceased had presented a pistol to his head with the apparent intention to shoot him, when in fact, he was only jesting, or if the supposed pistol, though sufficiently resembling a deadly weapon to be readily mistaken for one, was but an inoffensive toy.[8]

People are not legally responsible for what they do while sleepwalking, even though they may have a dream corresponding to what they are doing:

> Suppose that a mother dreams that her daughter is being seduced by a soldier; she gets up in her sleep, takes an axe, and kills her daughter, probably thinking that she is killing the supposed soldier. Here, according to the dream facts, the mother is killing a human being in circumstances that do not, even if true, constitute in themselves a defense. Nevertheless the mother is not guilty of murder, for dream knowledge is not knowledge for legal purposes.[9]

For there to be legal liability, there must be an act. In sleep there are bodily motions, but in the absence of any conscious awareness, there is (legally speaking) no act. The woman couldn't help what motions she went through in her sleep, for they were not directed by her conscious will.

Nevertheless, the law takes precautions about this general principle:

> A sleepwalker who kills another person with a revolver is not for that reason alone guilty of homicide; but if, knowing himself to be given to

[8]Judge Cofer, 78 Kentucky 183, 39 Am. Rep. 213 (1879).
[9]Glanville Williams, *Criminal Law, The General Part* (London: Stevens, 1953), p. 17.

sleep-walking, he had gone to sleep with the loaded revolver by his side, the putting it there would be an act that might well be sufficiently negligent to make him guilty of manslaughter. . . . It is possible for a man to enter another's house in a dream-state resulting from temporary mental disorder, such as epilepsy or hysterical ague, and such an entry is neither burglary nor housebreaking. To prevent abuse of this defense, it is necessary to allow the prosecution to put in evidence every fact tending to show that the alleged automatism is a fake.[10]

Cases involving other states of unconsciousness besides sleep have been heard as well. In England the driver of a van drove his car at high speed across a road junction where there was an illuminated "Halt" sign and collided with a car before overturning. In court he pleaded that he was not responsible for his action because he had become unconscious and remembered nothing from a short time before he reached the crossing until after the collision. The court accepted this plea and held that loss of memory could only be attributed to his being overcome with illness without warning. A higher court, however, held that he had not given enough evidence that he was in any state different from ordinary sleep.

One justice thought it relevant to observe that the British Road Traffic Act "contains an absolute prohibition against driving dangerously or ignoring 'Halt' signs. . . . It is no answer to a charge to say: 'I did not mean to drive dangerously' or 'I did not notice the 'Halt' sign." Another justice observed that in spite of this absolute prohibition, there are some states of unconsciousness which would exclude liability for dangerous driving. A man might be excused, for example, if he had a sudden stroke or epileptic fit, if he had a blow on the head from a stone, or if he was attacked by a swarm of bees "so that he is for the time being disabled and prevented from exercising any directional control over the vehicle, and any movements of his arms and legs are solely caused by the action of the bees."[11] Even so, if he drove knowing that he was liable to have an epileptic fit, his driving could be considered dangerous.

Why is a person legally responsible for falling asleep at the wheel but not for having a heart attack? Because, said the court, anyone who feels sleepy can stop beside the road and take a nap; there are precautions that can be taken against drowsiness, but not against a sudden stroke or the entry into the car of a swarm of bees. As a rule, people feel drowsy before falling asleep, and if a driver is drowsy, he or she is supposed to pull over to the side. (But what if the driver falls asleep without the prior warning sign of drowsiness?)

What about the acts of a person who is drunk? According to one authority:

[10] Ibid., p. 18.
[11] This case is described in H. L. A. Hart, *Punishment and Responsibility* (New York: Oxford University Press, 1968), pp. 93–94, where the quotes are found.

A drunkard who, in his partly insensate condition, does some injury is deemed to perform an act, though in fact his condition may be very like that of the sleep-walker. *Drunkenness is a self-induced condition;* sleep-walking is not. On the other hand, an injury done in a drunken *sleep* receives the same exemption as any other injury during sleep.[12]

With so much depending on the distinction between sleep and waking, what of acts performed under hypnosis? "When you awake," says a hypnotist, "you will be uncomfortable because the room is very stuffy and you will go to the window and open it." Although the room is cold and drafty, when the hypnotized subject awakens, she remarks on how stuffy it is and goes to the window and opens it. She believes that she is doing it "of her own free will," but every spectator recognizes that the idea was implanted in her during hypnosis. Is she responsible? Suppose that the hypnotist had instructed her to turn on a jet which would have filled the room with poison gas; or suppose that he had told her to jump out of the window. Isn't the hypnotist responsible, with the hypnotized subject acting only as a vehicle for his own will?

When an act occurs, the law turns to the last *voluntary agent* before the act. If an adult sells a child a gun and the child shoots someone with it, the law does not consider the child a voluntary agent but indicts the adult instead; but if an adult shoots the gun, the law holds him or her liable rather than the person who sold the gun. In the hypnosis case, is the subject or the hypnotist the last voluntary agent? Although it appears that the subject is merely the vehicle by which the hypnotist works his will, this is not quite the case. The subject has a part in it too, since she consented to be hypnotized in the first place; and if she had seen experiments in hypnosis before, she had some idea of what to expect. If she didn't want to be hypnotized, she could have said no. Moreover, there are some things which, if she was asked to do them under hypnosis, she would not do and would come out of the hypnotic trance immediately. Thus, the matter of responsibility in this case is not either-or: each one has a part to play, the importance of which varies from case to case. The prevailing legal opinion appears to be that hypnosis is not, like sleep, a state of unconsciousness: "While it is going on, it is a coherent conscious experience capable of being clearly remembered afterwards."[13] But it is not clear that any general conclusions can be reached about the hypnotized subject's responsibility.

F. Inner Compulsion

When Aristotle discussed compulsion as excusing, he meant the good old-fashioned variety of compulsion, which entails being compelled by another person to do certain acts. He was not aware of the modern concept of com-

[12] Williams, *Criminal Law,* p. 18. Emphasis mine.
[13] Robert W. White, *The Abnormal Personality* (New York: Ronald Press, 1956), p. 202.

pulsion from within. On the face of it, inner compulsion does sound absurd: How can one be compelled by oneself, or a part of oneself? Isn't this, at best, a misleading figure of speech?

It may be a figure of speech, but by whatever name we call it, it refers to something with which human beings have had to deal for many centuries, even in Aristotle's time. Not only can a person be a slave to another person, but a person can also be a slave to his or her own overpowering passions. Of such inner drives Aristotle must have been aware from reading the dramas of Euripides. A person may be in the grip of an impulse so powerful as not to be able to rid himself or herself of it, in spite of constant attempts. It is *as if* the individual was being forced to act in certain ways at gunpoint by someone else, except that no one else is using force; some part of the person seems incomprehensibly to be moving him or her powerfully and irrevocably toward certain actions.

Fyodor Dostoyevsky in his story *The Gambler* gives a memorable portrait of the compulsive gambler who, knowing that he will end up penniless, still cannot stop himself: he cannot stop while he is winning, for he always "believes" that he will win again, and when he is losing he must always recoup his losses; the result is that he cannot stop until he is broke. He may be perfectly aware of this pattern of behavior yet be unable to stop it. Dostoyevsky may not have known the cause of such behavior, but he knew from his own experience what the feeling was like and he was observant enough to record in the minutest detail the gambler's behavior—so much so that Sigmund Freud, in his little book *Dostoyevsky,* found the Russian novelist's portrait to be clinically accurate. Here is a case of "overwhelming impulse," where the gambler appears to be a passive victim, like a rowboat tossed about by a storm. As an explanation of such behavior some psychiatrists are inclined toward the view that the roulette wheel, where the results are a matter of chance, represents the infantile world to which the gambler desires to return, in opposition to the world of "order, logic, and reason," to which parents wish to acclimate their maturing child; the rebellion is symbolized in a pathological addiction to gambling.

Are such people to be held responsible for being addicted, or shall we say that they are simply passive instruments of inner urges too powerful to be consciously combated? The problem is not an easy one. At the moment they may be unable to conquer their impulses; but what if they gave in to them at an earlier period, when they could have conquered them (as other people did)? Then they are like drivers who, soused with liquor, have car accidents. In both cases, the individuals may be too far gone to be responsible, though they are responsible for getting into their condition in the first place. But unlike drunken drivers, it is far from clear at what point compulsives could have taken preventive measures, especially if they didn't see their addiction coming.

The law sometimes speaks of "irresistible impulses." If an impulse is irresistible, then of course it is (by definition) impossible to resist it; and if it is impossible to resist it, a person cannot be held responsible for not doing so. But the problem is, how do you know when an impulse is really irresistible? You may try and try and not resist it, but how do you know that you could not have resisted it if you had tried harder or tried some more? All that can really be known is, not that the impulse was irresistible, but that under the circumstances it was not in fact resisted. Thus, though "irresistible impulse" would be an acceptable way out of responsibility if it could be shown to exist in an individual case, there is no way of showing in any individual case that it really exists.

Most impulses, however strong, are not irresistible "no matter what": there are extreme conditions under which they can be and are resisted. A woman with agoraphobia (fear of open places) stays at home and doesn't care to venture into the street or mingle with crowds of people. As the condition intensifies it takes more and more to get her to leave her apartment. But if she were starving and couldn't get anyone else to go, she would go to the market and buy groceries; and if a fire broke out in her apartment building, she would exit into the street along with all the others, though she might be a psychological wreck the next day, trembling and perspiring. It's not that "when unconscious impulse A is present, behavior B inevitably occurs," but only that the tendency toward behavior B (when A is present) is so strong that only an especially potent stimulus will be sufficient to prevent it.

Moreover, most unconscious compulsions affect only a certain segment of a person's life; other parts are left untouched. A certain young woman has a fear of glass that she doesn't understand; she dares not touch glass tumblers, windowpanes, doorknobs, vases, and so on. This habit is annoying to her family, and they tell her to "just get over it." She tries but continues to panic every time she touches glass. Finally she is persuaded to see a psychiatrist; but while hanging up her coat, she accidentally upsets a glass vase on the shelf above, which breaks into a thousand fragments all over her mink coat, and she runs in terror out of the office, coatless, never to return. The fear of glass, especially after more description that could be added, seems a fair candidate for being irresistible. Yet in other aspects of her life she is quite normal, and aside from her inordinate fear of glass, her behavior is in no way unusual.

Such examples of unconscious motivation confront us all the time. We are all acquainted with people who can't stand to step on the cracks in the sidewalk, people who have to make sure that the sheets hang down from both sides of the bed to an exactly equal length, and people with a horror of certain colors and shapes. But these compulsions are fairly harmless, and we dismiss them as innocent peccadillos. Others, however, are not so harmless. Many people are extremely self-destructive in their behavior without realizing it.[14] There is the timid man who builds up his resentment and always

[14]See Edmund Bergler, *The Basic Neurosis* (New York: Grune and Stratton, 1949); and Edmund Bergler, *The Battle of the Conscience* (Washington, D.C.: Washington Institute of Medicine, 1948).

ends by telling the boss off and getting fired from his job; there is the enthusiastic cousin who always breezes into town at 3 A.M. and calls up all her friends, waking them from sleep, and wondering the next day why they are all so cool to her; and there are persons whose words always seem to come out in an insulting way (protesting "I didn't mean it that way," but nevertheless causing irritation). Such people see clearly that others react negatively to them, but they fail just as regularly to see what they themselves have done to provoke this reaction. The result is the deterioration of all their social and professional relationships. If the world does not provide them with a daily kick in the teeth, they will manipulate the world so as to provide the kick in the teeth themselves, by doing things (unconsciously) that can be counted on to provoke other people's anger and resentment, after which they will wonder, "What have *I* done?"

Unconscious motivations appear constantly when we dip just below the surface of human behavior, and once we see them, they alter our picture of what makes people "tick," as well as our assessment of their responsibility. A young man rings the doorbell of an apartment to make a delivery, and a girl answers the bell; he enters the apartment and within ten seconds stabs her to death with an ice pick that he finds lying on the refrigerator. "A brutal, savage murder," comments the newspaper; and so it is. But why did it occur? The girl was wearing a ring, and it resembled his mother's wedding ring; when he saw the ring, he was in an instant frenzy and couldn't control himself. He had revered his mother and dreamt of her even when she sent him to an orphanage to get rid of him, even when he was pushed around from one orphanage to another and no one wanted him. One day when he came to visit his mother unexpectedly, he found her in bed with a man, and in the course of time he discovered how she was making her living. His realization of what she was shattered all his cherished illusions about her, and for this he hated her, yet he wanted her love desperately as the only anchor in his life. He could not live with that ambivalence of feeling. Her wedding ring was the symbol of her sanctity: nobody else could wear one in his eyes because it threatened that image of her which he wanted desperately to preserve. Yet at the same time he hated her, and this symbol of her marriage vows was a mockery of what she really was. It all came back to him in one overpowering surge of emotion when he saw the girl's ring.[15] The impulse to kill, to rid himself forever of the terrible ambivalence he couldn't live with, was irresistible.

Or was it merely not resisted, or not resisted enough? If he had stopped for a moment to think, could he have resisted? But could he under the circumstances have stopped to think? Perhaps you or I could, but could he? It seems quite certain that no one knows the answer to that question. Until we do, psychiatrists will appear in court, one for the prosecution and one for the defense, one saying, "Yes, of course he's responsible," and the other saying, "No, under the circumstances he wasn't responsible, he was a prisoner of his

[15] This incident is described, along with many other case histories, in Robert Lindner, *The Fifty-minute Hour* (New York: Rinehart, 1954).

past." (But aren't there other people, equally prisoners of their past, who manage to get themselves out of the prison? Doubtless there are, but of course it doesn't follow that *he* could have.)

G. Insanity

If you ask a physician or psychiatrist, "Is this man insane?" he or she will be likely to respond, "I can't tell you. 'Insane' is a legal term, not a medical term." Nevertheless, physicians are required to testify in court whether or not in their opinion a defendant is insane. Anyone who is found insane will not be convicted for the crime, but since (because of the crime) the individual is considered "dangerous," he or she will probably be remitted to a mental institution, possibly for life.

"Insanity" is a very slippery term to get a hold on. When a man's behavior strikes others as especially peculiar or idiosyncratic, they are inclined to say "He's crazy." In the Soviet Union many political prisoners are not taken to jails but to mental institutions, where their "mental aberrations" (consisting of political dissent) are "treated" by deprivation of food and rest and various insidious kinds of torture until their "sickness" is cured by confession of their errors—exactly as in the Inquisition.

In the West the methods used are not as extreme, but not so different either. Most of the persons who are committed against their will to mental institutions (formerly called "insane asylums") are losers in a family battle— children who can't be handled by their parents, old people no longer wanted by their children. Even those who enter such institutions after being accused of crimes may remain there for more years than they would have served in prison for committing the crimes. The reason is that by law people cannot stand trial until they are found mentally competent to understand the charges against them, which must be attested to in writing by a psychiatrist; the temptation (particularly if they are good workers) is to keep them institutionalized year after year, with psychiatrists (who have generally not even seen the patients after the first commitment) testifying in their annual reports that the patients are "mentally incompetent" and hence cannot stand trial. So, those who are committed can't prove their innocence unless they stand trial, but they can't stand trial as long as they're still "mentally incompetent"—a Catch-22 situation.[16]

For our daily purposes it isn't important to decide whether a person should be classified as "insane"; we can describe the person's behavior and react to the individual accordingly. But for legal purposes it is of great importance: a convicted person who is declared sane goes to prison, whereas one who is

---

[16] See Bruce Ennis, *Prisoners of Psychiatry* (New York: Harcourt Brace Jovanovich, 1972); Thomas Szasz, *The Manufacture of Madness* (New York: Harper & Row, 1970); Thomas Szasz, *The Myth of Mental Illness* (New York: Harper & Row, 1974); and Thomas Szasz, *Psychiatric Slavery* (New York: Macmillan, 1977).

declared insane ("not of sound mind") goes to a mental institution. Since so much turns on the distinction, it is a matter of some importance to know by what criterion someone is to be declared sane or insane.

The classic criteria, called the McNaghten Rules, were set forth in 1843: "To establish a defense on the ground of insanity, it must be clearly proved that, at the time of committing the act, the accused was laboring under such a defect of reason, from disease of the mind, as not to know the nature and quality of the act he was doing, or, if he did know it, that he did not know he was doing what was wrong." But though the McNaghten Rules are sometimes used in courts to this day, several difficulties have arisen in using them to mark off the "sane" from the "insane."

1. The concept of "disease of the mind" or "mental disease" is far from clear. We know what a disease of the body is; we can often isolate the germ or the virus that is unique to the disease. But what is a disease of the mind? Perhaps it can be defined as one that keeps the mind from functioning properly, but what does "properly" denote? Besides, one principal cause of a mind not functioning is stupidity, which is hardly insanity. Many have thought of homosexuality as a "mental disease," for which people should be "put in a loony bin." But is every bit of idiosyncratic behavior, every aberration, every kind of tendency to action that is not statistically in the majority, to be called "mental disease"? If people feel strong antipathy to a certain kind of behavior, they will answer yes, and the person is likely to be put away. But if there is one thing that is aberrant, idiosyncratic, and statistically abnormal, it is genius; should the genius therefore be put away also? Many people throughout history have said yes to that one too.[17]

2. Many people who are declared insane, including many people whose behavior seems "crazy as a loon," *do* know the "nature and quality of their act." The ice-pick killer may have had an irresistible impulse, but didn't he know exactly what he was doing? Almost everyone who isn't unconscious knows what he or she is doing, though he may not appreciate or foresee its consequences.

3. Knowledge of an act being wrong can cause difficulties as well. "Wrong" is a moral term. Sociopaths who have no sense of right and wrong at all don't know that what they're doing is wrong; they know only that other people *call* their acts "wrong." Moreover, if the crime is political dissidence, it may not be wrong at all, but quite heroic. In any case, what one person considers wrong another may not; the McNaghten Rules seem to presuppose some uniform objective standard of right and wrong. For this reason some courts have preferred to interpret knowledge of wrong as meaning "wrong in the accused person's own opinion." But a religious zealot who believes he is commanded by God to kill all the children in the neighborhood does not "know that his act was wrong." He firmly believes what he does to be his sacred duty.

[17] See Szasz, *The Myth of Mental Illness.*

Because of these and many similar difficulties, the term "wrong" is sometimes construed as meaning the same as "illegal." The question then becomes, "Did the person know that his or her act was illegal?" The answer must be, sometimes yes and sometimes no. Sometimes a person is simply ignorant of the law, but what has that to do with insanity? (Apparently ignorance of the law is an excuse only if someone is declared insane.)

4. The main objection to the McNaghten Rules is that they present a *cognitive* criterion rather than a *volitional* one. They refer only to what defendants did not *know,* and not to what they could not *do.* For this reason the British Medical Association proposed that the McNaghten Rules be expanded to read that the accused "was laboring, as a result of disease of the mind, under . . . a *disorder of emotion* such that, while appreciating the nature and quality of the act, and that it was wrong, he did not possess sufficient power to prevent himself from committing it." [18] Thus, a killer may have known what he or she was doing and that it was wrong (illegal?) but could not prevent himself or herself from doing it.

As we have seen, it is difficult, if not impossible, to know whether at a particular moment an individual could have acted otherwise, but at least the criterion is clarified by introducing ability to so *act* (though the troublesome phrase "as a result of disease of the mind" still remains). Perhaps the Swiss Penal Code gives the best summation of all when it says succinctly that to be insane, the defendant must be "incapable of appreciating the unlawful nature of his act or of acting in accord with such appreciation."

Even so, there is doubt whether this or any definition succeeds in encapsulating what people want to distinguish when they use the term "insane." When a defendant flies into an incoherent rage before a jury, with wild movements of the hands and rolling of the eyes, it is easy for the jury to find the individual insane. But what of the cool, collected murderer, who carefully conceives and carries out an elaborate criminal plan over a period of time? Such a person shouldn't be called insane, we may say. Yet, though that individual knows the nature of the act and that it was wrong, is he really incapable of preventing himself from committing it? The British Medical Association, in considering one such case, answered in the following way:

> The answer depends on the interpretation put on the words "incapable of preventing himself." Ley [the killer], because of his insanity, lived in a twilight world of distorted values which resulted not so much in his being "incapable of preventing himself" from committing his crime . . . as in his being incapable of appreciating, as a sane man would, why he should try to prevent himself from committing it. . . . If each of Ley's acts is considered separately, it would be difficult to maintain that he could not have prevented himself from committing them. Yet if his course of conduct is looked at as a whole, it might well be argued that,

[18] Royal Commission Report (1953).

as a result of his insanity, he was incapable of preventing himself from conceiving the murderous scheme, incapable of judging it by other than an insane scale of ethical values, and, in that sense, incapable of preventing himself from carrying it out.[19]

In the end, a judge or jury's decision whether to call a person insane probably depends very little on whether his or her behavior accords with a specified set of criteria; during the course of the trial each member develops a gut feeling and judges accordingly. Lord Blackburn, giving evidence on a new homicide law, expressed this view in 1874:

I have read every definition which I ever could meet with, and never was satisfied with one of them, and have endeavored in vain to make one satisfactory to myself; I verily believe that it is not in human power to do it. You must take it that in every individual case you must look at the circumstances and do the best you can to say whether it was the disease of the mind which was the cause of the crime, or the party's criminal will.

Should there not be some yardstick to guide the jury? Another jurist at the same hearing thought not: "However much you charge a jury as to the McNaghten Rules or any other test, the question they would put to themselves when they retire is—Is this man mad or is he not?"[20]

Sometimes the condition that inclines people to call someone "insane" is something that pervades his or her entire life. Consider a man who is so paranoid that he trusts no one, even those who have proved themselves trustworthy for many years. In every action, no matter how innocent, he suspects a fiendish plot against him, and he responds accordingly by hatching fiendish plots against others and sometimes carrying them out. His hatred encompasses everyone, sometimes even himself; he would not mind seeing the entire world blown up, himself included. Killing other people means no more to him than swatting flies, and it is all justified in his mind by the fanatical belief that they have all either conceived of or are carrying out monstrous plots against him. That the hatred and paranoia pervade every nook and cranny of his life is clear enough. But because of this should he be called insane?

Sometimes the condition pervades only an aspect of the person's life, leaving the rest quite normal. A woman may be indistinguishable from everyone else in personal and social relationships, but when one or both of her parents are mentioned she flies into a rage. No amount of reasoning ("They were doing the best they could, by their own lights") moves her, no evidence

---

[19] Ibid.

[20] The last two quotes are from Minutes of Evidence of the Select Committee on the Homicide Law Amendment Bill (1874), Q. 274.

makes the slightest difference. The threat of punishment fails to deter her, and in the end she kills them both. Is she to be called insane?

Strangest of all is the phenomenon labeled "temporary insanity." The assumption here seems to be that someone can be "perfectly normal" all day long until one o'clock, then be insane for two minutes, and then sane again the rest of the day. Is there such a thing as temporary insanity? Most people are inclined to say no, but wasn't the ice-pick killer "temporarily insane" just at the moment he saw the ring and wielded the ice pick? Only then did the (real or alleged) irresistible impulse overcome him. Or was he insane all the time, and his insanity was only manifested in action at that moment?

Regardless of what we think in that case, "temporary insanity" is a convenient loophole in the law many times. In a well-known case during World War II, an American flyer in Burma was caught in the burning wreckage of his plane; there was no way of extricating him and in a minute or so he would burn to death. He saw this and cried, "Shoot me, somebody!" No one dared, until a friend carried out the request. For this the friend was court-martialed, and since the law of the armed forces permitted no other penalty than death for deliberate killing, there seemed no escape from this sentence, which everyone agreed he did not deserve. The man was therefore let off by being declared "temporarily insane." The irony is that he was probably never more sane than during the minute he took stock of the situation, rapidly but carefully weighed the consequences, and shot.

Yet, as usual with the law, every silver cloud has a dark lining. There are persons who have committed murder while high on LSD and who have been found innocent "by reason of temporary insanity" due to the influence of the drugs. Why does this verdict seem unjust? Perhaps it is the fact that a person who takes LSD does so voluntarily and is aware of possible consequences; there is also the utilitarian consideration that such a decision sets a precedent for more people to take LSD and commit murders under its influence knowing or believing that they will be let off.

The concept of insanity, if it is not too vague to be called a concept at all, becomes more elusive the more we look at actual cases, with the full facts of the history of the accused before us, and are asked to distinguish the sane from the insane. At best, there seems to be a spectrum of infinite shades of color, with white becoming gray and dark gray shading into black, though we are asked to call each case either white or black. It is no wonder, under these circumstances, that many states of the United States simply call persons insane—which means, for all practical purposes, that they can be committed to a mental institution—if they are proven to be a danger to themselves or to others. But is being a danger to oneself or others the same as being insane?

2. PATERNALISM

When you promise someone a favor, sign a contract, or consent to surgery, it is generally assumed that you do these things *voluntarily,* "of your own volition." What this means, according to judgments handed down at Nuremberg (which are typical of many formulations), is that you exercise "free power of choice without the intervention of any element of force, fraud, deceit, duress, over-reaching, or other ulterior form of constraint or coercion." As we indicated before, if you gave a robber your money at gunpoint, you did not give it voluntarily; you did it under threat of force: you would not have given over the money "of your own free will." You still exercised your choice (to surrender your money rather than be killed), but you had to make this unwelcome choice because someone else forced it on you. Similarly, if you gave money to a blackmailer upon threat of exposure of some secret which would have meant loss of your job or reputation, you did not give up the money voluntarily, but under threat.

But there are degrees of pressure, and hence degrees of voluntariness: one act may be more or less voluntary than another one. As we have seen, there are various kinds of pressure other than the threat of death (which is just the extreme case), and indeed there can be pressure without threats at all. A friend may "pressure" you into making a hasty decision, claiming that there is a dire emergency which calls for immediate actions; you don't deliberate (though, as it turns out, there was no emergency), and later regret your decision. You weren't forced to do what you did, yet doing it wasn't fully voluntary either. There does not seem to be a sharp line here: pressure of various kinds does cause people to do what they would not do "in a cool hour" in the light of their considered judgment.

In billionaire Howard Hughes's last years, he had been in the hands of the "Mormon Mafia" for some time and his tendencies toward secretiveness and paranoia were already well developed, but there were still times when he apparently yearned to escape from the psychological vise he had helped to construct. On one occasion, according to one account, Hughes and his entourage had moved to Bayshore Inn overlooking Vancouver Bay:

> When they took Hughes up the elevator to the suite they had picked out for him, Hughes went over to the window and looked out, instead of scuttling into his bedroom.
> "The aides had picked the big middle room for The Office," Margulis [one of the men] said. "The boss gazed out the window a little while and watched a seaplane landing in the harbor. He said he liked the view.
> "The aides didn't like that one bit," said Margulis. "They told me to get him away from the window and into his bedroom.
> "Then something happened that really frosted me. The boss said he liked the big room and the view and said it would make a nice sitting

room for him. He hadn't had a sitting room for years, and he'd always had the windows taped and never looked out.

"They warned him that somebody could fly past the sitting room in a helicopter and shoot his picture with a telephoto lens. 'Here's *your* room,' they told him, and took him into another little blacked-out bedroom, with the draperies all taped down tight. He just went along with them, and they had him back in the cave again. After a while he got into bed, and called for a movie, and everything was just the way it had been for years." [21]

Whenever Hughes showed glimmerings of a desire to escape, he was pushed back into his cocoon again. True, nobody *forced* him; his people conned him. They were afraid that if he went public again, they would be out of jobs and their importance to him (as well as their inflated salaries) would be over; so they worked on him mentally at what they knew was a weak spot and it worked. His consent to the arrangement described could hardly be called fully voluntary.

To be voluntary a decision should also be an *informed* decision. It should not be based on deceit, fraud, or the withholding of relevant information. If you go to buy a diamond and the merchant sells you a piece of glass, the sale was fraudulent, for it was not a voluntary exchange of your money for the product you asked to buy. The sale was based on deceit and misinformation: your decision to buy a diamond at that price may have been arrived at without coercion or pressure, but your buying a piece of glass at the price, nevertheless was not voluntary. If you asked for water and your host brought you a clear liquid that looked like water but contained poison, your drinking of the liquid was the result of deceit: you would not voluntarily have drunk the poison. When a patient consents to an operation, but the physician conceals the possible consequences of the operation from the patient, the patient's consent is not an informed consent. Some would say that what is required is consent that is both voluntary *and* informed; others would say that being informed is just part of what it *means* to speak of voluntary consent and that without full information the consent is not properly called "voluntary."

There is a problem, however, about how fully informed the consent should be. True, a patient should be told all the relevant facts prior to making a decision. But a physician could go on endlessly citing medical facts or theories which *might* be relevant to the case, and even if the physician does this, there may still be other unknown factors which could be highly relevant to the patient's decision. A patient can give *relatively* informed consent, but it would be difficult to give *fully* informed consent: information, too, is a matter of degree.

When inmates of prisons and mental institutions "give their consent" to psychosurgery or new experimental drugs and vaccines, it is extremely un-

[21] *Time,* December 13, 1976, p. 36.

likely that their consent is either informed or without pressure. Even if no threats are used, the prisoners know that if they do not participate in the experiment they will be penalized in some way, either through being denied early release or by the removal of certain privileges. Coercion always lurks in the background, even if the swords are not drawn. It is also unlikely that the consent elicited is even reasonably well-informed; the physicians may casually ask inmates, "How would you guys like to join an interesting experiment; it won't take much of your time," and in their anxiety to have guinea pigs for some new technique or product they may fail to mention the dangerous side-effects or possibly fatal consequences of what they are proposing. (They are not likely to get lawsuits from the spouses of dead prisoners, who in any case probably will never learn what has really happened.)

A third condition may also be mentioned which is distinct from the other two but is often found together with them: the person who consents must be in a *rational* psychological state—one in which he or she can deliberate coolly and weigh the alternatives on the basis of fully divulged information. There may well be occasions when the consenter is not pressured in any way and all the relevant facts have been clearly laid out, yet he or she is in no position to make a decision because of extreme depression, grief, great pain (the promise of relief predisposing the patient to sign anything), or mental confusion as to the importance of it all. Undertakers get grieving widows and widowers to buy expensive coffins when they are in such a state; and salespeople see an opening for a con-job when they can catch the unwary victim in a passive mental state. A person in a state of extreme depression may be quite lucid as to the facts, but in such a state a recital of facts that would ordinarily horrify (such as the prospect of his or her own imminent death or even the extinction of all life on the planet) would not move the individual to any kind of response to avoid it. A person in extreme depression may jump out of a high window, not through pressure, not because he or she doesn't know the fatal consequences, but because at the moment the individual simply doesn't care.

Regarding contracts the law requires that they be "voluntarily entered into"; and while there is seldom an attempt to define "voluntary," many contracts are declared null and void by the courts when there is a suspicion of deceit, fraud, coercion, or even great pressure. If you were disappearing into the quicksand and someone appeared with a long stick to rescue you but stopped a moment and said, "First I want you to sign this contract saying you'll give me everything you own," even if you do sign, such a contract would be null and void because it was signed "under duress." And without the quicksand, if you signed a contract consenting to be someone's slave for life, the courts will still declare it null and void, not because you had been pressured or coerced (you may not have been), not because you didn't know the relevant facts and consequences (you might have) but because such an agreement would put an end to all your freedom from that point on. Indeed, your doing so would be considered sufficient reason for believing that you were "not in a rational frame of mind." (It is a dubious empirical point, however; should the signing of such an agreement be taken as prima facie evidence of your being in a confused psychological state? And if not, should such a contract be honored?) Other contracts, such as suicide pacts, are also legally null and void, because, if honored, they would lead to the contractors' death, whereas legal contracts are supposed to be aids in the business of life; thus the State attempts to "protect people against themselves" by not honoring such contracts, often on the ground that contracts of that kind cannot be said to be fully voluntary.

"Protecting people against themselves" is the theme of *paternalism.* You act paternalistically toward someone when you do something for that person's benefit but against his or her will at the time. (It may not actually *be* to the individual's benefit, as long as you think it is when you perform the action.) We shall consider both *personal* paternalism and *legal* paternalism.

John Stuart Mill, along with most writers on ethics in Europe and America, was strongly against paternalism. In his work *On Liberty,* Mill wrote:

> Neither one person, nor any number of persons, is warranted in saying to another human creature of ripe years, that he shall not do with his life for his own benefit what he chooses to do with it. . . . The only purpose for which power can be rightfully exercised over any member of a civilized community, against his will, is to prevent harm to others. He cannot rightfully be compelled to do or forbear because it will be better for him to do so, because it will make him happier, or because, in the opinion of others, to do so would be wise, or even right.[22]

In general, thought Mill, people should be free to make their own mistakes and then hopefully profit by those mistakes and not repeat them later; and even if they do not profit by them, "there is a part of the life of every person who has come to years of discretion, with which the individuality of that person ought to reign uncontrolled either by any other person or by the public collectively." In saying these things Mill probably went far beyond any view that could be justified on strictly utilitarian grounds, for he said, "a man's mode of laying out his existence is the best, not because it is best in itself, but because it is his own mode. . . . It is the privilege and proper condition of a human being, arrived at the maturity of his faculties, to use and interpret experience in his own way."[23]

Yet there are occasions on which almost everyone would behave paternalistically. Suppose a friend says to you, "Be sure to wake me up at 6:00 A.M. for my new job," but when the time comes she doesn't want to get up and doesn't appear to care about the job. Thus, at time t_1 she wanted you to get her up, but at time t_2 she didn't want you to. Since you have to go against

[22]John Stuart Mill, *On Liberty* (1859), Chapter 1.
[23]Ibid.

one or the other of her wishes, what should you do? You would probably do the one that you believed would most benefit her, although it went against her wishes at the time that you did it. We usually believe that such paternalistic behavior (called *personal paternalism*) is justified, not only because it accords with a person's wishes at one of two times, but because (we believe) it will benefit the individual; in this case, by going against your friend's wishes at time t_2, you promote her long-term goals (keeping the job) and may even (eventually) receive her thanks for going against her wishes then. If you had acted against her wishes to promote your own goals, however, you would have been using her as a means to your ends, and in that case your paternalism might not have been justifiable.

Consider another case. A patient in a hospital is extremely depressed and refuses food; after several such refusals an attendant force-feeds the patient, thus keeping him alive. If we are totally antipaternalistic, we may say, "If the patient wants to die, let him die!" Yet, in many cases the patient will later thank the attendant for doing what he did. The attendant may have gone against the temporary wishes of the patient, but his action made possible the fulfillment of the long-term wish of the patient, namely, to stay alive (the wish to die being only a temporary aberration). Wasn't the attendant's action then justifiable? If the patient continues for some time to wish for death, he can bring this about in many ways; but as long as he desires life at times t_1, t_2, t_4, and t_5, and only desires death at t_3, it would seem preferable to place the continuing desire above the temporary one, not only because it is the "steady" desire of the patient, but because when there is a choice between life and death, it is always preferable to assume, unless there is overwhelming evidence to the contrary (such as continuing pain with no hope of recovery), that a person will opt for life. At least then the individual has a chance to exercise his or her choice again.

Personal paternalism is one thing, but *legal paternalism* is quite another. Legal paternalism occurs when laws are passed by the State limiting the freedom of action of individuals, not for the benefit of others, but for their own benefit (or what the State believes to be their own benefit). Most states in this country require motorcyclists to wear helmets, because of the high incidence of head injuries in motorcycle accidents: if a cyclist is too foolish to wear a helmet for protection, the states impose a penalty on him or her for failure to do so. Even if the cyclist doesn't want to wear one, the states require usage for the cyclist's own good. Many would say, "It's the cyclist's own business whether to wear one; it's his or her risk." The issue is complicated, however, by the fact that after an accident, the victim may have to be supported in a hospital at the taxpayers' expense for months or years, and the simple precaution of wearing a helmet would seem a small price to pay to prevent such a contingency.

If a police officer sees a person attempting to commit suicide by jumping into the river, one of the officer's duties, as a representative of the State, is to attempt to rescue the person if that is possible without substantial risk to himself. Why should the officer intervene, if the person wants to commit suicide? By rescuing the would-be suicide he or she is acting against the person's will (at the time) though for that individual's benefit (or so it is assumed). The police officer's actions (which are not legally required of the ordinary citizen) can be justified by saying that he or she is probably fulfilling the person's long-term wishes; that one should always assume that life is preferable to death, even for the person who is tired of life at the time; and that if the individual wants to commit suicide later, that option will still be available.

Legal paternalism, however, can easily get out of hand. Many people are moral busybodies, who want nothing more than for others to act in ways which they (the busybodies) think the other persons ought to—for the others' own good, of course. It is one thing for someone to be on the receiving end of a constant barrage of speeches beginning with, "It would be for your own good if you . . ."; it is another to be forced to accept such advice through legislation which authorizes penalties for not accepting it. "Adult bookstores and X-rated movies should be legally prohibited, for your own good, of course" and "Prostitution and homosexuality should be prohibited, even if people want to engage in them, because it would be better for people if they didn't" are examples of legal paternalism. Indeed, the full application of legal paternalism in a society results in *legal moralism*, the infliction of an entire moral code on a nation by law. In Moslem nations, for example, everyone is required to observe Moslem morality. Nothing is left to choice; everything—diet, sex, marriage—is controlled within the very narrow limits set by the law of the land. In more "liberal" nations, morality is a matter of choice, up to the point where a person attempts to violate the rights of others.

Nevertheless, there are persons who seem to leave no other alternative than to deal with them paternalistically, since they are unable to take care of themselves. One such group consists of persons who are well along into senility. When an elderly husband and wife can no longer take care of themselves but refuse to leave their home, either the State or their children (protected by laws enabling them to do this) must presumably intervene on the elderly persons' behalf. Suppose that an elderly couple "wants to get even with the power company" by refusing to pay the utility bills, with the result that gas and electricity are cut off. It isn't that the couple doesn't have the money, but that, out of a deep distrust of the utility company, the two have decided to "show them a thing or two" by refusing to pay. At this point the son or other relative gets power of attorney to write checks on their behalf to pay for the utilities. It is possible, of course, to say, "If they're so stupid as not to pay the utility bills, let them freeze!" But they would pay the bills if they were "of sound mind"; since they are not, someone must see to the matter for them, for their own good. When people no longer are able to foresee the consequences of their own actions, it would appear that someone else must do so on their behalf.

A second group for whom legal paternalism may be justified consists of those who are mentally incompetent, perhaps for their entire lives—idiots, imbeciles, people with severe mental handicaps, and (the most fluid group of all) "the insane." The reasons in this case are like the ones in the case of senility. But there is a danger in the fact that the authorities can place so many people in this category. If a married couple wants to get hold of parents' money a bit early, the two may have them declared mentally incompetent, which deprives the parents of their legal rights, including their bank account and property. Or if a somewhat cantankerous old woman lives alone in a cottage with numerous cats which annoy the neighbors, they may complain to the local authorities, who can ship the old woman to a mental institution and confiscate her property "to repay the state for her room and board." Such injustices are constantly committed by those who have the power of the law on their side, and any person who is a bit of a nuisance or is the subject of complaints by family or neighbors is fair game for institutionalization, which can be accomplished quite legally by having the person declared mentally incompetent.

The third and most difficult group which may sometimes require paternalistic behavior consists of infants and children. Parents must constantly act against the child's will for the child's benefit, since the child cannot appreciate the consequences of his or her own actions. Parents must pull a child out of the path of a speeding car, prohibit bicycling on a crowded highway, or require certain household tasks in order to accustom the child to the idea of work. But unlike senile persons, children will develop into adults, and the tendency of parents is to continue to behave paternalistically toward children even when they should be making their own decisions and profiting from their own mistakes. In such matters the law usually sides with the parents and requires children to remain under the parents' (real or imagined) "protective wing" until the children are legally of age (usually eighteen).

We have discussed some of the problems the parent-child relationship causes in the section on children's rights (see pp. 275–79). When should children be allowed full freedom of action? The ten-year-old son would like to try out some LSD; he would gladly give his voluntary consent (he isn't pressured, and so on), though at his age it could hardly be informed consent (with full knowledge of possible consequences). The parent feels justified in prohibiting the child from doing it, and the prohibition is for the child's own benefit. The twelve-year-old daughter is invited to go out on a sexual exploit with a man whom she knows; again, she would gladly give her consent, but is not the mother within her rights to say no? Still, despite these examples, parents are inclined to be paternalistic even when the time for it is past. There are cases when parents have prohibited a son or daughter from entering a certain trade or profession even though it's what the child wants and is also well suited for. A father may think he is acting for his son's benefit in such a case, but is he? Parents often think they are acting for their children's benefit when in fact they are only forcing on the child what *they* (the parents) want them to be or do. Even if children turn out to be mistaken, it is sometimes preferable to let them find out for themselves rather than to be prohibited with the words, "It's all for your own good."

But the line between paternalism and self-determination is very hard to draw: it varies from child to child, and from parent to parent (some parents being authoritarian, some permissive). Most parents don't know when to let go gracefully; but others let go too soon or never apply the reins at all, and by abdicating responsibility entirely they cause their offspring to go out into the world as spoiled brats unprepared for life. A very delicate balancing act must be performed here, and the only general rule that would seem applicable, both for the sake of utility and for protecting the children's rights, is "Prepare your children for life by letting them make their own decisions as much as possible; but remember that part of the children's preparation for life also consists of rules of behavior that they must learn to observe, whether or not they want to at the time."

Euthanasia

Euthanasia, or mercy killing, is the deliberate ending of a human life for reasons of mercy, such as to avoid pain and suffering from an incurable disease. *Voluntary euthanasia,* in which the patient makes the decision to end his or her life, is not paternalistic; but *nonvoluntary euthanasia,* when done on behalf of someone else for that person's own good but without that person's consent, is.

Voluntary euthanasia is like suicide, except that instead of the person causing his or her own death, others do it at the request of the sufferer. If a person has the right to life, it would seem, doesn't that individual have a right to death? Others, of course, have the right to refuse or deny the request. But if a patient requests a friend or physician to administer a painless but lethal pill, and the other person agrees, are anyone's rights being violated? Shouldn't such an action be permissible?

Voluntary euthanasia is more complicated than suicide, however. How can we be sure that the patient's request is fully voluntary? If a patient expresses a wish to die, we cannot be quite sure how to interpret the remark. Is it a carefully considered decision? Is it based on all the relevant facts of the case? (What if the patient has been told that there is no hope for recovery when there is?) Is it based on a momentary impression of the course of the illness? Is the remark perhaps made in a moment of great pain, and should it therefore be discounted? The wish to be quietly put to sleep, sincerely meant today in a mood of depression, may pass tomorrow. Should we, then, take the patient's word at time t_1 or at time t_2?

Even if the consent is fully voluntary, however, problems still arise about administering euthanasia to someone else. In most countries it is legally forbidden to cause the death of another person, even for the most humane of reasons and even if the patient repeatedly requests it. The main reason for this prohibition probably is that the precautions needed to be taken are so extensive that it would be virtually impossible to make them foolproof. Consider: (1) What if you told others that you would like to be painlessly put out of the way in case you became incurably ill rather than suffer protracted pain, but once you reached that state you changed your mind but were incapable of conveying to them your revised wishes? (2) What if *in their opinion* you were incurably ill, and they convinced you that it was true, but nevertheless it was not true? We never know for sure that someone is incurably ill until death occurs. Cases of spontaneous remission, in which even large malignant tumors disappeared and physicians couldn't figure out why, are common. Of course, even if you stood a slim chance of recovery, you might prefer to have others terminate your life to avoid further pain, but all such details—such as how slim the chance must be—would have to be arranged in advance, and even with extensive and careful prearrangements you still might change your mind later. (3) What would prevent relatives, eager for an inheritance, from killing you prematurely with the excuse that, after all, it was a mercy killing, to which you had agreed in advance in a signed document? A little "accident," an injection of a lethal drug, would do the job, and under the law they would only be carrying out your wishes as expressed in the document. No matter how many precautions had been taken, might you not have something to fear from such relatives? Perhaps this difficulty could be overcome if you and only you were permitted to self-administer the lethal dose. But you might be in no condition to carry out the act; you would have to take others' word for it what the dose contained; and in the face of what you thought was impending death you might be in a miserable and depressed frame of mind and take the lethal dose at once, even though, with time to think about it, you wouldn't have done it. (Relatives might even drug you into a state of depression in which you *would* do it.) (4) If euthanasia was legalized, patients might well fear to enter a hospital, believing that some way would be contrived to get them out of the way, perhaps by entering their rooms in the quiet of the night. There might not be enough evidence afterward to convict the guilty party. There are so many "slips between the cup and the lip" that the law may indeed be justified in prohibiting euthanasia no matter what the circumstances. Even if the patient signed a request in the presence of three witnesses, it is possible that such slips could occur.

If there are problems with voluntary euthanasia, they multiply when it is nonvoluntary. If the patient is able to consent or not consent in full knowledge of the facts, and does not consent, then, of course, killing him or her is outright murder. Even if it is done to spare the patient pain, killing someone without consent "for his own good" would seem to be about the least justifiable form of paternalism.

The difficult cases are those in which the person is not able to say either yes or no. Perhaps the patient is so far gone as to be unable to respond or to comprehend the question; in that case it would be difficult to find a justification for the killing. Or perhaps the patient is a newborn child. We would mercifully put an incurably ill pet out of the way to end its pain; would it be any the less humane to let a terminally ill infant die when what remained of his or her life would consist largely of suffering and pain? Most ancient peoples practiced infanticide, allowing malformed babies to die of exposure. Infanticide is no longer practiced, but many believe it might be the most merciful course: if the child could expect no happiness in life and parents could expect a great deal of unhappiness in spending all their time caring for the child, would death not be the preferable alternative? Might the infant, if he or she did grow up, even say, "Why did you let me live?" But, of course, we never know this; it is only speculation. Most persons are glad to be alive in spite of great physical handicaps.

Active euthanasia consists of taking active steps (such as administering a poison) to end a person's life. *Passive euthanasia* consists of simply letting the person die; it may include removing the artificial life-support systems until nature takes its course. A physician who actively does something to cause a patient to die can be charged with murder, whereas no such charge is usually brought if he or she declines to use "extraordinary means" to keep the patient alive. Even the Catholic Church does not require a physician to use extraordinary means, such as indefinite continuation of a patient on a respirator to sustain life.

Morally if not legally, however, the difference between killing and letting die is more tenuous. If there is a serious congenital disease which would cause a newborn distress and pain throughout life and render the child permanently incapable of attending to essential bodily functions such as eating, some say that a case can be made for doing something that will painlessly cause death:

> I can understand why some people are opposed to all euthanasia, and insist that such infants must be allowed to live. I think I can also understand why other people favor destroying these babies quickly and painlessly. But why should anyone favor letting "dehydration and infection wither a tiny being over hours and days"? The doctrine that says that a baby may be allowed to dehydrate and wither, but may not be given an injection that would end its life without suffering, seems so patently cruel as to require no refutation.[24]

If someone believes, with the Catholic Church, that killing, even mercy killing, is wrong because condemned by God but that letting die (under certain extraordinary circumstances) is not, then the two can be morally distinguished on theological premises. But for anyone who has no such theological beliefs, it is indeed difficult to see why the passive method is more acceptable than the active. Consider the following case:

[24] James Rachels, "Active and Passive Euthanasia," *Killing and Letting Die,* ed. Bonnie Steinbock (Englewood Cliffs, N.J.: Prentice-Hall, 1980), pp. 64–65.

"It's a condition called spina bifida," Dr. Savano said. "There's a hole in the baby's back just below the shoulder blades, and some of the nerves from the spine are protruding through it. The baby will have little or no control over her legs, and she won't be able to control her bladder or bowels." Dr. Savano paused to see if Mr. Blake was understanding him. "The legs and feet are also deformed to some extent because of the defective spinal nerves."

Mr. Blake was shaking his head, paying close attention but hardly able to accept what he was being told.

"There's one more thing," Dr. Savano said. "The spinal defect is making the head fill up with liquid from the spinal canal. That's putting pressure on the brain. We can be sure that the brain is already damaged, but if the pressure continues, the child will die."

"Is there anything that can be done?" Blake asked. "Anything at all?"

Dr. Savano nodded to Dr. Hinds. "We can do a lot," Dr. Hinds said. "We can drain the fluid from the head, repair the opening in the spine, and later we can operate on the feet and legs."

"Then why aren't you doing it?" Mr. Blake asked. "Do I have to agree to it? If I do, then I agree. Please go ahead."

"It's not that simple," Dr. Hinds said. "You see, we can perform surgery, but that won't turn your baby into a normal child. She will always be paralyzed and mentally retarded. To what extent, we can't say now. Her bodily wastes will have to be drained to the outside by the means of artificial devices that we'll have to connect surgically. There will have to be several operations, probably, to get the drain from her head to work properly. A number of operations on her feet will be necessary."

"Oh, God," Mr. Blake said. "Hilda and I can't take it. We don't have enough money for the operations. And even if we did, we would have to spend the rest of our lives taking care of the child."

"The child could be put into a state institution," Dr. Hinds said.

"That's even worse," Mr. Blake said. "Just handing our problem to somebody else. And what kind of life would she have? A pitiful, miserable life."

None of the rest of us said anything. "You said she would die without the operation to drain her head," Mr. Blake said. "How long would that take?"

"A few hours perhaps," Dr. Savano said. "But we can't be sure. It may take several days, and conceivably she might not die at all."

"Oh, God," Mr. Blake said again. "I don't want her to suffer. Can she just be put to sleep painlessly?" [25]

[25] From *Intervention and Reflection: Basic Issues in Medical Ethics* by Ronald Munson, ed. © 1979 by Wadsworth Publishing Co., Inc. Reprinted by permission of Wadsworth Publishing Co., Belmont, California 94002.

Legally, there might be problems with a physician doing this. But morally, would it not be preferable to letting the child die a slow painful death? The patient's death is just as intentional one way as the other. And would a physician be doing her a favor by letting her remain alive under these conditions?

It might be said in such cases that the death of the patient would *not* be intentional but a side-effect or incidental result of what was intended. Using this as a justification, a patient has the right to refuse treatment (and presumably a parent has the right to refuse treatment on behalf of a child). If the patient (or parent) requests that treatment be stopped, a physician, who is after all there to serve the patient's wishes, is surely obliged to do so—just as a surgeon must have the patient's consent before undertaking surgery. The right to refuse treatment in such cases is not the same as the right to voluntary euthanasia. According to one author, "The purpose of the right to refuse medical treatment is not to give persons a right to decide whether to live or die, but to protect them from the unwanted interferences of others."[26]

In cases in which continued treatment has no chance of improving the patient's condition and brings more pain and discomfort than it does relief, death can also be brought on by discontinuing the treatment. In such instances treatment is stopped in order to avoid the pain and discomfort, not directly for the purpose of letting the patient die.

The moral rule invoked in discontinuing treatment in these cases is called the "law of double effect," which is accepted by the Catholic Church as well as others. If you intend A (death), your act is a sin (or legally, a crime); but if you intend B and A is a by-product or unintended consequence of B, there is no sin and no crime. If you are caught on the twentieth floor of a blazing building and jump out of the window to escape the fire, you are not guilty of committing suicide even though you know that a consequence of escaping the fire will be your death from the fall. If your intention is not death but simply to refuse treatment ("to be protected from the unwanted interferences of others") or to relieve the great pain and distress which accompanies chemotherapy or some other form of treatment, then you have not done anything with the specific *intent* to cause death: death is only an indirect consequence of actions you undertake for other reasons.

The law of double effect, however, has itself been questioned. If you know that doing one thing will have something else as its effect, how is this really different from intending that effect? Still, it remains to be shown that a person's death, intended or not, is not sometimes the most desirable result. From a utilitarian point of view, if continued life would mean only continued pain, with no hope of cure, death would certainly be the preferable alternative; and from the vantage point of human rights, it would require a good reason to say that a person may not decide on the means—either quick ones, such as through a fatal injection, or slow ones, such as the pursuit of a drug

---

[26] Bonnie Steinbock, "The Intentional Termination of Life," in *Killing and Letting Die,* p. 71.

habit—that would bring about his or her own death. The choice of death for someone else, such as one's own newborn children, remains a far more difficult problem.

3. FREEDOM

We all want, or say we want, to be free. But it is not always clear what we are saying when we say this. If we heard a woman say "I'm free!" we wouldn't know what she was referring to: free from a dictatorship? from marriage bonds? from the irritations of the job? from addiction to alcohol? Or she might mean that she was free *to do* certain things: free to marry again, free to spend the money she just won, free to eat the foods she likes after a long diet. If we knew the full context of her remarks, we might know specifically what she was talking about. There are several distinct ways in which people talk about being free.

In one sense, people are free if they *have what they want;* and anything that stands in the way of getting what they want limits their freedom. For the Stoic, being free means paring down your desires so that you want no material things but only the inner peace and resignation of *apatheia.* For the adventurer, being free means leading a life as full of excitement and adventure as possible (and having the wherewithal to do this). For the hunter, being free means having many miles of wilderness in which to enjoy nature and live off the land. (Such a person could be free in the nineteenth century but would find it more difficult today.)

In another sense, people's freedom is proportional to the *range of choices open to them:* the more options they have, the freer they are. In this sense, being wealthy makes individuals freer, because they can have a lot more things than they can without it (even though there are things that money can't buy).

But already there is conflict. Suppose you can choose among a thousand things, none of which you want very much; on the other hand, suppose your choice is limited to one, which is just exactly what you want. In which of these situations are you freer? Suppose you are in a locked room (that you either don't know is locked or don't care) doing just what you want; you haven't many options but you have what you want. Are you freer than if you could go wherever you wanted but *not* do what you most desired? [27]

There are also people whom we may feel sorry for even though they do have what they want, because their range of wants is so limited. They can choose steak or lobster or crab or bouillabaisse, but all they want is hamburger: that's all they've had and they don't care to try anything else. Or, they are no longer under the dictatorship that restricted their activities, but all they want is life under the dictatorship: they love the dictator and don't want any other kind of life. They are like the caged lions that, after the cage

[27] See Joel Feinberg, *Social Philosophy* (Englewood Cliffs, N.J.: Prentice-Hall, 1973), Chapter 1.

is opened, still stay inside the cage. They are free to do or have many things, only they aren't disposed to avail themselves of the opportunities; the range of choices open to them is, as they are now, useless to them.

If you have everything you want (not just material things, but whatever it is you want), hopefully you will be happy; in this sense happiness is closely connected with freedom. On the other hand, if being free means having a maximum of choices open to you, then this does not guarantee happiness but only helps to provide the *means* to it: some people have an enormous range of choices open to them (through wealth, prestige, fame) and still aren't happy because they "don't have what they really want." In this sense, being free doesn't necessarily mean being happy. Indeed, many people don't want freedom all that much: they would prefer to be told what to do and not have to make choices but have most of their decisions made for them. People who enlist in the army for twenty years often belong in this category, and so do the people living under the Inquisition described in Dostoyevsky's "The Grand Inquisitor" in *The Brothers Karamazov.*

Perhaps the most fruitful way to approach claims about freedom is to distinguish first between *freedom from* and *freedom to,* and then ask individuals what they are (or are not) free from or free to do. Freedom from is called *negative freedom:* it is freedom from constraints that prevent the doing of certain things (usually, but not necessarily, the doing of things that people want to do). If a prisoner has been in chains and is released, he is now free from his chains. If a writer with writer's block goes through psychotherapy and now no longer has it, she has been freed from her inability to write. If a man has been prevented by his government from writing anything contrary to what the government says, and he escapes to another country, he is now free from the censorship that constrained him. If a woman was dominated by a tyrannical husband and succeeds in getting a divorce, she is now free from his domination. There are all kinds of things people may be free from, some of which they may not want to be free from (e.g., the bonds of marriage) and some of which they may not even realize they are free from (e.g., the bonds of dictatorship, for people living in the United States).

There is also freedom to, sometimes called *positive freedom.* We are all free to do many things, some of which we may have no desire to do, like eating pig's kidneys or trying to swim the Hellespont. We are free to spend our wages on various things, since stores here offer a wide range of choices. We are free to stay at home or go to the movies tonight. We are free to write a letter to an aunt, to phone her, or to ignore her entirely. We are free to do anything we can do by choosing to do it, and of course we are free to do it even if we do not choose to. We are free to walk across the room, but we are not free to fly in the air like birds; we are free to plunge into the water but not to stay under water for an hour (without scuba-diving or other equipment) while staying alive. Some have said that the inability to fly or to remain under water is no lack of freedom, but it is difficult to see why not, since it is something human beings cannot do, though it's a lack of freedom that we won't *miss* if we don't desire to fly like birds or swim like fish.

The two senses of freedom are related, of course: if you are in chains, you are not free to walk about in the streets; if you are not free from a dictatorship, you are not free to speak or write as you please; and so on. A considerable amount of freedom from is required before you are free to do many of the things you want to do. If you are locked up in jail and in chains, you are not free to do many things at all, even though, once released, you might fail to do (or not care to do) most of the things you would then be free to do.

Still, there are great differences in emphasis. A poor peasant is not free to do nearly as many things as a wealthy person in a metropolis with diverse cultural interests; but if the peasant lives under a benevolent government, in a fairly remote region where he is largely self-sufficient, he is free *from* rules and regulations imposed by others and can conduct his life pretty much as he likes. The army officer, by contrast, is free *to* do many more things: he can give orders and make sure that they are carried out; many conveniences are available to him that are not available to those of lesser rank; and yet he is himself hedged about by rules and regulations from above, a violation of which would quickly assure his loss of position and influence. He is not nearly as free from the commands and rules that bind him as is the peasant.

Where does "being a slave to one's passions" fit in? If a woman has an irresistible urge to gamble (assuming that it is really irresistible), she is not free *to* do certain things that she would have done (and presumably wanted to do) if she did not have the addiction. And because she cannot do those things, she is not free to do them until she is free *from* the addiction. When someone isn't free from whatever-it-is, it is like a stumbling block in the way of achieving certain goals which might be achieved if the stumbling block was not there.

The kind of freedom that is called *political freedom* has to do chiefly with freedom *from* one specific kind of constraint—the use of force, or threat of the use of force, against citizens by the government. The more a government imposes such constraints, the less citizens are free *to* live their life as they like. At the same time, some government constraints make civilized life possible: without a police force you may not be free to walk the streets in safety (though even with a police force you may not be able to do this). You are not free (without a penalty, at least) to drive on the right or left side of the road as you please; but because the law prescribes which side you should drive on, you may drive more safely than you could without the law. This is the truth embodied in the saying that freedom is possible only under law. The trouble is that in the guise of protecting you, there is often far too much law; when you are regulated to death, more freedom is lost than gained.

To complicate matters further, we sometimes speak not of individuals but of *nations* as being free: "It's a free country," or "Uganda is not a free nation." The latter means, as a rule, that the citizens of a given nation (or most of the citizens, perhaps everyone but the ruling hierarchy) are not free: they are not free from tyranny, not free to do many or most of the things they want to. What determines a nation's freedom is the nature of its political structure, which either places severe restrictions on the freedom of those who live there or permits citizens to make the most of their own choices without government intervention. A free country that did not contain free individuals would be a contradiction in terms; to speak of a free country is simply a shorthand way of speaking of the high degree of freedom the individuals in that country possess.

All these kinds of freedom can be distinguished from one another, and yet many philosophers have alleged that none of these distinctions cuts to the heart of the problem. To say that Mr. Smith is free to do a certain act, they say, is to say at least this: that he *could* have acted otherwise than he did— that, for example, he could have done *B* instead of *A*. And, they ask, what if it should turn out that nobody can ever act otherwise than he or she does? Wouldn't that mean that freedom is nothing but an illusion?

"But it's obvious," I may reply, "that I have real choices, that I can do either act *A* or act *B*. Suppose that act *A* is walking toward the door and act *B* is walking toward the window. Are you really prepared to say that I can only do *A* but can't do *B?* Do you want to place a bet on it? You bet me $1,000 that I will walk to the door, and I'll win the bet by walking to the window. Do you want to put your money where your mouth is?"

An opponent is not likely to take me up on this bet. "You don't get what I mean," he says. "I'm not saying you can't walk to the window if you choose or that you can't walk to the door if you choose. I'm saying that when you sat down at the table just now, you could not have done anything else but just that; no other course of action was possible for you." And if we reply, "I'll prove you wrong; I'll get up and go out of the room and *not* sit at the desk. You want to bet that I can't?" He will reply, "I'm not saying that you can't do it *now*. You'll do it just to win the bet if for no other reason. I'm saying that at the moment you sat down a while ago, you *could not* have done anything other than what you did."

But how is it possible to prove this? At first glance, at least, it seems to be obviously false. I did sit down at the table; but I could have gone to the refrigerator to make a sandwich instead. I almost did, then decided that I'd better sit down and get to work. But it seems perfectly plain to me that I could have done the other if I'd chosen to do it instead.

But this is just what the other person denies. "You could indeed have gone to the refrigerator *if* you had chosen to do so, but with you, just as you were at that moment, including your state of mind (your half-hunger which still wasn't sufficient to cause you to go to the refrigerator), you could not have done anything but what you actually did. If you say you could have, that's just because you—and I too—are ignorant of all the *causal factors* leading you to sit down at the table. We don't know whether the toss of the coin will turn up heads or tails, but that's not because if it comes out heads there are no causes for its doing so, but because we are ignorant of all the causal factors—the vigor of the toss, the amount of spinning, the distance from the table, the direction of the throw, and so on. Once we knew all the factors, we'd know that the coin could not have come down any way other than it did. I'm saying the same for your decision to sit down just now. The causes of it are much more complex than those involved in the throw, but the principle is the same."

The doctrine this person is voicing goes by the name of *determinism,* which, in its simplest form, is the view that every event that occurs in the universe has a cause and that human actions, being also events, also have causes. To say that event E has a cause is to say that there is a set of conditions, C_1, C_2, C_3, and so forth, such that if those conditions were exactly repeated, the event E would be repeated—that is, an event just like it would occur.

We now have three concepts to relate to one another—*responsibility, freedom,* and *determinism.* Determinism is a metaphysical doctrine, whose relevance to ethics is certainly not obvious: some say it has nothing to do with ethics at all. The other two, responsibility and freedom, are clearly of relevance to the analysis of human conduct. The issue of determinism has now come into the picture only because, at least in the opinion of some philosophers, the truth or falsity of it has important implications for the concepts of freedom and (indirectly) of responsibility. It is because we are concerned with freedom that we are led to discuss determinism, since, according to the philosophers in question, if determinism is true, then freedom is an illusion. But our focus is on freedom, and we are concerned with determinism only to the extent that it bears on the issue of freedom.

Since everything has a cause, says the determinist, human actions also have a cause (or causes). Human actions are caused (in part) by human decisions: no determinist denies that if you decide to do A, you may do A, and if you decide to do B, you may do B. But, continues the determinist, your decision to do A had causes. A man's decision to kill his wife's lover is caused by things like his anger, his jealous disposition, the assault to his masculine pride, and so on. If someone objects that many men in that situation have anger, pride, and jealousy, but don't commit murder, the determinist will reply that the causal conditions are not all the same. We may never know exactly the combination of factors that led this man to kill whereas another man, in much (though never exactly) the same situation did not; but we should not confuse our *ignorance* of the causal factors with the view that there *were* no causal factors.

If science is dedicated to anything, it is the idea that whatever happens has a cause. "Do you really want to deny this?" the determinist asks. "The fact that we haven't found the causes of many events doesn't show that there aren't any. Among the theories of the cause of cancer, would you really give any credence to a scientist who says that it *had* no cause? Because of the enormous complexity of causal factors, the total cause (or total set of conditions on which the event depends) is often extremely difficult to track down, but surely it is absurd to give up and say that the event 'just popped into existence from nowhere' and had no cause at all. And the same with human events: when we educate children, we *cause* them to learn certain things; when we try to reform people, we try to *cause* changes in their attitudes. We constantly assume, not only in science but in everyday life, that events have causes. It's not that we can always control the events with such knowledge of causes. (Solar eclipses are caused but we can't control them, and juvenile delinquency has causes and we can't always control that either.) But that they all *have* causes is something that I doubt you would care to disagree with. You would be flying in the face of all science and all evidence if you did."

This, in highly condensed form, is the determinist's position on causes. The determinist is not, however, a *fatalist*. Fatalism says that a certain outcome, a certain future event, is inevitable (unavoidable), *no matter what* you or anyone else may do. And of some future events, like eclipses, this is true, but not of human actions: many events, like polluting the air or cleaning it up again, occur *because* of what people do, not in spite of it. The grade you get on your next exam is largely up to you. The fatalist argues, "If I'm fated to pass my next exam, I'll pass it whether I study or not; if I'm fated to fail it, I'll fail it whether I study or not. In the first case, studying is unnecessary; in the second case, studying is futile; therefore I won't study." The determinist says nothing so foolish as that; rather, the determinist's position is that everything is caused, and of course human beings are the causes of many occurrences, such as devising examinations and passing them. Countless things in the world would not be as they are but for human decisions, but these decisions have causes too: "You can decide as you please but you can't please as you please."

There are objections, however, which have been made to the determinist's position. If we knew all the causal factors leading to event *E,* the determinist maintains, as well as the laws of nature involved, we could infallibly predict *E*'s occurrence. But though we can do this with many things in scientific laboratories, where we can control the conditions, and where what happens depends on a small number of factors (such as temperature and pressure in the case of the expansion of gases), we cannot do this to any great extent with events having highly complex causal conditions (such as what you are going to decide to do the night after you've finished your last final exam for the term). If people do predict this, and do so correctly, it's an "educated guess" based on incomplete information. Why can't we predict everything? Because we don't know all the causal factors. "If we knew *enough,* we'd be able to predict all future events," the determinist says. But suppose we can't predict them? "That's because we don't know enough." And when do we know enough? "Only when we were able to make all the predictions." (Compare: "If you read this long enough, you'd understand it." "I've read it fifty times and I still don't understand it." "Well, that's because you haven't read it long *enough.*" When would you have read it long enough? When you understand it. It wouldn't be called "enough" until you did.)

Suppose that you set up a laboratory experiment, twice in succession, making as sure as possible that all the factors—amount of material, temperature, and so on—are the same both times. Still, the experiment turns out very different the second time: the first time you got a precipitate and the second time you didn't. What does that show? "Well," the determinist says, "one or more of the causal factors *must* have been different." How do you know this? Have you any evidence? The determinist assumes that the mere fact that the experiment came out differently the second time is evidence *all by itself* that one or more of the causal factors was different. But what kind of reasoning is that? It begs the question (assumes the point at issue), just like some of the arguments for psychological egoism. You can't prove a position by assuming it in the process of trying to prove it. None of this argumentation shows that determinism is false, only that arguments for it are invalid.

The determinist says that the scientific evidence points to the conclusion that determinism is true. But there is a strange asymmetry in the reasoning here: if you find a cause for *E,* that confirms the conclusion that everything has a cause; if you don't find a cause for *E,* that doesn't confirm the conclusion that some events have no causes, but shows only that we haven't yet *found* the cause. What would ever show that it *had* no cause? Nothing, apparently; no matter how long you fail to find the cause the determinist will still say, "We haven't found it, but it's there all right." What kind of hypothesis is it when observations can count in favor of it but nothing whatever can count against it? For a long time people thought that all swans are white, because all swans that had been found were white; then black swans were discovered in Australia, and this proved once and for all that *not* all swans are white. What could prove that some events have no causes? If nothing could prove it, then the statement "All events have causes" has no intelligible opposite; and a statement that has no intelligible opposite is immediately suspect as far as its making any true claim about the universe is concerned.

For this reason some philosophers have held that the causal principle (determinism) is not a true statement about the universe at all, but not a false statement either; rather it is *no statement at all.* The causal principle is a kind of rule or regulative principle, a *heuristic* maxim, a rule of the scientific game, which presents the framework within which we conduct our scientific investigations; it is not a law of nature (like the one about swans) discovered within the frame. If this is so, then determinism itself is neither true nor false, just as the rules of a game (e.g., baseball, you can't have more than three strikes) are neither true nor false. Rules can be changed, but they can't be falsified by the further course of our investigations. And in that case there need be no worries about determinism being *true.* [28]

Some philosophers find this argument against determinism convincing and others do not. Let's leave open the question of the truth of determinism, then, and ask: *If* it is true, what are the implications of it for ethics? How does it make human freedom an illusion? The answer given by the determinist is simple: "If determinism is true, all your actions are caused, all the

[28] For a more extensive treatment of this, see John Hospers, *Introduction to Philosophical Analysis* (Englewood Cliffs, N.J.: Prentice-Hall, 1967), Chapter 5.

choices leading to your actions are caused, and all the desires (or whatever else) leading to your choices are caused. For every one of these occurrences there is a set of conditions which is sufficient to produce them. Your thoughts, your deliberations, your decisions are the inevitable result of causal factors leading back into your childhood and even your genetic makeup, over which you had no control. *A* is a sufficient condition for *B, B* for *C, C* for *D, D* for *E.* Given the set of previous conditions, the final outcome was inevitable, and *could not have been* different from what it was. You may *feel* that you are free to decide and act, but in reality each of your decisions and acts is the inevitable result of a large array of causal factors. Actually you are no more free than the hands of the clock as they move forward, driven by the inner mechanisms of the clock. So determinism, you see, *is* incompatible with freedom."

That is, in brief, the *incompatibilist view,* the view that determinism makes freedom impossible. But there is another view, called the *compatibilist view,* that even if determinism is true (which is not necessarily granted), it still does not disturb human freedom: such freedom exists whether or not determinism is true. The conclusion that freedom is incompatible with determinism is based, says the compatibilist, on several fallacies.

1. The determinist says that every event is unavoidable, given the causal conditions leading up to it. But this is a distortion of the meaning of the term "unavoidable." "Unavoidable" means that something cannot be avoided. Death is unavoidable, that is, no one can avoid it; but death by smallpox is avoidable if we are vaccinated for smallpox. A solar eclipse is unavoidable, that is, no one can stop it; but failing an exam is not unavoidable, for students can avoid that fate by preparing and studying. There are things we can do nothing about and things we can do something about. But it is absurd to say that everything, both eclipses and failures in exams, is unavoidable. This is simply not true, and there must be something wrong with a theory that yields such an obviously false conclusion.

The determinist will reply that everything is not unavoidable in the ordinary sense; it is only that a certain event is unavoidable *given* the sufficient condition (all the causal factors). Once factors *A, B, C, . . . ,* which together form the sufficient condition for *E,* have occurred, then *E* will inevitably occur, whether *E* is an eclipse or a decision to kill your wife's lover.

But how can the determinist know this? We know all the conditions for a solar eclipse but not for a human decision. How do we know that a uniform set of conditions exists which inevitably brings about a certain human decision? We are going far beyond the evidence if we say such a thing; indeed, once again, the deterministic principle may not be true at all; it may be simply a regulative maxim or rule of the game. In that case it isn't that there are no exceptions to it, but that we—or at least the determinists—just won't *count* anything that happens, no matter what it is, as an exception.

2. The determinist says that, given all the causal conditions leading up to *E* (*E* being a decision to walk to the window), you *could not* have done any-

thing else but walk to the window. But there is a confusion here. When we say you cannot do E, we normally mean that you will not succeed in doing E no matter how hard you try or no matter how much you want to. That's the ordinary meaning of "can" and "could": you can do certain things, like run a mile in ten minutes, but you cannot do other things, like run a mile in two seconds. "You could have done it" applies when you didn't try hard enough. "You couldn't have done it" applies when you tried your best but still didn't succeed. Now along comes the determinist and says that you couldn't have acted differently, *the conditions being just what they were.* And we can reply: "You mean I couldn't have done it, even if I had tried? But if I *had* tried, then one of the causal conditions *would have been different.*"

"You couldn't have acted differently than you did," says the determinist, "if *all* the causal conditions had been the same." But "could have acted differently" means *"would* have, *if* I had chosen to." And if I had chosen differently, one of the conditions would have been different. If the determinist says I couldn't have done differently even if all the causal conditions had been the same, he is guilty of a self-contradiction: he is saying that if *all* the causal conditions had been the same I would have done differently if one of the causal conditions had *not* been the same.

> I *couldn't* have done differently if all the causal conditions (leading to my action) had been the same

becomes

> I *wouldn't* have done differently even if I'd chosen to, even if all the causal conditions had been the same.

But this last sentence contradicts itself; if I had chosen to, then one of the causal factors, my deciding to do E (on which the occurrence of E very often depends), would have been different. Then of course not all the causal conditions would have been the same!

According to the compatibilist, the facts are these: sometimes by deciding to do E, I do E; deciding to do E is never a sufficient condition by itself (for I may decide to walk and suddenly have a paralytic stroke), but it is one of the members of a set of conditions that *is* sufficient. In many events—passing exams though not preventing eclipses—I can and do make the difference. My choices can lead to my actions: if I decide to do E, I'll do E, and if I decide not to, I won't. That's all we need for ethics—that my decisions are causally instrumental in producing my actions. And that remains true even if determinism is true. It is not *whether* an act is caused but *what kind* of cause it has that makes a difference between freedom and the lack of it: if a bomb explosion will occur regardless of what I do, I am not free to prevent it, but if I can defuse the bomb by cutting wires and so forth, then I am free to prevent it. There are some things we are free to do and some things we are not; no doctrine such as determinism can change that obvious fact. It's true that there are some actions that we are not free to prevent; perhaps the ice-pick killer was not free to refrain from stabbing the girl. If he *was* at that moment the victim of an irresistible impulse, he was not free with respect to his act. But that doesn't mean that none of us is *ever* free. Indeed, most of us *are* free with respect to most of our acts, in that we can do them or not do them, depending on which we choose. That's all we mean by freedom, and in that sense we obviously have it with respect to most of our actions.

Suppose a judge said to a woman, "Did you marry this man freely?" and the woman, fresh from an ill-digested course in philosophy, said, "No, your honor." If the judge then asked, "Did he force you into this marriage? Did he threaten you?" and she replied, "No, your honor, none of that. I married him because of my *desire* to marry him, and since my act (marriage) was caused by my desire to do it, I was not free," the judge no doubt would throw the case out of court at once. "If you did it from your own desire," he would say, "then you did it of your own free will, and if that's not a case of a free act I can't imagine what one would be like." And wouldn't he be right?

In this sense of freedom, the only sense relevant to ethics (whatever other ones philosophers may concoct), we all are free, at least with respect to most of our actions most of the time. And being free, we are also *responsible*. That term too has a usage and a significant opposite. If you hire a babysitter to take care of the children one evening while you and your spouse are away and you come back a bit earlier than expected and find the babysitter not in the house (because, it turns out, she thought she could steal away for two hours with her boyfriend and still be back before you returned), you may well say to her, "I hold you responsible!" What if she said, "I'm not responsible, because my going off for two hours was caused by the fact that my desire to go out with my boyfriend was stronger than my desire to tend the children in the house"? Would that let her off the hook? You might let her off if she had suddenly had a fainting spell or a heart attack, or even if she had become suddenly ill and the ambulance had taken her to the hospital; she was not responsible for suddenly becoming ill. But what she did "of her own free will" she was responsible for. She had the capacity to stay in the house as agreed, and though she knew it was important to do so, she still did not do it. She knowingly flouted explicit orders. If that isn't abdication of responsibility, what is? If she isn't responsible for this action, what can the word "responsible" ever mean applied to human action? If you can't blame her for what she did, when can you blame anyone for anything? If anyone still says, "Never, because everything is caused," we can reply, "Even if that's true, there is a difference between those states of affairs that you caused and could have prevented by taking appropriate action or making the appropriate decision, and those (such as having a fainting spell) which you could not." That is the important distinction for ethics. And the distinction remains, whatever may turn out to be the case with respect to determinism.

An incompatibilist may still reply, however, "You are using the term 're-sponsible' in its garden-variety, ordinary meaning. I was not using it in that sense. I meant *'ultimately* responsible.' I mean that given the complete set of conditions on which *E* depends, *E* (even when it is a decision) would not be other than it is. Given the babysitter's total state of mind and body at the time, it was inevitable that she would go out and leave the children." "But then," we might object, "we can't blame her for being in that frame of mind when she took the job for the evening." "No," the incompatibilist must reply, "we can't blame her for that either, because given the total set of causal conditions on which that state depends, it was inevitable that at that moment she would be in that state." (Of course none of this is proved; it is simply the deterministic *hypothesis.*)

If we accept this incompatibilist view, must we abandon the concept of responsibility entirely? No, but much of what is now included in it will drop out. If everything is "ultimately inevitable," there will be no justification for feelings of remorse or for believing we could and should have done some-thing other than we did.

We ordinarily believe that when we abdicate our responsibility there is some defect in us, which we could have altered by trying; because we could and should have been different we hold ourselves responsible. But incompat-ibilists will have none of this. Given that framework, the term "responsible" will have a very different meaning from the ordinary one. It will not refer to any past action, any blame, any desert, for under the incompatibilist theory, these concepts must disappear; it will be used only to guide and induce (or prevent) future actions. "I hold you responsible!" will then be a way of trying to make a person feel ashamed of what he or she did in order to prevent a recurrence. It will be no different from saying, "I hold you respon-sible!" to the dog when it climbs on the sofa while you are away and you catch it there when you return, with its tail between its legs, anticipating punishment. You cannot expect the dog to regret its past actions or to ac-knowledge a defect in its character that it might have avoided; you can only, by scolding it (and the word "responsible" will mean nothing, only your tone of voice in using it) get the dog (with luck) to refrain from doing the prohibited act again.

All this, however, is very different from the way in which we now hold our fellow human beings responsible. We use the word not so much to con-dition their future behavior as to take account of their past performance and acknowledge that they did something worthy of blame because they *could* have done differently. And this is just the part—"could have done differ-ently"—that incompatibilists will not assent to; that is why they must throw out the word "responsible" in the way we generally use it and substitute a different meaning which has little in common with the old. In doing this they are not simply remolding or reworking a traditional concept but scrap-ping it entirely and substituting something quite different, which has nothing much in common with the old word except the sound of the syllables.

EXERCISES

1. Do you consider the following to be acceptable excuses? Why or why not?
   a. "Of course I'm ignorant of the new law, your honor. I was out of the country when it was passed."
   b. "Of course I tried using the roof sprinkler when sparks from the forest started falling on the house. I suppose I could have figured out that it wouldn't do any good because every neighbor would be doing the same thing and the water pressure would be low. I just didn't think of that. Did you really expect me to figure that out?"
   c. "I thought that by clipping my dog's long hair, I would be making the dog cooler in the summer. I didn't realize that the long hair is protection against heat and that the dog doesn't sweat through its skin."
   d. "But it's so obvious. Naturally I thought that if one vitamin pill would do me some good, six of them would do me six times as much good."
   e. "When I'm uncomfortable, I go to bed and turn on the heating pad. So when she passed out from the pain I thought the heat would make her more comfortable. How was I to know she had appendicitis?"

2. Two bitter enemies meet in the desert and agree to bury their differences until they find the nearest water hole together. The water is poisoned, and the first man drinks it and dies. Later, the second man pleads that he should be excused for the death of the first man. What would you think of the following pleas as excuses?
   a. "I didn't know that the water was poisoned."
   b. "I knew the water was poisoned and I told him so, but he didn't believe me, and drank it anyway. Did you expect me to *force* him not to drink it?"
   c. "I knew the water was poisoned, but I said nothing. After all, I didn't actually *do* anything to kill him."
   d. "I knew the water was poisoned, but I told him it was O.K. He didn't have to believe me, did he?"

3. "I know I didn't stop my car at the stop sign, but the sign was down—it had been washed out in the recent cloudburst." What do you think of the following countercharges?
   a. "You should have known there was usually a stop sign there. You're a citizen of the community."
   b. "You should have known that wherever a small road leads into a highway, there is a stop sign."
   c. "You should have known that the law requires you to stop there, even though there was no sign. The sign is there only for your convenience in remembering, and if it happened to be down that's your tough luck. A city map containing the location of all the stop signs in town is posted in City Hall."

4. To what extent are you excusable in the following situations?
   a. Through carelessness you have neglected to have the brakes on your car fixed. While driving through an intersection you see, at the last moment, someone scurrying across the street against the red light. You slam down on the brakes, but they do not work properly, and as a result the pedestrian is killed.
   b. You are driving your car on ice for the first time, quite carefully, and step on the brake to avoid running into someone. You are ignorant of the fact

that brakes are worse than useless on ice; you skid into a pedestrian, who is killed.

   c. You know that brakes are useless while driving on ice, but your reflexes are conditioned to ordinary conditions, and before you think of it you have stepped on the brake, killing a pedestrian.

   d. You run over a dog on the highway. You could have avoided doing so, but you plead, "I don't see anything wrong with running over dogs."

5. After a person has taken hold of the wheel while intoxicated and killed a pedestrian, should the judge look more leniently on his case than she would if he had run down the pedestrian while sober? Or should she hold him responsible for two offenses instead of one—first that of becoming intoxicated and then that of running down a pedestrian while in an intoxicated state? Consider the following dialogue:

JUDGE: But you were responsible for getting drunk in the first place.

DEFENDANT: But I wasn't drunk at first, I just had one drink—I didn't know that the person who bought me the drink had made it a double, and he didn't know (what I could have told him beforehand if he'd asked me) that I am no longer master of myself if I have more than one normal-sized drink.

JUDGE: But you were responsible for taking more than one.

DEFENDANT: No, after that first one I didn't even know what was going on; I just drank the others automatically as he gave them to me, without knowing what I was doing.

JUDGE: But you are responsible for having driven a vehicle while intoxicated.

DEFENDANT: But I'm not—by the time I got to the car I was going by instinct and was in no fit state to judge anything. I don't even remember doing it.

What *is* the person responsible for, then? Nothing?

6. A man accidentally shoots someone. To what extent do you think the following considerations are (wholly or partly) excusing? Explain.

   a. "I was drunk and thought it was a squirrel."

   b. "I wasn't myself when I did it—I was irritable and depressed."

   c. "I did it in the heat of passion—I would never have done it ordinarily, and never before in my life was I in such a state."

   d. "I did it in the heat of passion." (But he is a person who regularly does things in the heat of passion. He is easily carried away.)

   e. "What I did was contrary to my usual nature."

   f. "I don't remember doing it, though I don't deny that I did it."

   g. "I remember doing it, but it was as if some demon got hold of me and made me do it. I tried to resist but couldn't."

   h. "I guess I just lost my head."

   i. "I'm just a person with unusually strong aggressive impulses."

7. To what extent, if any, do you think the following plea constitutes a legitimate excuse for an offense? "I admit that I did it and that I acted wrongly, but almost *anyone in my position would have done the same.*" (For example, the man came home, found another man committing adultery with his wife, and shot him.)

8. Evaluate the following excuses:

   a. "I told the lie, but I did it only halfheartedly."

   b. "I had my fingers crossed when I told her it."

    c. "I am naturally very shy, and I just couldn't make myself speak up."
    d. "I would ordinarily have spoken to protect her, but her husband was in the room and he's stronger than I am."

9. Which of the following, in your opinion, are mitigating circumstances in the commission of a crime? Why?
    a. The defendant was born in the slums.
    b. His parents never gave him any conception of right and wrong.
    c. Well, that's just the way he is, and you can't expect him ever to be any different.
    d. He was all right before he went to prison the first time (for a crime he didn't commit), but there he learned the techniques of crime from hardened criminals and learned to hate society for what it had done to him. Besides, no one would give him a job after he got out, so he had to turn to crime to stay alive.

10. To what extent, if any, do you think that people can be held responsible for (*a*) the thoughts or ideas that enter their minds? (*b*) their desires? (momentary ones? recurring ones?) (*c*) temperamental traits like having a quick temper? Justify your answers.

11. In John Steinbeck's novel *The Grapes of Wrath* (pp. 42–47) the tenant farmers who are evicted from their land try to place responsibility for their plight. They tried to attack the drivers of the bulldozers who were razing their houses. But the drivers said they were only hired for the job, obeying orders. "Get the men who hired us." But these men in turn were hired by the landlords. "So get the landlords." But the landlords hadn't been receiving their rent and couldn't pay their taxes, so they had sold their houses and farms at reduced rates to large corporations. "So get the corporations." But the corporations needed money to pay their bills in a declining economy, and their first duty was to provide some dividends for their stockholders, who were the actual owners of the corporations. "So get the stockholders." But there were thousands of them, scattered all over the country. Besides, what could be done to them? Sometimes the only income they had was from their stocks, and they had to survive too. Who, then, was to be held responsible?

    Steinbeck never hinted at the answer that (at least some) economists would give. After World War I, the Federal Reserve expanded the money supply, creating a "false prosperity," extending huge amounts of credit at artificially low rates of interest. When this bubble burst, it took virtually the whole economy with it. (See Murray Rothbard, *The Great Depression;* and Lionel Robbins, *The Great Depression.*) Assuming that this is the answer, do you hold the Federal Reserve (and the federal government which partially determined its policies) responsible? Was the Federal Reserve both *causally* and *morally* responsible? (Assume that the Federal Reserve did it with the best of motives.)

12. Does extreme need count as an excusing condition, in your opinion, for committing what would otherwise be a crime? Consider these cases:
    a. I am dying of hunger or thirst, or am in extreme pain, and I steal food, drink, or a medicine which may save my life.
    b. I am a heroin addict and have an urgent felt need for a fix. So I burglarize someone's house to get the money.
    (If there is a difference between the two cases, why?)

13. "X sets a trap for a trespasser, believing that he has the right to do so. Is this ignorance of fact or law if he does not have the right? X destroys certain goods

in the belief that he is their legal owner. His belief is erroneous. Is he ignorant of fact or law?" (Herbert Morris, *Freedom and Responsibility,* p. 344.)

14. Do you consider any of the following to be examples of justified paternalism? Why?
    a. "Of course I stopped the marriage. Why, the girl is only sixteen."
    b. "Eight times now he's tried to commit suicide by jumping out of the apartment window, and eight times I've rescued him."
    c. "No, I absolutely will not let her wash her hair twice every day. It's not good for her hair to do it that often."
    d. "I absolutely will not let the boy ride a motorcycle. Motorcycles are dangerous."
    e. "No, I will not let my daughter associate with that girl. Her parents are Jehovah's Witnesses, and I don't want my daughter to be tainted. It's for her own good."
    f. A baby is born both blind and deaf. Its parents give it a lethal dose of a painless drug.
    g. A law is passed prohibiting persons under 18 from posing nude for photographs.
    h. A law is passed prohibiting adults from engaging in dangerous activities, such as hang-gliding and motorcycle racing, "to protect individuals from the consequences of their own actions." An amendment is proposed to include activities such as fumigating houses, working with asbestos, and washing the windows of skyscrapers.
    i. Employers and employees are required to contribute payments to the Social Security fund, on the theory that doing so is for their own good, and that if left to themselves most people would not put away savings for their old age.

15. Can you think of any good reason why we should keep a person alive, even if he or she has become a "human vegetable," incapable of any distinctively human activity, and yet put a pet dog or cat "to sleep" if it is incurably ill and in pain? (A religious answer might be, "Because the person has an immortal soul and the animal doesn't." But try to avail yourself of an answer that doesn't involve any theological assumptions.)

16. Ernest Tidyman's book *Dummy* describes a young black man who is totally deaf and unable to learn language but who can do good manual work by imitating others if they show him how to do it. He goes to a hotel one day, shows a twenty-dollar bill to a prostitute, and accompanies her to a room. She is later found murdered. He is arrested but he cannot stand trial because the nature of the accusation against him cannot be communicated to him. So he is remanded to a state mental institution, where he spends several years. Through the influence of a Chicago attorney, however, he is let go because there is no evidence of "mental disease." After he has been back at his job for a few weeks, another prostitute is murdered and again he is the last person to be seen with her. He is arrested once more and this time put in state prison in spite of the fact that he is still ignorant of the accusation against him. What would *you* do with such a case?

17. Discuss this statement about compulsion by Patrick Devlin (*Enforcement of Morals,* 1882):

> The question whether liberty is a good thing is as irrational as the question whether fire is a good thing. It is both good and bad according to time, place, and circumstances. Compulsion is bad

(1) when the object aimed at is bad;

(2) when the object aimed at is good, but the compulsion employed is not calculated to obtain it;

(3) when the object aimed at is good, and the compulsion employed is calculated to obtain it, but at too great an expense.

Thus, (1) to compel a man to commit murder is bad, because the object is bad; (2) to inflict a punishment sufficient to irritate but not sufficient to deter or to destroy for holding particular religious opinions is bad, because such compulsion is not calculated to effect its purpose, assuming it to be good; and (3) to compel people not to trespass by shooting them with spring-guns is bad, because the harm done is out of all proportion to the harm avoided.

If, however, the object aimed at is good, if the compulsion employed such as to attain it, and if the good obtained overbalances the inconveniences of the compulsion itself, I do not understand how the compulsion can be bad.

Show how this view would have different consequences from those of (for example) Mill's *On Liberty,* in considering problems such as those in Exercise 14.

18. Evaluate the following comments:

   a. From Mark Twain, *What Is Man?* pp. 5–7: "Whatsoever a man is, is due to his *make,* and to the *influences* brought to bear upon it by his heredities, his habitat, his associations. He is moved, directed, *commanded,* by *exterior* influences—solely. He *originates* nothing, not even a *thought.* . . . A man's brain is so constructed that *it can originate nothing whatever.* It can only use material obtained *outside.* It is merely a machine; and it works automatically, not by will-power. *It has no command over itself, its owner has no command over it.*"

   b. From Clarence Darrow, "Crime and Criminals," *Attorney for the Dammed,* p. 6. To the prisoners in the Cook County Jail, 1902: "You may not yourselves see exactly why it was you did this thing, but if you look at the question deeply enough and carefully enough you will see that there were circumstances that drove you to do exactly the thing which you did. You could not help it any more than we outside can help taking the positions that we take."

   c. From Patrick Nowell-Smith, *Ethics,* p. 298: "Leopold Mozart was a competent musician; his son Wolfgang was given a good musical education and practised his art assiduously. Each of these facts helps to explain how he was able to compose and play so well. There is plenty of evidence that musical ability runs in families and still more of the effects of teaching and practice. But, having learnt these facts, we do not have the slightest tendency to say that, because Mozart's abilities were 'due' to heredity, teaching, and practice, his compositions were not 'really' his own, or to abate one jot of our admiration. In the same way, however a man came by his moral principles, they are still *his* moral principles and he is praised or blamed for them. The plea that, being what he is he cannot help doing what he does, will no more save the wicked man than it will save the bad pianist or actor who has the rashness to expose his incompetence in public. Nor is he saved by being able to explain how he has come to be what he is."

19. Resolve the following dispute:

A: I still think that a person's behavior is completely determined—a certain act is caused by a series of circumstances A, and A by a preceding set of circumstances B, and B by C, indefinitely back, including his or her power of resistance and other traits of character. Of course I know that we have (for practical reasons) to blame, to punish, to "hold responsible." But when we talk that language we are talking pragmatically only.

B: No, it's not pragmatic; responsibility refers to a *fact* of the moral life. And I hold that a person's acts are, though caused, *his* or *her own* and that the individual is personally responsible for them.

20. Here are two people, each equally addicted to smoking. It is equally hard for them to stop the habit. But one of them succeeds in stopping, and the other does not. Would you say that (a) here are two different effects of the same cause or that (b) here are two different effects to which two different causes correspond? (If the latter, what difference in causation might you point out?)

21. To what extent in the following examples would you say that (1) the act is voluntary, (2) the person is free, and in what sense?
   a. You knowingly take a pill which will keep you content and free of conflicts for the rest of your life.
   b. You knowingly submit to brain surgery which will make resistance to the regime under which you live impossible for you in the future.
   c. Under threat of punishment or death, you submit to the surgery (b).
   d. You knowingly take a "truth serum" which renders you incapable of lying.
   e. You perform an act as a result of posthypnotic suggestion.
   f. An enemy tortures you into giving away state secrets.
   g. You lock yourself in an upper story and throw away the key.
   h. Through habit and inertia, a slave refuses his freedom when it is granted.
   i. A woman accepts an LSD pill, not knowing its probable effects on her.
   j. A hungry dog smells meat on the table, almost takes the meat, but, on the command of its master, refrains.

22. Which of the following statements do you consider true, and why?
   a. "I could never have done anything other than what I actually did."
   b. "I could have done other than I did, if one or more of the causal conditions had been different."
   c. "I could have done other than I did, even if all the causal conditions leading up to my act had been the same."
   d. "I would not have done other than I did, if all the causal conditions leading up to my act had been the same."
   e. "Everything I do is compelled by previous events in my history."
   f. "If I was omniscient I could predict every act I would perform for the rest of my life."
   g. "Since an omniscient God could predict everything I am going to do, I am not free."
   h. "As long as I'm doing what I want to do, I'm free."
   i. "As long as I'm happy, I'm free."
   j. "The more choices I have available to me, the freer I am."
   k. "The fewer constraints or impediments there are to my action, the freer I am."

23. To what extent is freedom compromised by such techniques as behavior modification therapy, drug therapy, and psychosurgery? Consult such books as Maya

Pines, *The Brain Changers* (New York: Harcourt Brace Jovanovich, 1972); Vance Packard, *The People Shapers* (Boston: Little, Brown, 1977); and Ronald Munson, ed., *Intervention and Reflection: Basic Issues in Medical Ethics* (Belmont, Calif.: Wadsworth Publishing, 1979), Chapter 6.

24. Three practices are described in this excerpt from Maya Pines, *The Brain Changers*, pp. 231–32. Which do you find the most objectionable, and why?

> In France, where generations of peasant women have painstakingly force-fed geese by hand (to fatten their livers for good *foie gras*), surgeons have begun to take over the job, performing a delicate operation on the animals' hypothalamus to knock out their centers of satiety. This makes the geese eat incessantly—as if of their own free will—damaging their insides and consuming almost as much as when they were stuffed by hand. To top it all, a drug company is now developing a chemical that could be injected directly into the animals' brains to produce the same effect in only a few minutes, at negligible cost.
>
> In the case of human beings, which do you find most inimical to freedom—compulsory behavior modification, electro-shock therapy, or brain surgery (e.g., prefrontal lobotomy)?

SELECTED READINGS

Responsibility and Excuse

Aristotle. *Nicomachean Ethics*. Many editions. See Book 3.

Austin, John. "A Plea for Excuses." *Aristotelian Society Proceedings* 57 (1956–1957): 1–30.

Barnes, Wriston H. F., W. D. Falk, and A. Duncan-Jones. "Intention, Motive, and Responsibility." *Aristotelian Society Proceedings*. Supplementary Vol. 19 (1945): 230–48.

Beardsley, Elizabeth L. "Excusing Conditions and Moral Responsibility." In Sidney Hook, ed. *Determinism and Freedom*. New York: New York University Press, 1958.

Brandt, Richard. "Blameworthiness and Obligation." In Abraham Irving Melden, ed. *Essays in Moral Philosophy*. Seattle: University of Washington Press, 1958.

———. *Ethical Theory*. Englewood Cliffs, N.J.: Prentice-Hall, 1959. See Chapter 18.

Broad, C. D. "Conscience and Conscientious Action." In C. D. Broad. *Ethics and the History of Philosophy*. New York: Humanities Press, 1952.

Ewing, Alfred C. *Ethics*. New York: Macmillan, 1953. See Chapter 8.

Frankena, William K. "Obligation and Ability." In Max Black, ed. *Philosophical Analysis*. Ithaca, N.Y.: Cornell University Press, 1950.

Glover, Jonathan. *Responsibility*. London: Routledge & Kegan Paul, 1973.

Hart, H. L. A. "The Ascription of Responsibility and Rights." In Antony Flew, ed. *Essays in Logic and Language*. Vol. 1. New York: Philosophical Library, 1951.

———. "Legal and Moral Obligation." In Abraham I. Melden, ed. *Essays in Moral Philosophy*. Seattle: University of Washington Press, 1958.

———. "Legal Responsibility and Excuses." In Sidney Hook, ed. *Determinism and Freedom*. New York: New York University Press, 1958.

———. *Punishment and Responsibility*. New York: Oxford University Press, 1968.

Lewis, H. D., J. W. Harvey, and G. A. Paul. "The Problem of Guilt." *Aristotelian Society Proceedings*. Supplementary Vol. 21 (1947): 175–218.

Nowell-Smith, Patrick. *Ethics*. Baltimore: Pelican Books, 1954. See Chapters 19–20.

Nozick, Robert. "Coercion." In Sidney Morgenbesser, ed. *Philosophy, Science, & Method*. New York: St. Martin's Press, 1969.

Prichard, H. A. "Duty and Ignorance of Fact." In his *Moral Obligation*. Oxford, Eng.: Clarendon Press, 1949. Reprinted in Herbert Morris, ed. *Freedom and Responsibility*. Stanford, Calif.: Stanford University Press, 1961.

Vivian, Frederick. *Human Freedom and Responsibility*. London: Chatto & Windus, 1964.

Paternalism

Davidson, Henry. "Professional Secrecy." In E. Fuller Torrey, ed. *Ethical Issues in Medicine*. Boston: Little, Brown, 1968.

Downing, A. B., ed. *Euthanasia and the Right to Death*. London: Peter Owen, n.d.

Dworkin, Gerald. "Paternalism." *The Monist* 56 (1973).

Feinberg, Joel. "Legal Moralism and Free-floating Evils." *Pacific Philosophical Quarterly* 61 (1980): 122–55.

———. "Legal Paternalism." In his *Rights, Justice, and the Bounds of Liberty*. Princeton, N.J.: Princeton University Press, 1980.

Foot, Philippa. "The Problem of Abortion and the Doctrine of the Double Effect." In Bonnie Steinbock, ed. *Killing and Letting Die*. Englewood Cliffs, N.J.: Prentice-Hall, 1980.

Gert, Bernard, and Charles Culver. "Paternalistic Behavior." *Philosophy and Public Affairs* 6 (1976): 45–57.

Mill, John Stuart. *On Liberty* (1859).★ Many editions.

Munson, Ronald, ed. *Intervention and Reflection: Basic Issues in Medical Ethics*. Belmont, Calif.: Wadsworth Publishing, 1979. See Part 4.

Freedom

Austin, John. "Ifs and Cans." *Proceedings of the British Academy* 42 (1956): 102–32.

———. "A Plea for Excuses." *Aristotelian Society Proceedings* 57 (1956–1957): 1–30.

Ayer, Alfred Jules. "Freedom and Necessity." In his *Philosophical Essays*. New York: St. Martin's Press, 1954.

Beardsley, Elizabeth L. "Determinism and Moral Perspectives." *Philosophy and Phenomenological Research* 21 (1960): 1–20.

———. "Moral Worth and Moral Credit." *Philosophy and Phenomenological Research* 66 (1957): 304–28.

Berofsky, Bernard, ed. *Free-will and Determinism*. New York: Harper & Row, 1966.

Broad, C. D. "Determinism, Indeterminism, and Libertarianism." In his *Ethics and the History of Philosophy*. New York: Humanities Press, 1952.

Campbell, Charles Arthur. "Is Free-will a Pseudo-problem?" *Mind* 60 (1951): 441–65.

Dworkin, Gerald, ed. *Determinism, Free-Will, and Moral Responsibility*. Englewood Cliffs, N.J.: Prentice-Hall, 1970.

Enteman, Willard F., ed. *The Problem of Free Will*. New York: Charles Scribner's Sons, 1967.

★Dates in parentheses are dates of first publication.

Feinberg, Joel. "The Idea of a Free Man." In his *Rights, Justice, and the Bounds of Liberty*. Princeton, N.J.: Princeton University Press, 1980.

Hobart, R. E. (Dickinson Miller). "Free-will as Involving Determinism and Inconceivable Without It." *Mind* 43 (1934): 1–27.

Hook, Sidney, ed. *Determinism and Freedom*. New York: New York University Press, 1958. See Parts 1 and 4.

Hospers, John. *Introduction to Philosophical Analysis*. Englewood Cliffs, N.J.: Prentice-Hall, 1967. See Chapter 5.

Hunold, Albert, ed. *Freedom and Serfdom*. The Hague: Reidel & Co., 1961.

Kekes, John. "Freedom." *Pacific Philosophical Quarterly* 61 (1980): 368–83.

Kenny, Anthony. *Freewill and Responsibility*. London: Routledge & Kegan Paul, 1978.

Leoni, Bruno. *Freedom and the Law*. Los Angeles: Nash Publishing, 1961.

Matson, Wallace I. "The Irrelevance of Free-will to Moral Responsibility." *Mind* 65 (1956): 489–97.

Ofstad, Harold. *The Freedom of Decision*. London: Allen & Unwin, 1961.

Oppenheim, Felix. *Dimensions of Freedom*. New York: Macmillan, 1961.

Schlick, Moritz. *The Problems of Ethics*. Englewood Cliffs, N.J.: Prentice-Hall, 1939. See Chapter 7.

10

Morality and the State

1. AUTHORITY AND CONSENT

When you make a decision, whether a wise one or a foolish one, you take responsibility for your own actions; other people may be affected by your actions, and if as a result of your decision they are harmed, you are (morally and legally) responsible for that also. When you belong to a church, a club, a fraternity, or a chamber of commerce, you voluntarily join, assuming whatever duties and accepting whatever privileges are involved, and you are free to resign whenever you choose. If you are a stockholder in a corporation, you accept whatever procedures are part of the conditions of owning stock, such as determining corporation policy by a majority vote of members; if you don't like the procedures, you need not join or you can pull out whenever you choose.

The only exception to all this is the State. (When we are talking about the institution, we capitalize the S; when we talk about a state of the United States, such as Pennsylvania, we use a small s.) We are born into it, and we are required under penalty to obey its laws. We cannot pull out of it if we don't like it; we may be able to emigrate elsewhere, but that would only place us under the governance of another State, which might be worse than the one we left. It is the principal organization, or institution, to which we belong (as citizens) without having consented to membership in it, and we must perforce remain members as long as we are in the geographical area that is under its jurisdiction. It is the institution under whose governance we find ourselves without having given prior *consent* to doing so.

The situation is all the more troublesome because the State, unlike all other organizations, can use force to make us comply. The Catholic Church can excommunicate members, and a club can expel members, for violation of

417

rules on which such membership is dependent; but neither the church nor the club can detain people by force, arrest them, try them, convict and sentence them. (The Catholic Church could once do this, but only when the church was also the State.) General Motors is a powerful organization, but it cannot arrest you for not buying Chevrolets. But the State can arrest you for failing to obey one of its laws, even if the law you disobey is a foolish or vicious one. The State has a monopoly on the legal use of force within a specified geographical area; or, more accurately, since it may sometimes delegate the use of force to others (campus police can also detain you, then turn you over to the city police), it retains for itself the legal right to determine who may, and under what circumstances, employ the use of force against others.

Thus the power of the State is tremendous and all-encompassing. But where does it derive its *authority* to exercise that power? You have the authority to discipline your own children, while your neighbors have the authority with regard to their own children but not to yours. But what gives the institution we call the State the authority—not just the power, which it already has—to make laws governing your life, and then to arrest and try you for violating them?

Many political philosophers have held that the State has that right because of the *consent* of its citizens. Others have held that it has the right without consent, and still others that it has no such right at all. We shall now examine a few of the principal views that have been held on the issue of the State's authority over its citizens.

A. Plato: Government by the Elite

Governments arise chiefly through conquest. A coastal fishing village is attacked by raiders who outnumber the occupants in arms and conquer them. Rather than pillage them and leave, they find life more secure by remaining among them and sending their representatives to levy taxes (along with rules and regulations) on the inhabitants in exchange for their protection from outside aggressors. Repeatedly throughout history raiders and conquering armies have subdued a geographical area, and in the course of time they become the "legitimate government" of that area. They have the physical power—superiority in arms. But what *entitles* them to rule? The "tragedy of power" is that those who come into power in that way are seldom the same people who are worthy to *wield* power once they have it. People who have a talent for aggression, action, and risk taking are not thereby equipped to rule wisely or well. Napoleon, the conquerer of nations, denigrated the English as "a nation of shopkeepers," though in the end it was they who defeated him.

It was to correct the problem of rule by the incompetent that Plato, in his *Republic,* set forth a plan whereby those who ruled *would* be guaranteed to do so wisely and well. Rulers of states, he believed, must be experts in their field, for they require highly specialized knowledge to handle efficiently the complex problems confronting them daily. It is absurd, he thought, for law-yers and physicians to be required to go through an intensive course of train-ing for their professions while politicians, on whose wisdom the entire citizenry depends, have no special training at all.

But they must not only be experts: they must be wise and incorruptible men and women of the highest moral character, or they might use their specialized knowledge to advance their own interests instead of the interests of the people they are governing. They must be wise shepherds. To ensure the incorruptibility of their moral character once they are in office and have the powers of that office is a far more difficult task than to acquire specialized knowledge and skill. Once they are in positions of power, they will be strongly tempted to abuse that power for ends other than the welfare of those whom they govern. Thus, they must be protected from early youth against all corrupt moral influences, and their characters must be molded in such a way that they will be immune to the temptations of becoming corrupt and to the fawning admiration of flatterers. No effort should be spared to ensure that those who will govern will be both the best intellects and the most moral human beings. This combination is rare enough at best, and when it occurs in the young it must be nurtured and cultivated with the utmost care.

What, then, should their training be like? Briefly, children who show the slightest promise of being wise future rulers must be educated in body, mind, and spirit. The most important instrument for intellectual develop-ment is long and intensive training in mathematics, for in this such children learn the rigor of thinking and the demands of objectivity in reasoning. For the good of their souls, they must also be trained in mathematics, astron-omy, music, and poetry—so that they will become sensitive to the feelings and attitudes of others. They will also undergo a period of military training to make their bodies a fit vessel for their souls. Not until they are thirty will they be permitted to study philosophy, which combines intellectual rigor with moral commitment. If they come to it too early, Plato maintained, it will only corrupt them:

You must have seen how much harm is done now by philosophical discussion—how it infects people with a spirit of lawlessness.

Yes, I have.

Does that surprise you? Can you not make allowances for them? Imagine a child brought up in a rich family with powerful connections and surrounded by a host of flatterers; and suppose that, when he comes to manhood, he learns that he is not the son of those who call them-selves his parents and his true father and mother are not to be found. Can you guess how he would feel towards his supposed parents and towards his flatterers before he knew about his parentage and after learn-ing the truth? Or shall I tell you what I should expect?

Please do.

I should say that, so long as he did not know the truth, he would

have more respect for his reputed parents and family than for the flatterers, and be less inclined to neglect them in distress or to be insubordinate
in word or deed; and in important matters the flatterers would have less
influence with him. But when he learnt the facts, his respect would be
transferred to them; their influence would increase, and he could openly
associate with them and adopt their standards of behavior, paying no
heed to his reputed father and mother, unless his disposition were re-
markably good.

Yes; all that would be likely to happen. But how does your illustration apply to people who are beginning to take part in philosophical
discussions?

In this way. There are certain beliefs about right and honorable conduct, which we have been brought up from childhood to regard with
the same sort of reverent obedience that is shown to parents. In opposition to these, other courses attract us with flattering promises of pleasure; though a moderately good character will resist such blandishments
and remain loyal to the beliefs of his fathers. But now suppose him
confronted by the question, What does "honorable" mean? He gives the
answer he has been taught by the lawgiver, but he is argued out of his
position. He is refuted again and again from many different points of
view and at last reduced to thinking that what he called honorable might
just as well be called disgraceful. He comes to the same conclusion about
justice, goodness, and all the things he most revered. What will become
now of his old respect and obedience?

Obviously they cannot continue as before.

And when he has disowned these discredited principles and failed to
find the true ones, naturally he can only turn to the life which flatters his
desires; and we shall see him renounce all morality and become a lawless
rebel. If this is the natural consequence of plunging the young into philosophical discussion, ought we not to make allowances, as I said before?

Yes, and be sorry for them too.

Then, if you do not want to be sorry for those pupils of yours who
have reached the age of thirty, you must be very careful how you introduce them to such discussions. One great precaution is to forbid their
taking part while they are still young. You must have seen how young-
sters, when they get their first taste of it, treat arguments as a form of
sport solely for purposes of contradiction. When someone has proved
them wrong, they copy his methods to confute others, delighting like
puppies in tugging and tearing at anyone who comes near them. And
so, after a long course of proving others wrong and being proved wrong
themselves, they rush to the conclusion that all they once believed is
false; and the result is that in the eyes of the world they discredit, not
themselves only, but the whole business of philosophy. An older man
would not share this craze for making a sport of contradiction. He will
prefer to take for his model the conversation of one who is bent on

seeking truth, and his own reasonableness will bring credit on the pursuit. We meant to insure this result by all that we said earlier against the present practice of admitting anybody, however unfit, to philosophic discussions, and about the need for disciplined and steadfast character.[1]

Even after all this careful preparation, not completed until the age of thirty-five, those selected must spend fifteen years among the people they are to govern, in various humble positions, to make sure that they know what the life of ordinary people is like and how they can improve it. The majority of the trainees will fall by the wayside at one stage or another of this arduous process, being eliminated by difficult civil-service-style examinations. Only a few will survive to the end of the training, which terminates at the age of fifty, to take their position on the Council of Rulers.

The rulers will live simple lives, with no ostentation and only enough income to meet their needs; in that way, no one will be attracted to political office by hope of financial gain. So as not to distract their attention from statecraft, they will even have their spouses and children in common, so that family attachments will not get in the way of their sole purpose in life, which is rulership. But even if they are not corrupted by money, may they not be corrupted by power? This, too, Plato makes every effort to prevent. No one will be an absolute ruler; the Council of Rulers will consist of a comparatively small number of those who survive the long period of training. And because of the nature of that training, no one will use the high office for anything but the purpose of serving other citizens well. The only kind of impulse sufficient to carry people through all those years of training is complete dedication to the office of rulership.

What of the vast majority who never attain to rulership? They are governed—wisely, it is hoped, after all that training—by those equipped to rule. Political power is too important a thing to be in the hands of people untrained for the job. They are to be governed from above and can offer no input from below. The rulers are the wise shepherds, and the sheep, lacking wisdom, are better off not having any voice in how the nation is to be governed. The people have no right to consent to whoever rules them, nor have they any qualifications to do so. Their consent is not sought because it would not be wise for them to have such power: they would disagree among themselves, and whatever they did consent to would more likely be bad policy than good.

Criticisms of Plato's scheme have abounded through the centuries. Among the most important ones are:

1. Corruption may still leak in despite this scheme. Who, for example, makes out the civil-service examinations, which determine who is to survive in the long period of training? Wasn't Plato wrong in keeping from the rul-

[1] From *The Republic of Plato* translated by F. M. Cornford (1941), pp. 259–61. Reprinted by permission of Oxford University Press.

ers-to-be any immoral influences, such as sensuous strains of music and criticisms of the gods as found in Homer? Must they not be acquainted with
such things in order to attack them? Plato sometimes writes as if the rulers
must be nurtured like hothouse plants, rather than as men and women of the
world who must be acquainted with its evils.

2. The role of experts in government has often been questioned. Experts
are useful as efficient means to agreed-upon ends. But what equips the experts
to determine as well the *ends* which the State will serve? Since citizens' lives
are being affected, shouldn't they be permitted to determine their own ends,
rather than have them determined by the rulers? Plato *does* grant the populace
a large measure of freedom, but simply because the rulers in their infinite
wisdom *permit* it; the citizens do not possess freedom by right. If the rulers
decide to censor literature, for example, it's for the good of the people and
they have no cause to complain.

It is because it is their lives that are affected that they (the people) should
have a voice in the rulership. They may not express that voice wisely
(though they may learn); nevertheless, said John Stuart Mill, even a mediocre
government in which the people have a voice is preferable to a wise government in which they have none: "That a handful of human beings should
weigh everybody in the balance, and give more to one and less to another at
their sole pleasure and judgment, would not be borne unless from persons
believed to be more than men, and backed by supernatural terrors."[2]

B. Hobbes: Political Dictatorship

Thomas Hobbes (1588–1679), having lived through the civil war in England,
feared revolution and civil disorder above all else. For this reason he had a
very different idea of the State. In his *Leviathan,* he envisioned the condition
of human beings prior to the existence of any governments, which he called
a "state of nature." In this condition every person is the potential enemy of
every other: no one knows who may attack at any time, and since there is
no law, each person must defend himself or herself. There are no courts to
settle disputes, and if the parties to a dispute cannot resolve it, their only
recourse is to fight. All are in a constant condition of war; and in such a
condition, leisure and civilized life are impossible, and human life is, in
Hobbes's words, "nasty, brutish, and short."

Each person needs a strong government for protection, and each person
would be better off with such a government. Peace is necessary for the
achievement of all other goods, and peace can be assured only if there is a
strong State to keep people from harming one another and to ward off attacks from the outside. Seeing that they have need of a strong central authority, they get together (in a conclave at Stonehenge?) and decide that they

---

[2]John Stuart Mill, *Principles of Political Economy* (1848), Book 1, Chapter 2.

need a sovereign (who Hobbes probably thought of as one person, though it could just as well be several people ruling together), with whom they make a "compact"; in return for the protection that the sovereign can afford them through armies and the police, they consent to be ruled by him. They voluntarily give up most of the rights they had in a state of nature and trade it for peace in the form of "law and order." In doing so, Hobbes said, they give up much less than they gain in return.

What are the powers of the sovereign? They would strike most contemporary readers as quite considerable. The sovereign can do just about anything he likes in order to sustain peace in the kingdom. He can suppress freedom of speech, if he thinks it is leading to dissension among his subjects, and can assume a number of other powers as well:

> It is annexed to the sovereignty to be the judge of what opinions, and doctrines are averse, and what conducing to peace; and consequently, on what occasions, how far, and what men are to be trusted withal in speaking to multitudes of people; and who shall examine the doctrines of all books before they be published. . . . [There] is annexed to the sovereignty the whole power of prescribing the rules whereby every man may know what goods he may enjoy, and what this is men call *propriety*. . . . [There] is annexed to the sovereignty the right of judicature; that is to say, of hearing and deciding all controversies which may arise concerning law . . . or concerning fact. For without the decision of controversies, there is no protection of one subject against the injuries of another. . . . To the sovereign is committed the power of rewarding with riches or honor; and of punishing with corporal or pecuniary punishment, or with ignominy, every subject according to the law he hath formerly made; or if there be no law made, according as he shall judge most to conduce to the encouraging of men to serve the Commonwealth, or deterring of them from doing disservice to the same.[3]

Though Hobbes was skeptical concerning all religion, he granted the sovereign the power to institute a state religion and punish all dissidents—not because the official doctrine was true, but because a uniform teaching for all would promote peace and order.

But the sovereign is not to be a complete dictator: since the original purpose for making the covenant was protection of life and limb, the sovereign cannot command the surrender of life, since that goes against the very purpose for which the covenant was instituted:

> Covenants not to defend a man's own body are void. Therefore, if the sovereign command a man, though justly condemned, to kill,

---

[3] Thomas Hobbes, *Leviathan* (1651), Chapter 18.

wound, or maim himself; or not to resist those that assault him; or to abstain from the use of food, air, medicine, or any other thing without which he cannot live; yet hath that man the liberty to disobey. If a man be interrogated by the sovereign, or his authority, concerning a crime done by himself, he is not bound . . . to confess it; because no man . . . can be obliged by covenant to accuse himself. . . . When therefore our refusal to obey frustrates the end for which the sovereignty was ordained, then there is no liberty to refuse; otherwise, there is. . . . And when the defense of the Commonwealth requireth at once the help of all that are able to bear arms, every one is obliged; because otherwise the institution of the Commonwealth, which they have not the purpose or courage to preserve, was in vain. To resist the sword of the Commonwealth in defense of another man, guilty or innocent, no man hath liberty; because such liberty takes away from the sovereign the means of protecting us, and is therefore destructive of the very essence of government.[4]

But if the sovereign does not deliver protection, then the covenant becomes null and void: "The obligation of subjects to the sovereign is understood to last as long and no longer, than the power lasteth by which he is able to protect them. For the right men have by nature to protect themselves, when none else can protect them, can no covenant be relinquished."[5]

Hobbes, too, had his critics. Among the limitations of the theory that critics have commented on are the following:

1. It is questionable whether citizens really do gain more than they give up, if the covenant obliges them to give up freedom of speech and religion, freedom to resist the draft, freedom to conduct their lives in accord with their own choices rather than the sovereign's commands. But according to Hobbes, the end is so important that it justifies all those means: the end is peace and protection, and in order to attain personal security, it is worth giving up everything else. What good, after all, is freedom of speech if individuals are in imminent and constant danger of death? According to Hobbes, there is no alternative: if you want protection, you must accept all the conditions necessary to having it.

Many critics would say, however, that it is not necessary to pay such a high price for protection. Freedom of speech and press was preserved to a high degree in Great Britain even in World War II when the bombs were falling, and having it helped preserve the society rather than cause it to disintegrate in dissension. Here all the arguments Mill uses for freedom of speech in his *On Liberty* (see pp. 260–61) could be used to rebut Hobbes. (But, of course, Mill didn't live in the midst of civil war.)

2. There is a certain tension in Hobbes's theory: people are by nature self-

[4] Ibid., Chapter 21.
[5] Ibid.

ish, aggressive, and shortsighted, and they need a sovereign to keep them in line. (Hobbes's picture of human nature is not exactly a rosy one.) But if they are that shortsighted, can they be farsighted enough to *see* that they need a sovereign to rule them? In a state of nature they are in a state of "war of all against all," yet they peaceably congregate to get themselves out of this mess and elect themselves a sovereign.

3. The sovereign they elect turns out to be a dictator: once in power, with the army behind him, he is subject to no further restraints. (Hobbes didn't even make the sovereign a signatory to the contract, for what could citizens do if the sovereign violated it?) He can do whatever he likes—can violate every one of the citizens' rights and be a Nero or Caligula if he chooses. True, Hobbes conceded that people cannot contract away their right to life; but what if the sovereign takes it nonetheless? Ordinary citizens are disarmed victims, just as they are under any totalitarian government today. The contract binds the citizens but does not bind the sovereign. In the end the contract doesn't afford citizens very much protection. (Of course they have the *right* to resist the taking of their lives; but of what use is this right when the king's armies or police force are executing them?)

4. One further objection is that there never was such a state of nature as Hobbes described. And this is doubtless true: there is some kind of social organization, even if only a tribal chief, in every society anthropologists have ever encountered. But this objection is really not very serious. Hobbes did not claim that his story relates a historical event that occurred in the dim past. It is, rather, a myth—a kind of exercise in abstraction, saying to us, "See what life would be like if there was no strong central authority."

However, if the contract is a myth, what becomes of the contention that government is by consent? If we ask what justifies the State in ruling us, Hobbes's answer was that we all consented to it in the original compact: we saw that a strong central authority was necessary and we acted accordingly. But if the contract is a myth, then there was nothing to which we really consented. Hobbes might say that our continued residence in the country implies consent, but this is an extremely implausible argument: Does continued residence in a dictatorship from which you are forbidden to emigrate imply consent to its restrictive rules and its police state? Does the fact that you remain in East Germany because of the Berlin Wall imply that you consented to stay there?

Even if there were some original parties who consented, there are serious problems with government by consent. (a) If I consent to something, I can later (under certain conditions) revoke it, but once the Hobbesian contract is entered into, there is no getting out of it, unless the sovereign no longer offers protection. But then it is a bit late to get out: people may still have the right but lack the power. (b) What kind of consent is it that obliges not only the consenters but their descendants in perpetuity? Can we consent for somebody else? Can I consent to have *you* sign a document if you are unwilling? Surely we can consent only for ourselves, just as we can forgive only for ourselves, not on behalf of others. How does the fact that your great-great-great-grandparents once signed a document obligate *you* to live up to its terms? The fact still remains that *you* didn't consent. If your ancestors did, that's their problem; but you didn't, so how can you be bound by the contract that *they* signed?

C. Economic Dictatorship

Before we consider democracy as an alternative to the Platonic and Hobbesian concepts of the State, we may note one advantage of a dictatorship, or indeed any government in which there is a strong central authority which dictates to a large degree the course of citizens' daily lives. The dictator (or group that exercises dictatorial power) in such a government need not consult the citizens: if decisions are made that the people don't like, there's not much they can do. Still, sometimes the ruler's decisions may be wise ones, and if the ruler is in possession of a complex range of facts and the population isn't, he or she can act quickly and decisively without having to go through the painfully slow democratic process. In the event of invasion by another power, the nation's defenses can be mobilized quickly, without having to consult the populace. Such a State may thus be prepared for a catastrophe, and even ward it off, whereas in a democracy it may take months or years for a defense program to get through the legislature. In taking quick and decisive action, whether for good or for ill, a dictatorship can be much more *efficient*.

This efficiency in making instant decisions, however, is likely to be matched by an *inefficiency* in carrying them out. Slave labor is notoriously inefficient; and even when the citizens are not (strictly speaking) slaves, but unwilling subjects of a despotic government, they will defeat the purposes of the government when they can. It takes an enormous police force, including secret police (such as the KGB), to coerce the population into obeying commands, and it also may require a system of espionage, pitting one citizen against another: no one knows who may be a government agent, and no one dares speak freely to others for fear of arrest. (Parents may not even speak frankly to children for fear their own children may turn them in.) The dictator usually doesn't mind this invasion of freedom; indeed, a regime of terror is often welcome as a means of keeping the citizens in line. But there is nevertheless an enormous drain on the economy involved in this all-pervasive policing operation: resources that could otherwise be spent on consumer goods must be spent on the large and unwieldy apparatus of "internal defense." Even so, the moment the leash is loosened, the people defect, as millions of Soviet citizens defected to the Germans when they invaded in 1941.[6] Unless the dictator is unremittingly efficient in the policing operation,

---

[6] See Peter Huxley-Blythe, *The East Came West* (Caldwell, Idaho: Caxton Printers, 1968).

the citizens will be something less than efficient in obeying his commands.

The effects of such policing are soon evident throughout the economy, which is, of course, a "command" economy rather than a market economy. Unless the government leaves the economic lives of citizens alone (a rare phenomenon), one central economic plan is typically imposed on the entire nation: instead of leaving each citizen free to make his or her own plans, a central plan is imposed forcibly on everyone. No one may own a business; only the State may run stores and factories. And when this happens, tremendous inefficiency, waste, and corruption take place: tractors required for plowing the fields and threshers for harvesting the grain are in disrepair a hundred miles away until long after they are needed for the harvest, which meanwhile rots in the field. Since no one can make a personal profit from a harvest, it is not in anyone's interest to ensure the harvest of crops, most of which will be distributed elsewhere by the government planners.

Why not, then, permit individuals to make their own economic decisions? Because, at least according to Marxist theory, this would be "exploitation." According to Marx, any person who owns a business is in a position to exploit workers. To rescue workers from this fate, the State intervenes and permits no one at all to own businesses. After the Russian Revolution, all those who had employed six or more workers were considered "capitalists" and were shot as exploiters of the poor, or in some cases they were made to teach the business to the "new proletariat" and were shot after that. Never mind that in a free economy prices can be adjusted to what the competition may charge, whereas in an economic dictatorship there is no competition, so the State can charge what it likes; never mind that good workers in a free economy who are underpaid will be sought by competing firms and become gainfully employed there, whereas workers are assigned permanently to jobs in a command economy. According to Marxist theory, private ownership of the means of production will result in exploitation of the workers, and the State is needed to prevent this. The cure in this case, however, may be worse than the disease (if there is a disease). If private owners can exploit their workers, cannot the State do so also, with its huge coercive apparatus, such as summary arrests, secret trials, and slave labor camps? The State has this power, a power which private employers in a free economy do not have; what assurance is there, then, that the State will not use it?

It is part of the Marxist theory that "the State will wither away." But if no private ownership of the means of production is permitted, what fills the vacuum? "Public ownership"—ownership by the State—is the suggested alternative. It won't do to say "the people" own it: not all the people acting together can manage a factory or make decisions as to what and how much to produce and where to obtain the materials. "Publicly owned" factories in the Soviet Union are managed and controlled by a few bureaucrats, typically political appointees who have not worked their way up through the ranks and therefore do not know the business through and through, as the private entrepreneur does. Thus, when private ownership is forbidden, the State not

only operates the economy wastefully and inefficiently, but it becomes omnipotent: it owns everything, it controls everything, and it can deny access
to anything to any person for any reason it wishes.

This point is dramatically made in Henry Hazlitt's "futuristic" novel *Time
Will Run Back,* in which the dictator of a nation, Stalenin, suddenly dies and
his son is called home to rule. The citizens have no knowledge of a free
economy, all books about it having long since been burned. Now Peter Stalenin, the son, must try to restore prosperity to a ruined economy. At first
he tries to do it through dictatorship from above:

> "Of course people ought to consider it a privilege to work for the
> State, because when they work for the State they are working for them-
> selves; they are working for each other . . ."

Peter stopped. He found that he was mechanically repeating the arguments of Bolshekov.

"I agree that people ought to feel this way," said Adams, "but our
experience shows that they just don't. The hard fact is that some people
simply have to do more unpleasant chores than others, and the only way
we can get the unpleasant chores done is by compulsion. Not everybody
can be a manager, or an actor or an artist or a violin player. Somebody
has to dig the coal, collect the garbage, repair the sewers. Nobody will
deliberately *choose* these smelly jobs. People will have to be assigned to
them, forced to do them."

"Well, perhaps we could compensate them in some way, Adams—say
by letting them work shorter hours than the others."

"We thought of that long ago, chief. It didn't work. It unluckily
turned out that it was only the pleasant jobs, like acting or violin playing, that could be reduced to short hours. But we simply can't afford to
have people work only a few hours on the nasty jobs. These are precisely the jobs that have to be done. We couldn't afford to cut our coal
production in half by cutting the hours in half, for example; and we just
haven't got the spare manpower to rotate. Besides, we found that on
most such jobs a considerable loss of time and production was involved
merely in changing shifts."

"All right," agreed Peter; "so under our socialist system we can't have
freedom in choice of work or occupation. But couldn't we provide some
freedom of initiative—at least for those who direct production? Our propaganda is always urging more initiative on the part of commissars or
individual plant managers. Why don't we get it?"

"Because a commissar or plant manager, chief, is invariably shot if his
initiative goes wrong. The very fact that he was using his own initiative
means that he was not following orders. How can you reconcile individual initiative with planning from the center? When we draw up our Five
Year Plans, we allocate the production of hundreds of different com-
modities and services in accordance with what we assume to be the

needs of the people. Now if every plant manager decided for himself what things his plant should produce or how much it should produce of them, our production would turn out to be completely unbalanced and chaotic."

"Very well," Peter said; "so we can't permit the individual plant manager to decide what to produce or how much to produce of it. But this is certainly a big disadvantage. For if someone on the Central Planning Board doesn't think of some new need to be satisfied, or some new way of satisfying an old need, then nobody thinks of it and nobody dares to supply it. But I have in mind something different from that. How can we encourage individual plant managers to devise more efficient ways of producing the things they are ordered to produce? If these plant managers can't be encouraged to invent new or better consumption goods, at least they can be encouraged to invent new methods or machines to produce more economically the consumption goods they are ordered to produce, or to produce a higher quality of those consumption goods."

"You're just back to the same problem," Adams said. "If I'm a plant manager, and I invent a new machine, I'll have to ask the Central Planning Board to get somebody to build it, or to allocate the materials to me so that I can build it. In either case I'll upset the preordained central plan. I'll have a hard job convincing the Central Planning Board that my invention or experiment won't fail. If my invention does fail, and it turns out that I have wasted scarce labor and materials, I will be removed and probably shot. The member of the Central Planning Board who approved my project will be lucky if he isn't shot himself. Therefore, unless the success of my invention or experiment seems absolutely certain in advance, I will be well advised to do what everybody else does. Then if I fail, I can prove that I failed strictly according to the rules. . . . Now take your other suggestion, chief. Suppose I devise a more economical method of making the product assigned to my factory. I will probably need different proportions of labor and materals, or different kinds of labor and materials, than I would with the old method. And in that case I will again be upsetting the central plan."

Peter sighed. "That doesn't seem to leave much room under our system for initiative, improvement and progress."

Adams shrugged his shoulders. . . .

"Very well then, Adams. So under our socialist system we can't have freedom in choice of work or occupation; we can't have freedom of initiative. But can't we at least give people more freedom in the choice of what they consume?"

"How are you going to do that?" Adams asked. "We issue ration tickets for everything we produce, and we try to distribute them evenly—at least within each of the Four Functional Groups. We can't let people have ration tickets for more than we produce. They complain about that already."

"No, Adams; but some people like cigarettes and others don't; some like beer and others don't; some prefer spinach to potatoes, and some like it the other way round. Why not permit everyone his choice?"

"Well, maybe we could work out something better than the present rationing system, chief, but the fundamental problem remains. People can consume only what is produced. We must draw up our production plans in advance, on the basis of the known needs and assumed wants of consumers. And then . . . well, I repeat: people can consume only what is produced. So how can they have freedom of choice?"

"I think there are two answers to that," said Peter, after blowing a few more smoke rings. "We could still give consumers considerable freedom of choice *individually,* even if they did not have much when considered *collectively.* In other words, out of the stock of goods already produced, we could devise some method under which one person could get more spinach if he preferred, and the other more potatoes, instead of each having to take the exact proportion in which the total supplies of spinach and potatoes were raised."

"Well—maybe, chief. But I still insist that the fundamental problem would remain unsolved. Considered collectively, how can consumers have any freedom of choice? They have to take what there is."

. . .

". . . And I haven't even mentioned one problem. Suppose there is some product, or some potential product, which is not produced but which, if it were invented or discovered or produced, people would want in great quantities? How are you going to find by mathematics that people would want such a product *if* it existed? Or even that such a product is missing?"

Peter sighed. "It's all pretty discouraging. We seem to be reduced to the conclusion that under our socialist system we can't have freedom in choice of work or occupation and we can't permit freedom of choice for consumers. Is that right?"

"People are free to use or not to use their ration tickets," answered Adams.

"In other words," said Peter, "they are free to consume what we tell them they can consume. They are free to consume what we, the rulers, have decided to produce."

. . .

". . . I'm frankly bewildered. What did Friedrich Engels mean, anyhow, when he said that 'Socialism is an ascent from the kingdom of necessity to the kingdom of freedom?' "

"He was talking only of what conditions would be when the socialist heaven had finally been reached," Adams answered. "He was obviously not talking of the transitional period from capitalism into socialism. That period, as Marx very distinctly pointed out, would be marked by the 'dictatorship of the proletariat.' And when Marx said 'dictatorship' he meant *dictatorship*."

"How long was the transitional period supposed to take?"

" 'Until the resistance of the capitalists has been completely broken,' as Lenin said. Until the capitalists have disappeared, until there are no classes."

"How long was *that* supposed to take?"

"A few years . . . maybe even a few decades . . . I don't know."

"But we completely defeated the capitalists and the bourgeoisie more than a century ago!"

"I suppose Marx and Engels would argue, chief, if they were alive today, that the transitional period would go on until the last remnants of capitalist mentality had been stamped or educated out of people's minds, until each wanted to work for all and not for himself."

"But we have now had more than a century of daydreaming, pep talks, exhortations, denunciations, forced labor, shootings and torture—and we still don't seem to have brought about that transformation in human motives!"

"Human nature, chief, seems to be a little more stubborn than Marx and Engels supposed. They argued, of course, that it was not human nature that created human institutions, but rather that it was human institutions that created human nature."

"Doesn't that sound, Adams, like putting the cart before the horse? And even under capitalism, if a man really wanted to work primarily for humanity, instead of primarily for himself and his family, wasn't he free to do so?"

"But under capitalism, chief, he got the highest rewards by working for himself; therefore his biggest incentive was to work for himself and not for others."

"That's begging the question. If a man is not already selfish, he is not stimulated by selfish incentives. If he finds his greatest reward in advancing the welfare and happiness of others, that is what he will do; and selfish incentives will not divert him, because he will not feel them."

"Then I suppose the answer is, chief, to set up social institutions so as to harness even the self-regarding motives in such a way that when a man pursues his own welfare he will do most to promote the welfare of society."

"But socialism begins precisely at the other end, Adams! It argues that it is only by pursuing the welfare of society that a man can promote his own welfare. The appeal is still primarily selfish. But the argument, judging by results, appears to be unconvincing. . . . Let me put it this way: 'I want to get rich,' said the individual in the Dark Ages. 'Go ahead and get rich,' answered capitalism, 'and you will find, to your surprise, that you have also incidentally enriched society.' 'I want to get rich,' still says the individual today. 'Devote yourself to enriching society,' says socialism, 'and you will find, to your surprise, that this is also the surest way to enrich yourself.' "

"Isn't that the nobler appeal, chief?"

"I don't know. But it seems to me that the real question is which system actually works best."

"You started by asking me, chief, what Engels meant when he said that socialism was 'a leap from the kingdom of necessity to the kingdom of freedom.' "

"Ah, yes . . . and what *did* he mean?"

"He meant, I take it," answered Adams, "that under capitalism the individual was not free but enslaved, because one class was dominated and exploited by another; one man was dominated and exploited by another; the worker had to obey the orders of his employer or starve. And socialism means freedom from all this."

"I don't quite see it," Peter said. "Under any system of production whatever, there has to be social organization. There have to be those who direct the work and those who are directed; those who give orders and those who follow them; those who boss and those who are bossed. There has to be, in other words, a managerial hierarchy. If it is merely a question of building a single house, there has to be someone to decide that the house is to be put up, and what kind and where. There has to be an architect to design it, a builder to interpret the plans and to decide what workers to use and what to tell them to do—"

"But under socialism, chief, unlike capitalism, there is no exploitation of the workers for the profit of the employer."

"Under socialism," retorted Peter, "the State is the sole employer. If the worker fails to please the powers that be in the State, or if he arouses their active animosity, there is no one else to whom he can turn. A far greater tyranny may be exercised over him under socialism than I imagine was even possible under capitalism. For if a worker failed to please a particular employer under capitalism, I imagine he was free to go to another. And the fear of losing his exploited workers to some other employer must have mitigated the exploitation practiced by each employer. . . . But under socialism, if a worker falls out of favor with the powers that constitute the State, he can be forced to starve; there is no one else to whom he can turn."

"What I think Engels meant, chief, is that under capitalism the workers were exploited by the capitalist class, and crises and depressions seemed to come like visitations apart from anybody's wishes; while under socialism, society takes its destiny into its own hands and is in that sense free."

"I see," said Peter sarcastically. "And in practice, who constitutes 'society?' Who *is* 'society?' "

"Society is everyone."

"Oh, come now! *Everyone* can't make the decisions. No two persons' decisions would ever agree."

"Well, by society I mean the State."

"And by the State—?"

Adams grinned. "I mean us."

"Exactly. The hierarchy momentarily headed by me," said Peter. He had a sick feeling as he thought once more of his appalling responsibility. "What it comes down to is this, Adams. Society consists, and consists necessarily, of a small body of rulers and a large body of ruled. And this body of rulers itself consists of a hierarchy, finally topped by one man with the power to resolve disputes and make final decisions. So when we say that 'society' does this or that, we mean that the State does this or that. And when we say the State, we mean the ruling hierarchy. We mean the Protectors; we mean the Party; we mean the Central Committee; we mean the Politburo; we mean merely the Dictator himself—or," Peter grinned, "the Dictator's Deputy."

"But under socialism," protested Adams, "the State reflects not the will of the exploiters against the proletariat, but the will of the proletariat themselves. The State is just the mechanism by which the People express their will. It is a dictatorship of the proletariat—"

"Or a dictatorship *over* the proletariat? Let's face the real facts. Under our socialist system a few people—say the Central Planning Board—make the economic plan, and the rest of the people are ordered to carry out the plan. All initiative must come from the center, and none can come from the periphery."

"It *has* to be that way, chief. There would be no point in having a master overall plan, deciding just what goods should be produced, and just how much of each, and by just whom, if anybody anywhere were free to decide to make or do something else. That would be chaos."

"But isn't there any productive system that would allow more liberty, Adams? Isn't there any system that would allow more centers of initiative? What actually happened under capitalism? Were workers free to change from one job to another that they liked better? Was the individual capitalist free to decide to make what he pleased, and in the way he pleased? Was the consumer free to consume what he preferred, and to reject what he didn't like?"

"I don't know what happened under capitalism, chief. Nobody knows. And we destroyed the capitalist literature so completely that I don't see how we are going to find out. But surely we are not going to turn back to that discredited and vicious system—which the world got rid of at the cost of so much blood and sacrifice—to take lessons in how to improve socialism!"

"All right," agreed Peter, "let's forget about capitalism. But I still don't understand what Engels meant when he called socialism 'the kingdom of freedom.' I still don't know what Marx meant when he said that under socialism the State would 'wither away.' For it seems to me that it is above all under socialism, where the State owns all the means of production, does all the planning and assigns and controls all the jobs, that the State is and must be closest to omnipotence. . . ."

He gazed unseeingly out of the window.

"Adams, you have convinced me. It is precisely under a socialist State that the least liberty can exist. Under complete socialism, in fact, liberty for the individual is simply impossible."[7]

D. Democracy

We are so accustomed to the idea of democracy that the solution to the difficulties in the preceding positions seems obvious to us. In a small group every citizen participates in devising the rules (laws) that shall govern them, as in a New England town meeting, or in ancient Athens, where every citizen was a voting member; both of these are instances of *direct democracy*. In a large modern nation, however, direct participation in lawmaking is impossible, so governance is feasible only by means of a *representative democracy:* all who are eligible and care to may go to the polls and elect those who will make the laws.

It should be clear, however, that going to the polls and electing representatives isn't enough. In many dictatorships people go to the polls too, but the choice is always between, for example, one communist candidate and another communist candidate; there is no choice for anyone who wants to vote anticommunist. There is more of a choice in the United States, but still, if there are only two viable candidates for president and a voter doesn't like either one, he or she is in the unenviable position of either not voting or voting for someone he or she doesn't really want—the lesser of two evils. So there has to be a choice among candidates representing widely differing views, not merely differing personalities, in order for there to be a truly representative democracy.

Representative democracy is also limited if candidates of a diverse spectrum of opinion are chosen by certain high officials of the government who then have the power to determine who can be voted for. The final result may not be all that different from a dictatorship. There has to be some provision for *grass-roots* movements, starting from the bottom up and not coming from the top down. In other words, there must be room for initiatives and referendums, or the wishes of the majority of the people may still not be represented in government.

But even if there are initiatives and referendums, a truly representative democracy may still not exist. If the *channels of communication,* such as the press, radio, and television, are all either owned by the government or con-

---

[7] Henry Hazlitt, *Time Will Run Back* (Westport, Conn.: Arlington House, 1966), pp. 118–24, 129–33. (Also published under the title *The Great Idea*.) Reprinted by permission of Henry Hazlitt.

trolled by it so that the only information voters get on a candidate is from the censored press and it is all favorable, the majority may vote for that candidate but voters might not have done so if they had known the facts. Such a government would have the trappings of democracy but still fall short of representing the real wishes of the majority.

But now suppose all these conditions are fulfilled: there are many, diverse candidates selected from grass-roots movements who present their programs in a free press. There are still problems with democracy. Democracy, it is said, is "government by the people," "self-government," or "government with the consent of the governed." But all these stock phrases are somewhat confusing. When I speak of myself, I mean one person, an individual. When ten people each speak of themselves, they mean each one individually: *A* means *A*, *B* means *B*, and so on. But when we speak of democracy as "self-government," we are not talking about each of us governing himself or herself at all; we are speaking of a process in which the majority of the voters favors a certain candidate, who, together with others in Congress or the legislature, decides which bills will be enacted into law (a decision again made by a majority). You, as an individual, may be opposed to all of them. In this situation you are not governing yourself, but *they* are governing *you*. You do have a part in the election of these people, an infinitesimally small part (almost never enough to swing an election), but *you* are not determining policy: indeed, a certain policy may be imposed on you against your will, which is hardly a case of *you* governing *yourself*. The self is an individual, not a collective; and democracy is government by the majority of a collective, which may not accord with the needs or wishes of you as a self at all. You are governed by others whose tenure in office you may or may not approve.

In a representative democracy the will of the majority becomes law—not the majority of the citizens but the majority of the legislators at any particular time. But what of the minority? What if the majority votes to persecute or to discriminate against a minority, or even to kill off the minority group? In a democracy, whatever the majority says goes. If 51 percent say yes and 49 percent say no, the 49 percent have to live with a policy which may mean persecution or exile, confiscation of possessions, or even death in the gas chamber.

But the possible ill effect of democracy on the minority is not the only limitation of democracy. Even the majority may be harmed, for members of the majority may be easily persuaded, by lies, distortions, and propaganda, to do stupid, foolish, or shortsighted acts. Error times 100 million is still error. A majority voting on some national policy may be just as catastrophic as a majority voting what the proper cure for arthritis is. No special knowledge of statecraft is possessed by the majority—and that is precisely why Plato had only scorn for democracy:

> Imagine this state of affairs on board a ship or a number of ships. The master is bigger and burlier than any of the crew, but a little deaf and short-sighted and no less deficient in seamanship. The sailors are quar-

relling over the control of the helm; each thinks he ought to be steering the vessel, though he has never learnt navigation and cannot point to any teacher under whom he has served his apprenticeship; what is more, they assert that navigation is a thing that cannot be taught at all, and are ready to tear in pieces anyone who says it can. Meanwhile they besiege the master himself, begging him urgently to trust them with the helm; and sometimes, when others have been more successful in gaining his ear, they kill them or throw them overboard, and, after somehow stupefying the worthy master with strong drink or an opiate, take control of the ship, make free with its stores, and turn the voyage, as might be expected of such a crew, into a drunken carousal. Besides all this, they cry up as a skilled navigator and master of seamanship anyone clever enough to lend a hand in persuading or forcing the master to set them in command. Every other kind of man they condemn as useless. They do not understand that the genuine navigator can only make himself fit to command a ship by studying the seasons of the year, sky, stars, and winds, and all that belongs to his craft; and they have no idea that along with the science of navigation, it is possible for him to gain, by instruction or practice, the skill to keep control of the helm whether some of them like it or not. If a ship were managed in that way, would not those on board be likely to call the expert in navigation a mere star-gazer, who spent his time in idle talk and was useless to them? . . . But our present rulers may fairly be compared to the sailors in our parable, and the useless visionaries, as the politicians call them, to the real masters of navigation.[8]

Those worthy to occupy positions in government are not usually those who are attractive to the majority of the population. People are taken in by thirty-second television ads, which don't tell where a candidate stands on the issues or why, but only try to "con" the public into liking a candidate's face or demeanor. Voters go for charming personalities, whether or not they are qualified for the difficult job before them. They tend to prefer the candidates who promise the most, disregarding the question of where the money to pay for the proposals is to come from. They tend not to like really superior individuals, for the voters feel inferior to them and prefer someone mediocre ("one of us"). In democracy, said Plato, there is

a contempt for all those fine principles we laid down in founding our commonwealth, as when we said that only a very exceptional nature could turn out a good man, if he had not played as a child among things of beauty and given himself only to creditable pursuits. A democracy tramples all such notions under foot; with a magnificent indifference to

[8] From *The Republic of Plato* translated by F. M. Cornford (1941), pp. 195–96. Reprinted by permission of Oxford University Press.

the sort of life a man has led before he enters politics, it will promote to honor anyone who merely calls himself the people's friend.[9]

Suppose that a physician or nutritionist tries to tell a man what foods are good for him, what he should eat and not eat. But the man "knows what he likes" and prefers to eat what he likes rather than what is beneficial to him. Advertisements promoting the foods he likes, and pandering to his desires, extol the alleged virtues of the foods he prefers. It is more than likely that he will succumb to them, listening to the confectioner rather than to the nutritionist. According to Plato, democracy is government by confectioners.

The first president of Mexico, Benito Juárez, is said to have remarked, "Since democracy is government by the people, and the people do not vote themselves into slavery, freedom flows from democracy as water flows from the hills." But the people, collectively, sometimes do vote themselves into slavery—not wanting it, no doubt, but not seeing it as the end result of the policies they vote for. Spurred by politicians' promises, they vote more and more benefits for themselves, which mean higher taxes; and when taxes become so high that they will vote out of office any legislator who votes to increase them (though they still want the benefits), the only way to pay for the benefits is by printing money, with the result that the value of each unit of money declines and inflation starts spiraling upward. The majority of people don't want inflation, but they fail to see that outcome as the predictable result of the benefits they vote for. Or, they may think, "We'll take it from the rich." Then productive enterprises stop expanding, or are abandoned entirely, and massive unemployment results, necessitating increasing welfare benefits from a decreasing reserve: more and more people take cookies out of the jar, and fewer and fewer people put new cookies in, until after a time, the jar is empty. A "benevolent despot" who looked a few inches ahead of his nose would have known this and seen it coming, but the majority in a democracy turns instead to the confectioners.

And so in time democracy collapses into totalitarianism. Out of the chaos comes a Caesar who restores law and order at gunpoint, and on harsh terms. Democracy has self-destructed. This is not *necessarily* the fate of all democracies, but it has happened often enough in history to give us pause. Plato believed that democracy gives way to totalitarianism, and history has repeatedly borne him out.

E. A Constitutional Republic

The United States is not, strictly speaking, a democracy but a *constitutional republic;* that is, not anything that a majority of the members of Congress vote on can become law, because there is a constitution which limits the

---

[9] Ibid. p. 283. Reprinted by permission of Oxford University Press.

powers of the majority to enact laws. For example, the First Amendment says that Congress shall pass no law abridging freedom of speech or of the press; thus, if Congress passed a law banning the publication of information critical of the State, such a law might well be declared unconstitutional by the Supreme Court. If a law was enacted condemning prisoners without a trial, refusing them *habeas corpus,* or exacting torture or other "cruel and unusual punishment," all such laws would be declared unconstitutional and would be null and void.

Of course, a constitution can always be changed—in the case of the United States, by the concurrence of the legislatures of three-fourths of the states— but the amendment process is usually long and arduous, not the sort of thing that can be rushed like the passage of a law during the frantic closing days of a legislative session. An amendment cannot be passed without many millions of people knowing about it and heatedly arguing its pros and cons for a considerable period of time. At any rate, the design of a constitutional republic is to protect the rights and freedoms of citizens by *placing a limit* on what a majority of legislators may enact. But in what specific ways should a limit be placed on majority vote, and in what specific directions? On this question disagreement is considerable.

In John Rawls's book *A Theory of Justice* (1971), readers are asked to imagine a group of persons about to become the founders of a new nation somewhere on earth who wish to determine in advance the nature of the constitution which will determine what each of them will be legally permitted to do or prohibited from doing. All the prospective citizens are assumed to be ignorant of what their social status will be, what their position will be in the work force, even what race they will belong to and what sex they will be. Thus, it is not likely that discriminatory legislation will be permitted against any particular group (blacks, women, labor, farmers, etc.), since any person might find himself or herself in that group. The "veil of ignorance" concerning all such matters is meant to secure impartiality in each person's decision. The main principles which every impartial voter will accept, according to Rawls, are:

> First principle: Each person is to have an equal right to the most extensive total system of equal basic liberties compatible with a similar system of liberty for all.
> Second principle: Social and economic inequalities are to be arranged so that they are both (a) to the greatest benefit of the least advantaged, consistent with the just savings principle, and (b) attached to offices and positions open to all under conditions of fair equality of opportunity.[10]

Such principles, embodied in the constitution of a republic, involve a limitation on the powers of the State in some ways but an extension of them in

[10]John Rawls, *A Theory of Justice* (Cambridge, Mass.: Harvard University Press, 1971), p. 302. The "just savings principle" limits the amount of capital and resources that may be accumulated in one generation in view of the rights of subsequent generations.

others. Equality of opportunity would be embedded in the constitution by the *b* part of the second principle. It not only would require the enactment of what is now known as the Equal Rights Amendment, but (depending on how it is interpreted) would necessitate a large body of enforcers to ensure that everyone's opportunities were indeed equal; some would say that even a tightly run police State would not suffice to attain it (see p. 317.) The enactment of the *a* part of that principle would have even more profound consequences: if some technical innovation, such as the automobile, was introduced and did not improve the lot of everyone, including the buggy manufacturer, such an innovation presumably would not be permitted. How many innovations that have reduced drudgery and increased leisure in modern life would have been possible within such a restriction?

Is there any one kind of constitutional republic that a group of intelligent and impartial individuals would decide to create, particularly if a unanimous vote were required? In view of the countless utopias that have been spawned throughout the ages by writers who sincerely believed that intelligent and impartial persons, one and all, would choose the one that the author described, it seems highly improbable that any one constitution, Rawls's or any other, would receive the unanimous assent of any sizable group of human beings. Rawls's constitution-makers, for example, entrust enormous powers to the elected representatives of the State, as well as to the government bureaucracy; many others, viewing the abuses of power of governments throughout the ages, would entrust the State with far fewer powers.

The primary intent of the framers of the American Constitution was to *limit* the role of the State, so that individuals would be protected not only from harm done by other individuals but from harm done by the State itself. The Bill of Rights (the first ten amendments to the Constitution) endeavored to preserve freedom of speech and press, to make citizens secure against unwarranted search and seizure, to enable them to defend their lives and their homes, to ensure that no one was convicted of a crime without a fair trial, and so on. In a democracy such rights and liberties would not always be protected: the populace, often ignorant of the issues, inflamed by popular appeals, or thinking only of the immediate present and not of the long-term consequences of their recommendations, might overturn some of these rights and liberties; against such tendencies a constitution would stand as a bulwark to limit the power of the majority.

The U.S. Constitution says much about political freedom but little about economic freedom, though probably if a resolution had been introduced saying that "Congress shall pass no law abridging freedom of production and trade," it would have been viewed with favor. But it is economic freedom that the bulk of legislation in the twentieth century has served to curtail (for the most part without constitutional authority as far as the federal government is concerned). Advocates of limited government have thus been especially concerned to remove the countless limitations on freedom of production and trade already enacted into law.

Those economic measures, according to advocates of the free market, have had undesirable consequences for the consumer, although that was not the intention of the legislators at the time they enacted the measures. For example, Congress has passed minimum wage laws—a seemingly humane measure meant to ensure that workers have decent wages. But the main effect of such laws has been to create unemployment: the restaurateur and the owner of the corner shop who cannot afford the minimum wage have had to dismiss the employees they couldn't afford. The law thus has kept one group protected from the market at legislated wages, while keeping all others from getting employment at all. The apprenticeship system, which would enable persons to learn a trade, also has been destroyed, since it doesn't pay an employer to train someone for a job at the legislated wage. In addition, the "humane" legislation has discouraged expansion of production and has foreclosed jobs for future employees. The businesses that would have expanded if no such legislation had become law would have competed with each other for able workers, thus pushing wages up.

Consider another case—the passage of rent-control laws by legislatures and municipalities. In order to prevent people from having to pay unreasonable rents, rents have been frozen at a certain rate. But the result has been that the housing industry has died: it isn't worth anyone's while to build new housing at the legislated rents, and the building trades go to the areas of the country that do not have rent controls. The solution to the problem—having so many apartment units available that owners would have to compete to get renters—has been rendered impossible by the fact that the controls discourage, rather than encourage, new building. And since the owners often can't keep apartments up to standard at the required rental rates, they neglect them or abandon them, thus turning many cities into slums.

There are countless other examples of laws such as those mentioned, whose tendency is to deprive people of the very opportunities the legislation seeks to make available. Economic legislation of that sort also has expanded an already overblown bureaucracy, which raises everyone's taxes and requires huge increases in the money supply (inflation) to sustain it.[11]

Many persons care little about economic liberty, particularly if they are not themselves involved in economic activities: they don't care how much other people are controlled, although they themselves suffer in the form of higher taxes and higher prices for everything they buy. But economic liberty and political liberty are intimately connected. For example, the First Amendment guarantees freedom of the press; but what if the federal government, anxious to silence its critics in the press, was to own and distribute all supplies of wood pulp and paper, and to allot supplies of paper only to those

---

[11] For further discussion of the effects of such legislation, see, for example, Albert Lee, *Slumlord* (Westport, Conn.: Arlington House, 1975); Murray Rothbard, *For a New Liberty* (New York: Macmillan, 1973), Chapter 8; John Hospers, *Libertarianism* (New York: Laissez Faire Books, 1971), Chapter 4; H. B. Acton, *The Morals of Markets* (London: Longmans, 1971); and Milton Friedman and F. A. Hayek, eds., *Rent Control: Myths and Realities* (Hillside, N.J.: Enslow Publishers, 1981).

newspapers and magazines that refrained from criticizing the government? Such a move would silence the criticism as effectively as would a violation of the First Amendment through censorship. Being able to obtain paper independently of the government on the free market is thus just as essential to freedom of the press as the constitutional guarantees themselves.

Advocates of limited government constantly attack the intrusion of the State into enterprises which would be far more efficiently handled if the free market was permitted to operate. Consider, for example, the postal service. The U.S. government has a legal monopoly on the handling of first-class mail; no competition in this area is legally permitted. When no one else is permitted to provide the service, the present provider (the State) has no incentive to do its job well, or even adequately. Service deteriorates and costs rise. It was not always so: in the early nineteenth century private carriers of mail competed with one another; they carried the mails from one part of the nation to another more quickly and cheaply than the U.S. Postal Service. At one time the private agencies delivered mail at about one-fifth the cost of the government service. At last Congress cracked down and outlawed all private postal services, thereby creating a State monopoly of the postal system. Whatever rates it charged, no one would undercut its prices, for no compet itors were permitted.[12]

Control of the currency supply seems to many people to be an indispensable function of the State; and yet, advocates of limited government contend, there is even less excuse for government control of the currency than for government control of the postal system. Indeed, considering the historical record of governments in this respect—from the ancient practice of clipping coins to the continuous inflation of the money supply after the invention of paper—it is difficult to resist the conclusion that having the government control the money supply is rather like hiring the fox to guard the chickenhouse. As Congress appropriates more and more money to satisfy more and more lobbyists and pressure groups, the government runs its printing presses over time to pay the bills, which means that every dollar is worth less than before (inflation), and everyone who is on a fixed income or has a savings account is cheated just as much as if he or she had been robbed at gunpoint. Counterfeiters even of small amounts are prosecuted, but the State engages in the same activity in mind-boggling amounts quite legally. The effect in both cases is the same—"watering the stock," "diluting the martini." The Federal Reserve, which has charge of the money supply in the United States, has indeed become, as many predicted at its formation in 1913, an enormous engine of inflation.

The government was not always in such complete control of the currency. During the first century of America's history private minters of coins flourished, and they established such good reputations for their companies that their coins were universally accepted: if a coin said "one ounce of gold," people could depend on it containing an ounce of gold. The companies could also issue paper, but no one was forced to accept it. All this was done away with when the federal government reserved to itself the exclusive right to mint coins and to distribute paper substitutes (which once could be exchanged for gold or silver). Citizens are now required by "legal tender laws" to accept the paper currency in exchanges and in payments of debts, no matter how each unit may have deteriorated in value. How a monetary system could operate efficiently and reliably, without danger of inflation and, without any involvement of the State, has been worked out in numerous writings.[13]

As far as their freedom is concerned, people stand to gain much if government is limited. Instead of people having to use the "services" of a government monopoly such as the post office (and pay for its support whether or not they use it), they can choose which of several competitors to patronize; if they don't like one, they can use another. Competition makes for more efficiency (government monopolies like the post office and the Bureau of Motor Vehicles have no particular incentive to provide efficient service), and individuals also have greater freedom of choice.

What areas might be left to the State? The minimal State, or the "nightwatchman" State, as Robert Nozick calls it,[14] has the primary function of *protection*—not of compulsory redistribution (taking a dollar out of one person's pocket and transferring it to another's, minus the government's handling fee). The main subdivisions of the State would then be (1) the police, to protect citizens from aggressors within the country; (2) the armed forces, to protect citizens from aggressors outside the country; and (3) the courts, to adjudicate disputes involving harm (deliberate or inadvertent) inflicted by one citizen on another. In addition, the State could be charged with, for example, defenses against pollution, protection of the environment, protection against fraud and misrepresentation in consumer products, overseeing installment of safety equipment in factories and vehicles, and (according to some at least) protection of wildlife and endangered species of animals.

Reserving just those areas for the State means, of course, that individuals would have no choice in such matters: they would have to pay taxes to support those State enterprises whether they wanted them or not, and their consent would neither be asked for nor needed. If a local police force or court system was inefficient, unresponsive to demands, or corrupt, there would not be much citizens could do about it: they would still be required to pay taxes to support an organization they would not support voluntarily.

Suppose then that these functions too were placed in the "private sector."

[13] See, for example, Henry Hazlitt, *The Inflation Crisis and How to Resolve It* (Westport, Conn.: Arlington House, 1978); Martin A. Larson, *The Federal Reserve* (Old Greenwich, Conn.: Devin-Adair, rev. ed. 1978); Friedrich A. Hayek, *Choice in Currency* and *Denationalization of Money* (both published by the Institute of Economic Affairs, London, 1976); and Henry Mark Holzer, *Government's Money Monopoly* (New York: Books in Focus, 1981).

[14] Robert Nozick, *Anarchy, State, and Utopia* (New York: Basic Books, 1974).

What would be left for the State? Suppose that the post office started admitting competitors in the distribution of first-class mail; the competitors, always more efficient than the State, would soon capture the market (as happened in the 1840s before the government cracked down), leaving the tax-supported one without any clients. In the same way, suppose that the municipal police force started permitting competitors to "protect" citizens—not just as a *supplement* to the city's services (as in the hiring of a neighborhood patrol car to watch the neighborhood at night) but as a *substitute* for them. People might then say, "I find the Pinkerton Agency much more efficient, and I'd rather not pay taxes to support yours at all." Gradually, as more organizations arose to compete for the business of protecting citizens, the less efficient governmental organization would usually find itself without clients. At that point the State would probably opt for coercing its citizens, rather than to allow one government department after another to self-destruct as private competitors won out in open competition.

But what could justify such coercion? If the State is our servant and not our master, don't we have a right to dispense with its services? Who ever heard of a servant you couldn't let go if he lay down on the job and didn't do anything for you? Many would say, as nineteenth-century English philosopher Herbert Spencer did, that people have the perfect right to rid themselves of the services of such an employee; no one can rightly be forced to pay for such services. "Each man should be free to act as he chooses, provided he trenches not on the equal freedom of each other man to act as he chooses": this was Spencer's "Law of Equal Freedom." [15] Thus each resident, wrote Spencer in 1845, should have the right to employ or discharge whatever servants he or she wants to, including the State:

> We can not choose but admit the right of the citizen to adopt a condition of *voluntary outlawry.* If every man has freedom to do all that he wills, provided he infringes not on the equal freedom of any others, then he is free to *drop connection with the State*—to relinquish its protection and to refuse paying toward its support. It is self-evident that in so behaving he in no way trenches upon the liberty of others, for his position is a passive one, and while passive he cannot become an aggressor. . . . He cannot be compelled to continue one of a political corporation without a breach of the moral law, seeing that citizenship involves payment of taxes; and the taking away of a man's property against his will is an infringement of his rights. *Government being simply an agent employed in common by a number of individuals to secure to them certain advantages, the very nature of the connection implies that it is for each to say whether he will employ such an agent or not.* If any one of them determines to ignore this mutual-safety confederation, nothing can be said except that he loses all claim to its good offices and exposes himself to the danger of maltreat-

[15]Herbert Spencer, *Social Statics* (New York: Robert Schalkenbach Foundation, 1970; originally published in 1845), p. 95.

ment—a thing he is quite at liberty to do if he likes. He cannot be coerced into political combination without breach of the Law of Equal Freedom; he *can* withdraw from it without committing any such breach, and he has therefore a right so to withdraw.[16]

But if a person has the right to ignore the State and to opt for "voluntary outlawry," what would be the result? What if everyone took advantage of this option? Then indeed the State would wither away, and without the State there would be anarchy.

F. Anarchism

"Any undertaking that involves more than one person, requires the voluntary consent of every participant. Every one of them has the right to make his own decision, but none has the right to force his decision on the others."[17] But if this principle was followed, someone might object, wouldn't we end up with no government at all? That is precisely what the advocates of no government, or *anarchism,* want. Before we see how the function now discharged by the State could be handled noncoercively without the State, let us consider one writer's explanation of the moral principle underlying it:

> A group is composed of a number of individuals. If it is morally wrong for one individual to aggress against another, then it is also morally wrong for any group of individuals to do so—even if the group calls itself the government. The reason most people are not committed to this view is that they have not yet seen this logical connection between private aggression and governmental aggression. In fact, if a proponent of the former view is ever asked why he considers it immoral for an individual to aggress, but not immoral for a government, he usually replies in an incredulous tone, "but that's not aggression—we all had an equal chance to vote for our government, didn't we?"
>
> Consider what this view overlooks. Suppose an aggressor A is one of a gang of ten aggressors. He conducts a hold-up in a place of business and takes the proprietor's cash. There is no doubt his conduct is immoral. Suppose, however, the gang had conducted a vote by secret ballot before the hold-up, for the purpose of selecting their hatchet man. Does the fact that these nine people previously approved of the robber's actions justify them? Does the fact that a secret ballot was conducted make the robbery or intimidation moral? Suppose instead of nine people in the gang there were 999. Would this justify the robbery? Would 90 million

16 Ibid., p. 185. Italics added.
17 Ayn Rand, "Man's Rights," in *Capitalism, the Unknown Ideal* (New York: Signet Books, 1967), p. 325.

people justify it? It is apparent the immorality is not changed by numbers. Governmental aggression is no different in principle from this. . . .

At this point the reader might say, "Yes, I agree that aggression is wrong in any form at any time, but let's talk sense. I approve of what the government is doing. I give my consent to be taxed. How can it be theft or intimidation if I approve?" This argument is the basis for the fraudulent claim that a government exists because of "the consent of the governed."

There are some asking this question who are less innocent than others. A person may, in view of a moral alternative, choose to give his consent to allow another individual or group to deprive him of his own rightful values, and providing his choice affects only himself his behavior would be sacrificial. He can bring about his own self-destruction if he is stupid enough to do so, but he cannot morally grant consent to the destruction or deprivation of others. The moment he grants consent or approval in face of a moral alternative, to an organization which he knows will deprive even one other individual of his rightful values without that person's consent, he becomes a contributing cause to the aggression. He merely confesses by so doing that even if he is not yet an actual *formal* member of the aggressive gang, he is certainly a member in principle, a supporter and sympathizer. Such people put the gun in the hands of government because without their "approval" the aggressors would be unarmed.

. . . What then is the moral status of the government apologist who says that the government is not aggressing, since he gives his consent? Would such a person "consent" to have the A & P supermarket threaten and intimidate him, and throw him in jail if he did not financially support them? Does he really consent to government?

The question to ask such an individual is: *would he continue to give his consent to government's demands if they were not similarly made on others?* Let us suppose that government published a statement declaring that all others (except this individual who "gives his consent") who do not wish to pay taxes are free not to do so, without fear of intimidation or jail sentences. Suppose they further stated that no individual or company would be aggressively (by any laws or threats of intimidation) prevented from competing with government in all areas where they now hold an aggressive monopoly. Would the government apologist still consent to government forcing him, *and not the others,* to pay taxes? It is very unlikely that any intellectually honest person would still claim to give his consent to such an aggression against him. *And yet, as far as he is personally concerned, nothing has changed. So what exactly is it that he actually gives his consent to? He is giving his consent to aggression against others, otherwise he would have no objection to being the only one forced to do as government bids him do.* Nor could he claim that it would not be fair for him (a single individual) to be aggressed against, for then he would logically be opposed to aggression against any and all individuals. . . .

Some governmental apologist may still attempt to justify government's demand for taxes on the grounds that no government official or political representative intimidates him with a gun. Let us go back to our example of the robber, and let us suppose that he is a suave, soft-spoken, mild-mannered man. Would it make any difference if, instead of entering the premises with a gun, he phoned the proprietor and gently told him to have 10% of his receipts ready to hand over to him the following day at 4 p.m.? Let us further assume that the proprietor refused to comply. The mild-mannered man now informs the proprietor that he will have to pay more because he did not conform to the majority vote of his gang. Finally after the proprietor refuses all such demands, the soft-spoken robber pays him a visit. This time another man is with him who has a gun. They order the proprietor to appear before a committee set up by the gang. The committee orders the man to pay or go to jail. Has any of this changed the aggressive nature of the gang, or the nature of the mild-mannered robber's conduct? Not the slightest. His aggression has merely become more sophisticated and better disguised. We have already observed that aggression takes many forms and may be performed in numerous ways without the immediate presence of a gun. *What is clear about government and its method of extracting taxes, is that in the final analysis, it always relies on the gun.* Anyone wishing to test this statement need only consistently refuse to pay taxes.[18]

But how would anarchy work in practice? If there is no State, wouldn't anyone be able to do as he or she liked to others and get away with it? Wouldn't we have Hobbes's "state of nature" with us again? Isn't the State necessary—perhaps a necessary evil, but still necessary?

Anarchists reply that the State is an unnecessary evil and that all the essential functions of civilized life can be managed better without it. A government police force can be replaced by private defense agencies, and government court systems can be supplanted by private arbitration agencies. Let's say that the municipal tax-supported police force is disbanded; citizens can then get together and hire a private defense company to protect them. Persons who do not wish to join need not do so—no one else has the right to force them—but they will remain unprotected. The agency will fulfill the same function as the police force, except that its services can be terminated and a more efficient competitor hired. Different people will presumably avail themselves of the services of different agencies, just as they now use different insurance companies to insure their homes and their cars.

What if a man stole something from you and he belonged to a different agency? If a representative of your agency came to him to demand return of the stolen item, couldn't he say, "Your agency has no jurisdiction over me—so get lost"? What would happen then?

---

[18] Richard and Ernestine Perkins, "The Nature of Government," in their *Rational Anarchy* (New York: Laissez Faire Books, 1971), pp. 72–75. Some emphasis added. Reprinted by permission of the authors.

Inevitably, conflicts would arise between one protective agency and another. According to David Friedman, however, such conflicts could be resolved:

> I come home one night and find my television set missing. I immediately call my protection agency, Tannahelp Inc., to report the theft. They send an agent. He checks the automatic camera which Tannahelp, as part of their service, installed in my living room and discovers a picture of one Joe Bock lugging the television set out of the door. The Tannahelp agent contacts Joe, informs him that Tannahelp has reason to believe he is in possession of my television set, and suggests he return it, along with an extra ten dollars to pay for Tannahelp's time and trouble in locating Joe. Joe replies that he has never seen my television set in his life and tells the Tannahelp agent to go to hell.
>
> The agent points out that until Tannahelp is convinced there has been a mistake, he must proceed on the assumption that the television set is my property. Six Tannahelp employees, all large and energetic, will be at Joe's door next morning to collect the set. Joe, in response, informs the agent that he also has a protection agency, Dawn Defense, and that his contract with them undoubtedly requires them to protect him if six goons try to break into his house and steal his television set.
>
> The stage seems set for a nice little war between Tannahelp and Dawn Defense. . . .
>
> But wars are very expensive, and Tannahelp and Dawn Defense are both profit-making corporations, more interested in saving money than face. . . .
>
> The Tannahelp agent calls up his opposite number at Dawn Defense. "We've got a problem." . . . After explaining the situation, he points out that if Tannahelp sends six men, and Dawn eight, there will be a fight. Someone might even get hurt. Whoever wins, by the time the conflict is over it will be expensive for both sides. They might even have to start paying their employees higher wages to make up for the risk. Then both firms will be forced to raise their rates. If they do, Murbard Ltd., an aggressive new firm which has been trying to get established in the area, will undercut their prices and steal their customers. There must be a better solution.
>
> The man from Tannahelp suggests that the better solution is arbitration. They will take the dispute over my television set to a reputable local arbitration firm. If the arbitrator decides that Joe is innocent, Tannahelp agrees to pay Joe and Dawn Defense an indemnity to make up for their time and trouble. If he is found guilty, Dawn Defense will accept the verdict; since the television set is not Joe's, they have no obligation to protect him when the men from Tannahelp come to seize it.
>
> What I have described is a very makeshift arrangement. In practice, once (free market) institutions were well established, protection agencies would anticipate such difficulties and arrange contracts in advance, be-

fore specific conflicts occurred, specifying the arbitrator who would settle them.[19]

But how are arbitrators to make their decisions? Must there not be one
standard "code of law" on the basis of which they must decide?

> In [a free market] society, who would make the laws? On what basis
> would the private arbitrator decide what acts were criminal and what
> their punishments should be? The answer is that systems of law would
> be produced for profit on the open market. . . . There could be com-
> petition among different brands of law, just as there is competition
> among different brands of cars.
> In such a society there might be many courts and even many legal
> systems. Each pair of protection agencies agrees in advance on which
> court they will use in case of conflict. Thus the laws under which a
> particular case is decided are determined implicitly by advance agree-
> ment between the protection agencies whose customers are involved. In
> principle, there could be a different court and a different set of laws for
> every pair of protection agencies. In practice, many agencies would
> probably find it convenient to patronize the same courts, and many
> courts might find it convenient to adopt identical, or nearly identical,
> systems of law in order to simplify matters for their customers. . . .
> In such a society law is produced on the market. A court supports
> itself by charging for the service of arbitrating disputes. Its success de-
> pends on its reputation for honesty, reliability, and promptness and also
> on the desirability to potential customers of the particular set of laws it
> judges by. The immediate customers are protection agencies. But the
> protection agency is itself selling a product to its customers. Part of that
> product is the legal system, or systems, of the courts it patronizes and
> under which its customers will consequently be judged. Each protection
> agency will try to patronize those courts under whose legal system its
> customers would like to live.[20]

But couldn't criminals get together and form their own protective organization, looting and killing others and being defended by their own agency in
the process of doing so? According to Friedman:

> There would hardly be enough murderers at any one time to support
> their own protective agency, one with a policy of patronizing courts that
> did not regard murder as a crime. Even if there were, no other protec-
> tive agency would accept such courts. The murderers' agency would

[19] David Friedman, *The Machinery of Freedom* (Westport, Conn.: Arlington House, 1978), pp.
157–58. Reprinted by permission of Arlington House Publishers, Westport, Connecticut.
[20] Ibid., pp. 159–60. Reprinted by permission of Arlington House Publishers, Westport, Connecticut.

either accept a reasonable court or fight a hopeless war against the rest of society.[21]

But there are problems with anarchism also. Let us consider a few.

1. If there are different arbitration agencies, each one might have somewhat different rules it would enforce. All would presumably try to protect their members against such obvious offenses as murder, violence, and theft; they wouldn't get many clients if they failed to do that much. But what if some members wanted to be protected against the presence of adult bookstores or X-rated films and joined an organization that would raid such stores and burn the books? The defense agency to which the bookstore owners belonged would then attempt to locate and turn them over to its arbitration agency for trial. But the agency representing the store breakers would respond that by the rules of *their* agency no crime was committed and they therefore had every right to destroy the sources of such immoral influences. What next? A war between them would be expensive and would only encourage other agencies to enter the scene that could charge less because they did not have to absorb the costs of such a conflict. They would probably try to settle the matter by adjudication. But who would win? Probably the agency which had the largest clientele in the area. This solution would certainly not be satisfactory to all parties, but whenever there is a deep-rooted conflict of opinion satisfaction for all is not possible in any case. It is the same under government: passing a law prohibiting such bookstores is bound to be unpopular with some people, but not doing so is unpopular with others, and either there will be such bookstores or there won't; the wishes of both groups cannot be satisfied. Any individual client would get the defense agency, but not necessarily the result, he or she wants.

2. But what if an individual wanted protection but couldn't afford it? Some would say, "You only get what you pay for. If you're forced to provide something for another person for which that person won't or can't pay, you are to that extent enslaved to that person." Others would add that everyone pays for protection now, since everyone pays taxes: you pay a sales tax on every item you buy, and although only homeowners pay property taxes, renters are charged more because of the property taxes their landlords have to pay (among other things, to support the police). But let us consider the matter of the cost of protection a bit further:

Friedman might decide to purchase the Pinkerton "Paranoid Plan," while Joe might make do with a couple of locks and a little wire that turns on an "aa-oo-ga" horn when tripped. Governed, both Friedman and Joe will have no choice as to what agency they do business with— there would be only one. On the free market, one might decide that Tannahelp, Inc. was by far the most reliable name in the industry, while

[21] Ibid., p. 164. Reprinted by permission of Arlington House Publishers, Westport, Connecticut.

the other might prefer Dawn Defense. Finally, consider Maxine. She lives across the street from Friedman and next door to Joe. She would like the Paranoid Plan, but is able to afford only one small Yale lock. She is presently saving her money toward the day when she can afford an aa-oo-ga horn like Joe's. Under the governmental system, Maxine would be assured of getting the rough equivalent of one more lock *and* the horn, for the government would see to it that Friedman and Joe paid for it for her. This is not the case on the free market. Maxine must continue to scrimp and save, perhaps having to go without sufficiently nutritious meals, until she has managed to purchase the horn.

· · ·

The problem of Maxine is not unique to the free market arrangement. . . . Any plausible governmental solution is likely to have its Maxines too. There have always been groups of people who have been inadequately protected by their governments. Sometimes it has been ethnic groups, sometimes religious groups, sometimes just "non-conformists"; police services have, from time to time, been inadequately provided to people because of their sex, because of their social beliefs, because of their personal life-styles, because they are black, because they are white, because they are yellow, because they are red, because they are rich, because they are poor, because they believe in Jesus, and because they don't believe in Jesus. There have always been Maxines in governed societies. . . .

Maxine does, after all, have a recourse on the free market. She can get together with others in a similar situation to cooperatively provide the most important of defensive services, in a protective association. (It is also possible, of course, that defensive services may be sold on some sort of credit plan. . . .) Such communal solutions to defense problems are as readily available to people living in a market society as are the profit-seeking defense agencies, since the free market is the locus of *all* voluntary exchange, and not just the locus of monetary exchange for goods and services. There are advantages of agencies over associations for those who can afford them, of course, but these advantages do not necessarily include being adequately protected. Lacking the cash to pay an agency, Maxine may find herself devoting part of her time to participating in night patrols of the homes of association members. Indeed, she might find this method of defending herself philosophically more palatable than giving money to some greedy capitalist. In any case, she need not do without adequate protection.[22]

3. Wouldn't there be a tendency for one protective agency to dominate all the others and thus gradually bring about a monopoly of protection, like the

[22]John T. Sanders, *The Ethical Argument Against Government* (Washington, D.C.: University Press of America, 1980), pp. 128, 155–156. Reprinted by permission of the University Press of America and John T. Sanders.

present police force? For years, let's say, an agency has rendered efficient service for the lowest price and thus attracted more clients than any other. Let's say that it now has 80 percent of the protection business in a certain area. Isn't it likely to gobble up the rest? And if a difference of opinion breaks out between the dominant agency and a smaller one, wouldn't the smaller one, knowing it couldn't win an open fight, have to defer to the larger one, thus causing the larger one to get still more clients because it could protect them better? And wouldn't this create a monopoly of service and become in effect the State all over again?

Anarchists—and many others as well—would say that this conclusion is based on premises which, though popularly believed, are quite false. Large department store chains have competed for generations, yet continue to flourish, each satisfying the needs of some; the same is true of competing insurance companies and countless other enterprises. Protective organizations would follow the same pattern. No monopoly of goods or services can long be sustained without the coercive force of the State, not a monopoly of postal services or of laundry soaps or of anything else. This view goes contrary to the popular mythology but is nonetheless well substantiated by history.[23]

Even if one such organization became so efficient as to capture most of the market, this would be because the majority of the customers prefer it to its competitors. General Motors, for example, long controlled more than half the American car market for the simple reason that more people chose to buy General Motors products than Ford or Chrysler. But if General Motors suddenly started doubling its prices, it would lose its share of the market and those competitors that held the prices down would flourish.

4. The thorniest problem for anarchism is national defense. If there were no government of the United States to levy taxes for national defense, how would the territory of the United States (or what used to be that nation) be protected against foreign aggression? If the entire world were de governmentalized, there would be no national governments to make war on each other, and probably no hydrogen bombs or bacteriological agents for mass killings (the typical instruments of governments). But if the United States alone ceased to exist as a government, and its armed forces along with it, wouldn't it be fair game for predatory foreign powers that would see an unparalleled opportunity to fire a few missiles and take over?

It is everyone's interest to be protected against invasion, against being bombed and looted and killed; defense is one interest that is really common to all, and probably "the common defense" was the reason for having governments in the first place. Most people who see such a danger will be glad to pay for protection against it. But there is the notorious "problem of freeloaders." Jones says to himself, "Thousands of people are already making

---

[23] See Gabriel Kolko, *The Triumph of Conservatism* (New York: Free Press, 1963); Friedman, *The Machinery of Freedom,* Chapters 6 and 7; D. T. Armentano, *The Myths of Anti-Trust* (Westport, Conn.: Arlington House, 1973); John Hospers, *Libertarianism,* Chapter 4; and Sanders, *The Ethical Argument Against Government,* Chapter 8.

voluntary payments for defensive weapons like radar screens with which to
defend their lives and property against foreign aggression; *my* little contri-
bution won't make a difference to the whole defense effort, and I could use
the money for my own purposes. So I shall decline to contribute to it." If
your house is insured and mine isn't, the insurance company will cover the
loss of your house but not of mine; but with defense against foreign aggression, there is no such distinction: enemy bombers may level the house of the
one who has paid defense dues along with the one who hasn't, and if there
is no attack the person who hasn't paid will be protected along with the
person who has.

Numerous schemes for voluntary payments to defense against foreign
aggression have been worked out, such as making them part of the fees paid
for other purposes to insurance companies, or treating them like contribu-
tions to a charity or like tips at restaurants. It is not clear to what extent
these schemes would be effective. Even proponents of anarchism, such as
Friedman, concede the difficulty:

> What will I do if, when all other functions of our government have
> been abolished, I conclude that there is no effective way to defend
> against aggressive foreign governments save by national defense fi-
> nanced by taxes—financed, in other words, by money taken by force
> from the taxpayers? In such a situation, I would not try to abolish that
> last vestige of government. I do not like paying taxes, but I would rather
> pay them to Washington than to Moscow—the rates are lower. I would
> still regard the government as a criminal organization, but one which
> was, by a freak of fate, temporarily useful. It would be like a gang of
> bandits who, while occasionally robbing the villages in their territory,
> served to keep off other and more rapacious gangs. I do not approve of
> any government, but I will tolerate one, so long as the only other choice
> is another, worse government. Meanwhile, I would do my best to de-
> velop voluntary institutions that might eventually take over the business
> of defense.[24]

Whether the political (nonpolitical?) system (nonsystem?) of anarchism
could be made to work is a much discussed question; we barely have hinted
here at the array of arguments and counterarguments. If it could be made
practicable it would satisfy several goals at once: (1) ethical egoism, since
each person would choose to join or not join in accordance with what he or
she perceived as self-interest; (2) utilitarianism, since without the coercive
activity of the State, a large number of the ills of the world would no longer
exist, and the free market, unlike the State, would encourage competition
and reward inventiveness, increasing enormously the standard of living; and
(3) individual rights, since no one could be forced to accept protection or pay

[24]Friedman, *The Machinery of Freedom,* pp. 196–97. Reprinted by permission of Arlington House
Publishers, Westport, Connecticut.

for it nonvoluntarily. (Rights violators would be brought to trial without their consent in order to protect and vindicate the victims; nonviolators, however, would have no rights abridged and would be left free to live by their own choices.)

In any case, the world is so heavily populated with coercive governments that the prospects for the citizens of any nation on earth freeing themselves of governmental control seem quite remote. Moreover, if the citizens of one nation did succeed in doing so, that nation would be in grave danger if the other nations did not do so simultaneously—another extremely remote prospect. Accordingly, much of the thinking of anarchists has been directed toward a consideration of what moves can be made in the direction of the dissolution of governments, and by what stages it might gradually be achieved.[25]

2. THE ETHICS OF NATIONS

Whether one likes them or not, national governments exist, along with their apparatus for coercion and their huge military establishments. Since they exist and are not about to go away, certain important problems arise about what conduct is right or wrong in relation to them.

A. Prima Facie Duties to One's Country

Just as many persons believe that they have prima facie duties to members of their own family that they do not have to others, so, too, many believe that they have prima facie duties to their own nation (or citizens of it) that they do not have to other nations. "I'd rather help my fellow Americans than foreigners." "When there is a national crisis, I should help defend my own country, not other countries." These statements are manifestations of *patriotism*. What moral stance should be taken on patriotism?

If you help your fellow countrymen rather than people in Africa, it may not be because you believe your countrymen are better or more worthy of your efforts. They simply may be easier to help: you can go see them or write them a check, whereas it is difficult to do anything for people far away, even if you knew their names and could send them money, for you would not know into whose hands it might fall. Indeed, helping to defend your country in war does not necessarily mean you consider your fellow countrymen better or more worth defending than residents of other countries. Your

[25] See, for example, Rothbard, *For a New Liberty,* Epilogue; Sanders, *The Ethical Argument Against Government,* Chapter 9; Morris and Linda Tannehill, *The Market for Liberty* (New York: Laissez Faire Books, 1970), Part 3; James J. Martin, ed., *Men Against the State* (De Kalb, Ill.: Adrian Allen Associates, 1953); and Richard and Ernestine Perkins, *Precondition of Peace and Prosperity: Rational Anarchy* (New York: Laissez Faire Books, 1971).

position need not be "I'm defending America because it's America" but "I'm defending America because I value freedom above dictatorship," or "because I believe in the right of self-defense against outside attackers," and so on. You believe that the preservation of certain values can best be achieved by joining your countrymen rather than remaining aloof and possibly seeing those values destroyed by an aggressor.

If someone said, "I have duties to America just because it's America," a German could say, "I have duties to Germany because it's Germany." Such a position would be as difficult to defend as personal egoism (the view that others should serve me because I am I), for it presents no reason whatsoever for having duties to one's own country or countrymen rather than to others; the accident of where people happen to be born does not really offer any reason. But if someone said, "I value America for qualities A, B, C, . . ." and that person considered those qualities worth defending, even possibly dying for, because other countries (or their governments) lacked those qualities, then that individual at least would have defended his acts on behalf of other Americans by general principles and not by reference to geography.

> My attachment to these United States is wholly, entirely, absolutely to the Revolution, the real world revolution [the preservation of individual rights], which men began here and which has a foothold on earth here. If reactionaries succeed in destroying the revolutionary structure of social and political human life here, I care no more about this continent than about any other. If I lived long enough I would find and join the revival of the Revolution wherever it might be, in Africa or Asia or Europe, the Arctic or Antarctic. And let this country go with all the other regimes that collectivism has wrecked and eliminated since history began. So much for patriotism, mine.[26]

B. The Obligation to Obey the Law

Why should we obey a law that has been passed by our nation's government? Almost inevitably individual moral convictions and the law conflict: the State cannot permit ignorance of or disagreement with the law as a reason for disobeying the law, for this would put an end to law itself (see pp. 363–65). On the other hand, we feel bound to act in accord with our moral convictions, whether or not these agree with the law of the land. We want to act on our own judgments, but the law says, "No, if your judgment disagrees with the law, you are nevertheless bound under penalty to obey the law." The relationship of the law and the dictates of conscience is indeed complex.

1. There are many things we would do or not do on moral grounds alone, whether there was a law or not. The law prohibits us from committing mur-

[26] Rose Wilder Lane, in *The Lady and the Tycoon,* ed. Roger L. MacBride (Caldwell, Idaho: Caxton Printers, 1973), pp. 267–68.

der, but most of us, believing it wrong to commit murder, would not commit it in any case. When we go to a friend's dinner party, we do not even consider stealing the contents of the guests' pocketbooks where they lie unprotected in the bedroom; it's not so much that the law prohibits us from committing such a theft, but that we simply would not do it. (The law may, however, help to deter those who are tempted.)

2. There are many laws which it would not be immoral to break, but we usually obey them because not doing so is too much of a nuisance. Nobody would feel acute guilt at overparking for ten minutes, but we tend not to overpark anyway because we would have to pay a fine, which isn't worth the extra parking time. We also tend to drive over 55 miles an hour on highways where doing so seems quite safe; if we do not, it is for fear of being ticketed for speeding rather than because of any conviction of moral duty.

3. There are laws and regulations we believe to be unwise, unduly vague or detailed, unnecessary, more of a nuisance than they're worth, or simply better not to be on the books. We disobey them when we believe we can get away with it; occasionally we may obey them because we believe that disobedience to a bad law may serve to induce others (and perhaps ourselves) to disobey good ones. But we have no respect for them as laws. If you own a store or factory, you find yourself burdened by some 3,000 unindexed pages of regulations having the force of law, which tell you that you must paint the room a certain color, have a cafeteria if you employ more than nine people, have guardrails 42 inches high and the rungs in your ladders 12 inches apart (which contradicts some state laws that specify 14 inches), insist on employees wearing safety goggles even when no danger exists (or face a fine for not doing so), and so on. Some of the laws promote safety, but for every good rule there may be a thousand which are quite useless and waste employee time in keeping up with the required paperwork. The inspectors charged with enforcing the rules may themselves know nothing about the running of a plant. Under such circumstances widespread disobedience of "nuisance laws" like these, whose main purpose is to keep government employees paid at the taxpayers' expense, may be expected.

4. Finally, there are laws with which we disagree on moral grounds: we consider the law not only a nuisance, but immoral or vicious. Some parents strongly disapprove of some of the textbooks their children are required to read at public school but cannot afford a private school. Occasionally, because a neighbor issues some irrational complaint, a person is forcibly taken to a state mental hospital "for observation," in violation of what he or she considers basic rights. A man is drafted into the army to fight for a cause in which he does not believe. These are the troublesome cases where law and morality are in direct conflict. In this country we may agitate for a change in such laws, but the change may never be forthcoming. We may decide to obey, under duress, or we may decide to disobey and take the consequences, which may be extremely serious.

Many would say that whether we have an obligation to obey the law depends in part on what kind of government a nation has. Those who live in a dictatorship, where citizens may be made slaves in concentration camps or tortured and executed for trivial or trumped-up offenses, have no duty to obey the laws at all; the laws are there simply to keep them enslaved, to serve the State's purpose and not theirs. But those who live in a relatively free society, where people are generally free to do most of the things they want without interference, have an obligation, perhaps not to obey all the laws, but to obey more of them than their counterparts in totalitarian nations. If there is to be peace and safety within the society, people must refrain from doing at least those things which will disturb that peace. If others refrain, then so should we, in the spirit of fair play: we all get certain benefits (peace, safety, freedom of decision), and for the arrangement to work we should all share the burdens.

If we grant that there is a prima facie duty of fair play, is that duty the same in political as in personal relationships? Is it assumed voluntarily, that is, are certain burdens accepted in return for certain benefits? What if some don't want the benefits or don't consider them benefits? What if citizens have been taxed to the hilt (burden) in order to receive benefits they didn't want and didn't ask for, or what if the benefits went to some and not to others?

To the extent that we receive benefits, we are required to pay for them. If the benefits don't match the burdens, why should we not be free to opt out of the system? If, however, we try to reform the system from within, we may not be successful during our lifetime; and if we do go elsewhere, outside the country, we may fare even worse. Freedom to choose noncoercively is possible, if at all, only on a few unclaimed islands, and if we were to go to one of them seeking political freedom, we would probably be much less free to do other things, such as engage in cultural activities, which are also of great value to us. If you gain one freedom, you may lose another. The outcome will then depend on which freedom you value more.

C. International Relations

What justifies a nation's leaders in involving the nation in military activity? "Wars should be defensive, never aggressive" can be taken as morally axiomatic. The question is: When is it justifiable to involve a nation in a *defensive* war?

The situation is much the same with nations as with individuals. A person may be entirely peaceful yet face the choice of defending himself or herself or being killed. The people as well as the government of a nation may be peaceful, with no aggressive design on any other nation's territory, and yet if they are not prepared to respond to attack, they may be eliminated entirely. If the troops of another nation invade a country, kill or enslave the population, and seize their possessions, retaliation is clearly a case of self-defense.

Most situations, however, are not that clear-cut. What if the other nation doesn't attack but demands concessions, such as money, natural resources, or a strip of territory? Giving up property would amount to less than giving up lives. But the government of the hostile nation knows this, which is why they demand the concessions that they do. Besides, as Czechoslovakians learned in 1938, giving concessions generally leads the aggressor nation to "up the ante" and make new and greater demands. Where can the process stop short of total surrender? Isn't it better to take on an aggressor at the start rather than wait until a series of concessions has weakened a nation?

Or, what if the hostile nation doesn't attack, or hasn't yet attacked, but conquers surrounding territories, blocking off a nation's sea lanes, or conquering areas with essential natural resources? Finding no resistance, it may keep on conquering territories, strengthened by those it has already subdued, and in the end a country may be so weakened in comparison with the aggressor that when the ultimatum "Surrender or be destroyed" is presented, that nation will be forced to surrender because it no longer has the strength to retaliate successfully.

Often, the best way to prevent war is to be well prepared. A bully who doesn't think he can beat you is unlikely to attack. A nation that is not aggressive but simply uses its strength as a deterrent to attack by others is undoubtedly following wise and moral policy in that it may prevent attack entirely. Even so, such a move is double-edged: arming may itself lead the potential enemy to increase its own armaments, leading to an arms race. No assurance of peacefulness on one nation's part may be sufficient to convince another that it is not preparing to attack. The result may be mutual preparation for full-scale war, with each nation assuming the other a threat, and eventually one may initiate a pre-emptive strike against the other. In modern war the nation that strikes first has an enormous advantage: it can decimate an enemy before the latter has a chance to retaliate, and even if it does retaliate, much of the country may have been destroyed.

But should a country then anticipate an attack with a pre-emptive first strike, thus starting a war that just possibly might not otherwise have started at all? (If you see someone lighting a match in a gunpowder plant, should you wait, until you all go up in an explosion, or are you justified in taking a pessimistic view of the person's intentions and stop him forcibly on the spot?) It is possible that such a pre-emptive strike might (depending on the circumstances) save a free society from an outside aggressor. Yet there is an enormous danger in a strike of this sort: What if the potential victim only *thinks* that the other nation will strike? What if those in charge of its government are paranoid and thus start a war that would otherwise not have occurred? A utilitarian calculation of the consequences of each alternative, along with a fair estimate of their probability, would be quite impossible to make, especially in view of the probable mental state of the leaders of the nations involved. Moreover, an estimate of the situation in view of the probable violations of human rights would be even more difficult: if the hostile nation attacks, many thousands of innocent lives will be lost, but in the (perhaps improbable) event that it does not, no conflict will occur at all.

What, then, should be the stance of one nation toward another? No justification seems possible for one nation to attempt to police the world: What gives the government of one nation the right to keep the other ones in line according to its own lights? It seems plausible to believe, instead, that the only proper moral stance in international relations is some form of *isolationism,* or the noninvolvement of one country in the internal affairs of other countries, even though many people in those countries may be enslaved. Your government should not require you, with your taxes and perhaps your life, to pay for rescue operations that it may decide to embark on but of which you might not approve. It would be more desirable for any individual who so chooses, or for any group of individuals voluntarily banding together, to contribute to the liberation of subject peoples, or even to join foreign armies in order to help to achieve that result. Such an individual would be committing only himself or herself and, unlike the State, not pledging the lives of others.

But exactly what does a policy of isolationism—by governments, not individuals—involve? The term can be used to mean different things.

1. It can mean that a nation should be involved in no "entangling alliances." A nation that allies itself with another is committed to going to the other's defense if it is attacked, and wars often result. But on the other hand, war may result if alliances with other nations are avoided. The policy of noninvolvement with other nations may be a safer course for large and powerful nations such as the United States, which can be fairly self-sufficient without the rest of the world. But small nations not strong enough to resist aggression by a neighboring large nation have to have friends and allies. If Holland and Belgium and the Scandinavian countries had banded together to resist Nazi aggression when it first began, with the occupation of the Rhineland, Hitler's forces might have been defeated at once and World War II would never have occurred. Because they did not form an alliance, they were picked off one by one and conquered.

Alliances, then, may save the day. But on the other hand, alliances can be entangling: a nation that has a mutual protection alliance with another doubles its defenses but is then committed to going to war in case the other nation is attacked, in a cause that may be really none of its affair.

2. Isolationism can mean that a nation will take no action at all unless its own territory is attacked. But if the Soviets took over Mexico and constructed a missile base in Tijuana, that action would hardly be a matter of indifference to the residents of San Diego a few miles away. Should the government sit by and wait until San Diego or some other American city is attacked? (And if Mexico, how about Cuba?) By waiting the nation could become a sitting duck: others could attack and inflict such damage that retaliation would be either impossible or ineffective.

What if a predatory nation, such as the Soviet Union, marches into another country where there is civil strife or chaos and sets up a puppet government, which then shoots all dissenters and takes control? Suppose it happens in Hungary, and the United States does nothing, and it happens in Czechoslovakia and Afghanistan, and again there is nothing but the expected verbal protest. Suppose, then, that it happens with less fanfare in Africa, in various islands along the oil-shipping lanes from Arabia, and here and there like a rash all over the world. After this pattern has begun to develop, shall we still say, "It's none of our business—*we* haven't been attacked yet?" When a political vacuum arises, a totalitarian government generally fills it. Would we have no justification in trying to fill such a vacuum ourselves, not by taking over the unstable country but by keeping it from being overrun by others? If we did do this, the nation that was about to take it over could hardly complain about *its* rights being violated, since it was the principal rights violator. The United States would not be violating the rights of a people by protecting them from outside aggression, if we otherwise kept our hands off. Whether we *should* do it is a matter to be decided on the basis of facts that differ from case to case; but don't we have a *right* to do it as long as we only protect other countries and do not otherwise interfere with their lives? Surely we would not be violating the rights of a pedestrian by protecting him or her against a thug.

Even though the rights violator could hardly claim a violation of rights by our protecting the victim, other questions arise. If you go to the aid of the pedestrian, you do it of your own volition without involving someone else. But when a nation goes to the aid of another, it involves in the enterprise the money and lives of many of its own citizens, who, if they fail to support the cause, may face heavy fines and prison sentences. Morally there is an enormous difference between enlisting yourself voluntarily in a struggle and enlisting others nonvoluntarily. Besides, isn't there a suspicion of paternalism in the whole business? "We are going to help the victims of aggression"— but what if, to protect them against aggression by a left-wing dictatorship, we support a right-wing dictatorship which is also oppressing them? *We* may consider the left-wing dictatorship a greater evil, and perhaps indeed it is, but shouldn't the threatened *people* be the judge of that? Aren't we imposing on them *our* idea of what is for their good, rather than respecting their own? Such, at least, is the history of many interventions by one nation in the affairs of other nations that, officially at least, are only being protected. If we protect the pedestrian against the thug, does our action give us the right to determine the rescued person's subsequent life style?

3. Isolationism can mean that one nation should not extend to another country military or even economic aid. Money for such aid has been taken by force and threat of force from the taxpayers of the helping nation. But what if economic aid to a nation enables it to stave off an attack from a nearby totalitarian nation? Giving money is surely less costly than giving lives. Indeed, the economic aid may sometimes prevent a war from occurring. (It *may*, although usually it does not. American economic aid to nu-

merous nations has usually had the effect of solidifying the dictatorships which continue to crush the people; the money has lined the pockets of politicians and seldom gotten to the people who were supposedly being helped.)

What if certain essential elements—such as chromium, vanadium, and other metals without which the American steel industry would soon come to a stop—can be obtained only overseas, for example, in Africa, and that those markets are cut off by an aggressive power? Would the cutoff not defeat us as effectively as military invasion? If we took no steps to preserve the resources, we might indeed be militarily helpless against a possible future attack, and yet there seems no justification for going to war to retain them, since the metals don't belong to us. But if we can't buy them from the country that's taking them over are we justified in trying to take them? What rights could the aggressor nation claim that it has not already violated? Still, if the invading nation takes the resources by force, that action hardly justifies another nation (such as our own) in doing the same thing. We would be justified in *buying* them, provided that the owners of the resources were willing to sell them to us. If those resources had already been taken over by an invading power, we would be justified in returning them to their rightful owners, just as you would be justified in returning a stolen watch to its rightful owner. Unlike the case of the watch, however, the return probably could not be effected without war, and how could this be justified unless it penalized no one but the aggressors (never innocent bystanders), and was engaged in only by those who voluntarily chose to engage in it?

"Never fight, always negotiate" is doubtless a worthy saying, and if all nations followed this advice there would be no wars. But not all nations do so. It takes two to negotiate, and what if the other nation refuses to do so? If one government is bent on fighting, what can another government do but resist? If an aggressor isn't willing to negotiate or is willing only under impossible conditions ("The only thing we'll negotiate is *how* we take you over, not *whether* we do so, for we've already determined to do that, and that's nonnegotiable"), another nation's willingness to negotiate will only be interpreted as weakness, and in the end that nation will be forced to defend itself anyway.

If *one* side is bent on war, the other has the unpleasant choice of either defending itself or surrendering and suffering possible death or enslavement. Thus, *both* sides must be willing to negotiate, or negotiation cannot occur. Unfortunately, armed attack is the ultimate trump card: when negotiation fails, one or another party can always resort to war. The reverse (when war fails, negotiate) is not the case, since the victor in war no longer sees any need to negotiate with the vanquished: it can now impose whatever terms it wishes without negotiation. Might does not make right, yet it is might that in the end determines the fate of nations.

D. Trade and Diplomatic Relations

Should the government of a nation that is peaceful deal with the government of another nation that constantly violates the most basic rights of its citizens? It's true that all governments to some degree violate the rights of citizens, but there is an enormous difference of degree between a government that resorts to systematic torture, murder, and looting and one that does not. In personal relations, you wouldn't sit down at your dinner table with a murderer or a gangster; why should a nation's leaders do so in international relations?

For a utilitarian the answer is comparatively easy: it's only the future consequences that count, and more good may result from dealing with other governments than avoiding relations. Cooperation among nations to mutual advantage may, for example, prevent an arms race or keep it from getting out of hand. Since it is governments, not ordinary citizens, that launch wars, it is governments that must deal with one another to help prevent war. For the sake of peace, it is better for both sides to talk, even if neither side trusts the other, in the hope of working something out. True, past governmental actions may have brought on the situations requiring negotiations, but as utilitarians we are concerned only with future consequences and must let bygones be bygones.

If instead of taking a purely utilitarian approach we consider the matter in the light of rights and justice, the issue is more complex. Does a gangster government deserve recognition, not to mention its usual concomitant, trade? Haven't gifts to, and trade with, the Soviet government (no trade with individuals in the Soviet Union is permitted) propped up that government time and again, thus enabling it to continue to violate the rights of its citizens? American gifts of food during the famine of the 1920s undoubtedly saved many Russian lives, but it also kept afloat a dictatorship that has continued to violate the rights of its citizens to this day. So did the sales and loans of grain and advanced American technology during the 1960s and 1970s. By stabilizing the government of a country whose economy is so wasteful and inefficient that it cannot feed its own people without outside help, hasn't the American government (and other Western nations) been responsible for keeping the Soviet people in chains? If we had had no trade with the Soviets of any kind, not only would we have denied the government any moral sanction, but we might have enabled the people to overthrow the tyranny which victimizes them.

However, all this is water under the bridge. Just as it would be useless for a physician to recommend a preventive measure to someone who already was ill, so it would be futile to recommend how to avoid getting into a bad international situation when such a situation already exists. Granted that many mistakes were made in the past and that as a result we are in a situation now that we wouldn't have been in if these mistakes had not been made, what can we do now? That is always a difficult question, whether it concerns the

spread of a cancer in the body, the progressive influence of inflation throughout an economy, or the deterioration of international situations resulting in
the threat of war.

Often, however, it is possible to reverse course, even though belatedly.
Enormous evidence has accumulated that tyrannies such as the Soviet Union
would long since have collapsed without outside help: its technological progress, for example, has been achieved only by the nation's stealing, buying, or
accepting loans or gifts from other nations.[27] The Kama truck plant, the
largest in the world, which also builds tanks for the Soviet army, was designed by American companies. The vehicles manufactured there are also of
American design, and components were immediately incorporated into Soviet tanks.

> The first and second five-year plans were built by American compa-
> nies. . . . Trade with the U.S.S.R. was started over fifty years ago un-
> der President Woodrow Wilson with the declared intention of
> mellowing the Bolsheviks. The policy has been a total and costly failure.
> . . . We have built ourselves an enemy. We keep that self-declared en-
> emy in business. . . .
> We can stop the Soviets any time we want to, without using a single
> gun or anything more dangerous than a piece of paper or a telephone
> call. We have Soviet *technical dependence* as an instrument of world
> peace—the most humane weapon that can be conceived. We have always
> had that option. We have never used it.[28]

In a speech to the AFL-CIO, Aleksandr Solzhenitsyn said:

> It is necessary only that the West stop making concessions. . . . Our
> whole slave system depends on your economic assistance. It is American
> trade that allows the Soviet economy to concentrate its resources on
> armaments and preparations for war. Remove that trade, and the Soviet
> economy would be obliged to feed and clothe and house the Russian
> people, something our socialist economy has never been able to do. Let
> the socialists among you allow this socialist economy to prove the su-
> periority that its ideology claims. Stop sending them goods. Let them
> stand on their own feet, and then see what happens.[29]

---

[27] See, for example, Anthony Sutton, *Western Technology and Soviet Development,* 3 vol. (Stanford, Calif.: Hoover Institute, 1966–1972); and Werner Keller, *East Minus West Equals Zero*
(New York: Putnam, 1962).

[28] Anthony Sutton, *National Suicide: Military Aid to the Soviet Union* (Westport, Conn.: Arlington
House, 1973), pp. 262–63. Italics added.

[29] Aleksandr Solzhenitsyn, quoted in the *New York Times,* July 10, 1975.

E. Terrorism

When terrorists hijack a plane or hold hostages from another nation for ransom, what policy should be adopted? We can say, "Killers should be killed," but even if true, this statement is not helpful in such instances; if they were killed a great many innocent people would also be killed—the passengers in the plane, the civilian population of Iran if American bombs had dropped in order to free the hostages (and the hostages themselves, no doubt).

The policy of the Israeli government is not to pay one penny in ransom for the return of hostages. Not only has it announced this policy, but it has adhered to it. In this way terrorists are discouraged: they get nothing in return for their labors except the lives of those they captured (if the Israelis don't recapture them first as they did at Entebbi). From a utilitarian point of view at least, this policy is probably best: acts of terrorism are made unprofitable, and the terrorists must also cope with the fear of retaliation. The only fly in the ointment is that the hostages themselves may be killed. But, of course, this is a strong probability even without such a policy.

Doesn't the policy sacrifice the innocent? Israelis claim that their soldiers and espionage agents go out voluntarily, knowing that capture is possible and that no ransom will be paid in return for their lives. But some of them are draftees, who did not enlist voluntarily, and some are innocent civilians who did not agree to any such policy. In any case, it may be that any practice that discourages the taking of hostages saves more human lives than other policies.

The American policy, by contrast, has been to pay the ransom in order to save the hostages' lives, as was done in Iran. Let us assume (which is not certain) that the hostages would have been killed if the ransom had not been paid. With the hostages home and films shown on television of the happy reunited families we are likely to say, "The lives were more important than the money." But that ends only the first chapter, for now terrorists are on notice all over the world that they can take hostages and collect ransom. "If the Americans consider lives more valuable than money," they might reason, "let's take from them what's most valuable by their own pronouncement, and see what we can hold them up for in exchange." An ominous precedent has thus been set. It is possible that by the short-range saving of lives, there will be more long-range taking of lives, as the word spreads that Americans will pay ransom to any terrorist who chooses to hold American citizens hostage.

The policy of trying to rescue hostages is also troublesome. When attempts are made to rescue hostages, more lives may be lost—as was the case in the abortive rescue attempt of American hostages in Iran. Then it becomes a matter of balancing one set of lives against another, which is always one of the most agonizing decisions that can be made. Those taken hostage have a right to their lives, but so do the rescuers. The rescue of hostages is one of the most difficult of situations, in which the attempt to preserve one person's or group's right to life jeopardizes that of another.

F. Revolution

There are some persons in every generation who are so unhappy with the
existing order of things that they undertake violent means to change it.
Sometimes the impulse toward violence is itself so powerful that the causes
on behalf of which the violence is proposed become merely pretexts for its
use: if people can't find one reason to express violence, they can always find
another.

When the grievance is imaginary, or when it is relatively trivial and the
proposed retaliation is extreme, then it can hardly be argued that the revolutionists are engaged in self-defense: they are engaged in outright aggression
against others. But when the grievance is extreme, when people are hunted
down by secret police or interrogated and tortured for dissent, then the
grievance is genuine enough, and their actions can be construed as the defense of themselves and others against oppression. But granting all this, some
questions arise concerning their proposed revolutionary actions.

1. What will be achieved by the violence? In many cases the revolutionists
will simply meet death by their enemies' guns. Perhaps they may achieve
martyrdom, and their cause will triumph in the end through this martyrdom.
But even martyrdom requires that oppressors grant them publicity. Ma-
hatma Gandhi won millions to his cause because the British permitted him
access to the press and the media; had he tried to spread his views in the
Soviet Union or China or any of an ugly assortment of African and Latin
American dictatorships, he would have been taken out and shot, and no one
would ever have heard of his existence.

2. Who are the enemies of the revolution? Often the revolutionists' retaliation is not against just a few persons (oppressors) but against the whole of
society: virtually everyone is the "enemy." They would kill all if they could
in order to establish a "new order." What is the probability of everyone's
deserving death, as opposed to the probability that the revolutionists' view
of the world is a delusion?

3. Who is expendable? This is the most important moral question that
revolutionists have to face. They know that before their cause can succeed
many people will die. Many of these people do not agree with the revolutionists' views or aims. By what right do the revolutionists draw others who
are unwilling into their battle? People may risk their own lives, but have
they the right to risk the lives of others who do not favor their aims or
methods? "The cause I believe in is so important that I'd gladly sacrifice your
life for it" is a dubious moral rule on which to act.

Suppose the revolutionists are utilitarians. They will then make a careful
calculation of the probable consequences of their revolutionary cadre's actions. They must be careful, as most revolutionists are not, not to stack the
cards in favor of their own view of the outcome, though rationalization in
such a situation will be almost irresistible. It is possible that if they fairly
calculate the value of the end (which according to them at least would be

very great) against the suffering and loss of life involved in the means required to achieve the end, they may come to the conclusion that suffering and death are worth it. Most revolutionists *believe* this to be the case, and sometimes it may actually *be* the case, though the probabilities are against it. (Most revolutionists who succeed in toppling one tyranny institute a regime as oppressive as the one which preceded it. The American Revolution, by contrast, was achieved with minimal loss of life and by ill-equipped volunteer armies.[30])

Let us suppose that in this case the revolutionists are right (although they could hardly know this in advance) and that the cost of their enterprise is minimal in human life. Would the sacrifice be worth it? From the utilitarian point of view the answer would quite surely be yes, especially if those lives were snuffed out without pain. The utilitarian considers the sum total of happiness and misery, without considering *by whom* it must be borne. Human beings are to the utilitarian mere means to heightened utility.

But now let us consider the question in light of the concept of human rights. Consider just one person who disapproves of the revolution and is nevertheless caught up in it against his or her will and killed. Should the future happiness of others, if indeed that comes to pass, be built upon the nonrevolutionary sacrifice of this life, or even a small number of lives of dissenters? If so, what happens to the belief in the rights of the individual? Perhaps even the right to life (in its minimal sense) should sometimes be overridden by considerations of utility; but once a move in this direction is begun, it is difficult to see where the list of sacrificial victims will stop, as long as total utility is maximized.

"But antirevolutionists will be better off if the revolution succeeds; they just don't know it," it may be objected. Let us suppose that in a particular case this is true (though it is also possible that the person making this objection is simply carried away with revolutionary fervor and has little conception of what things would really be like after the revolution has succeeded). Even if the dissenters *mistakenly* believe that the success of the revolution would be bad, has anyone the right to use a gun, as opposed to an argument, to change their minds? If revolutionists are willing to trample on the rights of those who do not agree with them, how many other persons' rights will they be willing to violate before the conflict is over? Are the lives of other people theirs to be disposed of as they wish? And if not, by what right can revolutionists sacrifice the life of even one person who disagrees with the cause?

Just what is one human life worth? Kant held that the individual life is of infinite value. But the meaning of this dictum is not clear. If we accept it, must we believe that the loss of one life, which would have expired in six months anyway, is of greater importance than, for example, having a telephone system by which a person could dial another person almost anywhere

---

[30] For a classic analysis of why this was so, see Friedrich Gentz and Stefan T. Possony, *Three Revolutions* (Chicago: Regnery, 1959).

in the world? Should millions be willing to give large amounts of their time just to save one human life somewhere in the world? If one human life is of "infinite value," it would seem that the answer would have to be yes.

If we are placed in a situation where we have to choose between two alternatives, *A* and *B,* and *A* involves the death of ten people and *B* the death of twenty, and these are the only choices, then presumably we should sacrifice the ten, because the other alternative would be even worse; it would not be wrong to do this, because we would be doing the best possible act under the circumstances. But does one human life weigh so heavily on the scale as to outweigh thousands of material benefits? Should we give up a reasonably decent standard of living for the rest of our lives in order to save the lives of people in India whom we do not know? Should you give up having electric power for the rest of your life in order to save the life of your ill grandmother?

Human life is admittedly of great value, but is there no limit to its worth? Some people do not place great value even on their *own* lives; should others place more value on them than they do themselves? In utilitarianism, if one person is pretty sure to be miserable for the limited remainder of his life, and many others would be made happier by the person's early death (perhaps just because of the immense expense of continued hospital care), it would be justifiable to administer a painless death potion to that person, provided that others did not know of it and would therefore not dread the same fate for themselves; but, of course, this ignores the view that a person has a right to life, as well as the traditional view of justice (since the person does not deserve to die).

Consider the amount of joy that has been given to people for the last 200 years by hearing the compositions of Mozart: in view of the fact that this is virtually pure enjoyment with very little admixture of distress or pain, the amount of intrinsic good resulting from that one composer's works must be enormous. And now consider a group of, say, a hundred persons who have produced in their lives very little but unhappiness for themselves and for those around them. Would you, if you could do so by pressing a button, put them painlessly out of existence if thereby you could create another Mozart? Fortunately no such choices can be made, since there is no known causal connection between getting rid of one person and giving rise to a genius. But if it was possible, it would surely seem that on utilitarian principles it should be done, though on Kantian principles it should not: human lives are not negotiable, and your life is not the property of others, to be continued or extinguished without your consent.

Revolutionists, if they think in terms of general ethical concepts at all, are likely to be utilitarians, since they thereby can get over the hurdle of sacrificing others' lives against their will as long as it is "for the greater good." Perhaps they themselves would be willing to be sacrificed for the greater good of others if it came to that; if they would not, their view would not be a consistent application of their own principles. But if they really carefully weigh the alternatives, they usually will conclude that peaceful change, though slower, is best for everyone, themselves included; education may be slow, as is evolving a political system, but it is far more likely not to reap the bitter fruits of pain and death. And in the small proportion of cases in which peaceful change is not possible, at least not foreseeable in any considerable span of time, then the use of force against others should be only in response to genuine violations of rights, and only against those who have violated them. If no such limitation is placed on revolutionary action, revolutionists themselves may fall into the same trap in which they have enmeshed others: if they do not hesitate to expend the lives of others, it is their own lives that in the end may be expended, and in a cause that is not their own.

EXERCISES

1. An individual is ordinarily said to be bound by a promise to someone else unless there is some good reason for breaking it. Is a nation (the administration now in office) bound by a treaty which was signed by the previous administration, and of which the present officials (then not yet in power) disapproved at the time?

2. Discuss the following statement by Frederic Bastiat from *The Law* (1848): "How is legal plunder to be identified? Quite simply. See if the law takes from some persons what belongs to them, and gives it to other persons to whom it does not belong. See if the law benefits one citizen at the expense of another by doing what the citizen himself cannot do without committing a crime. Then abolish this law without delay."

3. Either each person should be free to choose for himself or herself, or some person or group in political power makes the decision for him or her. Given these alternatives, consider the following specific issues. Since your answer will probably not be the same in all cases, why do you decide one way for one issue and another way for another?

   a. Should laws be passed banning certain foods from the market? For example, candy and cake can be harmful to health, so should you be prohibited by law from consuming them? Similarly, cigarettes are unhealthful, so should a law be passed prohibiting anyone from having them?

   b. Should the Food and Drug Administration have authority to declare certain substances harmful and take them off the market?

   c. Should the State determine which drugs and medications should be "by prescription only," or should all be available for anyone to purchase?

   d. Should marijuana, cocaine, heroin, amphetamines, and other now illicit or restricted drugs be available on the market for purchase, or should the State have power to prohibit their use? (See Thomas Szasz, *Ceremonial Chemistry.*)

   e. Should the State be empowered to freeze wages and prices during an inflationary period? (See George Reisman, *The Government Against the Economy.*)

   f. Should the State have the power to enact antitrust laws in order to protect competition? (See D. T. Armentano, *The Myths of Antitrust.*)

g. Should the State have the power to license physicians, set the conditions under which they must deal with patients, and subsidize medical schools as well as patients? (See Marvin Edwards, *Hazardous to Your Health;* and John Hospers, *Libertarianism,* pp. 180–87.)

h. To what extent, if any, should the State have the power to regulate business enterprises? (See Robert Poole, ed., *Instead of Regulation;* and Dan Smoot, *The Business End of Government.*)

i. Should the State provide jobs to ease the unemployment problem? (See George Gilder, "The Make-work Economy," *Harpers,* Nov. 1979, and "Gambling on Truth," *Reason,* Oct. 1981.)

j. Should the State appropriate funds to ease the energy crisis? (See C. V. Myers, *Money and Energy;* and Lindsey Williams, *The Energy Non-Crisis.*)

4. Could the following activities be carried out without a State? Consider not only efficiency but morality in your answers.

a. Care for the needy

b. Wills and estates

c. Operation of roads and railroads

d. A system of coinage

e. A banking system

f. Preservation of natural resources

g. Preservation of endangered species

h. Police protection

i. Arbitration of disputes

j. Creation and maintenance of prisons and work farms

k. Defense against external aggressors

(See, for example, James R. Dunn, "Back to the Land: Environmental Suicide," *Reason,* March 1978; John Baden and Richard Stroup, "Saving the Wilderness," *Reason,* July 1981; Samuel Blumenfeld, Robert Michaels, and R. W. Johnson, "Energy Self-Defense," *Reason,* January 1980, as well as the references listed in Exercise 3.)

5. Discuss the following remarks on terrorism:

> Do you really believe that the professional terrorist thinks that any given act of terror will alter the features of the society, bringing in peace on earth? Of course not. The terrorist uses terror to create a loss of faith in the existing order, or to strike out at the leaders of a political order. The act of terrorism is useful only if your political philosophy makes the destruction of society a blessing in itself. If you resent signs of other men's economic superiority, or social superiority, then terrorism is one way of striking out at what you resent. It's not that the terrorist believes that his acts of violence are furthering a better society as such; it's that he sees a burnt-down society, a blown-up society, and a leveled society as a legitimate goal. Terrorism is made legitimate as a means because only terror and destruction can possibly bring such a burning society into being.
>
> Now consider some of the implications of this. As envy is loosed on the land, we have to devise policies to combat it. How? Can we legislate new wealth-distribution programs? The guilt-ridden capitalists have believed they could buy off the jealousy-dominated socialists with such programs. You

know the slogans: "FDR saved capitalism from itself." "We need a government-business partnership." "Every society needs an economic safety net." But these slogans are meaningless to the envious man. It's not redistribution that he wants. He knows that we cannot redistribute the wealth so that the rich man's luxuries are made available to the masses. Even if he didn't know, he wouldn't care. What he wants to see is a society in which nobody has access to the luxuries. He's not trying to "get his" at your expense. He's trying to "smash yours" at your expense. His motivation is utterly perverse: it's the act of taking away yours, destroying yours, which gives him his kicks.

. . .

The awful truth about envy is that *it cannot be placated.* If you try to buy off the envious man, your very ability to buy him off—the existence of excess capital for you to buy him off, to delay your day of judgment—repulses him. Who was it that the Red Brigades got? Aldo Moro, a long-time socialist. Every public official becomes a target, not because of his ideology, but because of his high position as an official. Every sign of success makes you a potential target.

Henry Fairlie, writing in *The New Republic* (Sept. 17, 1977), made some incisive comments about the nature of envy. He stresses the fact that men refuse to admit that they are envious, even to themselves. He quotes La Rochefoucald: "Few are able to suppress in themselves a secret satisfaction at the misfortune of their friends." (From Gary North, "The Politics of Envy," *Remnant Review,* August 15, 1980. Reprinted by permission of Gary North.)

6. You are at war. The enemy systematically resorts to the torture of spies and captured prisoners to gain the information it desires, a practice which gives it a tactical advantage over your side and probably costs your side many lives because of your own unwillingness to use such methods to obtain any information from the enemy. Moreover, some neutrals are likely to be lost to your side as a result of the enemy's practice: if they side with the enemy but fall into your hands, they won't be tortured anyway, but if they side with you and fall into your enemy's hands, they will be tortured mercilessly. Unless you change your tactics, therefore, you may lose the war, or at any rate many thousands of lives. Under these circumstances, are you justified in using torture to expedite victory for your side?

7. Consider this report from *Newsweek,* May 19, 1980:

In an old Jewish cemetery outside the West Bank town of Hebron, Israeli settlers buried another victim of Arab terrorism last week. Then some of them went on a rampage. Shouting "Revenge now!" they stormed into Arab Hebron firing submachine guns into the air, hurling stones through windows, breaking into shops and smashing parked cars. "It's not enough to take an eye for an eye," said Rabbi Meir Kahane; "we have to take two!"

Three days earlier Palestinian gunmen ambushed a group of Israelis who had been praying in Hebron, killing six and wounding sixteen. Israel responded with a swift and ruthless crackdown. Houses from which the gunmen fired were blown up, scores of suspects were arrested, an indefinite curfew was clamped on Hebron and the town's mayor was deported, along with two other West Bank leaders. Israel also launched a seaborne commando raid against Palestinian positions in Lebanon, killing three commandos of the PLO. The Israeli chief of staff, Lt. Gen. Rafael Eitan, warned that his men would strike again "at any time, any hour, any place."

Much of the rest of the world thought that Israel had overreacted.

Was the Israeli reaction out of proportion to the offense? Why or why not?

8. Terrorists from across the Lebanese border conduct raids into Israel, killing numerous women and children. Israel launches counterstrikes into southern Lebanon, devastating airfields and parts of towns. The people killed had nothing to do with the raid into Israel. Justice demands that "only the guilty be punished." But, reply Israeli leaders, without these retaliatory raids—which admittedly are bound to kill innocent people—there is no way to stop the raids from Lebanon, which killed many innocent Israeli families before the retaliatory strikes from Israel began.

The victims of these raids were innocent of any violation of the rights of Israelis. How would you respond to the remark, "If even *one* innocent person was killed, conducting the raid was an immoral act"? Yet it was a retaliatory raid, and if the Israelis had not conducted it (let us assume), the raids against Israeli towns and villages would have continued, killing ever more Israelis who were not guilty of any rights-violations either. Is there any moral way out of this dilemma?

9. In the novel and subsequent film *The Night People,* the Russians hold the son of an American in captivity, threatening to kill him unless the American authorities turn over several people the Russians want, who have escaped to America from behind the Iron Curtain. The man wants his son back at all costs, even if it means returning the other people unwillingly to Russia. What will happen to them if they are sent back? Without doubt, like thousands of others who were "forcibly repatriated" back to Russia by American military authorities after World War II, they will be tortured and then killed. Those who will be tortured and killed if sent back to Russia are many; the man's son is only one person. Should the Americans consent to the exchange?

10. In June 1981 the Israeli air force conducted a pre-emptive strike against an atomic plant near Baghdad, citing evidence that the plant was to be used for the nuclear extermination of Israel. (France had offered to supply a low-level atomic fuel usable for industry but not for bombs, but Iraq refused it, insisting on nuclear fuel that could be used for bombs, and France finally granted the request.) Should the Israelis have waited until they were sure? Was their move a case of justified self-defense?

11. Under what conditions, if any, and why, would you consider it justifiable for a head of State or legislature to do the following:
    a. Impose martial law
    b. Imprison suspects without a trial
    c. Censor the press and media
    d. Engage in compulsory redistribution of land
    e. Declare war on another nation
    f. Permit a county or state to secede from the nation

12. Winston Churchill said that democracy is the worst form of government—until you examine all the others. Do you agree?

13. Assume that you have inherited the rulership of a nation and have the power to change the course of the government from totalitarianism to maximum individ-

ual freedom. Your aims are misunderstood by some of the citizens, however. In the northern provinces there is a spreading movement to unseat you by force of arms. If you don't put down the rebellion by force, your regime of liberty will be at an end; if you do, your dedication to liberty will be questioned, and more rebellions are likely to break out elsewhere. As a champion of freedom, what should you do?

14. In the situations described below, consider the morality of truth telling and promise keeping. Are Kantian moral rules geared to a more civilized world than the one described in these examples? Also, how many of the atrocities described can be attributed to the coercive power of governments? (How many would have occurred without governments, committed through the treachery of individuals acting without government coercion?)

   a. "Yuzhakov was arrested during the day, and at night they came for his wife. They presented her with a list of names and demanded that she sign a confession that they had all met in her house at a Menshevik-SR meeting (of course, they had not). They promised in return to let her out to be with her three children. She signed, destroying all the persons listed—and, of course, she herself remained in prison." (From *The Gulag Archipelago 1918– 1956: An Experiment in Literary Investigation I–II,* Volume One, by Aleksandr I. Solzhenitsyn, p. 74. Copyright © 1973 by Aleksandr I. Solzhenitsyn. English translation copyright © 1973, 1974 by Harper & Row, Publishers, Inc. Reprinted by permission of the publisher.)

   b. "A streetcar motorwoman of Krasnodar was returning on foot late at night from the car depot; on the outskirts of the city, to her misfortune, she passed some people working to free a truck that had gotten stuck. It turned out to be full of corpses—hands and legs stuck out from beneath the canvas. They wrote down her name and the next day she was arrested. The interrogator asked her what she had seen. She told him truthfully. Anti-Soviet Agitation—ten years." (From ibid., Reprinted by permission of the publisher.)

   c. "The mildest and at the same time most widespread form of betrayal was not to do anything bad directly, but just not to notice the doomed person next to one, not to help him, to turn away one's face, to shrink back. They had arrested a neighbor, your comrade at work, or even your close friend. You kept silence. You acted as if you had not noticed. (For you could not afford to lose your current job.) And then it was announced at work, at the general meeting, that the person who had disappeared the day before was an inveterate enemy of the people. And you, who had bent your back beside him for twenty years at the same desk, now by your noble silence (or even by your condemning speech), had to show how hostile you were to his crimes. (You had to make this sacrifice for the sake of your own dear family, for your own dear ones! What right had you not to think about them?) But the person arrested had left behind him a wife, a mother, children, and perhaps they at least ought to be helped? No, no, that would be dangerous: after all, these were the wife of an enemy and the mother of an enemy, and they were the children of an enemy—and your own children had a long education ahead of them!" (From *The Gulag Archipelago 1918– 1956: An Experiment in Literary Investigation III–IV,* Volume Two, by Alek-

sandr I. Solzhenitsyn, p. 637. Copyright © 1974 by Aleksandr I. Solzhenitsyn. English language translation copyright © 1975 by Harper & Row,
Publishers, Inc. Reprinted by permission of the publisher.)

d. "When the city of Kiev surrendered to the Bolshevik troops, it was on the
specific promise of Voroshilov, advanced to induce the surrender, that the
thousands of loyal Czarist army officers in that city, with their wives and
children, would be allowed peacefully to leave for their homes or wherever
they wanted to go. Instead, the minute the surrender was complete, Voroshilov had all of the men shot forthwith, and put their wives and daugh-
ters in brothels 'for the health of his army.' When he actually boasted of
this foul treachery fifteen years later to William Bullitt, and Bullitt could
not refrain from commenting on the treatment of the women, Voroshilov
explained that it didn't make any real difference that they too had not been
shot at once, for they were all dead within three months anyway." (From
Robert Welch, *The Politician,* p. 209.)

e. "The permanent lie becomes the only safe form of existence, in the same
way as betrayal. Every wag of the tongue can be overheard by someone,
every facial expression observed by someone. . . . A shake of the head
instead of a nod might well cost you resettlement in the Archipelago. . . .

"But that was not all: your children were growing up. If they weren't
yet old enough, you and your wife had to avoid saying openly in front of
them what you really thought; after all, they were being brought up to . . .
betray their own parents. . . . And if the children were still little, then you
had to decide what was the best way to bring them up; whether to start
them off on lies instead of the truth (so that it would be *easier* for them to
live) and then to lie forevermore in front of them too; or to tell them the
truth, with the risk that they might make a slip, that they might let it out,
which meant that you had to instill into them from the start that the truth
was murderous, that beyond the threshold of the house you had to lie, only
lie, just like papa and mama." (From *The Gulag Archipelago 1918–1956: An
Experiment in Literary Investigation III–IV,* Volume Two, by Aleksandr I.
Solzhenitsyn, pp. 646–48. Copyright © 1974 by Aleksandr I. Solzhenitsyn.
English language translation copyright © 1975 by Harper & Row, Publishers, Inc. Reprinted by permission of the publisher.)

f. In "Operation Keelhaul" at the end of World War II, by Allied agreement
with Stalin all nationals were to be repatriated to their native countries
whether they wanted to go or not. Thousands of Russians (including Lat-
vians and Lithuanians, now a part of the Soviet Union) who had escaped
during the German invasion were rounded up by British and American
soldiers and forced at gunpoint into trains bearing them back to the Soviet
Union and certain death. Many slit their wrists and jumped from the trains
to their deaths crossing high bridges. Seeing their resistance, American and
British soldiers, under orders to send them back, promised them that they
were going to the West; the train would start and a few minutes later, going
east, it would be taken over by Soviet troops, who accompanied the prisoners to Russia to be shot. (See Jules Epstein, *Operation Keelhaul;* and Peter
Huxley-Blythe, *The East Came West.*)

15. Frederic Bastiat wrote of individuals, "Let a merchant begin to sell his goods on
the principle of brotherly love, and I do not give him even a month before his

children will be reduced to beggary" (*Economic Sophisms,* 1850). What could be said for or against the conduct of international relations on "the principle of brotherly love"?

16. Organic theory of the State: "The individual is to the State as the organ of a body is to the body. Remove an organ and the body can no longer function adequately. Separated from the body, it dies. An individual is a part of the State, with no separate existence as an individual." Examine and evaluate.

SELECTED READINGS

Authority and Consent

Bastiat, Frederic. *The Law* (1848).★ Irvington, N.Y.: Foundation for Economic Education, 1962.

―――. *Selected Essays on Political Economy* (1850). Princeton; N.J.: Van Nostrand, 1964.

Benn, S. I., and Richard Peters. *Social Principles and the Democratic State.* London: Allen & Unwin, 1955. Published in the United States as *Principles of Political Thought.* New York: Collier Books, 1965.

Bowie, Norman, and Robert Simon, eds. *The Individual and the Political Order.* Englewood Cliffs, N.J.: Prentice-Hall, 1979.

Friedman, David. *The Machinery of Freedom.* Westport, Conn.: Arlington House, 1978.

Harris, R. Baine, ed. *Authority: A Philosophical Analysis.* Tuscaloosa, Ala.: University of Alabama Press, 1976.

Hayek, F. A. *The Constitution of Liberty.* Chicago: University of Chicago Press, 1960.

―――. *Law, Legislation, and Liberty.* 3 vols. Chicago: University of Chicago Press, 1973.

―――. *The Road to Serfdom.* Chicago: University of Chicago Press, 1944.

Hobbes, Thomas. *Leviathan* (1651). Many editions.

Hospers, John. *Libertarianism.* New York: Laissez Faire Books, 1971.

Kadish, Mortimer, and Sanford Kadish. *Discretion to Disobey.* Stanford, Calif.: Stanford University Press, 1973.

La Boetie, Etienne de. *The Politics of Obedience* (1577). New York: Free Life Editions, 1975.

Locke, John. *Second Treatise on Civil Government* (1691). Many editions.

Marx, Karl. *Selected Writings,* ed. David McLellan. New York: Oxford University Press, 1977.

Mill, John Stuart. *Principles of Political Economy* (1848). Many editions.

Mises, Ludwig von. *Omnipotent Government.* New Haven: Yale University Press, 1944.

Nock, Albert Jay. *Our Enemy, the State* (1935). New York: Arno Press, 1972.

Nozick, Robert. *Anarchy, State, and Utopia.* New York: Basic Books, 1974.

Paterson, Isabel. *The God in the Machine.* New York: Putnam, 1943. Reprinted by Caxton Printers, 1964.

★Dates in parentheses are dates of first publication.

Perkins, Richard, and Ernestine Perkins. *Rational Anarchy*. New York: Laissez Faire Books, 1971.

Plato. *Republic*. Many editions.

Rand, Ayn. "The Nature of Government." In her *Capitalism the Unknown Ideal*. New York: Signet Books, 1967.

Rothbard, Murray. *For a New Liberty*. New York: Macmillan, 1973.

————. *Man, Economy, and the State*. Princeton; N.J.: Van Nostrand, 1962.

Sanders, John. *The Ethical Argument Against Government*. Washington, D.C.: University Press of America, 1980.

Schwartz, Thomas, ed. *Freedom and Authority*. Belmont, Calif.: Wadsworth Publishing, 1973.

Shafarevich, Igor. *The Socialist Phenomenon*. New York: Harper & Row, 1980.

Singer, Peter. *Democracy and Disobedience*. New York: Oxford University Press, 1974.

Spencer, Herbert. *The Man vs. the State* (1884). Caldwell, Idaho: Caxton Printers, 1944.

————. *Social Statics* (1845). New York: Robert Schalkenbach Foundation, 1970.

Tannehill, Morris, and Linda Tannehill. *The Market for Liberty*. New York: Laissez Faire Books, 1970.

Taylor, Richard. *Freedom, Anarchy, and the Law*. Englewood Cliffs, N.J.: Prentice-Hall, 1973.

Wolff, Robert Paul. *In Defense of Anarchism*. New York: Harper & Row, 1970.

Wooldridge, William. *Uncle Sam the Monopoly Man*. Westport, Conn.: Arlington House, 1973.

The Ethics of Nations

Bedau, Hugo, ed. *Civil Disobedience*. New York: Pegasus Books, 1969.

Care, Norman, and Thomas Trelogan, eds. *Issues in Law and Morality*. Cleveland: Case Western Reserve University Press, 1973.

Cohen, Carl. *Civil Disobedience*. New York: Columbia University Press, 1971.

De George, Richard, ed. *Ethics and Society*. New York: Macmillan, 1968.

Downie, R. S. *Government Action and Morality*. New York: Macmillan, 1964.

Fuller, Lon. *The Morality of Law*. New Haven, Conn.: Yale University Press, 1964.

Lane, Rose Wilder. *The Discovery of Freedom*. New York: Arno Press, 1943.

Murphy, Jeffrie, ed. *Civil Disobedience and Violence*. Belmont, Calif.: Wadsworth Publishing, 1971.

Roche, George C. III. *Legacy of Freedom*. Westport, Conn.: Arlington House, 1969.

Schaffer, Jerome, ed. *Violence*. New York: David McKay, 1971.

Templeton, Kenneth, ed. *The Politicization of Society*. Indianapolis: Liberty Press, 1979.

Wasserstrom, Richard, ed. *Morality and the Law*. Belmont, Calif.: Wadsworth Publishing, 1971.

————. *War and Morality*. Belmont, Calif.: Wadsworth Publishing, 1970.

Index

F
G 8
H 9
I 0
J 1